SIDONIUS APOLLINARIS
SELECTED LETTERS

EDITED BY

JOOP VAN WAARDEN
Radboud Universiteit Nijmegen

Shaftesbury Road, Cambridge CB2 8EA, United Kingdom

One Liberty Plaza, 20th Floor, New York, NY 10006, USA

477 Williamstown Road, Port Melbourne, VIC 3207, Australia

314–321, 3rd Floor, Plot 3, Splendor Forum, Jasola District Centre, New Delhi – 110025, India

103 Penang Road, #05–06/07, Visioncrest Commercial, Singapore 238467

Cambridge University Press is part of Cambridge University Press & Assessment, a department of the University of Cambridge.

We share the University's mission to contribute to society through the pursuit of education, learning and research at the highest international levels of excellence.

www.cambridge.org
Information on this title: www.cambridge.org/9781316514504

DOI: 10.1017/9781009083485

© Cambridge University Press & Assessment 2026

This publication is in copyright. Subject to statutory exception and to the provisions of relevant collective licensing agreements, no reproduction of any part may take place without the written permission of Cambridge University Press & Assessment.

When citing this work, please include a reference to the DOI 10.1017/9781009083485

First published 2026

A catalogue record for this publication is available from the British Library

A Cataloging-in-Publication data record for this book is available from the Library of Congress

ISBN 978-1-316-51450-4 Hardback
ISBN 978-1-009-08762-9 Paperback

Cambridge University Press & Assessment has no responsibility for the persistence or accuracy of URLs for external or third-party internet websites referred to in this publication and does not guarantee that any content on such websites is, or will remain, accurate or appropriate.

For EU product safety concerns, contact us at Calle de José Abascal, 56, 1°, 28003 Madrid, Spain, or email eugpsr@cambridge.org

CONTENTS

List of Maps and Figures	page viii
Preface	xiii
Conventions, Abbreviations and Editions	xv
General Introduction	1
1 Biography	1
2 Works	4
2.1 Works That Have Come Down to Us	4
2.2 Works That Were Lost or Can Be Assumed to Have Existed	5
3 Context	6
3.1 Late Antiquity	6
3.2 Politics	7
3.3 Society	8
3.4 Philosophy and Religion	12
3.5 Literature	14
3.6 Letter Writing	15
4 The Correspondence: A Work of Art and Strategy	16
4.1 Structure and Aims of the Collection	16
4.2 Epistolary Conventions and Politeness	19
4.3 Text Linguistics and Narratology	20
4.4 Intertextuality	22
4.5 Vocabulary, Syntax and Style	23
5 Afterlife	25
6 Manuscript Tradition and Text	26
SIDONIUS APOLLINARIS: SELECTED LETTERS	31
Epistula 1.1	33
Epistula 1.5	33
Epistula 1.9	36
Epistula 2.9	37
Epistula 2.10. Carmen 27	39

Epistula 2.12	41
Epistula 3.9	42
Epistula 3.12. Carmen 28	42
Epistula 4.19	44
Epistula 4.20	44
Epistula 5.5	45
Epistula 5.16	45
Epistula 6.11	46
Epistula 7.1	47
Epistula 7.7	48
Epistula 7.17. Carmen 33	49
Epistula 7.18	51
Epistula 8.3	51
Epistula 8.15	53
Epistula 9.16. Carmen 41	53
Commentary	57
Letter 1.1: Dedication	57
Letter 1.5: Travelling to Rome	70
Letter 1.9: Becoming City Prefect	88
Letter 2.9: Villa Life	101
Letter 2.10 with Poem 27: A Poem for the Cathedral of Lyon	120
Letter 2.12: His Daughter's Illness	138
Letter 3.9: Supporting a Slave-Owner	144
Letter 3.12 with Poem 28: Restoring Grandfather's Grave	148
Letter 4.19: Coming Soon	159
Letter 4.20: Exotic Pageantry	161
Letter 5.5: A Roman Speaking Burgundian	167
Letter 5.16: Excellent News for the Family	175
Letter 6.11: Recommending a Jew	182
Letter 7.1: The Resistance of Clermont and the Rogations	185
Letter 7.7: Clermont Surrendered	198

CONTENTS vii

Letter 7.17 with Poem 33: Clermont and the Monks 208
Letter 7.18: Envoi for the Seven-Book Collection 222
Letter 8.3: Sending a Life of Apollonius of Tyana 228
Letter 8.15: In Praise of the Bishop of Orléans 245
Letter 9.16 with Poem 41: His Spiritual Testament 250

Appendix: Sidonius' (Presumed) Epitaph and Death Date 265

Bibliography 267
Index 294

MAPS AND FIGURES

Map 1	Gaul *c.* 380–*c.* 480	*page* ix
Map 2	Lyon *c.* 470 (churches, cemeteries, highways)	x
Map 3	Sidonius' voyage to Rome in 467	xi
Figure 1	Dolveck's stemma, simplified (according to Marolla 2023, 19)	27

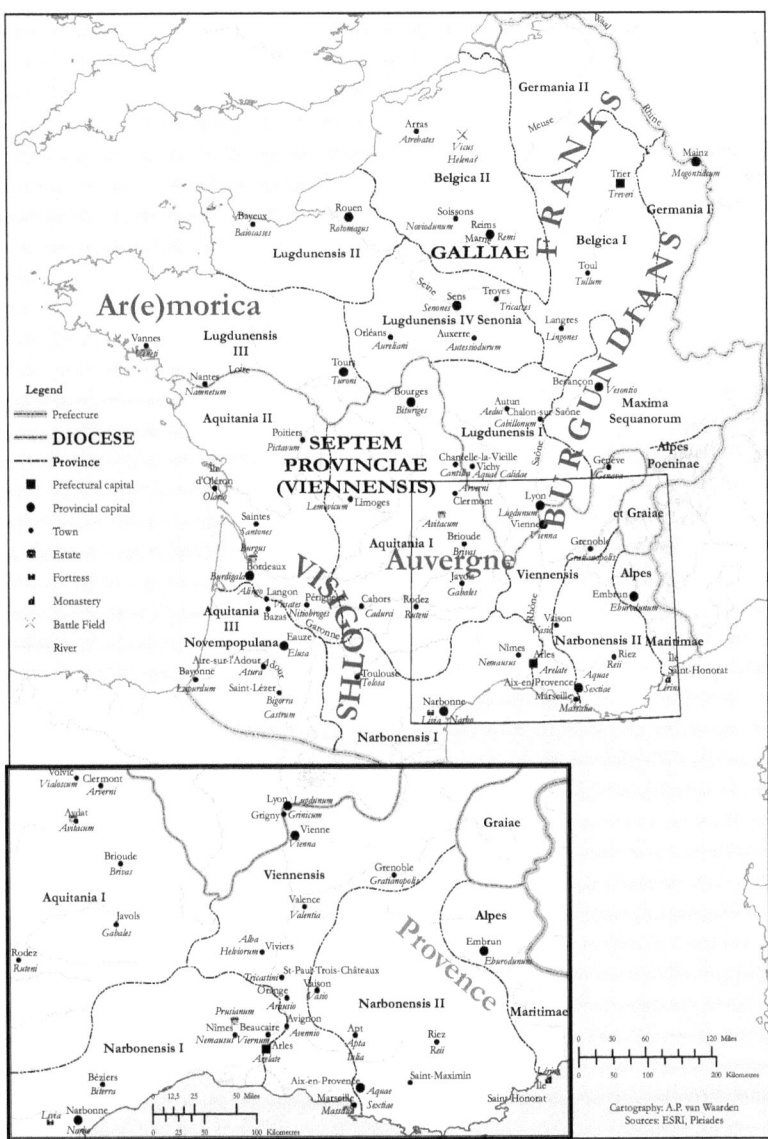

Map 1 Gaul c. 380–c. 480

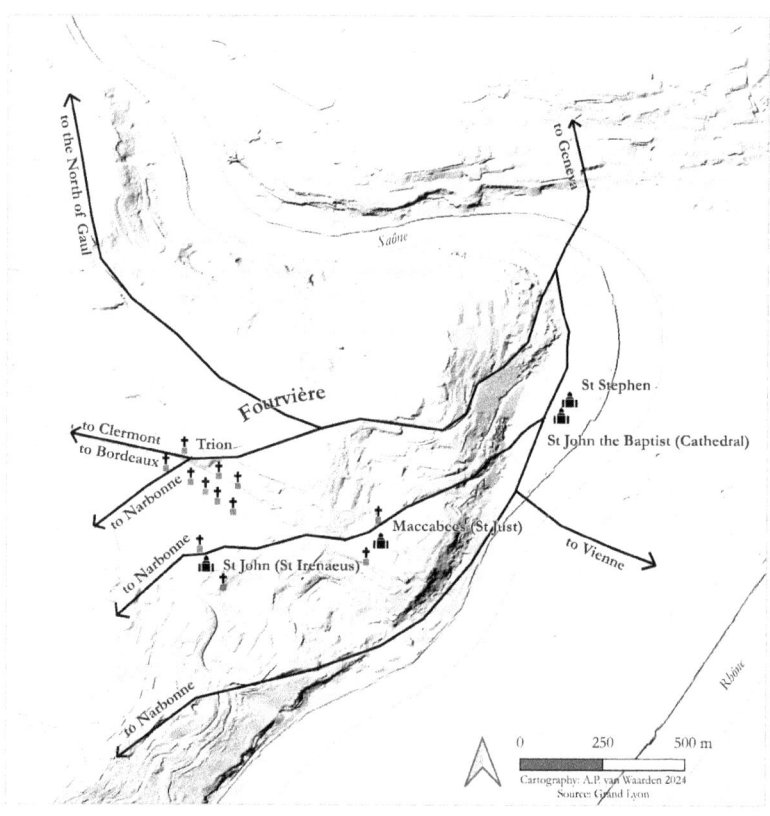

Map 2 Lyon *c*. 470 (churches, cemeteries, highways)

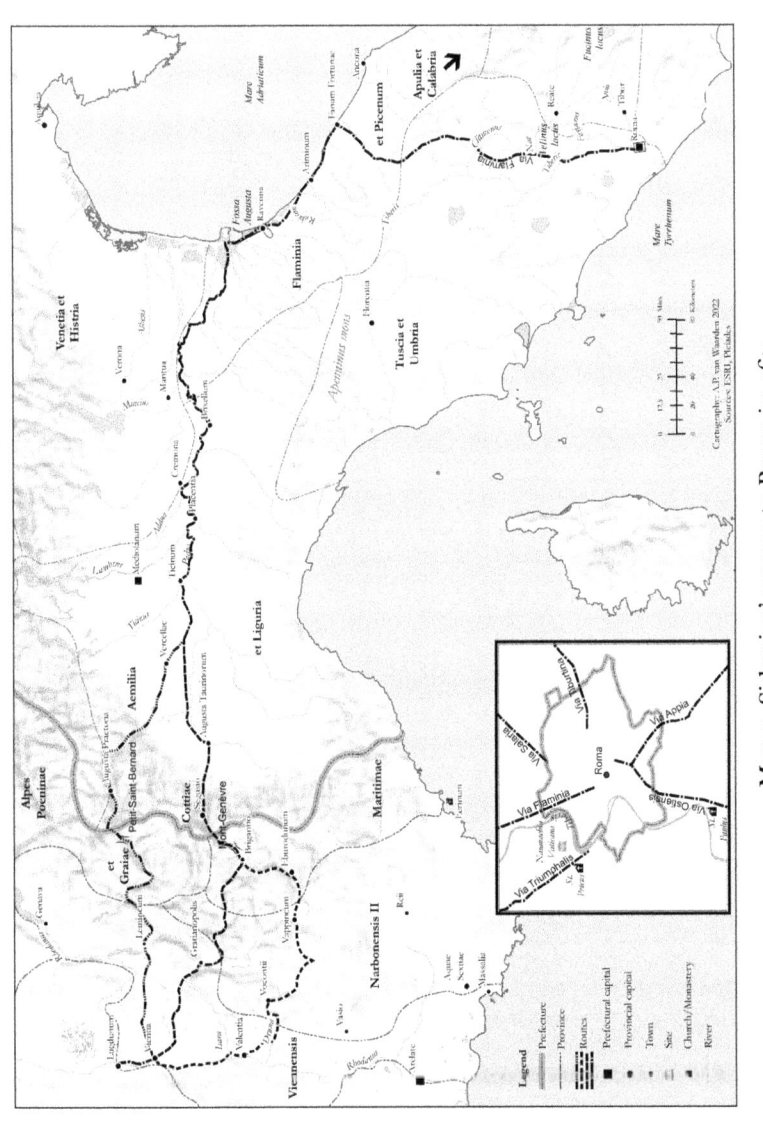

Map 3 Sidonius' voyage to Rome in 467

PREFACE

The grand arc of Latin literature, from the third century BCE to the eighteenth century CE, reached one of its highpoints in the fifth century in the oeuvre of Sidonius Apollinaris, a body of highbrow aristocratic poetry and prose on the cusp of Antiquity and the Middle Ages. His work so far was not represented in the Cambridge Greek and Latin Classics. This selection of twenty of his letters aims to offer a first introduction to his person and his world, the world of late antiquity, as well as to his virtuoso prose style, in keeping with its own time and yet tenaciously rooted in classical examples. The selection pays attention to a broad range of themes covering his career, his network, his thinking and beliefs. Gaul and Rome, Romans and 'barbarians', resistance and cooperation, prefecture and episcopate, family and friends, riches and asceticism, villas and books, pride and prejudice, despondency and hope – together, they outline a life lived to the full in turbulent times. For this, we have Sidonius' own words – no more, no less. His carefully crafted correspondence is a self-portrait and a targeted literary influencing tool. Therefore, it is important for the selection to cover the whole of it and to enable an in-depth linguistic and intertextual assessment. Picks from the letters, however, tend to privilege the customary bits. A case in point is Book 1, letter 2, about the Visigothic king Theoderic, which has been anthologized over and over again. Out of context, however, it gives a very skewed picture of Sidonius' relationship with the Visigoths. Because of this and the obviously limited size of the volume, not everybody will find their favourite letters, but I hope that the coherence of the selection will make up for this. Sidonius has certainly not been understudied in the past decades. Nevertheless, on the shoulders of giants, this commentary attempts to take a fresh look at the matter and comes up with a number of new solutions.

Warmest thanks are due to the chair holders of Latin, Marc van der Poel, sadly missed since 2022, and Bé Breij at the Department of History, Art History and Classics of Radboud University, Nijmegen, for enthusiastically providing me with an institutional home as a Research Fellow. The collections of the University Library of Amsterdam again proved inexhaustible. Over the years, many fine colleagues spoiled me with generous help, in particular Gavin Kelly and two fellow commentators of Sidonius' letters, Filomena Giannotti and Giulia Marolla. I am grateful to the perceptive readers of the draft General Introduction, Daniël den Hengst, Gavin Kelly and Stefania Santelia. The series editors, initially Philip Hardie and Stephen Oakley, then, for the greater part of the book, Philip Hardie and

Chris Whitton, made an invaluable contribution to the commentary by their learned, detailed and unrelenting comments, which certainly took it to the next level. Wherever this is not the level of perfection, that is my fault. I thank Cambridge University Press and their dedicated staff for accepting and flawlessly producing this book. My son Pieter, a land surveyor and a keen outdoor sportsman, contributed the maps and Giulia Marolla kindly permitted me to use her stemma of the MSS.

This volume of selected letters somehow feels like a conclusion to twenty years of Sidonius research. Therefore, I dedicate it to the eminent Latinists who cradled my Sidonian infancy, my former doctoral supervisors Daniël den Hengst and, unfortunately no longer among us, Jan den Boeft.

CONVENTIONS, ABBREVIATIONS AND EDITIONS

CONVENTIONS

Ancient authors and their works are cited according to the *Thesaurus Linguae Latinae*. The poems in the letters are numbered continuously from 25 to 41, in accordance with Christiansen and Holland's 1993 *Concordantia in Sidonii Apollinaris carmina*. See *The Edinburgh Companion to Sidonius Apollinaris*, pp. xiii–xiv.

In cross-references to letter-writers, the indication '*Ep.*' is left out wherever possible without creating misunderstanding, e.g. 'Plin. 1.1.1' (= Plin. *Ep.* 1.1.1), but: 'Sidon. *Carm.* 24.34–43, *Ep.* 7.12.1'. 'Sidon.' is also omitted if possible: '7.1.2' = Sidon. *Ep.* 7.1.2. The indication 'Intro', followed by a section number, refers to the General Introduction.

ABBREVIATIONS

Barrington Atlas	R. J. A. Talbert (ed.), *Barrington Atlas of the Greek and Roman World*, Princeton 2000
BEEC	D. G. Hunter, L. J. Lietaert Peerbolte, and P. van Geest (eds.), *Brill Encyclopedia of Early Christianity*, Leiden 2024
Blaise	A. Blaise and H. Chirat, *Dictionnaire latin–français des auteurs chrétiens*, Turnhout 1954
BNP	H. Cancik, M. Landfester, and H. Schneider (eds.), *Brill's New Pauly: Encyclopaedia of the Ancient World*, Leiden 2002–11
BNP Atlas	A. Wittke, E. Olshausen, and R. Szydlak (eds.), *Historical Atlas of the Ancient World*, *BNP* Suppl. 3, Leiden 2010
*CAH*² 14	Av. Cameron, B. Ward-Perkins, and M. Whitby (eds.), *The Cambridge Ancient History*, vol. 14: *Late Antiquity: Empire and Successors*, A.D. 425–600, Cambridge 2000
CC SL	*Corpus Christianorum: Series Latina*, Turnhout
CDS	*Brepols Cross Database Searchtool*, https://clt.brepolis.net/cds/pages/Search.aspx

CIL	T. Mommsen et al. (eds.), *Corpus Inscriptionum Latinarum*, 17 vols, Berlin 1863–, https://cil.bbaw.de/en/
CSEL	*Corpus Scriptorum Ecclesiasticorum Latinorum*, Vienna 1866–
DAGR	C. Daremberg and E. Saglio (eds.), *Dictionnaire des antiquités grecques et romaines*, 10 vols, Paris 1877–1919
Duchesne	L. Duchesne (ed.), *Fastes épiscopaux de l'ancienne Gaule*, 3 vols, Paris 1907–15
Forcellini	E. Forcellini, *Totius Latinitatis lexicon*, rev. G. Furlanetto and V. De-Vit, 6 vols, Prati 1858–79
Geisler	E. Geisler, 'Loci similes auctorum Sidonio anteriorum', in Lütjohann's edition, pp. 351–416
G–L	B. L. Gildersleeve and G. Lodge, *Gildersleeve's Latin Grammar*, 3rd ed., London 1895
Griffe	É. Griffe, *La Gaule chrétienne à l'époque romaine*, 3 vols, Paris 1964–6
Heumann–Seckel	H. Heumann and E. Seckel, *Handlexikon zu den Quellen des römischen Rechts*, 10th ed., Graz 1958
H–S	J. B. Hofmann and A. Szantyr, *Lateinische Syntax und Stilistik*, Munich 1965
ICVR	*Inscriptiones christianae urbis Romae*, www.edb.uniba.it/search/basic
Keil	H. Keil (ed.), *Grammatici Latini*, 8 vols, Leipzig 1855–80
K–S	R. Kühner and C. Stegmann, *Ausführliche Grammatik der lateinischen Sprache*, part 2 *Satzlehre*, 3rd ed., rev. A. Thierfelder, Leverkusen 1955
Le Blant	E.-F. Le Blant (ed.), *Inscriptions chrétiennes de la Gaule antérieures au VIIIe siècle*, 3 vols, Paris 1856–92
LRE	A. H. M. Jones, *The Later Roman Empire, 284–602: A Social, Economic and Administrative Survey*, Oxford 1964
L–S	C. T. Lewis and C. Short, *A Latin Dictionary*, Oxford 1879
LSJ	H. G. Liddell, R. Scott, and H. Stuart Jones, *A Greek–English Lexicon*, 9th ed., Oxford 1940

MGH	Monumenta Germaniae Historica: AA (Auctores antiquissimi), LL nat. Germ. (Leges nationum Germanicarum), SS rer. Merov. (Scriptores rerum Merovingicarum), Berlin 1826–, www.dmgh.de/
Niermeyer	J. F. Niermeyer and C. van de Kieft, *Mediae Latinitatis lexicon minus*, Leiden 1976
NLS	E. C. Woodcock, *A New Latin Syntax*, London 1959
OCD	T. Whitmarsh (ed.), *The Oxford Classical Dictionary*, 5th ed., https://oxfordre.com/classics/
ODCC	A. Louth (ed.), *The Oxford Dictionary of the Christian Church*, 5th ed., Oxford 2022
ODLA	O. Nicholson (ed.), *The Oxford Dictionary of Late Antiquity*, Oxford 2018
OLD	P. G. W. Glare, *Oxford Latin Dictionary*, 2nd ed., Oxford 2012
OLS	H. Pinkster, *The Oxford Latin Syntax*, vol. 1: *The Simple Clause*; vol. 2: *The Complex Sentence and Discourse*, Oxford 2015–21
ORBIS	*The Stanford Geospatial Network Model of the Roman World*, https://orbis.stanford.edu
PCBE 4	L. Pietri and M. Heijmans (eds.), *Prosopographie chrétienne du Bas-Empire*, vol. 4 *Prosopographie de la Gaule chrétienne, 314–614*, Paris 2013
Pleiades	*Pleiades: A Gazetteer of Past Places*, https://pleiades.stoa.org/home
PLRE	*The Prosopography of the Later Roman Empire*, vol. 1 A. H. M. Jones, J. R. Martindale, and J. Morris (eds.), A.D. 260–395; vol. 2 J. R. Martindale (ed.), A.D. 395–527, Cambridge 1971–80
RE	A. F. von Pauly, G. Wissowa et al. (eds.), *Paulys Realenzyklopädie der classischen Altertumswissenschaft*, 50 vols, Stuttgart 1894–1997
RGA²	H. Beck, D. Geuenich, and H. Steuer (eds.), *Reallexikon der germanischen Altertumskunde*, 2nd ed., 37 vols, Berlin, 1973–2008

RICG	H.-I. Marrou, et al. (eds.), *Recueil des inscriptions chrétiennes de la Gaule antérieures à la Renaissance carolingienne*, Paris 1975–
SEP	*Stanford Encyclopedia of Philosophy*, https://plato.stanford.edu/
Sidonius Companion	G. Kelly and J. van Waarden (eds.), *The Edinburgh Companion to Sidonius Apollinaris*, Edinburgh 2020
Sidonius website	J. van Waarden (ed.), *Sidonius Apollinaris: Your Research Companion*, https://sidonapol.org; from 1 May 2025, it is essentially continued on the Propylaeum Platform, www.propylaeum.de/themen/sidonius-apollinaris, to which it links for the various parts.
Souter	A. Souter, *A Glossary of Later Latin to 600 A.D.*, Oxford 1949
TCCG	N. Gauthier, J.-C. Picard et al. (eds.), *Topographie chrétienne des cités de Gaule des origines au milieu du VIIIe siècle*, 16 vols, Paris 1972–2023
TLL	F. Vollmer et al. (eds.), *Thesaurus Linguae Latinae*, Leipzig/Munich 1900–, https://tll-open.badw.de/de/thesaurus/lemmata

EDITIONS, TRANSLATIONS AND COMMENTARIES

For an overview of editions, see Furbetta 2020, Condorelli 2020c, 566–8 and the Sidonius website. In this commentary, references are made to the following editions:

Anderson	W. B. Anderson, W. H. Semple, and E. H. Warmington, *Sidonius: Poems and Letters*, 2 vols, Cambridge, MA, 1936–65 (with English translation)
Bellès	J. Bellès, *Sidoni Apol·linar: Lletres*, 3 vols, Barcelona 1997–9 (with Catalan translation)
Ketelaer & van Leempt	N. Ketelaer and G. van Leempt, Utrecht 1473/4 (*editio princeps*)
Loyen	A. Loyen, *Sidoine Apollinaire: Poèmes et lettres*, 3 vols, Paris 1960–70 (with French translation)

CONVENTIONS, ABBREVIATIONS AND EDITIONS

Lütjohann	C. Lütjohann et al., *Gai Sollii Apollinaris Sidonii epistulae et carmina*, MGH AA 8, Berlin 1887
Mohr	P. Mohr, *C. Sollius Apollinaris Sidonius*, Leipzig 1895
Pio	G. B. Pio, *Sidonii Apollinaris poema aureum eiusdemque epistole*, Milan 1498 (with commentary)
Savaron	J. Savaron, *Caii Sollii Apollinaris Sidonii Aruernorum episcopi opera*, 2nd ed., Paris 1599 (with commentary)
Sirmond	J. Sirmond, *Caii Sollii Apollinaris Sidonii Aruernorum episcopi opera*, 2nd ed., Paris 1652 (with commentary)

For an overview of translations, see Green 2020 and the Sidonius website. In this commentary, I refer to the above mentioned translations by Anderson, Bellès and Loyen, to those in the commentaries of Köhler 1995, Hindermann 2022b, Giannotti 2016, Amherdt 2001 (lemmas only) and Marolla 2023 (on Books 1–5 respectively) and also to Dalton 1915 (English), Köhler 2014 (German) and Mascoli 2021 (Italian) (see the Bibliography).

In cross-references, these specific editions are used:

Avitus of Vienne (Alcimus Avitus)	Peiper = R. Peiper, *Alcimi Ecdicii Auiti Viennensis episcopi opera quae supersunt*, MGH AA 6/2, Berlin 1883
	M-R = E. Malaspina and M. Reydellet, *Avit de Vienne: Lettres*, Paris 2016
Ausonius	Green = R. P. H. Green, *Ausonii opera*, Oxford 1999
Ennodius	Vogel = F. Vogel, *Magni Felicis Ennodi opera*, MGH AA 7, Berlin 1885
Fronto	vdH = M. P. J. van den Hout, *M. Cornelius Fronto: Epistulae*, Leipzig 1988
Paulinus of Nola	Hartel = W. von Hartel, *S. Pontii Meropii Paulini Nolani opera*, vol. 1 *Epistulae*, vol. 2 *Carmina*, CSEL 29–30, Vienna 1894
	Dolveck = F. Dolveck, *Paulini Nolani carmina*, CC SL 21, Turnhout 2015

GENERAL INTRODUCTION

1 BIOGRAPHY

Gaius Sollius Modestus Apollinaris Sidonius,[1] usually referred to since the Renaissance as Sidonius Apollinaris, is among the most prominent witnesses of the fifth century in Gaul. A virtuoso poet and prose writer, he combines autobiography with political influencing, nostalgia for the Roman past with promotion of the new generation, and aristocratic panache with Christian piety. In a Gaul that is being progressively lost to the Roman empire, with many Romans around him conforming to the new Germanic order, he makes carefully calibrated opposition his hallmark.[2] It is these tensions that spark his artistry.[3]

The main stages of Sidonius' life are as follows:[4]

429/32	Born in Lyon from high-ranking Gallo-Roman nobility. His father serves as *praefectus praetorio Galliarum* in 448/9, like his grandfather Apollinaris (who had been the first of his line to embrace Christianity) in 408/9. His mother is from the family of the Aviti.[5]
	Continuing his education in Arles, the capital of the prefecture of the Gauls, he forges connections with important families in Narbonne among other places.
452–5	Returns to Lyon. Marries Papianilla, daughter of the Auvergnat nobleman Eparchius Avitus, *praefectus praetorio Galliarum* 439 and instrumental, thanks to his connections with the Visigoths, in the coordinated

---

[1] In late antiquity, the *tria nomina* system was no longer the norm. While the use of *praenomina* declined, various *cognomina* were added to commemorate one's ancestors, followed by a nickname (*signum*, ending in *-ius*) and/or a personal diacritic (often a former *signum*). Sidonius went by his *nomen gentile* Sollius and by his *signum* or diacritic Sidonius; cf. 1.9.6n. *Solli meus*. See Marolla 2024, 797–801, with literature.

[2] Kulikowski 2020, 203–4 points out how, in Sidonius' lifetime, Gallo-Roman identity underwent a fundamental shift of loyalty from the Emperor to the Gothic or Burgundian kings, but Sidonius 'was never able to reconcile himself to it'.

[3] The tension styled 'Writing to Survive' in the title of my commentaries on Book 7, van Waarden 2010 and van Waarden 2016.

[4] For details, see van Waarden 2020b.

[5] For his father (called Alcimus?), see Mathisen 2020a, 134 'Anonymus 8'; for his grandfather, Mathisen 2020a, 80, and letter 3.12 in this volume with his epitaph; for his mother (Avita?), Mathisen 2020a, 128 'Anonyma 4'. For a family tree, see *PLRE* 2, 1317.

January 456	defeat of Attila's Huns in 451. The dowry includes the estate of Avitacum near Clermont.[6] Four children are known: a son Apollinaris, and the daughters Severiana, Alcima and Roscia.[7] In Rome. Recites the panegyric (*Carm.* 7) for his father-in-law, who became emperor the year before, put forward by the Gallo-Roman nobility and with Visigothic support. Rewarded with a statue in the 'poets' corner' of the Forum of Trajan. Avitus is forced out of office soon after and dies, defeated in battle by the *magister militum* Ricimer. He is buried in the family shrine of St Julian in the Auvergne.[8]
Late 458	Panegyric (*Carm.* 5) at the reception of the emperor Majorian and his troops in Lyon, after they break Gallic resistance to his government. Their personal relationship restored thanks to Majorian's policy of appeasement.[9]
460s	Period of aristocratic leisure in Lyon and at Avitacum, devoted to travelling, literary activity and preparing for baptism under the direction of Faustus, bishop of Riez.[10]
Autumn 467	Leads an Arvernian delegation to Rome to welcome the emperor Anthemius.[11]
January 468	Panegyric (*Carm.* 2) in Rome celebrating Anthemius. Subsequent promotion to the rank of *patricius* and appointed *praefectus urbi*.[12]
469	Avoids presiding over the trial for high treason of the *praefectus praetorio Galliarum* Arvandus because of conflicting loyalties to the accused and the Gallic

---

[6] Alternatively, she inherited Avitacum from her father. See below 3.3 with n. 44.

[7] For Papianilla and Roscia, see letter 5.16 in this volume; for Apollinaris, Intro 3.3 n. 46 and 5 n. 114, letters 3.12 Introduction, 7.17 Discussion, 9.16 Introduction and 9.16.1n.; for Eparchius Avitus, *Carm.* 28.1n. (in letter 3.12). See further Mathisen 2020a, also in what follows.

[8] For the panegyric, see letter 1.9 in this volume; for the statue, *Carm.* 41.25n. (in letter 9.16); for Ricimer, 1.5.10n.; for Julian, 7.1.7n.

[9] See Harries 1994, 86–95.

[10] For Faustus, see 8.3.2n. For the period of retirement from public life, Harries 1994, 103–24.

[11] See letter 1.5 in this volume.   [12] See letter 1.9 in this volume.

1 BIOGRAPHY

	plaintiffs, a reflection of divergent interests of the Auvergne and Provence.[13]
469/70	Appointed bishop of Clermont.[14]
471–5	Changing sides from Visigoths to Burgundians, fuels the resistance in Clermont against the expansion of the Visigoths under their king Euric. In 473, introduction of the ceremony of the Rogations to boost morale.[15]
Mid-475	The imperial government surrenders the Auvergne to the Visigoths.[16] Provence is overrun a year later, the end of Roman rule in Gaul.
475–6	Exiled to the fort of Livia, near Carcassonne.[17]
476/7	Pardoned with the help of the royal adviser Leo and after paying his poetic respect to Euric.[18] Reinstated as bishop in a precarious balance of power with the *comes ciuitatis*, a Visigothic appointee.[19]
479/86	Death and burial, possibly in the Church of St Saturninus in Clermont. Fragments of his tombstone were identified in 1991.[20]

In drawing up Sidonius' biography, we should always keep in mind that we largely depend on his own words and on the form in which he chose to present his output. External sources are few and he is reticent about much we would like to know, be it for political reasons or due to social conventions.[21]

---

[13] Narrated in letter 1.7. See 7.7.2n.
[14] Sidonius is silent about this nomination (Harries 1994, 15: 'a gap in the record'), but letters 5.3 and 6.1 testify to his perplexity at his new office. Letter 3.12 (see commentary) arguably signposts his departure from Lyon to start a new life in Clermont.
[15] See letter 7.1 in this volume.   [16] See letter 7.7 in this volume.
[17] See letter 8.3 in this volume.   [18] See letters 8.3 (in this volume) and 8.9.
[19] See letter 7.17 in this volume.
[20] The death date is debated. The year 479, which follows from one version of the epitaph, is probably too early. Book 9 of the correspondence was conjecturally published in 482 (see below 2.1). The *terminus ante quem* is given by Gregory of Tours, who says (*Hist.* 23) that Sidonius died *cum iam terror Francorum resonaret in his partibus*, which could point to the Battle of Soissons 486/7. On the dating problem, see Mathisen 2020c, 61–4, Kelly 2020, 188–9. The attribution of the tombstone is controversial. The full text of the (presumed) epitaph is preserved in two manuscripts. For its attribution, see van Waarden 2020b, 14–15. For its text and further reading, see the Appendix. For Sidonius and St Saturninus, *Carm.* 41.65–8n. (in letter 9.16).
[21] See van Waarden 2020b, 14–26.

2 WORKS

Sidonius himself selected and edited his work for publication as is apparent from the openings and closures of the various collections.[22]

2.1 Works That Have Come Down to Us

His oeuvre includes poetry and prose:

- 3 imperial panegyrics in hexameters in the vein of Claudian's fusion of epic and panegyric, with prefaces and dedications (*Carm.* 1–8);[23]
- 16 occasional poems in various metres (*Carm.* 9–24), ranging from short epigrams to substantial epithalamia and celebratory writing, the so-called *Carmina minora*, written in the tradition of Martial, Statius' *Siluae* and Claudian's shorter poems;[24]
- 17 more poems in the letters in various metres (*Carm.* 25–41), among them those included in this selection: an inscription for a church in Lyon (27), the epitaphs of Apollinaris the Elder (28) and of the monk Abraham (33), and the autobiographical final poem (41);[25]
- 147 letters (*Epistulae*) divided into 9 Books, in the tradition of Pliny the Younger and Symmachus – 146 by Sidonius to 106 different addressees, 1 by a correspondent (letter 4.2);[26]
- 2 more letters introducing *Carm.* 15 and 22;
- 1 speech given in Bourges in 470 when presiding over the election of its bishop (included in 7.9.5–25).

In dating the individual pieces and the collections, one should allow for a considerable margin of uncertainty, especially in the letters, which have a dramatic date, a date of writing and a date of (revised) publication. The panegyrics will have circulated separately immediately after performance (from 456 to 468) and possibly also as a group, considering

---

[22] For publishing, see below 3.3.
[23] See Stoehr-Monjou 2020 and, for their dates, Kelly 2020, 167–70.
[24] See Consolino 2020 and, for their dates, Kelly 2020, 170–7. Sidonius uses the word *epigramma* to indicate, beyond the short, witty pieces à la Martial and inscriptions, all kinds of longer occasional poetry (Mondin 2008, 467–87, Consolino 2015), in line with late antique generic experimentation (see below section 3.5; for late antique epigram, Mondin 2019). Note, in this volume, letter 4.19, an epigram in prose.
[25] See Consolino 2020 and, for their dates, Kelly 2020, 177–8. The continuous numbering 25–41 was introduced by Christiansen and Holland 1993.
[26] See Gibson 2020b and, for their dates, Loyen's 1970 edition (which is nowadays thought to be over-confident in its detailed dating), Harries 1994, 7–10, Mathisen 2013 and Kelly 2020, 179–93.

the arrangement of the dedicatory material. The *Carmina minora* have clear opening and closing poems as a collection (9 and 24), dedicated to Magnus Felix in Narbonne, and were arguably published together in the 460s.[27] A comprehensive publication in 469 of the Panegyrics, the *Carmina minora* and Book 1 (or 1 and 2) of the *Epistulae*, by means of which Sidonius accounted for his behaviour prior to the episcopate, has become something of a given in scholarship, but is not unassailable.[28] The general view of the publication of the correspondence is for Book 1 (or 1 and 2) to have been published in *c.* 469, as they contain no references to the episcopate, Books 1–7 after the return from exile in 477/8 and Books 8 and 9 individually at later dates, conjecturally 480 and 482. This chronological layout was established on internal cues, but must be qualified by artistic compositional considerations, as we will see.[29]

2.2 *Works That Were Lost or Can Be Assumed to Have Existed*

Our picture of Sidonius is one-sided because his religious output has been lost. As a bishop, he must have delivered numerous sermons, but only the stylized speech in Bourges has been preserved. Gregory of Tours says he prefaced a volume of liturgical prayers (*missae*) by Sidonius, which may be identical with the collection of prayers for which 7.3 was the cover letter. Letter 8.15 and *Carm.* 41 in letter 9.16 suggest the output of hagiography and hymns. The selected correspondence is of course a fraction of the letters he wrote during his lifetime. One quotation from such a letter has survived. Likewise, more occasional poetry – his favourite pastime and an asset in society – very probably existed, as he himself hints.[30]

---

[27] Much ingenuity has gone into refining the dating of the individual pieces and partial collections, instigated by Loyen 1, xxxi–xxxv, who saw three consecutive editions. Though incremental publication is not to be excluded (for instance with the later addition of the longish pieces 22 and 23, as surmised by Schetter 1992), Mondin 2008 has been influential in considering one single publication, lately dated to the early to mid-46os by Kelly 2020 and to 468/9 by Condorelli 2023, xxv. The MSS tradition provides no arguments either way (Dolveck 2020b, 484).
[28] For a coordinated publication, see for instance Harries 1994, 6–7 and 10 and Delaplace 2015, 245–6. Objections are raised by Kelly 2020, 167–77 and 185–93. Cf. Intro 4.1 and letter 1.1 Discussion; this letter strongly suggests Sidonius' apologetic intentions in publishing at least Book 1.
[29] See below, section 4.
[30] For details and references, see van Waarden 2020b, 17–18. For the *missae*, see Greg. Tur. *Hist.* 2.22. For letters 8.15 and 9.16, see in this volume. The quotation is to be found in Alc. Avit. *Ep.* 48 M-R (51 Peiper) (discussion in van Waarden 2020b, 16 n. 21). The hint is in Sidon. 2.8.2 *ceteris epigrammatum meorum uoluminibus* (discussion in van Waarden 2020b, 18 n. 35).

3 CONTEXT

Sidonius was a Roman and a writer in the mainstream of Latin literature, but he needs to be understood within a literary and historical paradigm that goes beyond the Roman and the classical.

3.1 Late Antiquity

Late antiquity in the Roman Empire is a half millennium of political innovation, demographic and social rearrangement, religious transformation and cultural experimentation. It is, in the words of Henri Irénée Marrou, 'a different antiquity, a different civilization', while Averil Cameron summarizes its grand project as 'remaking the past'.[31] Extending from the near-collapse of the Empire in the third century, reshaped by Diocletian's administrative reorganization resulting in a western and an eastern half, to the advent of Islam in the seventh century, it turned a crisis of identity into a creative fusion of traditional Graeco-Roman culture and the theology and ethics of unfolding Christianity – the Empire's only state-sponsored religion from the end of the fourth century. In the West, as Germanic successor kingdoms progressively ousted imperial rule (in Gaul, by the end of the fifth century), the otherness of the 'barbarians' challenged the inherited identities of the original populations. Sidonius' life took place precisely between these three poles of classical culture, a transformative worldview and the antagonistic other, within a significantly shrunken (essentially Gallic) horizon. His generation experienced an overriding feeling of belatedness as the past they revered seemed as distant as it was indispensable. Personally, however, he does not hesitate to trust in the young to carry on his legacy – the very note on which the correspondence ends.[32]

---

[31] Marrou 1977, 13 'une autre antiquité, une autre civilisation', Cameron 1999.
[32] Established as a separate field of study at least since the Second World War, late antiquity boasts a huge bibliography. For delimitation and general characteristics, see, for instance, Demandt 1997, Bowersock et al. 1999a, Inglebert 2012. The presumed 'fall of the Western Empire' has fascinated historians ever since Edward Gibbon's *Decline and Fall*. In recent years, the idea of a more or less peaceful accommodation of the newcomers has been defended by Goffart 1980, but a violent breakdown is seen by Ward-Perkins 2005 and Heather 2005. Wickham 2005 refines the picture for individual regions as these were differently affected. For an overview of theories and their ideological roots, see Demandt 1984, Lançon 2017. For the notion of belatedness, see Kulikowski 2020, 197. For the confident conclusion of the correspondence, see 9.16 Introduction.

3.2 *Politics*

For Gaul, the fifth century was a period of insecurity and change of statehood as the influx of Germanic populations solidified into independent Burgundian, Visigothic and Frankish polities. On New Year's Eve 406, Germanic tribes – among them the Vandals – crossed the Rhine and, in the ensuing years, caused havoc as they moved through the country all the way to Spain, from where the Vandals later crossed to Africa, the vital granary of Rome, capturing Carthage in 439 and developing into a naval power that sacked Rome in 455. What enabled the advance through Gaul was the weakness of the regime of the western emperor Honorius (regnal years 395–423) and a series of civil wars, especially after the execution in 408 of the strongman behind the throne, Stilicho. In Gaul, the usurper Constantine came close to legitimacy, rallying support among the Gallic aristocracy including Sidonius' grandfather Apollinaris who served as *praefectus praetorio* to his son Constans. The situation was further destabilized by another usurper, Gerontius, who exposed southern Gaul to the invaders. Meanwhile an eastern wave of Visigoths, under Alaric, threatened Milan in 402 (causing the imperial residence to be moved to Ravenna) and sacked Rome in 410. In 411, Constantine was defeated and killed by Honorius' troops led by Flavius Constantius. Gerontius committed suicide. In the same year, a Gallic aristocrat, Jovinus, was proclaimed emperor with backing from many of his peers but was suppressed by the loyal praetorian prefect of Gaul Claudius Postumus Dardanus with the help of the Visigoths in 413. A wave of revenge ensued, which most likely also took Apollinaris with it. This conflict of loyalties was to haunt the family for generations.[33] In 418, the Visigoths, with their king Theoderic, were allocated the region from Bordeaux to Toulouse, based on an alliance (*foedus*) with the Roman state, initiated by Constantius, as a buffer against the remaining invaders in Spain.

The situation in Gaul more or less cooled down while at the court in Ravenna, after a brief interlude following Honorius' death, the son of his sister Galla Placidia and Constantius, Valentinian III, was reinstalled on the throne in 425. New strongmen came with them: Bonifatius and Aëtius, of whom the latter prevailed. In southern Gaul, Theoderic became a trusted authority figure, close to Sidonius' father and his future father-in-law Eparchius Avitus among others, and an indispensable ally of Aëtius in countering the invasion of the Huns in 450. The Visigothic tryst with

---

[33] Letter 3.12 is the near-certain proof of his death, as is argued in this volume on the basis of an allusion to the parallel fate of Pompey in Lucan's *Pharsalia*. See my commentary, sections 1 and 4, and van Waarden 2024.

the Gallic nobility continued under Theoderic's successor Theoderic II (453–66/7; see 1.5 Introduction). With his support, the Gallic Council of the Seven Provinces propelled Avitus to his ephemeral, essentially usurping, emperorship in Rome in 455/6. This move exposes the enduring conflict of loyalty of the Gallic provincials vis-à-vis the central government, which, in the 470s, was to be decided in favour of their local interests, embedded in the successor Visigothic and Burgundian kingdoms.[34] The relatively stable and personally profitable political situation of Sidonius' youth goes a long way to explain his eventual fury as King Euric, from 466/7 onwards, undermined the *foedus* and worked towards an independent Visigothic polity from the Loire to the Strait of Gibraltar. As bishop of Clermont, Sidonius switched his support to the Burgundians who, based in his hometown Lyon since 456, were more obviously working within a Roman framework, with some members of the royal house acting as *magister militum*. As indicated above in Sidonius' life, a quick succession of short-lived and largely ineffective Western emperors hastened the end, among them Majorian (reigned 457–61), victim of civil war with Ricimer, Anthemius (467–72), an Easterner backed by Constantinople, whose expedition against the Vandals failed (he too defeated was by Ricimer, his son-in-law), and Julius Nepos (474–5, died 480) who negotiated a peace treaty with Euric and ceded the Auvergne. Provence followed in 476. In Italy, the general Odoacer sent the Western imperial regalia back to Constantinople, thus sealing the 'fall of the Western Empire'.[35]

3.3 Society

A few topics with particular relevance to the present selection from the correspondence may serve to illustrate the society in which Sidonius and his fellow Gallo-Romans lived.[36]

Coexistence with 'barbarians' was an overriding preoccupation. Romanized ever since Caesar's campaigns, Gallic society was now defined by the tensions created by the influx, settlement and progressive domination of newcomers. The original settlement with the Visigoths, called *hospitalitas*, provided for the billeting of immigrant troops in a number of

---

[34] See Kulikowski 2020, 203–4.
[35] For the history of the fifth century, in Gaul in particular, see Cameron and Garnsey 1997 (*CAH* 13), Cameron et al. 2000 (*CAH* 14, including Collins 2000, 112–16), Demandt 2007, Delaplace 2015, Kulikowski 2020; also van Waarden 2010, 10–14.
[36] For overviews, see Jones 1964 (*LRE*), Brown 1971b, Mratschek 2020a, Mratschek 2020b; also van Waarden 2010, 15–16.

cities and the redistribution of land in a 2:1 proportion in favour of the newcomers, though probably on a modest scale.[37] Cultural differences (habits, language, religion) were a target of condescension on the part of highly educated Romans.[38] On the other hand, the Germanic kings needed Romans to run the state, which resulted in successor kingdoms that were clearly 'sub-Roman'.[39]

Defining a hierarchical society, **social strata** were very distinct. Sidonius' own milieu of blue-blooded Gallo-Roman aristocrats, administrators, intellectuals and bishops is prominent in the correspondence. In addition we get glimpses of ordinary people like the professional crews of oarsmen on the River Po (1.5.5), a chef and his footman (2.9.6), enslaved people fleeing for protection (3.9.2), gravediggers (3.12.1), attendants in a cavalcade (4.20.1) or charioteers and barge haulers (*Carm.* 27 in 2.10.4).[40] Dependencies are interlinked in webs of patronage, both between equals (e.g. senators in 1.9, bishops in 7.1) and unequals (Sidonius writing to the slave owner in 3.9, the Jewish client in 6.11). A town's bishop will direct and protect his flock (e.g. Mamertus and Sidonius in 7.1, Sidonius in 7.7) in much the same way as noblemen had always offered their communities patronage.[41] Messengers and letter bearers, recruited across all social classes, form the connecting threads of all networks.[42]

In a male-dominated society, **women** were largely kept out of the spotlight. Their position must be teased out between the lines. In the imperial

---

[37] The nature of the treaty with the Visigoths is still controversial (for a summary, see Halsall 2007, 422–54). Goffart 1980 argued that, instead of being massively expropriated, the Roman landowners paid two-thirds of their tax levy to the Visigoths (see n. 32; cf. Collins 2000, 112). Subsequent research favours an overall more gradual balancing of Roman and Visigothic interests, e.g. Heather 1991, 221–2, Delaplace 2015, 171–83. The outcome at the end of the century was a legal situation in which the Romans had their own law-codes within the new polities (*Lex Romana Visigothorum* and *Burgundionum*); see Charles-Edwards 2000, 282–6.

[38] In this volume, see e.g. letters 4.20 and 5.5. For the 'barbarians' in Sidonius' view, see Kaufmann 1995, 79–219, Fascione 2019, Egetenmeyr 2022 (who sees them as the 'others', staged to demarcate Roman high culture, rather than as the intrinsically objectionable). For the Gallo-Roman elite's ways of coping with the consequences, see Mathisen 1993 (among them, moving eastward: see 2.9.1n. *Apollinarem*).

[39] Thus Heather 2005, 421. See letters 5.5 and 8.3 in this volume for the Romans Syagrius and Leo in their roles as royal counsellors and juridical experts.

[40] See Kaufmann 1995, 221–68, Mathisen 2020c, 64–8, Grig 2024.

[41] In post-Roman Gaul, bishops assume this once secular role (though in tandem with the king's governor, the *comes ciuitatis*; see letter 7.17), not least pressured by the loss of imperial career opportunities; see Mathisen 1989 and Mathisen 1993. Its capacity to become a decentralized legal entity was one of the crucial success factors of the Gallic Church (see Fischer and Lind 2017, 117–19).

[42] See Mratschek 2020b, 227.

age, married women remained in the legal power of their father rather than their husband. Once their father died, they were legally independent. The dowry, which could be used by their husband, remained their property.[43] We see this reflected in the estate of Avitacum, Sidonius' second home, but still Papianilla's property.[44] Within the scope of this volume, she legally shares in her husband's advancement (5.16.3) and benefits from the careers and status of her own family (5.16.3–4).[45] Other noteworthy aspects include common parental care (2.12, 5.16.5) and the role of grandmother and aunts in education (5.16.5, among other things training their little niece's *ingenium*). Reading is a gendered activity, women occupying themselves with devotional books (2.9.4). When it comes to creative writing, they are typically inspirational to their husbands, but sometimes also contribute themselves (2.10.5–6). At the other end of the social spectrum, two old Gothic women are drunk and loud, robbing Sidonius of his concentration (8.3.2).

When it comes to **elite status**, there are broadly two elites in Sidonius' days: a practical-oriented administrative elite and an intellectual elite, of which Sidonius is an iconic representative. They build on the same literary-oriented school system and are not mutually exclusive.[46] For both, office-holding is an essential gauge of status in a profoundly hierarchical society (5.16). Sidonius will hold to task anyone who neglects their

---

[43] See Harper 2012, 672.
[44] See 2.2.3 *Auitaci sumus: nomen hoc praedio, quod quia uxorium, patrio mihi dulcius*. Alternatively, the estate belonged to her as an inheritance from her father; see n. 6.
[45] For sharing status, cf. *Dig.* 1.9.8 *Feminae nuptae clarissimis personis clarissimarum personarum appellatione continentur*. This is actually a reciprocal process, as the ideal bride impersonated the best from both families (cf. 7.9.24). Papianilla's family of the Aviti was even more prestigious than the Apollinares (Harries 1994, 23–35). For the female members of the family, see Mascoli 2010, 35–45. For the legal status of women, marriage and family, see e.g. Arjava 1996, Hemelrijk 1999, 7–16, Nathan 2000, Evans-Grubbs 2009, Harper 2012. Sidonius broadly shares the mainstream classical view of women rather than the Christian misogynous tendency present in his age (see Santelia 2011).
[46] See Schwitter 2015, 80–93, John 2026, 51–2. Sidonius' son Apollinaris might be an example of the first category, to his father's disappointment. Sidonius characterizes him as *in hac* [i.e. literary matters] *certe neglegentissimus, quippe qui perexiguum lectione teneatur uel coactus uel uoluntarius* (9.1.5, in the early 480s). He is absent from the concluding letters of the collection, which are addressed to his friends and peers on whom Sidonius puts his hopes (see 9.16 Introduction and Addressee; cf. 3.12 Introduction). His further career is marked by enthusiasm for the Visigoths (Heather 2005, 420), a hazardous flight to Italy and activities as a warlord. See further Prévot 2004, Mascoli 2010, 23–33, Mathisen 2020a, 81; cf. Intro 1 n. 7 and 5 n. 114.

3 CONTEXT   11

duties to the state.⁴⁷ For the likes of him, however, culture is more than just an asset: it is the apex of humanity and the condition for the survival of *Romanitas*.⁴⁸ The prime marker of such elite status is *doctrina*, the acquired perfection of knowledge and utterance, complementing one's natural predisposition.⁴⁹ It is manifested in many ways: literary production and patronage (1.9), copying and disseminating manuscripts (8.3), participation in intellectual and literary networks, and letter writing.⁵⁰ The representation of status includes villa life (2.9, *otium* balancing *negotium*) and communal building initiatives (2.10).⁵¹

During the fourth and fifth centuries, office-holding gained added weight over birth for the aristocracy. The number of **senators** was substantially enlarged, while the equestrian order all but disappeared. The title of *clarissimus* designated the lowest rank of senator, *spectabilis* the middle tier and *illustris* the highest one, reserved for those who had held the praetorian or city prefecture or had been *magister militum*, plus the principal palatine ministers. On top of this, the former consuls and those carrying the honorific, non-hereditary title of *patricius* formed the peak of the pyramid.⁵² Coming from a family of praetorian prefects of the Gauls, Sidonius was high up in this pyramid, perfectly qualified for the level of city prefect and *patricius* that he was eventually to attain. Even so, he had to look for a patron when he arrived as an envoy in Rome (1.5), as the Senate of the City was a class of its own, in addition bolstered by the residencies of several emperors during the fifth century.⁵³

A central notion in **social conventions**, *amicitia* is the untranslatable term for the blend of business interest and personal goodwill holding together networks, regulated by an extensive code of politeness, the essence of which consists in belittling one's own worth and contribution (*uerecundia, pudor*) while magnifying the partner's stature. *Amici* have the reciprocal obligation (*officium*) of keeping the relationship alive by frequent (epistolary) contact and giving presents.⁵⁴

⁴⁷ See e.g. 1.6, 8.8.
⁴⁸ Sidonius harked back to the golden times of Trajan in particular (see Mratschek 2008) and to Roman history at large (Mratschek 2013, Mratschek 2020a), creating identity from the past.
⁴⁹ Cf. 7.9.18 *certat natura doctrinae* [in a nobleman's personality]. For the knowledge of Greek as an element of *doctrina*, see 2.9.5n. *interpretatus* and 8.3 Discussion.
⁵⁰ See John 2026, 7.
⁵¹ Incidentally, Sidonius is not known for having exercised euergetism through building (Harries 1994, 179).
⁵² See *LRE* 1, 527–35; also van Waarden 2010, 393.
⁵³ See Gillett 2001, McEvoy 2010.
⁵⁴ See Wood 2012, Mathisen 2020c, 29–42 (and, for Social Network Analysis, 68–74), Mratschek 2020b, 218–22. For the terminology of *amicitia*, Hellegouarc'h

Gift-giving is central to the functioning of late antique aristocracy and an obligation of *amicitia*. In Sidonius' correspondence – as befits a littérateur – the gifts are mainly poems included in the letters. There is also a gift of a nightcap to a monk and of books requested by friends: a copy of the *Heptateuch* sent to Ruricius along with 5.15 and of Varro's *Libri logistorici* and Eusebius' *Chronographia* and *Canones* to Namatius along with 8.6. As to his own work, he provided *Carm.* 15 with a prose cover letter, while sending a copy of his liturgical production attached to 7.3 (lost) and of his election speech in Bourges following 7.9 (extant). Entire books of letters, with their accompanying letters, went to the dedicatees Constantius (1.1n., 7.18n., 8.16), Petronius (8.1) and Firminus (9.1, 9.16n.).[55]

Publishing in antiquity was essentially a matter of starting an exponential cascade of copies and distributions of one's work within social networks. The first draft or copy would be sent to the work's dedicatee who was expected to play his part in the process, correcting scribal errors, mending verbal and stylistic lapses, and applying interpunction, followed by copying and distribution, but could also be consulted on substance.[56]

3.4 Philosophy and Religion

Late antique philosophy is largely synonymous with **Neoplatonism**, a synthesis of the ideas of Platonists, Stoics, Aristotelians and Pythagoreans.[57] Neoplatonism views the multiplicity of things as derived (emanated) from the transcendent First Principle, the One, and tainted in the process. The aim is for individual souls to return to, and ultimately reunite with, the One. Asceticism, astrology and ritual are instrumental to this end. In Sidonius' circle, the Platonist position of the incorporeality and eternity of the soul was a matter of debate.[58] He refers to his philosophical friends

---

1963, Bruggisser 1993. For *uerecundia*, see Kaster 2005, 13–27; for *pudor*, Kaster 2005, 28–65. For politeness in letter writing, below 4.2.

[55] See Williams 2014, van Waarden 2016, 183–5 with literature; also Intro 3.6. Cf. 2.12.1n. *cum piscibus*.

[56] Cf. e.g. Plin. 1.2.1 *hunc rogo ... et legas et emendas*, Sidon. 9.11.6 *aut distinctionum raritas aut frequentia barbarismorum* '[a work revised by you is certain not to contain] either a lack of interpunction or an excess of barbarisms'. The honour of receiving a dedication is also a burden: Sidon. 8.16.1 *correctionis labor ... honor editionis*. For the commonplace of asking for correction, see Janson 1964, 141–3; it developed into an independent subject of letters (Köhler 1995, 112–3); it is considered to be a polite fiction by some (Kelly 2020, 182). Further reading: Kenney 1982, 10–22, Gillett 2012, 839, Mathisen 2018, Hanaghan 2019, 171–6.

[57] See *ODLA* 1066–7 'Neoplatonism'.

[58] Mamertus Claudianus embraced it in his *De statu animae*, dedicated to Sidonius (see letters 4.2 and 4.3), whereas the latter's spiritual mentor Faustus opposed

as the 'Platonic brotherhood'.[59] Rooted in Narbonne, and boasting members such as the erudite poet Consentius and Euric's counsellor Leo, this group was particularly fascinated by the teachings ascribed to Pythagoras, uniting a mystical worldview and a modest lifestyle, embodied in the figurehead Apollonius of Tyana, whose biography Sidonius had copied for Leo from his book holdings (8.3).[60]

In Sidonius' milieu, this brand of philosophy peacefully coexisted with a non-polemical orthodox **Christianity**, tinged with asceticism and amalgamated with aristocratic pride in humility. After the emperor Constantine embraced Christianity in 312 and Theodosius I excluded pagan cult from the public sphere and established Christian orthodoxy as the only licit religious practice in the 390s, the church became a dominant factor in society, with bishops everywhere providing secular and spiritual authority on the local level.[61] In Gaul, the confrontation of the orthodox Nicene belief of the Gallo-Romans and the homoean variant of the Visigoths and Burgundians was not very virulent, although Sidonius could deploy it to confront Euric's aggression.[62] Much more pervasive was the penchant for asceticism and monasticism, and their theological underpinning, which, in Gaul, began with St Martin of Tours (d. 397). Radiating mainly to the west, his movement was paralleled in the east (Provence, Rhône corridor, Jura and Valois) by the spirituality of the island monastery of Lérins (off Cannes), founded by Honoratus (d. 429/30), followed by other aristocratic refugees. Sidonius and many of his circle, among them in the first place Faustus, who had been abbot of Lérins before he became a bishop in the late 450s, were influenced by Lérins. Its moderate asceticism suited the nobility looking for a new orientation in the troubles of the time.[63]

---

it in favour of the orthodox Christian view of the soul being created and subject to time and space. See van Waarden 2010, 18–19.

[59] *Carm.* 14.*ep.* 1 *Complatonicis tuis, Ep.* 4.11.1 *a collegio ... Complatonicorum.*

[60] See further 8.3 Discussion and van Waarden 2010, 17–19.

[61] On the role of bishops, see Rapp 2005, Lizzi Testa 2009, Gwynn 2012. For Gaul and its peculiarity of aristocratic bishops, Mathisen 1993; also van Waarden 2010, 22–4. On their interaction with the Visigoths, including exile, see Stadermann 2023. In this volume, see letters 6.11, 7.1 and 7.17 for the bishop in action. For ecclesiastical factionalism in Gaul, see Mathisen 1989.

[62] See 7.6.2 and 6, 7.8.3. Euric used it too. The Nicene creed, formulated under the auspices of Constantine, held that Christ was of the same essence (Gr.: *homoousios*) as God the Father, whereas the Germanic peoples adhered to the belief that he was 'of a similar essence' (Gr.: *homoiousios*) – a conviction that is often crudely called 'Arian'; see *ODLA* 126–7 'Arians and Homoeans in the West'.

[63] For early Gallic monasticism, also comprising the austere variant in Cassian's monastery in Marseille (cf. 2.9.5n. *ad uerbum*), see van Waarden 2016, 2–17 with literature. In this volume, see 7.17.3n. (including the development of monastic rules) and 8.15.1n. For aristocratic reorientation, Mratschek 2020b, 222–6; a

Another essential novelty was the cult of the saints and the concomitant interest in hagiography (saints' lives), combined with the attraction of relics and miracles.[64] Jews were a tolerated but disdained minority, best if converted.[65] Meanwhile, the ancient opposition of Christianity vs paganism had lost its poignancy as a cultural marker. Intellectuals could safely explore and exploit classical literature and mythology on a par with innovative Christian reading.[66]

3.5 Literature

Late antique literature lives from the paradox of harking back to the classical past – exemplary, unsurpassed – and producing anti-classical works instead – hybrid, unstable.[67] Mixing genres and tonalities, as it were creating textual mosaics from heterogeneous fragments,[68] it is a reflection of the mentality of the ages that ultimately shaped the form and extent of the classical legacy as it has come down to us, not least determined by its Christian component. Miniaturization, interpretation and metaliterariness are among its most prominent characteristics. Miniaturization is seen in the attention to word selection, in the resorting to variation and figures of parallelism, and in the fragmentation of discourse into short units of composition. A concurrent phenomenon is a preference for visual effects by means of detailed descriptions (*ekphrasis*).[69] Attention to both tradition and interpretative detail lies behind the vast output of critics, compilers and commentators of pagan as well as biblical texts.[70] Late antique writers tend to have a keen metaliterary self-awareness, manifest, for example,

---

follower of the new lifestyle was called a *conuersus*. For a general overview, Rousseau 2000. For the theological rationale, traditionally called Semipelagianism, which maintained that man, while dependent on God's grace for salvation, must still do the first step of their own free will, see *ODCC* 1481 'Semipelagianism'.

[64] See in this volume, for saints' lives, 8.15, for relics and miracles, 7.1. The seminal study is Brown 1981. For Sidonius and religion, see Bailey 2020.

[65] See 6.11.

[66] See the library described in 2.9.4–5: Augustine alongside Varro, Horace alongside Prudentius.

[67] For an introduction, see Formisano 2007, Elsner and Hernández Lobato 2017.

[68] Thus the groundbreaking observations of Jean Fontaine who coined the phrase 'mélange des genres et des tons' (Fontaine 1977).

[69] This complex of characteristics has been described by Michael Roberts, of what he called the 'jewelled style' (Roberts 1989). Rhetorical education enabled and strengthened this basic attitude.

[70] See Zetzel 2018, and, for Bible commentary (with its penchant for allegory in the wake of Origen, see 2.9.5n.), Young 1997.

in the proliferation of prefaces,[71] and indeed one of the key structural elements in Sidonius' correspondence.

In their artistic dialogue with the past, the intertextual strategy of late antique poets is distinctive.[72] In classical intertextuality, when an earlier passage is integrated in a new context, the meaning of the new passage will typically depend heavily on the earlier one.[73] In late antique poetry, however, in addition to this, there is also the possibility that an allusion is applied as a formal, decorative feature. Late antique poets can be ranged accordingly in a continuum. Sidonius' allusions often appear to go beyond mere reminiscences, which puts him at the 'classical' end of the range.[74]

3.6 Letter Writing

Letter writing in antiquity was an indispensable tool of day-to-day exchange and letter collections could enshrine the fame of their authors. Late antiquity from the fourth to the sixth centuries is the golden age of letter writing, featuring extensive collections by the likes of Libanius and John Chrysostom in the East and Symmachus and Augustine in the West, to name but a few. Looking back (in the west) on the famous correspondences of Cicero, Seneca, Pliny the Younger and Fronto in particular, wider cultivated elites, in a wave of communication among the expanding civilian and military bureaucracies across the empire, came to see collected letters as a means of creating public personae.[75] The epistolary genre is eminently flexible, serving ends as wide apart as an invitation and a theological tract. In all cases it supports the process of social bonding between sender and recipient. In collections like Sidonius', this process is taken to an elitist level as the letters' literary sophistication reflects and enhances the genius and exquisite taste of both sides.[76] Such letters sometimes contain poems, a social convention and (in terms of literary criticism) an

---

[71] See Pelttari 2014, 45–72.

[72] The same is valid for prose writers, albeit with the greater formal freedom of the genre. Cf. e.g. G. Kelly 2008, 161–221.

[73] This is Gian Biagio Conte's trailblazing 'allusion as a trope' (Conte 1986), inspired by Giorgio Pasquali's 'allusive art' (Pasquali 1942).

[74] See Pelttari 2014, Kaufmann 2017; for Sidonius in particular, Gualandri 2020, 280–3. Hardie 2019, however, questions a distinctive late antique style in poetry. For Sidonius' prose, see 4.4 below.

[75] See Sogno et al. 2017a (esp. Sogno et al. 2017b, 6–7), featuring, for Sidonius, Mratschek 2017. For an overview, also Sykutris 1931, Zelzer 1997; cf. van Waarden 2010, 30–4.

[76] Sidonius calls such letters *litterae paulo politiores* (1.1.1n.) or *litteras litteratas* (4.17.2). Pliny set the standard: Plin. 1.1.1 *epistulas, si quas paulo curatius scripsissem*. See further below 4.2.

instance of the mixture of genres.⁷⁷ This mixture may create a meaningful dialogue between both elements.⁷⁸
In ancient rhetorical handbooks, epistolography is little more than an appendix. Letters – they say – must be concise, straightforward and perspicuous (unless there is a secret), attuned to the current needs of the recipient as though talking to them. Depending on the communicative situation, different types are distinguished, such as friendly, blaming, consoling, advisory, commendatory, jesting. Covering letters accompany a piece of writing, either one's own as a gift, for revision, or a copy of a text from one's library upon request (e.g. 8.3). The *salutatio* type simply fulfils the social obligation of keeping in touch.⁷⁹

4 THE CORRESPONDENCE: A WORK OF ART AND STRATEGY

4.1 Structure and Aims of the Collection

Sidonius' body of correspondence does not exist in a void. It is an instance of senatorial correspondences in the tradition of Cicero, Pliny the Younger, Fronto and Symmachus, projecting the prestige and values of their class in writing to a large number of correspondents on a variety of subjects (familial, social, political, literary) at the height of their prestige.⁸⁰ More specifically, Sidonius draws inspiration from Pliny and Symmachus, as he states right at the beginning (1.1.1 *Quinti Symmachi rotunditatem, Gai Plinii disciplinam maturitatemque ... insecuturus*), and from Pliny in particular (4.22.2 *ego Plinio ut discipulus assurgo*). The initial seven-book unit reflects the number of books created by Symmachus and his son (the edition which Sidonius knew⁸¹), while the total of nine books is sanctioned by Pliny's example (9.1.1 *liber nonus ... eo quod Gaius Secundus, cuius nos orbitas sequi hoc opere pronuntias, paribus titulis opus*

---

⁷⁷ Sections 3.3 and 3.5 above.
⁷⁸ Letters 2.10, 3.12, 7.17 and 9.16 in this volume are cases in point. For the phenomenon, see Neger 2020, Hindermann 2022b, xxi–xxiv; cf. Pabst 1994, 310–11. See further 2.10 Discussion 'A Poem in a Letter'.
⁷⁹ For a collection of epistolary theorists, see Malherbe 1988, among them the 4th-cent. Julius Victor. A letter is one half of a dialogue (Dem. *De eloc.* 223, citing Aristotle), a voice in *amicorum colloquia absentium* (Cic. *Phil.* 2.7), and reflects the mind of the writer (see 7.18.2n.). For epistolary types, see Cugusi 1983, 106–15, Malherbe 1988, Fögen 2018, Gibson 2020b, 383–5. For adapting one's message and style to the hearer/reader and the occasion, cf. Cic. *Orat.* 123, *De orat.* 3.210, Quint. *Inst.* 11.1.4. For embedded poetry in dialogue with the context, see further 2.10 Introduction. For cover letters and gift exchange, see Intro 3.3 'Gift-Giving'.
⁸⁰ See White 2018.   ⁸¹ See Gibson 2020b, 390–1.

epistulare determinet). The grand arc of Sidonius' correspondence begins with a dedicatory letter to Constantius, 'the constant one', and ends with a valedictory epistle to Firminus, 'the firm one', imitating and, at the same time, contrasting Pliny's example, who starts with Clarus, 'clear', and ends with Fuscus, 'dark', both pairs of names beginning with C–F. However, whereas Sidonius projects steadfastness despite everything (cf. 7.18.3n. *numquam*), Pliny gives in to pessimism.[82]

Book 1 centres on Rome and Sidonius' political vicissitudes and can be seen as a defence of his work and political choices before becoming a bishop in 469 (Delaplace 2015, 245; cf. Intro 2.1 with n. 28 and letter 1.1 Discussion). Book 2 is the book of aristocratic leisure (*otium*), complementing Book 1. In Book 3, the war in Auvergne emerges with Sidonius as the defender of Clermont in his new role as bishop.[83] Together, Books 1–3 form a triad under the keywords 'career', 'leisure' and 'crisis'.[84] Books 4 and 5 address a variety of themes and make for a middle ground as, starting with Book 6, letters to bishops gain prominence. They take up the whole of Book 6, which features mainly letters of recommendation, and the first half of Book 7 (letters 1–11), which in a way is the highpoint of the collection as it fiercely exposes the abandoning of the Auvergne by the imperial government to the Visigoths. In a comforting gesture, the remainder of Book 7 explores the Christian lifestyle of laymen and monks. The last letter of the Book is addressed to Constantius and explicitly refers back to the opening letter of Book 1: the reader has in their hands what is arguably the first comprehensive 'edition' of the Correspondence in seven books.[85] Two more consecutive books complete the collection. In Book 9, poetry, which Sidonius had earlier rejected as unsuitable for a bishop, makes a conspicuous comeback and youthful addressees make for hope.[86] The final letter 9.16 takes up the dedication

---

[82] Signposting his debt to Pliny, Sidonius, in 1.1, conflates Pliny's letters 1.1, 1.2 and 1.5; see van Waarden 2022a and 1.1 Discussion. For the meaningful names, see Gibson 2011, 657–9. For Pliny's darkening mood (only relieved in Book 9 by the perspective of literary survival), see Gibson 2015. However, Fuscus stands not only for darkness, but was also a promising young man. Sidonius probably sensed this, as he ended Book 9 with letters to young Firminus and others of the next generation – a sign of continuity and hope (see the introduction to 9.16).

[83] Gibson 2012, 69 draws a parallel with Pliny's accession to the consulate in his Book 3.

[84] In the words of Hindermann 2022b, xi.

[85] See commentary on 7.18 in this volume.

[86] See 9.12.1 *ab exordio religiosae professionis huic principaliter exercitio* [i.e. writing verse] *renuntiaui* (the *leuitas uersuum* is not in keeping with the *grauitas actionum*) and 2 *in silentio decurri tres olympiadas* (which, incidentally, dates the letter to twelve years from the beginning of his episcopate, to *c*. 482). This 'silence' may have

to Constantius and subsumes the entire nine-book collection.[87] Although Sidonius frames both Book 8 and 9 as additions made upon request,[88] it is not improbable that, for artistic reasons, he had eyed these later moves from the very beginning. It has even been argued that these are two false closures imitating Pliny.[89]

Within individual books, patterning, apart from catering for variety,[90] creates meaningful subplots. For instance, in Book 1, three letters stressing the importance of public service (nos 3, 4 and 6) dovetail with two on Sidonius' journey to Rome (5 and 9) and, in Book 7, letters concerning the ideal bishop (4) and the case in point of such a nomination (5, 8 and 9) surrounding the letters on Sidonius' defence of Clermont and its demise (6 and 7).[91]

Individual letters were adapted for publication or even written specially for the collection.[92] Sidonius' meticulous capitalization on the concept of 'books'/scrolls (at a time when the codex had made such subdivisions superfluous) stands out when compared to, for instance, Jerome, Augustine and Paulinus of Nola whose letter collections had no canonical ordering in late antiquity.[93] The artistic rationale is akin to the meaningful structure of the Augustan poetry book, emulated by Pliny as well.[94]

Strategy – whether in maintaining *amicitia* and family relationships or in wielding political influence – is a pervasive aim of the correspondence. Self-fashioning is an important means to this end, such as (as illustrated in this volume) Sidonius the career man at the imperial court (1.5, 1.9), the

---

been consciously modelled on the *interuallum lyricum* between Horace's first three and fourth book of *Odes* (Egelhaaf-Gaiser 2010, 268–9). Already Book 8 contains two occasional poems. For the youthful addressees, see Intro 3.1 and letter 9.16 Introduction.

[87] See commentary in this volume. [88] See 8.1.1 and 9.1.1.

[89] For the former idea, see Kelly 2020, 187, for the latter, Gibson 2013, who re-evaluates his argument at Gibson 2020b, 390.

[90] *Varietas* of themes and moods is a leading principle both for portraying the author and to make for entertaining reading. See 1.1.n. *uaria occasione*, 2.9.6n. *uarietur*, 7.18.2n. *uarios ... motus ... hortando* etc.; cf. 9.11.3 *uario ... congestu*; on keeping the reader's attention: 7.18.4n. *ante legere cessabis quam lecturire desistas*. For *uarietas*, see Fitzgerald 2016; for the overarching idea of *concordia discors* (unity in variety) and the jewelled style as its literary embodiment, see Roberts 1989, 144–6. Cf. Pliny's requirement of a good collection of poetry: Plin. 4.14.3 *ipsa uarietate temptamus efficere, ut alia aliis quaedam fortasse omnibus placeant* and Auson. *Epigr.* 1.1–4 Green *Non unus uitae color est nec carminis unus | lector: habet tempus pagina quaeque suum. | ... laetis | seria miscuimus.*

[91] See Harries 1994, 13 and 16; in this volume, the commentary on letters 1.5/1.9 and 7.7. In contrast with this allusive take on the collection, Mathisen 2013 defends an ordering based on 'dossiers' and 'dockets' in Sidonius' archive.

[92] See Kelly 2020, 181–5. [93] See Gibson 2012.

[94] See Gibson 2020, 375; cf. above n. 90.

family man (2.9, 2.12, 3.12), the versatile littérateur (2.10, 8.15, 9.16), the champion of Roman culture (5.5), the effective bishop (7.1, 7.7), the pious Christian (7.17) and the victim of barbarian ascendency (8.3). The alternately smooth and convoluted style, in all its aspects of 'coded communication',[95] heightens the elite sense of belonging together and serves the diplomatic aim of blurring or hiding the inopportune.[96]

4.2 Epistolary Conventions and Politeness

As indicated above,[97] the principal lubricant in social intercourse in Sidonius' hierarchical world is for people, albeit fully aware of their own and their interlocutor's ranks and worth, to be overly modest themselves and extol the other. Politeness determines epistolary conventions.[98] Here are some recurrent conventions in the letters:

As to **address and valedictory lines** (*inscriptio* and *subscriptio*), Sidonius' greeting formula is invariably of the type *Sidonius Constantio suo salutem* (1.1) to laymen and *Sidonius domino papae Mamerto salutem* (7.1) to bishops. He possibly shortened and normalized the headings across the collection as, in his day, longer formulas were the rule, including the addressee's full titles and qualifications. The greeting tags are *uale* and *memor nostri esse dignare, domine papa* 'be so kind as to remember me, lord bishop', respectively. In the body of the text further markers are *domine fili, domine frater* and *domine maior*, for a younger, an equal and a senior person respectively, *domine* identifying the person concerned as a member of the senatorial aristocracy.[99]

Sidonius has a specific way of handling the first and second persons singular and plural to manage the dialogical situation, the **'you' and 'I'**. He will use the singular (*ego, tu*; also possessive pronouns and the finite verb) to fill the foreground of the scene, whereas the plural (*nos, uos*) projects the same persons ('I', 'you') into the background. The singular is direct and active, suggesting responsibility and certainty, whereas the plural is indirect and passive, making for non-responsibility and doubt. The choice is subjective, although objective data such as the addressee's rank and the closeness or distance of the relationship play a role. A letter

---

[95] See below, section 4.2.
[96] Which he describes with the words *praesentia semiplene ... dicuntur* (4.22.5). For examples, see Schwitter 2015, 259–80.
[97] Section 3.3.
[98] For politeness theory, see Brown and Levinson 1987, summarized in van Waarden 2020e, 422–3.
[99] For *papa*, see also 2.10.2n. For instances of *domine*, 1.1.1n., 7.17.1n., 9.16.1n. For forms of address, see Dickey 2002.

to relatives will normally use straightforward *ego* and *tu*. In a letter of apology, the sender will modestly 'hide' behind a plural (*nos*), while giving the recipient a generous *tu* (e.g. 4.19). Literary matters also trigger this constellation (e.g. 1.9.7 *collata uestris mea carmina*: the addressee's poetry is obviously *hors concours* and must be spared the comparison with Sidonius' poems). In letters between bishops, a complex alternation, within one and the same letter, of *ego/nos* and *tu/uos* will negotiate the hurdles of piety and authority.[100]

In dedicatory and covering letters as well as in letters containing a poem, the author stresses (or pretends) that he wrote the book or poem in obedience to the addressee's order, or else apologizes for not being able to comply with the request (e.g. 8.15) – the so-called ***iubes–pareo*** motif.[101]

The message of the letters is often aesthetically wrapped up or pragmatically concealed. The late antique elite fashion of *obscuritas*, often dubbed '**coded communication**', especially in evidence in epistolography, is two-sided. It serves the purpose of enhancing social cohesion among an educated in-crowd (e.g. 1.9.1n. *aenigmata*, praising the host for making his statements satisfying by complicating them). It also enables criticism, whenever free speech is inhibited by political pressure (e.g. 1.1.2, where a seemingly otiose discussion of the history of rhetoric hides Sidonius' nonconformism; 7.17.2, where one reads his displeasure as an official between the lines; 8.3.5, which can be interpreted as a mirror of princes indirectly held up to Euric).[102]

4.3 Text Linguistics and Narratology

The conventions discussed in the previous section, linguistically speaking, belong to the domain of **pragmatics**, the branch of **text** (or **discourse**) **linguistics** studying how textual elements are embedded in the situational context and how context contributes to meaning. Text linguistics is broadly concerned with text as an information structure, as communication.

In this commentary, attention is also given to word order and particles. **Word order** as a communicative tool creates 'topic' and 'focus' in a clause. Topic is the element about which the clause is going to provide

---

[100] Outside the selection in this volume: see examples in van Waarden 2010, 588–9. For full discussion, see van Waarden 2020e (for the diachronic perspective, also van Waarden 2021 and van Waarden 2023).
[101] See Janson 1964, 116–19.
[102] See Harries 1994, 11–19, van Waarden 2010, 39–40 and 61–6, Schwitter 2015, 126–297. See also 4.1 above.

information, while focus is this very information, characterized by its relevance and 'newness'. The first position in the clause is typical for topics (though certainly not exclusively). See e.g. 4.20.1 *illum ... equi ... antecedebant*: *illum* is existing information (referring back to prince Sigismer), becoming topic of the new sentence, and *equi antecedebant* is new information (focus) about Sigismer. The opposite is also seen, e.g. 2.12.2 *ipsa uegetatio* in last position as topic (Severiana's illness), preceded by the new information of prayers for her well-being. Both topic and focus elements can be contrasted, e.g. the contrastive topic in 2.9.2 *praediorum ... hospitalitatis* ('enough of the estates: let's now talk hospitality') and contrastive focus in 8.3.2 *philosophi uitae* (topic) *scriptor ... lector*. An important means of creating contrast and emphasis is hyperbaton (also called 'discontinuity'), often in combination with placing the contrastive or emphasized element in an early position ('fronting'), e.g. 7.18.2 *commendo igitur uarios iudicio tuo nostri pectoris motus*. Other topics include the order of noun and adjective in a noun phrase, which may be significant, e.g. 1.5.2 *publicus cursus* (see n.). A finite verb in first position (verb initial) serves to mark (immediate) progress, e.g. 1.9.3 *parui ego praeceptis*.

Besides serving communicative goals, word order is also determined by artistic factors, among them the increasingly pronounced tendency to end a sentence by bringing forward the verb form, creating so-called verbal hyperbaton, e.g. 1.5.1 *fideliore didicisse memoratu*, 7.1.1 *importuna deuorauit impressio*.[103]

Particles help to establish text cohesion as well as communication. Particles highlighted in the commentary include, among others, *nam(que)* and *enim* (the former giving subsidiary information or introducing a new topic, the latter involving the addressee's judgement), *uidelicet* and *scilicet* (factual evidence vs intersubjective conclusion), *quippe* (developing from explanatory to connective), *autem* (providing background information or a new consideration) and *tamen* (developing from contrast to continuation).[104]

Key structures of **narrative**, such as the relationship narrator–narratee (who tells to whom?), focalization (from whose point of view is the story told?), time and space, underpin the letters' development and their mutual coherence.[105] The **narrator** is not necessarily identical with the author. In 7.7.1, the story of the plight of Clermont is framed as a

---

[103] For word order, see *OLS* 2, 948–1137; for topic/focus and contrast/emphasis, ibid. 829–65.

[104] For particles, see *OLS* 2, 1164–1216, Kroon 1995, Schrickx 2011.

[105] See the innovative publication Hanaghan 2019. For an introduction to narratology and classics, see de Jong 2014.

messenger tale by Sidonius' intermediary, who is normally associated with fun. The tragedy is all the more poignant for it. In 7.1.3–6, the alarming events in Vienne are told as the result of information, understandably so, as the **narratee** is the bishop of Vienne himself. In 7.17.1, interpretative 'telling' is preferred over 'showing' in a direct way. **Focalization** is explicitly addressed in 1.5.1 as preference is given to autopsy (by the narrator) over bookish knowledge (by the narratee). In 7.18.2, a subjunctive signposts the perspective of the narrator. **Time** has two different aspects. Firstly, manipulating the ratio of story time (the time the events take) vs discourse time (the time telling takes), the narrator speeds up or slows down tempo, influencing the perception of the narratee. Secondly – an aspect specific for letters – epistolary time has three interrelated layers: the moment the events took place (the dramatic date), the moment of writing and the moment of reading. This is further complicated by the moment of publication (entailing revision) and the intended readership (the primary and secondary readers of the original letters and the readers of the letter collection). Dating individual letters is consequently a slippery undertaking.[106] **Space** may be more than background. In 1.5, the spatial dimension of the journey to Rome creates a psychological envelope for Sidonius' self-understanding. In 4.20, the description of the parade visualizes the consequences of admiring the barbarians.

4.4 Intertextuality

Anchored in tradition, Sidonius must be read with ears open to a host of hypotexts. His poetry relies in varying degrees on Catullus, Virgil, Horace, Ovid, Lucan, Martial, Statius, Juvenal, Ausonius, Claudian and Prudentius. In the correspondence, intertextuality, though unmistakable, is sparser and it is not always easy to judge its contribution to the creation of meaning.[107] Pliny the Younger and Symmachus are always present for style and composition. Plautus and Terence supply archaic language, which is both a recherché treat for the literary in-crowd and a narrative means of creating comic effects. Back-reaching encyclopaedism (Varro, first century BCE) and the archaizing second-century trend CE (Fronto, Apuleius, Gellius) serve as cultural anchors. Occasional glimmers of Cicero, Sallust, Livy and Suetonius are less essential than recurrence to epic, Lucan in particular. Finally, the Bible is an important point of reference.[108] In the selection

---

[106] For an example of epistolary time, the writer anticipating the reader's reaction, see 2.12. For dating, see Kelly 2020, 179–85.
[107] See the general discussion in 3.5 above.
[108] For Sidonius' intertextuality, see Gualandri 2020. For Pliny and Symmachus,

4 THE CORRESPONDENCE

in this volume, allusions are particularly essential in letters 1.1 and 7.18 (Statius and Pliny for prefatory material), 1.5 (a travelogue inspired by Horace, including allusions to Virgil, Martial, Pliny and Claudian), 2.9 (the biblical story of Tobias and his cousins), 2.10 (in *Carm.* 27, where Martial sets the scene), 3.12 (where Lucan furnishes the clue to deciphering the letter), 4.20 (a possible allusion to the Vicus Helena carnage via Martial), 7.1 (Lucan for framing the war with the Visigoths), 7.7 (again Lucan and also Silius Italicus), 7.17 (Ausonius and Horace in the embedded *Carm.* 33), 7.18 (Pliny for the variety of emotions in letter writing), 8.3 (touches of Pliny and a conclusion referring to Livy), 9.16 (Pliny for the letter's season and addressee, Horace and Prudentius for the equilibrium prose–poetry, and Horace, Ovid and Prudentius in the embedded *Carm.* 41; the letter's last words are a silent salute to Cicero).

4.5 Vocabulary, Syntax and Style

When Sidonius' lifelong friend from Vienne, the priest Mamertus Claudianus, dedicated his *De statu animae* to Sidonius, he addressed him not only by his full titles and qualifications, *praefectorio patricio doctissimo et optimo*, but also with the specific claim to fame *ueteris reparator eloquentiae* (*Anim.* praef.). Thus, a contemporary acknowledges Sidonius' genius for restoring the Latin language to its old lustre. His syntax is almost wholly classical, and prose rhythm as well as versification adhere to hallowed standards.[109] In word choice and word formation, his 'restoration' draws on the **archaizing** tendency of the age which, paradoxically, inspires him to invent freely what he needs.[110] His stylistic palette is extensive and essentially bipartite: **smoothness** and regularity on the one hand, **complexity** and irregularity on the other. The main feature of the first category is sequencing: the stringing together of parallel words, phrases or clauses (*cola*), in principle of the same length (*isocolon*). At their most compact, such sequences consist in strings of words (verbs, nouns, names, adjectives or adverbs) in pairs or triplets, optionally combined into higher order (often asyndetic) pairs or triplets: 8.3.2 *litigiosius bibacius uomacius*, 1.5.10 *theatra macella, praetoria fora, templa gymnasia*. This develops into composite

---

also Gibson 2020b, 389–91. For Sidonius' archaisms, Wolff 2020, 402; for second-century archaism, *OCD* 'Archaism in Latin', Holford-Strevens 2003.

[109] For syntax, see Wolff 2020, 397, for prose rhythm, van Waarden and Kelly 2020, for versification, Condorelli 2020a.

[110] For vocabulary (neologisms, hapax legomena, archaic words, etc.), see Gualandri 1979, 143–81, Wolff 2020, 397–405. Cf. Sidonius' own appraisal of these new-old words: *noua … uerba quia uetusta* (4.3.3).

lists of the type 1.5.1 *fluuios ... poetarum carminibus illustres aut urbes moenium situ inclitas aut montes numinum opinione uulgatos aut campos proeliorum replicatione monstrabiles.* Parallel clauses are the most extensive manifestation, e.g. 7.1.5 *indicis ieiunia interdicis flagitia, supplicia praedicis remedia promittis.* Essential features of this style include polyptoton (the same word or root in different forms), paronomasia (cognate or similar words), alliteration, assonance, homoeoteleuton ((near) rhyme). Parallelism is varied by means of chiasmus, equal *cola* length by diversifying the last member. There is an overall effect of redundancy and formulaic recycling.[111]

Regularity is offset by complexity, for instance in the opening sentence of 5.1 where a long, winding introduction serves to take the addressee off guard by the straightforward conclusion. Another example is the description of the plight of Clermont's defenders (7.7.3). After an opening in the 'regular' style, it unfolds the full extent of their despair in a labyrinthine conceit. The 'irregular' style is the prime means of putting the reader on edge.

Irregularity is connected with a tendency towards **hyperbole** and 'manneristic' extremes in sentiment and expression, and – in general – the tension between the poignancy of an episode and the elegance of its wording (e.g. 1.5.7n., 2.12.3n., 2.9.10n., 7.1.2n., 7.7.3n.).[112]

Sidonius' prose is consistently **rhythmical**, with varying emphasis but few exceptions.[113] Most later Latin art prose adopts a system in between the classic metrical clause endings (*clausulae*) and the accentual system

---

[111] For style, see van Waarden 2010, 55–9 and Wolff 2020, 405–15. 'Smoothness' in rhetoric goes back to the fifth century BCE: see Sloane 2001 'Gorgianic figures'. For an overview of figures of style, see e.g. Rowe 2001. For an overview of the compact type of sequences, see van Waarden 2010, 570–5. The so-called 'law of rising members' describes the tendency for enumerations to have shorter constituents first and end with (a) longer one(s), e.g. 7.2.7 *solus tenuis peregrinus*, 7.1.2n. *aut ambustam murorum faciem aut putrem sudium cratem aut propugnacula uigilum trita pectoribus*, and 1.1.1n., 1.5.10n., 2.9.6n. (the opposite also occurs to surprise effect). A few examples among many of verbal abundance (redundancy) include 2.9.6 *insitum institutumque*, 2.9.9 *salsis iocularibusque*, 8.3.6 *metimur aestimamusque*.

[112] See Gualandri 1979, 35–74. 'Manneristic' denotes stylized exaggeration; the term mannerism is used in particular in art history to label the 16th-cent. style of painting and sculpture, which broke with the poise and naturalism of the Renaissance.

[113] For prose rhythm, see van Waarden and Kelly 2020. The commentary points out some special, potentially meaningful cases. The order shown is based on a complete inventory of clause and sentence endings (before comma, (semi)colon and full stop; n=590) in the letters in this selection. Oberhelman's requirements for prose to be intentionally metrical are almost met for the proportion of the four standard classical clausulae (60%; indicated with an * in the following table) and amply so for all types of clausula together (almost 100%).

that would be used in the Middle Ages (*cursus*). Sidonius is much closer to the former than most of his contemporaries. His preferred rhythms, together covering more than four-fifths of cases, include:

* cretic + spondee	–⌣– –×	28%
paeon IV/choriamb + spondee	⌣⌣⌣– –×	17% (12% and 5% resp.)
* double trochee	–⌣ –×	13%
* double cretic	–⌣– –⌣×	12%
* cretic + tribrach	–⌣– ⌣⌣×	7%
paeon I + spondee	–⌣⌣⌣ –×	6%

5 AFTERLIFE

The first posthumous traces of Sidonius occur in the fifth-/sixth-century correspondences of his slightly younger friend Ruricius of Limoges and of the next generation, his nephew (?) Alcimus Avitus of Vienne and his more distant kinsman Ennodius of Pavia.[114] In his late-sixth-century *Histories*, Gregory of Tours, himself a native of Clermont, repeatedly drew on Sidonius' correspondence in his account of the latter's life.[115] Sidonius as a letter writer had a distinct impact on the Middle Ages, with his works represented in libraries in ever increasing numbers. Although he was already a traceable influence in the ninth century, his heyday came at the outset of the High Middle Ages, during the so-called 'Renaissance of the twelfth century', which saw a surge in the study of Latin classics in the cathedral schools of Chartres and Canterbury, among others. Sidonius was imitated for his ornate style and was mined for moral examples.[116] In fourteenth- to sixteenth-century Renaissance humanism, Sidonius – and late antique taste in general – became controversial in the competition with Ciceronianism. Petrarch acknowledged his 'boldness', but misunderstood Sidonius' attitude towards Cicero.[117] Eclecticists, however, embraced him, notably Coluccio Salutati, chancellor of Florence in the late fourteenth

---

[114] All three men corresponded with Sidonius' son Apollinaris (see Intro 1 n.7 and 3.3 n. 46). Sidonius himself and Ruricius had been correspondents (see Mathisen 1999, 114–20) and Sidonius had written the latter's epithalamium (*Carm.* 10–11). For details of this first stage of Sidonius' reception (including the partial index of his letters in the Codex Sangallensis 190), see Furbetta 2013, 41–65, Mathisen 2020b.

[115] Greg. Tur. *Hist.* 2.21–5, also *Iul.* 3, *Vit. patr.* 3. See Mathisen 2020b, 633–5; in this volume, 7.1.7n. and 7.17 Discussion.

[116] For Sidonius in the Middle Ages, see Chronopoulos 2020 and Hernández Lobato 2020, 665–71, with literature. For a multifaceted appraisal of the 'long twelfth century', see Noble and Van Engen 2011.

[117] See in this volume, 1.1.2n.

century, and the late fifteenth-century School of Bologna, represented by Filippo Beroaldo and his student Giovan Battista Pio (*c.* 1475–1540), who put out the first commented edition in print.[118] After that Sidonius fades as a literary point of reference, only to become a landmark for historians. Two French editions with important commentaries are a monument to this new role, one by the Clermontois magistrate Jean Savaron (second, enlarged edition 1599), which places the emphasis on interpretation with constant attention to his sources, the other by the Jesuit priest Jacques Sirmond (1614), mainly geared towards history and prosopography.[119] Never entirely absent in the intervening centuries, Sidonius nowadays enjoys a twofold popularity. On the one hand, he is prominent in scholarship as a beneficiary of the comeback of late antiquity since the 1970s, on the other he is a rewarding subject for fiction on whom to project feelings of decadence and decline, cast among 'the last of the Romans'.[120]

6 MANUSCRIPT TRADITION AND TEXT

The study of the manuscript tradition of Sidonius has two pivotal points. The first is Christian Lütjohann's 1887 edition in the *Monumenta Germaniae Historica*, the second Franz Dolveck's extensive revision and new stemma in the 2020 *Edinburgh Companion to Sidonius Apollinaris*. In this volume, I follow Dolveck's lead.

We possess over a hundred witnesses of Sidonius' work – seventy-seven MSS when we exclude anthologies and fragments – which makes him a well-diffused author, but the situation differs from period to period. All MSS in existence must have had one common archetype (Dolveck calls it the *Ur-Archetyp*), tentatively datable to the seventh or eighth century, which contained both his letters and his poetry, but did not necessarily reflect Sidonius' own take on the composition of the corpus. Later splits in the tradition also generated separate MSS of the *Epistulae* or the *Carmina*. The oldest MSS known to us were written in the ninth century,[121] while the rich production of the twelfth century yields no fewer than fifty MSS.[122]

---

[118] For Humanism and Sidonius, see Hernández Lobato 2020, 671–85, with literature. Pio's edition was printed in Milan in 1498, a quarter century after the *editio princeps* (text only) curated by Nicolaes Ketelaer and Geraert van Leempt (Utrecht, 1473/4).

[119] For links to editions which can be accessed online, see the Sidonius website.

[120] For early modern to contemporary reception, see van Waarden 2020d and Giannotti 2020. For scholarship, Furbetta 2020 and Condorelli 2020c.

[121] ***L*** preserved in Oxford and ***R*** in Reims: see n. 123.

[122] For links to manuscripts which can be accessed online, see the Sidonius website.

6 MANUSCRIPT TRADITION AND TEXT

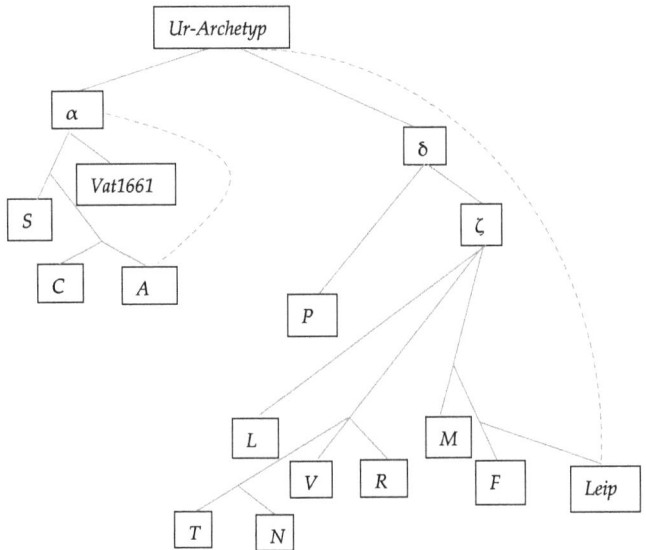

Figure 1 Dolveck's stemma, simplified (according to Marolla 2023, 19).

The stemma of the letters is bipartite. We are concerned with an α-branch, recognizable by its specific ordering of Book 7 (*Vat1661*, important though late, and *SCA*), and a δ-branch. Within the δ-branch, *P* occupies a prominent place. Sub-branches of δ include the so-called 'fourth family' (*L* and *VRTN*) and *MFLeip*. Both *A* and *Leip* preserve older readings thanks to edits. As a rule of thumb, if a reading in α agrees with *P* (or *PL*), it is the reading of the archetype.[123]

The Latin text in this volume is based on Lütjohann's seminal edition, reconsidered in the light of Dolveck's stemma. The following table documents the differences and the MS support. The aim is to approximate the

---

[123] Branch α: *Vat1661* = Vatican Library Vat. lat. 1661 (#69 in Dolveck's census, Dolveck 2020a, late 12th/early 13th cent.), *S* = Paris, IRHT private collection 347 (#53, formerly Schøyen collection, second half 12th), *C* = Madrid, National Library 9448 (#25, second half 11th), *A* = Vat. lat. 3421 (#71, 11th). Branch δ: *P* = Paris, National Library Par. lat. 2781 (#43, late 10th), *L* = Oxford, Bodleian Library Laud. lat. 104 (#37, first half 9th), *V* = Vat. lat. 1783 (#70, 10th/early 11th), *T* = Florence, Medicean Library Plut. 45.23 (#13, 12th), *R* = Reims, Municipal Library 413 (#56, 9th), *N* = Paris, Par. lat. 18584 (#52, 10th), *M* = Florence, S. Marco 554 (#16, second half 11th), *F* = Paris, Par. lat. 9551 (#49, 13th), *Leip* = Leipzig, University Library Rep. I 48 (#21, late 12th or 13th).

Ur-Archetyp as closely as possible. The text is deliberately conservative and avoids conjectures that go beyond this archetype.[124]

	Van Waarden	Lütjohann
1.1.2	silere me in stilo epistulari melius puto, quem δ	silere melius puto, quem in stilo epistulari *Wilamowitz*
1.1.3	\<lucubratiunculas\> *Leip in margine*	\<litterulas\>
1.1.4	anchora *codd.*	ancora
1.1.4	scaturientia *codd.* (sca turpentia *L*)	scaturrientia
1.5.1	nominum *codd.*	numinum *Wilamowitz*
1.5.5	Padi certa, pars *codd. plerique*	Padi, † certa pars
1.5.6	hic cum *codd.*	hic [cum]
1.5.6	lintrium *codd. plerique*	lyntrium *L*
1.5.8	Fucini *P¹LVRTM*	Velini *Mommsen*
1.5.9	diuersorii α*P alii plerique*	deuorsorii
1.9.1	eo *codd. plerique*	eodem *M²T¹*
1.9.6	*nullam lacunam ante quamquam indicant codd. nisi L*	\<agedum\> *Wilamowitz*
1.9.7	ipsas *codd.*	istas
2.9.5	sermocinabantur α	sermocinabamur δ
2.9.6	parapsidibus *codd.* (-bs- *LM*)	paropsidibus
2.9.7	diuersorium *codd.*	deuorsorium
2.9.7	nuncupatur α*PM*	nuncupabatur *LeipFT*
2.10.6	rem oratoriam *codd. plerique N¹*	oratoriam *LN*
3.12.1	sed tamen *codd.*	sed iam

[124] The MSS almost always assimilate prefixes (e.g. 1.1.2 *illustrium*, 1.9.7 *collata*), which is reflected in this volume (for a single exception, see 8.15.2n. *inreposcibile*). Lütjohann creates an ahistorical situation by assuming *inlustrium, conlata*, etc. throughout (these differences are not listed below); cf. Quint. *Inst.* 1.7.7 and the ancient writers on orthography (Keil vol. 7). In the list, a superscript 1 (e.g. *P¹*) indicates a correction by the first-hand scribe, a superscipt 2 (e.g. *M²*) a correction by a second hand.

6 MANUSCRIPT TRADITION AND TEXT

	Van Waarden	Lütjohann
3.12.2	et superueni *codd.*	superueni
4.20.1	arma et armatum et armatos *codd. plerique*	arma et armatos *L*
4.20.1	conciperes *codd. plerique*	conceperas *LRN*
4.20.1	inspiciebatur *codd. plerique N¹*	conspiciebatur *LVRN*
5.5.2	Harilao *LR¹TN Heraeus*	† harilao
5.5.2	Fago *Heraeus* (faccho *L*: facco *R:* facho *R¹*)	falco *MF*
5.5.4	operis *codd.*	operae
5.16.2	citerior *codd.*	citior
5.16.5	alienis *codd.*	alendis *Wilamowitz*
7.1.2	tamen *codd.*	iam
7.1.3	nullam lacunam ante primis indicant *codd.*	<quod> primis
7.1.3	cuiuscemodi *PLeipMF*	cuiusque modi
7.1.3	saepe *Pio* (sepe *codd.*)	sulpure
7.1.4	inusitato *codd.*	inuisitato *Haupt*
7.7.1	si tamen cataplus *M¹FLeip*	si tamen <…> aut cataplus
7.7.1	melior *FLeip*	minus <tristis>
7.7.3	tamen *codd.*	tam
7.7.3	nostris *codd.*	nostri
7.18.1	relectis *ACSPMFVR* (relictis *Vat1661Leip*)	electis *LTN*
8.3.1	parere *codd. plerique*	parare *LN¹*
8.3.1	distractus *codd. plerique* (destrictus *LN¹*)	districtus
8.3.2	diuersorium *codd.*	deuorsorium
8.3.5	fuisse suspectui *codd.*	[fuisse] suspectui
8.15.1	Anianum *codd. plerique*	Annianum *L*
9.16.1	dictatus *codd.*	dicatus
9.16.2	diocesibus *codd.*	dioecesibus
9.16.3 v. 44	possit *codd.*	posset
9.16.4	finem *codd.*	fine

SIDONIUS APOLLINARIS
SELECTED LETTERS

SIDONIUS APOLLINARIS
SELECTED LETTERS

Epistula 1.1

SIDONIVS CONSTANTIO SVO SALVTEM.

Diu praecipis, domine maior, summa suadendi auctoritate, sicuti es in 1
his, quae deliberabuntur, consiliosissimus, ut, si quae litterae paulo politiores uaria occasione fluxerunt, prout eas causa persona tempus elicuit, omnes retractatis exemplaribus enucleatisque uno uolumine includam, Quinti Symmachi rotunditatem, Gai Plinii disciplinam maturitatemque uestigiis praesumptuosis insecuturus. nam de Marco Tullio silere me in 2
stilo epistulari melius puto, quem nec Iulius Titianus sub nominibus illustrium feminarum digna similitudine expressit. propter quod illum ceteri quique Frontonianorum utpote consectaneum aemulati, cur ueternosum dicendi genus imitaretur, oratorum simiam nuncupauerunt. quibus omnibus ego immane dictu est quantum semper iudicio meo cesserim quantumque seruandam singulis pronuntiauerim temporum suorum meritorumque praerogatiuam.

sed scilicet tibi parui tuaeque examinationi has <lucubratiunculas> 3
non recensendas (hoc enim parum est) sed defaecandas, ut aiunt, limandasque commisi, sciens te immodicum esse fautorem non studiorum modo uerum etiam studiosorum. quam ob rem nos nunc perquam haesitabundos in hoc deinceps famae pelagus impellis. porro autem super hui- 4
usmodi opusculo tutius conticueramus, contenti uersuum felicius quam peritius editorum opinione, de qua mihi iam pridem in portu iudicii publici post liuidorum latratuum Scyllas enauigatas sufficientis gloriae anchora sedet. sed si et hisce deliramentis genuinum molarem inuidia non fixerit, actutum tibi a nobis uolumina numerosiora percopiosis scaturientia sermocinationibus multiplicabuntur. uale.

Epistula 1.5

SIDONIVS HERONIO SVO SALVTEM.

Litteras tuas Romae positus accepi, quibus an secundum commune con- 1
silium sese peregrinationis meae coepta promoueant sollicitus inquiris, uiam etiam qualem qualiterque confecerim, quos aut fluuios uiderim poetarum carminibus illustres aut urbes moenium situ inclitas aut montes

nominum opinione uulgatos aut campos proeliorum replicatione monstrabiles, quia uoluptuosum censeas quae lectione compereris eorum, qui inspexerint, fideliore didicisse memoratu. quocirca gaudeo te quid agam cupere cognoscere; namque huiuscemodi studium de affectu interiore proficiscitur. ilicet, etsi secus quaepiam, sub ope tamen dei ordiar a secundis, quibus primordiis maiores nostri etiam sinisteritatum suarum relationes euoluere auspicabantur.

2 egresso mihi Rhodanusiae nostrae moenibus publicus cursus usui fuit utpote sacris apicibus accito, et quidem per domicilia sodalium propinquorumque; ubi sane uianti moram non ueredorum paucitas sed amicorum multitudo faciebat, quae mihi arto implicita complexu itum reditumque felicem certantibus uotis conprecabatur. sic Alpium iugis appropinquatum, quarum mihi citus et facilis ascensus et inter utrimque terrentis latera praerupti cauatis in callem niuibus itinera mollita. fluuiorum quoque,

3 si qui non nauigabiles, uada commoda uel certe peruii pontes, quos antiquitas a fundamentis ad usque aggerem calcabili silice crustatum crypticis arcubus fornicauit. Ticini cursoriam (sic nauigio nomen) escendi, qua in Eridanum breui delatus cantatas saepe comissaliter nobis Phaethontiadas

4 et commenticias arborei metalli lacrimas risi. uluosum Lambrum caerulum Adduam, uelocem Athesim pigrum Mincium, qui Ligusticis Euganeisque montibus oriebantur, paulum per ostia aduersa subuectus in suis etiam gurgitibus inspexi; quorum ripae torique passim quernis acernisque nemoribus uestiebantur. hic auium resonans dulce concentus, quibus nunc in concauis harundinibus, nunc quoque in iuncis pungentibus, nunc et in scirpis enodibus nidorum strues imposita nutabat; quae cuncta uirgulta tumultuatim super amnicos margines soli bibuli suco fota

5 fruticauerant. atque obiter Cremonam peruectus adueni, cuius est olim Tityro Mantuano largum suspirata proximitas. Brixillum dein oppidum, dum succedenti Aemiliano nautae decedit Venetus remex, tantum ut exiremus, intrauimus, Rauennam paulo post cursu dexteriore subeuntes; quo loci ueterem ciuitatem nouumque portum media uia Caesaris ambigas utrum conectat an separet. insuper oppidum duplex pars interluit Padi certa, pars alluit; qui ab alueo principali molium publicarum discerptus obiectu et per easdem deriuatis tramitibus exhaustus sic diuidua fluenta partitur, ut praebeant moenibus circumfusa praesidium, infusa

6 commercium. hic cum peropportuna cuncta mercatui, tum praecipue quod esui competeret deferebatur; nisi quod, cum sese hinc salsum portis pelagus impingeret, hinc cloacali pulte fossarum discursu lintrium uentilata ipse lentati languidus lapsus umoris nauticis cuspidibus foraminato fundi glutino sordidaretur, in medio undarum sitiebamus, quia nusquam

CAMBRIDGE GREEK AND LATIN CLASSICS

GENERAL EDITORS

P. E. EASTERLING
Regius Professor Emeritus of Greek, University of Cambridge

PHILIP HARDIE
Fellow, Trinity College, and Honorary Professor of Latin Emeritus, University of Cambridge

† NEIL HOPKINSON

RICHARD HUNTER
Regius Professor of Greek Emeritus, University of Cambridge

S. P. OAKLEY
Kennedy Professor of Latin, University of Cambridge

OLIVER THOMAS
Associate Professor in Classics, University of Nottingham

CHRISTOPHER WHITTON
Professor of Latin Literature, University of Cambridge

FOUNDING EDITORS

P. E. EASTERLING

† E. J. KENNEY

uel aquaeductuum liquor integer uel cisterna defaecabilis uel fons irriguus uel puteus illimis. unde progressis ad Rubiconem uentum, qui originem nomini de glarearum colore puniceo mutuabatur quique olim Gallis cisalpinis Italisque ueteribus terminus erat, cum populis utrisque Hadriatici maris oppida diuisui fuere. hinc Ariminum Fanumque perueni, illud Iuliana rebellione memorabile, hoc Hasdrubaliano funere infectum: siquidem illic Metaurus, cuius ita in longum felicitas uno die parta porrigitur, ac si etiam nunc Dalmatico salo cadauera sanguinulenta decoloratis gurgitibus inferret. hinc cetera Flaminiae oppida statim ut ingrediebar, egressus laeuo Picentes, dextro Vmbros latere transmisi; ubi mihi seu Calaber Atabulus seu pestilens regio Tuscorum spiritu aeris uenenatis flatibus inebriato et modo calores alternante, modo frigora uaporatum corpus infecit. interea febris sitisque penitissimum cordis medullarumque secretum depopulabantur; quarum auiditati non solum amoena fontium aut abstrusa puteorum, quamquam haec quoque, sed tota illa uel uicina uel obuia fluenta, id est uitrea Fucini gelida Clitumni, Anienis caerula Naris sulpurea, pura Fabaris turbida Tiberis, metu tamen desiderium fallente, pollicebamur. inter haec patuit et Roma conspectui; cuius mihi non solum formas uerum etiam naumachias uidebar epotaturus. ubi priusquam uel pomeria contingerem, triumphalibus apostolorum liminibus affusus omnem protinus sensi membris male fortibus explosum esse languorem; post quae caelestis experimenta patrocinii conducti diuersorii parte susceptus atque etiam nunc istaec inter iacendum scriptitans quieti pauxillulum operam impendo.

neque adhuc principis aulicorumque tumultuosis foribus obuersor. interueni etenim nuptiis patricii Ricimeris, cui filia perennis Augusti in spem publicae securitatis copulabatur. igitur nunc in ista non modo personarum sed etiam ordinum partiumque laetitia Transalpino tuo latere conducibilius uisum, quippe cum hoc ipso tempore, quo haec mihi exarabantur, uix per omnia theatra macella, praetoria fora, templa gymnasia Thalassio Fescenninus explicaretur, atque etiam nunc e contrario studia sileant negotia quiescant iudicia conticescant, differantur legationes uacet ambitus et inter scurrilitates histrionum totus actionum seriarum status peregrinetur. iam quidem uirgo tradita est, iam coronam sponsus, iam palmatam consularis, iam cycladem pronuba, iam togam honoratus, iam paenulam deponit inglorius, et nondum tamen cuncta thalamorum pompa defremuit, quia necdum ad mariti domum noua nupta migrauit. qua festiuitate decursa cetera tibi laborum meorum molimina reserabuntur, si tamen uel consummata sollemnitas aliquando terminauerit istam totius ciuitatis occupatissimam uacationem. uale.

Epistula 1.9

SIDONIVS HERONIO SVO SALVTEM.

1 Post nuptias patricii Ricimeris, id est post imperii utriusque opes euentilatas, tandem reditum est in publicam serietatem, quae rebus actitandis ianuam campumque patefecit. interea nos Pauli praefectorii tam doctrina quam sanctitate uenerandis laribus excepti comiter blandae hospitalitatis officiis excolebamur. porro non isto quisquam uiro est in omni artium genere praestantior. deus bone, quae ille propositionibus aenigmata, sententiis schemata, uersibus commata, digitis mechanemata facit! illud tamen in eo studiorum omnium culmen anteuenit, quod habet huic eminenti scientiae conscientiam superiorem. igitur per hunc primum, si quis quoquo modo in aulam gratiae aditus, exploro; cum hoc confero, quinam
2 potissimum procerum spebus ualeret nostris opitulari. nec sane multa cunctatio, quia pauci de quorum eligendo patrocinio dubitaretur. erant quidem in senatu plerique opibus culti genere sublimes, aetate graues consilio utiles, dignitate elati dignatione communes, sed seruata pace reliquorum duo fastigatissimi consulares, Gennadius Auienus et Caecina Basilius, prae ceteris conspiciebantur. hi in amplissimo ordine seposita praerogatiua partis armatae facile post purpuratum principem principes erant. sed inter hos quoque quamquam stupendi tamen uarii mores et genii potius quam ingenii similitudo. fabor namque super his aliqua suc-
3 cinctius. Auienus ad consulatum felicitate, Basilius uirtute peruenerat. itaque dignitatum in Auieno iucunda uelocitas, in Basilio sera numerositas praedicabatur. utrumque quidem, si fors laribus egrediebantur, artabat clientum praeuia pedisequa circumfusa populositas; sed longe in paribus dispares sodalium spes et spiritus erant. Auienus, si quid poterat, in filiis generis fratribus prouehendis moliebatur; cumque semper domesticis candidatis distringeretur, erga expediendas forinsecus ambientum
4 necessitates minus ualenter efficax erat. et in hoc Coruinorum familiae Deciana praeferebatur, quod qualia impetrabat cinctus Auienus suis, talia conferebat Basilius discinctus alienis. Auieni animus totis et cito, sed infructuosius, Basilii paucis et sero, sed commodius aperiebatur. neuter aditu difficili, neuter sumptuoso; sed si utrumque coluisses, facilius ab
5 Auieno familiaritatem, facilius a Basilio beneficium consequebare. quibus diu utrimque libratis id tractatus mutuus temperauit, ut reseruata senioris consularis reuerentia, in domum cuius nec nimis raro uentitabamus, Basilianis potius frequentatoribus applicaremur. ilicet, dum per hunc amplissimum uirum aliquid de legationis Aruernae petitionibus elaboramus, ecce et Kalendae Ianuariae, quae Augusti consulis mox futuri repe-
6 tendum fastis nomen opperiebantur. tunc patronus: 'heia', inquit, 'Solli

meus, quamquam suscepti officii onere pressaris, exeras uolo in obsequium noui consulis ueterem Musam uotiuum quippiam uel tumultuariis fidibus carminantem. praebebo admittendo aditum recitaturoque solacium recitantique suffragium. si quid experto credis, multa tibi seria hoc ludo promouebuntur.' parui ego praeceptis; fauorem ille non subtraxit iniunctis et impositae deuotionis adstipulator inuictus egit cum consule meo, ut me praefectum faceret senatui suo.

sed tu, ni fallor, epistulae perosus prolixitatem uoluptuosius nunc opusculi ipsius relegendis uersibus immorabere. scio, atque ob hoc carmen ipsum loquax in consequentibus charta deportat, quae pro me interim, dum uenio, diebus tibi pauculis sermocinetur. cui si examinis tui quoque puncta tribuantur, aeque gratum mihi ac si me in comitio uel inter rostra contionante ad sophos meum non modo lati claui sed tribulium quoque fragor concitaretur. sane moneo praeque denuntio quisquilias ipsas Clius tuae hexametris minime exaeques. merito enim collata uestris mea carmina non heroicorum phaleris sed epitaphistarum neniis comparabuntur. attamen gaude, quod hic ipse panegyricus, etsi non iudicium, certe euentum boni operis accepit. quapropter, si tamen tetrica sunt amoenanda iocularibus, uolo paginam glorioso, id est quasi Thrasoniano fine concludere Plautini Pyrgopolinicis imitator. igitur cum ad praefecturam sub ope Christi stili occasione peruenerim, iubeas ilicet pro potestate cinctuti undique omnium laudum conuasatis acclamationibus ad astra portare, si placeo, eloquentiam, si displiceo, felicitatem. uidere mihi uideor ut rideas, quia perspicis nostram cum milite comico ferocisse iactantiam. uale.

7

8

Epistula 2.9

SIDONIVS DONIDIO SVO SALVTEM.

Quaeris cur ipse iam pridem Nemausum profectus uestra serum ob aduentum desideria producam. reddo causas reditus tardioris nec moras meas prodere moror, quia quae mihi dulcia sunt tibi quoque. inter agros amoenissimos, humanissimos dominos, Ferreolum et Apollinarem, tempus uoluptuosissimum exegi. praediorum his iura contermina, domicilia uicina, quibus interiecta gestatio peditem lassat neque sufficit equitaturo. colles aedibus superiores exercentur uinitori et oliuitori: Aracynthum et Nysam, celebrata poetarum carminibus iuga, censeas. uni domui in plana patentiaque, alteri in nemora prospectus, sed nihilominus dissimilis situs similiter oblectat. quamquam de praediorum quid nunc amplius positione, cum restet hospitalitatis ordo reserandus? iam primum sagacissimis in hoc exploratoribus destinatis, qui reditus nostri iter aucuparentur,

1

2

domus utraque non solum tramites aggerum publicorum uerum etiam calles compendiis tortuosos atque pastoria diuerticula insedit, ne quo casu dispositis officiorum insidiis elaberemur. quas incidimus, fateor, sed minime inuiti iusque iurandum confestim praebere compulsi, ne priusquam septem dies euoluerentur, quicquam de itineris nostri continuatione meditaremur.

3   igitur mane cotidiano partibus super hospite prima et grata contentio, quaenam potissimum anterius edulibus nostris culina fumaret; nec sane poterat ex aequo diuisioni lancem ponere uicissitudo, licet uni domui mecum, alteri cum meis uinculum foret propinquitatis, quia Ferreolo praefectorio uiro praeter necessitudinem sibi debitam dabat aetas et dignitas primi inuitatoris praerogatiuam. ilicet a deliciis in delicias rapieba-

4   mur. uix quodcumque uestibulum intratum, et ecce huc sphaeristarum contrastantium paria inter rotatiles catastropharum gyros duplicabantur, huc inter aleatoriarum uocum competitiones frequens crepitantium fritillorum tesserarumque strepitus audiebatur, huc libri affatim in promptu (uidere te crederes aut grammaticales pluteos aut Athenaei cuneos aut armaria extructa bybliopolarum), sic tamen quod qui inter matronarum cathedras codices erant, stilus his religiosus inueniebatur, qui uero per subsellia patrumfamilias, hi coturno Latiaris eloquii nobilitabantur; licet quaepiam uolumina quorumpiam auctorum seruarent in causis disparibus dicendi parilitatem: nam similis scientiae uiri, hinc Augustinus

5   hinc Varro, hinc Horatius hinc Prudentius lectitabantur. quos inter Adamantius Origenes Turranio Rufino interpretatus sedulo fidei nostrae lectoribus inspiciebatur; pariter et, prout singulis cordi, diuersa censentes sermocinabantur, cur a quibusdam protomystarum tamquam scaeuus cauendusque tractator improbaretur, quamquam sic esset ad uerbum sententiamque translatus, ut nec Apuleius Phaedonem sic Platonis neque Tullius Ctesiphontem sic Demosthenis in usum regulamque Romani ser-

6   monis exscripserint. studiis hisce dum nostrum singuli quique, prout libuerat, occupabantur, ecce et ab archimagiro aduentans qui tempus instare curandi corpora moneret, quem quidem nuntium per spatia clepsydrae horarum incrementa seruantem probabat competenter ingressum quinta digrediens. prandebamus breuiter copiose, senatorium ad morem, quo insitum institutumque multas epulas paucis parapsidibus apponi, quamuis conuiuium per edulia nunc assa, nunc iurulenta uarietur. inter bibendum narratiunculae, quarum cognitu hilararemur institueremur, quia eas bifariam orditas laetitia peritiaque comitabantur. quid multa? sancte pulchre abundanter accipiebamur.

7   inde surgentes, si Vorocingi eramus (hoc uni praedio nomen) ad sarcinas et diuersorium pedem referebamus; si Prusiani (sic fundus alter nuncupatur), Tonantium cum fratribus, lectissimos aequaeuorum

nobilium principes, stratis suis eiciebamus, quia nec facile crebro cubilium nostrorum instrumenta circumferebantur. excusso torpore meridiano paulisper equitabamus, quo facilius pectora marcida cibis cenatoriae fami exacueremus. balneas habebat in opere uterque hospes, in usu neuter; sed cum uel pauxillulum bibere desisset assecularum meorum famulorumque turba compotrix, quorum cerebris hospitales craterae nimium immersae dominabantur, uicina fonti aut fluuio raptim scrobis fodiebatur, in quam forte cum lapidum cumulus ambustus demitteretur, antro in hemisphaerii formam corylis flexibilibus intexto fossa inardescens operiebatur, sic tamen, ut superiectis Cilicum uelis patentia interualla uirgarum lumine excluso tenebrarentur, uaporem repulsura salientem, qui undae feruentis aspergine flammatis silicibus excuditur. hic nobis trahebantur horae non absque sermonibus salsis iocularibusque; quos inter halitu nebulae stridentis oppletis inuolutisque saluberrimus sudor eliciebatur; quo, prout libuisset, effuso coctilibus aquis ingerebamur harumque fotu cruditatem nostram tergente resoluti aut fontano deinceps frigore putealique aut fluuiali copia solidabamur: siquidem domibus medius it Vardo fluuius, nisi cum deflua niue pastus impalluit, flauis ruber glareis et per alueum perspicuus quietus calculosusque neque ob hoc minus piscium ferax delicatorum. 8 9

dicerem et cenas et quidem unctissimas, nisi terminum nostrae loquacitati, quem uerecundia non adhibet, charta posuisset; quarum quoque replicatio fieret amoena narratu, nisi epistulae tergum madidis sordidare calamis erubesceremus. sed quia et ipsi in procinctu sumus teque sub ope Christi actutum nobis inuisere placet, expeditius tibi cenae amicorum in mea cena tuaque commemorabuntur, modo nos quam primum hebdomadis exactae spatia completa uotiuae restituant esuritioni, quia disruptum ganea stomachum nulla sarcire res melius quam parsimonia solet. uale. 10

Epistula 2.10. Carmen 27

SIDONIVS HESPERIO SVO SALVTEM.

Amo in te quod litteras amas et usquequaque praeconiis cumulatissimis excolere contendo tantae diligentiae generositatem, per quam nobis non solum initia tua uerum etiam studia nostra commendas. nam cum uidemus in huiusmodi disciplinam iuniorum ingenia succrescere, propter quam nos quoque subduximus ferulae manum, copiosissimum fructum nostri laboris adipiscimur. illud appone, quod tantum increbruit multitudo desidiosorum, ut, nisi uel paucissimi quique meram linguae Latiaris proprietatem de triuialium barbarismorum robigine uindicaueritis, eam breui abolitam defleamus interemptamque; sic omnes nobilium sermonum purpurae per incuriam uulgi decolorabuntur. 1

2   sed istinc alias: interea tu quod petis accipe. petis autem, ut si qui uersiculi mihi fluxerint, postquam ab alterutro discessimus, hos tibi pro quadam morarum mercede pernumerem. dicto pareo; nam praeditus es quamquam iuuenis hac animi maturitate, ut tibi etiam natu priores gerere morem concupiscamus. ecclesia nuper exstructa Lugduni est, quae studio papae Patientis summum coepti operis accessit, uiri sancti strenui, seueri misericordis quique per uberem munificentiam in pauperes humanitatemque non minora bonae conscientiae culmina leuet.
3   huius igitur aedis extimis rogatu praefati antistitis tumultuarium carmen inscripsi trochaeis triplicibus adhuc mihi iamque tibi perfamiliaribus. namque ab hexametris eminentium poetarum Constantii et Secundini uicinantia altari basilicae latera clarescunt, quos in hanc paginam admitti nostra quam maxume uerecundia uetat, quam suas otiositates trepidanter edentem meliorum carminum comparatio premit.
4   nam sicuti nouam nuptam nihil minus quam pulchrior pronuba decet, sicuti, si uestiatur albo, fuscus quisque fit nigrior, sic nostra, quantula est cumque, tubis circumfusa potioribus stipula uilescit, quam mediam loco, infimam merito despicabiliorem pronuntiari non imperitia modo sed et arrogantia facit. quapropter illorum iustius epigrammata micant quam istaec, quae imaginarie tantum et quodammodo umbratiliter effingimus. sed quorsum ista? quin potius paupertinus flagitatae cantilenae culmus immurmuret.

Quisquis pontificis patrisque nostri
collaudas Patientis hic laborem,
uoti compote supplicatione
concessum experiare quod rogabis.
aedes celsa nitet nec in sinistrum   5
aut dextrum trahitur, sed arce frontis
ortum prospicit aequinoctialem.
intus lux micat atque bratteatum
sol sic sollicitatur ad lacunar,
fuluo ut concolor erret in metallo.   10
distinctum uario nitore marmor
percurrit cameram solum fenestras,
ac sub uersicoloribus figuris
uernans herbida crusta sapphiratos
flectit per prasinum uitrum lapillos.   15
huic est porticus applicata triplex
fulmentis Aquitanicis superba,
ad cuius specimen remotiora
claudunt atria porticus secundae,
et campum medium procul locatas   20

uestit saxea silua per columnas.
hinc agger sonat, hinc Arar resultat.
hinc sese pedes atque eques reflectit
stridentum et moderator essedorum,
curuorum hinc chorus helciariorum 25
responsantibus alleluia ripis
ad Christum leuat amnicum celeuma.
sic, sic psallite, nauta uel uiator;
namque iste est locus omnibus petendus,
omnes quo uia ducit ad salutem. 30

ecce parui tamquam iunior imperatis. tu modo fac memineris multiplicato 5
me faenore remunerandum, quoque id facilius possis uoluptuosiusque,
opus est ut sine dissimulatione lectites, sine fine lecturias; neque patiaris,
ut te ab hoc proposito propediem coniunx domum feliciter ducenda
deflectat, sisque oppido meminens, quod olim Marcia Hortensio, Terentia
Tullio, Calpurnia Plinio, Pudentilla Apuleio, Rusticiana Symmacho legen-
tibus meditantibusque candelas et candelabra tenuerunt. certe si praeter 6
rem oratoriam contubernio feminarum poeticum ingenium et oris tui
limam frequentium studiorum cotibus expolitam quereris obtundi, rem-
iniscere quod saepe uersum Corinna cum suo Nasone compleuit, Lesbia
cum Catullo, Caesennia cum Gaetulico, Argentaria cum Lucano, Cynthia
cum Propertio, Delia cum Tibullo. proinde liquido claret studentibus
discendi per nuptias occasionem tribui, desidibus excusationem. igitur
incumbe, neque apud te litterariam curam turba depretiet imperitorum,
quia natura comparatum est, ut in omnibus artibus hoc sit scientiae preti-
osior pompa, quo rarior. uale.

Epistula 2.12
SIDONIVS AGRICOLAE SVO SALVTEM.

Misisti tu quidem lembum mobilem solidum lecti capacem iamque cum 1
piscibus; tum praeterea gubernatorem longe peritum, remiges etiam
robustos expeditosque, qui scilicet ea rapiditate praeteruolant amnis
aduersi terga, qua deflui. sed dabis ueniam, quod inuitanti tibi in pisca-
tionem comes uenire dissimulo; namque me multo decumbentibus nostris ualidiora maeroris retia tenent, quae sunt amicis quoque et externis
indolescenda. unde te quoque puto, si rite germano moueris affectu, quo
temporis puncto paginam hanc sumpseris, de reditu potius cogitaturum.
Seueriana, sollicitudo communis, inquietata primum lentae tussis impulsu 2
febribus quoque iam fatigatur, hisque per noctes ingrauescentibus;

propter quod optat exire in suburbanum; litteras tuas denique cum sumeremus, egredi ad uillulam iam parabamus. quocirca tu seu uenias seu moreris, preces nostras orationibus iuua, ut ruris auram desideranti salubriter cedat ipsa uegetatio. certe ego uel tua soror inter spem metumque suspensi credidimus eius taedium augendum, si uoluntati iacentis obsti-
3 tissemus. igitur ardori ciuitatis atque torpori tam nos quam domum totam praeuio Christo pariter eximimus simulque mediocrum consilia uitamus assidentum dissidentumque, qui parum docti et satis seduli languidos multos officiosissime occidunt. sane contubernio nostro iure amicitiae Iustus adhibebitur, quem, si iocari liberet in tristibus, facile conuincerem Chironica magis institutum arte quam Machaonica. quo diligentius postulandus est Christus obsecrandusque, ut ualetudini, cuius curationem cura nostra non inuenit, potentia superna medeatur. uale.

Epistula 3.9
SIDONIVS RIOTHAMO SVO SALVTEM.

1 Seruatur nostri consuetudo sermonis: namque miscemus cum salutatione querimoniam, non omnino huic rei studentes, ut stilus noster sit officiosus in titulis, asper in paginis, sed quod ea semper eueniunt, de quibus loci mei aut ordinis hominem constat inconciliari, si loquatur, peccare, si taceat. sed et ipsi sarcinam uestri pudoris inspicimus, cuius haec semper uerecundia fuit, ut pro culpis erubesceretis alienis.
2 gerulus epistularum humilis obscurus despicabilisque etiam usque ad damnum innocentis ignauiae mancipia sua Britannis clam sollicitantibus abducta deplorat. incertum mihi est an sit certa causatio; sed si inter coram positos aequanimiter obiecta discingitis, arbitror hunc laboriosum posse probare quod obicit, si tamen inter argutos armatos tumultuosos, uirtute numero contubernio contumaces, poterit ex aequo et bono solus inermis, abiectus rusticus, peregrinus pauper audiri. uale.

Epistula 3.12. Carmen 28
SIDONIVS SECVNDO SVO SALVTEM.

1 Aui mei, proaui tui tumulum hesterno (pro dolor!) die paene manus profana temerauerat; sed deus affuit, ne nefas tantum perpetraretur. campus autem ipse dudum refertus tam bustualibus fauillis quam cadaueribus nullam iam diu scrobem recipiebat; sed tamen tellus, humatis quae superducitur, redierat in pristinam distenta planitiem pondere niuali seu diuturno imbrium fluxu sidentibus aceruis. quae fuit causa, ut locum

auderent tamquam uacantem corporum baiuli rastris funebribus impiare. quid plura? iam niger caespes ex uiridi, iam supra antiquum sepulchrum glaebae recentes, cum forte pergens urbem ad Aruernam publicum scelus e supercilio uicini collis aspexi meque equo effuso tam per aequata quam per abrupta proripiens et morae exiguae sic quoque impatiens, antequam peruenirem, facinus audax praeuio clamore compescui. dum dubitant in crimine reperti dilaberentur an starent, et superueni. confiteor errorem, supplicia captorum differre non potui, sed supra senis nostri ipsum opertorium torsi latrones, quantum sufficere posset superstitum curae, mortuorum securitati. ceterum nostro quod sacerdoti nil reseruaui meae causae suaeque personae praescius, in commune consului, ne uel haec iusto clementius uindicaretur uel illa iusto seuerius uindicaret. cui cum tamen totum ordinem rei ut satisfaciens ex itinere mandassem, uir sanctus et iustus iracundiae meae dedit gloriam, cum nil amplius ego uenia postularem, pronuntians more maiorum reos tantae temeritatis iure caesos uideri.

sed ne quid in posterum casibus liceat, quos ab exemplo uitare debemus, posco, ut actutum me quoque absente tua cura sed meo sumptu resurgat in molem sparsa congeries, quam leuigata pagina tegat. ego uenerabili Gaudentio reliqui pretium lapidis operisque mercedem. carmen hoc sane, quod consequetur, nocte proxima feci, non expolitum, credo, quod uiae non parum intentus. quod peto ut tabulae, quantulumcumque est, celeriter indatur; sed uide, ut uitium non faciat in marmore lapidicida; quod factum siue ab industria seu per incuriam mihi magis quam quadratario liuidus lector adscribet. ego uero, si pio studio rogata curaueris, sic agam gratias, quasi nil tibi quoque laudis aut gloriae accedat, quem patruo tuo remoto solida praesentis officii sollicitudo mansisset pro gradu seminis.

>Serum post patruos patremque carmen
>haud indignus auo nepos dicaui,
>ne fors tempore postumo, uiator,
>ignorans reuerentiam sepulti
>tellurem tereres inaggeratam.   5
>praefectus iacet hic Apollinaris
>post praetoria recta Galliarum
>maerentis patriae sinu receptus,
>consultissimus utilissimusque
>ruris militiae forique cultor,   10
>exemploque aliis periculoso
>liber sub dominantibus tyrannis.
>haec sed maxima dignitas probatur,

> quod frontem cruce, membra fonte purgans
> primus de numero patrum suorum 15
> sacris sacrilegis renuntiauit.
> hoc primum est decus, haec superba uirtus,
> spe praecedere quos honore iungas
> quique hic sunt titulis pares parentes,
> hos illic meritis superuenire. 20

6 noui quidem auctoris nostri non respondere doctrinae epitaphii qualitatem, sed anima perita musicas non refutat inferias. tibi quoque non decet tardum uideri quod heres tertius quartusque dependimus, cum tot annorum gyro uoluto magnum Alexandrum parentasse manibus Achillis et Iulium Caesarem Hectori ut suo iusta soluisse didicerimus. uale.

Epistula 4.19

SIDONIVS FLORENTINO SVO SALVTEM.

Et moras nostras et silentium accusas. utrumque purgabile est; namque et uenimus et scribimus. uale.

Epistula 4.20

SIDONIVS DOMNITIO SVO SALVTEM.

1 Tu cui frequenter arma et armatum et armatos inspicere iucundum est, quam uoluptatem, putamus, mente conciperes, si Sigismerem regium iuuenem ritu atque cultu gentilicio ornatum, utpote sponsum seu petitorem, praetorium soceri expetere uidisses! illum equus quidem phaleris comptus, immo equi radiantibus gemmis onusti antecedebant uel etiam subsequebantur, cum tamen magis hoc ibi decorum inspiciebatur, quod cursoribus suis siue pedisequis pedes et ipse medius incessit, flammeus cocco rutilus auro lacteus serico, tum cultui tanto coma rubore cute

2 concolor. regulorum autem sociorumque comitantum forma et in pace terribilis, quorum pedes primi perone saetoso talos adusque uinciebantur; genua crura suraeque sine tegmine; praeter hoc uestis alta stricta uersicolor uix appropinquans poplitibus exertis; manicae sola brachiorum principia uelantes; uiridantia saga limbis marginata puniceis; penduli ex umero gladii balteis supercurrentibus strinxerant clausa bullatis

3 latera rhenonibus. eo, quo comebantur, ornatu muniebantur; lanceis uncatis securibusque missibilibus dextrae refertae clipeis laeuam partem adumbrantibus, quorum lux in orbibus niuea, fulua in umbonibus ita

censum prodebat ut studium. cuncta prorsus huiusmodi, ut in actione thalamorum non appareret minor Martis pompa quam Veneris. sed quid haec pluribus? spectaculo tali sola praesentia tua defuit. nam cum uiderem quae tibi pulchra sunt non te uidere, ipsam eo tempore desiderii tui impatientiam desideraui. uale.

Epistula 5.5

SIDONIVS SYAGRIO SVO SALVTEM.

Cum sis consulis pronepos idque per uirilem successionem (quamquam id ad causam subiciendam minus attinet), cum sis igitur e semine poetae, cui procul dubio statuas dederant litterae, si trabeae non dedissent (quod etiam nunc auctoris culta uersibus uerba testantur), a quo studia posterorum ne parum quidem, quippe in hac parte, degenerauerunt, immane narratu est, quantum stupeam sermonis te Germanici notitiam tanta facilitate rapuisse. atqui pueritiam tuam competenter scholis liberalibus memini imbutam et saepenumero acriter eloquenterque declamasse coram oratore satis habeo compertum. atque haec cum ita sint, uelim dicas, unde subito hauserunt pectora tua euphoniam gentis alienae, ut modo mihi post ferulas lectionis Maronianae postque desudatam uaricosi Arpinatis opulentiam loquacitatemque quasi de Harilao uetere nouus Fago prorumpas? aestimari minime potest, quanto mihi ceterisque sit risui, quotiens audio, quod te praesente formidet linguae suae facere barbarus barbarismum. adstupet tibi epistulas interpretanti curua Germanorum senectus et negotiis mutuis arbitrum te disceptatoremque desumit. nouus Burgundionum Solon in legibus disserendis, nouus Amphion in citharis, sed trichordibus, temperandis amaris frequentaris, expeteris oblectas, eligeris adhiberis, decernis audiris. et quamquam aeque corporibus ac sensu rigidi sint indolatilesque, amplectuntur in te pariter et discunt sermonem patrium, cor Latinum. restat hoc unum, uir facetissime, ut nihilo segnius, uel cum uacabit, aliquid lectioni operis impendas custodiasque hoc, prout es elegantissimus, temperamentum, ut ista tibi lingua teneatur, ne ridearis, illa exerceatur, ut rideas. uale.

Epistula 5.16

SIDONIVS PAPIANILLAE SVAE SALVTEM.

Rauenna ueniens quaestor Licinianus, cum primum tetigit Alpe transmissa Galliae solum, litteras aduentus sui praeuias misit, quibus indicat esse se gerulum codicillorum, quorum in aduentu fratri etiam tuo Ecdicio, cuius aeque titulis ac meis gaudes, honor patricius accedit, celerrime, si cogites eius aetatem, si merita, tardissime. namque ille iam pridem suffragium dignitatis ineundae non soluit in lance sed in acie aerariumque publicum ipse priuatus non pecuniis sed manubiis locupletauit. hoc tamen sancte Iulius Nepos, armis pariter summus Augustus ac moribus, quod decessoris Anthemii fidem fratris tui sudoribus obligatam, quo citerior, hoc laudabilior absoluit; siquidem iste compleuit, quod ille saepissime pollicebatur. quo fit, ut deinceps pro republica optimus quisque possit ac debeat, si quid cuipiam uirium est, quia securus, hinc auidus impendere, quandoquidem mortuo quoque imperatore laborantum deuotioni quicquid spoponderit princeps, semper redhibet principatus.

interea tu, si affectum tuum bene colligo, hisce compertis magnum solacium inter aduersa maxima capis nec animum tuum a tramite communium gaudiorum uicinae quoque obsidionis terror exorbitat. noui enim probe ne meo quidem te, quem ex lege participas, sic honore laetatam, quia, licet sis uxor bona, soror optima es. qua de re propitio deo Christo ampliatos prosapiae tuae titulos ego festinus gratatoriis apicibus inscripsi, pariter absoluens sollicitudinem tuam, fratris pudorem; quem nil de propria dignitate indicaturum, si uerecundum forte nescires, nec sic impium iudicares. ego uero non tantum insignibus uestris, quae tu hactenus quanto liberius, tanto impatientius praestolabare (quamquam his quoque granditer), quantum concordia fruor; quam parem nostris suisque liberis in posterum exopto, uotis in commune deposcens, ut sicut nos utramque familiam nostram praefectoriam nancti etiam patriciam diuino fauore reddidimus, ita ipsi, quam suscipiunt patriciam, faciant consularem.

Roscia salutat, cura communis; quae in auiae amitarumque indulgentissimo sinu, quod raro nepotibus contingit alienis, et cum seueritate nutritur, qua tamen tenerum non infirmatur aeuum sed informatur ingenium. uale.

Epistula 6.11

SIDONIVS DOMINO PAPAE ELEVTHERIO SALVTEM.

Iudaeum praesens charta commendat, non quod mihi placeat error, per quem pereunt inuoluti, sed quia neminem ipsorum nos decet ex asse damnabilem pronuntiare, dum uiuit; in spe enim adhuc absolutionis est cui suppetit posse conuerti. quae sit uero negotii sui series, ipse rectius praesentanea coram narratione patefaciet. nam prudentiae satis obuiat epistulari formulae debitam concinnitatem plurifario sermone porrigere. sane quia secundum uel negotia uel iudicia terrena solent huiuscemodi homines honestas habere causas, tu quoque potes huius laboriosi, etsi impugnas perfidiam, propugnare personam. memor nostri esse dignare, domine papa.

Epistula 7.1

SIDONIVS DOMINO PAPAE MAMERTO SALVTEM.

Rumor est Gothos in Romanum solum castra mouisse: huic semper irruptioni nos miseri Aruerni ianua sumus. namque odiis inimicorum hinc peculiaria fomenta subministramus, quia, quod necdum terminos suos ab Oceano in Rhodanum Ligeris alueo limitauerunt, solam sub ope Christi moram de nostra tantum obice patiuntur. circumiectarum uero spatia tractumque regionum iam pridem regni minacis importuna deuorauit impressio. sed animositati nostrae tam temerariae tamque periculosae non nos aut ambustam murorum faciem aut putrem sudium cratem aut propugnacula uigilum trita pectoribus confidimus opitulatura; solo tamen inuectarum te auctore rogationum palpamur auxilio, quibus inchoandis instituendisque populus Aruernus, etsi non effectu pari, affectu certe non impari coepit initiari, et ob hoc circumfusis necdum dat terga terroribus.

non enim latet nostram sciscitationem: primis temporibus harumce supplicationum institutarum ciuitas caelitus tibi credita per cuiuscemodi prodigiorum terriculamenta uacuabatur. nam modo scaenae moenium publicorum crebris terrae motibus concutiebantur; nunc ignes saepe flammati caducas culminum cristas superiecto fauillarum monte tumulabant; nunc stupenda foro cubilia collocabat audacium pauenda mansuetudo ceruorum, cum tu inter ista discessu primorum popularium que statu urbis exinanito ad noua celer ueterum Niniuitarum exempla decurristi, ne diuinae admonitioni tua quoque desperatio conuiciaretur. et uere iam de deo tu minime poteras absque peccato post uirtutum experimenta diffidere. nam cum uice quadam ciuitas conflagrare coepisset, fides tua in illo ardore plus caluit; et cum in conspectu pauidae plebis obiectu solo corporis tui ignis recussus in tergum fugitiuis flexibus sinuaretur, miraculo terribili nouo inusitato affuit flammae cedere per reuerentiam, cui sentire defuit per naturam. igitur primum nostri ordinis uiris et his paucis indicis ieiunia, interdicis flagitia, supplicia praedicis, remedia promittis; exponis omnibus nec poenam longinquam esse nec ueniam; doces denuntiatae solitudinis minas orationum frequentia esse amoliendas; mones assiduitatem furentis incendii aqua potius oculorum quam fluminum posse restingui; mones minacem terrae motuum conflictationem fidei stabilitate firmandam. cuius confestim sequax humilis turba consilii maioribus quoque suis fuit incitamento, quos cum non piguisset fugere, redire non puduit. qua deuotione placatus inspector pectorum deus fecit esse obsecrationem uestram uobis saluti, ceteris imitationi, utrisque praesidio. denique illic deinceps non fuere uel damna calamitati uel ostenta formidini.

7 quae omnia sciens populus iste Viennensibus tuis et accidisse prius et non accessisse posterius uestigia tam sacrosanctae informationis amplectitur, sedulo petens, ut conscientiae tuae beatitudo mittat orationum suarum suffragia quibus exempla transmisit. et quia tibi soli concessa est post auorum memoriam uel confessorem Ambrosium, duorum martyrum repertorem, in partibus orbis occidui martyris Ferreoli solida translatio adiecto nostri capite Iuliani, quod istinc turbulento quondam persecutori manus rettulit cruenta carnificis, non iniurium est quod pro compensatione deposcimus, ut nobis inde ueniat pars patrocinii, quia uobis hinc rediit pars patroni. memor nostri esse dignare, domine papa.

Epistula 7.7

SIDONIVS DOMINO PAPAE GRAECO SALVTEM.

1 Ecce iterum Amantius, nugigerulus noster, Massiliam suam repetit, aliquid, ut moris est, de manubiis ciuitatis domum reportaturus, si tamen cataplus arriserit. per quem ioculariter plura garrirem, si pariter unus idemque ualeret animus exercere laeta et tristia sustinere. siquidem nostri hic nunc est infelicis anguli status, cuius, ut fama confirmat, melior
2 fuit sub bello quam sub pace condicio. facta est seruitus nostra pretium securitatis alienae. Aruernorum, pro dolor, seruitus, qui, si prisca replicarentur, audebant se quondam fratres Latio dicere et sanguine ab Iliaco populos computare. si recentia memorabuntur, hi sunt qui uiribus propriis hostium publicorum arma remorati sunt; cui saepe populo Gothus non fuit clauso intra moenia formidini, cum uicissim ipse fieret oppugnatoribus positis intra castra terrori. hi sunt qui sibi aduersus uicinorum aciem tam duces fuere quam milites; de quorum tamen sorte certaminum si quid prosperum cessit, uos secunda solata sunt, si quid contrarium, illos aduersa fregerunt. illi amore rei publicae Seronatum barbaris prouincias propinantem non timuerunt legibus tradere, quem conuictum deinceps
3 res publica uix praesumpsit occidere. hoccine meruerunt inopia flamma, ferrum pestilentia, pingues caedibus gladii et macri ieiuniis proeliatores? propter huius tamen inclitae pacis expectationem auulsas muralibus rimis herbas in cibum traximus, crebro per ignorantiam uenenatis graminibus infecti, quae indiscretis foliis sucisque uiridantia saepe manus

fame concolor legit? pro his tot tantisque deuotionis experimentis nostris, quantum audio, facta iactura est? pudeat uos, precamur, huius foederis, nec utilis nec decori. per uos legationes meant; uobis primum pax quamquam principe absente non solum tractata reseratur, uerum etiam tractanda committitur. ueniabilis sit, quaesumus, apud aures uestras ueritatis asperitas, cui conuicii inuidiam dolor eripit. parum in commune consulitis; et, cum in concilium conuenitis, non tam curae est publicis mederi periculis quam priuatis studere fortunis; quod utique saepe diuque facientes iam non primi comprouincialium coepistis esse, sed ultimi. at quousque istae poterunt durare praestigiae? non enim diutius ipsi maiores nostri hoc nomine gloriabuntur, qui minores incipiunt non habere. quapropter uel consilio, quo potestis, statum concordiae tam turpis incidite. adhuc, si necesse est, obsideri, adhuc pugnare, adhuc esurire delectat. si uero tradimur, qui non potuimus uiribus obtineri, inuenisse uos certum est quid barbarum suaderetis ignaui.

sed cur dolori nimio frena laxamus? quin potius ignoscite afflictis nec imputate maerentibus. namque alia regio tradita seruitium sperat, Aruerna supplicium. sane si medicari nostris ultimis non ualetis, saltem hoc efficite prece sedula, ut sanguis uiuat quorum est moritura libertas; parate exulibus terram, capiendis redemptionem, uiaticum peregrinaturis. si murus noster aperitur hostibus, non sit clausus uester hospitibus. memor nostri esse dignare, domine papa.

Epistula 7.17. Carmen 33

SIDONIVS VOLVSIANO FRATRI SALVTEM.

Iubes me, domine frater, lege amicitiae, quam nefas laedi, iam diu desides digitos incudibus officinae ueteris imponere et sancto Abrahae diem functo neniam sepulchralem luctuosis carminibus inscribere. celeriter iniunctis obsecundabo, cum tua tractus auctoritate, tum principaliter amplissimi uiri Victorii comitis deuotione praeuentus, quem iure saeculari patronum, iure ecclesiastico filium excolo ut cliens, ut pater diligo; qui satis docuit, quae sibi aut qualis erga famulos Christi cura ferueret, cum torum circa decumbentis antistitis, non dignitatem minus quam membra curuatus ac supra uultum propinqua morte pallentem dolore concolor factus, quid uiro uellet lacrimis indicibus ostenderet. et quia sibi maximas humandi funeris partes ipse praeripuit, totum apparatu supercurrentis impendii quod funerando sacerdoti competeret impertiens, saltim ad obsequium, quae remanserunt, uerba conferimus, nihil aliud

exaraturi stili scalpentis impressu quam testimonium mutuae dilectionis.
ceterum uiri mores gesta uirtutes indignissime meorum uilitate dictorum
ponderabuntur.

 Abraham sanctis merito sociande patronis,
  quos tibi collegas dicere non trepidem
 (nam sic praecedunt, ut mox tamen ipse sequare),
  dat partem regni portio martyrii.
 natus ad Euphraten, pro Christo ergastula passus   5
  et quinquennali uincula laxa fame,
 elapsus regi truculento Susidis orae
  occiduum properas solus ad usque solum.
 sed confessorem uirtutum signa sequuntur
  spiritibusque malis fers, fugitiue, fugam.   10
 quaque uenis, Lemurum se clamat cedere turba;
  daemonas ire iubes exul in exilium.
 expeteris cunctis, nec te capit ambitus ullus;
  est tibi delatus plus onerosus honor.
 Romuleos refugis Byzantinosque fragores   15
  atque sagittifero moenia fracta Tito.
 murus Alexandri te non tenet Antiochique;
  spernis Elisseae Byrsica tecta domus.
 rura paludicolae temnis populosa Rauennae
  et quae lanigero de sue nomen habent.   20
 angulus iste placet paupertinusque recessus
  et casa, cui culmo culmina pressa forent.
 aedificas hic ipse deo uenerabile templum,
  ipse dei templum corpore facte prius.
 finiti cursus istic uitaeque uiaeque: 25
  sudori superest dupla corona tuo.
 iam te circumstant paradisi milia sacri;
  Abraham iam te comperegrinus habet;
 iam patriam ingrederis, sed de qua decidit Adam;
  iam potes ad fontem fluminis ire tui.   30

3 ecce, ut iniunxeras, quae restant, sepulto iusta persoluimus; sed, si uicissim caritatis imperiis fratres amicos commilitones obsequi decet, ad uicem, quaeso, tu quoque, quibus emines, institutis discipulos eius aggredere solari fluctuantemque regulam fratrum destitutorum secundum statuta Lirinensium patrum uel Grinincensium festinus informa; cuius discipli-
4 nae si qui rebelles, ipse castiga; si qui sequaces, ipse collauda. praepositus illis quidem uidetur sanctus Auxanius, qui uir, ut nosti, plusculum iusto et

corpore infirmus et uerecundus ingenio eoque parendi quam imperandi promptior exigit te rogari, ut tuo ipse sub magisterio monasterii magister accedat et, si quis illum de iunioribus spreuerit tamquam imperitum uel pusillanimem, per te unum sentiat utrumque non impune contemni. quid multa? uis ut paucis quid uelim agnoscas? quaeso, ut abbas sit frater Auxanius supra congregationem, tu uero et supra abbatem. uale.

Epistula 7.18

SIDONIVS CONSTANTIO SVO SALVTEM.

A te principium, tibi desinet. nam petitum misimus opus raptim relectis exemplaribus, quae ob hoc in manus pauca uenerunt, quia mihi nil de libelli huiusce conscriptione meditanti hactenus incustodita nequeunt inueniri. sane ista pauca, quae quidem et leuia sunt, celeriter absolui, quamquam incitatus semel animus necdum scripturire desineret, seruans hoc sedulo genus temperamenti, ut epistularum produceretur textus, si numerus breuiaretur. pariter et censui librum, quem lector delicatissimus desiderares, et satis habilem nec parum excusabilem fore, si, quoniam te sensuum structurarumque leuitas poterat offendere, membranarum certe fascibus minus onerarere. commendo igitur uarios iudicio tuo nostri pectoris motus, minime ignarus, quod ita mens pateat in libro uelut uultus in speculo. dictaui enim quaepiam hortando, laudando plurima et aliqua suadendo, maerendo pauca iocandoque nonnulla. et si me uspiam lectitauisti in aliquos concitatiorem, scias uolo Christi dextera opitulante numquam me toleraturum animi seruitutem, compertissimum tenens bipertitam super his moribus hominum esse censuram. nam ut timidi me temerarium, ita constantes liberum appellant. inter quae ipse decerno satis illius iacere personam, cuius necesse est latere sententiam.

ad propositum redeo. interea tu, si quid a lectionis sacrae continuatione respiras, his licebit neniis auocere. nec faciet materia ut immensa fastidium, quia cum singulae causae singulis ferme epistulis finiantur, cito cognitis in quae oculum intenderis ante legere cessabis quam lecturire desistas. uale.

Epistula 8.3

SIDONIVS LEONI SVO SALVTEM.

Apollonii Pythagorici uitam, non ut Nicomachus senior e Philostrati sed ut Tascius Victorianus e Nicomachi schedio exscripsit, quia iusseras, misi; quam, dum parere festino, celeriter eiecit in tumultuarium exemplar turbida et praeceps et Opica translatio. neque mihi rem credito diuturnius elaboratam uitio uertas: nam dum me tenuit inclusum mora moenium Liuianorum, cuius incommodi finem post opem Christi tibi debeo, non ualebat curis animus aeger saltim saltuatim tradenda percurrere, nunc per nocturna suspiria, nunc per diurna officia distractus. ad hoc, et cum me defetigatum ab excubiis ad diuersorium crepusculascens hora reuocauerat, uix dabatur luminibus inflexis paruula quies; nam fragor ilico, quem mouebant uicinantes impluuio cubiculi mei duae quaepiam Getides anus, quibus nil umquam litigiosius bibacius uomacius erit. sane, cum primum reduci aliquid otii fuit, impolitum hunc semicrudumque et, ut aiunt, tamquam musteum librum plus desiderii tui quam officii mei memor obtuli.

3 quocirca sepone tantisper Pythicas lauros Hippocrenenque et illos carminum modos tibi uni tantum penitissime familiares, qui tamen doctis, ut es ipse, personis non tam fonte quam fronte sudantur. suspende perorandi illud quoque celeberrimum flumen, quod non solum gentilicium sed domesticum tibi quodque in tuum pectus per succiduas aetates ab atauo Frontone transfunditur. sepone pauxillulum conclamatissimas declamationes, quas oris regii uice conficis, quibus ipse rex inclitus modo corda terrificat gentium transmarinarum, modo de superiore cum barbaris ad Vachalin trementibus foedus uictor innodat, modo per promotae limitem sortis ut populos sub armis, sic frenat arma sub legibus.

4 exuere utcumque continuatissimis curis et otium tuum molibus aulicis motibusque furare. historiam flagitatam tunc recognosces opportune competenterque, si cum Tyaneo nostro nunc ad Caucasum Indumque, nunc ad Aethiopum gymnosophistas Indorumque bracmanas totus lectioni uacans et ipse quodammodo peregrinere. lege uirum fidei catholicae pace praefata in plurimis similem tui, id est a diuitibus ambitum nec diuitias ambientem; cupidum scientiae continentem pecuniae; inter epulas abstemium, inter purpuratos linteatum, inter alabastra censorium; concretum hispidum hirsutum in medio nationum delibutarum atque inter satrapas regum tiaratorum murrhatos pumicatos malobathratos uenerabili squalore pretiosum; cumque proprio nihil esui aut indutui de pecude conferret, regnis ob hoc, quae pererrauit, non tam suspicioni quam fuisse suspectui; et a fortuna regum sibi in omnibus obsecundante illa tantum beneficia poscentem, quae mage sit suetus oblata praestare quam sumere.

6 quid multis? si uera metimur aestimamusque, fors fuat an philosophi uitae scriptor aequalis maiorum temporibus accesserit, certe par saeculo meo per te lector obuenit. uale.

Epistula 8.15

SIDONIVS DOMINO PAPAE PROSPERO SALVTEM.

Dum laudibus summis sanctum Anianum, maximum consummatissimumque pontificem, Lupo parem Germanoque non imparem, uis celebrari fideliumque desideras pectoribus infigi uiri talis ac tanti mores merita uirtutes, cui etiam illud non absque iustitia gloriae datur, quod te successore decessit, exegeras mihi, ut promitterem tibi Attilae bellum stilo me posteris intimaturum, quo uidelicet Aurelianensis urbis obsidio oppugnatio, irruptio nec direptio et illa uulgata exauditi caelitus sacerdotis uaticinatio continebatur. coeperam scribere; sed operis arrepti fasce perspecto taeduit inchoasse; propter hoc nullis auribus credidi quod primum me censore damnaueram. dabitur, ut spero, precatui tuo et meritis antistitis summi, quatenus praeconio suo sub quacumque et quidem celeri occasione famulemur. ceterum tu creditor iustus laudabiliter hoc imprudentiae temerarii debitoris indulseris, ut quod mihi insolubile uidetur tibi quoque uideatur inreposcibile. memor nostri esse dignare, domine papa.

Epistula 9.16. Carmen 41

SIDONIVS FIRMINO SVO SALVTEM.

Si recordaris, domine fili, hoc mihi iniunxeras, ut hic nonus libellus peculiariter tibi dictatus ceteris octo copularetur, quos ad Constantium scripsi, uirum singularis ingenii, consilii salutaris, certe in tractatibus publicis ceteros eloquentes, seu diuersa siue paria decernat, praestantioris facundiae dotibus antecellentem. sponsio impleta est, non exacte quidem, sed uel instanter. nam peragratis forte diocesibus cum domum ueni, si quod schedium temere iacens chartulis putribus ac ueternosis continebatur, raptim coactimque translator festinus exscripsi, tempore hiberno nil retardatus, quin actutum iussa complerem, licet antiquarium moraretur insiccabilis gelu pagina et calamo durior gutta, quam iudicasses imprimentibus digitis non fluere sed frangi. sic quoque tamen compotem officii prius agere curaui, quam duodecimum nostrum, quem Numae mensem uos nuncupatis, Fauonius flatu teporo pluuiisque natalibus maritaret. restat, ut te arbitro non reposcamur res omnino discrepantissimas, maturitatem celeritatemque. nam quotiens liber quispiam scribi cito iubetur, non tantum honorem spectat auctor a merito quantum ab obsequio. de reliquo, quia tibi nuper ad Gelasium uirum sat benignissimum missos iambicos placuisse pronuntias, per hos te quoque Mytilenaei oppidi uernulas munerabor.

Iam per alternum pelagus loquendi
egit audacem mea cymba cursum
nec bipertito timuit fluento
    flectere clauum.
soluit antemnas, legit alta uela,   5
palmulam ponit manus, atque transtris
litori iunctis petit osculandum
    saltus harenam.
mussitans quamquam chorus inuidorum
prodat hirritu rabiem canino,   10
nil palam sane loquitur pauetque
    publica puncta.
uerberant puppim, quatiunt carinam,
uentilant spondas laterum rotundas,
arborem circa uolitant sinistrae   15
    sibila linguae.
nos tamen rectam comite arte proram,
nil tumescentes ueriti procellas,
sistimus portu, geminae potiti
    fronde coronae,   20
quam mihi indulsit populus Quirini,
blattifer uel quam tribuit senatus,
quam peritorum dedit ordo consors
    iudiciorum,
cum meis poni statuam perennem   25
Nerua Traianus titulis uideret,
inter auctores utriusque fixam
    bybliothecae;
quamque post, uisus prope, post bilustre
tempus accepi, capiens honorem,   30
qui patrum ac plebis simul unus olim
    iura gubernat.
praeter heroos ioca multa multis
texui pannis; elegos frequenter
subditos senis pedibus rotaui   35
    commate bino.
nunc per undenas equitare suetus
syllabas lusi celer atque metro
Sapphico creber cecini, citato
    rarus iambo.   40
nec recordari queo, quanta quondam

scripserim primo iuuenis calore;
unde pars maior utinam taceri
　　possit et abdi!
nam senectutis propiore meta, 45
quicquid extremis sociamur annis,
plus pudet, si quid leue lusit aetas,
　　nunc reminisci.
quod perhorrescens ad epistularum
transtuli cultum genus omne curae, 50
ne reus cantu petulantiore
　　sim reus actu;
neu puter solui per amoena dicta,
schema si chartis phalerasque iungam,
clerici ne quid maculet rigorem 55
　　fama poetae.
denique ad quoduis epigramma posthac
non ferar pronus, teneroque metro
uel graui nullum cito cogar exhinc
　　promere carmen: 60
persecutorum nisi quaestiones
forsitan dicam meritosque caelum
martyras mortis pretio parasse
　　praemia uitae.
e quibus primum mihi psallat hymnus 65
qui Tolosatem tenuit cathedram,
de gradu summo Capitoliorum
　　praecipitatum;
quem negatorem Iouis ac Mineruae
et crucis Christi bona confitentem 70
uinxit ad tauri latus iniugati
　　plebs furibunda,
ut per abruptum boue concitato
spargeret cursus lacerum cadauer
cautibus tinctis calida soluti 75
　　pulte cerebri.
post Saturninum uolo plectra cantent,
quos patronorum reliquos probaui
anxio duros mihi per labores
　　auxiliatos, 80
singulos quos nunc pia nuncupatim
non ualent uersu cohibere uerba;

> quos tamen chordae nequeunt sonare,
> corda sonabunt.

4 redeamus in finem ad oratorium stilum materiam praesentem proposito semel ordine terminaturi, ne, si epilogis musicis opus prosarium clauserimus, secundum regulas Flacci, ubi amphora coepit institui, urceus potius exisse uideatur. uale.

COMMENTARY

LETTER 1.1: DEDICATION

Outline

Sidonius sends Constantius the volume of his selected letters he had asked for. The comparison with Symmachus, Pliny and ultimately Cicero is inevitable, and daunting. It would have been wiser to confine himself to the success of his poetry. On the other hand, should this selection also prove a success, then Constantius can expect more.

Introduction

The opening letter of Book 1 serves as both a dedicatory and a prefatory letter for Sidonius' letter collection – originally for Book 1, or Books 1 and 2, as a try-out (§4 'if jealousy does not take hold of it'), but later for its first seven. It accompanies the letters which, at the behest of his senior soulmate and supporter, the Lyonese aristocrat Constantius, Sidonius selected from his archive for being especially worthwhile and meriting broader circulation. It functions as a dedication by naming the initiator and dedicatee, presenting him with the work, and asking him for correction, and it serves as a preface by exploring its literary pedigree and playing down expectations – with an ominous twist. It is part of a series of prefatory and concluding letters that bind the collection together and articulate it into 7 + 1 + 1 books: 7.18, 8.1, 8.16, 9.1, 9.16 (see Intro 4.1). Of these, 7.18 and 8.16 are also addressed to Constantius: the former closes the edition of the first seven books with a forceful look back and an accolade for its dedicatee, while the latter gives him credit for the extension. The final letter of the collection, 9.16, does not fail to mention him again for his defining role in the entire project.

Discussion

Sidonius takes care that he is in good company, choosing Pliny the Younger's sophisticated nine-book correspondence as his model, along with the correspondences of Symmachus and, in a special way, of Cicero. He thus self-consciously inscribes himself into the tradition of senatorial letter writing (Intro 4.1). Something new is happening here, as there are no traces of an explicit and accepted canon in earlier letter collections, except for Cicero's canonical status as a letter writer (Gibson 2020b, 386–8; cf. Intro 3.6).

Sidonius' opening letter is explicitly reminiscent of Pliny's letter 1.1 (text Mynors 1963):

C. Plinius Septicio <Claro> suo s.

1 Frequenter hortatus es, ut epistulas, si quas paulo curatius scripsissem, colligerem publicaremque. collegi non seruato temporis ordine – neque enim historiam componebam –, sed ut quaeque in manus uenerat. 2 superest ut nec te consilii nec me paeniteat obsequii. ita enim fiet, ut eas quae adhuc neglectae iacent requiram et si quas addidero non supprimam. uale.

They have in common the so-called *iubes–pareo* motif (the publication is requested by the dedicatee, the author obeys; see Intro 4.2), they promise that, in case of success, more is to follow and they point out that the selection is from the group of stylistically refined letters (Intro 3.6 n. 76) and is diverse (Intro 4.1 n. 90). Two further elements in Sidonius' letter, however, at first sight are absent from Pliny: (1) Pliny says nothing about his literary pedigree, whereas Sidonius is explicit about Symmachus and Pliny, and about Cicero (*hors concours*) with a certain Titianus in his wake, and (2) Pliny does not dwell on anything concerning copy-editing and circulation, which for Sidonius, by contrast, is a matter of deep concern, especially the threat of hostile criticism. On closer inspection, Sidonius found these topics, reading on so to say, in Pliny's letters 1.2 and 1.5 (as argued in van Waarden 2022a, cf. Hanaghan 2017b, 252–5). In letter 1.2, Pliny highlights three models for his speeches: Demosthenes and Calvus, plus Cicero in a special position. And he asks for help in copy-editing the drafts before publication. More than being only a formal parallel, both elements in Sidonius make sense in light of Pliny's letter 1.5.

Here, Pliny introduces his *bête noire*, colleague and antagonist, the lawcourt orator Marcus Aquilius Regulus, steeped in the murky waters of criminal prosecution since the days of Nero. Reading this letter with Sidonius' letter in mind, we are struck by the following elements:

- §2: a friend of Pliny is reviled by Regulus as 'ape of the Stoics' (*Stoicorum simiam*). Cf. Sidon. 1.1.2 *oratorum simiam*, applied to Titianus by 'all Fronto's other followers'.
- §11–13: Regulus once criticized one of Pliny's co-advocates for being satisfied with contemporary oratory (*eloquentia saeculi nostri*) instead of vying with Cicero (*cum Cicerone aemulatio*). Pliny stresses his veneration for Cicero. Cf. Sidon. 1.1.2, where Titianus *does* imitate Cicero, while the modernist Frontonians, out of jealousy (*aemulati*), criticize him for copying 'a worn-out style' (*ueternosum dicendi genus*). Sidonius expresses his deepest respect for the old masters.

These elements implicitly link rhetorical nonconformism to political risk. In Regulus' day, under emperors like Nero and Domitian, adhering to Stoic doctrine was synonymous with opposition and equivalent to a death sentence, as for the famous Thrasea Paetus (Tac. *Ann.* 16.21–35) and for Regulus' dupe. 'Aping' the Stoics in words and deeds could be fatal. Likewise, the distinction between *cum Cicerone aemulatio* and *eloquentia saeculi nostri* was a political litmus test, contra or pro the regime: the conformist co-advocate remained on the safe side by adhering to 'contemporary oratory', whereas a preference for old-fashioned republican oratory, 'vying with Cicero', was playing with fire. Linguistic choices and socio-political adherence overlapped.

In Sidonius' opening letter the 'ape of the orators' and the high esteem for Cicero are not trivial either: their echo of Pliny lends them the full force of socio-political nonconformism. Hence his maniacal attention to hostile criticism, which goes beyond the fear of being trapped in a discussion of linguistic do's and don'ts (serious enough, though, 'in a world in which the proper use of language was a prerequisite for success and distinction in the public forum' (Zetzel 2018, 9)). It hints at the underlying party strife and contested loyalties around the Visigothic presence and the failure to stabilize Gallic interests in Rome (which makes at least Book 1 into a defence of his conduct prior to the episcopate (see Intro 2.1 with n. 28 and Intro 4.1). What he says is this: like this freaky Titianus, my ultimate solidarity is with Cicero, that is, with a past that bears the hallmark of genuine Romanness against all social and political rot; like Cicero, I am in the middle of political turmoil; like his letters, mine bear witness to our struggle for survival. My opponents are no better than the horde of little Frontonians, unable to rise above the level of contemporary conformism.

Addressee

Constantius, probably a *uir clarissimus* (Intro 3.3), belonged to the lay elite of Lyon. He likely became a *conuersus* (Intro 3.4 n. 63) as can be inferred from the adjective *sanctus* at 3.2.1 *sanctum pedem* and from the descriptions at 3.2.3 *religione uenerabilis* and 7.18.4n. *si quid a lectionis sacrae continuatione respiras*. A distinguished poet (2.10.3n.) and an outstanding orator (9.16.1) in Sidonius' view, he actively supported the goals of bishop Patiens of Lyon, contributing a poem to his new church, for which Sidonius also wrote an inscription (*Carm.* 27 in 2.10, in this volume). He authored a *Life of Germanus* (*MGH SS rer. Merov.* 7, 225–83, ed. Levinson), the emblematic bishop of Auxerre (d. ?448), written *c.* 480 as part of 'a co-ordinated effort [by Auxerre and Lyon] to counter the vigorous promotion of St Martin by Perpetuus of Tours' (Harries 1994, 121–2; Gillett 2003, 115–38; see 2.10 Addressee (Patiens), 8.15.1n.). Germanus had maintained contacts with members of the ascetic Lérins group (Intro 3.4) and with towns such as Lyon, Arles and probably also Clermont as a promoter of St Julian of Brioude (Harries 1994, 41–2 and 202; cf. Intro 1 'January 456'). Consequently, in choosing his hagiographer as the chief inspiration for his letters, Sidonius lends his correspondence the stamp of the Lérinian aristocratic religious revival. Or it might have been the other way round: Constantius (and the church of Lyon) pushed Sidonius to the fore as their figurehead in order to boost this revival through his collected correspondence.

Whatever the case, it was Constantius' idea to publish a collection of the letters and he helped disseminate them. Lyon supported Clermont during the war with the Visigoths: Patiens by sending food supplies in 471 (6.12) and Constantius by visiting the town despite his advanced age and boosting its morale in the winter of 473–4 (3.2). Constantius lived to see Book 9 of the Letters being circulated (he is spoken of in the present tense in 9.16.1n.), at more or less the same time as his own *Life of Germanus* was published. He died at the age of 84 and was buried in Saint-Irénée in Lyon, if the epitaph Le Blant 34 can be ascribed to him (Prévot in *PCBE* 4, 521–2). For all the importance attached to him, however, he remains a relatively modest figurehead, certainly no power broker. Thus, Sidonius' whole project of maximizing influence is held together by this local representative of the Lyon church and intimate friend rather than by a high-profile grandee or metropolitan bishop. In this respect, Constantius is comparable to Pliny's dedicatee Clarus, a '(relatively) modest addressee', whose being selected shows 'the writer's affection even for his social inferior' (Gibson and Morello 2012, 160; cf. Intro 4.1): Sidonius, too, as a former city prefect and a *patricius*, was socially senior to Constantius (cf. Constantius' relatively unconnected position in Sidonius' network (Mathisen 2020c, 73, figure 2.7; cf. Mratschek 2020b, 219–20)). It puts the actual scale of Sidonius' undertaking into a more modest perspective (on the ever more restricted scale of Gallo-Roman networks, see Wickham 2005, 170).

Prosopography: Mathisen 2020a, 89; cf. van Waarden 2016, 253–6.

Date and place

Written specifically for the collection, in principle for Book 1 (Kelly 2020, 181–2), it must be dated to 469/70 and probably originated in Lyon (Loyen 2, 2).

Literature

This letter is discussed in every publication on the structure of the letter collection. Commentary: Köhler 1995, 99–119. On dedication, see van Dam 2008; on prefaces, Janson 1964.

Commentary

Sidonius Constantio suo salutem: for address line conventions, see Intro 4.2.

1 Diu praecipis: it is a commonplace in dedications for the author to stress that the dedicatee has long been urging him (e.g. Plin. 1.1 *Frequenter hortatus es*, Tac. *Dial.* 1.1 *Saepe ex me requiris*) or that he himself has long been hesitating whether or not to publish (e.g. Cic. *Orat.* 1 *diu multumque ... dubitaui*, Stat. *Silv.* 1 praef. *Diu multumque dubitaui*, Sidon. 7.3.1 *Diu multumque deliberaui*). For the *iubes–pareo* motif in dedicatory letters, see Intro 4.2. For the first and second persons singular in this motif, see van Waarden 2020e, 436. **domine maior:** see Intro 4.2 'Address'. **summa suadendi auctoritate:** the phrase is only found elsewhere at Tac. *Germ.* 11.2 *audiuntur auctoritate suadendi magis quam iubendi potestate*. The same distinction between persuasive authority and discretionary power is made here. **sicuti es ... consiliosissimus:** *sicuti* (or *sicut* elsewhere, without appreciable difference but for rhythm (van Waarden 2010, 202), or *ut*) + finite form of *esse* indicates the state in which someone or something finds themselves when the action begins, and is often causal 'as', 'since' (K–S 2, 451–2). *consiliosus* is an archaism from Cato (*c.* 200 BCE) which Sidonius must have found in Aulus Gellius' *Noctes Atticae*, a treasure trove of ancient lore, or in (excerpts from) Fronto's archaizing correspondence (Gell. 4.9.12 and Fronto 128.5 vdH respectively, both authors second century CE); see Wolff 2020, 398–9 and 402; for archaism, Intro 4.4 and 4.5. The impressive long superlative stylishly closes the phrase with the rare clausula choriamb + cretic (–⏑⏑– –⏑×; see Intro 4.5). **si quae litterae paulo politiores uaria occasione fluxerunt:** *si quae* = *quaecumque*, see K–S 2, 430. For the concept of 'polished letters', see Intro 3.6 with n. 76. *uaria occasione* is further developed in 7.18.2n. *dictaui enim quaepiam hortando, laudando plurima et aliqua suadendo, maerendo pauca iocandoque nonnulla*. Attention to different situations, moods and addressees, required by literary theorists (see Intro 3.6), results in alternating moods (and letter lengths) in individual books of letters (Intro 4.1 with n. 90). *fluxerunt*, of unbridled eloquence and abundant literary production, is answered by *scaturientia* 'gushing' at the end of this letter; the phrase echoes Stat. *Silv.* 1 praef. *hos libellos, qui mihi subito calore et quadam festinandi uoluptate fluxerunt*; for the flow of eloquence, cf. e.g. 4.3.10 *arentem uenulam rarius flumini tuo misceo*, 4.17.1 *fonte facundiae*, 8.3.3 *perorandi ... flumen*, 9.7.2 *flumen in uerbis*; in Hor. *Sat.* 1.4.11 *cum flueret* [sc. Lucilius] *lutulentus*, proficiency has become a vice. Recent editors prefer the emendation *fluxerint* (subjunctive in a clause dependent on another clause with a subjunctive, parallel to 2.10.2 *si qui uersiculi mihi fluxerint*), unnecessarily so, for Sidonius (like others) just as easily picks the indicative, as at 6.3.2 *fastidit*, 6.7.2 *dignabitur*, 7.8.2 *uoles* and 8.16.3 *placemus* (see *OLS* 1, 666–71; cf. van Waarden and Kelly 2020, 473 n. 31). **prout eas causa persona tempus elicuit:** cf. 9.11.3 *scripseram librum ... plenum onustumque uario causarum temporum personarumque congestu* (for variety, see Intro 4.1 with n. 90). *causa persona tempus* is an asyndetic triplet of nouns, characteristic of Sidonius' smooth stylistic register (Intro 4.5). **omnes ... uno uolumine includam:** is applicable both to the edition of Book 1 (or Books 1–2) and Books 1–7 (see above Introduction). The word *uolumen* ('book', 'volume', originally a 'scroll', from *uoluere*) lays stress on the book's material aspect, a book as something you can hold in your hand; the choice between *liber, libellus, opus, opusculum* and *uolumen* – all frequent in Sidonius – depends on which particular function of the book the author has in mind (see van Waarden 2016, 32–40). In §4, the same collection is referred to as *opusculo*; cf. 7.18.1n. *libelli*. For the train of thought, cf. Stat. *Silv.* 1 praef. *an hos libellos ... congregatos ipse dimitterem,* Sidon. *Carm.* 9.11 *in formam redigi iubes libelli* 'you demand [that my occasional verse] be put into book form' (in the dedicatory poem of his *Carmina minora*). **retractatis exemplaribus enucleatisque** 'after revising and clarifying the originals': the sender kept the originals (*exemplaria*) of his correspondence in his files, which enabled him to revise and reuse them (see Cugusi 1983, 139–41 and 190, for Sidonius in particular Mathisen 2013; see also Intro 2). *enucleare*, lit. 'to bring out the kernel', fig. 'to remove obscurities', 'to explain' (*OLD* 2, cf. *TLL* 5/2.615.54–76), is here used for the process of clarifying the original letters, which included the removal of most, if not all, specific information; this is the same as expressed in 8.16.5 *nihil inditum non absolutum* 'there is nothing contained in [the letters] which is not clear', in accordance with the theoretical requirement of *perspicuitas* (Quint. *Inst.* 8.2.22) and *lux* (Iul. Vict. *Rhet.* 27; cf. Intro 3.6). Sidonius is fond of the one-word cretic + spondee clausula: *e-nucleatisque*, and below *ma-turitatemque, insecuturus, nuncupauerunt, praerogatiuam, haesitabundos, mul-tiplicatisque* (van Waarden and Kelly 2020, 472). **Quinti Symmachi rotunditatem, Gai Plinii disciplinam maturitatemque** 'Quintus Symmachus' smoothness, Gaius Plinius' skill and perfection': in the typical fashion of the *grammaticus*, authors are labelled and catalogued according to a variety of styles. Other such lists include Quint. *Inst.* 12.10.10–11, Tac. *Dial.* 26–7, Front. *Ad Marc. imp.* 133.11–134.6 vdH, Macr. *Sat.* 5.1.7, 16–17, not forgetting Sidonius' own parody of a literary catalogue, *Carm.* 9.211–317 (see Winterbottom 1982, 44). *rotunditas* is the stylistic quality of being 'smooth and finished', 'well-rounded' (*OLD rotundus* 3), applied by Sidonius to a speaker: 8.11.5 *acer rotundus, compositus excussus* 'sharp or smoothly rounded, quiet or energetic' and to a metre: 8.4.2 *rotundatos hendecasyllabos* 'shapely hendecasyllables' (tr. Anderson). There is an additional element of ideas being 'neatly wrapped up', 'rounded-off' (cf. Cic. *Fin.* 4.7 [maxims] *breviter, … apte ac rotunde*, Quint. *Inst.* 8.5.27 [notions] *rotunda et undique circumcisa*). Symmachus typically is the writer of short, elegantly formulated notes. *disciplina* is 'mastery', 'know-how' as the result of study (cf. *TLL* 5/1.1318.62). *maturitas* in Sidonius is 'seriousness' (4.3.4), 'perfection' (5.2.2), 'finish' (9.16.3n.). As a quality of style, it has slightly diverging connotations with theorists, from 'maturity' (Cic. *Brut.* 8), 'opulence' (Quint. *Inst.* 12.10.11), 'breadth' (Tac. *Dial.* 26.1) to 'seriousness' (Macr. *Sat.* 5.1.16). Sidonius sees in Pliny a combination of rhetorical expertise and flawless execution. Symmachus' and Pliny's qualities obey the 'law of rising members' (Intro 4.5 n. 111; cf. 1.5.10n., 2.9.6n., 7.1.2n.), which lends greater weight to the latter, the parallelism being underscored by the rhyme *rotunditatem-maturitatem* (Intro 4.5). For Quintus Aurelius Symmachus (*c.* 340–402), leading Roman senator, orator, and epistolographer (nine books of letters to private persons and a number of letters and official reports to the emperor, which can be considered as a tenth book), city prefect of Rome 384–5, consul 391, one of 'the last pagans of Rome', see *PLRE* 1, 865–70, *ODLA* 1436–7, Cameron 2011, Sogno 2017. For Gaius Plinius Caecilius Secundus (Pliny the Younger, 61/2–?113), born into an equestrian family, adopted by his maternal uncle Gaius Plinius Secundus (Pliny the Elder, the author of the *Natural History*), advocate, senator, consul in 100, provincial governor and epistolographer (nine books to private persons plus a book of official correspondence with the emperor Trajan), see *OCD* 'Pliny (2) the Younger', Gibson and Morello 2012, Salzman 2017b, 21–3, Gibson 2020a. **uestigiis praesumptuosis insecuturus** 'which would mean that I follow … with arrogant steps': predicative future participles with final or consecutive meaning like *insecuturus* are common in later Latin (H–S 390); examples abound in Sidonius, e.g. 1.2.9 *excubaturus*, 1.10.2 *commendaturus*. With this phrase, focalization shifts from Constantius' argument to Sidonius' misgivings. The clausula *insecuturus* is the preferred cretic + spondee (see Intro 4.5).

2 nam de Marco Tullio silere me in stilo epistulari melius puto: *nam* 'clearly', 'obviously' is so-called 'forward-linking *nam*', providing an afterthought to the preceding clause while at the same time introducing a new topic (Kroon 1995, 129–209 on *nam* and *enim*, esp. 157–8; for another example, see 1.9.2n. *namque*); it here serves as an ellipsis ('I do not mention Cicero') and an anticipation of an expected objection by the reader ('But what about Cicero?'), a figure of style called *occupatio*; see K–S 2, 117–18, H–S 505–6 (cf. Sal. *Jug.* 19.2 below). After Symmachus and Pliny, it is Cicero's turn, in reversed temporal order (Köhler 1995, 106). Marcus Tullius Cicero, 106–43 BCE, politician, orator, writer on oratory and philosophy, letter writer. A defining political figure during the demise of the Roman republic and one of the most prolific writers of Roman literature, he acquired lasting influence as the orator par excellence (e.g. Quint. *Inst.* 12.10.12 *in omnibus … eminentissimum*). About nine hundred of his letters have been preserved, published posthumously, among them the collections *Ad familiares* and *Ad Atticum*. See *OCD* 'Tullius (*RE* 29) Cicero, Marcus'; for his letters, White 2010; the intellectual context, Rawson 1985; Cicero in late antiquity, MacCormack 2013. Cicero is one of the authors mentioned the most by Sidonius, seventeen times in all. The last words of the collection are a silent salute to him (see 9.16.4n. *exisse uideatur*). He is *oratorum princeps* (5.13.3), especially featuring in lists of emblematic authors – among them Virgil and Horace, mentioned nineteen and fourteen times respectively – and typically matched with Demosthenes. For the verbosity of his speeches, see 5.5.2n. *opulentiam loquacitatemque*. In light of the frequency of mention, Symmachus (four times) and Pliny the Younger (six times) are clearly authors whom Sidonius introduces for a specific purpose, whereas Cicero seems to be part of a generalized canon. In what follows, the MS readings diverge slightly concerning *me*: *me* is omitted in the α branch and the sentence is garbled in *LR*. Wilamowitz's reshuffling in the Lütjohann edition (see Intro 6) disturbs the balance of the sentence, where, right at the outset, *in stilo epistulari* 'when it comes to letter writing' provides the topic, together with the two persons concerned, Cicero and Sidonius. For *silere* out of respect, cf. Sal. *Jug.* 19.2 *nam de Carthagine silere melius puto quam parum dicere* (cited by Quint. *Inst.* 2.13.14); concerning Cicero, cf. Plin. 9.26.8 *quamquam hunc omitto; neque enim ambigi puto*. Petrarch notoriously misunderstood *silere* as if Sidonius meant to reject Cicero's style and oeuvre: *Inuentum esse hominem Latinum qui … eloquentiam aut stilum aut omnino dicendi genus Ciceronis irrideat!* (*Epistolae familiares* 1.1, in the intermediate version (β), not in the original (γ) nor in the definitive (α) ones; see Intro 5). *stilus* occurs frequently in late antique epistolographers, meaning literally 'stylus', hence 'writing' and 'style' (*OLD* 4), here equivalent to 'genre' (cf. 3.3.2 and 9.16.4n. *oratorio stilo* 'prose', 3.14.1 *poetarum stilo* 'poetry', 4.22.1 *stilum historiae* 'historiography'); see 8.15.1n. *stilo*. **quem nec Iulius Titianus sub nominibus illustrium feminarum digna similitudine expressit** 'as not even Julius Titianus, in his *Letters of Famous Women*, adequately reproduced that model': *nec* is ironical. Titianus is a shadowy Gallic rhetor and antiquarian (*c.* 200 CE), an imperial tutor who sank to itinerant provincial schoolmaster, author of a *Geography* and a prose paraphrase of Aesop's *Fables*, a versatile speaker (*fandi artifex*, Ausonius says in *Ep.* 9b.81 Green) with a talent for imitation demonstrated – according to Sidonius here – by a *Letters of Famous Women*, reworking something like Ovid's *Heroides* in the style of Cicero's correspondence. In the *Historia Augusta, Max.* 27.5, he is a man *qui dictus est simia temporis sui, quod cuncta esset imitatus*. For the complex sources, see *PIR*^{2} I 604–5, *PLRE* 1, 875 'Tatianus 1', *BNP* 'Titianus. 1. Iulius Titianus' (Zelzer), *OCD* 'Iulius Titianus' (Holford-Strevens). *sub nominibus* indicates fictitious authors, e.g. Aug. *Civ.* 15.23 *sub nominibus apostolorum*, 'supposedly written by the Apostles'. For the phrase *digna similitudine expressit*, cf. Quint. *Inst.* 2.13.12 *siue exprimi pro dignitate non possunt* (in the same paragraph where he cites Sallust: see above). *exprimere* is 'to reproduce', 'to copy' (*OLD* 6a), here only in Sidonius, but frequently in Pliny, e.g. Plin. 4.7.5 *Cato ... uerum oratorem ... expressit*. **ceteri quique Frontonianorum:** second/third-century archaizing mannerists, nominally associated with Fronto, not necessarily his pupils (Holford-Strevens 2003, 354–63, *OCD* 'Frontoniani'); for Fronto and the archaizing tendency of Sidonius' age, see 8.3.3n. *Frontone*, Intro 4.4 and 4.5. These archaizing orators preferred the unpolished style of preclassical orators to the balanced prose of Cicero's speeches, lacking attention to the *mot juste*. Fronto himself, however, admired Cicero's pithier style as a letter writer: Fronto *Ep. Ant.* 3.10.1, p. 104.12–14 vdH *epistulis Ciceronis nihil est perfectius*. By Sidonius' time, *quisque* 'every single' freely combines with adjectives, whether in the positive, comparative or superlative degree, singular or plural; see H–S 170. **utpote consectaneum aemulati** 'wrangling with a member of their own school, as one might expect': *utpote* reinforces an explanatory clause, 'as is natural' (*OLD*). A *secta* is a 'line of teaching', 'system of ideas or principles', in specialized disciplines such as philosophy, oratory and medicine (*OLD secta*^{1} 2ab). *aemulati* 'animated by rivalry', 'jealous' (*OLD* 3), a distorted form of *aemulatio* of great men, gleaned from Plin. 1.5.11–13, as argued in Discussion above. **cur ueternosum dicendi genus imitaretur** 'because he allegedly imitated a worn-out literary style': the reason why they called him *oratorum simia*. *cur* + subjunctive in later Latin introduces a causal or factual subordinate clause, instead of *quia* or *quod* (H–S 541); in Sidonius' usage, it may connote a subjectivity that is not necessarily shared by the author (Köhler

1995, 108–9; cf. e.g. 1.11.12 *cur ... anteferretur*). *ueternosum* 'exhausted', 'spiritless' (L–S II) returns in the last books, 8.16.4, 9.16.2n. **oratorum simiam nuncupauerunt:** grafted on Plin. 1.5.2 *Stoicorum simiam*; see Discussion above. For the clausula, see above §1 *enucleatisque*. **quibus omnibus ego immane dictu est quantum semper iudicio meo cesserim** 'I have always, in my judgement, fallen awfully short of all of these men': Sidonius maximizes the qualitative distance between Cicero, Pliny, Symmachus and himself, and extols their status as the foremost exponents of their times. Cf. Plin. 1.2.2 *uim tantorum uirorum 'pauci quos aequus ...'* [Verg. *Aen.* 6.129] *adsequi possunt* in Discussion above. This is the prime trope of modesty in which an author proclaims their incompetence (Curtius 1990, 83–5, Janson 1964, 124–40), here leaning towards comic hyperbole, veiling serious intention with banter spilling over from the Titianus vignette. There is a slightly archaic and emphatic feel to *immane dictu est quantum*: see van Waarden 2022a, 1030 with n. 25. *quibus omnibus* and *ego* are fronted as topic (see Intro 4.3). **seruandam singulis pronuntiauerim temporum suorum meritorumque praerogatiuam:** *pronuntiauerim* 'pronounce a judicial decision' (*OLD* 3). *temporum*, i.e. their precedence in time, cf. 4.3.1 *si me decursorum ad hoc aeui temporum praerogatiua non obruat*. *meritorum* 'achievements', 'accomplishments', in the idiom of the likes of Sidonius, is not primarily a moral quality but one's objective career successes (see van Waarden 2016, 66–7 and 150). The notion of *praerogatiua* 'precedence' occurs no fewer than nineteen times in the correspondence, testifying to the crucial importance of social distinction in Sidonius' world, cf. Intro 3.3. The object phrase *seruandam ... praerogatiuam* is split, indicating postponed *temporum ... praerogatiuam* as the focus constituent ('new information'); see Intro 4.3. For the clausula, see §1n. *enucleatisque*.

3 sed scilicet tibi parui: *scilicet* 'of course', 'obviously' is a modal particle marking the intersubjectivity of the evidence which is supposed to be shared by the addressee, as opposed to, for instance, *uidelicet* 'clearly', where the logic is all the sender's own; see Schrickx 2011, 143–84. *tibi parui* 'I have done as you asked', gathering the letters.   **tuaeque examinationi has <lucubratiunculas> non recensendas ... sed defaecandas, ut aiunt, limandasque commisi:** *examinationi* 'scrutiny', 'judgement', usually *examen* (e.g. 1.9.7n.). After *has*, a noun seems to have gone missing. Lütjohann supplemented *litterulas*, followed by modern editors. However, as pointed out by Dolveck 2020b, 503 n. 61, the word *lucubratiunculas* 'little night labours', added in the margin of MS Leipzig, UB, Rep. I 48 (Dolveck #21), maybe by the scribe's hand, could be a better candidate. It makes excellent sense and is idiomatic (attested in Fronto (Marcus Aurelius),

Gellius, Ausonius and Jerome, *TLL* 7/1.1745.65–84; diminutives of modesty in *-iuncula* four times in Sidonius, e.g. 2.9.6n. *narratiunculae*). It would be a surprising scribal conjecture, and the Leipzig MS, besides being probably collated against the archetype, seems to have had access to a different source (Dolveck 2020b, 495 and 503). *recensendas* in the technical sense of 'revising', 'correcting' proofs (*TLL* 11/2.296.73–297.13). *defaecandas* graphically and emphatically 'to be cleared', like wine strained of dregs. *limandas* 'filing', 'polishing', 'fine-tuning', i.e. removing any verbal or stylistic infelicities in copy-editing. Also of honing one's style, see 2.10.6n. *limam*; cf. Janson 1964, 142. *commisi* 'I submit' is the typical epistolary perfect amounting to a present tense: the sender, as it were, takes up the reader's position, for whom the dispatch of the attachment is in the past. **te immodicum esse fautorem non studiorum modo uerum etiam studiosorum:** the patron's care for the authors themselves, beyond a shared passion for literature, is a safeguard against the risks of publication and a 'mutual reassurance among those of one's rank as to the value of the shared cultural tradition' (Mratschek 2020a, 238). For *fautorem*, cf. Plin. 6.23.5 [about himself] *fautor ... commendatorque* 'a patron and supporter'. *studiorum* is synonymous with *studium litterarum* as often in Pliny (e.g. 4.28.2, 6.6.3, 8.12.1; see van Waarden 2016, 157 and cf. 1.9.1n. *studiorum*, 2.10.1n. *studia*). The wordplay imitates Plin. 6.6.3 *erat non studiorum tantum uerum etiam studiosorum amantissimus*; for the commonplace, see also e.g. Quint. *Inst.* 1 praef. 6, Plin. 4.28.2, Sidon. 5.10.4 (where the wordplay is *artes–artifices*). For the publication process and its social implications, see Intro 3.3. **nos ... haesitabundos ... impellis:** cf. 9.11.9 *in audentiam sermocinandi quem non ipse compellas?* The plural *nos* for 'I' underscores the hesitancy with which the author faces publication; see Intro 4.2. The *litteratus* is wary per definition, and only the prodding of his patron can help him overcome his diffidence. **in hoc deinceps famae pelagus:** the adverb causes discontinuity (hyperbaton) of the noun phrase, cf. 3.2.1 *tua deinceps exhortatio*, 7.15.2 *hac deinceps condicione*; see *OLS* 2, 1102–3 (alternatively, *deinceps* is attributive). Publishing is a risky affair like going on a sea voyage. Sailing is an established metaphor, since Pindar, for the process of creative writing or, more rarely as here for the first time, publishing a literary work; see Janson 1964, 146–7; Lieberg 1969; Curtius 1990, 128–31; Harrison 2007b; for Sidonius in particular, Gualandri 1979, 105–7; Santelia 2002, 40–3; Hanaghan 2017b, 255–61; Wolff 2020, 413–14. Cf. the sustained nautical metaphor in *Carm.* 41 (in 9.16, with commentary). The phrase *famae pelagus* 'sea of ambition' is particular to Sidonius, cf. *Carm.* 35, 7.15; for general studies of *fama* in (Roman) literature, see Hardie 2012 and Guastalla 2017. The clausula *pelagus impellis* is the frequent paeon IV + spondee; see Intro 4.5.

4 porro autem super huiusmodi opusculo tutius conticueramus: *porro autem* introduces a new consideration with an implied contrast; occurring regularly in Sidonius, it is typical of later Latin (source *CDS*). The term *opusculum* denotes the result of the writing process, with due modesty; see §1 *uolumine* and van Waarden 2016, 32–40. *tutius conticueramus* (indicative) works in the same way as modal expressions like *melius fuerat* 'it would have been better': 'it would have been safer for me to keep silent' (*OLS* 1, 460). **uersuum felicius quam peritius editorum opinione** 'the critical acclaim of my poetry published successfully rather than skilfully': a modest twist to the commonplace that competence and success are different things, cf. e.g. Plin. 4.22.2 *egit ipse causam non minus feliciter quam diserte*, Ennod. 8.37 *plus felicibus epistolis debetur laudatio quam peritis*. The opposition *felix–peritus* was evidently an issue in the glossaries listing *differentiae* (pairs of words that should be distinguished) in use in schools (see Zetzel 2018, 104–6), as Servius takes Virgil to task for using *felicior* where he meant *peritior* (Serv. *ad Aen.* 9.772). For the attention to symmetry and sound (rhyme) in *felicius quam peritius*, see Intro 4.5; for the idiom [comparative] *quam* [comparative], see K–S 2, 473–4. *editorum* 'put out', 'circulated' is Sidonius' preferred term for publication (4.10.2, 8.1.3, 8.16.1, 9.1.2, 9.11.4); see Intro 3.3. *opinione* 'reputation (for a quality)' (*OLD* 5b), cf. 1.5.1n. *opinione*. The noun is a so-called *vox media*, 'good/bad reputation', like, for example, *fortuna* 'good/bad luck', *ualetudo* 'good/ bad health'; cf. *iudicii* in the ensuing clause. **de qua mihi iam pridem in portu iudicii publici ... sufficientis gloriae anchora sedet:** cf. *Carm.* 2.538–9 asking the Muse to grant the finished poem a favourable reception] *portumque petenti | iam placido sedeat mihi carminis anchora fundo* and *Carm.* 41.19–20 *sistimus portu, geminae potiti | fronde coronae* (cf. Plin. 8.12.1 where a patron of the arts is said to be the *portus* of all literati). Both metaphors *portus* and *anchora* are explained by a noun phrase in the genitive, like *famae pelagus* above: sea, harbour, anchor – the picture is complete. *iudicii* 'favourable opinion', 'esteem' (*OLD* 10). *anchora* is the MS reading (also 8.6.15, *Carm.* 2.539, 24.101); the spelling with *h* is defended by Servius at *Aen.* 1.169 *anchora: hoc nomen cum in Graeco, unde originem ducit, aspirationem non habeat, in Latino aspiratur. sedet* 'sticks' (*OLD* 9), also of vessels drawn ashore in a harbour (Verg. *Aen.* 7.201 *portuque sedetis*, Sidon. 1.8.2 *naues sedent*). **post liuidorum latratuum Scyllas enauigatas** 'after sailing past Scyllas with their envious barkings', cf. 7.9.8 *obloquiorum Scyllas et ... linguarum, sed humanarum, latratus* (van Waarden 2010, 461– 3). For *liuidorum* of jealousy in literary matters, cf. 3.12.5n. *liuidus lector*. *latratuum* creates the association with dogs, prototypes of spiteful aggression (Otto 1890, 69), cf. *Carm.* 41.9–10n. (in 9.16) *chorus inuidorum | ... hirritu ... canino*. Scylla is the proverbial personification of aggressive jealousy, especially popular in late antiquity (cf. Hier. 125.2 *Scyllaei obtrectatorum canes*). The plural means 'the likes of Scylla', 'instances of Scylla' (cf. Lucr. 5.893; H–S 19). As a literary motif, Scylla has a complex history, especially in Hellenistic and Augustan poetry, embodying cultural preoccupations with the canine, the marine, and the feminine; see Hopman 2012; Lowe 2015, 73–84; *OCD* 'Charybdis, Scylla'. The topos proliferated in the Middle Ages: Lake 2023. **sed si et hisce deliramentis genuinum molarem inuidia non fixerit** 'but if jealousy should not dig its grinding teeth into these absurdities either': The pointing suffix *-c(e)*, in classical Latin only admitted selectively, is an archaizing revival of the practice in early Latin, where it can suffix all case endings; Sidonius employs it only when the next word begins with a consonant, evidently for euphonic and rhythmic reasons (van Waarden 2010, 95–6n. *harumce*); cf. 2.9.6n., 5.16.3n. *deliramentis* serves politely to denigrate one's own work (cf. Symm. 5.43 *nugas suas et deliramenta* 'one's bagatelles and absurdities'; see Intro 3.3 'Social Conventions'), which may serve – as here – the ulterior purpose of veiling criticism (see Discussion above and Intro 4.2 'Coded Communication'). The noun is among the words revived from early Latin by the second-century archaizing authors (Mannheimer 1975, 160; see Intro 4.5). *genuinum molarem* is close to a tautology, each word meaning 'back tooth', 'molar', *molaris* also 'wisdom tooth' (Lucarini 2002, 377–8, indeed, would delete one of them as a gloss); both are used as metaphors for jealousy and criticism, e.g. Hier. *Chron.* 2 praef. *multos ... qui ... huic uolumini genuinum infigant*, Sidon. 4.22.6 *colubrinis oblatratorum molaribus fixi*; cf. Hor. *Carm.* 4.3.16 *et iam dente minus mordeor inuido*; see Otto 1890, 107 *dens*. **actutum tibi a nobis uolumina numerosiora percopiosis scaturientia sermocinationibus multiplicabuntur** 'volume shall immediately follow upon volume in greater numbers, to you from me, all brimful with the most copious flow of correspondence': this sentence made up of long words and a pleonasm (*numerosiora ... multiplicabuntur*), suggesting the boundless nature of the author's promise, brings the letter effectively to a close (Wolff 2020, 411). *actutum*, because politeness requires a promise to be fulfilled as soon as possible, cf. the dedicatory letter of Book 9, which Sidonius says he will 'promptly append to the margins of the eighth book' (9.1.4 *marginibus octaui celeriter addemus*; van Waarden 2020a, 157). By *tibi a nobis* the addressee is foregrounded, the author modestly withdraws (Intro 4.2). *scaturientia* is an intensified form of *scatere* 'to gush' (for the productivity of the verbal suffix -*urire* in Sidonius, see Wolff 2020, 399). It picks up *fluxerunt* in §1. The words *sermo* and *sermocinatio* 'conversation' came to mean 'correspondence', 'letter' in later epistolographers; for letters as a conversation, see Intro 3.6 with n. 79. The clausula *multiplicabuntur* (choriamb + spondee, $-\cup\cup- -\times$) is among the less frequent ones in Sidonius (van Waarden and Kelly 2020, 474–5). This ending mirrors the concluding paragraph of Pliny's opening letter (Plin. 1.1.2) in a more elaborate and poignant form. Sidonius is deeply indebted to Pliny, yet his creative impulse, in a new setting and in different times, is fundamentally different, filled by a sense of 'belatedness' and the related 'manneristic' complexity of his prose style (see Intro 3.1 and 4.5 respectively).

uale: for valedictory conventions, see Intro 4.2.

LETTER 1.5: TRAVELLING TO ROME

Outline

Sidonius writes from Rome evaluating his travels from Lyon as an envoy to the emperor Anthemius (§1). After a remarkably easy crossing of the Alps (§2), the countryside with its rivers, where the imperial boat service takes Sidonius down the Po (§3–4), is gradually enveloped by violent Roman history while the prosperity of Ravenna appears endangered by its foul waters (§5–7). The last overland part of the journey is nightmarish as Sidonius is afflicted by a bad fever and cannot quench his thirst for fear of being poisoned by the springs they encounter. Only when he visits the tombs of Peter and Paul, upon arrival prior to entering the city, is he miraculously cured. Biblical reminiscences of vivifying spiritual water take over from classical allusions (§8–9). Waiting to be admitted to the emperor, Sidonius observes the carefree bustle in the town as the wedding of the magister militum *Ricimer with Anthemius' daughter Alypia runs on and on (§10–11).*

Introduction

After the dedicatory first letter, Book 1 sets out with letter 1.2 in praise of the Visigothic king Theoderic II, who reigned in Toulouse from 453 to 466. Sidonius describes him as the ideal cultivated barbarian ruler. Theoderic, indeed, had supported Sidonius' father-in-law Eparchius Avitus, who had excellent long-standing connections in Toulouse, to seize the imperial throne for Gaul in 455. In 466, Theoderic was murdered by his brother Euric, who initiated a quite different policy towards Rome, intent on creating a comprehensive Visigothic kingdom (see Intro 3.2). At the time of publication of Book 1, *c.* 469, Theoderic's portrait stands out as a manifest of Gallo-Roman–Visigothic cooperation and a warning against Visigothic aggression. Then follow two series of letters on the theme of Rome (Mathisen 2013, 235–8, Kelly 2020, 179–81), conveying both the strength and the weakness of the capital, which Sidonius dubs *domicilium legum, gymnasium litterarum, curiam dignitatum, uerticem mundi, patriam libertatis, in qua unica totius orbis ciuitate soli barbari et serui peregrinantur* (1.6.2).

Letters 1.5 and 1.9 together give an account of Sidonius' travels and second visit to Rome on a diplomatic mission on behalf of the Auvergne to the new emperor in 467–8 (see 1.9.5n. *legationis Aruernae*), and his successful quest for protection resulting in the Panegyric of Anthemius and his city prefecture. They arguably are one original letter split for the purpose of publication (letter 1.9 has a concluding section, but no formal opening, whereas the opposite is the case in 1.5: Köhler 1995, 265, Kelly 2020, 184, who compares Pliny's Vesuvius letters 6.16 and 6.20). Intertwining with letters about the first visit in 455–6 and the 469 trial for alleged treason of the Gallic prefect Arvandus, which happened during Sidonius' term in office and directly affected him as head of the senate and as an interested party in Gallic factional strife, they establish the theme of civil service in Rome and the divided loyalties in Gaul (see Intro 1 and 4.1).

Discussion

This letter is modelled on Horace's poetic account of his voyage to Brindisi in *Sat.* 1.5 on a diplomatic mission leaving Rome (Sidonius, as an envoy, is travelling towards it) and continues a literary tradition which goes back to Lucilius' *Voyage to Sicily* (*Sat.* 3, 119/116 BCE). It pairs the attractiveness of a travelogue with the deeper layers of a personal, a religious, and a political message, abounding in allusions and allowing a variety of readings from literal to allegorical. Throughout, potentially disruptive tensions lurk: between Gaul and Italy, Ravenna and Rome, Anthemius and Ricimer. Rome is unstable for all its glory (cf. 1.6.2 *domicilium legum, gymnasium litterarum, curiam dignitatum, uerticem mundi, patriam libertatis*). If read as an inward journey of conversion, preparing the reader for the future bishop (as does Eigler 1997), the overriding presence of water, and the lack of it, develop their full allegorical potential (below and van Waarden forthcoming). In contrast to the Horatian hypotext, there are few signs of interaction in detail with other, more recent travel accounts like Ausonius' *Mosella* and Rutilius Namatianus' *De reditu suo* (though there is a parallel with Claudian's *Panegyric on the Sixth Consulship of Honorius*). The religious element fits in with the Christianizing trend in travel literature favouring pilgrimage accounts (*BNP* 'Travel Literature', Soler 2005).

The Italy through which Sidonius travels as well as the Rome where he comes to stay had suffered considerably from barbarian incursions, Rome having been looted in 410 by the Visigoths and in 455 by the Vandals. Disrepair of the main roads and the strategic relocation of the court to

Ravenna had redefined the overall transport system, favouring travel by water (see already Rutilius in the 410s, Fo 1991). Sidonius' itinerary shows that this was even the case for the imperial postal service, the *cursus publicus* (Franceschelli and Dall'Aglio 2014). The city of Rome was in decline, its population reduced to half or less of what it had been in the Augustan period (*BNP* 'Rome IIA Population') and much of its built environment subject to destruction and progressive abandonment and spoliation (Harries 1994, 155–8). Among the public buildings still in use – as far as Book 1 is concerned – were sections of the imperial palace (§10 below), parts of the senatorial complex (1.7.9; Machado 2019, 119–20), the *rostra* and the Capitol (1.7.4 and 8, 1.11.3); in addition, a variety of public spaces (§10, 1.10.2), port facilities (1.10.2), travellers' lodgings (§9), senatorial mansions (1.9.5n.), aqueducts and the Aurelian Walls (§9). In the fifth century, new building projects were mainly Christian foundations (taken as an indication of a developing 'temple society' economy by Wood 2022: S. Maria Maggiore and S. Stefano Rotondo are cases in point), which gave the city a decidedly Christian character (Machado 2019; the classic survey is Krautheimer 1980, ch. 2). Characteristically, throughout the letter, Sidonius ignores mundane material inconveniences in his devotion to the grand ideas of *Romanitas* and *Christianitas* in addition to keeping silent about his inevitably traumatic memories of the botched year with Avitus in Rome (455–6).

Addressee

Heronius, also the addressee of 1.9, is otherwise unknown. He could have been born in Lyon (§2 *Rhodanusiae nostrae*). As a participant in Arvernian decision-making (§1 *commune consilium*), he may well have been a *uir clarissimus*, as Mathisen thinks. He wrote poetry (1.9.7); cf. Intro 3.3 'Elite Status'. Prosopography: Mathisen 2020a, 99; cf. Marolla 2024, 809.

Date and Place

The narrated time is the autumn of 467, before the celebration of Anthemius' second consulship on 1 January 468 where Sidonius is to pronounce the Panegyric (*Carm.* 2). The time of writing may be the same but could well be months later, in combination with 1.9, after the panegyric and Sidonius' promotion. The letter's open end, amid the uncompleted marriage of strongman Ricimer, is, above all, a narratological 'cliffhanger' suggesting a politically uncertain future (Hanaghan 2019, 63; cf. Intro 4.3).

Literature

Commentary: Köhler 1995, 183–215. Studies: Uggeri 1987, esp. 325; Gualandri 1979, 49–55; Uggeri 1990, esp. 177–8; Fo 1991, esp. 64–5; Fernández López 1994, 204–29; Eigler 1997; Percival 1997; Piacente 2005; Soler 2005; Mazzoli 2006; Wolff 2012; Longobardi 2014; Franceschelli and Dall'Aglio 2014; Fournier and Stoehr-Monjou 2014; Fournier and Stoehr-Monjou 2015; Wolff 2016; Hanaghan 2017a; Fascione 2018; Hanaghan 2019, 39–42 and 61–3; Oppedisano 2020; Gualandri 2020, 310–12; Herrin 2020b; Stoehr-Monjou 2021; Urlacher-Becht 2023, 312–19; van Waarden forthcoming.

Commentary

1 Litteras tuas Romae positus accepi: an epistolary formula, cf. e.g. Cic. *Att.* 6.1.1 *Accepi tuas litteras ... Laodiceae*. In this polite interactive opening paragraph the sender and the addressee are referred to in the singular (*tuas ... accepi*), as they are at the end of the combined letter 1.9.7–8 (but see 1.9.7n. *uestris*, 8 *nostram*), which makes for an uncomplicated exchange (Intro 4.2). *positus* 'living', 'finding oneself', of individuals largely from 2nd cent. onwards (*TLL* 10/1.2663.51–4), e.g. 7.7.2n. *positis intra castra*. **secundum commune consilium:** probably the joint agenda of the Arvernian leadership which had sent Sidonius as its delegate. **peregrinationis** 'foreign travel' (*OLD* 1), acquiring overtones of a pilgrimage in §9 (healing at the sanctuaries: Eigler 1997, 176) and denouncing the lack of seriousness in politics in §10. **sollicitus** 'meticulous', 'in detail' (L–S IIE). **uiam ... fluuios ... urbes ... montes ... campos:** the list of a travelogue, cf. Apul. *Mund.* praef. *moenia urbis ... amnis fluenta ... magnitudines montium*, Sidon. 3.2.3 *aggeres ... fluuios ... colles ... ualles* (cf. Ov. *Ars* 1.220 *loca ... montes ... aquae*). The sentence unfolds in four parallel noun phrases (*isocolon*: Intro 4.5). **fluuios ... poetarum carminibus illustres:** the reader is introduced to a literary landscape; cf. 2.9.1 *celebrata poetarum carminibus iuga*. Descriptions and catalogues of rivers are a staple of poetry from Homer (*Il.* 12.19–24) onward: Ovid *Met.*, for instance, contains four such catalogues (1.568–87, 2.241–59, 14.326–34, 15.270–95) and Ausonius' *Mosella* is entirely devoted to the description of one river. **urbes moenium situ inclitas:** so-called *laudes urbium* are part of rhetorical teaching (Menander Rhetor §346–51, ed. Russell and Wilson 1981). Examples include Ausonius' *Ordo urbium nobilium*, paralleled by Sidonius' *Carm.* 33.15–24 (in 7.17, see commentary), who also praises Rome (1.6.2), Constantinople (*Carm.* 2.31–67) and Narbonne (*Carm.*

23.37–68): van Waarden 2016, 224–5. **moenium situ** 'the layout of the buildings', 'townscape': for *moenia* in this sense, see *TLL* 8.1327.43–58; cf. 7.1.3n. *moenium*. For *situs*: *OLD* 3; cf. 2.2.3 *agri … situs*, Plin. 5.6.3 *regionis situm* 'landscape'. **montes nominum opinione uulgatos** 'mountains widely known due to the suggestiveness of their names': *opinione* 'reputation' (*OLD* 5d), cf. 1.1.4n. *uersuum … opinione*. As a case in point, Sidonius will cross the Alps with all the famous associations evoked by that name. Wilamowitz' emendation *numinum* is unnecessary (Mossberg 1934, 1). **campos proeliorum replicatione monstrabiles:** *replicatione* 'repetition' (L–S IV), i.e. 'recollection', 'recalling to mind'; cf. 2.9.10n., 7.7.2n. *si prisca replicarentur. monstrabiles* 'remarkable' is rare: also 3.7.2, 4.3.5, borrowed from Pliny 6.21.3 with identical construction; Wolff 2020, 400. **uoluptuosum** 'pleasurable' (*OLD* 1) returns in 1.9.7 where the addressee is supposed to have had enough of the (cover)letter, deeming it *uoluptuosius* to read the Panegyric itself. **inspexerint** with the nuance of 'observing' (*OLD* 3), 'seeing with one's own eyes'; cf. 4.20.1 *inspiciebantur*; cf. 8.3.4n. *peregrinere*. **fideliore didicisse memoratu:** seeing for oneself or having a first-hand account from someone is more reliable than reading, and indeed a basic incentive to travelling: cf. e.g. *Hist. Aug. Hadr.* 17.8 *peregrinationis ita cupidus, ut omnia quae legerat de locis orbis terrarum praesens uellet addiscere*, Mart. Cap. 2.149 *at iam fas puto quicquid … lectitans intellexeram conspicari*, Hier. 53.1 *ut eos quos ex libris nouerant coram quoque uiderent*, and implicitely Plin. 2.3.8–9; cf. 8.3.4n. *ipse … peregrinere. didicisse*: perfect for present infin. governed by verbs of desiring is a poeticism (*OLS* 1.539–40). Hyperbaton of the noun phrase is common in sentence endings to round off and create specific rhythms (*OLS* 2.1104–6), here a paeon I + spondee clausula (Intro 4.5). **namque:** frequent in Sidonius as an alternative to *nam*, mainly for reasons of euphony (cf. 1.9.2n., 2.10.3n., 3.9.1n., 7.1.1n.. 7.7.6n.). Unlike *nam*, it may occupy the second or third position in the sentence, creating room for a topic constituent (*OLS* 2, 1197–8, van Waarden 2010, 85–6 and 394–5; for topic, Intro 4.3). **huiuscemodi:** see 1.1.4n. *hisce*. **de affectu interiore:** cf. 1.7.2 *ab affectu profundiore*. The preposition *de* gradually ousts *ex* and *ab* in later Latin (cf. 7.1.1n.). *affectus* 'attachment', 'sympathy' is one of the many words which designate friendship in social relations, like *amicitia, gratia, necessitudo, caritas* and *amor* (van Waarden 2010, 189; Intro 3.3 'Social Conventions'). **ilicet** 'therefore', 'consequently' (Serv. *Aen.* 8.223 *potest 'ilicet' accipi pro 'igitur' aut 'continuo'*), signposting the next step in a reasoning or narrative (*TLL* 7/1.329.59–75); also 1.9.5n., 2.9.4n. **etsi secus quaepiam** 'although some things went wrong' (*OLD secus* 3) is a reminder that the confidence projected by the first stages of the journey is not all there is. For the ellipse of *fieri*, see K–S 2, 553–4. **sub ope …**

dei: cf. 1.9.8n. *sub ope Christi.* Sidonius' epistles are scattered with similar devout phrases (van Waarden 2010, 88), here specifically the wish for an auspicious start under the protection of the deity, cf. e.g. Liv. *praef.* 13 *cum ... precationibus deorum dearumque ... inciperemus,* Plin. *Paneg.* 1.1 *initium ... nihil ... sine deorum immortalium ope.* In the course of the letter, it will become apparent that Sidonius really needs (and, when in Rome, receives) divine assistance in his illness. **ordiar a secundis:** words of good omen first, cf. Symm. 4.19.1 *a prosperis ordiendum est.* **maiores nostri:** cf. e.g. Cic. *Div.* 1.102 *maiores nostri,* Plin. *Paneg.* 1.1 *maiores* in a comparable context. **sinisteritatum** 'misfortunes' is rare, modelled on Plin. 6.17.3, 9.5.2 (Wolff 2020, 400). **euoluere auspicabantur:** *euoluere OLD* 7. *auspicari OLD* 3a. The clausula cretic + spondee is by far the commonest in Sidonius, though grander as a single word (Intro 4.5).

2 egresso mihi Rhodanusiae nostrae moenibus: programmatic opening words, referring to Hor. *Sat.* 1.5.1 *egressum magna me accepit Aricia Roma*; see Discussion above. *Rhodanusiae nostrae* 'our <town> on the Rhône', i.e. Lyon, an idiosyncratic word formation, establishing rivers and water as the literal and metaphorical theme of this letter. *nostrae* either inclusive (mine and my family's) or sociative (mine and yours), in which case Heronius would have been a native of Lyon, too. **publicus cursus** 'state transport': a courier service and transport system across the empire, available only on warrant from the emperor, as was the case for Sidonius (*BNP* 'Cursus publicus', *OCD* 'Postal service', *ODLA* 440; Corsi 2000, Crogiez-Pétrequin 2021). Anteposition of *publicus* lends it the contextual role of highlighting Sidonius' privilege, the neutral order being *cursus publicus* (Intro 4.3). **usui fuit** 'was at my service': *usui* is a predicative dative (*NLS* §68); see below §7 *diuisui.* **sacris apicibus** 'an imperial missive': a so-called *euectio,* granting permission to send a requested embassy (Oppedisano 2022, 70); for the diplomatic mission, see 1.9.5n. *legationis Aruernae. sacer* 'holy', 'hallowed' is an attribute of the emperor (*OLD* 7; cf. *Cod. Iust.* 2.7.25.4 *per augustos apices*); it sets apart people and objects that belong to the divine sphere, opp. *profanus* (Ulp. *Dig.* 1.8.9). *apices* (pl.) 'letter' or any other piece of writing (later Latin: *TLL* 2.227.81, L–S IIE); also 5.16.3n. **per domicilia sodalium propinquorumque:** Sidonius initially takes his time visiting friends and kinsfolk, in the aristocratic way (cf. letter 2.9), no doubt also to create understanding for his embassy. This could offer an indication of where Sidonius crossed the Alps – a much-debated issue to date – as this part of his network extended mainly south of Lyon into Provence, with the Rhône as its backbone (Crogiez-Pétrequin 2010, 37–9; Mratschek 2020b, 218–22). The *Tabula Peutingeriana* (medieval copy of a third-/fourth-century map of the road system for the *cursus* *publicus*, *OCD* 'Peutinger Table') delineates three possible routes starting from Vienne, which would have been Sidonius' first stop, and leading to two Alpine passes, the northerly Alpis Graia Pass (Petit-Saint-Bernard, leading to the Aosta Valley) or, via two alternative roads, the southerly Alpis Cottia/Matrona Mons Pass (Mont-Genèvre, leading to the Susa Valley) (see Map 3). Fournier and Stoehr-Monjou 2014, Fournier and Stoehr-Monjou 2015 opt for the Petit-Saint-Bernard, Crogiez-Pétrequin 2010 and Wolff 2016, 196 n. 9 for the Mont-Genèvre. The latter gained importance in late antiquity generally, but the *Peutingeriana* does not indicate a postal road. **non ueredorum paucitas:** despite strict regulations, lack of horses (light *uerēdi*) was a notorious pain at the postal stations, which were bound to provide from five to ten each (*Cod. Theod.* 8.5.49; Crogiez-Pétrequin 2021). **arto implicita complexu:** for hugging on taking leave, cf. e.g. Hor. *Sat.* 1.5.43, Rut. Nam. 1.35–6, Sidon. 4.8.1. **itum reditumque:** for wishes for safe journey and return, cf. e.g. Cic. *Att.* 15.5.3 *noster itus reditus*, Suet. *Tib.* 38 *uota pro itu ac reditu suo*. **sic Alpium iugis appropinquatum:** this reminds the reader of the classic crossing of the Alps by Hannibal, cf. Liv. 21.35.4 *nono die in iugum Alpium peruentum est*. Whereas the story as a whole is told in the first person, two impersonal verbs punctuate the journey, *appropinquatum* at the Alps and *uentum* at the Rubicon (§7). Kelly (van Waarden and Kelly 2020, 472) points out the four roughly even, rhythmically marked clauses which make up the sentence. **citus et facilis:** unlike Hannibal's struggling and the terrifying reputation of the Alps in general (Sil. 3.476–99, Amm. 15.10.2), Sidonius pretends it was easy going. The literary landscape so far suggests that man (Roman) has tamed nature. **terrentis … praerupti:** cf. Liv. 21.32.9 *inter confragosa omnia praeruptaque*. The hyperbaton graphically illustrates the slopes on both sides, as does *cauatis … niuibus* for the heaps of snow. **itinera mollita** 'trails made less steep', cf. Liv. 21.37.3 *molliuntque … cliuos*.

3 uel certe peruii: *OLD certe* 2c, *OLD peruius* 1. **antiquitas:** the ancestors are praised for installing robust structures where nature fell short; cf. Agenn. *Grom.* p. 53, 8 [boundaries] *quae aut loci natura aut sollers procurauit antiquitas*. Couched in apposite technical language, this graphic vignette closes the first stage of the journey. **aggerem calcabili silice crustatum** 'the roadway coated with sturdy gravel': *agger* 'road' *OLD* 4b, see 2.9.2n., *Carm.* 27.22n. (in 2.10.4). *calcabilis* 'walkable', 'rideable' is rare, possibly a Sidonian neologism (Wolff 2020, 397–405, also for the following). **crypticis arcubus fornicauit** 'has vaulted with covered arches' is a verbal tour de force with the rare graecism *crypticus* (*TLL* 4.1261.47–54; *cryptoporticus* 'covered gallery', though, is in normal use) and *fornico*, in

Sidonius only (*TLL* 6/1.1123.51–4; also *Carm.* 23.319). **Ticini:** *Ticinum*, modern Pavia, on the River Ticino, not far from its confluence with the River Po, connected with the Adriatic Sea by land (the *Via Aemilia* to Rimini) or by water (Sidonius' route via the Po to Ravenna; Uggeri 1990, 178); see *ODLA* 1153 'Pavia'. **cursoriam ... escendi:** Sidonius explains the technical term *cursoria* 'boat of the *cursus publicus*', 'express boat' (*TLL* 4.1528.75–8; Uggeri 1990, 188). *escendi* 'I boarded' (not 'disembarked') *TLL* 5/2.857.47–59. **Eridanum:** the Greek name for the Po (*Padus* below §5), in poetry (from Verg. *Georg.* 4.372 onward), suits the mythical setting now evoked; cf. Plin. *Nat.* 3.117 *Eridanus ... poena Phaetontis illustratus*. The name also signposts Sidonius' hypotext, Claud. *VI Hon.* 146–209, with the landscape of the Po (v. 148 *Eridanus*) as the backdrop for the defeat of Alaric's Goths. **cantatas saepe comissaliter nobis Phaethontiadas:** at parties, guests used to recite poetry (Apul. *Apol.* 10). *comissaliter* 'in party mood' is a hapax (L–S s.v., Wolff 2020, 398 for Sidonius' coinage of adverbs in *-ter*). *Phaethontiadas*: Phaethon's sisters (first named thus Verg. *Ecl.* 4.63) mourn their brother who, unable to steer the sun's chariot, crashed into the Po. They are turned into poplar trees, their tears into amber (Ov. *Met.* 1.750–2.366). Claudian, *VI Hon.* 159–92, evokes their appearance and their brother's hubris. Unlike Claudian, who is serious about the fate of those, like Alaric, who dare to jeopardize Rome (they will meet their end like Phaethon), Sidonius seems to treat the episode in a light-hearted way, but a case can be made that this is hidden criticism of Ricimer as another Alaric (Fournier and Stoehr-Monjou 2014 §34, Hanaghan 2017a, 638–9), especially as Ricimer must have haunted Sidonius for personal reasons in these regions (below §4n. *in suis ... inspexi*). **arborei metalli:** cf. Ov. *Met.* 2.365 *de ramis electra*, 10.262–3 *ab arbore lapsas | Heliadum* [= Phaethon's sisters] *lacrimas*, Claud. *VI Hon.* 163–4 *rami caput umbrauere uirentes | Heliadum totisque fluunt electra capillis. metallum* for any extracted substance, *TLL* 8.874.68–83. **risi** echoes Hor. *Sat.* 1.5.97–103, where the company makes merry (v. 98 *risusque iocosque*) at local superstition. As a Christian, Sidonius will reject all pagan myth dealt with in poetry as *poetarum figmenta* (Arnob. *Nat.* 4.32, Aug. *Conf.* 1.17). *lacrimas risi* is the final pun.

4 Sidonius' progress is measured by means of a list of tributaries, Lambro, Adda, Mincio and Adige, inspired by Claud. *VI Hon.* 195–7 where the *Ligures Venetosque ... amnes* appear as follows: *pulcher Ticinus et Addua uisu | caerulus et uelox Athesis tardusque meatu | Mincius inque nouem consurgens ora Timauus*. Cf. also the generic model of the full-blown catalogue of tributaries of the Moselle in Auson. *Mos.* 349–80 (Dräger 1997, 15–21). The journey took about five days (Cassiod. *Var.* 4.45). **uluosum Lambrum:** the

Lamber joins the Po opposite *Placentia* (Piacenza). *uluosus* 'abounding in sedge [*ulua*]' (Sidonius only, also *Carm.* 7.324). **caerulum Adduam:** the *Addua* (Adda) flows into the Po near Cremona. *caerulus* 'greenish-blue' (*OLD* 2), as in Claudian above. The pair is opposed for their light and dark colours, respectively. **uelocem Athesin:** a traveller on the imperial boat service would not have encountered the *Athesis* (Adige), which is further north. Sidonius' literary borrowing from Claudian sits uneasily with his actual journey. *uelocem* is consistent with *Paneg.* 12(9).8.2 *Athesis ... asper ... uorticosus ... ferox*, but the river is *amoenus* in Verg. *Aen.* 9.680, Ambr. *Hex.* 5.2.6, Cassiod. *Var.* 3.48. **pigrum Mincium:** the Mincio reaches the Po below Mantua. Geographically, it runs west of the Adige: the inverse order is due to Claudian. For *pigrum*, cf. Verg. *Georg.* 3.14–15 *tardis ingens ubi flexibus errat | Mincius*. For the pair *Athesis* and *Mincius*, cf. also Claud. *Carm. min.* 12.11–13. Again an opposed pair, slow-fast, both pairs asyndetic (Intro 4.5). **Ligusticis Euganeisque montibus** broadly indicates the Alpine mountain range from west to east, synonymous with Claudian's *Ligures Venetosque* (cf. Claud. *Carm. min.* 12.6–7 *Ligures fauete campi, | Veneti fauete montes*). The ancient Euganei were driven out by the Veneti; their region comprised Verona, Aquileia and Padua, among other settlements (*BNP* 'Euganei'). **aduersa** 'upstream' (*OLD* 6). **in suis etiam gurgitibus inspexi:** *gurgitibus* poetical (*OLD* 2). The autopsy (*inspexi*) serves to visualize the lifelike *locus amoenus*. Peace reigns in a landscape that has had its share of war and injustice – the first of a series of allusions that bemoan war in Italy. The infamous distribution of lands in Virgil's time is duly mentioned, but – significantly – the defeat and death of Sidonius' own father-in-law Avitus in the war with Ricimer at nearby Piacenza a mere eleven years before is not (Intro 1). **ripae torique:** *torus* 'bank' (L–S v), cf. Verg. *Aen.* 6.674 *riparumque toros*. **quernis acernisque:** for the oaks, Verg. *Aen.* 9.680–1 *siue Padi ripis Athesim seu propter amoenum | consurgunt geminae quercus*; maple-trees do not belong in these riparian forests (Regato 2022) and are a literary invention, added as a poetic rarity for sonic reasons. **auium ... concentus:** cf. e.g. Cic. *Leg.* 1.21, Verg. *Georg.* 1.422. **dulce** adverbial. **in concauis harundinibus ... in iuncis pungentibus ... in scirpis enodibus:** triple parallelism with variation and rhyme (Intro 4.5). *scirpi* 'bulrushes' are proverbially smooth (*OLD* 1b). **nidorum strues** 'nest structure': this meaning of *strues* is rare, Tert. *Adv. Val.* 15 *struem mundi*, *CIL* 8.647. **tumultuatim** 'profusely': Sidonius only (4.11.2, 8.6.6). **amnicos margines:** later Latin favours attributive adjectives over the possessive (and, more rarely, objective) genitive (H–S 60); cf. *Carm.* 27.27n. *amnicum*. **soli bibuli suco:** *bibuli* 'spongy' *OLD* 2a, e.g. Mart. 11.32.2 *de bibula ... palude* (of reeds); *suco OLD* 4.

5 obiter: probably 'soon' with verbs of motion (van Waarden 2010, 174). **Cremonam:** first stop, corresponding to the River Adda above. **Tityro Mantuano:** i.e. Virgil, born in Mantua and disguised as Tityrus in the *Eclogues* (*Ecl.* 1.1, Sidon. *Carm.* 4.1); the case is dat. of agent. **largum suspirata proximitas:** *largum* as an adverb, 'copiously', is rare (*TLL* 7/2.974.79–83). Mantua is pitied for its vicinity to Cremona at Verg. *Ecl.* 9.28 *Mantua uae miserae nimium uicina Cremonae* (cf. Mart. 8.55.7 *iugera ... miserae uicina Cremona*). Having defeated Brutus and Cassius at Philippi (42 BCE), the veterans were assigned the lands of Cremona among other towns. As this proved insufficient, Mantua, forty miles distant, was expropriated as well. **Brixillum:** present-day Brescello, halfway between Cremona and Mantua on the right bank of the Po, apparently the harbour where crews changed between the western (*Aemiliano*) and eastern (*Venetus*) sections (*BNP* 'Brixellum'; for the late-Roman provinces of *Aemilia et Liguria* and *Venetia et Histria*, *LRE* 1069 Map II, *BNP Atlas* 224–5). **Rauennam:** the main imperial residence for the first half of the fifth century, as the capital Milan had become unsafe due to the invading Goths, it continued to serve strategic and ceremonial functions between 450 and 476, when the emperors predominantly resided in Rome (Gillett 2001; see 1.9.1n. *gratiae aditus*). The town consisted of three parts: the town proper, its harbour *Classis* to the south and the suburb *Caesarea* in-between. It was linked to the southern branch of the Po by the *Fossa Augusta* (*BNP* 'Ravenna', *OCD* 'Ravenna', *ODLA* 'Ravenna and Classe'; Mauskopf Deliyannis 2010 (map p. 42), Herrin 2020a). **paulo post ... subeuntes:** the distance from Brixillum obviously being considerable, this looks like a wink at Hor. *Sat.* 1.5.25–6 *milia tum tria repimus atque subimus | ... Anxur*, where Horace 'crawls on' only three miles to arrive at Anxur. **cursu dexteriore** 'bearing to the right', via the canalized connection with the Po. **quo loci** = *ubi* (Wolff 2020, 397). **ueterem ... nouumque:** Augustus indeed built a new port to create an Adriatic naval base, connecting it to the old town by means of the *Via Caesaris* and further north to the Po through the *Fossa Augusta* flanking the older *Via Popilia*, but this binary opposition is also a favourite stylistic device in Sidonius (Intro 4.5, cf. 5.5.2n., 7.1.3n.). **ambigas utrum:** a favourite Sidonian phrase, again creating an opposition (cf. 3.11.2, 7.6.6, 8.4.2); it is the rhetorical device of *dubitatio* (see e.g. *Rhet. Her.* 4.40). Sidonius' Ravenna is an ambiguous town, both thriving and unhealthy, defended as well as split by its canals. This is developed in what follows, not least stylistically. Metaphorically, Ravenna is a *locus horridus* – no doubt court intrigues and all – though not without hope, as against Rome which is spiritually healing but unbalanced on a daily basis. Strikingly, Sidonius entirely concentrates on the town's briny and filthy waters, whereas he could, for instance, have highlighted its fine churches as he does elsewhere for other churches (e.g. letter 2.10), among them bishop Ursus' Basilica with the new (still existing) Baptistry of Neon and the Church of the Holy Cross with its equally new (and surviving) oratory, the so-called Mausoleum of Galla Placidia. In his framing, however, the town is infested with mosquitoes and constitutes an upside-down world (see 1.8.2). **oppidum duplex:** the old town, divided by a branch of the Po (Padenna), was successively provided with canals within and around its (archaeologically elusive) walls (Mauskopf Deliyannis 2010, 53–5). The phrase echoes Auson. *Mos.* 481 *duplicemque per urbem* [Arles], *Ep.* 24.73 *duplex Arelas.* **pars ... Padi certa:** for *certus* 'fixed', 'regulated', of a river, cf. Mela 3.24 *Rhenus ... diu solidus et certo alueo lapsus haud procul a mari huc et illuc dispergitur.* The chosen interpunction is supported by most manuscripts; however, there is some discussion among editors: Lütjohann distrusted *certa*. **molium publicarum discerptus obiectu:** for *molium* (*OLD* 3d) *publicarum*, cf. 2.9.2 *aggerum publicorum. discerpo OLD* 2. The ramification of this sentence mirrors the intricacy of Ravenna's water management. **exhaustus** 'drained': *OLD* 1a.

6 hic cum ... tum praecipue ... deferebatur: probably – in this stylistic context – best taken as parallel clauses, with both *cuncta* and *quod* as subjects of *deferebatur*, agreeing in number with the nearest subject, as usual (*OLS* 1, 1248). Alternatively, supply *essent* with *peropportuna. hic* indicating direction is a feature of later Latin (*TLL* 6/3.2763.34–65); MSS *MTF* changed to *huc*. **esui:** food supply being the crucial factor in public well-being as Sidonius himself experienced as town prefect (see letter 1.10). **salsum ... pelagus:** *salsum*, by being fronted, stresses the water's undrinkability. *pelagus* 'sea', 'sea-water' is predominantly found in poetry, but in prose it is a sober technical term (cf. e.g. Colum. 12.24.1, Vitr. 8.2.2). **hinc ... sordidaretur:** a single virtuoso string of nouns and adjectives makes the sticky blubber tangible. The subject phrase *ipse ... umoris* is surrounded by two phrases in absolute ablatives: *cloacali ... uentilata* and *nauticis .. glutino.* **pulte:** *puls* in the sense of 'sludge', 'pulp' occurs only in Sidonius, also *Carm.* 41.76n. (*TLL* 10/2.2603.43–6). **sordidaretur** 'was dirtied', 'was polluted', late Latin (see L–S); cf. 2.9.10n. **discursu lintrium:** *discursu OLD* 3, e.g. Amm. 23.6.11 *nauium crebri discursu. linter* 'pirogue', a long canoe, poled standing up, archaeologically well documented for Cisalpine Gaul (Uggeri 1990, 188–91), and suited for a variety of transport (Serv. *Georg.* 1.262). **languidus lapsus:** *lapsus OLD* 2a; cf. 2.2.1 *aqua ... labens ... languescit.* The sluggishness is illustrated by the hyperbaton *lentati ... umoris.* **nauticis cuspidibus:** for *nauticis*, cf. §4n. *amnicos. cuspis* 'pole' *TLL* 4.1554.53. **foraminato ... glutino:** *foramino* 'to pierce'

Sidonius only, also 2.2.4, 3.3.5. *glutinum* here 'sticky mud' (see *OLD*). **in medio undarum sitiebamus:** the oxymoronic plight of Tantalus, cf. e.g. Ov. *Am.* 3.12.30 *in medio Tantalus amne sitit*; of Ravenna, also *Carm.* 9.298 [someone heading for the town] *undosae petiit sitim Rauennae* (water there is more expensive than wine: Mart. 3.56 and 57). At the same time, the transition is made to water bearing existential overtones in the rest of the letter, spiritual thirst being only quenched *apostolorum liminibus* (§9). The association is with the biblical episode of Jesus and the Samaritan woman at the well, Vulg. *Ioh.* 4.13 *omnis qui bibit ex aqua hac* [from the well], *sitiet iterum; qui autem biberit ex aqua quam ego dabo ei, non sitiet in aeternum*. The reader may remember Sidonius' recent *conuersio* and baptism by bishop Faustus at Riez (*Carm.* 16.71–90; Intro 1 and 3.4), which took place in the heat of summer amid *sitientes... agros*. In the letter's hypotext, Hor. *Sat.* 1.5.7 *propter aquam, quod erat deterrima*, Horace decides not to eat only that evening. **uel ... uel ... uel ... uel**, four times emphatically the need for pure water. **aquaeductuum:** at the time in bad condition, restored under Theoderic the Great in 502 (Cassiod. *Chron. MGH AA* 11.160). **defaecabilis** 'filtering': so Köhler 1995, 201 correctly; for active *-bilis*, cf. 2.2.16 *peruagabilis* 'flitting about' (Wolff 2020, 398). **illimis** 'free from mud': only other instance Ov. *Met.* 3.407 *fons erat inlimis*. For an altogether more positive assessment of Ravenna's climate in ancient sources, see Pellizzari 2003, 36 with n. 8.

7 unde progressis ad Rubiconem uentum: formulated like a military campaign, cf. *Bell. Afr.* 25.3, *Epit. Alex.* 35.11, with unusual construction of abl. abs. and impersonal verb, introducing the next stage, for which Sidonius may have had in mind the description of the emperor Honorius' travels from Ravenna and his *aduentus* in Rome in Claud. *VI Hon.* 494–522 (cf. Kelly 2016). The Rubicon, not unequivocally identified with any modern river, was a reddish stream (hence its name) flowing into the Adriatic between Ravenna and Rimini, marking the boundary between Italy and Cisalpine Gaul. In 49 BCE, Caesar crossed it, unleashing civil war. **puniceo:** cf. Luc. 1.214 *puniceus Rubicon*. **diuisui fuere** 'were divided', with the notion of plunder (*OLD*). The noun *diuisus* is found only in dat., in Livy and once in Gellius. *fuere*: the ind. perf. 3rd pers. plur. ending *-ēre* is found in Plautus, Terence and poetry, and employed for its poetic flavour by Livy and Tacitus in parts of their work; in later prose. *-ēre* and *-ērunt* are applied depending on the desired rhythm (Löfstedt 1956, 2, 295–6, H–S 720). In his letters, Sidonius uses *-ērunt* twice as often as *-ēre*, but always writes *fuere*. Perf. forms in *-ēre* tendentiously take up the last or the penultimate position in the clause. **Ariminum Fanumque:** in Rimini, civil war began with Caesar occupying it, establishing his headquarters there and building up his forces (Caes. *Civ.* 1.11, Flor. *Epit.* 2.13.18). For Sidonius, when later defending Clermont, it will acquire the bleak connotation of the complaint of its inhabitants in Luc. 1.248–57: *o male uicinis haec moenia condita Gallis … nos praeda furentum primaque castra sumus … hac iter est bellis* (7.1.1n. *nos miseri Aruerni ianua sumus*). The *Via Flaminia* runs 209 miles from Rimini to Rome. At *Fanum Fortunae* (modern-day Fano), the road turns inland along River Metaurus. **Iuliana rebellione** is a one-off characterisation of Caesar's coup-d'état, in parallel with the next phrase; the adj. also at 2.14.1 *legionum Iulianarum*. In late antique perception, Caesar's image was generally positive, as the founder of the imperial dynasty; Sidonius shows this tendency at 8.6.1, 9.14.7 (Mratschek 2024). **Hasdrubaliano funere:** in the Second Punic War, in 207 BCE, the Carthaginian general Hasdrubal was defeated by the Romans at the Metaurus, a turning point in the war against Hannibal (Liv. 27.39–52, Sidon. *Carm.* 2.532 *improbus ut rubeat | Barcina clade Metaurus*; cf. Hor. *Carm.* 4.4.38–41 *testis Metaurum flumen et Hasdrubal | deuictus et pulcher fugatis | ille dies Latio tenebris, | qui primus alma risit adorea*). **ita … ac si:** *OLD ita* 1c. **uno die parta porrigitur:** cf. Horace's *ille dies … qui primus.* **Dalmatico salo:** the Adriatic Sea. The province of Dalmatia roughly comprised present-day Croatia and Bosnia-Herzegovina, capital Salona (*Carm.* 23.497 *Dalmaticae … Salonae*). *salum* with adj. for a particular sea is poetic (*OLD* 2b; *Carm.* 7.370 *Britannum,* 9.19 *rubrum*). **cadauera … inferret,** an epic motif from Homer *Il.* 21.218–20 onwards (Gualandri 1979, 54 with n. 65), also as an emotional argument in oratory (Cic. *Sest.* 77 *corporibus ciuium Tiberim compleri*). For Sidonius' 'manneristic' taste in describing emotions through stylistic and conceptual extremes, see Intro 4.5 'Hyperbole'. **decoloratis gurgitibus:** cf. (for bloodshed in the civil war) Hor. *Carm.* 2.1.33–6 *gurges … decolorauere*; cf. also Ov. *Trist.* 4.42 *decolor ipse suo sanguine Rhenus.* With this reminder of the pernicious effects of (civil) war (perhaps hinting at a potential conflict Ricimer–Anthemius, see Fournier and Stoehr-Monjou 2014, §39; Hanaghan 2017a, 642–4), the tone is set for the following setback.

8 statim ut ingrediebar egressus: inverting §5 *tantum ut exiremus intrauimus.* **Picentes … Umbros:** for the provinces *Flaminia et Picenum* and *Tuscia et Umbria,* see *LRE* 1069 Map II, *BNP Atlas* 224–5. **mihi:** ethic dative (*OLS* 1.932–2). **Caleber Atabulus** 'the sirocco from Calabria': from Hor. *Sat.* 1.5.77–8 *incipit ex illo montes Apulia notos | ostentare mihi, quos torret Atabulus*; cf. Sen. *Nat.* 5.17.5 *Atabulus Apuliam infestat.* The sirocco is most felt in spring and autumn. The province of *Apulia et Calabria* is present-day Puglia. As Sidonius refers to Horace with *Caleber ille* in this very book (1.11.1), the intertextuality is even more intricate: 'Horace's sirocco' (cf. Gell. 2.22.3 *Horatianus* ... *ille Atabulus*).   **pestilens regio Tuscorum:** the coastal morasses of Tuscany were infamous for their malaria (Plin. 5.6.2 *est sane grauis et pestilens ora Tuscorum*; Sallares 2002). Actually, as both the sirocco and these morasses are a long way off from Umbria, the description is a rather grandiose way of evoking the elusive atmospherical threats from east and west to which the traveller is exposed.   **spiritu ... infecit:** contagion was thought to be air-borne from poisonous evaporations in hot and cold mists ('bad air' in Hippocrates and Galen; Nutton 1983): cf. Colum. 1.5.4 and, of malaria in particular, Vitr. 1.4.1, Varro *Rust.* 1.12. *spiritu aeris ... inebriato et ... alternante* 'with a current of air intoxicated ... and alternating between ...'. *modo calores ... modo frigora*: on the effects of hot and cold winds in general, already Hipp. *Aer.* 3–6; on the dangerous effects of alternating warmth and cold, especially in autumn, Cels. 2.2, cf. Ov. *Ars* 2.317–8 *modo frigoribus ..., modo ... aestu.* Cf. 2.12.2n. *salubriter*.   **uaporatum** 'heated', 'feverish', proleptic.   **febris sitisque:** Cels. 3.6.1 *de potione uero ingens pugna est eoque magis quo maior febris est. haec enim sitim accendit e tum maxime aquam exigit, cum illa periculosissima est.* Celsus goes on to explain that the thirst will abate as soon as the fever goes down.   **cordis medullarumque secretum** 'the hidden parts of my heart and marrow', heart and marrow being one's vital and emotional core, affected by hunger and thirst (Sen. *Thy.* 97–9) and anger (Sen. *Ag.* 132), or comforted by friendship (Ruric. *Ep.* 2.10.3 *usque ad medullas cordis uestri dilectio nostra peruenit*, 2.19.17). In Christian idiom, God knows man's heart and marrow, e.g. *Hebr.* 4.12 [God] *pertingens usque ad diuisionem ... medullarum et discretor cogitationum et intentionum cordis.* God's knowledge of the *secreta cordis* is a commonplace throughout late antiquity. Hence, in an allegorical interpretation, Sidonius' heartrending thirst is also a longing for spiritual water (see above §6n. *in medio undarum sitiebamus*).   **amoena fontium aut abstrusa puteorum:** so-called inverse genitive, the characteristic late-Latin usage of an abstract noun or substantivized neuter adjective with a modifier in the gen. instead of a noun with an adjectival modifier (*amoena fontium* = *fontes amoeni*) (H–S 152).   **tota** 'all': *OLD* 6. The narrative pace quickens: we are nearing Rome.   **uitrea Fucini** opens an asyndetic paired list of six (3×2; Intro 4.5) lakes and rivers, carefully ordered ab ab ba ba ab ab with inverse gen. (*uitrea Fucini* = *Fucinus uitreus* etc.). All but Clitumnus are found in *Aeneid* 7, the prelude-*cum*-catalogue to the war between Aeneas and Turnus. Bellès 1, 166 n.59 stresses its hyperbolic character; Köhler 1995, 206 sees it as a humorous representation of Sidonius' extreme thirst. *uitrea Fucini:* the Lacus Fucinus, nowadays drained, south of L'Aquila, cf. Verg. *Aen.* 7.759 *uitrea ... Fucinus unda.* The reading *Fucini* is uncertain: the archetype seems to have read *sucini* (found in α *PNFLeip*), which is meaningless.

P adds *fu* above the line and the remaining MSS have *fucini*. Mommsen (followed by all modern editors except Köhler and Bellès) replaced it by *Velini* attested in *Aen.* 7.517 *fontesque Velini*, the *Velinus lacus* being north of Rieti, which is closer (*uicina*) to the Flaminia than Lake Fucinus (see Map 3). However, as shown in §4n. *uelocem Athesin*, Sidonius is not necessarily guided by geographical concerns (cf. Gualandri 1979, 54–5 with n. 66). **gelida Clitumni:** river in Umbria, ultimately flowing into the Tiber, mentioned Verg. *Georg.* 2.146, its source described Plin. 8.8 (§2 *purus et uitreus*). *uitreus* and *gelidus* of streams also combined at Hor. *Carm.* 3.13.1 and 6, Auson. *Mos.* 28 and 30. **Anienis caerula:** the river *Anien/Anio* (mod. Aniene) rises in Sabine country and falls into the Tiber (cascades at Tivoli), Verg. *Aen.* 7.683 *gelidumque Anienem*, Sil. 10.363 *gelidis Anien ... caerulus undis*. **Naris sulpurea:** the *Nar* (mod. Nera), sulphurous tributary of the Tiber rising in Umbria, Enn. *Ann.* 260 *sulphureas ... Naris ad undas*, Verg. *Aen.* 7.517; cf. Plin. 8.20.4 [Lago di Bassano] *color caerulo albidior ... sulpuris odor*. All south-east Tuscany is rich in sulphurous thermal springs. **pura Fabaris:** identified by Serv. *Aen.* 7.715 *qui Tiberim Fabarimque bibunt* with the *Farfarus* (mod. Farfa), which flows into the Tiber midway between the Nera and the Aniene. **turbida Tiberis:** turbid and irregular, the Tiber carries silt with it, choking its mouth (*OCD*); cf. Verg. *Aen.* 7.31 [the mouth of the Tiber] *uerticibus rapidis et multa flauus harena*, Ps.-Acro ad Hor. *Carm.* 1.2.13 '*uidimus flauum Tiberim*': *aut turbidum aut colore limi flauum*, referring to Virgil. The phrase is climactic, playing on sound *t-r-b-t-b-r*. **fallente** *OLD* 7a. **pollicebamur:** the plural for 'I' minimizes the rashness of this promise (Intro 4.2).

9 patuit et Roma conspectui 'there Rome came into view': *TLL* 10/1.661.42–63. Cf. Claud. *VI Hon.* 530–1 *se Roma uidendam | obtulit. et* makes for liveliness, cf. 1.9.5n. *ecce et*, 2.9.4n. *et ecce*, 2.9.6n. *ecce et*, 3.12.2n. *et superueni* (Merchie 1922, 147). **non solum formas uerum etiam naumachias:** water is all that occupies his mind; only here will his thirst be quenched. *forma*: masoned channel of an aqueduct (*OLD* 16d). *naumachia*: artificial lake for exhibiting mock sea-fights (*OLD* 2). Although these battles had long been obsolete, traces of the basins subsisted into late antiquity. The *Naumachia Traiani* or *Vaticana*, in particular, right behind the *Mausoleum Hadriani*, is reasonably well known from excavations (Richardson 1992, 265–6), giving its name to the *regio naumachiae*. This – and its dedicated aqueduct – is exactly where Sidonius must have passed by en route to St Peter's (also Eigler 1997, 175). Cf. Claud. *VI Hon.* 521–2 for the arches and other magnificent structures welcoming one when approaching Rome. **pomeria:** the *pomerium* is Rome's sacral boundary (Richardson 1992, 293–6), gradually enlarged but not coinciding with its expanding walls. For Sidonius, however, the *pomerium* and the walls (the *Muri Aureliani*, begun 271/2 and finished *c.* 10 years later; Richardson 1992, 260–2) seem to be identical. He may use the word *pomeria* to evoke the spiritual Christian 'refoundation' of Rome by the apostles (for the latter, see Harries 1994, 157; Hunsucker 2025, 233–305). Before entering the town and going about his business, he first goes to the sanctuaries of St Peter and St Paul – martyrs' churches in the cemeteries outside the walls. The habit is time-honoured, cf. *Pan.* 2(12).21.1 *sed quod facere magnas urbes ingressi solemus, ut primum sacras aedes et dicata numini summo delubra uisamus.* **triumphalibus apostolorum liminibus affusus:** *triumphalibus* because the martyrs were considered triumphant heroes (e.g. Damas. *Carm.* 23.7 *Christi meruere triumphos*, Prud. *Perist.* 2.3–4 *festus apostolici ... hic dies triumphi | Pauli atque Petri nobilis cruore*). Probably not quite incidentally, the road leading to the Vatican hill from the north is the *Via Triumphalis* (today Via Trionfale), whose name has not been adequately explained so far (*BNP* 'Vaticanus') but may well have had this association for Sidonius (Savaron, p. 36; Eigler 1997, 175). *apostolorum*: saints Peter and Paul, the successors of Romulus and Remus as Rome's patrons, according to Prudentius (*Perist.* 2.459–60 *hic nempe iam regnant duo | apostolorum principes*; *Perist.* 12 is entirely dedicated to them, both sentenced and buried near the Tiber, and venerated on either side; cf. Euseb. *Hist. eccl.* 2.25.5–8). *limen* 'home' *OLD* 2c, specifically 'area around the tomb of a saint', 'martyr's church', pilgrimages to Rome being called *ad limina apostolorum*. Peter's basilica was built on the Vatican Hill by Constantine in the 320s, while the chapel dedicated to Paul on the *Via Ostiensis* was replaced by a large church in the 380s (nowadays S. Paolo fuori le Mura). The first pilgrim guides that have come down to us, dating to the seventh century, describe the same circular movement to visit the cemeteries as Sidonius makes (Birch 1998, 6–7, 12–14, 27–37; esp. 29 for Peter and Paul's earliest memorial site, S. Sebastiano on the Via Appia; text Valentini and Zucchetti 1942; see Map 3). *affusus OLD* 7, cf. e.g. 4.23.3, Prud. *Cath.* 9.5. Sidonius professes his unworthiness (see Bailey 2020, 270). **omnem ... languorem:** miraculous healings will be immediate (*protinus*) and comprehensive (*omnem ... explosum OLD* 2), e.g. *Vitae patr. Iurens.* 146 *ut ... explosa omni inaequalitate* ['illness'], *confestim sanitatis pristinae commodis redderetur*. Sidonius' recovery implicitly also quenches his thirst. He has found his spiritual centre in the Rome of the apostles. Now, after some rest, he is ready for the unholy Rome of politicians. **post quae caelestis experimenta patrocinii:** cf. 7.1.3n. *post uirtutum experimenta* and 7n. *pars patrocinii*. With heavenly patronage secured, the quest for human patronage is opened. **conducti diuersorii:** despite his invitation, Sidonius has to hire his own lodging, as was usual for provincial envoys to the western court (Gillett 2003, 238–9). There is not even a hint at his having been here before: all previous contacts have apparently faded or are off-limits (see 1.9 for his being subsequently hosted by a private citizen as a springboard for securing patronage higher-up; van Waarden 2020b, 22–3; cf. Le Guennec 2017). Cf. 2.9.7n. *diuersorium* as 'guest room', 8.3.2n. 'living quarters'. **scriptitans**, with frequentative infix -*tit*-, but 'writing at one's will', 'privately' rather than 'frequently' (L–S II); only here in Sidonius who, however, uses *lectito* ten times, primarily as an alternative to *lego* (2.9.4n. *lectitabantur*, 7.18.3n. *lectitauisti*). **quieti** is opposed to *operam*, an opportunity for punning never lost on Sidonius. **pauxillulum** is an archaism from comedy (Mannheimer 1975, 169; Wolff 2020, 402; see Intro 4.4 and 4.5), also used at 2.9.8n., 8.3.3n.

10 tumultuosis foribus: the bustle of petitioners and *aulici* at the gate of the Visigothic court of Toulouse is no different, as the reader already knows (1.2.8–9), identical, for that matter, to any patron's morning audience (cf. e.g. Claud. *Olybr*. 43–7 *populus undare penates, adsiduos intrare*). **nuptiis patricii Ricimeris:** the *magister utriusque militiae* and *patricius* Flavius Ricimer played a defining role in the complex history of the years 456–72 in the west, a period of de facto civil war, supporting and eliminating emperors at will, among them Avitus, Majorian and Anthemius (prosopography Mathisen 2020a, 117–18; studies Anders 2010, Roberto 2020; historical overview Kulikowski 2020, 207–11). In the spring of 467, after an interregnum of a year and a half, he half-heartedly accepted the imperial nominee of the eastern emperor Leo I, Anthemius. The marriage of Anthemius' daughter and Ricimer was meant to provide stability; however, as an encoded reading of §§10–11 makes plausible (Hanaghan 2017a), Sidonius doubted a good outcome. He even dared to publicize his misgivings by circulating Book 1 not long after, as relations remained delicate. *patricius*: honorific, non-hereditary title for the highest-ranking civil officers (*ODLA* 1144); Sidonius himself got it thanks to his prefecture (5.16.4n., Claud. Mam. *Anim. praef.*). **filia perennis Augusti:** she was called Alypia (Mathisen 2020a, 127 'Anonyma 2'), but is clearly considered as no more than a pawn and remains anonymous, also at 1.9.1n. and *Carm.* 2.483–6 (*regia uirgo*). Only one quarter of women are given names in Sidonius as against three quarters of men (Mathisen 2020c, 44–5; for Sidonius' own awareness, see 7.9.24). *perennis* 'immortal' of emperors, *TLL* 10/1.1322.67–1323.7. **in spem publicae securitatis copulabatur:** in his Panegyric on Anthemius, Sidonius will say: *adice praeterea priuatum ad publica foedus* (*Carm.* 2.483). **ordinum partiumque** 'classes and walks of life': *ordo* 'social class', in the civil (senators, decurions etc.) as well as in the ecclesiastical domain (clerics, monks, widows etc.) (*OLD* 4; also *Carm.* 41.23n.; van Waarden 2010, 109–10, Mathisen 2020c, 33–8).

partes probably envisages the social division *pars ciuilis* and *pars armata*, the latter being particularly prominent under Ricimer (1.9.2n. *partis armatae*, *Carm.* 5.565–6 *ciuilis ... partis ... | ... armati*). **Transalpino tuo:** as a 'northerner' he is an outsider (1.8.3 *innoxiis Transalpinis*), aptly referring back to the initial passage of the Alps. **latere conducibilius uisum:** *latēre* is subject. *conducibilis* 'advisable' is an archaism (Mannheimer 1975, 158). **exarabantur** 'were written', 'were penned' (*OLD* 4); this is the 'epistolary imperfect', in the past from the perspective of the future reader; cf. e.g. Cic. *Att.* 5.20.5 *cum haec scribebam*. **theatra ... gymnasia:** Köhler 1995, 211 compares Plaut. *Amph.* 1011–13 and points out the run of seven endings in *-a*. **Thalassio Fescenninus explicaretur:** 'T(h)alassio' is the ritual cry as, after the ceremony and dinner, the bride is accompanied to the bridegroom's home (*BNP* 'Wedding Customs and Rituals III. Rome'). *Fescenninus* (*OLD* 2) of lewd songs sung at weddings, e.g. Catul. 61.120 *procax Fescennina iocatio*, Sidon. *Carm.* 14.*ep.* 1 [introducing a wedding poem] *quatenus ... Fescennina cantarem. explicaretur* 'died away' (*OLD* 9; cf. 2.1.4 *moras tuas ... explica*). **studia sileant:** here begins another list, this time divided into 2×3 cola (silence first: *sileant, quiescant, conticescant*, then suspension of activities: *differantur, uacet, peregrinetur*); verb-final, then verb-initial, with the last colon extended ('law of rising members', Intro 4.5 n.111; also 1.1.1n., 2.9.6n., 7.1.2n.). *studia* probably 'schools' (Haarhoff 1958, 111; cf. 4.21.4 *disciplinis grammatici rhetorisque studia*). Schools could be loud: Mart. 9.68. **iudicia conticescant:** cf. Cic. *Pis.* 26 *cum ... iudicia conticuissent*. **differantur legationes:** the Gallic embassy is a case in point. **scurrilitates histrionum:** cf. Aug. *Civ.* 6.1 *mimicae scurrilitati*. Already condemned by Quint. *Inst.* 11.1.30, *scurrilitas* 'bad language' is among the vices regularly denounced by Christian moralists (e.g. Caes. Arel. *Serm.* 6.1 *turpiloquia et scurrilitates*). All shows went counter to the seriousness of God's creation, inducing uncontrollable emotions in the spectators (fundamental is Tertullian's treatise *De spectaculis*, c. 200 CE). Sidonius combines a reminiscence of Plin. 4.25.3 *qui in tanta re tam serio tempore tam scurriliter ludat?* with Christian rigour. **peregrinetur:** the catchword of this letter; see §1n. *peregrinationis*.

11 iam six times, heightening anticipation; for repeated *iam*, cf. e.g. Hor. *Carm.* 3.29.17–24, Petron. 26.1. **uirgo tradita:** a woman is 'handed over' in marriage to another household in an act called *deductio in domum mariti*, making it a *matrimonium iustum* (cf. Quint. *Decl.* 306.5 *uirginem quam pater tradidit*; *OLD traditio* 5c; *BNP* 'Marriage III. Rome'. **coronam sponsus ... deponit:** cf. Ricimer's earlier counterpart Stilicho as bridegroom at Claud. *Carm. min.* 30.184–5 *iugalem | promeruit Stilicho socero referente coronam*. Wreaths were worn on festive occasions; at weddings, bride and groom were wreathed (*BNP* 'Wreath, Garland'). **palmatam consularis:** the *tunica palmata* is among the distinctions of consular dignity; cf. Sidon. *Carm.* 5.5 *post palmam* ['triumph'] *palmata uenit* (*BNP* 'Ceremonial dress', *ODLA* 1530 'tunica palmata'). *consularis*: besides designating ex-consuls and certain provincial governors, also an honorific title, conferred by the emperor; see *ODLA* 408 'consularis'. **cycladem pronuba:** the *cyclas* was an outer garment having a decorative border, often of gold, worn by women as a sign of wealth (Olson 2008, 51–2, e.g. Prop. 4.7.40 *aurata cyclade*). It marks the bridesmaid (*OLD pronuba* a; *BNP* 'Wedding Customs and Ritual' III. Rome'; also at 2.10.4n.) out as a high-ranking *matrona*. The *pronuba* assisted in the *dextrarum iunctio* and their reciprocal declaration of *consensus*. **togam honoratus:** by Sidonius' time, the *toga* is the dress for *honorati* (senators) on high-profile occasions (*BNP* 'Toga'). All MSS have *senator* before *honoratus*, which must be an ancient gloss, rightly excised by Lütjohann. **paenulam ... inglorius:** *paenula* 'cape', 'hooded cloak' (*OLD* 1), common piece of clothing, could be worn by both men and women (*Dig.* 34.2.23.2; Olson 2017, 10). *inglorius* 'undistinguished' (*OLD*), cf. e.g. 1.6.4 *inglorium ... pauperis*, Hier. 118.5 *ex diuitibus ... inglorii*. **thalamorum** 'wedding', 'marriage' (sg. and plur., *OLD* 2b), poetic in origin (Verg. *Aen.* 10.649 and later), enters prose from *c.* 400 CE onwards (e.g. Aug. *Civ.* 3.13, Alc. Avit. *Ep.* 2.7 (ed. M-R); in Sidonius, 4.20.3, 5.8.1, 7.2.7). **necdum:** narratologically, the unconsummated marriage is a cliff-hanger, potentially conveying Sidonius' unease over a happy end (see above 'Date and Place'). **laborum meorum molimina:** this one-off pleonasm (cf. Aug. *In psalm.* 103.1.7 *magno molimine, magno labore*) may be playful or sarcastic. *molimen* in prose not before 3rd cent. (except Liv. 2.56.4). **reserabuntur:** *OLD* 4b, van Waarden 2010, 366. **occupatissimam uacationem:** oxymoron expressing the author's annoyance, after Plin. 9.6.4 *otiosissimis occupationibus*, conveying Pliny's irritation at the futile circus games hampering his routine. It provides the final *pointe*, with the superlative penultimate and a clausula consisting of two double trochees (Intro 4.5).

LETTER 1.9: BECOMING CITY PREFECT

Outline

This letter picks up where letter 1.5 left off. The wedding of Ricimer and Alypia over, life resumes its ordinary course. Now finally Sidonius can turn to the business for which he came to Rome. In consultation with his host Paulus, he surveys the senators who have the most influence on the emperor and selects Caecina Basilius as his patron, with whom he then fine-tunes the Arvernian petition (see §5n. legationis Aruernae). Basilius also makes it clear that Sidonius' interests would be furthered if he wrote the panegyric for the upcoming ceremony of Anthemius' second consulate in January. *Things go according to plan: the petition gets Basilius' decisive backing and, thanks to the same, the panegyric earns Sidonius no less than the city prefecture. In its final paragraphs (§§7–8), the letter turns out to be the cover letter for the copy of the panegyric (*Carm. *2 with its preface* Carm. *1) that Sidonius is sending to Heronius, with all due modesty and high regard for the addressee. Be it thanks to his talent or due to chance, Sidonius concludes, his pen got him the office (§8* cum ad praefecturam … stili occasione peruenerim*).*

Introduction

Letters 1.5 and 1.9 may originally have formed one whole, as pointed out in the introduction to 1.5. In the intervening letters, the probing story of the alleged treason of the Gallic prefect Arvandus in 1.7 determines how readers react to 1.9, where they are confronted with Sidonius' carefree pride in being appointed as city prefect. This is an example of the rule in Sidonius that it is not dating or chronology that determines the order of the letters, but aesthetics and content (Intro 4.1).

Discussion

Pliny's cover letters for his acceptance speech to Trajan (3.13 and 3.18) may have influenced Sidonius in including 1.9. Comparing 1.5 and 1.9, it is striking how easily the former lends itself to complex, layered interpretation, whereas the latter stands out for stylistic elaboration.

Addressee

The same addressee as 1.5.

Date and Place

Written in early (?) 468, after the panegyric had been prepared for publication. Possibly revised at a later stage of publication. See introduction 1.5 'Date and Place' and below §1n. *post imperii.*

Literature

Commentary: Köhler 1995, 265–82. History: Stevens 1933, 93–101; Harries 1994, 142–50; Delaplace 2015, 244–5 (clashing clan interests in Gaul, Sidonius' Book 1 as a defence). Court ritual: MacCormack 1981; for consular ceremonies in particular Mitchell 2018. For cover letters of literary works, Janson 1964, 106; for Pliny's cover letters as a model, Köhler 1995, 265, Condorelli 2008, 59–65, Stoehr-Monjou 2020, 319.

Commentary

1 Post nuptias patricii Ricimeris seamlessly links to 1.5.10n. *nuptiis patricii Ricimeris*. **post imperii utriusque opes euentilatas:** *imperii utriusque* denotes the eastern and western halves of the Empire. *euentilatas* 'squandered', a figurative meaning found repeatedly in Sidonius (Wolff 2020, 403; lit. 'to winnow thoroughly' (*OLD*)). Sidonius does not mince words. This criticism sits slightly uneasily with the political vulnerability in 468 of Sidonius as an official in relation to the emperor Anthemius and to the powerbroker Ricimer, who lived on until July and August 472, respectively. This sheds some doubt on an early publication date of Book 1 (Kelly 2020, 192, Intro 2.1). **publicam serietatem** 'seriousness in public affairs': *serietas* is rare (first at Auson. *Parent.* 2.6), but *–(i)tas* is among the most productive suffixes for creating abstract nouns in later Latin (Wolff 2020, 399). **rebus actitandis** 'doing (extensive) business': for the frequentative infix *–tit–*, see 1.5.9n. *scriptitans*. Having answered Heronius' second question about his travels (1.5.1 *uiam*), Sidonius now turns to the first question concerning the realization of the embassy's goal (1.5.1 *coepta*; for this order, Köhler 1995, 265). **Pauli praefectorii:** identification is uncertain, either Fl. Synesius Gennadius Paulus (according to *PLRE* 2, 855 'Paulus 36' and Mathisen 2020a, 113) or the Fl. Paulus who was city prefect in 438 and in the 440s (see *PLRE* 2, 854 'Paulus 31'). Gillett 2003, 239 n.72 notes that, if the former identification is correct, it is odd that Gennadius Paulus directed him to the patronage of Caecina Basilius, not Gennadius Avienus (§2), who would have been his relative. **tam doctrina quam sanctitate:** learning and integrity commend the aristocratic intellectual (see Intro 3.3 'Elite Status'; cf. Cic. *Fam.* 4.4.5 *probitate ... uirtute ... doctrina*), here without overtones of the slippage in contemporary usage for this pair to denote Christian orthodoxy and piety (e.g. Paul. Nol. *Ep.* 31.5, Vincent. Ler. *Comm.* 2; cf. Sidon. 9.9.16 *conscientiae ... doctrinae*); cf. 3.12.6n. *doctrinae* and 2.9.6n. *sancte*. **hospitalitatis:** as envoys had to procure their own lodging and food (1.5.9n. *conducti diuersorii*), Paulus' hospitality is abundantly praised (*uenerandis, comiter, blandae*). **excolebamur:** plural of modesty like §5 *elaboramus* (Intro 4.2); or did Paulus host all the ambassadors? The size of the embassy is unknown: Sidonius may even have been alone (1.5.2 suggests a personal invitation), which was not unusual (see Oppedisano 2022). Nor does Sidonius mention the nature of the request: see §5n. *petitionibus. excolebamur* chimes with *excepti*. The sentence ends with the main clause, which is a distinctive feature of this letter: on average, main clauses are at the end just as often as subordinate clauses (154 vs 160 respectively in this selection). **in omni artium genere:** varies 2.10.6n. *in omnibus artibus.* In attributing the same wide range of learning to another friend, Mamertus Claudianus, in 5.2.1, Sidonius specifies these *artes: grammatica, arithmetica, geometrica, musica, dialectica, astrologia, architectonica, metrica* – essentially the medieval *trivium* and *quadrivium* (cf. Cic. *Fin.* 3.2.5). In another case (Lampridius in 4.1.2), it is a more exclusively literary range: *heroicus* (epic), *comicus, lyricus, orator, historicus, satiricus, grammaticus, panegyrista, sophista, epigrammatista, commentator, iurisconsultus.* **deus bone:** the interjection suggests a lively oral exchange; cf. 4.3.2 in a similar context (cf. Intro 3.6). **propositionibus aenigmata** starts a carefully ordered asyndetic list of four items, each consisting of a Latin and a Greek noun, specifying Paulus' prowess. Sidonius often clusters Greek technical terms, rather to flaunt his verbal versatility than to provide exact definitions (Gualandri 1979, 145–63), although in this case we can probably recognize dialectic and rhetoric, followed by versification and metre. A *propositio* is 'a case proposed for discussion' (*OLD* 4c), closely related to logic (*OLD* 4a, b), cf. 9.9.15 *syllogismis tuae propositionis uncatis. aenigma* 'riddle', one of seven types of allegory (Char. *Gramm.* 276.8, frowned upon by Quint. *Inst.* 8.6.52). Paulus is praised for making his statements of problems satisfying by complicating them, so-called *obscuritas* (Schwitter 2015, Intro 4.2). **sententiis schemata:** *sententia* 'opinion', 'point of view' (*OLD* 1) is also the usual meaning in Sidonius. Greek σχῆμα (Latin *figura*) is a 'figure of speech', 'rhetorical figure', lending a poetical quality to the enunciation (Quint. *Inst.* 9.1.13; van Waarden 2010, 422); also *Carm.* 41.54n. (in 9.16). **uersibus commata:** *comma* 'part of a line of verse', delimited by a caesura (*TLL* 3.1816.71–1817.38); also *Carm.* 41.36n. **digitis mechanemata:** probably 'technical highlights in his metres'. The sense is not straightforward: a medieval glossator already struggled to explain it (Chronopoulos 2020, 652–3). For *digitis*, cf. Schol. Hor. *Ars* 274 *digitis autem pro arte rithmica et numeris. mechanema* 'artifice', 'work of art' is only found here and Aug. *Civ.* 21.6; in Greek, it refers most often to a non-mechanical contrivance of some kind (cf. LSJ μηχάνημα II). Sidonius himself applies the same twin criterion of caesura and metre in his critical appraisal of Mamertus Claudianus' poetry (4.3.8): [*hymnus*] *commaticus est … seruatis metrorum pedibus.* For the crucial importance of versification and metre for the likes of Sidonius, see Condorelli 2020a, 440–2. **illud … studiorum omnium culmen anteuenit, quod** 'this stands out as the summit of all his pursuits, that …': for *studia*, see 1.1.3n. *studiorum. culmen:* reaching the top, whether in politics or private life, or indeed surpassing oneself, is among Sidonius' most cherished values; cf. 1.11.17 *potestatum* *dignitatumque culmina*, 2.13.1 *rei publicae ... culminibus*, 7.14.7 *scientiae dignitas ... cuius ad maximum culmen ... ascenditur.* **huic eminenti scientiae conscientiam superiorem** 'a character surpassing this brilliant erudition': his personality is even more eminent than his erudition, manifest in the four aspects of prose and poetry just (*huic*) mentioned. The opposition in the clause is enhanced by chiasmus and polyptoton. In Sidonius, *scientia*, besides meaning 'knowledge', 'know-how' (e.g. 3.14.2 *scientia ... linguae Latinae*; *OLD* 2), above all indicates mastery of the entire cultural domain as an essential asset of top-level Romans (synonymous with *doctrina*, *disciplina*; cf. 2.9.4n. *similis scientiae uiri*, 2.10.6n. *scientiae ... pompa*; *OLD* 3 'learning', 'erudition'), while *conscientia* has connotations ranging from '(Christian) conscience' to 'character', 'personality' (van Waarden 2010, 234). The play on *scientia–conscientia* is a favourite of Sidonius (also 6.3.1, 9.2.3, 9.4.2; Wolff 2020, 410) and of Augustine (e.g. *Civ.* 20.14 *ut accuset uel excuset scientia conscientiam*). **gratiae aditus** 'access to favour': *gratiae* is an objective gen.; cf. Liv. 41.23.4 *praetorem qui priuatae gratiae aditum apud regem quaerebat*. The omission of the verb 'to be' contributes to the swift pace of the description, as in the next paragraph (G–L §209). Despite the imperial consent and Sidonius' past experience in Rome, access to court to be effective must evidently be backed by apposite patronage. From the 450s until 476, as the last western emperors returned to Rome for their residence, the Roman senatorial aristocracy played a key role at the imperial court (Gillett 2001, Salzman 2017a; see 1.5.5n. *Rauennam*). Sidonius' poor network outside Gaul – witness his correspondence – comes as a reminder that even provincial grandees were dependent on securing senatorial advocacy once in Rome (Mratschek 2020b, 220–1). **exploro:** the verbal tense changes to a lively historic present (*OLS* 1, 401–10). **quinam ... spebus ualeret nostris opitulari:** the word order serves a communicative goal (so-called verbal hyperbaton *spebus ualeret nostris* lending *spebus* emphasis: *OLS* 2, 1104–5, Intro 4.3; for its function of demarcating clauses, see 2.12.1n. *germano* and e.g. 7.1.1 *importuna*) as well as creating a good clausula (paeon I + spondee: Intro 4.5). *spebus ... nostris*: possibly 'my expectations' (putting the 'I' in the background; Intro 4.2 'You and I') or 'our (personal) expectations' (i.e. Heronius' and Sidonius'), but best taken as referring to the interests of the Auvergne as a whole represented by the embassy (cf. Delaplace 2015, 245). The plural *spebus* is found from the 4th cent. onwards; in Sidonius also 3.6.3.

2 nec ... dubitaretur: the selection process was straightforward because few candidates qualified for discussion. For *dubito* in a positive sense ('to discuss', 'to consider'), see L–S ɪʙ, cf. *TLL* 5/1.2093.31–6. **quidem** is concessive ahead of *sed.* **opibus culti genere sublimes** is the first of three asyndetic pairs of adjectival phrases, each phrase consisting of an adjective qualified by an ablative noun. Such lists in a variety of combinations of verbs, nouns and adjectives are typical of personal descriptions: 1.2, 2.1, 3.13 and 7.9.5–25 contain the most virtuoso examples (cf. van Waarden 2010, 571–84). The highlighted aspects are the usual ones in a *laudatio*: ancestors and family assets, position in society, character (van Waarden 2010, 440–1). **utiles** 'helpful': *OLD* 4; cf. *Carm.* 28.9n. (in 3.12). **dignitate ... dignatione** 'dignity ... repute': with paronomasia (Wolff 2020, 411–12). *dignatio* is the esteem one enjoys (*OLD* 2). A gentleman will be conscious of his rank, yet not be stand-offish for it, cf. 7.4.1 *cum sitis opinione* ['reputation'] *magni, gradu* ['rank'] *maximi, non tamen esse uos amplius dignitate quam dignatione laudandos*. The social ideal is a combination of power and affability in order to be an effective partner in the patronage system (*amicitia*; see Intro 3.3). **fastigatissimi consulares** 'the most eminent consulars': for *fastigatus*, see L–S *fastigo*, *TLL* 6/1.325.40–6; Sidonius has a certain preference for this verb and its cognates (van Waarden 2010, 486). For *consularis*, see 1.5.11n. **Gennadius Auienus:** consul in 450, in 452 he accompanied bishop Leo of Rome on an embassy to Attila (*PLRE* 2, 193 'Gennadius Avienus 4'). His clan the Corvini (§4), like the Decii and the Anicii, were among the major families in offices of senatorial rank in the fifth and early sixth centuries, the Corvini lagging slightly behind precisely in the decade dominated by Ricimer (456–72 CE) (Barnish 1988, esp. 125; for a critical reconsideration, see Cameron 2012). **Caecina Basilius:** praetorian prefect of Italy in 458 and 463–5, consul in 463 (*PLRE* 2, 216–17 'Fl. Caecina Decius Basilius 11'), belonging to the *gens Decia* (§4). In the past decades, he had advocated a policy of total concentration on the Vandals and been a driving force in ousting Avitus and Majorian, whose political efforts were largely directed towards Gaul. He was an extremely versatile politician intent on securing the participation of the senate in government under all circumstances. His protection of Sidonius comes as a volte-face for both men – though plausibly not as unprepared as Sidonius suggests in 1.5 and 1.9. Anthemius was proclaimed emperor on 12 April 467 and will have used his time well to ease the relationship with the rival factions in Gaul as a backing (see Oppedisano 2020, 106–7; cf. Delaplace 2015, 244–5). **in amplissimo ordine:** the senate (standard usage since the Republic). **partis armatae:** 'the military' as against the *pars ciuilis* (cf. *Carm.* 5.565–6). The military was a key power factor (hence *praerogatiua* 'privilege') in the years under consideration. It included the *magister militum* Ricimer in the first place but also two other *magistri militum*, Basiliscus, commander of the eastern expedition against the Vandals in 468 and usurper in the east 475–6, and Marcellinus, commander of the western forces against the Vandals in 468, and perhaps involved in the elusive *coniuratio Marcelliniana* (1.11.6) after the demise of Avitus in 457 (Henning 1999, 253–4). **post purpuratum principem principes:** the point is marked by alliteration and polyptoton. *purpuratus* of an emperor: *TLL* 10/2.2706.66–2707.7; cf. 7.9.19 *principes purpuratos*, see 8.3.5n. *inter purpuratos*. **mores** 'personality' is a central notion in the correspondence. It denotes a person's character as apparent from his conduct, a combination of moral principles and behaviour in society. Evaluating a person's *mores* is a constant concern (van Waarden 2010, 233). **genii ... ingenii** 'dignity ... disposition' (tr. Anderson): paronomasia. For *genius* in this sense, *TLL* 6/2.1841.52–65 (5th/6th-cent. usage). **fabor namque** 'I will next say': *namque* here is 'forward-linking', introducing a new statement (see Kroon 1995, 152–63, *TLL* 9/1.37.11–20; see also 1.1.2n. *nam*), in this case connecting the statement of the difference between the two men with the following detailed comparison.

3 §§3 –4 are a formal *synkrisis* or *comparatio*, a comparative juxtaposition of people (*BNP* 'synkrisis') – a technique which inevitably creates a polarized picture. The comparison between Caesar and Cato at Sall. *Catil.* 54 is an obvious model, with closely similar phrasing (so Köhler 1995, 270). **felicitate** 'good fortune' (*OLD* 1). We cannot verify this claim; in any case, Avienus had been consul together with none less than the emperor Valentinian. The opposition with *uirtute* 'merit' is a rhetorical commonplace (cf. e.g. *Rhet. Her.* 4.20.27). **numerositas:** we do indeed know of considerably more posts held by Basilius than by Avienus. **praedicabatur:** the dominant clausula from here on is cretic + spondee (Intro 4.5). **fors:** adverb 'happened to ...'. **artabat** is emphasized by being fronted (see Intro 4.3). **praeuia pedisequa circumfusa** 'preceding, following and surrounding'. **populositas** 'multitude': for the system of *clientela*, see *BNP* 'cliens, clientes'. A large following is obviously desirable; the opposite bodes ill: 1.7.3 *pati de occurrentum raritate suspicionem*. Later Latin has a preference for abstract nouns, cf. 1.5.8n. *amoena*, 2.9.4n. *competitiones*. **sodalium:** *sodalis*, like *amicus*, is a slightly more veiled term than the outspoken *cliens* (Henriksén 2012, 21 for Martial). Wordplay (*in paribus dispares*) and sound effects (*s–sp–sp*) continue. **fratribus** in this context probably means 'cousins' (*OLD* 2). **domesticis ... forinsecus:** the reach of patronage is essential, preferably beyond one's own family as well as across regional boundaries (for the latter, van Waarden 2010, 235–6 on 7.4.3 *longe positorum*). **ualenter efficax:** cf. 3.1.1 *quod est ad amicitias ampliandas ... ualidius efficaciusque*, for redundancy and formulaic recycling as stylistic means, Intro 4.5.

4 et in hoc ..., quod 'also in this respect ... that'.   **cinctus ... discinctus** 'in office ... out of office/retired/private': a peculiarly Sidonian use of the opposition (found with different forces at 1.7.3, 5.7.3); cf. 7.2.5 *priuati ... cincti* (*TLL* 3.1124, 5/1.1316.7–16 and 57–9). In late antiquity, *cingulum* is the (sword)belt or uniform indicating a public office (*TLL* 3.1068.81–1069.32; cf. Niermeyer for the medieval usage *cingulum* 'function').   **totis** = *omnibus* 'all', becomes common in later Latin; earliest instances include Plin. *Nat.* 7.97, Apul. *Met.* 7.12.2 (*OLS* 1, 992).   **aditu difficili** is an ablative of quality (G–L §400). The same phrase occurs 8.11.4. As accessibility is an essential quality of any *patronus* (above §2n. *dignitate*), the opposite does not go unnoticed; cf. 7.4.3 for criticism of a patron *qui se ambientibus rigidum reddit*.   **sumptuoso:** benefits in a patronage relationship being mutual, clients could be required to pay in return for a favour (Bowersock et al. 1999b, 637–8 'Patronage').   **si utrumque coluisses, ... consequebare** 'had you courted both [which is unlikely], you got ...': the pluperfect subjunctive in the *si*-clause expresses the irreality of the condition, while the imperfect indicative in the main clause states the reality of the possibility (G–L §597, 3). *consequebare* with the second person singular passive alternative ending *-re* instead of *-ris*.

5 id tractatus mutuus temperauit 'our joint discussion arrived at this compromise': *tractatus OLD* 3a. *mutuus* in the weakened sense of *communis* (*TLL* 8.1738.52–8), cf. *Cod. Iust.* 10.65.5 pr. *communi consilio tractatuque*. *id temperauit*, followed by *ut*, is unusual (cf. *OLD tempero* 9); it is more often seen in the form of *hoc temperamentum, ut* 'a compromise to the effect that', first found in Plin.1.7.3, 10.115, then (perhaps as a borrowing) in Sidon. 7.18.1, 9.11.3.   **senioris consularis:** having been the first to hold a consulate and probably being the elder, Avienus came first in rank (for precedence among officials, *Cod. Iust.* 12.3.1.1, cf. Auson. *Ep.* 18.3–4). Seniority of age and/or office (for bishops also time in office) was a crucial social ordering principle, recurring throughout the correspondence (the noun *praerogatiua* 'precedence' alone occurs no less than nineteen times).   **nec nimis raro:** lit. 'not too seldom', is a litotes (G–L §700).   **Basilianis potius frequentatoribus applicaremur:** as to *Basilianis*, the classical rule holds that the adjective defines a category, whereas the genitive of the proper name would have put the stress on the owner himself (Spevak 2014, 175–82). It can be usefully applied here as well, although in later Latin attributive adjectives tend to replace genitives anyway, for which see 1.5.4n. *amnicos*. Anteposition of the adjective in combination with *potius* creates contrast. *frequentatoribus* 'frequent visitors' is attested in Tert. *Monog.* 8 and then from the 4th cent. onwards (*TLL* 6/1.1305.46–54). *applicaremur* 'I should attach myself' (*OLD* 8).   **ilicet** 'so' (Anderson translates: 'well') signposts the next step in the narrative; see 1.5.1n. *ilicet.*   **de legationis Aruernae petitionibus:** as pointed out at §1n. *excolebamur,* the size of the embassy is not specified. The nature of the request is not mentioned either, as both were known to the addressee.   **ecce et Kalendae Ianuariae:** for *ecce et,* see 1.5.9n. *patuit et Roma.* During work on the petition, the conversation turned to the upcoming (see following *mox* and *opperiebantur*) Kalends of January Festival, running from 31 December to 3 January, 1 January being the day for the annually appointed magistrates to assume office and 3 January for the emperor to be offered oaths of loyalty and best wishes (for the Kalends, Meslin 1970, for the popular celebrations, Grig 2024, 173–218). There must have been enough time left for Sidonius to write the panegyric – he was not completely unprepared mentally either, as the change of imperial policy towards Gaul had been in the making in the preceding half year (see n. on §2 *Caecina Basilius*; misreading the phrase, as though the date had already arrived, Stevens 1933, 98 n. 1 and Köhler 1995, 273 are unduly concerned about the lack of preparation time, the latter suggesting that Sidonius had written the complex parts beforehand).   **repetendum fastis nomen** 'the second mention on the magistrates' list': see *BNP* 'Fasti'. Anthemius had held his first consulate in 455, when still in Constantinople. The panegyric begins, addressing Anthemius: *annum pande nouum consul uetus (Carm.* 2.3).

6 With increasing liveliness by means of direct speech, the climax of the narration is reached.   **heia:** exclamation expressing urgency (*OLD* d); cf. e.g. Plin. 4.29.1 *Heia tu.*   **Solli meus:** Sidonius is addressed variously by his *nomen gentilicium* (5.17.9 *domine Solli*) or his diacritic (1.11.13 *comes Sidoni*); see Intro 1 n. 1.   **suscepti officii:** the embassy.   **exeras uolo:** *exeras* from *ex(s)ero* 'to show' (*OLD* 3). For *uolo* with simple subjunctive, without *ut,* in an emphatic wish, see G–L §546 remark 2.   **noui ... ueterem:** cf. 1.5.5n., 7.1.3n. Sidonius had contributed a panegyric for the emperor Avitus in 456 and for Majorian in 458 (Intro 1 and 2.1).   **uotiuum quippiam ... carminantem** 'reciting something expressing good wishes': *uotiuum* refers to the vows, best wishes and compliments (*uota*) made on occasions such as New Year (see above *Kalendae Ianuariae*) directed at the emperor (Iust. *Dig.* 50.16.233.1 *post Kalendas Ianuarias die tertio pro salute principis uota suscipiuntur*) and at the start of the tenure of higher officials (*uotorum nuncupatio, uota publica*); see *BNP* 'Vota', *ODLA* 594–5 'Festivals and calendars, secular and political'. The rare verb *carmino* 'to sing' (*TLL* 3.474.29–45) is used by Sidonius also at *Carm.* 37.82, 40.25; the adjective *carminabundus* at 8.11.6.   **uel tumultuariis fidibus** 'even on improvisatory strings': *tumultuarius* occurs several times in Sidonius, e.g. 2.10.3n. *tumultuarium carmen,*

COMMENTARY: 1.9:6–7   97

8.3.1n. *tumultuarium exemplar*, where it is part of the modesty topos, pretending that a work is hasty and slipshod whereas, in reality, it is carefully executed. In this case it is politeness on Basilius' part, tongue-in-cheek, pretending not to put too much pressure on the poet. The tone of the conversation is both informal (*uotiuum quippiam*) and ironically high-brow (*uel tumultuariis fidibus carminantem*). *fidibus* is a poetical metaphor for (a piece of) poetry (cf. *OLD fides²*). **admittendo sc.** *tibi* 'for you to be admitted' or 'for you about to be admitted': in later Latin the gerundive develops into a future passive participle (H–S 312–3, *OLS* 1, 435 and 551–2); see also 2.10.5n. *ducenda*, 2.12.2n. *augendum*, 5.5.1n. *subiciendam*, 7.1.5n. *amoliendas*, 7.7.6n. *capiendis*, *Carm.* 33.1 *sociande* (in 7.17). With following *recitaturo* and *recitanti* a logical sequence is laid out. **solacium ... suffragium:** *solacium* from 'relief' tends towards 'help', 'support' in later Latin (Tert. *Virg. uel.* 9 *consilio et solacio iuuare*, and later; see 7.7.2n. *solata sunt*). *suffragium* 'influence' on behalf of a candidate (*OLD* 5), here, specifically, support organized by a claque (Köhler 1995, 275). **si quid experto credis** is proverbial, e.g. Verg. *Aen.* 11.283 *experto credite* (Otto 1890, 127). **seria ... ludo:** a serious spin-off from something playful, i.e. from a piece of poetry (*lusus* and *ludere* in this sense, *OLD lusus* 4, *ludo* 8). A related thought and wordplay in Plin. 7.9.10 [*carmina*] *lusus uocantur; sed hi lusus non minorem interdum gloriam quam seria consequuntur*. **parui ego praeceptis ... iniunctis:** the *iubes–pareo* motif, omnipresent in correspondence (see Intro 4.2), is here seen in daily life. Verb initial serves to mark (immediate) progress from the preceding (*OLS* 2, 1016–7); see Intro 4.3. **deuotionis adstipulator inuictus:** *deuotio* 'promise', 'obligation', specifying the terms of a loan and requiring a borrower (*promissor*) to pay back a lender (*stipulator*) by a specified period of time. *adstipulator* 'one who joins in the stipulation', a supporter (*TLL* 5/1.880.35–50 *deuotio*, *OLD stipulator*, *adstipulator*; Heumann–Seckel s.v.). *inuictus* 'unbeatable', 'matchless', cf. *Carm.* 2.353 *inuictus Ricimer* (admiringly), *Ep.* 7.2.8 *praestigiator inuictus* (ironically). **consule meo ... senatui suo:** stresses both the constitutional element (the nouns) and the personal relationship with the emperor (the pronouns). The *praefectus urbi* also presided over the senate. **praefectum faceret:** paronomasia.

7 epistulae perosus prolixitatem: epistolary theory prescribes *breuitas*. It is one of the most common topoi in letters as is the play on the excuse for exceeding the ideal length (Intro 3.6). Hyperbaton emphasizes *epistulae*: 'in the case of a letter ...'; see n. at §1 *spebus*. **uoluptuosius** 'with greater pleasure': closing the ring with the opening 1.5.1n. *uoluptuosum*. **opusculi:** diminutive of modesty (cf. 1.1.4n. *opusculo*). The panegyric counts no fewer than 548 lines (*Carm.* 2), preceded by a preface of 30 lines (*Carm.* 1). **loquax ... charta** repeats the idea of excessive length. *charta* (lit. 'paper') is first found in the sense of 'letter' at Cic. *Att.* 2.20.3 (*TLL* 3.999.8–25).   **in consequentibus** 'in the continuation': for the terminology in cover letters, see van Waarden 2010, 430–1.   **pro me ... sermocinetur:** cf. e.g. the narrative justification of letter 2.9 (§1 *reddo causas reditus tardioris*, §10 *ipsi in procinctu sumus teque ... nobis inuisere placet*), intended to fill the gap of Sidonius' absence until his meeting again with the addressee, and 4.19n. *et uenimus et scribimus*.   **dum uenio, diebus ... pauculis** kindly conceals that Sidonius' return will take considerably longer than the couple of days that Heronius can while away reading the poem.   **examinis tui:** cf. 1.1.3n. *tuaeque examinationi.*   **puncta** 'votes', 'good marks': see *OLD* 2; also at *Carm.* 41.12n. (in 9.16.3); in both cases, Sidonius may have specifically in mind the Horatian examples of *puncta* awarded for poetic performance, e.g. *Ars* 343.   **in comitio uel inter rostra:** the *comitium* is the chief place of political assembly in Republican Rome occupying an area north of the Forum Romanum at the foot of the Capitoline, while the *rostra* is the speaker's platform on the south side of the *comitium*, adorned with the prows (*rostra* – hence *inter*) of ships captured from the city of Antium, 338 BCE, during the Roman expansion in Italy (see *OCD*). Rather than a contemporary reality, the vignette of a city prefect speaking to the people is a reminder of good old Rome and enhances Sidonius' newly acquired office (Köhler 1995, 277). Public gatherings in late antiquity typically took place in theatres or the circus (cf. Rutil. 1.202 *nuntiat accensus plena theatra fauor*, Sidon. 1.10.2 *populi Romani theatralis caueae fragor* and *Carm.* 8.10, cited below), more often than not in the form of orchestrated shows of allegiance to the emperor and his representatives (MacCormack 1981, Mitchell 2018).   **sophos meum** 'a "bravo" for me': *sophōs* (Gr. σοφῶς lit. 'cleverly') as a noun is first found in Martial, who uses it repeatedly (*OLD sophos*²); in Sidonius, among other places, at *Carm.* 8.10 *ad nostrum reboat concaua Roma sophos*, about himself being applauded by the people and senate.   **lati claui ... tribulium** 'senators ... common people': the *latus clauus* is a broad purple stripe on the tunic, indicating senatorial rank (*OCD* 'Clavus angustus, latus'). A *tribulis* is a fellow tribesman, member of a *tribus*, the Roman territory being originally divided into thirty-five geographically defined tribes, voting units in political assemblies, forming the basis of army recruitment and taxation (*OCD* 'Tribus', *BNP* 'Tribus'). In late antiquity, under completely altered circumstances, with the people reduced to applauding the emperor's decisions, the notion of 'neighbourhood resident' survived (Amm. 15.7.5), along with the weakened meaning 'commoner' (only Mart. 9.49.7 before late antiquity; Sidonius may have had an eye on this usage in Martial in combination with *sophos*). In his panegyrics, Sidonius maintains the fiction that the people voted for a new emperor (Anthemius: *Carm.* 2.19–20 *te curia plausu, | te punctis* *scripsere tribus*; Avitus: 7.567 *concurrunt ad puncta tribus*). **moneo praeque denuntio** = Claud. Mam. *Anim.* 2.9 (Engelbrecht p. 137.9). *prae* is probably an adverb, an archaism from comedy: 'in advance' (*TLL* 10/2.372.55–69; discussion in Köhler 1995, 278; on archaisms, see Wolff 2020, 402). **quisquilias ipsas** 'this rubbish': polite self-debasement; the noun of poetry elsewhere only Auson. *Praef.* 4.5. *ipse* is developing into a demonstrative pronoun, well established in Romance languages (*OLS* 1.1162–4). **Clius:** Greek genitive of Clio, the Muse often associated with history or heroic poetry (e.g. Hor. *Carm.* 1.12.2 *quem uirum aut heroa ... sumis celebrare, Clio?*, cf. Sidon. *Carm.* 5.568). **collata uestris mea:** in the comparison, *uestris* creates respectful distance as opposed to neutral *mea* (van Waarden 2020e, 425). **heroicorum phaleris** 'trappings of epic poets': substantivized *heroicus* and *epitaphista* (below) are Sidonian hapax legomena (cf. 4.1.2 for a longer series in the same vein; Gualandri 1979, 148 n. 19); cf. *Carm.* 41.33n. *heroos* 'hexameters'. *phaleris* 'ornaments (of (war) horses and soldiers)', metaphorically of rhetorical embellishments (L–S II, e.g. Symm. 1.89.1 *loquendi phaleras*), but particularly apt in the context of epic; cf. *Carm.* 41.54n. **epitaphistarum neniis** 'trash from tombstone poets': *nenia* (*OLD* 1) is the Roman ritual lament following the eulogy of the deceased, a song at a funeral, a funerary poem (Mogen 2020, 250–1; cf. 2.8.2 *neniam funebrem*, 7.17.1n. *neniam sepulchralem*), then also a rhyme, a jingle, and – as here – literary 'rubbish' (cf. 7.18.4n. *neniis*; *OLD* 1, 4, 5).

8 hic ipse panegyricus: the Panegyric of Anthemius and its Preface, possibly in a revised version (*Carm.* 1–2) (for the genre of panegyric, see *ODLA* 'Panegyric' and 'Panegyric, Latin'). **si tamen** 'if indeed': *tamen* makes the conditional relation more restrictive (late Latin; *OLS* 2.323–4, cf. ibid. 308; cf. 7.1.2n. *tamen*). **tetrica sunt amoenanda iocularibus** refers to the proverbial closeness and alternation of seriousness and mirth, continuing the tone of *seria ... ludo* above (Otto 1890, 176–7 'iocus', e.g. Plin. 2.13.5 *cum hoc seria, cum hoc iocos miscui*, Sidon. 2.12.3 *si iocari liberet in tristibus*, 7.18.2n. *maerendo ... iocandoque*). *tetrica* 'stern', 'uncompromising' (also 4.9.2 *seueritas ... non ... taetra sed tetrica*, 8.16.4 *loquendi tetricum genus ac perantiquum*, 9.11.4 *tetricis ... censoribus*), in this context seems to denote the tough character of the negotiations and of the high stakes of the panegyric (rather than Köhler's interpretation (p. 280) that the embassy was a failure). *amoenanda* 'to be brightened', late and rare (*TLL* 1.1961.81–1982.9; Wolff 2020, 402). Montaigne quotes this maxim in his *Essais* (4th ed. 1588, bk 3, ch. 5). **uolo:** combine with *concludere*. **paginam:** another metonym for 'letter', already at Cic. *Att.* 6.2.3 *quoniam respondi postremae tuae paginae prima mea*. **glorioso ... Thrasoniano fine** 'a boastful, Thraso-like ending': Thraso is a boastful soldier in Terence's *Eunuchus. glorioso* anticipates Plautus' title. **Plautini Pyrgopolinicis:** Pyrgopolinices is a comparable character to Thraso in Plautus' *Miles gloriosus*. Early comedy was in vogue among archaizing writers, beginning in the second century CE (Intro 4.5). Terence developed into a standard school author, along with Cicero, Sallust and Virgil (for Sidonius, see 4.12.1 where he is reading Terence with his son; quotations from Terence in 2.2.2 and 7.9.19; John 2026, 167). The pomposity of the lengthy words *Thrasoniano* and *Pyrgopolinicis* speaks for itself. **sub ope Christi** 'with Christ's help': a favourite of Sidonius to underscore a promise, something he hopes for, or – as here – gratitude; also 2.9.10n., 7.1.1n. (and similar 1.5.1n., 2.12.3n., 5.16.3n., 8.3.1n.). **stili occasione** 'thanks to my pen', i.e. thanks to my talent for writing (*OLD occasio* 2c 'the circumstance, etc., that provides the opportunity'). The same thought at Symm. 1.20.1 *iter ad capessendos magistratus saepe litteris promouetur*. Mratschek 2020b, 220 points out that Sidonius' 'ironic comment that he owed the city prefecture ... purely to "the good style" of his panegyric veils the harsh reality that the emperor Anthemius badly needed endorsement by the Gallo-Roman aristocracy'; the award is described in *Carm.* 41.29–32 (in 9.16). For the social position of panegyrists and their remuneration with offices, see Schindler 2009, 55–6; cf. Cameron 1970, 22–4. For the intimate link between classical education, literary activity and a career in the civil service, see John 2026, 24–35. **iubeas ilicet pro potestate cinctuti** 'order at once on the authority of an official' i.e. order as though you are an official (*cinctuti TLL* 3.1061): a tricky business – both for Heronius and for Sidonius – as this entails capital punishment by law (Iust. *Dig.* 48.4.3). If we assume that Heronius was a private man at the moment, his performing an act of authority is punishable and so is Sidonius' incitement. The fun is in the transposition of a private literary exchange between friends to the level of alleged state interest between an official and a private citizen forced into a role of authority. As to the reading *iubeas ilicet*, the MSS are unanimous. The partial lacuna in L does not warrant the emendations *iubeo te* (Mohr, Köhler) and *iuberis* (Anderson, Loyen, Bellès). **conuasatis acclamationibus** 'huzzas heaped together': *conuaso* 'to pack up' (and doing so in an underhand way) is a verb derived from comedy and lends the passage its specific tone (cf. 7.2.8 and van Waarden 2010, 180–1). *acclamationibus*: ritual chanting in public to express support, at all levels but specifically for the emperor (*ODLA* 'acclamation'). The latter association magnifies the clownish exaggeration. **uidere mihi uideor:** the sender imagines the reaction of the addressee, a typical epistolary turn of phrase of the kind advised in ancient theory (Iul. Vict. *Rhet.* 27 (Malherbe 1988, 64)). The phrase is first attested at Cic. *Att.* 7.1.2, also found at Sidon. 4.7.2, cf. 1.4.2 *spectare* *mihi uideor*, Plin. 1.6.1 *Ridebis, et licet rideas*. **ferocisse iactantiam** 'my arrogance has gone wild': *ferocio* is an archaic verb revived in the second century (Gel. 1.11.2 and 15, Apul. *Met.* 9.2). The final word *iactantiam* stays with the reader: indeed, the entire undertaking has been a huge gamble and Sidonius' attitude verges on hubris. The clausula is a firm double cretic (Intro 4.5).

LETTER 2.9: VILLA LIFE

Outline

Sidonius apologizes for the delay in visiting the addressee in Nîmes: he has been entertained, delightfully and at length, by two of his relatives on their respective estates, but he is on his way now (§§1–2). On a typical day, he says, the company indulged in sporting activities, including a bout of 'rugby', dice playing or reading and discussions in the well-stocked library – devotional holdings for the ladies, Latin and Christian classics for the gentlemen. One such discussion turned to a translation of Origen and Christian orthodoxy. After luncheon, there was more wine and story-telling (§§3–6). After the siesta, the guests went riding and, as both baths were under construction, an open-air sauna was put up for the occasion to the delight of everybody (§§7–9). Sidonius does not elaborate on the lavish dinners, which he reserves for their meeting soon (§10).

Introduction

Book 2 is Sidonius' book of *otium* (Hindermann 2020a, Hindermann 2022b, viii–xv). With its subject matter of aristocratic leisure, family affairs, estates and religious pursuits, it perfectly balances Book 1, the book about career in government and changing geo-political loyalties in Gaul. If Book 1 can be seen as a defence of Sidonius' work and political choices before becoming a bishop in 469, Book 2 is a visiting card for his lifestyle as a literate *grand seigneur* (see Intro 4.1).

Two lengthy letters on the theme of life on a large country estate (*uilla*) mark the two halves of the book, 2.2 with a description of the architecture of Sidonius' own Avitacum near Clermont and 2.9 with the landscape and a model day of aristocratic *otium* in the domains of Vorocingus and Prusianum near Nîmes, belonging to his relatives Apollinaris and Tonantius Ferreolus respectively. These letters unmistakably rely on the example of Pliny the Younger and his villa letters, two long ones, 2.17 and 5.6, describing the buildings and gardens of his Laurentinum and Tusci, and two shorter ones, 9.36 about a day on Tusci in summer and 9.40 about pastimes in winter on Laurentinum. Reasons for pride and markers of identity par excellence, the *uillae* of the likes of Sidonius, passed down through generations and kept going despite the barbarian invasions, acquire additional lustre as oases of *Romanitas* through this connection with the golden age of Pliny and Trajan (see Intro 3.3 'Elite Status' with n. 48, Mratschek 2008; Mratschek 2020b, 216–18).

Discussion

The Narration

The specifics of this narration, for one, flesh out the self-presentation of the author and his warm relationship with his kin, who, like himself, are as much civilized *bons vivants* as they are cultural connoisseurs. It has biblical overtones to boot, as the story of Tobias celebrating *per septem dies* in the company of his two cousins sets the tone (§2).

The impromptu open-air sauna has led to some discussion. It is striking because, earlier on, Sidonius had at length advertised his own superlative bath complex in 2.2.4–8. Were the hosts improving their baths or even building new ones, or only patching them provisionally – proof of a declining economic climate? Or, as sometimes argued, does Sidonius promote his status at the expense of his hosts – albeit amicably – in order to defend his family-in-law (the Aviti: Avitacum was their property) against presumed animosity on the part of the Apollinaris clan? Whatever the case (see further §8n. *in opere*), the overall atmosphere is one of great admiration and feeling good. If Sidonius wanted to tease his hosts at all for their slipshod baths, he is unsparing in his enthusiasm for their library, which is notable because in 2.2 he made no mention of his own estate library.

Eating and drinking are never far off the agenda. The letter reveals a senatorial aloofness from vulgar excess, combined with a practice that comes close to denying the ideal – a theme that will be addressed in later books when asceticism begins to infiltrate aristocratic milieus. The letter ends meaningfully with the word *parsimonia* 'temperance' – for now only to be able to face the next lavish invitation though.

Verb Tenses

The present tenses used in the exchanges between sender and addressee – in §§1 and 10 – create the framework for the story to develop. The perfect tenses in §2 serve to narrate the events leading up to the visit. The imperfects in §§3–9, by means of their typically 'in progress' aspect, describe the various situations occurring during the visit, not primarily as a temporal succession of events but as a spatial continuum of tableaux

(*OLS* 1, 416). Time does pass outwardly from morning till evening (§3 *mane*, 6 *tempus, clepsydrae, horarum spatia, prandebamus*, 7 *inde, meridiano*, 9 *horae*, 10 *cenas*), but essentially stands still in the perpetual present of *otium*. Sentence rhythm is obsessive throughout these paragraphs, almost all clauses ending in verb forms resembling the initial *rapiebamur* (§4) and, consequently, being heavily clausulated (paeon IV + spondee and related, and cretic + spondee; see Intro 4.5).

Readerly Focus

Donidius, the primary addressee, defines the focus of beginning and end. Being a senator himself, he is of course acquainted with elite hospitality and is, no doubt, himself preparing a lavish reception for Sidonius (though the bar is set high!). Any secondary addressee, reading this letter within the collection, will at least know the essence of this milieu. So its aim is not to provide an insight into senatorial *otium*, but – through the lens of the narrator – to create a well-wrought and diverting story for senators about senators. It is, by the very attention given to the minutest detail, a valuable gift of *amicitia* to the addressee and an entertaining piece of table-talk to be retold elsewhere (for the social aspect, see Intro 3.3; for narrative, Intro 4.3).

Addressee

Donidius was a *uir spectabilis*, as Sidonius points out in 5.1.1. This intermediate degree of senatorship (see Intro 3.3) suggests he had held a second-grade imperial office, either civil (for instance *proconsul* or *uicarius*) or military (such as *comes rei militaris* or *dux*); see *LRE* 528–9. In 5.1.3, Sidonius goes on to describe him as *meus aetate frater professione filius, loco ciuis fide amicus* 'my brother in age, my son in profession [Sidonius is then bishop], my fellow-citizen by domicile, my friend by his loyalty', which links Donidius to Clermont. At the time of writing, he apparently lived in Nîmes (§1). In letter 5.1, Sidonius supports him in the thorny question of retrieving part of an old family estate 30 miles north of Clermont. In 6.5, Sidonius recommends a *cliens* and slaves of Donidius, punning on his title: *uenerabilis Donidius dignus inter spectatissimos quosque numerari*. Prosopography: Mathisen 2020a, 90–1.

Date and Place

The letter is unanimously ascribed to Sidonius' first period of retirement, 461–7 CE. Sidonius' hosts Tonantius Ferreolus and Apollinaris figure also in *Carm.* 24, where the description of Apollinaris' garden possibly has a link with letter 2.9 (see below §8n. *antro*). *Carm.* 24 was published before 467 (Kelly 2020, 173–4). The publication of Book 2 is probably to be dated to 469 at the latest (Mathisen 2013, 225–7; Kelly 2020, 191; Intro 2.1).

Literature

Commentaries: Lucht 2011, Hindermann 2022b, 246–89. Studies: Stevens 1933, 68–74; Montone 2017, 26–8; Morvillez 2017; Hanaghan 2020.

Commentary

1 Quaeris cur ... Nemausum: combines the opening words of two of Pliny's villa letters, 2.17 *Miraris cur ... Laurentinum* and 9.36 *Quaeris quemadmodum in Tuscis* (see Introduction above). The phrasing goes even further back to Propertius' *Elegy* 2.31, which begins: *Quaeris cur ueniam tibi tardior?* Question and answer mimic a live meeting, a letter being 'one half of a conversation' (Intro 3.6 n. 79). Nemausus is present-day Nîmes with the iconic first-century Pont du Gard supporting its aqueduct. An important stage on the Via Domitia connecting Italy and Spain, it was conquered a few years later, in the early 470s, by the Visigoths (*BNP* 'Nemausus'). **uestra ... desideria producam:** *uestra* 'of you all', fronted with contrastive topic to *ipse*. The second person plural is typical of letters concerning travelling and visiting, involving those who accompany the addressee (often paired with a first person plural, 'I and my people'), e.g. Symm. 1.7.1 (to his father) *Bono animo sumus, cum uiam promissi memores inchoastis* (van Waarden 2021, 151–2). *desideria*: longing for one's friend is a commonplace in contexts of *amicitia* (cf. 7.10.1 *desiderio de uobis meo ... satisfacere*; Cugusi 1983, 77). *producam* 'I prolong' (*OLD* 10). **reddo causas reditus tardioris nec moras meas prodere moror:** densely stylized by means of chiasmus (*reddo causas – moras ... moror*), wordplay (paronomasia *reddo – reditus*, polyptoton *reddo – prodere*, oxymoron *nec moras ... moror*) and alliterations. Cf. 4.19n. *moras nostras*. **quae mihi dulcia sunt tibi quoque:** the classic formulation of friends being each other's *alter ego* is Sall. *Catil.* 20.3 *nam idem uelle atque idem nolle, ea demum firma amicitia est*, quoted by Sidonius in 5.3.2. **inter agros amoenissimos, humanissimos dominos** thematizes the interconnectedness of cultivated countryside and congenial owners. For what such 'most charming estates' (*OLD ager* 3; superlative *amoenissimus* is used often of fields, estates etc., especially in Pliny) comprise, cf. 8.4.1 (about another estate) *agris aquisque, uinetis atque oliuetis, uestibulo campo colle amoenissimus* (for villas and their settings, see Morvillez

2017) – an instance of the set description of the idealized countryside, the so-called *locus amoenus* (*OCD* and Grafton et al. 2010 s.v.), typically featuring fertile fields, shady trees, hills with a view, running water and bird song. In this letter, §1 mentions hills and agriculture (*colles, uinitori, oliuitori*), the view across the plain (*prospectus*), woods (*nemora*) and §9 running water (*it Vardo fluuius*). For Pliny, this landscape is ultimate bliss (5.18.1 *uilla amoenissima* and *homo … felicissimus*); for Salvianus (5th cent.), it is paradise in Aquitaine (*Gub.* 7.8). Horace, however, at *Ars* 17 *properantis aquae per amoenos ambitus agros*, warns against any otiose use of the topos. **humanissimos**: in Sidonius' usage *humanus* means 'generous', 'hospitable' (cf. van Waarden 2016, 164 on 7.14.11 *humanissimus esse narraris*; see Raga 2016) rather than 'cultured' (*OLD* 5, preferred by Hindermann 2022b, 251). This is made explicit in §2 *hospitalitatis ordo*. **Ferreolum:** A relative of Sidonius via their respective wives, Tonantius Ferreolus was a central figure in Gaul in the 450s and 460s, *praefectus praetorio Galliarum* from 451 to 452/3 and as such engaged in the military campaign that expelled Attila's Huns from Gaul and was responsible for the diplomatic success that led the Visigoths to lift the siege of Arles. In 469, he was a member of the embassy to Rome accusing the Gallic prefect Arvandus of treason, which involved Sidonius, then city prefect of Rome, in a conflict of loyalties (described in letter 1.7; see Intro 1 and letter 1.5 Introduction). He owned the estates of Prusianum near Nîmes – the one in this letter – and Trevidon near Rodez (see map in Santelia and Condorelli 2023, 269). He is among the recipients of Sidonius' *carmina minora* collection (*Carm.* 24.34) and received the flattering letter 7.12 from him. Prosopography: Mathisen 2020a, 95–6. **Apollinarem:** Apollinaris may have been a paternal cousin of Sidonius together with his brothers Thaumastus and Simplicius (as argued by Mathisen 2020c, 58–9, modified for Simplicius by Marolla 2022), although the siblings have traditionally been held to be Sidonius' uncles. This trio is among Sidonius' frequent correspondents (3.11, 4.4, 4.5, 4.7, 4.12, 5.3, 5.4, 5.6, 5.7). Apollinaris is another addressee of the *carmina minora* (*Carm.* 24.48–74, where he is singled out with a lyrical description of his estate Vorocingus near Nîmes – the same as in this letter). After the Visigothic advance, he went to live in Vaison in Burgundian occupied territory in the 470s (see for a similar case, 7.1 Discussion 'Vienne and Mamertus'; see Intro 3.3 n. 38). In 474–5, he was suspected of involvement in a plot to restore Roman rule in Vaison (Harries 1994, 231–3). Prosopography: Mathisen 2020a, 80–1. **tempus uoluptuosissimum exegi:** a third superlative, making for an extremely complimentary atmosphere. Gleaned from Plin. 3.1.1 *nescio an ullum iucundius tempus exegerim.* **praediorum his iura contermina, domicilia uicina:** *praediorum* 'as to their estates', fronted, is topic. *iura* 'property', 'ownership' (as in 3.5.2 *praedii* ... *iura*, *OLD* 10), i.e. the land they own. *domicilia*, also a legal term, denoting stable residence (*Cod. Iust.* 10.40), alternating below with *aedibus* (the building) and *domui* (the house and its inhabitants) (Lucht 2011, 34–5). Their estates border each other while the manors are situated at some distance. The formulation is the result of Sidonius' stylistic urge to create oppositions. **gestatio** 'walk', 'drive', see Sherwin White 1966, 194: 'The *gestatio* is a formal walk set in shrubberies and often connected with a colonnade'. Pliny mentions a *gestatio* for his villas Laurentinum (2.17.13) and Tusci (5.6.17), and for his neighbour's estate at Comum (1.3.1). **peditem ... equitaturo:** the clause varies Plin. 2.17.2 *iunctis* ['by carriage'] *paulo grauius et longius, equo breue et molle* (see Whitton 2013, 226). *equitaturo* 'for someone who would go on horseback' is substantival use of the future participle (G–L §437 n. 1). **exercentur uinitori et oliuitori:** *exercentur* 'are cultivated' (*OLD* 3b). *oliuitori* 'olive grower' is a hapax, coined to rhyme with *uinitori*, both dative of the agent, associated with recherché prose style (G–L §354, H–S 97); cf. 8.4.1 *uinetis atque oliuetis*. These farmhands – like most of the servants mentioned throughout the letter – would have been enslaved people (Kaufmann 1995, 240–1). There is no archaeological confirmation so far of olive groves in these regions (Brun 2005, 98); cf. the praise of Narbonne, *Carm.* 23.47 *palmite ... trapetis* 'vine ... olive mills', which is above all a stylistic bravura piece rather than an accurate geographical description. **Aracynthum et Nysam:** placed chiastically in relation to *uinitori et oliuitori*. Mount Aracynthus is variously located in western or central Greece, but for Sidonius (as for Verg. *Ecl.* 2.24 *Actaeo Aracyntho*) it is in Attica and dedicated to Pallas Athena and the olive tree (Ravenna 1990, 62), cf. *Carm.* 15.32–3 *hastam ... quam ualle Aracynthi | ipsa sibi posita Pallas protraxit oliua*. Nysa is the mythical mountain where Dionysus was reared (e.g. Verg. *Aen.* 6.804–5), and is thus associated with the vine. **celebrata poetarum carminibus iuga:** a literary landscape is the best landscape, cf. 1.5.1 *fluuios ... poetarum carminum illustres*. *iuga* 'ridges', *pars pro toto* for *montes*, is itself a poeticism. **dissimilis ... similiter:** the same polyptoton is found in 7.6.9, 8.6.2, appealing to later writers in particular (van Waarden 2010, 328), strengthened to the ear by added *situs*. The entire introductory paragraph has been dominated by binary oppositions.

2 quamquam 'however' introduces the main clause: *OLD* 3. **de praediorum ... positione:** *praediorum* is extremely contrastive topic in a bold hyperbaton (Intro 4.3) in order to express: 'Why talk any longer about the estates? We must concentrate on hospitality'. Elliptical interrogative sentences with *quid* are quite common: the verb can easily be inferred from the immediately following context (*OLS* 1, 346). **hospitalitatis**

ordo reserandus 'the course of my visit to be disclosed': *OLD ordo* 9, *resero* 4b.   **sagacissimis ... exploratoribus** 'keen-scented scouts', like hounds. The humorous flourish that begins here plays on the metaphor of hunting (a seigneurial pastime if any, the hunter becoming the hunted), flooding the landscape with scouts and ambushes, all intent on intercepting Sidonius on his way home (Gualandri 1979, 132–3). Humour is one of the registers a letter writer – and indeed a gentleman – must master, cf. 7.18.2n. *dictaui ... iocando ... nonnulla* and typical stories for entertainment at dinner such as this one.   **reditus nostri:** Sidonius is on his return journey from the valley of the Gardon via Nîmes to Lyon, logically. *nostri*: the author, his family and retinue.   **aucuparentur** 'had to be on the lookout for', like bird-catchers (< *auis* + *capio*).   **aggerum publicorum** 'public highways': see 1.5.3n. *aggerem*.   **compendiis** 'short cuts' (*OLD* 3a).   **pastoria** = *pastorum*: the adjective is rare, also at 4.18.5 *fistulas ... pastorias*. For the late Latin preference for an attributive adjective instead of a possessive genitive, see 1.5.4n. *amnicos*; also below §4 *aleatoriarum* and *grammaticales*, §6 *senatorium*, §7 *cenatoriae* and often, e.g. 3.12.1n. *bustualis*.   **insedit, ne ... insidiis elaberemur** 'occupied, lest we evaded the ambushes' (e.g. Verg. *Aen.* 7.478).   **officiorum** 'services', 'courtesy' as an act of friendship (Intro 3.3), an oxymoron in combination with *insidiis*.   **priusquam septem dies euoluerentur:** the explicit duration of seven days could be a biblical reminiscence. A standard amount of time for any consequential activity in biblical thinking, it is also the duration of Tobias' celebration of his healing in the company of his two cousins: *Vulg. Tob.* 11.20–1 *ueneruntque Achior et Nabath consobrini Tobiae ... et per septem dies epulantes omnes cum gaudio magno gauisi sunt*. *euoluerentur* 'passed', 'elapsed' (of time) is later Latin (*TLL* 5/2.1067.66–1068.20). Thus the visit would begin with an insider's joke.

3 mane cotidiano is a one-off phrase, the usual expression being *cotidie mane* (Cato *Agr.* 156.6 and after); cf. 4.8.1 *mane primo*, 5.17.10 *mane nouo*.   **partibus super hospite ... contentio:** *partibus* '(both) sides' (*OLD* 16) is dative of possession (G–L §349), with ellipsis of the verb 'to be'. *super* is increasingly used instead of *de* in later Latin (H–S 281). *contentio* 'rivalry' (*OLD* 3).   **quaenam ... anterius ... culina fumaret:** the entire visit is dominated by eating and drinking, with its opposite in the final words, §10n. *parsimonia*. For the close connection between eating and hospitality, 8.4.1 *ager tuus ... hospites epulis, te pascit hospitibus*. For food as a means of distinction, see *ODLA* 'Dining' and Raga 2019. *anterius* 'earlier', 'first', is used as an adverb from fourth century onward, repeatedly in Sidonius (*TLL* 2.159.55–62). As breakfast consisted of cold food (bread or porridge), the 'smoking kitchen' is a metonym for preparing food, apart from the fact that the fires were probably kindled first thing in the morning (Hindermann 2022b, 257–8). For the smoke, cf. *Carm.* 35.44 (in 8.11.3) *fumificas ... culinas*, where the joke is that Sidonius, if not welcomed by his friends, has to make do with damp and smelly inns (cf. Grig 2024, 11). The motif goes back to Martial's *nigra culina* (e.g. Mart. 1.92.9). **lancem ponere** 'keep the balance': a collocation found elsewhere only at Manil. 4.775 *lancibus ... positis* (v.l. *-as*), Cypr. Gall. *Lev.* 153 *posita ... lance.* **uicissitudo** 'alternation': *OLD* 2, van Waarden 2010, 305. **licet** 'although' (*OLD* 4) with imperfect subjunctive is usual in later Latin (first seen at *Rhet. Her.* 4.5 *licet ... eligerent*; see H–S 605). It was impossible to keep the balance although the relationship was so close on both sides (Apollinaris was a cousin on Sidonius' side of the family (*mecum*), Tonantius Ferreolus was related to Sidonius' wife, part of his family-in-law (*cum meis*)), which in principle should have made it easy. However, Ferreolus' seniority (*aetas*) and rank of prefect (*dignitas*) tipped the scales in his favour. **necessitudinem** '(the respect owed to) his family relationship' (cf. *OLD* 1). **praerogatiuam** 'privilege', 'first choice' (*OLD* 3). Precedence (see 1.1.2n. *praerogatiuam*) through age and career is an iron law in all circumstances. The paragraph ends on the most important notion, emphatically one entire word, with the clausula cretic + spondee, like 1.1.2n. (Intro 4.5).

4 ilicet: 1.5.1n., 1.9.5n. **rapiebamur:** the sustained use of the imperfect tense binds the ensuing descriptive section §§4–9 together (see Discussion 'Verb tenses'). The various activities and localities are not specifically attributed to either villa. **et ecce:** cf. 1.5.9n. *et.* **huc ... huc ... huc** is equivalent to *hic ... hic ... hic* when looking in some direction, like 8.6.14 *huc ... huc prospici*, 8.13.3 *huc ... contemplans, huc ... praeuidens* (cf. *TLL* 6/3.3070.42–5). Ball playing, dice and a reading room are the activities on offer. The first two are described at some length in 5.17.6–7, where Sidonius styles himself as an avid sportsman as much as a reader (*sphaerae primus ego signifer fui, quae mihi, ut nosti, non minus libro comes habetur*). It is only logical that in our case, too, the gentlemen should have participated in the games that had evidently been started by assistants. The ball game in question possibly is the popular *harpastum*, a kind of rugby, or its three-player variant *trigon* (*BNP* 'Ball games', Weiler 1981, 212 and 266–7). The description is marked out by the use of Graecisms (*sphaeristarum, catastropharum, gyros*), of which Sidonius is fond (and which is also markedly Plinian), especially for technical terms, usually in clusters (Gualandri 1979, 145–63, esp. 159 n.53 for this passage, Wolff 2020, 405; using Greek terms is optional: 2.2.8 *si graecari mauis*). By contrast, the ensuing dice playing is described in Latin terms. **sphaeristarum constrastantium paria**

'pairs of opposing ball players': *sphaerista* only in Sidonius (also 5.17.7). Ball courts (*sphaeristeria*) belonged to the standard facilities of villas (Stat. *Silv.* 1.5.57–8, Plin. 2.17.12, 5.6.27 (mentioning the game as such only generically: 3.1.8 *deinde* [after a bath] *mouetur pila uehementer et diu*), and Sidonius' own at 2.2.15). **inter rotatiles catastropharum gyros** 'amid rapid circles of dives': *rotatilis* 'turning fast', 'swift' (Blaise) is very rare, four occurrences in all (the first being Prud. *Praef.* 7 *rotatiles trochaeos*). *catastropharum,* lit. 'falling down', as a sports term only here and 5.17.7 (*TLL* 3.598.50–4). For *gyrus,* see also 3.12.6n. **duplicabantur** 'double up', 'bend over' (*OLD* 1), in other words in 5.17.7 *cum ... per catastropham saepe pronatus aegre de ruinoso flexu se recolligeret* (cf. Schol. Stat. *Theb.* 1.420 FLEXOQUE GENU: *duplicato*). **aleatoriarum uocum competitiones** 'the rival cries of the dice players': for *competitiones,* as the usual, juridical meaning 'claim' will not do, 'competition', 'rivalry' (Blaise, Souter) seems preferable to 'harmony' (*TLL* 3.2064.52–4). For the abstract noun, cf. 1.9.3n. *populositas.* When tired of playing at ball, people used to turn to dice (2.2.15 *aleatorium lassis consumpto sphaeristerio*); for the combination, cf. e.g. *Carm.* 23.490–1 *pilas ... talos* 'balls ... dice' and 3.3.2 *pila pyrgus* 'ball and dice-box'. Dice playing is absent from Pliny. **fritillorum:** a *fritillus* is a dice-cup, a convex shaking-cup with a wide rim and internal ringed grooves. Alternatively, standing dice-towers were in use with an internal system of steps (*turricula, pyrgus,* 3.3.2, 5.17.6, 8.12.5). For both, *BNP* 'Fritillus'. **tesserarum:** 'dice-cubes' (*OLD* 1b). The sound of rattling dice (cf. Mart. 4.14.8 *sonat ... fritillis*) is imitated with a string of *fr, cr, fr, str,* and *t*-sounds. **libri:** a library is indispensable as a marker of elite status (e.g. Pliny 2.17.8 and his circle 3.7.8, 4.28.1) as well as a last resort against decline for a now endangered nobility (8.2.2 *solum erit posthac nobilitatis indicium litteras nosse,* with Mratschek 2020a, 256–7). For Roman private and public libraries, their collections, layout and administration, see Blanck 1992, 152–222. The library of Sidonius' host is furnished with plenty (*affatim*) of books – so many, the aside grandiosely proclaims, that one might have believed (*crederes*; G–L §258) it to be a professional library. For the ideal of a rich *uilla* library, cf. 8.4.1 *thesauris bibliothecalibus large refertus.* **grammaticales pluteos** 'the shelves of grammarians': *pluteus* basically 'screen', 'plank', here 'shelf', 'case' (Iuv. 2.7, *Dig.* 29.1.17; *TLL* 10/1.2470.39–52). **Athenaei cuneos** 'the wedge-shaped blocks of the Athenaeum': cf. 9.14.2 *Athenaei subsellia cuneata*; the lecture hall of the Athenaeum was built in the form of a theatre. The emperor Hadrian had endowed Rome with this school for the free arts and sciences (Aur. Vict. *Caes.* 14 *ludum ingenuarum artium;* it has been recently discovered under modern Piazza Venezia) as he had Athens with the famous library and conference centre (*BNP* 'School' IIIC' for other similar imperial initiatives). **armaria ... bybliopolarum:** for *armaria* 'bookcases', cf. Plin. 2.17.8 *in bibliothecae speciem armarium. bybliopolarum* 'booksellers', elsewhere in Sidonius (2.8.2, 5.15.1, 9.7.1) 'secretary', 'librarian'; see Santelia 2000. Booktrade (e.g. Mart. 4.72., Plin. 1.2.6, 9.11.2) existed alongside private copying rooms: Kleberg 1967, Blanck 1992, 120–9. **sic tamen quod:** *tamen* 'namely', explicative function specifically in late Latin (Spevak 2005, 208; see 7.1.2n. *tamen*; cf. van Waarden 2010, 396, van Waarden 2016, 152). *quod* + ind. = consecutive *ut* (4th cent. and later; H–S 581C2, Blaise 3). Devotional reading associated with women is contrasted with works meeting high literary standards associated with men: along with classical authors, eminent Christian writers may also meet these standards (Eigler 2013). **cathedras** 'armchairs' for women, as opposed to *subsellia* 'low seats', 'benches' for men: reading is a gendered activity (cf. *Carm.* 24.95, Sidonius' cousin Eulalia reading his *Carmina minora* in her home library; cf. Santelia and Condorelli 2023, 282 and see Intro 3.3 'Women'). **codices** 'books' made of vellum or papyrus, cf. Ulp. *Dig.* 32.1.52 *in codicibus ... membraneis uel chartaceis*. The library is provided with state-of-the-art editions. Though occasionally used for publishing as early as the first century CE (Mart. 2.1.3), the codex only became really successful thanks to Christian scribes from 300 CE onward; for classical works, it took even longer for the innovation to take hold (Kleberg 1967, 75–101, Harnett 2017). **stilus ... religiosus** 'religious genre', cf. 1.1.2n. *in stilo epistulari*. **coturno Latiaris eloquii** 'the grandeur of Latin eloquence': *cot(h)urnus* properly the thick-soled boot worn by tragic actors (*OLD* 1b), metaphorically 'grand style', 'grandeur' (*OLD* 2b, *TLL* 4.1088.7–32). Recherché *Latiaris* instead of *Latinus* adds to the elevated tone (also combined with *eloquii* at Symm. 1.3.2, Ennod. 7.26; cf. Sidon. *Carm.* 14.*ep.* 2 *Latiari lingua*, *Ep.* 2.10.1 *linguae Latiaris*, 4.3.1 *sermocinari Latialiter*). **quaepiam uolumina** 'some titles': the slightly archaic form *quaepiam* (G–L §107) is coveted by Sidonius and other archaizing authors (Intro 4.5). *uolumina* denotes books in their concrete, material aspect (Ulp. *Dig.* 32.52 pr. *omnia uolumina siue in charta siue in membrana sint*; van Waarden 2016, 38–9). **disparibus ... parilitatem:** characteristic polyptoton (cf. e.g. 7.1.2 *pari ... non impari*, 7.14.7 *dispari ... pari*; Wolff 2020, 410). **scientiae:** see 1.9.1n. *scientiae*. **Augustinus ... Varro:** Augustine (354–430; Mathisen 2020a, 83, *ODLA* 178–80 'Augustine of Hippo'), in his *De ciuitate dei*, copiously mined the antiquarian and prolific writer M. Terentius Varro (116–27 BCE; *BNP* 'Varro 2'; his works are mostly lost, unlike the other three authors mentioned). For Sidonius, too, Varro is the standard encyclopaedist and warrant of the Roman tradition, featuring in his library (*Carm.* 2.190, 14.*ep.* 3, *Ep.* 4.3.1, 8.6.18). He was actually not much prized for his style (Quint. *Inst.* 10.1.95 *plus scientiae collaturus quam eloquentiae*, Aug. *Civ.*

6.2 *minus est suauis eloquio, doctrina tamen ... refertus est).* These expert prose authors are chiastically (Christian–pagan) juxtaposed with two accomplished poets. **Horatius ... Prudentius:** Horace (Q. Horatius Flaccus, 65–8 BCE; *BNP* 'Horatius 7') is omnipresent in Sidonius as a model (Stoehr-Monjou 2013), for instance for *Ep.* 1.5 (see its Discussion) and for *Carm.* 41 in *Ep.* 9.16 where the collection is rounded off *secundum regulas Flacci* (9.16.4n.), rated among the greatest poets ever (e.g. *Carm.* 4.15–6, *Ep.* 8.11.7). The Christian poet Prudentius (Aurelius Prudentius Clemens, 348–c. 410; Mathisen 2020a, 117; *ODLA* 1245–6 'Prudentius'), often dubbed *Horatius Christianus* (for the Christian appropriation of pagan literature by Augustine and Prudentius among others, Pollmann 2017, 34–5), though not explicitly mentioned elsewhere by Sidonius, left traces throughout his work (among other things, in the genre of hymn: see again *Carm.* 41, with *Ep.* 9.16 Discusssion). **lectitabantur:** possibly another trace of Pliny's villa library, Plin. 2.17.8 *quod non legendos libros sed lectitandos capit*; for the form, see 1.5.9n. *scriptitans*, 7.18.3n. *lectitauisti*; it creates a one-word clausula, cretic + spondee (Intro 4.5).

5 quos inter: postponed preposition (G–L §413). **Adamantius Origenes:** the Greek Christian scholar and prolific writer Origen of Alexandria (184/5–253/5; *ODLA* 1107 'Origen', *BEEC* 'Origen'), highly controversial for the presumed unorthodoxy of his theological views and allegorical interpretation of the Bible (see Clark 1992), was nicknamed Adamantius ('Man of Steel') for his unbelievable productivity (Euseb. *Hist. eccl.* 6.14.10, Hier. *Vir. ill.* 54, *Ep.* 33.4 (Jerome lists both Origen's and Varro's works to prove that Origen surpassed even the latter in his output), 43.1). Sidonius also mentions him at 9.2.2 (*allegoricus Origenes*) as a paragon of *doctrina salubris* 'sound doctrine', together with Jerome and Augustine. Other than being a general reference to Origen and his work, *Adamantius Origenes* could also refer specifically to the protagonist of the dialogue *De recta in Deum fide*, also known as *Dialogue of Adamantius*, wrongly ascribed to Origen in antiquity, but close to his ideas, debating the crucial tenets of orthodox Christianity (Ilaria Ramelli in *BEEC* 'De recta in Deum fide'). Hence Anderson (Loeb edition 1, 454) attractively suggested the emendation *Origenis*: 'the *Adamantius* of Origen'. **Turranio Rufino:** Rufinus of Aquileia (*c.* 345–*c.* 410; Mathisen 2020a, 118; *ODLA* 1310–1) was a priest and a translator of Greek texts into Latin, among them Eusebius' *Church History* and Origen's *On First Principles*. His translations of Origen, purged to underpin the latter's orthodoxy, led to a conflict with that other great translator Jerome to whom it was an *infamis interpretatio* (*Ep.* 127.7). Jerome came up with a translation of his own to reveal the heretical passages. The case of *Turranio Rufino* is dative of the agent: see

§1n. *uinitori.* **interpretatus:** translation interested men like Sidonius, cf. 4.12.1–2 (comedy), 8.3.1 (the *Life of Apollonius*, a vexed question though among scholars: see letter 8.3 Discussion), 9.2.2 *Hieronymus interpres*. Their own knowledge of Greek was probably sufficient (John 2023, John 2026, 167–8), but see Denecker 2017, 150–96 for the experts such as Rufinus and Jerome. **fidei nostrae** 'our faith': meaning the orthodoxy of Sidonius and friends as opposed to the various heretical opinions that circulated – precisely what the Origenist debate was about; cf. 7.8.3 *fidem ... Arrianorum*, 7.9.1 *fidei catholicae* (not 'Christian belief' as opposed to 'paganism', as everybody was Christian). **pariter et** 'at the same time', 'as well': a favourite conjunction in Sidonius; see van Waarden 2016, 188. **sermocinabantur** 'they discussed': reading complex texts and then discussing them in philological detail to establish their meaning was common practice in intellectual circles, and indeed constitutive of such 'reading communities' (see Johnson 2010, Johnson 2011). *sermocinabantur* is the reading of the α MS-branch, whereas δ reads *sermocinabamur* (*T -àtur*, *LVRN* have a lacuna between §1 *Apollinarem* and 8 *in quam*), which is printed by Lütjohann. In the narrative context, *sermocinabantur* is more logical. The various activities are observed from a distance (passive, third person), enclosed by the first persons §4 *rapiebamur* and 6 *nostrum*. **protomystarum** 'foremost initiates': graecism (πρωτομύστης 'one just initiated') with altered meaning, only here and 4.17.3, where it qualifies two bishops who are experts in biblical exegesis. Jerome is certainly among the critics targeted here (cf. Hindermann 2022b, 269). **scaeuus cauendusque tractator** 'a misguided and dangerous author': *OLD scaeuus* 3. *tractator* in patristic idiom is 'author' (e.g. Hier. *Adv. Ruf.* 1.30 *inter ecclesiasticos tractatores*), 'exegete' (e.g. Aug. *Trin.* 2.1.2 *Scripturarum tractatores*) (Blaise 3). **ad uerbum sententiamque** 'faithful to the letter and the spirit': Rufinus' meticulous translation is there to disprove the allegations against Origen. The underlying discussion turns on the principle of translating in conformity with either the source or the target language as set out by Jerome in his *Ep.* 57, which informs this passage. In 57.5, Jerome argues that it is misleading to translate *uerbum uerbo* (citing Hor. *Ars* 133–4) due to the differences in languages: what counts is retaining the *uim uerborum*. He corroborates his argument with two examples of such a 'free' translation: Apuleius' of Plato's *Phaedo* and Cicero's of Demosthenes' *In Defence of Ctesiphon On the Crown*, both now lost (although Cicero discusses his in *De optimo genere oratorum*, esp. §14 *non uerbum pro uerbo ... sed ... uerborum uim*). Sidonius sides with Rufinus, apparently on account of the latter's stress on the orthodoxy of Origen: by translating Origen *ad uerbum* and not only *ad sententiam*, Rufinus does one better than Apuleius and Cicero. The actual purport of the discussion among the guests at Nîmes remains implicit.

Origen was an essential author for Provençal monasticism (Cassian and Lérins: Intro 3.4 with n.63) which struggled with possibly heretical traits in this incomparably great master (cf. Vincent. Ler. *Comm.* 24–7). The present passage shows how this argument even fed into the leisure activities of the laity. **exscripserint** 'have translated': as at 8.3.1 (with the proviso of the interpretative conundrum there, see above), 9.16.2. For the entire passage, Pricoco 1965b, 141–50.

6 hisce: 1.1.4n. *hisce.* **ecce et ... aduentans** 'look, someone arriving': for *ecce et*, see 1.5.9n. *patuit et.* The participle is used as a substantive (G–L §437). **archimagiro** 'chief cook': also Iuv. 9.109, Hier. *Quaest. hebr. in Gen.* 37.36 (*CC SL* 72 p. 45). **curandi corpora** 'refresh ourselves', doing anything conducing to physical health (Page at Verg. *Aen.* 3.511n.) **per spatia clepsydrae** 'by means of the intervals of the water-clock': probably, together with *quinta* below, a reworking of Plin 2.11.14 *dixi horis paene quinque; name duodecim clepsydris, quas spatiosissimas acceperam, sunt additae quattuor.* Water-clocks measured time by the flow of water from a vessel, ranges of marks indicating the time of the day, adjusted to the varying length of hours through the year (*OCD* 'Clocks', *BNP* 'Clocks IIB'; cf. Ker 2023). *clepsydra* also 2.13.4 *per horarum ... clepsydras.* **seruantem** 'keeping an eye on': *OLD* 2. **ingressum ... digrediens:** polyptoton: the boy enters as time departs; the entire sentence is as meticulously ordered as the water-clock itself. **quinta:** the fifth hour, about eleven o'clock, midday dinner time; cf. Mart. 8.67.1–2 *Horas quinque puer nondum tibi nuntiat et tu | iam conuiua mihi, Caeciliane, uenis.* For Pliny in his summer resort, *hora quarta uel quinta* (9.36.3) is the time to have some movement after his early-morning meditation. **senatorium ad morem:** Anderson (Loeb 1, 456 n. 1) plausibly suggests that this is a reference to the long (and unsuccessful) history of legislation against luxury, in particular the intervention by the censor of 275 BCE which set a limit to the possession of silver tableware. To this we should add the much more contemporary voice of Macrobius. In *Sat.* 3.13–17, the excessive display of wealth and the various *leges sumptuariae* of the past (*OLD* 'Lex (2)') pass in review, to end in a sigh of relief: *hoc saeculum ad omnem continentiam promptius* 'our own time is much more self-disciplined' (3.17.12). In the same spirit, Sidonius next claims that inhibition is now *insitum institutumque* 'rooted and anchored'. Compare his approval of Theoderic's dinner table, 1.2.6 *cibi arte, non pretio placent, fercula nitore, non pondere,* and his own invitation to dinner (*Carm.* 17), which promises restraint in tableware and food. In his later work, display of wealth and copious dining will be problematized from the viewpoint of asceticism (Intro 3.4; archaeological discussion of silver plate, Cameron 1992, Painter 1993, Baratte 2019 with illustrations;

on social aspects of dining, Raga 2009, Raga 2019; for the entire scene, cf. Stevens 1933, 69; for Sidonius selling his tableware, see 2.10.2n. *munificentiam*). **multas epulas paucis parapsidibus apponi:** the accusative and infinitive is the subject of the clause (G–L §535); late antique authors have a marked preference for the (already classical) use of passive infinitives in such cases (H–S 353). The oxymoronic opposition *multas–paucis* follows up on *breuiter–copiose*. *epulas* 'types of food', 'specialities', *OLD* b. *parapsidibus* 'dishes': this is the MS reading, also found as a variant at Petron. 34.2 (see Löfstedt 1985, 209). The more usual spelling is *-ops-*: *OLD paropsis*; cf. Iuv. 3.142 [people are not interested in one's character, but only ask questions like] *quam multa magnaque paropside cenat?* **assa ... iurulenta** 'roasted ... stewed': the meal is modest, yet varied in the manner of cooking. Apul. *Apol.* 39.4 proves that the question of which preparation tastes best was a matter of serious debate for Ennius in his didactic poem on gastronomy (*Hedyphagetica*). In Cels. 2.18.10 a similar trade-off is made for health. **uarietur:** *uarietas delectat* is an axiom encountered as early as Cicero (e.g. *De orat.* 3.100). It is found at every level, from gastronomy to aesthetics (for the latter, cf. e.g. Plin. 2.5.7), and is addressed by Sidonius himself as a dominant motif for his letter collection (Intro 4.1 with n. 90; cf. 7.18.2n. *uarios*). **inter bibendum:** also 9.13.2 [lines of poetry] *inter bibendum pronuntiandis*. **narratiunculae:** diverting stories accompanied drinking (for their sources, van Waarden 2010, 133–5; letter 7.2 is a case in point for Sidonius). The diminutive denotes not so much that they were short, but rather light and unpretentious (cf. 1.1.3n. *lucubratiunculas*). **hilararemur institueremur:** table talk should be delightful and instructive, not about controversial matters or business: Varr. *Sat.* 337 *sermones ... non super rebus anxiis aut tortuosis, sed ... uoluptate utiles*, 340 *in conuiuio legi ... potissimum quae simul sint* βιωφελῆ ('useful for life') *et delectent* (cf. for poetry, Hor. *Ars* 333 *aut prodesse uolunt aut delectare poetae*, 343 *omne tulit punctum qui miscuit utile dulci*). **bifariam orditas** 'begun in two ways' (*OLD ordior* 2b): the same elements e.g. Plin. 1.15.3 *lusissemus risissemus studuissemus* (in addition to a 'simple', refined meal), Sidon. 5.17.5 *distincta narratio ... laetitia permixta*. **quid multa?** addressed to the reader, it lends a colloquial tone to the letter; it is found as far back as Plautus, e.g. *Bac.* 1162 *quid multa? ego amo*, is frequent in Cicero's correspondence and in Sidonius' too; cf. 7.17.4n., 8.3.6n. (van Waarden 2016, 250; Intro 3.6). **sancte pulchre abundanter** 'responsibly, stylishly, lavishly': asyndetic tricolon obeying the 'law of rising members' (Intro 4.5 n. 111), cf. 7.3.2 *sancte facunde uenerabilis* (van Waarden 2010, 210). Connotations of *sanctus* range from 'decent', 'responsible', 'faithful' to 'holy': see van Waarden 2010, 163; in this volume also 2.10.2, 3.12.3, 5.16.2, 7.17.1 and 4, 8.15.1.

7 Vorocingi ... Prusiani 'at Vorocingus ... at Prusianum': locative case. They are Apollinaris' and Tonantius Ferreolus' properties, respectively: cf. §1n. *Ferreolum et Apollinarem*. Prusianum is named after Dion of Prusa, *c.* 40–after 111 CE, the most famous orator of the times of the emperor Trajan (Mratschek 2020a, 255). **praedio ... fundus:** neatly exchanges grammatical gender, neuter *praedio* referring to masculine *Vorocingus* (sc. *fundus*) and masculine *fundus* to neuter *Prusianum* (sc. *praedium*). **ad sarcinas et diuersorium:** the guests retire for the siesta. The precise situation is not clear. Did Vorocingus have a guest wing (*diuersorium*), whereas Prusianum had not (Carrié 2010, accepted by Hindermann)? It would indeed seem improbable that Sidonius had to make do with an inn (as in 1.5.9n. *conducti diuersorii*). On the other hand, Sidonius' company seem to have their own bedding with them (*sarcinas* and *instrumenta* below; 4.8.2 *sarcinulis* is a case in point for the cumbrous train of a travelling aristocrat) and building activities are going on in both houses (§8). For discussion, Anderson 1, 456–7 n. 2; Percival 1997, 284–6; Lucht 2011, 67–9; Hindermann 2022b, 276–7. **Tonantium cum fratribus:** Tonantius Jr (*Carm.* 24.34 *docti ... Tonantii*; Mathisen 2020a, 125, though not the owner of Prusianum) and his brothers leave their rooms to Sidonius and company. **lectissimos ... principes:** Lucht 2011, 70 may well be right that this has an epic ring, e.g. Verg. *Aen.* 5.729 *lectos iuuenes* and 7.468 *primis iuuenum*. *lectissimos* 'most honourable', 'excellent' (*TLL* 7/2.1133.72–1134.5). **nec** instead of *non*, lending it an energetic nuance, is a feature of archaic and late Latin (G–L §442 n. 3, Löfstedt 1956, 338–42). **instrumenta** 'equipment': specified by *cubilium nostrorum* (G–L §361). **equitabamus:** cf. Pliny on his Tuscan estate: Plin. 9.15.3 *equum conscendo* (for relaxation after doing some work), 9.36.5 *equo gestor* (reinvigorating after a meal). **pectora marcida cibis:** the breast as a receptacle or channel for food: *OLD pectus* 2a. *marcida* 'languid', cf. 1.6.3 *pingui otio marcidus*, 5.17.5 *otio diu marcidis aliquid agere uisum*. **cenatoriae** (rare, from Apul. *Met.* 5.3.2 *instrumentum cenatorium* onward) instead of *cenandi*; see §2n. **pastoria**. Whetting one's appetite through physical exercise, e.g. Cic. *Fin.* 2.62, *Tusc.* 5.97.

8 After the siesta and a ride on horseback, it is time for the daily bath, cf. Plin. 3.1.8 *hora balinei nuntiata est* (*est autem hieme nona, aestate octaua*) (followed by a ball game: *deinde mouetur pila uehementer et diu*), 9.36.3 *exerceor, lauor. cenanti mihi ...* (exercise, bath, dinner). Private baths are the crowning feature of a *uilla*. Sidonius is particularly proud of his huge bath complex at Avitacum, described at length in 2.2.4–8, provided with indoor facilities (*balneum*) and an outdoor *piscina*, and praised in *Carm.* 18 *De balneis uillae suae* and 19 *De piscina sua*. In comparison, the description by Pliny of his Laurentinum and Tusci villas with *balneum* plus *piscina* (Plin.

2.17.11 and 26, 5.6.25–6) is succinct. On Roman baths: Brödner 1983, esp. 186–97 on private baths, Yegül 2009.   **in opere uterque ... in usu neuter** 'both under construction ... neither in use': an amicable quip at the expense of his kin whose bathhouses compare poorly with Sidonius' own – as the reader of letter 2.2 will remember. There is more construction work going on in Apollinaris' villa: *Carm.* 24.55 [marble wall cladding]; cf. 8.6.10 [to another landowner] *aedificas?* As explained in the Discussion above, we can only guess at what exactly is the case (which would reflect the economic situation): are the baths being improved (Lançon 2017, 193–5) or are they in need of repair (Percival 1992, Percival 1997)? Harries 1994, 131–3 concludes with a *non liquet*. Or is there any family rivalry involved (Hanaghan 2019, 25–7 and 56 and Hanaghan 2020)? Grig 2024, 87–91 gauges the vitality of villas at the time, which was considerable in Aquitaine (Balmelle 2001) but less so elsewhere.   **uel pauxillulum** 'ever so little', 'at least briefly': *uel* (*OLD* 6) 'at any rate', 'even if only'. *pauxillulum*, from comedy, underscores the playful register of this passage; cf. 1.5.9n. *pauxillulum*.   **bibere:** there is drinking and drinking, the masters' *bibendum* (§6) being perfectly in order, the servants' a reason for condescending humour (cf. 8.3.2n. *nil umquam litigiosius bibacius* ('more tipsy') *uomacius* than two Gothic women who hamper Sidonius' creativity).   **assecularum meorum famulorumque:** Sidonius' attendants and the local household staff. Aristocrats never travelled alone, e.g. 4.8.2 where the servants prepare lunch on the road; accompaniment by no more than one slave and one client (4.18.2) was exceptional. For the status of these servants, probably mostly slaves, Samson 1992, Kaufmann 1995, 237–54. Interestingly, their socializing is allowed up to a certain point to dictate the schedule of the masters.   **compotrix** as an adjective only here; the noun *compotor/ –trix* 'drinking companion' e.g. Cic. *Phil.* 2.4.2, Ter. *An.* 232.   **cerebris ... dominabantur:** cf. Petr. *Sat.* 41.12 *uinus mihi in cerebrum abiit*, Macr. *Sat.* 7.5.14 *potus ut natura leuior ... petit ... cerebrum*.   **hospitales craterae** 'the wine-bowls of our hosts': the servants take advantage of the occasion.   **uicina:** the description of the erection of one or more open-air saunas in one long, contorted sentence up to the end of the paragraph is an example of the 'dense' strand of Sidonius' bipolar style (Intro 4.5). It makes the complexity of the construction tangible, sacrificing straightforwardness to stylistic brilliance (as Roberts 1989, 11 puts it while illustrating the 'jewelled style' (see Intro 3.5 n. 69): 'the more difficult and prosaic a subject, the better it was suited to display a writer's talents'). A hole is dug near water, a pile of heated stones dumped into it, a dome of plaited twigs built over it and covered with sturdy rugs. Then water is poured on the hot stones (cf. the permanent sauna in Vitr. 5.10.5; for a picture of a medieval open-air sauna, Cod. Bodmer 135, f. 6r, https://arqueotoponimia.blogspot.com/2017/12/saunas-improvisadas-los-sudatoria-del.html).   **forte** 'at some point' (cf. *OLD* 2). **lapidum cumulus ambustus:** with enallage of the adjective (*OLS* 1, 1051–3); cf. Plin. 6.16.11 *ambusti et fracti igne lapides* (emitted by Vesuvius). **antro ... corylis flexibilibus intexto:** *antro* 'a cave affording shelter', 'a hollow place with overarching foliage', with numerous poetical associations (*OLD* 1, 2). *corylis* 'hazel branches': pliable (Cato *Agr.* 18.9, Plin. *Nat.* 16.228) and also typical of pastoral scenery (Verg. *Ecl.* 5.3 and 21, 7.63–4). The phrase signposts the structure as a variant of the pastoral dell with shady foliage (Calp. *Ecl.* 1.8–12 is a particularly elaborate example). Apollinaris actually had a lush garden on his estate (*Carm.* 24.56–68) with plenty of shade, 'the trees creating not a grove but a cave' (68 *non lucum arboribus facit, sed antrum*). This cave is paradoxically turned into a receptacle for the heat and a sort of *antrum Vulcani* (Verg. *Aen.* 8.417–21, Iuv. 1.8–9). Later on, in Book 7, the reader may remember this ambivalent pastoral idyll when taken to the darkest days of Clermont and its decrepit defences: 7.1.2 *aut ambustam murorum faciem aut putrem sudium cratem* 'the scorched surface of the walls [the only other instance of *ambustus* in Sidonius] or the palisades of rotting wickerwork'. **sic tamen, ut:** see §4n. *sic tamen quod*. **Cilicum uelis** 'Cilician cloths': a *cilicium* is 'a rug or blanket of goat's hair (app. originating in Cilicia)' (*OLD*); at 4.24.3 they are used as curtains. **undae feruentis aspergine flammatis silicibus excuditur** 'is emitted by red-hot stones when pouring water on them that comes to a boil': for *undae ... aspergine*, cf. Plin. 2.17.14 *aspergine maris. feruentis* is proleptic. The phrase is modelled on Verg. *Georg.* 1.135 *ut silicis uenis abstrusum excuderet ignem* (of sparks struck from flintstone) and Ov. *Met.* 7.107–8 *aut ubi terrena silices fornace soluti | concipiunt ignem liquidarum adspergine aquarum* (of lime being produced by burning limestone and make it react with water (*BNP* 'Lime')). Ovid compares the roar of the fire-breathing bulls of Aeëtes, in the story of Jason and Medea, to the din of fire and steam when water is poured on red-hot limestone. In the sauna, the metamorphosis of the quiet pastoral into an uproar is complete.

9 non absque sermonibus salsis iocularibusque: *non absque* 'with plenty of' (< 'not without', litotes), found from the fourth century onward, e.g. Amm. 24.1.8 *non absque discriminibus multis*. Sidonius and his hosts having a good time in the hazelwood cave is the buffoonish version of the classic pastoral ambience of the singer-songwriter under the hazel and the elm: Verg. *Ecl.* 5.1–3 *Cur non, Mopse, boni quoniam conuenimus ambo, | tu calamos inflare leues, ego dicere uersus, | hic corylis mixtas inter consedimus ulmos?* **halitu nebulae stridentis** evokes the associated uproar (Verg. *Aen.* 8.420–1 *stridunt ... anhelat* in Vulcan's cave). **saluberrimus sudor:** a sweating out before dinner is medically required, cf. Cels. 1.3.4 *cibum sumpturis ... si balneum non est, calido loco ... sudare.* **quo ... effuso:** referring to *halitu*, cf. Verg. *Aen.* 6.241 *talis sese halitus ... effundens* (cf. Plin.

2.17.23 *hypocauston ... calorem ... effundit*). **coctilibus aquis ingerebamur:** the vapour bath is followed by the hot bath. It is not clear whether this is in the same ditch; cf. the indoor hot bath in Avitacum, 2.2.4 *hinc aquarum surgit cella coctilium. coctilis* 'hot' for water is unique as it is commonly said of bricks, 'fired' (e.g. Varro *Rust.* 1.14.4 *e lateribus coctilibus*). *ingerebamur* reflexive: 'we plunged into' (*OLD* 2c). **fotu ... tergente** 'purging (*OLD tergo* 2) balm', cf. e.g. Claud. Mam. *Stat. an.* 2.12 *caloris ac frigoris alterno fotu. tergente* 'purging' (*OLD* 2). **fontano ... puteali ... fluuiali:** now for the cold bath 'from a spring, a well or in the river'. For a well for cooling down, Plin. 5.6.25 *puteus ex quo possis rursus adstringi*. The situation is somehow different from one domain to the other, cf. §8 *uicina fonti aut fluuio*. Anyway, this looks rather like a stimulating *embarras du choix* (with the positive conclusion *solidabamur* 'we were invigorated') than a tedious, repetitive search as Hanaghan 2020, 128 thinks in his effort to read this open-air bathing in a negative light. **siquidem** 'namely' (*OLD* 4). **domibus medius** 'between the houses': the dative also 4.20.1n. *cursoribus medius* (*OLD medius* 3, *TLL* 8.582.77–9). **Vardo,** nowadays called River Gard or Gardon, flows into the Rhône east of Nîmes (this is the only mention in antiquity; *BNP* 'Vardo', *Pleiades* https://pleiades.stoa.org/places/253855601). The description develops the *locus amoenus* motif (§1n. *inter*). **defluo** 'flowing down': first attested in Statius (*Silv.* 1.3.53, *Theb.* 9.325); here of meltwater, cf. Symm. *Or.* 2.23 [the Rhine] *Alpinae niuis defluo liquore cumulatus*. **flauis ruber glareis** 'with a red tinge from the brownish shingle' (after Anderson). From its upper reaches in the Cevennes, the river carries copper and iron particles (*RE* 8A1.372.52–7 'Vardo'). **piscium ferax delicatorum:** *piscium ferax* only here and Avien. *Ora* 518–9 *piscium semper ferax | stagnum*. Cf. Plin. 2.17.15 *arborum ... ferax* and 28 *pretiosis piscibus. delicatorum* of taste 'delicate', 'exquisite', also Mart. 4.30.16 *pisces ... delicatos* (*OLD* 6b). The disposition of the attributes of the river is sophisticated: *ruber* surrounded by adjective plus noun, the triple sequence *perspicuus quietus calculosusque* and *ferax* surrounded by noun plus adjective – perhaps mimicking the river bed and its banks. All three parts have rhythmical endings: a double cretic and twice cretic + spondee (Intro 4.5). The description is a miniature version of the clarity of the water and the fish catalogue in Ausonius' *Mosella* (*Mos.* 55–149): for *perspicuus*, cf. 55–6 *uitreo ... profundo | secreti nihil amnis habens* (in Sidonius also *Carm.* 24.47 *perspicua ... in unda*); for *quietus*, cf. 61 *uada lene meant*; for *calculosus*, cf. 66–7 *lucetque latetque | calculus*; for *glareis*, cf. 67 *glarea*; for *delicatorum*, cf. 115 *delicias mensarum*.

10 dicerem et cenas ... unctissimas: dinner is touched upon only in passing (*praeteritio*). In oratory, omitting an element from the *narratio*, or postponing it, obviates boredom (*taedium*; Quint. *Inst.* 4.2.48). Here, the effect is twofold: the sudden stop dovetails with the epistolary convention of avoiding overlong letters (or pretending to do so; Intro 3.6) and morphs into the friendly gesture of singling out the imminent tête-à-tête of Sidonius and the addressee as a much better occasion for telling the story. **unctissimas** 'extremely rich': *OLD unctus* 1b, see above §6 *copiose* of the lunch. The restraint professed there (*insitum institutumque* n.) does not go a long way yet. Later, as asceticism gains traction, the host may have turned to fasting and vegetarianism, only compromising *si quid in cibis unctius* (4.24.4) on behalf of his guests. **nostrae loquacitati** 'my talkativeness': polite self-deprecation, cf. e.g. 6.3.2 *nostram loquacitatem*, 1.9.7 *loquax ... charta*, Plin. 5.20.8, Symm. 3.82.1. *nostrae* and the first person plural verb forms that follow blur the 'I' somewhat for his breaking epistolary etiquette, the 'you' remaining a straightforward *tu* (Intro 4.2 '"You" and "I"', van Waarden 2020e). **uerecundia** 'respect', elsewhere also 'modesty' and 'diffidence', 'restraint' (see 2.10.3n., cf. *uerecundus* at 3.9.1n., 5.16.3n., 7.17n.), a key concept in social intercourse (Intro 3.3 'Social Conventions' with n. 54). **charta** 'sheet' of papyrus for writing a letter on, 'stationery', cf. Mart. 14.11 *Chartae epistolares*. **quoque** 'indeed', does not express addition, but highlights one of several instances (van Waarden 2010, 236–7). **replicatio** 'recollection': see 1.5.1n. *proeliorum replicatione*. **epistulae tergum madidis sordidare calamis:** suggesting that it is not stylish to write on the back of the papyrus sheet, let alone when one is the worse for drinking. The back side was in principle avoided as its vertical fibres hampered the pen and were more liable to cause inkblots. In practice, however, sheets were used recto and verso, margins and all, people turning the letter over and writing the response on the back, squeezing an overlong work into a reasonably sized scroll (Iuv. 1.5–6 *plena iam margine libri | scriptus et in tergo*) or removing a previous text and reusing the sheet in case no new papyrus was to be had (Plin. 8.15.2) or out of parsimony (Cic. *Fam.* 7.18.2) (*ODLA* 1138 'Papyrus and Papyrology', Blanck 1992, 56–62). *madidis* plays on the meanings 'dripping' and 'drunk' (*OLD* 1, 6). *sordidare* 'to dirty', 'to spoil', cf. 1.5.6n. *sordidaretur*, cf. Auson. *Praef.* 5.1–2 for supposedly spoiling the sheet by writing on it. **in procinctu** 'ready (to leave)' (*TLL* 10/2.1531.33–7; cf. *OLD* 1b). Cf. the narrative situation in 1.9.7n. *dum uenio* and 4.19n. *uenimus*. **sub ope Christi:** see 1.9.8n. **expeditius** 'more readily' (*OLD* 3): unobtrusively linked with *in procinctu* as both have the basic meaning of 'ready for (military) action' (e.g. Cypr. *Fort.* 8 *expeditos in procinctu firmiter stare*). **hebdomadis exactae spatia completa** 'the days that remain until the end of the week': the noun *hebdomas* (gen. *-adis*) denotes any group of seven, also specifically seven consecutive days, 'a week', cf. 1.7.12 *per* *hebdomadam duplicem* 'during a fortnight' (*TLL* 6/3.2578.1–18). The week during which Sidonius promised to stay (§2 *septem dies*) is running out. He hopes that the end will be less exuberant. Some would take this to mean that Sidonius inserts another week to recover before he goes to Donidius (translations Anderson; Köhler 2014; Hindermann 2022b, 289). This would come entirely unexpectedly and would deal another blow to the addressee. **uotiuae ... esuritioni** 'the hunger I wish for': *uotiuae* 'wished for', 'longed for' is later Latin, e.g. Apul. *Met.* 7.13 *ad uotiuum conspectum*, Prud. *Perist.* 2.330 *uotiua mors* (L–S 11). **disruptum ganea** 'burst by gluttonous eating': *disruptum* is a strong expression (see Intro 4.5 'Hyperbole'), as *intestina rupta* is the medical term for intestinal rupture (Plin. *Nat.* 28.210, Marcell. *Med.* 28.49 [features *disrupta* besides]). *ganea OLD* b. **sarcire** 'heal', 'restore': e.g. Plin. *Nat.* 28.210 *rupta intestina sarcire*. **parsimonia** 'temperance' (*OLD* 2a): alternatively, remedies were advised for restoring the appetite, e.g. Plin. *Nat.* 20.34 *siser ... stomachum excitat* 'parsnip stimulates the appetite'. Comparing the conclusion of letter 2.2 to this one, one finds that 2.2 ends with an invitation by Sidonius to Avitacum vaunting its vastness (*spatia, grandem*: room for a big party). Here, on the other hand, Sidonius makes good on an invitation, whilst leaving Vorocingus and Prusianum on a note of after-party inhibition: expansivity in the first case vs restraint in the latter.

LETTER 2.10 WITH POEM 27: A POEM FOR THE CATHEDRAL OF LYON

Outline

In §1 Sidonius compliments his young friend Hesperius on his uncommonly serious literary interest. Hesperius has asked him for a recent poem (§2). Sidonius selects his dedicatory poem for bishop Patiens' new cathedral of Lyon while apologizing at length for its poor quality (§3–4). The poem describes the church's striking exterior and glittering interior, inviting everybody to enter and take the road to salvation. The finale (§§5–6) reminds Hesperius that now Sidonius expects a poem in return. It becomes apparent that Hesperius is about to marry. Sidonius warns him not to let his marriage come in the way of continuous study. Two series of historical exempla are there to prove, conversely, that a supportive partner enhances a man's literary capability.

Introduction

Poems in letters as an extra gift for the addressee – in addition to the letter itself (Intro 3.3) – are a distinctive feature of later epistolography in particular, an instance of the late antique mixture of genres (Fontaine

1977; see Intro 3.6). Sidonius has seventeen of these, comprising a total of 558 verses (Consolino 2020, 342–3), increasing in number in the later books (modelled no doubt on Pliny: Sherwin White 1966, 289), held back only by the taboo on light verse for clerics (see 7.17.1n. *diu desides* and e.g. 9.12.1). He calls such letters *litterae bimetrae* (9.15.1, *Carm.* 37.89; the modern term is *prosimetra*, see Pabst 1994, 310–11). Whether and how a particular poem relates to its letter (Harrison 2007a, 16 speaks of the 'guest' and the 'host' genres) is a matter of debate and taste. In Sidonius, metapoetical self-awareness and conscious self-presentation by means of these poems are evident (Mratschek 2017, Hindermann 2020b, Neger 2020, Hindermann 2022b, xxi–xxiv).

Two of his inserted poems are epigraphs for churches, the other one written for the basilica of St Martin of Tours (*Carm.* 31 in 4.18). The epigraph for Patiens' cathedral consists of 30 verses in Phalaecian hendecasyllables (– – –⏑⏑ –⏑ –⏑ –×). emulating the meter of Martial's epigram 4.64 from which it also takes its cue for the din and bustle surrounding the church (vv. 22–7); discussion in Consolino 2020, 362. At the poem's core is a description (*ekphrasis*: *BNP* 'Ekphrasis', Elsner 2002, Webb 2009) of the church that evokes metaphysical associations of sunlight and radiant gems: its richness is a foretaste of paradise as much as it is a tribute to Patiens (Hernández Lobato 2010). For texts inscribed in churches, see Leatherbury 2019 (for Sidonius, pp. 191 and 196).

Discussion

It is inevitably subjective to go beyond the obvious observation that Sidonius sends Hesperius a recent occasional poem embedded in a letter stimulating literary excellence. Nevertheless, the letter strongly suggests a more far-reaching intention. Here are some thoughts towards a coherent interpretation (the one by Egelhaaf-Gaiser 2014 is the most sustained to date; see vv. 22–7n. below):

1. The praise for Hesperius' enthusiasm is set against the background of Sidonius' cultural pessimism: Latin is sinking. Belonging to the happy few is an ambivalent accolade. Hesperius, however, is a hopeful successor (§3 *adhuc mihi iamque tibi*).
2. Only the very best is good enough. The letter itself sets the standard by its virtuosity: an extended depreciation of his own poem by the author (§§3–4), an original, atmospheric dedicatory poem and a carefully laid out series of *exempla* of marriage and literature (§§5–6).
3. The poem develops another counterpoint to pessimism, as Patiens is praised for his piety and his munificence. There is (implicitly) hope

for the future thanks to an energetic episcopate. This idea emerges here for the first time, in the middle of the book of *otium* and private affairs.

4. Unlike literary pursuits for an elite (§1 *paucissimi*), the Church is there for all (v. 29 *omnibus*). The aristocratic disdain for the *turba imperitorum* (§6) is counterbalanced by the 'democratization' of life around the new church (vv. 22–30).

5. The intertextuality of vv. 22–30, inverting motifs of Martial, Ausonius and Horace in a Christian sense, challenges the reader's literacy.

6. The final paragraphs stage the poem as a wedding gift and the future bride and groom as a literary tandem in the best Roman tradition. The scene is suffused with lamplight (§5 *candelabra*), harking back to the sunlight flooding the variegated interior of the church (vv. 8–15). I would suggest that the combination of literature with marriage is akin – perhaps even indebted – to Martianus Capella's *Philologia* in which Mercury presents his bride with the liberal arts as a wedding gift amid a profusion of light and colour (it was a standard work by the time of Gregory of Tours, *Hist.* 10.31.18).

Addressee

Hesperius was a younger friend of Sidonius (§1 *initia tua, iuniorum ingenia*), arguably also an inhabitant of the Auvergne (in 4.22.1 he is shown returning from Toulouse with a request for Sidonius, then bishop of Clermont). Praised for his literary interests by Sidonius, he became the teacher of the sons of Ruricius, a relative and close friend of Sidonius (Mathisen 2020a, 118). In Ruricius' letter collection, three epistles go to Hesperius (1.3–5) bearing on the subject of education. Both Sidonius (in 4.22) and Ruricius warmly qualify him as *magnificus* – possibly his nickname in their circle. Prosopography: Mathisen 2020a, 100.

The commissioner of the embedded poem is Patiens, bishop of Lyon from 449/50. Lyon being Burgundian territory by then, Patiens fostered the relationship with the royal family (6.12.3). Apparently wealthy, he sponsored church-building activities (this letter and 6.12.3) – no doubt in the context of the reconstruction of Lyon after the 458 rebellion (Santelia 2007, 319–20) – and sent food supplies to war-stricken zones in the years 472–5 (6.12.5, Greg. Tur. *Hist.* 2.24). His influence as a bishop ranged from supervising a problematic episcopal election in his diocese (4.25) to promoting Catholic orthodoxy (6.12.4) while supporting the typical Gallican stance in the theological debate on predestination (Intro 3.4). The last approximately datable event is his being one of two dedicatees of Constantius' *Life of Germanus* (*c.* 475–80, 1.1n. *Constantius*).

Sidonius assists at the feast day of St Just presided over by Patiens (probably 469, 5.17.10) and apologizes for using force in defence of his grandfather's tomb (see 3.12.3n.). He frames him as his mentor in preparation for the episcopate 469/70 (4.25.1 *pater noster in Christo*; Patiens will have ordained him as deacon, Harries 1994, 176) and sends him an exuberant letter of thanks for his war aid (6.12). Prosopography: Mathisen 2020a, 112; John 2026, 211. For his function in the structure of the epistles: Hanaghan 2019, 129–33.

Date and Place

The poem, followed by the letter, can be safely dated to the 460s (Kelly 2020, 178. Establishing a more precise date seems possible, *c.* 469, with Sidonius still in the company of Patiens in Lyon immediately prior to his episcopate (see also letter 3.12 Date and Place). Some see a confirmation in §3n. *adhuc*, interpreting it as proof that Sidonius recently stopped writing (light) verse upon switching to a clerical way of life (*conuersio*) (Loyen 2, 247; Wolff 2014, 212 n. 10).

Literature

The letter and the poem have generated a rich bibliography. In addition to the commentary by Hindermann 2022b, 290–343, a selection includes Santelia 2007, Hernández Lobato 2010 (repr. Hernández Lobato 2012, 493–518); van Waarden 2011, 102–3; Hecquet-Noti 2013; Egelhaaf-Gaiser 2014; Herbert de la Portbarré-Viard 2014, 381–9; Wolff 2014, 212–13; Schwitter 2015, 157–60; Montone 2017, 33–6; Consolino 2020, 362; Onorato 2020, 86–9; Hindermann 2022a. As for archaeology, excavations were supervised by Jean-François Reynaud (Reynaud 1998, Reynaud 2014, Reynaud and Prévot 2014 (an update of Février et al. 1986)).

Commentary

1 Amo in te quod litteras amas: *amo amas* is the most apt opening imaginable, applying the basic verbal paradigm (e.g. Char. *Gramm.* p. 216, 6) in a letter to a schoolmaster. The sentence immediately establishes the personal tie and states the theme. Such direct openings, often with a verb in first position (e.g. 1.7.1 *Angit me*, 3.8.1 *Veneror antiquos*), are frequent throughout epistolary literature (e.g. Cic. *Fam.* 9.22.1 *Amo uerecundiam*, Plin. 6.26.1 *Gaudeo et gratulor*); see van Waarden 2010, 46–8. Cf. a similar phrase 5.10.1 *amore studiorum te singulariter amat* (cf. also 8.10.1 *Esse* *tibi ... cordi litteras granditer gaudeo*). *amo* and its cognates *amor, amicus, amicitia* are keywords in the vocabulary of social interdependency (van Waarden 2010, 16; Intro 3.3 'Social Conventions' with n. 54; e.g. Cic. *Att.* 1.1.5, Plin. 6.8.2, Symm. 4.35, Sidon. 5.11.1). **usquequaque ... generositatem:** in contrast with the pithy opening words, this clause mimics the spreading of Hesperius' fame through extended word length. **excolere:** here 'to praise', 'extol' (as at 7.14.7 *miseriam praeferunt excoluntque*; cf. *OLD* 4) instead of the usual meaning 'to cultivate', 'improve' (hence the normalizing reading *extollere* in *T*). **diligentiae** 'diligence' is the quality needed for study (7.14.10 reading, 8.1.3 writing, 8.11.10 astrology); opp. *desidia* 7.14.10, see below *desidiosorum*. **generositatem** 'excellence' is a code word for senatorial status (Mathisen 2020c, 35). **nobis ... initia tua ... studia nostra commendas:** the 'I' turns from the first person singular (*amo, contendo*) to the plural, displaying modesty in comparing the achievements of the addressee to his own. Sidonius' interest in promoting talented young people echoes Pliny's, e.g. Plin. 6.23.2. For *studia*, see 1.1.3n. *studiorum*. **disciplinam** 'learning', 'skill': see 1.1.1n. *disciplinam*. **nos quoque subduximus ferulae manum** is from Juv. 1.15 *et nos ergo manum ferulae subduximus* (*subduco* 'withdraw' *OLD* 2c; *ferula* 'rod' cf. 5.5.2n. *post ferulas lectionis Maronianae*), proverbial for the painful effort of studying (Hier. 57.12, Macr. *Sat.* 3.10.2). **multitudo ... paucissimi:** this motif of a careless and ignorant majority as against an elite of last-ditch initiates recurs at the end of the letter in a somewhat broader perspective (§6n. *turba*). **meram linguae Latiaris proprietatem** 'the uncontaminated proper nature of the Latin language': Sidonius' programme of upholding Roman culture in the face of barbarian onslaught and the carelessness of Latin speakers themselves hinges upon the meticulous preservation of Latin idiom. He will eulogize any supporters he comes across (e.g. 3.3.2, 4.17.1, 8.2) and warn people who learn Germanic (like Syagrius in 5.5, where see Discussion). Further reading: Mathisen 1988; Banniard 1992; Denecker 2015, 410–18; Wolff 2020, 395–6; Hindermann 2022b, 297–9. The copious contemporary output of grammarians proves the broader social embedding of this elitist stance (Kaster 1988, Zetzel 2018, esp. 159–200). What counts in the first place are the very basics of language: thus, in Sidonius' own circle, Agroecius (plausibly identified with the addressee of 7.5; Zetzel 2018, 279) wrote an *Ars de orthographia* and Consentius the Elder (the father of Consentius, the dedicatee of *Carm.* 23; Zetzel 2018, 291) an *Ars de barbarismis et metaplasmis* among other things. *meram* 'pure', 'standard', cf. Diom. *Gramm.* 1.299.2 *artem merae Latinitatis*. *Latiaris*: see 2.9.4n. *Latiaris*. **proprietatem** 'proper nature', cf. 3.14.2 *proprietas linguae Latinae* as Sidonius' own yardstick; to Jerome, the *proprietas* of the target language is essential in translating (*Ep.* 106.55). **de triuialium**

barbarismorum robigine: Quint. *Inst.* 1.5 discusses the fundamental mistakes at word level, *barbarismus* (in single words) and *soloecismus* (in combining words) (Lausberg 1990, 257). Audiences used to react sharply to them (Apul. *Flor.* 9 *quis enim uestrum mihi unum soloecismum ignouerit? quis uel unam syllabam barbare pronuntiatam donauerit?*, Alc. Avit. *Ep.* 54 (ed. M-R); on the existence of an important Latinophone middle class at the time, Banniard 1992, 422). *triuialium* 'vulgar' (*OLD*). *barbarismorum*: see also 5.5.3n. *barbarismum. robigine* 'rust' for want of practice, cf. 8.6.18 *ori ... loquendi robiginem summouere.* **uindicaueritis** 'rescue', 'defend' (*OLD* 4a); plural: 'the like of you', i.e. 'the younger generation'. **interemptamque:** the killing is underscored by the cretic + spondee clausula. **nobilium ... uulgi**, making superior linguistic competence the exclusive domain of the nobility (Intro 3.3 'Elite Status'). **purpurae** 'purple', i.e. 'ornaments', 'beauty', a rare metaphor to qualify language (*TLL* 10/2.2705.12–21, e.g. Auson. *Mos.* 398; at 2.2.8 of architectural ornament); cf. Sidonius' ideal of poetic beauty residing in variety: *Carm.* 22.6 *purpureis ... pannis* 'purple patches (of digressions)' (going back to Hor. *Ars* 15–6 *purpureus ... pannus*; discussion Pelttari 2016).

2 istinc 'thereof', 'about that' is a later development (first certain attestation Aug. *C. Acad.* 2.4.10; *TLL* 7/2.517.44–9). **interea tu** 'as for you', rounding off and turning towards the addressee, cf. 2.10.2n., 7.18.4n. (cf. *OLD interea* c). **petis ... pareo:** see Intro 4.2 '*Iubes–pareo*'. **uersiculi mihi fluxerint:** the diminutive *uersiculi* is (self)depreciating (tongue-in-cheek), used of light verse in a tradition which includes Catullus, Martial, Pliny the Younger and Ausonius; see Condorelli 2008, 195–6. *fluxerint*: see 1.1.1n. *fluxerunt*. **dicto** 'order' (*OLD dictum* 1b). **ecclesia:** in §3 designated as *aedes* and *basilica*. For *ecclesia*, see Herbert de la Portbarré-Viard 2014, 252–73, esp. 265. Built next to the small first church on this site, St Stephen's, which probably took on the function of baptistry, this must have been the cathedral church, dedicated to St John the Baptist, whose foundations lie under the present cathedral (Reynaud 1998, Reynaud 2014, Reynaud and Prévot 2014; see Map 2). A festive week accompanied its consecration in which the invited speaker was Faustus, bishop of Riez (9.3.5). **papae** 'bishop': always in the vocative except here and 7.9.6. It is standard in the formulas of greeting and leave-taking of all of Sidonius' episcopal letters (Intro 4.2). Others words for 'bishop' in Sidonius' letters include *antistes, episcopus, pontifex* and (*summus*) *sacerdos* (van Waarden 2010, 569). **summum ... accessit** 'reached completion': simple accusative without *ad* only here and Claudian. Mam. *Stat. anim.* 2.6 (p. 119.5 ed. Engelbrecht; *TLL* 1.264.74–6). **sancti strenui, seueri misericordis:** a double asynctic pair of opposing adjectives, increasing in length. *sancti* 'holy' because of his ecclesiastical office (also of Patiens at 3.12.3n.; cf. 2.9.6n. *sancte*). *strenui* 'energetic', combining realism with piety, the ideal mix for a bishop (cf. the trade-off concerning the choice of a bishop in 7.9.9, who must be able to both *intercedere pro animabus apud caelestem* and *pro corporibus apud terrenum iudicem*; cf. *Vita abb. Acaun.* 3 *MGH SS rer. Merov.* 3.176.12 *sanctitate ... strenuitate*). *seueri misericordis* 'strict but merciful': not 'severe' opp. 'lenient' (as 7.9.10 *seuerum ... indulgentem*), but strict without being harsh. The core equilibrium coveted by the nobility in social intercourse is being approachable while remaining in control (letters 7.4 and 7.13 are cases in point; cf. the aristocratic bishop at 3.12.3n. *suaeque personae*). **munificentiam in pauperes humanitatemque:** the care of the poor is at the heart of the biblical message, and indeed of a bishop's tasks; classical municipal euergetism is also weighted with care for the underdogs (van Waarden 2010, 486–8). The lay *conuersus* will do the same (4.7.2 *pauper ad mensam*, 6.2.1 *pauperes pascit*; see Intro 3.4 n.63). In the hagiographical tradition, Sidonius sells his silver tableware for the benefit of the poor, Greg. Tur. *Hist.* 2.22. *humanitatem* 'generosity': see 2.9.1n. *humanissimos*. **culmina** 'roof', 'peak', playing on the literal and metaphorical meanings; see 1.9.1n. *culmen* and *conscientiam*, where a good conscience is also the highest achievement. The loftiness of the building mirrors the stature of its builder (Onorato 2020, 89; below v. 5n. *celsa*).

3 aedis 'church': see Herbert de la Portbarré-Viard 2023, 274–84, esp. 277. **extimis** 'the far end': this is usually thought to be the apse, although the text seems almost too long (139 words) to fit there, being twice as long as already impressive inscriptions in e.g. S. Agnese fuori le mura in Rome (*ICVR* VIII, 20757.0) and Paulinus' memorial church of Felix (Paul. Nol. *Ep.* 32.10). Normally, short texts, if at all, would accompany the portrayal of the founders in apse mosaics. The poem seems better suited to the entrance wall, also because of the invitation to approach the church with which it ends (cf. similar inscriptions on the counter-façade in contemporary churches like S. Sabina (still *in situ*) and S. Maria Maggiore in Rome). **praefati** 'above-mentioned' is post-classical (3rd cent. and later). **tumultuarium carmen:** see 1.9.6n. *tumultuariis fidibus*. **inscripsi** 'I have written for inscription on' + dat., cf. 4.18.4 *parietibus inscribere* of the other commissioned epigram for the church of St Martin in Tours. Such texts, called *tituli*, could be cut in stone, painted in fresco technique or executed as mosaics (Lansford 2009, x; Leatherbury 2019, 21 (n. 37), 191, 196). **trochaeis triplicibus:** the Phalaecian hendecasyllable, which ends with three trochees (see above 'A poem in a letter'). It is Sidonius' favourite lyrical metre (Condorelli 2020a, 453–5). *triplicibus* instead of *tribus* is later usage (van Waarden 2016, 63). **adhuc mihi iamque tibi:** an accolade for the junior poet who is allowed to take over the relay. Egelhaaf-Gaiser 2014, 386–8 and Hindermann 2022b, 305 think that *adhuc* conveys secrecy: the poem has not yet been published. Loyen 2, 247 and Wolff 2014, 212 n. 10 hold that it refers to the ban on light verse imposed by *conuersio* and becoming a bishop (see above Date and Place). **namque** introduces background information (Kroon 1995, 147–8); see also 1.5.1n. **Constantii**: the dedicatee of Sidonius' correspondence; see 1.1 Addressee. **Secundini**: the addressee of 5.8 according to which he was a specialist of the hexameter (§1 *te hexametris familiarius inseruientem*) and a satirist of the Burgundian court in Lyon. Prosopography: Mathisen 2020a, 120. **basilicae** 'church': see Herbert de la Portbarré-Viard 2023, 252–73, esp. 265. **clarescunt** 'shine', both literally and metaphorically (for the latter, cf. e.g. 1.8.3), like *micant* in §4. Execution in gold mosaic would match this idea, and fits the tenor of the following epigram, centred on light and colour in the building. Cf. *Carm.* 15.128 *lucebat in auro* for a similar effect in embroidery. **uerecundia** 'feeling of shame' (*OLD* 1), an essential element in polite social intercourse: modesty and a sense of shame in one, e.g. when receiving a compliment (Symm. 4.26 *uerecundiam tuam nimio laudis excursu non oportet onerari*) or failing to adhere to protocol (Symm. 7.60.1 *onerabat uerecundiam meam, quod prior scripseras*); see Intro 3.3 'Social Conventions' with n. 54; 2.9.10n. **suas otiositates** 'the fruits of its leisure', possibly recalling Ov. *Trist.* 2.224 *otia nostra*, is a one-off noun (Wolff 2020, 403). **premit** 'belittles', 'depreciates', cf. L–S B2; cf. Hor. *Ep.* 1.19.35–6 *mea ... opuscula lector | ... premat* (opp. *laudet ametque*).

4 nouam nuptam foreshadows Hesperius' upcoming marriage, to be revealed in §5. **pronuba** 'bridewoman': see 1.5.11n. **si uestiatur albo, fuscus quisque fit nigrior** 'any dark-skinned man looks even blacker when clothed in white': writers tend to be depreciatory of a dark skin (although not necessarily so, e.g. Ov. *Ars* 3.191 *alba decent fuscas* with Gibson 2003, 171). Cf. 4.18.5, where the dedication to St Martin is said to be probably *ut niger naeuus candido in corpore*, marring the beauty of the building. *quisque = aliqui(s)*, a feature of later Latin (van Waarden 2010, 268–9). **nostra, quantula est cumque, ... stipula**: *nostra*: self-effacing plural. *quantula ... cumque* is a wilful tmesis (Löfstedt 1985, 211) with expressive effect. *stipula* 'reed', 'pipe' (*OLD* c), taken from Verg. *Ecl.* 3.27 *stridenti miserum stipula disperdere carmen* 'ruin a poor song with a shrill pipe', in a pastoral poetical contest. The modest reed pipe is opposed to the trumpet (*tuba*), associated with the grand style of oratory (e.g. Fronto 35.22 vdH *tubae*, opp. *tibiarum*; Sidon. 4.3.10 *tuam tubam*) or epic (e.g. Mart. 8.3.22, opp. *auena*). Cf. the dedication of *Carm.* 23 (lines 4–5), where Sidonius makes a trade-off between his own *cantum ... pauperis cicutae* and the *tubam* of his friend. **uilescit** 'loses its value', 'pales': see van Waarden 2010, 474 *uilescunt*. **mediam loco:** i.e. between the other two on the sidewalls (§3 *latera*). **despicabiliorem** 'more contemptible', first found in fourth cent. (*TLL* 5/1.742.49–743.4). *-bilis* is a productive suffix in later Latin (Wolff 2020, 398–9), cf. e.g. 1.5.3n. *calcabilis*, 1.5.6n. *defaecabilis*, 1.5.10n. *conducibilis*. **epigrammata micant:** for *epigramma*, see Intro 2.1 n. 24; cf. *Carm*. 41.57n. *epigramma. micant* 'shine' in a metaphorical sense, but also literally, if we imagine them executed in radiant gold letters in well-lit mosaic panels in the altar space; cf. §3 *clarescunt*. **istaec:** for *-c*, see 1.1.4n. *hisce*. **imaginarie** 'as a semblance': *TLL* 7/1.402.60–5 'i.q. simulate, per speciem'. **umbratiliter** 'as a shadow': Sidonius' work has no substance as opposed to the eye-catching presence (*micant*) of the other two (it is also literally less well lit if placed on the entrance wall); cf. the combination of *imago* and *umbra* as opposed to reality in e.g. Cic. *Off*. 3.69, *Rep*. 2.52, Stat. *Silv*. 1.3.18–9, Verg. *Aen*. 2.772–3. This adverb and its meaning are one of Sidonius' private creations, primed by *quodammodo*; a rare adjective anyway, *umbratilis* elsewhere means 'artificial', 'over-protected' (L–S, Forcellini). **effingimus** 'I am the maker': this use of the present tense is called 'registrative' by H–S 306 (cf. e.g. Verg. *Aen*. 9.266 *cratera .... quem dat Sidonia Dido*, Prop. 4.1.77 *me creat Archytae suboles*). The matter is debated among linguists: Pinkster 1999, 715. **flagitatae cantilenae** 'the requested song': *cantilena* possibly with a slightly pejorative connotation, 'doggerel'. For the combination, cf. 5.17.11, 8.11.2. **culmus** 'straw', yet another synonym for 'pipe', chosen for the onomatopoeia on *-mu-* together with *immurmuret*.

Poem 27: Dedication

1–4: Apostrophe of the reader and praise of bishop Patiens
5–21: Description of the church (exterior, interior and annexes)
22–27: Description of the church's environment and the passers-by
28–30: Exhortation to join them towards the church and salvation.

1–2 Quisquis ... collaudas: the opening address is a common epigraphic device, especially in epitaphs (e.g. Mart. 11.13.1–2 *Quisquis Flaminiam teris, uiator,* | *noli nobile praeterire marmor*, *Anth. lat*. 429.1–2 Riese *Quisquis es, en hospes quaeso lege*). Various roles are involved in this dedication: of the narrator-focalizer, who is admiring the church and puts his experience into words (i.e. the authorial 'voice' behind the poem); of the observer, who shares the narrator's perspective (*collaudas*) and is guided around the building (i.e. the visitor/believer); of the commissioner (i.e. Patiens); and of the narratee, both the primary (= the observer) and the secondary one (the reader). On these narratological aspects of an *ekphrasis*, see de Jong 2014, 120–2. **Patientis ... laborem**: the three opening verses are distinguished by soundplay on Patiens' name, *p – t – s* (Hernández Lobato 2010, 302). There may also be wordplay on the meaning of *Patientis* in *laborem*. Patiens probably completed the renovation of a preceding church (6.12.3 *opera ... uetusta reparentur*), which involved its orientation (below), creating a prestigious cathedral as part of the episcopal group which also comprised a chapel and a baptistry with annexes (possibly also a *domus ecclesiae* accommodating the bishop and administrative functions). Only traces of the cathedral's eastern apse have been found so far. Its entrance was possibly at the western end giving out onto the thoroughfare (v. 22 *agger*), but Sidonius' description is too vague for certainty (literature Reynaud 1998, 43–86; Reynaud 2014; *TCCG* 4 (1986) 15–35, updated in 16 (2014) vol. 1, 146–57; see Map 2).

3–4 uoti compote 'having obtained its wish' is a set phrase (*OLD compos* 1). **supplicatione** 'prayer' in Christian usage, e.g. Cassian. *Inst.* 2.7.2 *stantes in supplicatione* (syn. *orant*) (Blaise). **experiare** 'may you be granted': in exchange for praise of the builder.

5–7 celsa: height (*celsus*, *culmen* and similar) is a common compliment for villas, here directly from the poem's hypotext Mart. 4.64 (see below vv. 22–7n.), v. 10 *celsae culmina ... uillae* (also e.g. Stat. *Silv.* 2.2.3, Auson. *Mos.* 320, Sidon. *Carm.* 22.119–20), transferred to the church that mirrors Patiens' stature (v. 2n. above) in the same way as the villas do for their owners. As the commonplace comes to attach to churches, the glory of God and of the saints becomes central (e.g. Paul. Nol. *Natal.* 10.5 Dolveck (*Carm.* 28 Hartel) (church of St Felix), Ven. Fort. *Carm.* 10.6.13 and 20 (church of St Martin)). **nitet** 'shines', 'stands out' (*OLD* 3, 5): this and synonyms like *micat* describe the overwhelming outward impression of exceptional buildings such as villas (e.g. Sidon. *Carm.* 22.120), temples (e.g. Mart. 8.65.2) and churches (e.g. Ven. Fort. *Carm.* 10.6.13). As to dimensions, contemporary churches would typically measure 150/160 x 60 feet and contain from 70 to 120 columns (Greg. Tur. *Hist.* 2.14 [Perpetuus' church of St. Martin in Tours], 2.16 [Namatius' cathedral of Clermont]; Duval 1991, 192–4). **in sinistrum aut dextrum:** i.e. 'to the south or the north', looking from the east, in astronomy and geodesy: Vitr. 9.4.6 *ad dextram orientis ... ad sinistram orientis* [about the northern and southern hemispheres]; Frontin. *Grom.* p. 27,15 *dextram* [sc. *partem orbis terrarum*] *appellauerunt <quae> septentrioni subiaceret*; Lucan. 9.417–20, Macr. *Sat.* 1.21.18; cf. *TLL* 5/1.921.15–75. **arce frontis** 'with the top of its façade' or 'with its high-rising façade': *arx* is rare in this sense (*TLL*

2.742.24–31; cf. Prud. *Ham.* 268 *frontis in arce* 'on top of her forehead'; metaphorically, *Carm.* 23.142 *residens in arce fandi* 'situated at the top of oratory'). There is a possible reminiscence of Prop. 2.31.11 [the high-rising temple of Apollo on the Palatine] *in quo Solis erat supra fastigia currus* (cf. Egelhaaf-Gaiser 2014, 385). The situation is unclear. The phrase may refer to either the front or the rear façade facing east. Herbert de la Portbarré-Viard 2023, 388 stresses the aspect of the church rising above the existing buildings. **ortum prospicit aequinoctialem** 'looks towards sunrise at the equinox', i.e. faces due east. Part of the foundation of an eastern apse (36 feet in diameter) has been found under the present cathedral, but this is not decisive for Patiens' church to have been oriented or occidented, i.e. built with its choir to the east or to the west (Reynaud 1998, 52–3). Churches were increasingly oriented (Paul. Nol. *Ep.* 32.13 [about St Felix' church] *prospectus uero basilicae non, ut usitatior mos est, orientem spectat*), as the coming of Christ was interpreted as the rising sun: Vulg. *Mal.* 4.2 *et orietur uobis ... Sol iustitiae, Luc.* 1.78 *uisitauit nos oriens ex alto*, and prayer was performed in that direction (*ODCC* 'Orientation', Vogel 1962, Wallraff 2004). *ortum ... aequinoctialem*: cf. e.g. Colum. 1.5.7 *ut frons eius* [sc. *uillae*] *ad orientem aequinoctialem directa est. aequinoctialis* in poetry is only in Catull. 46.2, likewise in the second half of a hendecasyllable (cf. Condorelli 2020a, 455). For *ortum prospicit*, cf. Stat. *Silv.* 2.2.45–6 *haec domus ortus | aspicit.*

8–10 As the sun has risen, the interior is shown in a profusion of light and colour. The lyrical 'impressionism' of the description excludes precision in detail, which is often difficult to tease out (see Roberts 1989, 73). **micat**: the radiance of the interior symbolically lends a foretaste of Paradise, dissolving the boundaries between matter and spirit (Roberts 1989, 76; Roberts 2011; Miller 2009). **bratteatum ... lacunar** 'the ceiling covered with gold leaf': cf. Sen. *Ep.* 115.9 *lacunaribus ornamentum ... bratteata felicitas*, Prud. *Perist.* 3.196–7 *tecta corusca super rutilant | de laquearibus aureolis*, 12.49–50 *bratteolas trabibus subleuit, ut omnis aurulenta | lux esset intus ceu iubar sub ortu*. **sollicitatur** 'is tempted', 'is drawn' (*OLD* 6), embedded in an expressive *s*-alliteration suggesting the path of the sunlight, with *sol-* mirroring *sōl* (Hernández Lobato 2010, 303). **fuluo** 'tawny' (brown-yellow), characteristic of gold, e.g. Verg. *Aen.* 11.776 *fuluo ... auro*; cf. Prud. *Perist.* 12.51 *fuluis laquearibus*, Sidon. *Carm.* 22.146–7 *aurea | tecta ... fuluo nimis abscondenda metallo.* **concolor:** cf. Stat. *Silv.* 4.7.16 *pallidus ... concolor auro.* The word is a favourite of Sidonius for describing pale matching hues, e.g. light green like grass (7.7.3n., van Waarden 2010, 362), deathly pale (7.7.3n., 7.17.1n.), blue-green like seaweed (*Carm.* 34.33 in 8.9.5) and reddish of skin (4.20.1n.).

11–15 The gaze turns towards the vault of the apse, the floor and the window zone – or so at least can one interpret these densely packed lines (see Herbert de la Portbarré-Viard 2014, 382–9). The dominant motif is the colourful diversity and brilliance of marbles, whether in slabs or in mosaic (Herbert de la Portbarré-Viard 2023, 220–1; for *uarietas*, see Intro 4.1 n. 90). By this time a standard way of looking at church interiors, this *ekphrasis* is inspired by first-century predecessors like Lucan (e.g. 10.111–21) and Statius (*Silv.* 2.2.83–94) and has its immediate predecessors in such passages as Prud. *Perist.* 3.198–200 [in the church of St. Eulalia] *saxaque caesa solum uariant, | floribus ut rosulenta putes | prata rubescere multimodis* 'shaped stones diversify the floor so that it looks like rosy meadows full of all kind of flowers glowing red', 12.53–4 [in S. Paolo fuori le mura] *tum camiros hyalo insigni uarie cucurrit arcus: | sic prata uernis floribus renident*, 'then he coated the curves of the arches with splendid glass of different hues, like meadows bright with spring flowers', Paul. Nol. *Ep.* 32.10 [in St Felix' church] *absidem solo et parietibus marmoratam camera musiuo inlusa clarificat* 'the apse whose floor and walls are clad in marble gets its light from the vault inlaid with mosaic'. **distinctum** 'embellished', 'variegated' (*OLD* 2), cf. e.g. Sen. *Ep.* 86.6, Stat. *Silv.* 1.5.41. **cameram** 'vault' (*OLD camara/camera*): Sidonius' bath has a similar combination of a wooden *lacunar* and a masoned vault (2.2.5); cf. Sen. *Ep.* 86.6 *nisi uitro* ['glass mosaic'] *absconditur camera*. **sub uersicoloribus figuris** 'in the shape of multicoloured patterns/figures', changing depending on the light or with multiple colours in their texture, cf. Sen. *Nat.* 36.44 and 46. *sub* 'subject to', 'shaped into': L–S 1c3, *OLD* 11a; alternatively, *sub* is taken locally, which presupposes two zones: the figural one above and a lower, blue-and-green one. **uernans herbida crusta:** *uernans* 'spring-like', 'light green', cf. Prud. *Psych.* 862–3 (a meadow), Sidon. *Carm.* 22.139 (columns). *herbida* 'grass-green', cf. Stat. *Silv.* 2.2.91 (a type of marble), Prud. *Psych.* 863 (light), Sidon. *Carm.* 5.39 (in pavement). *crusta* 'slab of marble', 'coating' (*OLD* 3), either entire or figurative (*opus sectile*), cf. *Carm.* 22.146 *paries tabulis crustatus*. **sapphiratos** 'sapphire-coloured' (a saturated blue), a Sidonian hapax. **flectit per prasinum uitrum** 'lays out in a curve along (or: across) the leek-green glass': *flectit*, in garlands across the wall or in a belt along the window-frames or the vaulted arcades of the nave. *uitrum* denotes either glass mosaic tiles or the glass of the window panes (various interpretations listed in Hindermann 2022b, 322).

16–21 The layout of the structures attached to the church remains unclear, as no material traces have been detected yet (Reynaud 1998, 66–78; we cannot even be completely certain that *porticus* and *atria* do not denote the interior of the church, see Herbert de la Portbarré-Viard

2023, 367). The text speaks of two identical porticos and an enclosure (*atria*, either an open space or a hall). These may have been two successive courtyards at the entrance (or a *narthex* and a forecourt?) or separate ones with different functions (as cloisters?) to the south side or at both ends of the church (see Herbert de la Portbarré-Viard 2023, 394, 404). Speaking of the nearby funerary church of St Just, *Ep.* 5.17.3 suggests that one purpose of such porticos was to accommodate worshippers if the capacity of the church fell short.   **porticus ... triplex** 'a triple colonnade', i.e. one with three rows of columns or with three passages, possibly also conveying the symbolic overtone of the Divine Trinity (Herbert de la Portbarré-Viard 2023, 243).   **fulmentis Aquitanicis:** *fulmentis* 'supports', i.e. columns; cf. *Carm.* 22.136 (ceiling) *fulta columnis*. *Aquitanicis*: of marble from the quarries of Aubertin in the western Pyrenees, patterned black and white; cf. *Lib. pontif.* 48.4 *columnis Aquitanicis*.   **campum medium:** probably the courtyard which is surrounded by the colonnade, cf. Paul. Nol. *Natal.* 9.366 Dolveck *medio ... campo* (*Carm.* 27 Hartel) (Herbert de la Portbarré-Viard 2023, 57 n. 306), or else the hall where both porticos meet (*campum* taken as 'built space', cf. 2.2.3 *uestibuli campus*, Auson. *Mos.* 49 *marmoreum ... campum*; *TLL* 3.215.33–40), rather than the nave of the church, as is usually thought (see Hindermann 2022b, 324), because it is illogical for the description to turn back to the church interior.   **uestit saxea silua:** *uestit* 'cover', 'clothe' (*OLD* 2c). *silua* 'a "forest"', of things thickly distributed (*OLD* 4). The phrase *saxea silua* is also in *Carm.* 22.206; cf. Stat. *Theb.* 4.220–1 *ferrea ... silua*, 5.533 *harundineam ... siluam*.

22–27 The hypotext here is Mart. 4.64.18–22, praising a friend's villa on the Janiculus Hill in Rome for its view and its quiet far above the hubbub of the town: *illinc Flaminiae Salariaeque | gestator patet essedo tacente, | ne blando rota sit molesta somno, | quem nec rumpere nauticum celeuma | nec clamor ualet helciariorum* 'on the other side the traveller on the Flaminian and Salarian Way is in view; but his carriage makes no sound, lest the wheel disturb soothing slumbers that neither boatswain's call nor bargee's shout can interrupt' (tr. Shackleton Bailey). Sidonius turns the motif upside down: the cathedral of Lyon finds itself enveloped by the noises of travellers and barge haulers, and is open to everyone. Auson. *Mos.* 161–8 paints a similar picture: hills and river, farmers, travellers and boatmen, calls and echoes. To Egelhaaf-Gaiser 2014, 384–5, the rude language employed there, together with the drunkenness in Hor. *Sat.* 1.5.16 (see below *nauta atque uiator*), determines the atmosphere of Sidonius' imitation. It is questionable whether this does justice to Sidonius' mindset, who may strip classical material of its original meaning in a Christianizing rewriting (see Intro 3.4 and 3.5, with Gualandri 2020, 281–2).

hinc agger ... hinc Arar: the church is built close to the embankment of the Saône, the road running along its western end (the entrance?), the river along the eastern end (the chancel?). Cf. Plin. 9.39.5 *solum templi hinc flumine et abruptissimis ripis, hinc uia cingitur*. On *agger*, see 1.5.3n. *aggerem*. **sese ... reflectit** 'takes the bend' in order to go round the building; the church also sits in a curve of the river. The meaning is not quite clear: it is sometimes taken as 'turns around' (Anderson), while Wolff 2014, 213 thinks that the travellers stop and turn towards the church in admiration. Certainly, their curved trajectory is answered by the curved backs of the haulers (and later opposed to the uplifting invocation of Christ). **stridentum ... essedorum:** for the sound of these travelling carriages, cf. Sen. *Ep.* 56.4 *quae me ... circumstrepunt essedas*, Claud. *Carm. min.* 18.18 *esseda ... multisonora*; for its absence, Mart. 4.64.19 (above). The drawn out phrase, carried on in the next line, reflects the slow progress made. **curuorum ... chorus helciariorum:** based on *clamor ... helciariorum* in Martials' hypotext. A similar scene is painted in Auson. *Mos.* 41–2 *per ripas ... | intendunt collo malorum uincula nautae. chorus* 'group', 'band' (*OLD* 5a) with overtones of 'choir' (+ gen. first time in Hor. *Ep.* 2.2.77 *scriptorum chorus*; cf. Sidon. *Carm.* 41.9n. *chorus inuidorum* in 9.16). Centrally located, Lyon was an important freight port. United in *collegia nautarum*, the hauliers wielded considerable influence (Bérard 2012). **responsantibus alleluia ripis**, obviously as an echo (cf. Claud. *Carm. min.* 25.49 *redituraque rupibus Echo*; Shakespeare *Twelfth Night* 1.5 *Halloo your name to the reverberate hills*). In the liturgy, *alleluia* is sung in response to a reading, while *amen* is the spoken confirmation (e.g. Aug. *In epist. Ioh.* 5 *respondeant omnes amen, cantent omnes alleluia*); cf. Hier. 77.11 *reboans* [against the ceiling] *in sublime alleluia*, Paul. Nol. *Ep.* 32.5 v. 26 '*alleluia*' *... balat ouile*. **ad Christum leuat:** *leuare (manus)* is the typical gesture of prayer, metaphorically 'to dedicate' in a higher sphere, e.g. Vulg. *Ps.* 24.1 *Ad te Domine leuaui animam meam*. **amnicum celeuma:** *amnicum* 'connected with the river' (see 1.5.4n. *amnicos*) replaces Martial's *nauticum*. *celeuma* 'call' giving the time to the haulers (elsewhere rowers or sailors weighing the anchor or hoisting the sails) (Sheerin 1982), cf. Rutil. 1.370 *resonat ... celeuma*; Sidon. 8.12.5 *celeuma* turned into a welcome greeting, Paul. Nol. *Carm.* 17.109–12 turned into a hymn.

28–30 psallite: in Christian usage 'sing psalms, hymns' (L–S II, Blaise 2). **nauta uel uiator** recalls Hor. *Sat.* 1.5.16 *nauta atque uiator* (also at the end of the line), while the apostrophe is reminiscent of the proverbial *siste uiator* on tombstones (cf. v. 1n.). **iste** = *hic* 'this': *iste* from early times encroaches more and more on the territory of *hic* and *ille* (H–S 184, van Waarden 2010, 116). **omnibus ... omnes:** the promise of salvation through faith is universal, based on Jesus' last words in Vulg. *Matth.*

28.18–20, *Marc.* 16.15–16 (van Waarden 2011, 103). **uia ... ad salutem:** the road to salvation leads through the church, cf. e.g. *Anth. lat.* 2042.1 Riese *Ecce do*[*mus*] *domini que ducit* [*ad atria celi*], Paul. Nol. *Ep.* 32.12 [above one of the entrances of the church of St Felix] *caelestes intrate uias ... huc ingressus*, Faust. Rei. *Grat.* 1.34 *uia quae ducit ad uitam* (but also Apul. *Met.* 5.20 *uiam quae sola deducit iter ad salutem*).

5 ecce parui: *ecce* 'here you are', lively confirmation of the fulfilment of an obligation, e.g. 7.2.10 *ecce parui*, 9.11.9 *ecce habes litteras*. Rare in Pliny's and Symmachus' letters, *ecce* abounds in Cicero's, there expressing delight at new developments, e.g. *Att.* 9.14.1 *ecce ... litteras accepi*. **tamquam iunior:** whereas in reality Hesperius is *iunior* (§1). **imperatis** is a double trochee clausula, the type that dominates §§5–6. **fac** + subj.: circumlocution of the imperative (G–L §271.1). **faenore** 'interest' (*OLD faenus* 1), as writing a letter or sending a poem automatically imposes a debt on the addressee (cf. Intro 3.3 'Social Conventions'), cf. e.g. Symm. 1.14.1 [you cannot claim an extensive answer] *qui nihil litterati faenoris credidisti* 'as you have not made a loan carrying literary interest', i.e. you have not sent me something yourself. **dissimulatione** 'negligence', later Latin (L–S IIB, *TLL* 5/1.1479.70–1480.13). **lectites ... lecturias:** *lectites* 'read often, with eagerness, or with attention' (L–S II); cf. 4.17.2 *frequenti lectione*. For *lecturias* 'long to read', cf. 7.18.4n. *lecturire* and 7.18.1n. *scripturire*. **propediem coniunx domum feliciter ducenda:** this is a typical instance of the information gap between the primary and the secondary reader, and their different expectations. Only now do we, secondary readers, hear that Hesperius is about to be married and that this letter is something of a wedding present – which sheds new light on the entire letter. Sidonius had composed full-blown wedding poems (*epithalamia*) for Ruricius and Hiberia (*Carm.* 10–11) and Polemius and Araneola (14–15). In the epistle introducing the latter, he had also highlighted the bridegroom's learning in relation to his marriage (*Carm.* 14 *ep.* 1 *magis ... doctrinae quam causae tuae*). For 'wife', *coniunx* is the preferred term in Sidonius' poetry as against *uxor* in his prose (see Hindermann 2022b, 225). **ducenda:** for the gerundive, see 1.9.6n. *admittendo*. **oppido** 'utterly', one of the archaisms revived in the 2nd cent. and favoured by later writers (Wolff 2020, 402, Intro 4.5). **meminens** 'mindful', a rare participle, synonym for *memor*, used five times by Sidonius (*TLL* 8.646.6–8, van Waarden 2010, 293). There follow two lists to make the point, first, that wives may assist their husbands in studying, with five illustrations from oratory, second, that they may even contribute to their output, with six cases in point in poetry. For the key role of models from the past (*exempla*) in Roman culture, see Roller 2018 (another instance is 3.12.6n.); for lists as a substantive and stylistic element in Sidonius, Hindermann 2022b, 292–3, Wolff 2020, 407–8, Intro 4.5. For educated women and women writers, see Snyder 1989, Hemelrijk 1999, Santelia 2005 (on the only late antique poem by a woman that has come down to us), Intro 3.3 'Women'. Though it is not made explicit, the orators – in chronological order – may represent the different stylistic registers on which Sidonius draws: Hortensius flowery (4.3.6 *uernat*), Cicero grand (*Carm.* 7.175 *tonas*, 35.22 *tonante lingua*), Pliny finished (1.1.1n. *disciplinam maturitatemque*), Apuleius noble (4.3.1 *ponderis*), Symmachus smooth (1.1.1n. *rotunditatem*). As a sixth element, Sidonius could have added Fronto who is another source of inspiration (4.3.1 for his *grauitas*, 8.3.3, 8.10.3; cf. 1.1.2n. *Frontonianorum*), with his wife Cratia (van den Hout 1999, ix–x). **Marcia Hortensio:** Marcia left Cato Uticensis for Cicero's rival orator Hortensius on the latter's request (between 55 and 52) and married Cato again after Hortensius' death – she now being a rich widow (*BNP* 'Marcia 4', 'Hortensius 7'). The moral issue – not addressed by Sidonius – was the subject of rhetorical exercises (Quint. *Inst.* 3.5.11). **Terentia Tullio:** Terentia married Cicero between 80 and 77. An independent personality, she intervened in political life and lobbied for his return from exile. Financial disagreements led to the breakdown of the marriage in 46 (*BNP* 'Terentia 1'). She is mentioned often in Cicero's letters but is not known for having assisted in his literary production (Hier. *Adv. Iovin.* 1.48 hints that she profited by his *sapientia*). On Cicero's role in Sidonius' correspondence, see 1.1.2n. *Marco Tullio*. He is mentioned in two more catalogues of great Roman authors, *Carm.* 2.186 and 23.146, as *Arpinas* 'the man from Arpinum'. **Calpurnia Plinio:** Calpurnia was the second or third wife of Pliny the Younger. She accompanied him to Bithynia (*BNP* 'Calpurnia 6'). Pliny praises her for her keen interest in his work and reputation (Plin. 4.19). On Pliny and the exemplarity of his correspondence for Sidonius, 1.1.1n. *Gai Plinii*. **Pudentilla Apuleio:** a rich widow, Pudentilla married the writer and orator Apuleius. He was accused of winning her favours with magic. His defence speech from 158/9 is preserved (*De magia*). For Apuleius as a translator, see 2.9.5n., as a stylist, 4.3.1, as a neo-Platonic philosopher, 9.13.3 *Madaurensi*. He is important to Sidonius and other late antique authors for his archaisms (Intro 4.4, 4.5). **Rusticiana Symmacho:** the noblewoman Rusticiana (mentioned by name only here and Symm. *Rel.* 34.12) was married to Symmachus (*PLRE* 1, 786–7 'Rusticiana'). For Symmachus as a stylistic model for Sidonius, 1.1.1n. *Quinti Symmachi.* **candelas et candelabra tenuerunt:** by providing light for their husbands' study themselves (instead of having the slaves do it), the wives not only more than take their responsibility for the household but also put it at the service of intellectual pursuits (see Hindermann 2022a; cf. *Carm.* 24.37–8 for a wife supporting her husband's business pursuits). The female component in a marriage enriches any husband's study, is what Sidonius wants to impart to his friend. So-called *lucubratio* (working or studying by night, either late at night or before sunrise) lengthens the day and bears connotations of diligence and frugality; see e.g. Cic. *Fam.* 9.2.1, Sen. *Ep.* 8.1, Plin. *Nat. praef.* 18, Quint. *Inst.* 10.3.25–7, Plin. 3.5.7–13, 9.40.2, Gell. *Praef.* 4, Auson. *Praef.* 5.5–8, Aug. *Ord.* 1.3.6; cf. Sidonius about himself at 7.9.4 *duabus uigiliis* (van Waarden 2010, 432); literature: Janson 1964, 147–8, Ker 2004.

6 rem oratoriam 'the domain of oratory': a unique expression, but cf. *OLD res* 8a, e.g. Gell. 16.10.4 *rei grammaticae*. **contubernio feminarum** is wilfully paradoxical: *contubernium* is comradeship among men (*OLD* 1, 2; e.g. 5.9.2) or cohabitation with a woman (*OLD* 3; e.g. 9.6.1). It opens up a third possibility: an intellectually rewarding marriage, equivalent to the *contuberniis eruditorum* in 7.14.10. Of the six women mentioned, the first and the last two are among the pseudonymous representatives in Roman love elegy of the type of *docta puella*, who enhanced their sexual attraction with cultural accomplishments. Originally incompatible with the idea of the chaste upper-class *matrona*, the combination gradually became acceptable, definitely so in Pliny the Younger with Calpurnia (Hemelrijk 1999, 79–81). Cf. the similar catalogue in Prop. 2.34.85–94; also Ov. *Trist.* 2.422–68. Five poets are also listed at *Carm.* 9.259–70; cf. Ov. *Am.* 3.9.61–6. For the poetic influence on Sidonius of poets in this list, Gualandri 2020, 285. For the motif of the weakening effect of marriage, cf. Mart. Cap. 1.36 *ne uxoris Cyllenius fotibus repigratus ... torperet*. **oris tui limam ... expolitam:** i.e. your polished, refined style; cf. *Carm.* 2.187–8 *polita | eloquiis ... lingua*, 23.143 *oris ... expolire limam*, and, for metrical refinement, 4.8.5 *asprata lima poliri*; Hor. *Ars* 291 *labor limae* (Banniard 1992); for copy-editing, 1.1.3n. *limandasque*. **uersum ... compleuit** 'finished a verse', i.e. she completed lines where the poet's inspiration left off; cf. Don. *Vita Verg.* 34 (Virgil) *duos dimidiatos uersus complesse ex tempore*; on the technical aspect, Ps. Mar. Victorin. [Aphthonius] *Gramm.* 6 Keil p. 65.6, 152.1, 152.17, 169.2. **Corinna cum suo Nasone:** the initiative is now on the side of the women. Ovid's muse in the *Amores* is named after the Greek lyric poet Corinna. Ovid's relegation in 8 CE for an indiscretion involving the imperial family defines Sidonius' perception in *Carm.* 9.269–70 and 23.158–61, where 'Corinna' is fictitiously identified with Augustus' daughter Julia. **Lesbia cum Catullo:** the pseudonym Lesbia refers to the poet Sappho of Lesbos. Catullus' affair with 'Lesbia' defines an important part of his production. Sidonius also mentions him at *Carm.* 9.266; cf. Ov. *Trist.* 2.427–8, Prop. 2.34.87–8, Apul. *Apol.*

10.3. **Caesennia cum Gaetulico:** Apronia Caesennia (*BNP* 'Apronia 2') married Cn. Cornelius Lentulus Gaetulicus (put to death by Caligula in 39; *BNP* 'Cornelius II.29'), who wrote erotic epigrams among other things. Sidonius probably couples Gaetulicus with Catullus in the wake of Martial who, in the preface to book 1, stages them as a justification for his own poetry (cf. Plin. 5.3.5). Martial also mentions Marsus and Pedo, who return, together with Gaetulicus, in Sidon. *Carm.* 9.259–60. **Argentaria cum Lucano:** Argentaria Polla was a recipient of Martial's poetry (Mart. 10.64). She married Lucan, author of the historical epic *Pharsalia* (see Intro 4.4). Statius wrote a poem for her at Lucan' death, in which he styles her *doctam atque ingenio tuo decoram* (*Silv.* 2.7.83; see also Sidon. *Carm.* 23.165–6 and van Waarden 2020d, 697 with n. 44). **Cynthia cum Propertio:** the pseudonym Cynthia derives from the epithet *Cynthius* of Apollo who was born on Mount Cynthos on Delos. 'Cynthia' is omnipresent in the love elegies of Propertius, who calls her a *docta puella* (1.7.11 and elsewhere): she inspires his poetry (2.1.4 *ingenium nobis ipsa puella facit*) and is a poet in her own right (1.2.27 *cum tibi praesertim Phoebus sua carmina donet*). Together they constitute the self-referential closure of Book 2 (34.93–4). Sidonius also mentions Propertius in *Carm.* 9.263; cf. extensively Ov. *Trist.* 2.447–64. **Delia cum Tibullo:** the pseudonym refers again to Apollo, born on Delos. Her identity is shadowy; she may even be fictitious. She had a problematic love affair with the elegiac poet Tibullus. Tibullus was in high esteem among contemporaries (Hor. *Carm.* 1.33 and *Ep.* 1.4 are addressed to him; Ov. *Am.* 3.8 is his obituary; cf. *Trist.* 2.465–6); Quint. *Inst.* 10.1.93 thinks him the best elegist. Sidonius also mentions him *Carm.* 9.260. **liquido claret** 'it is crystal-clear', an expression in vogue in the fourth/fifth cent. (Ambrose, Augustine, Macrobius, Mamertus Claudianus). **litterariam curam** 'cultivation of literature' (tr. Anderson): cf. 7.14.10 *litterariae artis*. *litterarius* 'pertaining to written language, literature' (cf. *TLL* 7/1.1529.57–1530.2). **turba ... imperitorum** 'the ignorant majority', analogous to the idea in 7.14.10 *turba quamlibet magnam litterariae artis expertem maxumam solitudinem appello*. Elite thinking is at the core of Sidonius' value system, and here links back to the beginning of the letter, where the *multitudo desidiosorum* is opposed to the *paucissimi* who care for Latin (cf. e.g. about public speakers 4.3.10 *turba ... pauci*). The preservation of culture depends on a threatened minority. Letter 7.14 lays out the pyramid of being, where inanimate matter is inferior to animal vitality, which, in its turn, is surpassed by the human mind. In humans, there is a sharp divide between the natural wisdom of the many, the *imperiti* or *rustici*, and the superior insight of the sophisticated few, the *periti*: §8 [*animae*] *quae sola naturali sapientia uigent ... peritarum se meritis superueniri facile concedunt*. This difference is comparable to the difference between man and beast: §2 *quanto antecellunt beluis homines, tanto anteferri rusticis institutos* (Intro 3.3 'Elite Status'; further on this theme, Kaufmann 1995, 221–68). **natura comparatum est, ut** is a Plinian phrase, Plin. 2.19.5, 5.19.5, 8.20.1. **in omnibus artibus** varies 1.9.1n. *in omnium artium genere.* **scientiae ... pompa:** a unique phrase. For *scientiae* 'erudition', see 1.9.1n. *scientiae. pompa* 'splendour', 'grandeur' (cf. *TLL* 10/1.2597.6–20), e.g. 3.14.2 *pompa ... linguae Latinae,* 4.20.3n. *Martis pompa.* The letters ends on a double cretic: *pompa quo rarior.*

LETTER 2.12: HIS DAUGHTER'S ILLNESS

Outline

Sidonius, to his regret, has to decline an invitation to a fishing trip from his brother-in-law Agricola, because his daughter Severiana is ill and the family is departing for the countryside. As the doctors have been of no avail, prayers for Severiana's recovery are much needed.

Introduction

This letter combines the epistolary motifs of replying to an invitation and of discussing health, including the conventional opposition of unwholesome town vs healthy countryside. It is also a document of family life and the role of women.

Discussion

Gibson 2020b, 389–90 has pointed out that this letter is addressed to 'Agricola', while the preceding one went to 'Rusticus'. Pliny, he says, is very careful never to write two letters in sequence to the same addressee. He breaks this rule only once, in letters 2.11–12. Sidonius evidently noticed this and went one better: in *no* instance does he address two successive letters to the same correspondent. But he signals that he knows he has gone one better by coming close, addressing his own letter 2.11 to Rusticus and letter 2.12 to Agricola, the 'countryman' and the 'farmer' respectively.

Addressee

Agricola was a son of the emperor Eparchius Avitus and brother of both Sidonius' wife Papianilla and Ecdicius (Intro 1; letter 5.16 Addressee). He married a daughter of Ruricius of Limoges (the family relationship is difficult to pin down: alternatively, he had a daughter who married a grandson of Ruricius, cf. Ruric. 2.32 addressed to Agricola, §3 *ancillam uestram*, Neri 2009, 340 n. 29). He became a *conuersus* in later life (see this same letter, §§1–2; see Intro 3.4 n. 63). Sidonius also wrote 1.2 to Agricola, in fact the prestigious first letter of the collection after the dedicatory letter to Constantius. Prosopography Mathisen 2020a, 77.

Date and Place

Dating must remain vague as many letters in Book 2 'simply belong to some point in the 460s' (Kelly 2020, 191). We can hypothesize a date between Sidonius' forced retirement to Gaul and his embassy to Rome, between 461 and 467. Severiana is old enough to decide what she wants to be done. Sidonius and Papianilla married *c.* 452–5. There is a faint chance that Severiana is the member of the family who turned sixteen and gave a party (below §2n. *Seueriana*).

As the letter speaks of the heat and oppressiveness of the town and the invigorating atmosphere in the countryside, the setting would seem to be either Lyon or Clermont. Sidonius was born in Lyon and had a pied-à-terre there. Papianilla may have possessed one in Clermont, but we do not know. The family can be supposed to have had a country house close to either town. Lyon has plenty of water to explain the fishing boat and the fast-flowing stream while Clermont has the Allier. As Agricola is intimately connected with Clermont and the Auvergne, Clermont is most plausible.

Literature

Studies: Montone 2017, 31–3; Hanaghan 2019, 79–81. Commentary: Hindermann 2022b, 350–61.

Commentary

1 tu quidem ... sed: *tu* is redundant but serves as a prop for the bifurcation *quidem ... sed* (K–S 1, 623–4; Whitton 2013, 119 on Plin. 2.5.11 *tu quidem*). **lembum:** a small fast-sailing boat (*RE* 12/2.1894–6, *DAGR* 3/2.1099). **iamque cum piscibus** 'indeed even when loaded with fish': *iam* is counter-presuppositional (Kroon and Risselada 2002), thwarting the expectation that the ship would be just big enough for the catch of fish. For epexegetic *-que* 'to be precise', see *OLD* 6a. There is an alternative translation: 'and already loaded with fish', as a foretaste of the fish they are going to catch on the proposed fishing trip (thus Loyen and

Hanaghan 2019, 80, among others; for gift exchange, including fresh fish, see Williams 2014, Intro 3.3 'Gift-Giving'; cf. Sidonius' epigram on sending fish, half of what he has caught, *Carm.* 21). **longe** 'especially' (*OLD* 7b). **remiges:** the plural suggests a relatively large boat, as one oarsman was in principle sufficient for this type of vessel. **expeditosque:** most clausulae in this letter are cretic + spondee (together with a strong presence of the double cretic). **amnis aduersi terga:** for rowing laboriously upstream and being dragged along in the opposite direction, cf. Verg. *Georg.* 1.201–3 *non aliter quam qui aduerso uix flumine lembum | remigiis subigit, si bracchia forte remisit, | atque illum in praeceps prono rapit alueus amni* (see Montone 2017, 32); cf. Liv. 24.40, Plin. 8.8.3. *terga* 'surface' is poetical usage, and somewhat elevated (*OLD* 8); cf. 9.14.6 *per turbulenti terga torrentis.* **dissimulo** 'I refuse', 'decline', late usage (Blaise 3, van Waarden 2010, 486). **multo ... ualidiora:** strong hyperbaton (*OLS* 2.1081–2) makes *multo* emphatic. **decumbentibus** 'lying ill' (*OLD* 2). **maeroris retia:** *rete* 'net', applied as a metaphor of deceit concerning property (Plaut. *Persa* 74) or love (e.g. Prop. 3.8.37), only here of grief, obviously suggested by the context. Even (or especially) in an emotional context, Sidonius indulges in artificiality, as also in §3, albeit there with an apology (Intro 4.5). **indolescenda** 'to be grieved at', with passive subject: cf. Min. Fel. 5.4 *indolescendum est* + accusative and infinitive (L–S II, *OLD* 2). **rite** 'duly' (*OLD* 3a), only here in Sidonius, and also rare in contemporaries. **germano moueris affectu:** the verbal hyperbaton, constantly used by later authors to signal the end of a clause rhythmically (*OLS* 2.1104, Intro 4.3), is noteworthy as the letter largely dispenses with this device; see e.g. 7.1.1n. *importuna* (cf. also 1.9.1n. *spebus*). **quo temporis puncto paginam hanc sumpseris:** the sender anticipates the moment of reading; on epistolary time, see Intro 4.3; for this letter in particular, Hanaghan 2019, 79–81. For *paginam* 'letter', 1.9.8n. For the later development of *sumere* to mean 'receive', van Waarden 2010, 430.

2 Seueriana: daughter of Sidonius and Papianilla (Intro 1). She might be the family member turning sixteen in *Carm.* 17 (see above Date and Place), although other identifications have been suggested (Kelly 2020, 172–3). She became a nun at some later point together with female relatives of bishop Avitus of Vienne (closely connected, possibly Sidonius' nephew; Mathisen 1981, 100), probably in the nunnery founded there by Avitus (Alc. Avit. *Carm.* 6.83–94 *mater Seueriana*). Prosopography Mathisen 2020a, 121. Children are almost completely absent in the works of Sidonius. Three of his own are the exception (Mathisen 2020c, 45; see 5.16.5n.). **sollicitudo communis** 'our common cause of anxiety', cf. 5.16.5n. to Papianilla about another daughter: *Roscia salutat,* *cura communis*. For *communis* of something shared by the sender and the addressee, see van Waarden 2010, 280–1. **lentae tussis** 'prolonged coughing': *lentae OLD* 5b, cf. Cels. 3.2.1 *lenti dolores lentaeue febres*. Illness is a frequent topic in correspondence, e.g. Cicero about his daughter (*Att*. 11.6.4 *Tulliae meae morbus et imbecillitas corporis me exanimat*), Pliny about a friend (1.22.1 *perturbat me longa et pertinax ualetudo Titi Aristonis*; Hindermann 2022b, xvii for other parallels), Fronto and Marcus Aurelius about their respective health (a dominant theme, e.g. 5.21–36 vdH; van den Hout 1999, 691–3 for an overview), Symmachus about himself (2.49 *Scribere hucusque non libuit obstrepentibus inbecillitatum querellis*). **febribus:** cf. Sidonius' own bouts of fever 1.5.8n., 5.3.3. **ingrauescentibus:** the one-word double cretic clausula represents the serious situation. **exire in suburbanum:** Montone 2017, 32–3 points out the similarity with Catull. 44, who is cured in his country house of a cough he incurred in town: 6–7 *fui libenter in tua suburbana | uilla malamque pectore expuli tussim* and 13–4 *hic* [i.e. in town] *me grauedo frigida et frequens tussis | quassauit usque dum in tuum sinum fugi*. For the opposition town/countryside in the context of health, see Hindermann 2022b, 96 on 2.2.2 *quin tu mage*. The opposition is also found in the call of duty requiring someone to return from his farmstead to town, e.g. 7.15.1 *ciuitatis habitatio* opp. *suburbanitatis*, or the opposite, urging someone to take some time-off from work in town, sometimes bringing up health again, e.g. 2.2.2 *si quid tibi salubre cordi* opp. *anhelantibus angustiis ciuitatis*. **denique** 'actually' (*OLD* 5). **sumeremus … parabamus** slips from the direct first person singular in §1 to the plural, first to a more blurred 'I', then to the collective plural 'I and my wife/ family/ household' that is standard in describing aristocratic travelling (van Waarden 2021, 151–2). For travelling nobility and their retinue, Mathisen 2020c, 64–5. **ad uillulam:** the same as the *suburbanum*; the diminutive denotes endearment, 'small but beautiful', cf. e.g. Catull. 26.1 *uillula nostra* (variant reading *uestra*), Plin. 2.17.29 *uillulae nostrae*. **preces … orationibus:** both in the Christian sense of 'prayer'; *prex*: L-S IIA, *OLD* 2c, Blaise; *oratio*, ecclesiastical Latin only: L-S IIIE, Blaise 5. Sidonius often thematizes the power of prayer, e.g. 9.3.4 [to his confessor, bishop Faustus] *animam* [sc. *meam*] … *frequentissimis tuis illis et ualentissimis orationum munerare suffragiis, precum peritus*; Bailey 2020, 272–3. **auram … salubriter:** for the combination, cf. e.g. Cypr. *Demetr*. 8 *aurae salubres* [necessary for agriculture], Amm. 22.16.8 [Alexandria] *inibi aurae salubriter spirant*. Hindermann 2022b, 356–7 plausibly links this to miasma theory which held that poisonous vapours of the soil (supposed to cause malaria among other things) were carried away by the air, thus limiting the spread of diseases. Vitruvius, for one, begins with the healthy location of the built environment (1.4, 6.1). Cf. 1.5.8n. *spiritu*

... *infecit.* **uegetatio** 'invigorating activity', 'stimulus', first found at Apul. *Met.* 1.2 and rare. Taking up the last position in the clause, this notion is its focus (*OLS* 2, 1038–41). The short syllables in the unusual clausula *ipsa uegetatio*, paeon I + cretic (van Waarden and Kelly 2020, 474), make for liveliness. **tua soror:** Sidonius' wife Papianilla. Her dowry or inheritance comprised the estate of Avitacum (2.2.3 *uxorium*; Intro 1 with n. 6). Cf. 5.16 in this volume, addressed to her (the only letter directed at a woman) in which Sidonius congratulates her on the promotion, *c.* 475, of her brother Ecdicius to the rank of *patricius*: §3 *uxor bona, soror optima*. This letter also mentions Roscia by name, as signalled above (Mascoli 2010, 38–42). See also Intro 3.3 'Women' and 2.10.5–6n. **inter spem metumque suspensi:** also Liv. 8.13.17. **taedium** 'discomfort' (*OLD* 3b). **augendum** (sc. *fuisse*) is a gerundive used as fut. pass. part.; see 1.9.6n. *admittendo.* **iacentis** 'lying ill' (*OLD* 2c).

3 torpori 'lethargy', due to heat and anxiety; cf. 2.9.7, 5.17.6, *Carm.* 2.9 (due to inactivity); *Carm.* 5.521, 'numbness' (due to freezing). **praeuio Christo** 'under Christ's guidance', also 4.10.2; cf. 3.7.2 *praeuio Deo*, 4.15.3 *Deo praeuio* – all concerning movement or development; see also 3.12.2n. *praeuio*; for similar formulas, see 1.5.1n. *sub ope ... dei*, 1.9.8n. *sub ope Christi*. The appeal to Christ returns at the end, framing the episode of the incompetent doctors. **simulque ... occidunt:** highly stylized clause with paronomasia and oxymoronic oppositions. **dissidentum:** doctors were notorious for disagreeing, cf. Plin. *Nat.* 23.32 *discordibus medicorum sententiis.* **parum ... satis** 'poorly ... very': respectively *OLD* 3b and *OLD* 9b; cf. 6.11.2n. *satis*, 7.18.2n. *et satis habilem*; also 9.16.3n. *sat*(*is*) + superlative. **officiosissime occidunt:** ignorant doctors and their 'licence to kill', e.g. Plin. *Nat.* 29.18 *medicoque tantum hominem occidisse impunitas summa est*, cf. Mart. 1.47, Auson. *Epigr.* 79 Green. Sidonius' phrase was proverbial in the Middle Ages as evidenced by John of Salisbury, *Policraticus* 2.29, and Vincent of Beauvais, *Speculum maius* 5.96. Savaron (p. 159) suggested as hypotext Hor. *Ep.* 1.7.8–9 *officiosaque sedulitas et opella forensis* | *adducit febres et testamenta resignat,* transferred from the 'killing' social obligations in town to the nefarious zeal of doctors. Horace also there speaks of withdrawing to the countryside (v. 1 *rure*), of health and sickness (v. 3 *sanum recteque ualentem,* v. 4 *aegro ... aegrotare*) and a heatwave in town (v. 5 *calor*). All this pays its due to satirical discourse about doctors, as in reality, in the medical profession, ethical behaviour and successful practice were stimulated and guaranteed wherever possible through education, organization and legislation (*BNP* 'Medical ethics' C Roman). **iure amicitiae** 'by right of friendship', cf. Sen. *Ben.* 6.16 on devoted doctors who become friends (§1 *ex medico ... in amicum transeunt*). For the expression, and the rights and duties of friendship, van Waarden 2010, 279–80 7.6.1n. *amicitiarum* *uetera iura*, van Waarden 2016, 212 7.17.1n. *lege amicitiae*. Cf. Intro 3.3 'Social Conventions'. **Iustus**, otherwise unknown (Mathisen 2020a, 103). **si iocari liberet in tristibus:** cf., in a similar vein, 7.7.1n. *ioculariter plura garrirem, si pariter ... ualeret animus exercere laeta et tristia sustinere*, 9.3.3 *quidam barbarismus est morum sermo iucundus et animus afflictus*. Wit is de rigueur in polite conversation and correspondence (Intro 3.6), the lack of it must be justified (Sidonius here nevertheless indulges in it; see Intro 4.5 'Hyperbole'). For the topos, cf. e.g. Cic. *Att.* 5.5.1 *nec iocandi locus est, ita me multa sollicitant*, Symm. 1.101.2, 3.21. **Chironica ... Machaonica:** The centaur Chiron is a complex character (*BNP* 'Chiron'), known for his healing expertise and his initiating young heroes in the art, among them Achilles (Hom. *Il.* 11.830–2, Hyg. *Fab.* 274.9 *artem medicinam chirurgicam ex herbis primus instituit*). Later tradition makes him invent veterinary medicine (Isid. *Orig.* 4.9.12, who explains: *inde pingitur dimidia parte homo, dimidia equus*). Sirmond (p. 35) suggests another pun on Greek for 'worse', χείρων, as in Diogenes the Cynic's famous question, while looking at two badly painted Centaurs: 'Which one is Chiron/ worse?' (Diog. Laërt. 6.51). Machaon, son of Asclepius, was a physician of the Greeks in the Trojan War, curing Menelaus, among others, with herbs obtained from Chiron (Hom. *Il.* 4.188–219, 11.833). I think there may be a nod to Virgil who, among the Greeks exiting the Trojan Horse, calls Machaon *primus* (either because he comes out first or as an honorific epithet: *Aen.* 2.263 *primusque Machaon*). So the humorous trade-off is between the veterinarian and the physician, the worst and the best. The adjectives *Chironica* and *Machaonica* are both hapax, instead of the proper names in the genitive: Wolff 2020, 405, cf. 2.9.2n. *pastoria*. **postulandus est Christus obsecrandusque:** *postulandus ... obsecrandusque* echoes the apostle Paul's much-cited phrase Vulg. *1 Tim.* 2.1 *obsecrationes, orationes, postulationes, gratiarum actiones*. The closure of the letter introduces the *Christus medicus* concept, Christ healing the sick, in its simplest, literal form. It is most often used as a metaphor of Christ healing mankind's spiritual diseases (after Vulg. *Matth.* 9.12) which is particularly frequent in Augustine (e.g. *Nupt. et concup.* 2.3.9 *humanam naturam ... peccato uitiatam Christo medico indigere*). In Sidonius' circle, this takes the form of a saintly cleric mediating or administering Christ's spiritual medicine, e.g. Sidon. 4.14.3 [we clerics reveal human sins to] *Christo res humanas uitasque medicaturo*, 7.6.1 *mederi ... tuae supplicationis efficacia*, Ruric. 1.1.3 [be harsh with my sins which] *nec a me posse curari ... Domino donante iam sentio* (Neri 2009, 168–9 n.39). **curationem cura:** wordplay on medical cure and lay concern. **potentia superna medeatur:** *potentia superna* is a recherché collocation for the much more common *potentia diuina*. The clausula is of the famous type *esse uideatur*, paeon I + trochee (see 9.16.4n. *exisse*, Intro 4.5).

LETTER 3.9: SUPPORTING A SLAVE-OWNER

Outline

Sidonius supports the complaint of one of his parishioners against the Briton chieftain Riothamus whose troops have apparently enticed away the plaintiff's slaves.

Introduction

This is a letter of recommendation – one of the most important applications of the epistolary genre (Cugusi 1983, 111–14; Furbetta 2015b (pp. 349–53 on Sidonius); Westenholz 2023 (for Sidonius in particular); see also Intro 3.6 with n. 79). They are part and parcel of the patronage of the likes of Cicero, Pliny, Fronto, Symmachus and Sidonius. Rather than urging for a job or another favour for his clients, Sidonius usually makes recommendations in juridical affairs, both before and after his consecration as bishop. Recommendations are either made in the absence of the person(s) in question, the letter being delivered by an external letter carrier (e.g. 6.2 in which Sidonius intercedes for a widow from his diocese), or take the form of a request handed in by the person interested himself, as in this letter and in 6.11 (cf. 6.10.1 and e.g. Cic. *Fam.* 13.6, Fronto 81.22 vdH). The recommended person is always evaluated in terms of the sensibilities of the addressee and his ties to the author (Cugusi 1983, 113; see §2 below and in another letter of recommendation, 6.11 Discussion). The same applies to letter carriers in general, who embraced all classes, but high-ranking correspondents preferably had their messages delivered by people of equal standing (Mratschek 2020b, 227).

Discussion and Addressee

The letter's addressee, Riothamus, was chieftain of a federate war-band composed of troops described as *Britanni* or *Brittones* in the sources. Its core may well have come from insular Britain, perhaps escaping from the Saxon incursions, gathering strength in continental Brittany (Armorica) and assimilating further elements in Gaul north of the Loire, which was dominated by the Franks and various Roman warlords. He is visible to us *c.* 469–72 as he was engaged by the imperial government to check the northward Visigothic pressure in the Auvergne, established his headquarters in Bourges but suffered a crushing defeat at nearby Déols. With the remains of his troops, he retired to the Burgundians. As bishop of Clermont, Sidonius was directly involved in the war (Intro 1 and 3.2; see *Ep.* 7.7), familiar with Bourges (see his intervention there in *Epp.* 7.5,

7.8, 7.9) and increasingly relying on the Burgundians (Delaplace 2015, 249–50). Hence his acquaintance with Riothamus comes as no surprise. It has even been suggested that Riothamus' remaining forces may have joined Clermont's defences.

Riothamus is a rendering of Brittonic *Ri(g)otamos 'most kingly', 'great king', and is a personal name rather than a title, as Arthurian scholarship would have it (Birks 2004, 124–5; see Literature below). Two more Britons/Bretons figure in the correspondence: first and foremost Faustus, the influential bishop of Riez, Sidonius' spiritual mentor (Mathisen 2020a, 95), and the cleric and monk Riochatus who visited Sidonius while carrying books from Faustus to Faustus' 'native Britons' (9.9.6 *Britannis tuis*; Mathisen 2020a, 118). Prosopographical entry for Riothamus: Mathisen 2020a, 118.

Date and Place

The letter was probably written in the early 470s, with Sidonius bishop of Clermont and Riothamus' troops looking for profitable deals in the neighbourhood, plausibly before their defeat (no earlier than 471, Delaplace 2015, 280). It is connected with the other letters related to the war in book 3, nos 2, 3, 4 and 7, and counts among the 'historically-dated letters' (Mathisen 2013, 222, Kelly 2020, 179).

Literature

Commentary: Giannotti 2016, 195–201. Primary sources on Riothamus and the Britons include Sidonius (also 1.7.5 *Britannos supra Ligerim sitos*), Jord. *Get.* 237–8 *Brittonum ... rex Riotimus* etc. and Greg. Tur. *Hist.* 2.18 *Brittani de Bituricas a Gothis expulsi sunt, multis apud Dolensim vicum peremptis*. See Wood 2000, 507–8; Egetenmeyr 2022, 336–40; monograph: Birks 2004.

Among students of Arthurian lore, Riothamus is seen as a possible source of the story of the legendary king. For sober discussions, see Halsall 2013, 365–7; Higham 2018, 152–4; cf. van Waarden 2020d, 699.

Commentary

1 Seruatur nostri consuetudo sermonis: cf. similar openings 9.3.1 *Seruat consuetudinem suam ... facundia uestra*, Symm. 9.15.1 *Consuetudinem meam seruo*; going back to Plin. 9.15.3 *tu consuetudinem serua, nobisque ... perscribe*. *nostri* 'my', as explained van Waarden 2020e, 431, is part of a diplomatic exchange, where the sender is only foregrounded in the actual request (§2 *incertum mihi est* and *arbitror*) and the addressee receives a cautious *uos* throughout. As writing letters is conversing at a distance (Intro 3.6 n. 79), *sermo* 'conversation' develops the meaning 'correspondence', 'letter' (van Waarden 2010, 152–3). **namque:** see 1.5.1n. *namque*. **querimoniam:** i.e. the complaint which is subsequently brought to the attention of the addressee (cf. e.g. 4.6.4, 4.21.3, 6.12.2). Letters of commendation will typically begin with an accolade of the addressee (*salutatio*) prior to bringing up the problem. **stilus** 'writing': see *OLD* 3b, 1.1.2n. *in stilo*. **in titulis:** *titulus* is the heading or salutation of a letter as opposed to its actual content, cf. 7.12.1 *titulorum ... sermonum* (van Waarden 2016, 60). **loci mei aut ordinis:** i.e. social rank and clerical profession, cf. 7.5.4 *locum statumque pontificis* 'the position and standing of a bishop' and 4.14.3 and 7.1.5 *in nostri ordinis uiris* 'in men of our (priestly/ episcopal) profession'; for the central notion of *ordo* 'social class', see 1.5.10n. *ordinum*. **inconciliari** 'incur unpleasantness' (tr. Anderson): a bishop cannot but give a judgement, but in doing so is vulnerable. The verb is a rare borrowing from early Roman comedy, of slightly slippery meaning (*TLL* 7/1.998.44–55); for Sidonius' archaisms, see Intro 4.5, Wolff 2020, 402. On the bishop's role as mediator and arbitrator, see Intro 3.4 and 6.11 Discussion. **ipsi** 'in person', i.e. from experience (*OLS* 1.1152). **sarcinam** 'burden': metaphorical use first found in Ovid (e.g. *Her.* 4.24), then in later Latin, e.g. 7.9.7 *publicae opinionis sarcinam*, Ambr. 5.18.5 *peccatorum sarcina*, Aug. 101.3 *curarum ecclesiasticarum sarcina*, Ennod. 6.13 *conscientiae meae sarcinam*. **pudoris ... uerecundia** 'sense of propriety (*OLD* 2a) ... sensitivity (cf. *OLD* 1)': an appeal to the addressee's sense of social norms (strikingly placing him on the same level as Sidonius' Gallo-Roman upper class) to ensure his willingness to look into the question; on socially constructive emotions, see Intro 3.3 'Social Conventions' with n. 54; 2.9.10n.

2 gerulus epistularum: see introduction. **humilis obscurus despicabilisque** 'lowly, obscure and undistinguished': cf. Cic. *Ver.* 5.181 *humili atque obscuro loco natus*. *despicabilis*: lit. 'to be looked down upon' in social perspective, 'low-ranking'; cf. 4.7.3 *personae despicabiles* in a similar context. The adjective is later Latin with the productive *-bilis* suffix (Wolff 2020, 398). The third element of the list is longest: see Intro 4.5 with n. 111. **etiam usque ad damnum innocentis ignauiae** 'even to the point of causing damage through innocent insipidity': the phrase plays on the judicial notion of *damnum iniuria datum* or *damnum iniuriae* 'damage caused by unlawful behaviour' (e.g. *Dig.* 2.13.10.3, 4.4.9.2; see *OLD* 1c, Heumann–Seckel 120 s.v. *damnum*, Valditara 2018). Substituting *innocentis* for *iniuria*, it creates the oxymoron of innocent inactivity doing harm; cf. Claud. *Ruf.* 2.198 *ignauo tantum licuisse nocenti*. **mancipia sua:** though low on the social ladder, he still possesses slaves. Slave-owning being a marker of status at every level, even modest households owned a couple of slaves (*OCD* 'Slavery, Roman', *ODLA* 'Slavery, Roman and post-Roman'). **Britannis clam sollicitantibus:** Riothamus' Britons enticing Roman slaves away is no doubt one of innumerable border disputes in a deeply divided Gaul where lawlessness was endemic (Harries 1994, 209). **incertum ... certa:** polyptoton (Wolff 2020, 410). **causatio** 'complaint' (*TLL* 3.702.59–69, cf. 74–5). **inter coram positos** 'in a face-to-face meeting', cf. 6.4.2 in a comparable situation. **discingitis** 'unravel', 'decide': a juridical term, e.g. *Cod. Theod.* 1.16.3 pr. *causis*, 1.16.9 *litibus*, 2.26.4 *iurgium*, Sidon. 2.7.2 *disceptationem* (*TLL* 5/1.1316.25–37). **hunc laboriosum** 'this poor fellow': *laboriosum* 'suffering hardship' (*OLD* 3b), cf. the person struggling to obtain justice in Plin. 4.9.1 *homo laboriosus et aduersis suis clarus*; also Sidon. 6.11.2 *huius laboriosi*. **inter argutos ... contumaces:** the Brittonic troops are described by means of the tripartite asyndeton *argutos armatos tumultuosos*, with an appended *contumaces* defined by another triad: *uirtute numero contubernio* (see Intro 4.5). The opposition to the overpowering barbarians typically serves to arouse sympathy for an endangered minority (Egetenmeyr 2022, 174–5; see also Intro 3.3 'Coexistence with "Barbarians"'). *argutos*, in this context, has a negative connotation: 'cunning', 'shrewd' (L–S B2); cf. positive 'subtle' at 9.9.10 *argute illa nec callide*. **ex aequo et bono** 'according to what is equitable and good': i.e. on the merits of the case, when a matter is to be decided according to principles of equity rather than by points of law (Merriam-Webster Dictionary Online; cf. Heumann–Seckel 49 s.v. *bonus*; e.g. Sen. *Clem.* 2.7.3 *clementia liberum arbitrium habet: non sub formula, sed ex aequo et bono iudicat*, *Cod. Theod.* 3.5.11, *Dig.* 17.1.12.9. For the trade-off between the letter and the spirit of the law, cf. e.g. Cic. *Caec.* 51 *ad uerba ... consilium autem eorum qui scripserunt*, Sen. *Contr.* 1.1.13 *diuisit in ius et aequitatem*). In the layout of the sentence, this 'fair judgment' sits as it were between the two sides. **solus ... pauper:** the plaintiff is characterized in a tripartite paired asyndeton: *solus inermis, abiectus rusticus, peregrinus pauper*. **solus inermis**, typically of the underdog: Liv. 7.5.6, Caes. Arel. *Serm.* 119.1 (Samson), Anon. *C. Iud.* 1 p. 11 (David); cf. 7.2.2 *solus tenuis peregrinus*. **abiectus** 'inferior', cf. e.g. Cic. *Deiot.* 30 *uestram familiam abiectam et obscuram*, rather stronger than *humilis*, cf. 7.9.10 *si eligimus humilem, uocatur abiectus* (by malevolent critics). **rusticus** 'uneducated': see Kaufmann 1995, 254–9, van Waarden 2010, 140–1 at 7.2.1 *stilo rusticante*. **peregrinus pauper**, closely connected in Jewish and Christian parlance as groups entitled to protection, e.g. Vulg. *Lev.* 19.10, Ambr. *Ep.* 9.68.5. In Sidonius' ethics too, the stranger merits care on an equal footing with one's own

148   COMMENTARY: 3.9:2–3.12

people, cf. 7.9.19 *si humanitas requirenda est ciui clerico peregrino*. The man whom Sidonius recommends is arguably one of his parishioners, but will be a stranger among the Britons. The poor deserve generous support as well: cf. e.g. 2.10.2 *per uberem munificentiam in pauperes*, 4.7.2 *cum inuitabitur ... pauper ad mensam*, 6.2.1 *cibis pauperes pascit*. *pauper* can mean either 'utterly destitute' or (as here) 'poor' (i.e. 'lower class') as opposed to 'rich' (Brown 2012, 343; see further Intro 3.3 'Social Strata'). **audiri** meaningfully is the last word.

LETTER 3.12 WITH POEM 28: RESTORING GRANDFATHER'S GRAVE

Outline

Departing from Lyon for Clermont, Sidonius approaches an old, overgrown graveyard, where the tomb of his grandfather is scarcely recognizable. Indeed, some gravediggers think they have hit upon a vacant spot and have begun digging a pit. Sidonius has them beaten up. Patiens, the town's bishop, accepts his apologies for this flare of temper. Sidonius asks his nephew Secundus to take care of the restoration of the burial mound and to provide for a gravestone at his expense. He also supplies the text to be engraved upon it, which involves a public rehabilitation of his grandfather as a second Pompey. Secundus must see to it that the engraver commit no errors. So belated a tribute has august precedents in Alexander the Great and Julius Caesar.

Introduction

Following a number of shorter letters, this vivid and elaborate account, which also includes a poem, opens the concluding part of Book 3 (Giannotti 2016, 212). At the letter's centre is the public rehabilitation of Sidonius' grandfather Apollinaris (see van Waarden 2024), proof of the author's self-confidence as a responsible heir and intended to boost family cohesion, arguably at his crucial transition from civil to ecclesiastical status. In the toxic political climate of the early fifth century, Apollinaris, as one of Gaul's principal civil officers, had not escaped the raging conflict of loyalties concerning emperors and usurpers (see commentary). Though still with due political prudence, Sidonius, in the inserted funeral poem, identifies the dangers of those times and honours his grandfather as *liber sub dominantibus tyrannis* (v. 12). He now finally lifts Apollinaris' grave out of its anonymity by providing it with a proper tombstone with this poem on it. The wording in §4 is modelled on Lucan's lament for Pompey's paltry grave in Egypt: a dilapidated tomb cannot diminish his glory – and better times are ahead. The same goes for Apollinaris, intimates Sidonius. This renewed confidence in the family expressly involves the next generation, for which, however, Sidonius has recourse to his nephew, appropriately named 'Secundus', without so much as mentioning his son Apollinaris the Younger, who, in the following letter, is warned to avoid bad company (see Intro 3.3 n. 46; van Waarden 2024, 6). Hope inspired by the young will turn out to be the guiding idea in the letters which conclude the collection (see 9.16 Introduction).

Subject and form are inspired by Pliny the Younger's letter 6.10, in which the author goes to visit the grave of his admired Verginius Rufus. To his dismay, it is still unfinished and anonymous ten years after. He cites the epigraph (a single couplet) which Rufus himself had composed (Henke 2012, 122).

Sidonius' letter is an example of compelling storytelling such as gentlemen were used to display on social occasions and, indeed, in their letters (see van Waarden 2010, 133–5; Henke 2012, 123–5; Risselada 2013, 300).

Discussion

Where exactly was Apollinaris the Elder buried? The Gallo-Roman town of Lugdunum was built on Fourvière (from *forum uetus*) Hill, its north–south *cardo* continuing, outside the enclosure, as the high road leading south to Narbonne, its east–west *decumana* extending west to the Auvergne and Aquitaine. Beginning in the third century, occupation gradually shifted from the hill to the banks of the Saône. Lyon's cemeteries extended along the western and southern slopes of Fourvière Hill, from the Saddle of Trion on the road to the west to the churches of St Irenaeus and St Just on the road to the south. Excavations have found remains of incineration and inhumation from the first century onward. Elements of older graves were often reused in later ones. The area of Trion is richest in more monumental tombs from the earliest period (Wuilleumier 1953, 74–5), while around St Irenaeus (in the fifth century still dedicated to St John, not to be confused with the cathedral; see Griffe 3, 54; also letter 2.10) and St Just (in Sidonius' time dedicated to the Maccabees, containing Just's tomb; see 5.17.10 for Sidonius attending the saint's day) Christian burials *ad sanctos* came to overlay earlier pagan ones. After 334, all datable graves are situated there, on the road to Narbonne (Audin 1952, 136; Reynaud 1998, 94–108 and 178; see Map 2; atlas Lenoble 2019).

It is usually thought that Apollinaris was buried at St Irenaeus or St Just (Loyen 2, 224 n. 34). There is reason for doubt, however. It is improbable that in these busy places his grave would have escaped Sidonius' attention or, for that matter, the gravediggers would have had free rein. The less visited and unkempt Trion graveyard (see Raynaud 2006, 137–9 and 141) is a better candidate. A burial away from the focus of attention would square with Apollinaris' vulnerable profile at his death (see, however, Stein 2015, who argues that the Gallic nobility preferred low-profile graves until the turn of the 4th to the 5th century). The site also fits Sidonius' direction of travel, along the road to the Auvergne (see further below §§1–2n.).

Addressee

Secundus is a nephew of Sidonius (§5 *patruo tuo*). His father, Sidonius' anonymous brother, had been educated under the care of Faustus of Riez (*Carm.* 16.71–7). His name can be considered as telling (Sidonius' 'back-up' family member): see above on Apollinaris Jr. Prosopography: Mathisen 2020a, 120 (Secundus); Mathisen 2020a, 138 ('Anonymus 35', Secundus' father).

Date and Place

Internal evidence converges on 469 for the date of writing (Loyen 2, 250; see below v.2n. *haud indignus*). It is worth trying to fit this into the historical context as well. I would argue that it was written when Sidonius left Lyon to take up his position as bishop of Clermont at some point in 469/70. Purportedly written *ex itinere* (§3), the letter's first circulation and the restoration of Apollinaris' tomb must have occurred at a moment chosen by Sidonius to further his interests by re-aligning the family, in which interests clashed all the time between the Auvergne and Provence, where its members oscillated between loyalty to the emperor and siding with the local powerbrokers, the Burgundians (for an historical overview, see Intro 3.2). The unpalatable Arvandus affair of 468/9 brought this to a temporary climax and was a factor in Sidonius' decision definitively to abandon his administrative career. We can imagine that, upon return, he felt the need to flag his own position as the foremost heir to Apollinaris' legacy (see Harries 1992, 304) and to restore family cohesion from a position of strength. In Lyon, he had prepared for his new ecclesiastical office with bishop Patiens who probably ordained him as a deacon. Gaudentius (see §4) would easily fit into this company. Patiens' excellent relationship with the Burgundians may, at the same time, have laid the groundwork for Sidonius' later political switch to their side (Delaplace 2015, 249–50). It is attractive to suppose that this letter was written at the very moment when Sidonius moved to Clermont, the watershed in his career (see further van Waarden 2024, 5–6).

The final redaction and the circulation to a broader audience as part of the collection took place *c.* 477 (Intro 2.1, van Waarden 2024, 6).

Literature

Commentary: Giannotti 2016, 212–26. Studies: Henke 2012, Colafrancesco 2013; Condorelli 2008, 198–200 (incorporated in Condorelli 2013, 268–70); Stein 2015, 199–203; Hanaghan 2019, 69–72; Consolino 2020, 360–1; Giannotti 2021a (included in Giannotti 2021b, 41–57); van Waarden 2024.

Commentary

1 Aui mei, proaui tui tumulum: states the theme at the outset; in pragmatic terms, the phrase is topic (*OLS* 2, 949–52). Sidonius' paternal grandfather, the first member of the family to be baptized, as Sidonius stresses in the epitaph, served as *praefectus praetorio Galliarum* in 408/9. He seems not to have survived the purges which followed the fall of the usurper Jovinus in 413 (see 5.9.1; for confirmation based on §4 below, see van Waarden 2024) – a usurpation which deeply divided Gallic loyalties and set a precedent for the political opportunism and estrangement from Italy defining Sidonius' own times (Kulikowski 2020, 200–1, van Waarden 2020b, 19; prosopography: Mathisen 2020a, 80; see family tree in *PLRE* 2, 1317). **hesterno (pro dolor!) die:** *pro dolor* 'how sad' (*OLD pro*² 2a) creates hyperbaton, highlighting *hesterno*, cf. 7.7.1 *Aruernorum (pro dolor!) seruitus* 'the slavery of the Arvernians, of all peoples – so sad'. Was the day before perhaps Apollinaris' birth- or death day? Hanaghan 2019, 69–70 stresses the narratological function of collapsing time into one day, making for excitement (see also §3 *ex itinere*). **autem** introduces background information, something like: 'the cemetery *happened* to be full' (for uses of *autem* other than contrastive, see *OLS* 2, 1180–1). **bustualibus fauillis** 'the ashes from tombs': the rare *bustualis* (*TLL* 2.2255.71–5) is one of many new adjectives in *-alis* (Wolff 2020, 398); for adjective instead of genitive, see 1.5.4n. *amnicos*. For *bustum* 'cremation tomb', see Reynaud 1998, 96. From the third century onward, inhumation was the norm in the Latin West, confirmed by Christian practice (*ODLA* 463–4 'dead, disposal of, Roman and Byzantine'). It is striking that Sidonius should mention cremation (*fauillis*) on a par with inhumation (*cadaueribus*). Unless the graveyard had centuries-old cremation tombs still on display, this would be no more than a rhetorical way of picturing the desolation of the spot. This trait rather underpins the supposition below (§2) that it was not one of the more popular and well-kept cemeteries *ad sanctos* of the town.

Apollinaris was not buried in full actual view. **sed tamen** 'but even so', i.e. despite the fact that there had been no human disturbance. **sidentibus aceruis:** possibly an allusion to Luc. 7.791 *sidentes … aceruos* (Giannotti 2016, 216), which would unobtrusively introduce the main allusion in §4. *sidentibus* 'sinking', 'subsiding' (*OLD* 3a), cf. e.g. Stat. *Silv.* 5.3.200 *rogus.* **corporum baiuli** 'corpse bearers': elsewhere Sidonius uses *baiulus* of a letter carrier (4.7.1, 6.4.1). **rastris funebribus:** a *raster/rastrum* is a digging tool, combining the functions of a fork, a rake and a hoe; see Rich 1901, 546–7. *funebribus* 'used for burying' (*OLD* 1). As said earlier, it was not uncommon for (elements of) older graves to be reused.

2 iam … iam: anaphora and ellipsis of the verb accelerate the pace of the narration. **niger caespes:** cf. *Cod. Theod.* 9.17.5 pr. *cum et lapidem hinc mouere et terram sollicitare et caespitem uellere proximum sacrilegio maiores semper habuerint.* **urbem ad Aruernam:** the capital of the people of the *Aruerni* (Auvergne, see *BNP* 'Arverni'), present-day Clermont-Ferrand, Roman *Augustonemetum*, in Sidonius' day called *ciuitas Aruernorum* or *Aruerni* for short. The delicate word order provides a cretic + spondee clausula (with elision of *-em*). If he took the usual road, Sidonius will have left Lyon (for his residences, see Intro 1) via the west end at the Saddle of Trion and passed through the age-old burying fields there. The journey would take three days (estimated with *ORBIS*, for private transport at 50 km/day); see §3 *ex itinere*. **publicum scelus** 'public offence', 'crime', as opposed to private or civil wrongs such as contract breach; the collocation is rare, cf. Ps.-Quint. *Decl.* 12.11 *in iudicium perduxi publicum scelus,* Aur. Vict. *Caes.* 11.1 *priuato scelere publicoque.* **e supercilio uicini collis** 'from the brow of the neighbouring hill': *OLD supercilium* 3, cf. 3.3.4 *in supercilium collis abrupti.* From Fourvière Hill (Loyen 2, 224 n.34), the traveller will look down on the cemeteries on its slopes; see Map 2 and Discussion above. **effuso** 'giving rein to' (*OLD* 14a). **sic quoque** 'even so', i.e. despite my haste. **praeuio** 'ahead', i.e. 'warning': cf. e.g. 5.16.1 *litteras aduentus sui praeuias*; see also 2.12.3n. *praeuio Christo.* *praeuius* tends to precede its head noun, highlighting the movement (resulting in a chiasmus with *facinus audax*; on word order in noun phrases, see *OLS* 2, 1076–80). **et superueni:** *et* in a lively way introduces the apodosis; see 1.5.9n. *patuit et Roma.* **supplicia** 'corporal punishment', probably flogging them (see §3 *caesos*). Whereas Savaron, p. 205, argued for the wrongdoers being killed, in accordance with ancient Roman law, current practice was probably far milder. By the fourth century, the law did not go beyond fines for grave robbery, the present case being an even lighter offence (*Cod. Theod.* 9.17 *De sepulchris uiolatis*). Even so, however, article 9.17.4 (356/7 CE) stipulates that these fines do not replace traditional severity: *quae poena* *priscae seueritati accedit, nihil enim derogatum est illi supplicio quod sepulchra uiolantibus uidetur impositum.* A century later, as Christian notions of the body and the hereafter are gaining ground, law enforcing is strict again, demanding capital punishment for disturbing graves: *Novell.* 23 (447 CE, also incorporated in the *Lex Romana Visigothorum* and arguably valid in Roman Burgundian law) *eorum qui sepulcra violassent capita persequendo*, for slaves as well as plebeians, while the upper classes are to be punished with infamy and clerics are to be removed from office; cf. *Dig.* 47.12.11 (Nehlsen 1978, 119–23). **opertorium** 'cover', 'lid', of the coffin (rare in this sense: *TLL* 9/2.701.27–33). **torsi** 'I had them tortured': the verb (*OLD* 3) suggests not just any beating-up, but the torture inflicted on enslaved people and *coloni* (*Novell.* 23.3 *seruos colonosque ... ad tormenta*) to get the truth out of them. **superstitum curae, mortuorum securitati:** cf. Auson. *Comm. prof.* 26.7–8 *et si qua functis cura uiuentum placet | iuuatque honor superstitum. curae* 'concern' (*OLD* 5). *securitati* 'peace in the grave' is an explicit wish on many tombstones (*OLD* 1d). The polyptoton *curae ... securitati* fittingly concludes the sentence.

3 nostro ... sacerdoti: i.e. Patiens, for whom see 2.10 Addressee. *sacerdoti* 'priest' is one of the terms used to indicate a bishop (van Waarden 2010, 569). **quod** 'as to the fact that' (G–L §525). **nil reseruaui:** not letting the local bishop, under whose jurisdiction this incident clearly falls, have the final say is a breach of protocol. On other occasions, Sidonius will deploy due diplomacy, e.g. having made a preliminary selection of episcopal candidates, 7.5.4 *nullus a me hactenus nominatus ... omnia censurae tuae salua ... seruantur.* **suaeque personae:** for the non-reflexive use of *suus* (= *eius/eorum/earum*) in later Latin, see L–H 175. *personae* 'role', 'position', 'dignity', cf. e.g. 7.4.2 *pontificali ... personae* 'priestly dignity' (van Waarden 2010, 228). The bishop's role is being both resolute and empathetic; cf. e.g. 6.1.3 [to bishop Lupus] *censurae tuae adtremat ... turba collegii* and *tu ... ultimos ... non despicis.* **in commune consului** 'I acted in the interest of both': see 5.16.4n. *in commune*, cf. 7.7.4n. *in commune consului.* **haec ... illa** 'the former ... the latter', indicating that the part with *haec* is the more important (G–L §307 R1). **ex itinere** 'while still underway', cf. e.g. Cic. *Verr.* II 3.154 [*epistula*] *missa ex itinere*, Sidon. 4.24.2 *ad amicum ... ex itinere perrexi* (the alternative 'immediately upon arrival' (e.g. Caes. *Gall.* 3.21.2) does not tally with the context). This temporal marker adds to the pace of the narrative (Hanaghan 2019, 69–72; see §1 *hesterno ... die*). **sanctus** because of his office; see 2.10.2n. *sancti* (also of Patiens). **amplius** (*quam* or + abl.) instead of *plus* (found from Cato *Agr.* 146.1 onward) is a favourite of Sidonius. **more maiorum reos tantae temeritatis iure caesos uideri:** Patiens says as much as: 'You have been very kind. According to ancient law, they would have been killed'. For the age-old sentiment likening this offence to sacrilege, see above §2n. *niger caespes*. The phrase *iure caesus* 'rightfully killed' is legal jargon, starting in the Law of the Twelve Tables as reported by Macr. *Sat.* 1.4.19 *si nox furtum faxit, si im occisit iure caesus esto* 'if he has stolen at night and has been killed, he was rightly killed'; cf. e.g. Liv. 1.26.9, Suet. *Caes.* 76.1. The verb *uideri* 'be deemed' (*OLD* 22) is also part of the formula, e.g. Cic. *De orat.* 2.106, *Cod. Iust.* 9.16.3. For the Roman reliance on violent judicial measures, see Lintott 2023.

4 ne quid ... casibus liceat 'to leave nothing to chance', a rare phrase, cf. *Pan.* 12[IX].9.6 *ut quicquam in te belli casibus liceat;* cf. e.g. Sen. 47.1 *in utrosque licere fortunae*, Plin. 4.8.2 *fortunae ... licet*. **ab exemplo** 'with this warning example in mind' (*OLD* 3a). **resurgat in molem sparsa congeries**: the wording is strikingly over-the-top for restoring a modest earth mound (Colafrancesco 2013, 71–2 already pointed out that *molem* is normally used of sizeable stone structures, e.g. Cic. *Phil.* 14.33, Verg. *Aen.* 6.233, and suggested that *resurgat* may hint at the 'renaissance' of the deceased and his family). All pieces fit together when we realize that the phrase recalls Lucan's lament for Pompey and his paltry burial in Egypt, predicting, however, a rehabilitation: *Phars.* 8.865–9 *proderit hoc olim, quod non mansura futuris | ardua marmoreo <u>surrexit</u> pondere <u>moles</u>. | pulueris exigui <u>sparget</u> non longa uetustas | <u>congeriem</u> bustumque cadet mortisque peribunt | argumenta tuae. ueniet felicior aetas.* Like another Pompey, Apollinaris has fallen an innocent victim to tyranny, but his time will come. Sidonius even sees to it that a more durable monument be immediately erected. For this reminiscence, see van Waarden 2024; see also Introduction above. Lucan is one of Sidonius' most important intertextual anchors; see Intro 4.4; 7.7.2n. *audebant*. **leuigata pagina** 'a smooth page', for the inscription to be incised on the marble slab; cf. Paul. Nol. *Natal.* 13.588–9 Dolveck (*Carm.* 21 Hartel) *pagina quaedam | marmoris*, Sidon. 2.2.7 *nihil illis paginis impressum* (i.e. on the virgin walls of his swimming pool; cf. *pagina* 'letter', 1.9.8n. *paginam*; Colafrancesco 2013, 72–4). The flatness of the stone is in subtle contrast to the elevation of the mound. **uenerabili Gaudentio:** *uenerabili*, in Sidonius' idiom, is usually connected with being a Christian, see e.g. 3.2.3 *religione uenerabilis*. This Gaudentius is generally thought to be the man mentioned in 1.3.2 and the addressee of 1.4, a medium-grade state official, who perhaps reached the rank of *uicarius septem prouinciarum* in late 467 (*PLRE* 2, 495; Mathisen 2020a, 98). The qualification *uenerabilis* could point at a *conuersio*, as often, after a worldly career, in the circle of bishop Patiens together with Sidonius. Loyen 2, 224 n.37 and 250 n. 12 rather ascribes the qualification to rank and seniority, which would establish a date after 467 for the letter. **sane** 'admittedly', 'at any rate', toning down expectations (*OLD* 8).   **quod consequetur:** for the 'pleonastic' future tense found from the 3rd cent. onwards, cf. e.g. Aquila *Rhet.* 30 *quae consequentur*, Macr. *Sat.* 7.12.10 *quod sequetur*.   **nocte proxima** 'last night': creative writing is done at night (cf. 2.10.5n. *candelas*); compressing it into one night only is both an excuse and a reason for hidden pride (see van Waarden 2010, 432 on *duabus uigiliis unius noctis aestiuae*; cf. Stat. *Silv.* 1 praef. *nullum ... biduo longius tractum, quaedam et in singulis diebus effusa* (see 7.18.1n. *celeriter absolui*)).   **non parum** 'not a little', litotes: 'considerably'.

5 tabulae ... indatur: *tabula* 'tablet', set up as a permanent record (*OLD* 5a), e.g. Cic. *Verr.* 2.189 *tabulas in foro ... exscribo, CIL* 2.1131 *tabulam marmoream.* For the legally binding function of *tabulae*, see Meyer 2004, 22–43.   *indatur* 'be applied to', 'be recorded on': a highly unusual verb for creating such records (cf. *Hist. Aug. Comm.* 11.11 *publicis monumentis indi iussit*; more common 2.10.3 *inscripsi*, Plin. 8.6.14 *incisa et insculpta*), it adds to the solemn, official atmosphere.   **ut ... non** supersedes *ne* in later Latin (H–S 535 and 643–4), cf. e.g. 4.13.3, 7.4.4.   **lapidicida** is a Sidonian hapax for *lapicida* 'stone-cutter'. marmore lapidicida is metrically undetermined (–∪∪ ∪∪∪–x).   **ab industria** 'from overzealousness': i.e. from hypercorrection, as opposed to *per incuriam* (the generally accepted translation 'deliberately' would imply a strange degree of malevolence).   **quadratario:** strictly the designer who drew the letters before they were carved, here apparently synonymous with *lapidicida* (Susini 1973, 14; see also Colafrancesco 2013, 75 and *OLD*, L–S s.v.).   **liuidus lector** 'spiteful reader': any artistic product is liable to (malevolent) criticism, see 1.1.4n. *liuidorum latratuum*.   **accedat** 'accrues to', 'is given to' (*OLD* 15c): cf. e.g. Cic. *Fam.* 1.7.9 *aliquantum ... laudis accesserit*, Symm. 5.42 *mihi ... plurimum honoris accedit*; repeatedly in Sidonius, 1.7.1, 4.1.1, 7.1.6n., 7.11(10).2, 7.14.12, 8.3.6n., 8.6.2, 8.14.2. The subjunctive is part of a conditional sentence of comparison (*sic ... quasi* 'with the result ... as if'; G–L §602). The thanks paid to Secundus for doing his uncle a favour will (inevitably and unduly) give the impression as though the former had no personal claim to praise.   **remoto** 'eliminated' has a sinister overtone, cf. e.g. Cic. *Mil.* 34 *Clodio remoto*, Nep. *Dion* 7.1 *aduersario remoto.* Sidonius had retired into political anonymity after the death of Majorian in 461. He might well have become a victim of the instability in Gaul himself. A similar crucial moment came in 468/9 with the trial of Arvandus for high treason (for both see Intro 1 and 3.2). Sidonius now seems to feel confident enough to assert his status as head of the Apollinaris faction.   **solida** 'entire' (*OLD* 8).   **seminis** is slightly unusual for 'family', 'relationship' (cf. Cic. *Leg. agr.* 2.95 *a stirpe generis ac seminis*), but appears several times in Sidonius, e.g. 1.6.2 *senatorii seminis homo*, 4.1.1 *affectus a semine* (a revealing analysis of family ties). Secundus lives up to his name by representing the next generation.

Poem 28: Epitaph

1–5: the dedicator addresses the passer-by
6–12: the deceased and his worldly credits
13–20: the deceased and his conversion to Christianity

The epitaph is written in Phalaecian hendecasyllables; see *Carm.* 27 in letter 2.10 with Introduction, Consolino 2020, 360–1 and Intro 3.6. Compare Sidonius' (presumed) epitaph in the Appendix.

1–5 Serum post patruos patremque 'Belated, now that my uncles and father are no more': that generation had evidently refrained from vaunting Apollinaris' merits. Their position had been a delicate one as, after the failure of Apollinaris and his allies siding with usurpers, they had been allowed to realign Gallic interest with the legitimate emperors Honorius and Valentinian III, with Sidonius' father eventually serving as *praefectus praetorio Galliarum* in 448–9 (below on vv. 6–12; see above Introduction, van Waarden 2020b, 19). The turbulent years around 450 ending with the murder of Valentinian in 455, followed by the coup of Sidonius' father-in-law Avitus and his ill-fated reign in Rome (Kulikowski 2020, 205–7), again postponed rehabilitation. It is now up to the third generation. Sidonius' father has remained anonymous (Mathisen 1981 thinks his name may have been Alcimus; Mathisen 2020a, 134 'Anonymous 8'). As to the uncles, they have long been thought to be identical with Sidonius' correspondents Apollinaris, Thaumastus and Simplicius. Mathisen 2020c, 58–9, however, has convincingly argued that these men belong to Sidonius' own generation (further 2.9.1n. *Apollinarem*). The anonymous uncles will have died and are no longer able to perform their familial duty (Mathisen 2020c, 58). For the concise use of *post* ('after the death of'), see Whitton 2013, 210 on Plin. 2.14.11n. *post silentium*; cf. Plin. 7.18.1 *post te*. For the phrase *patruos patremque*, cf. 7.12.1 *patrem … patruosque*. **haud indignus** possibly implies Sidonius' 468 city prefecture, which put him on a par with his grandfather, as Loyen 2, 250 n.12 points out. Alternatively it marks Sidonius out as a worthy heir because he fulfils his obligations, cf. 7.2.9 *digno herede* (see further Giannotti 2021b, 50–2). **uiator:** see 2.10.4 vv.1–2n. *Quisquis*. **tellurem tereres inaggeratam:** 'you trample the ground not raised to a mound': *tellurem tereres* is a Sidonian collocation; cf. *Carm.* 9.83 *tellurem pede proterens uoraci* (cf. *OLD* 3b); note the sound effects. *inaggeratam* is hapax.

6–12 iacet hic is among the most emblematic formulas in epitaphs. **post praetoria recta Galliarum:** i.e. after holding the office of praetorian prefect (*praetoria* = *praefectura praetorio*, *TLL* 10/2.1073.50–10) of the Gauls. The empire was split in four prefectures, two in the East and two in the West (Italy *cum* Africa and the Gauls) (*ODLA* 1220–1 'Praefectus Praetorio and Praetorian Prefecture'). The Gauls were divided between two *dioeceses*, Galliae in the north and Viennensis or Septem Provinciae in the south (*ODLA* 642–6 'Gaul'). In the fifth century the Gauls fragmented, losing their northern parts and harbouring ever more self-confident Visigothic and Burgundian *foederati* in the south and east. By Apollinaris' time the offices of the prefecture of the Gauls had already been transferred from Trier to Arles. **maerentis patriae sinu receptus:** *patriae sinu* is already in Cic. *Verr.* 5.125 *ex sinu patriae*, *Cael.* 59 *e sinu gremioque patriae*. The motive for *sinu receptus* is piety or friendship, also *Carm.* 24.31 *horum ... sinu receptus*, cf. Symm. 2.79 *amicitiae sinu receptandus*. **consultissimus** 'highly judicious' in administration, cf. e.g. *Eutr.* 4.10.3 [Scipio] *et paratissimus ad dimicandum et consultissimus*, and of the emperor for his administrative measures, *Hist. Aug. Pert.* 7.6, Auson. *Grat.* 2.7. **utilissimusque** 'and extremely effective', of persons (*OLD* 4): cf. e.g. Cic. *Inv.* 1.1.1 *uir et suis et publicis rationibus utilissimus*, cf. 1.9.2n. *utiles*, van Waarden 2010, 479n. *utilitatem*. **ruris militiae forique cultor:** for *ruris cultor* 'farmer', cf. Aug. *C. Iulian* 6.12, Euseb. *Gallic. Hom.* 43, l. 1 (and more usually *rus colere*). For commanders, first of all modestly taking care of their homestead is an ancient republican virtue, embodied, for instance, in Cincinnatus whom Sidonius likes to adduce (*Carm.* 2.527–9 *a rastris ad rostra*, 7.382–7 *pauper arator* and *triumphalis ... purpura*). With a slight shift in the notion of 'cultivating', *cultor* also combines with *militiae forique* 'military and civil service', cf. Ov. *Fast.* 2.508 *patrias artes militiamque colant*; for the thought, cf. Sidonius' own presumed epitaph, v. 4 *rector militiae forique iudex* (Appendix). **exemploque aliis periculoso | liber sub dominantibus tyrannis** 'and as an example for others at his own peril, a free man under high-handed tyrants': amid the internecine mayhem of strongmen (*tyrannis*), from usurpers to (semi-)legitimate heirs to the throne and high officials, in the decade *c.* 405–*c.* 415 (Kulikowski 2020, 199–201), Apollinaris had steered his own exemplary but risky course (alternative interpretation: 'perilous to others', cf. Anderson; *exemplo ... periculoso*, an echo of Mart. 1.27.4 *exemplo nimium periculoso*), as a free man (*liber*) (reminiscent of Sidonius' epitaph v. 5 *mundi inter tumidas quietus undas*). *Libertas* as a traditional Roman value is embraced by Sidonius: Rome as *patriam libertatis* in 1.6.2, free speech in satire at 5.8.2 *eloquii salsa libertas*; cf. 7.18.3n. *numquam me toleraturum animi seruitutem*; cf. *libertas* 'outspokenness' in 7.9.11, 7.13.5. The term *tyrannus* denotes a usurper in later Latin (see *ODLA* 1543 'Usurpers'), but here seems to comprise all political rivals of the time (specified in 5.9.1). For the collocation with *dominantibus*, cf. the pejorative qualification in 2.1.2 *indicit ut dominus, exigit ut tyrannus*.

13–16 frontem ... fonte: the paronomasia underscores the unity of the immersion of baptism and the ensuing rites of anointing in the sign of the cross and laying on of hands (*BEEC* 'Baptism'; Herbert de la Portbarré-Viard 2023, 333); cf. 8.3.3n. *fonte* ... *fronte* in a different context. **primus:** enshrined in law by the emperor Theodosius in a decree of 380 (*Cod. Theod.* 16.1.2) which made Christianity according to the Nicene Creed binding on all subjects, the turn from 'pagan' to Christian religion first took hold among officials (cf. Cameron 2011). **sacris sacrilegis** 'unholy worship', a phrase found first in the 3rd cent. (Comm. *Apol.* 673, Cypr. *Patient.* 4) and repeatedly in Augustine (e.g. *Civ.* 4.2).

17–20 superba 'that is a source of pride' (*OLD* 3). **spe:** Christian hope of salvation, resurrection and afterlife, cf. NT passages such as Vulg. *Act.* 24.15 *spem habens in Deum, Tit.* 3.7 *spem uitae aeternae.* **iungas** must mean 'equal' in this context, a meaning not recorded in any dictionary. **hic ... illic** in the Christian sense of 'on earth' and 'in heaven'; cf. e.g. Hier. 39.3 *quamdiu hic moramur* (cf. Cic. *Cluent.* 171 *illic* [in the underworld] ... *hic* [among the living]). **titulis pares parentes:** in Sidonius' aristocratic world, it is essential for children to equal or better their parents, especially in rank; cf. e.g. 5.16.4n. *sicut* (Sidonius' and Papianilla's generation having climbed from praefectorian to patrician rank, he hopes for their children to reach consular dignity); see 7.9.24 *filios ... quibus comparatus pater inde felicior incipit esse, quia uincitur* and van Waarden 2010, 528n. For *titulis pares*, cf. 3.6.3 *titulorum parilitate.* **meritis** 'merits' in the Christian sense, good deeds done for and rewarded by God; see *ODCC* s.v. 'Merit'. A common accolade in pre-Christian epitaphs (*ob merita, bene meritae* etc.), it is easily adapted to the new religion, e.g. *RICG* 1.106 [Trier c. 431–500] *egregiis caelum <...> meritis non posse negari*; cf. Sidonius' epitaph v. 2 *uiuit sic meritis Apollinaris*. The belief that personal merit helps in the achievement of salvation is especially in evidence in Gallican theology (see Intro 3.4 n. 63).

6 doctrinae 'learning': see Intro 3.3 'Elite Status', 1.9.1n. *doctrina.* **perita** 'qualified', 'knowledgeable': see 1.1.4n. *peritius.* **musicas ... inferias** 'a poetic funeral offering', cf. e.g. *CIL* 12.103 *tibi hasce grates dedicamus musicas* (*OLD musicus* 1). *inferiae* 'offerings to the dead' is largely absent from Christian parlance as is the rite (Hier. 77.12 is a rare exception, a metaphor as here). **heres tertius quartusque:** i.e. the third and fourth generations, Sidonius and Secundus respectively. **dependimus** 'we pay' (tribute, honour); see *TLL* 5/1.569.32–4. **annorum gyro uoluto:** cf. e.g. Sen. 12.6 *annus ... mensis ... angustissimum habet dies gyrum*, Pan. 8[V].3.1 *annorum uoluentium*, Aug. *Civ.* 15.27 *per uolumina tot annorum.* For *gyrus* 'circle', see also 2.9.4n. **magnum Alexandrum parentasse manibus Achillis:** Alexander the Great visited Troy in 334 BCE and honoured Achilles' tomb (Plu. *Alex.* 16, Arr. *An.* 1.12; Latin authors especially report Alexander's quote that he envied Achilles for having his fame spread by Homer, e.g. Cic. *Arch.* 24, Hier. *Hilar.* praef., Symm. 72). *parentasse* 'to have sacrificed' (strictly, to deceased parents). The verb is appropriate for Sidonius (and Caesar below), but Christians abolished the ritual: Tert. *Spect.* 13 *non parentamus*. **Iulium Caesarem Hectori ut suo iusta soluisse:** Luc. 9.964–99 tells how Caesar stumbled upon Hector's overgrown tomb and sacrificed to his Trojan ancestors. This time Sidonius does not create another intertextual link to Lucan, but fashions the story in his own way. *ut suo*: *ut* is causal, 'inasmuch as' (*OLD* 21). As a member of the *gens Iulia*, he traced his pedigree back to the royal family of Troy (e.g. Verg. *Aen.* 1.286–8, Suet. *Iul.* 6). *iusta soluisse* 'to have performed obsequies' (*OLD iustum* 3b 'what is due to the dead', *soluo* 21a) is Sidonius' standard formula, see *Carm.* 26 (2.8.3).15 *tibi iusta persoluta, Ep.* 3.3.8 *mortuis ... iusta soluentes*, 7.17.3n. *sepulto iusta persoluimus*. For the function of such *exempla*, see 2.10.5n. *meminens*. The lack of a clausula in the final words *soluisse didicerimus* (—⏑ ⏑⏑⏑×) is striking.

LETTER 4.19: COMING SOON

Outline

Fulfilment of the promise to write and visit.

Introduction

This is the shortest letter in the collection. It belongs to the subgenre of *salutatio* (see Intro 3.6). It immediately follows another also bearing on a delay (*mora*) in visiting and the role of correspondence – letter 4.18 being circumstantial, targeting the addressee's negligence, whereas 4.19 is short, with Sidonius as the culprit (Giannotti 2021b, 63–4).

Discussion

The letter is a prose epigram. Epigram is akin to letter writing of the sort practised by Sidonius, characterized by what Wolff 2020, 413 calls his 'art of "point"', the great attention given to formal perfection and ending the letters in a pun or another witty or striking formula. Epigrams will outline a situation and provide an unexpected solution, in its shortest form e.g. Mart. 1.110 *Scribere me quereris, Velox, epigrammata longa.* | *ipse nihil scribis: tu breuiora facis,* and 7.77 *Exigis ut nostros donem tibi, Tucca, libellos.* | *non faciam: nam uis uendere, non legere.* The groundwork for their prose counterparts was laid in rhetorical education. Training in argumentation included formulating *sententiae* carrying a special punch when neatly summarizing an argument (Winterbottom 1974, xii). In epistolary practice, short notes, covering the whole range of social activities, from invitations to news items, would be conceived in this way – the medium being at least as important as the message. The prime representative of this type of letter is Symmachus who boasts the shortest average letter length by far among epistolographers (Cavuoto-Denis 2022; statistics van Waarden 2022b). His shortest pieces (Symm. 4.13 and 8.72) have 22 and 19 words respectively, second only to this 14-word note by Sidonius. Pliny is never as concise, yet he too incorporated several 'epigrammatic' letters (e.g. 1.11, 5.2, 7.13, 9.32; see Fögen 2024). For a Greek example, see Libanius *Ep.* 7 Foerster.

Addressee

Florentinus is otherwise unknown. Prosopography: Mathisen 2020a, 96.

Date and place

Probably written when Sidonius was still a layman, travelling freely and visiting his friends.

Literature

Commentary: Amherdt 2001, 418. Studies: van Waarden 2020e, 423–4, Giannotti 2021b, 62–64.

Commentary

moras nostras … accusas: the first person plural for the 'I' and the second person singular for the 'you' stress the addressee's point of view and the sender's acquiescence (see Intro 4.2 '"You" and "I"'): Florentinus is simply right, humility suits Sidonius. For *moras nostras,* cf. 2.9.1n. *moras meas.* **purgabile** '(something which) can be made up for' (*TLL* 10/2.2674.64–72, cf. *impurgabilis TLL* 7/1.725.12–15), rare (prior to

COMMENTARY: 4.19–4.20   161

Sidonius only Plin. *Nat.* 15.93) but not unexpected on account of the productivity of the suffix -*bilis* in later Latin (Wolff 2020, 398). **et uenimus et scribimus** 'I am both coming and writing': continues in a toneddown vein of obedience (plural), as if to say 'I'm coming and writing, as indeed I should'. These plurals in addition provide a good clausula (double cretic). See the analysis in van Waarden 2020e, 423–4. As to *scribimus*, writing a letter is half a conversation and a stand-in for the sender's absence, cf. 1.9.7n. *charta ... quae pro me interim, dum uenio, diebus tibi pauculis sermocinetur* (cf. 2.9.10n. *in procinctu sumus*). Hanaghan 2019, 179 sees a piece of comedy: 'one can envisage Sidonius arriving immediately after his letter carrier or perhaps even delivering the letter himself'.

LETTER 4.20: EXOTIC PAGEANTRY

Outline

To his correspondent, who is a lover of pageantry, Sidonius describes the arrival of the Germanic prince Sigismer with his retinue at the palace of his future father-in-law in Lyon. The scene is as colourful and martial as it is romantic. Seeing what his friend loves, Sidonius sorely misses his presence.

Introduction

This letter is famous for the rare first-hand knowledge it provides about the appearance of Germanic tribes in Gaul. It paints a lively tableau of prince Sigismer, who has come to Lyon to woo a Burgundian princess as his bride, parading to the palace with his retinue, all in colourful attire and heavily armed. Close reading reveals another layer of the author's ironic distance as a senator from such display, but perhaps also of an undercurrent of uneasiness at a potential military conflict.

Discussion

This letter has much to tell about the clothes and weapons of Sigismer and his retinue. Historical and archaeological research has tried to pinpoint the ethnic identity of the company (Frankish?) and its effect on the lookers-on (awe at the barbarian danger?). This ethnic discourse is thoroughly questioned by von Rummel 2007, who argues that the alleged *habitus barbarus*, seen through the eyes of a culturally conservative civil Roman elite who fostered the antiquated ideal of Romans as the *gens togata*, had in reality long become the habitual outfit of the military elite and been adopted by the imperial court. Any interpretation of the sources, he says, will have to negotiate the trade-off between propaganda and reality (pp. 376–400). The discussion continues: see e.g. Liebeschuetz 2015 for a defence of the visual otherness of the barbarian *gentes*. A reconstruction of the episode thus, of necessity, rests on a variety of elements, both historical and ethnological, that are ambiguous in themselves, and remains hypothetical. It runs as follows.

Having been relocated by the Romans to Sapaudia (Geneva), the Burgundians extended their rule south to include Lyon in the 450s (briefly interrupted by the capture of the town by the emperor Majorian in 458), followed by their taking of Vienne in *c.* 470 (see 7.1 Introduction). The Roman powerbroker Flavius Ricimer, *magister militum* 456–72, was connected with the Burgundian royal family through his sister who was married to King Gundioc. Ricimer stripped his opponent Aegidius of his command as *magister militum Galliarum* in 463, which passed to Gundioc and remained with his successors. Aegidius stayed put and carved out a territory of his own north of the Loire with the support of the Salian Franks, who lived in modern-day northern France and Belgium. The Rhineland or Ripuarian Franks to the east, however, opposed him and formed an alliance with the Burgundians, possibly also to counter the Alemans. This alliance may well have been sealed with the marriage (no later than 469) of the Frankish prince Sigismer with a Burgundian princess which forms the background of this letter (Ewig and Nonn 2006, 15; see also Zöllner 1979, 33; Krüger 1983, 2.438; Harries 1994, 223–4; *CAH*² 14, 114–15 and 518–19; Kulikowski 2020, 209).

The letter can also be read as a mild rebuke by Sidonius of his friend Domnitius' liking for military display. Sidonius' correspondence is saturated with the cultural ideal of literary education, the essential senatorial status marker besides birth and wealth. Militarized aristocracies are a feature of the barbarian takeover and, indeed, the post-Roman era (Wickham 2009, 28–31). Conspicuously free of Sidonius' usual anti-barbarian language (for which see Egetenmeyr 2021; for Sidonius' attitude towards the barbarian 'others', see Fascione 2019, Egetenmeyr 2022, Intro 3.3 'Coexistence with "Barbarians"' with n. 38), this epistle shares Domnitius' interest (though with reserve: §3 *quae tibi pulchra sunt*) and, as it were, looks with his eyes. The parade is a feast of colour and brilliance (Schwitter 2015, 164–5), an exemplary *ekphrasis* (Intro 3.5, 2.10 Introduction), while criticism remains implicit and only serves the aim of strengthening the ties between friends with partly diverging interests. All the same, uneasiness perspires at the military potential of the barbarians via an allusion to Martial's line *sumus Martis turba sed et Veneris*, which may recall the bloodily disrupted wedding in *Carm.* 5.213–54 (see commentary below).

Addressee

Domnitius emerges from Sidonius' letters as a leading citizen of Lyon (see Loyen 2, 155 n.70). In 5.17.6, we get a vignette of him at an outing on St Just's day in Lyon, enthusing the dice players while Sidonius leads ball playing. All participants belong to the *ciuium primis* (§4, i.e. the leading group of local senators and the richest councillors, together with the town's bishop, see Wickham 2009, 24–5). Sidonius dubs him his friend and equal, a charming and witty man: *frater meus, homo gratiae summae summi leporis*. Prosopography: Mathisen 2020a, 90.

Date and Place

The Burgundian court in Lyon and Sidonius' relaxed attendance suggest a dramatic date between the stable presence of the Burgundians after 463 and Sidonius' more restricted sojourns during his episcopate beginning 469/70. Scholars point out the phrase §2 *in pace* – a period which ended in 469 with the Frankish participation in the fighting against the Visigoths at Angers to defend the Loire boundary (Zöllner 1979, 39, *CAH*² 14, 116). They date the letter to *c.* 469 (Stevens 1933, 94 n. 7), 469 at the latest (Loyen 2, 155 and 254 n. 20) or *c.* 470 (Mratschek 2020b, 235 n.168).

Literature

Commentary: Amherdt 2001, 421–32. Studies: Kaufmann 1995, 151–62; von Rummel 2007, 171–81; Mratschek 2020b, 235–6. Frankish history and Germanic realia: Girke 1922; Zöllner 1979; Krüger 1983, 2.379–442; Ewig and Nonn 2006; Wood 2014; *RGA*² 2, 361–482 'Bewaffnung'; 9, 373–461 'Franken'; 16, 603–25 'Kleidung'; 30, 372–92 'Textilien'; 31, 110–18 'Tracht und Trachtsmuck'.

Commentary

1 arma et armatum et armatos 'arms and armour and armed men': a playful portrayal of Domnitius endless (preceding *frequenter*) fascination with weaponry. Such longer polysyndetic sequences are rather exceptional (see van Waarden 2010, 575). The noun *armatus* does not occur exclusively in the ablative (as L–S, *TLL* and *OLD* would have it): see Aug. *Divers. quaest.* 73 l.3, Paul. Nol. *Ep.* 9.5. The manuscript tradition is not unequivocal. Although α and basically also δ support this reading, δ also bears traces of *animatos* ('spirited', 'courageous') instead of *armatos*. Savaron, pp. 274–5, compared Plaut. *Bacch.* 941–2 *hoc in equo* [i.e. the Trojan horse] *insunt* *milites* | *armati atque animati probe*. Lütjohann, followed by all later editors, opted for the reduction *arma et armatos* in L (also in T with variant *animatos* in the same hand, and in N with *armatos* corrected to *armatum et armatos* by a later hand). **inspicere iucundum est** contains a paeon IV + spondee clausula (for aphaeresis *iucundumst*, see G–L §719.2), the first of six in this letter, which is more than twice its average frequency (see Intro 4.5). **putamus:** the plural makes the 'I' unemphatical. **conciperes, si ... uidisses** 'you could have felt, had you been present' combines a potential subjunctive of the past in the apodosis with an unreal subjunctive of the past in the protasis. *conciperes* should be restored as the reading of the archetype, as only *LNR* read *conceperas* (changed to *conciperes* by N^1), which is, however, adopted by Lütjohann and all later editors (as for syntax, the ind. plpf. is indeed widely used in the apodosis of this type of unreal conditional, especially in later Latin (H–S 328); cf. e.g. 5.5.1 *dederant*). **Sigismerem:** could be a Frank, judging by the clothing of his retinue (tight-fitting, short sleeves and trouser legs) and their weapons (barbed lances, throwing axes), which correspond to the description of the Franks in *Carm.* 5.237–54; see Loyen 2, 231 n.71, Zöllner 1979, 33; Kaufmann 1995, 158–9; Amherdt 2001, 423; Mratschek 2020b, 235 n. 167; prosopography: Mathisen 2020a, 121. **ritu atque cultu gentilicio** 'according to the practice and fashion of his people': for *ritu atque cultu*, cf. near-synonymous 4.13.1 *habitu cultuque*. *gentilicio* in this sense is rare (*OLD* 2, *TLL* 6/2.1866.23–8). **utpote sponsum seu petitorem:** Sidonius does not know exactly, the case is intriguing to him, cf. e.g. 9.7.1 *scribam tuum siue bybliopolam pretio fors fuat officione demeritum*, where the puzzling questions (was it the scribe or the secretary? was he bribed with money or a favour?) add to the liveliness of the sudden appearance of a new book. The usual interpretation that Sidonius vents his indifference (Kaufmann 1995, 158; Amherdt 2001, 422; cf. Mratschek 2020b, 235) is out of tune with the sympathetic spirit of the letter. **praetorium soceri:** *praetorium* 'palace' (*OLD* 3: e.g. Juv. 10.161 *ad praetoria regis*). *soceri*: his (future) father-in-law plausibly was the Burgundian king Gundioc (436–73/4), for whom see Discussion above. The Burgundians were ruled by a principal king in Lyon and secondary kings in Geneva, Vienne and Valence (RGA^2 4, 246). **illum** in first position is topic of the sentence, its focus first of all the horses. **equus ... immo equi:** graphically zooming out from a close-up to the entire cavalcade. Amherdt 2001, 423 compares the description of Constantius II's *aduuentus* in Rome in Amm. 16.10.7–8 for layout and colourful detail. **phaleris comptus ... radiantibus gemmis onusti:** at parades, the horses' harnesses would be lavishly decorated with metal disks and gems among other ornaments, cf. e.g. Verg. *Aen.* 5.310 *phaleris*, Claud. *IV Hon.* 549–50 *phalerae ... gemmae* (see Toynbee 1973, 171–2). **uel** instead of *et* is frequent in later Latin (H–S 502, *OLS* 2,

679). **inspiciebatur** must be the reading of the archetype (only *LVR* read *conspiciebatur* (also *N*, changed to *inspiciebatur* by *N*[7]), which is preferred by Lütjohann and subsequent editors); for the nuance of 'seeing with one's own eyes', see 1.5.1n. *inspexerint*. **cursoribus suis siue pedisequis pedes et ipse medius:** *cursoribus* 'footmen' (who run ahead of a carriage etc., *OLD* d) and *pedisequis* 'attendants' (see *RGA*² 10, 534 'Gefolgschaft b3') functionally are near-synonymous, but echo *antecedebant* and *subsequebantur*, *pedisequis* being chosen to chime with *pedes*. *siue* is often equivalent to *et* in later Latin (H–S 504). *pedes et ipse*: Sigismer too goes on foot, no doubt out of deference for his father-in-law; cf. Liv. 28.9.15 *etiam si pedes incedat* for going on foot as a sign of modesty compared with riding on horseback or being driven in a chariot; the motif is worked out at length in Plin. *Paneg.* 24 *incedebas pedibus*. *medius* + dat.: see 2.9.9n. **flammeus cocco rutilus auro lacteus serico:** asyndetic triad of the colours of his garments: scarlet red, ruddy gold and silk white. The generalization that Germanic clothes were colourful (Zöllner 1979, 240–1) is not evident from the archaeological remains; these do at least support, however, the use of precious fabrics and costly embroidery (e.g. gold on purple) as markers of status and rank (*RGA*² 31, 113). **tum** 'moreover', *OLD* 9. **coma rubore cute:** the colours of his hair, face and skin match his clothes; for hues of white and red in one's complexion, cf. 1.2.3 *lactea cutis ... rubore suffunditur*. For colour, see Bohîlțea-Mihuț 2024, 397. **concolor:** see *Carm*. 27.10n. *concolor* (in 2.10).

2 regulorum ... sociorumque 'chiefs and attendants', a loosely defined escort of chieftains (see *TLL* 11/2.857.24) and guards, cf. 1.2.4 where the Visigothic king Theoderic is surrounded by *comes armiger* 'nobles in armour' and *turba satellitum* 'a crowd of guards' (tr. Anderson). For the retinue of Germanic princes, see Zöllner 1979, 138; *RGA*² 10, 533–54 'Gefolgschaft': free-born men devoted part of their lives to the personal service and protection of a leader in a mutual pledge of fidelity, cf. Tac. *Germ.* 13 on the Germanic *comitatus*. **forma et in pace terribilis:** *forma* 'appearance' (*OLD* 2). For the opposition in the one-off oxymoron *in pace terribilis*, cf. e.g. 4.6.3 *horumce terrorum sub pacis amoenitate meminisse*, 7.10.1–2 *belli terrore ... libertas pace*, Ennod. *Opusc.* 1 (*Panegyricus dictus Theoderico*) 92 *aut pacem blanda promittit effigies aut bella terribilis*. The military lifestyle of the Germans in war and peace was a commonplace, cf. e.g. Tac. *Germ.* 13.4 *in pace decus, in bello praesidium*. For the implications as to dating this letter, see Date and Place above. **pedes primi** 'fore-feet', 'toes', cf. Ov. *Am.* 3.2.64, Sen. *Tro.* 1081. The retinue's appearance is described from the feet up, contrary to customary rhetorical practice in physiognomical handbooks (e.g. the 4th-cent. *Anonymus de physiognomonia* 14–72), biography and portrayal (e.g. Suet. *Aug.* 79–80 from *capite* to *crure*, *Nero* 51 from *capillo* to *cruribus*, Amm. 25.4.2 [Julian] *ab ipso capite usque unguinum summitates*, and, indeed, Sidonius himself, *Ep.* 1.2.2–3 [Theoderic], 3.13.6–9 [Gnatho]); see Evans 1935, Rohrbacher 2010. **perone** 'a thick boot of raw hide' (*OLD*), cf. e.g. Verg. *Aen.* 7.690, Isid. *Orig.* 19.34.13. **genua … sine tegmine:** probably specific for the occasion, as (at least partial) leg covering was standard (Zöllner 1979, 241). **uestis alta stricta:** the same tight-fitting Frankish garment, with short trousers and sleeves, is described at *Carm.* 5.243–4; cf. e.g. Tac. *Germ.* 17 *ueste … stricta*. At 4.13.1, *uestis adstricta* denotes elegance from a Roman point of view (Amherdt 2001, 329–30). **poplitibus exertis:** Sidonius repeatedly visualizes bare knees (and, implicitly, shorter breeches) as a striking characteristic of the Germans, see e.g. *Carm.* 5.244 *patet … poples*, 7.456 *poplite nudo*; cf. *Ep.* 1.2.3. Originally an un-Roman wardrobe staple (Cic. *Fam.* 9.15.2 *bracatae et transalpinae nationes*, Tac. *Hist.* 2.20.1 *in superbiam trahebant quod …* [the Roman general Caecina] *bracas barbarum tegmen indutus togatos adloqueretur*), long and short trousers had been adopted long ago by the military (as late as 397, Honorius and Arcadius attempted to ban trousers from Rome (*Cod. Theod.* 14.10.2 and 4)); see Girke 1922, 2, 43–45, *BNP* 'Clothing: 4 Rome'. **saga** 'cloaks', worn by barbarians and soldiers (*OLD*); *BNP* 'Sagum'. **gladii**, either single- or double-edged, the latter called *spatha* (Zöllner 1979, 157–60, *BNP* 'Sword', *RGA*² 2, 430–3). **balteis supercurrentibus** 'baldrics running across (their shoulders)': at *Carm.* 5.245, *balteus* refers to a 'waistband'. *supercurrentibus* in this sense is a hapax. **strinxerant** 'pressed against', 'were tightly fitted to': the pluperfect indicates a resulting condition in the past (G–L §241.3). **bullatis … rhenonibus** '(belts from) studded reindeer skins': the equivalent of the *balteus* of *Carm.* 5.245. For *rhenones* (often cloaks) as typical of the Germans, cf. Caes. *Gall.* 6.21.5, Sall. *Hist.* frg. 3.104.

3 lanceis uncatis 'barbed lances': in combination with throwing axes, a recurrent Frankish armament; see Zöllner 1979, 157, von Rummel 2007, 177–9. *uncatis*: rare adjective (in Sidonius, also metaphorically 9.9.15 *syllogismis … uncatis*) for *uncus*. **securibusque missibilibus:** the so-called *francisca* throwing axe is typical of late antique Frankish weaponry (though not limited to the Franks; *RGA*² 9, 470–6 'Franziska') and is frequent among burial gifts; cf. *Carm.* 5.246 *citas … bipennes* (Zöllner 1979, 154–6, von Rummel 2007, 174–7). The adjective *missibilis* is rare, instead of *missilis*; Sidonius affects such forms, cf. e.g. 4.13.4 *plectibilibus*, 9.14.2 *plausibilibus*. **clipeis … adumbrantibus.** Frankish shields were round, with a central metal boss; cf. *Carm.* 5.247–8 *clipeosque rotare | ludus* (Zöllner 1979, 160–1). *adumbrantibus* 'overshadowing' (*OLD* 1, *TLL* 1.885.11–21), again a slightly contrived qualification. **ita censum … ut studium** 'both their wealth and their passion': cf. Manil. 5.369 *studium censusque* 'pleasure and profit' (tr. Goold). **in actione thalamorum** 'in the staging of the wedding': *in actione* + gen. denotes the implementation of something, e.g. Symm. 5.66 *gratiarum actio* 'giving thanks', Sidon. 6.8.1 *mercandi actione* 'by acting as a merchant', Cassiod. *In psalm.* 9 *in actione facinorum* 'in committing crimes'. Anderson p. 139 and Amherdt 2001, 431 follow the suggestion in *TLL* 1.441.9–10 where *actio* is interpreted as 'theatre play', 'drama'. **non ... minor Martis pompa quam Veneris:** after Mart. 5.7.6 [we Romans] *sumus Martis turba sed et Veneris*. Sidonius first applied it in the episode of the Roman raid on the Frankish wedding at Vicus Helena in *Carm.* 5.213–54, which culminates in the frenzy of Mars and the War Goddess crushing the bridal torches (*thalami ... faces*), a clash worse than in examples from myth (230–3): *non sic ... Venerem Martemque cient*. The allusive comparison of Sigismer's pageant with the Vicus Helena episode makes it clear how close affection and aggression are and how easily a feast can turn into carnage. Not for nothing does Sidonius qualify the trappings of Sigismer's retinue as *et in pace terribilis* (the lookers-on will have shared this feeling of unease, Harries 1996, 36). Read with Vicus Helena in mind, this letter is anything but innocent. *pompa* 'splendour', 'pageant', see 2.10.6n. *pompa*. **sed quid haec pluribus?:** this rhetorical question is one of the epistolary devices to suggest a conversation; see Intro 3.6. Attention turns back towards the addressee. **ipsam ... desideraui:** closing the letter with a complex punch line, Sidonius sacrifices clarity to wit. There are broadly two ways of looking at this, in which *desiderii tui* is either '(my) longing for you' (from nom. *desiderium tui*, objective genitive) or 'your longing (for the spectacle)' (nom. *desiderium tuum*); see G–L §364). In the former interpretation, the meaning boils down to 'at that moment I wanted not to feel the want of you' (Anderson p. 139, Köhler 2014, 133). In the latter, we get something like 'at that moment I missed the impatience of your desire' (Dalton; Loyen 2, 156; Amherdt 2001, 432; Mascoli 2021, 180). Either way, the sentence rounds off with a personal compliment. The clausula is a double trochee, one of Sidonius' commonest clausulae (van Waarden and Kelly 2020, 474, Intro 4.5), here preceded by another double trochee, which is remarkable (cf. e.g. Cic. *De orat.* 1.248 *scientiam desiderasse*).

LETTER 5.5: A ROMAN SPEAKING BURGUNDIAN

Outline

Descended from a consul who was also an excellent poet, the addressee Syagrius was a brilliant student of rhetoric, Sidonius remembers. Strangely enough, he is now an interpreter and adviser at the Burgundian court, having mastered Burgundian to the point of shaming native speakers. Sidonius warns him not to neglect reading and practising Latin.

Introduction

Book 5 is a middle book, not only for its position in the collection, but also for the diversity of its themes (the bishopric remaining in the background, to come all the more forcefully into evidence in the next books) and for its muted, 'autumnal' mood (see Marolla 2023, 8–17). This letter belongs to the subgenre of literary admonition (for epistolary types, see Intro 3.6). Another in this genre follows soon, letter 5.8.

Discussion

The tone is slightly ironical: admiring, on the one hand, on account of Syagrius' impeccable pedigree and linguistic brilliance; concerned, on the other, for the future of Latin. Denecker 2015, 410–18 points out the three strains of Sidonius' linguistic thinking: (1) upholding the purity of Latin requires a constant effort (cf. the same reasoning in 2.10.1n. as to the *meram linguae Latiaris proprietatem*), (2) Germanic is a backward language lacking euphony and the ability to express – indeed develop – full-fledged thoughts, and (3) undue contact with Germanic affects one's command of Latin. The reflex is the same as Ovid's in his *Tristia* and *Epistulae ex Ponto* about learning Gothic and losing one's Latin (see Williams 2002, 238–9; see commentary §1 below). Sidonius takes this one further in 4.17.1–2, with the pessimistic belief that Roman culture and the spendour of Latin speech (*sermonis pompa Romani*) are continually deteriorating but for the tough resistance of the happy few; the gap is absolute: 'the educated are as superior to the boors (*rusticis*) as men are to beasts'. Further reading: Mathisen 1988; Banniard 1992; Wolff 2020, 395–6; Hindermann 2022b, 297–9. The copious contemporary output of grammarians proves the broader social embedding of this elitist stance (Kaster 1988, Zetzel 2018, esp. 159–200). What counts in the first place are the very basics of language: thus, in Sidonius' own circle, Agroecius (plausibly identified with the addressee of 7.5; Zetzel 2018, 279) wrote an *Ars de orthographia* and Consentius the Elder (the father of Consentius, the dedicatee of *Carm.* 23; Zetzel 2018, 291) an *Ars de barbarismis et metaplasmis* among other things.

According to Sidonius, Syagrius acts as an interpreter, an arbitrator and an adviser at the Burgundian court. He may have been involved in the early stages of the development of Burgundian law (he is grandiosely dubbed *nouus Burgundionum Solon* in §3; for his role, Liebs 1998, 271–2; Wood 2016, 5; Wood 2017; for the intricate development of Burgundian sovereignty, Frye 1990). The Burgundian rulers, King Gundioc, d. 473, and his brother Chilperic, though Roman officials as well (see 4.20 Discussion, Marolla 2023, 194–9), knew no Latin (only Gundioc's son Gundobad did), so they would have needed regular advice on Roman law and interpreter services. This resulted, decades later, in the complementary *Lex Burgundionum* (or *Liber constitutionum*) and *Lex Romana Burgundionum* (see *ODLA* 903 s.v., *RGA*² 18, 315–7 and 322–3; cf. *BNP* 'Volksrecht' IV for the parallel *Lex Romana Visigothorum*; see Intro 3.3 n.37), which were probably compiled in the early sixth century, respectively a collection of Burgundian royal edicts (published under King Sigismund in 516–17 or even earlier, under his predecessor Gundobad, reigned *c.* 474–516) and a collection of abbreviated and modified Roman laws. While Sidonius professes diffidence at Syagrius' undertaking, 'there may even have been a generational element in the alertness of the younger men to the fact that the end of the old regime was nigh' (Heather 2005, 420; cf. John 2026, 230). Porena 2023 observes that, for all the influence ascribed to Syagrius, his (and Sidonius') horizon is a shrunken Gallic one if compared to the scale on which his forefather operated (see below; cf. Intro 3.1).

There is an attractive hypothesis that Sidonius may have played the same role of legal adviser as Syagrius, either at the Burgundian (Wood 2016, 5; Wood 2017, 12–14) or the Visigothic (van Waarden in the epitaph section of sidonapol.org; cf. Prévot 1993, 228) court, on account of his epitaph, line 7 *leges barbarico dedit furori* (van Waarden 2020b, 14–15; see Appendix); discussion in Marolla 2023, 146–8. A similar role is attested of Leo of Narbonne, counsellor of Euric at the court of Toulouse (letters 4.22, 8.3; see 8.3 Addressee and 8.3.3 [on Leo's advice, Euric] *frenat arma sub legibus*).

Addressee

Syagrius is also the recipient of letter 8.8, another letter of admonition, this time political, in which Sidonius urges him to pursue consular ambitions instead of farming his estate. He was a great-grandson of the consul of 382, Flavius Afranius Syagrius, who was a poet as well (§1 *e semine poetae*) and was buried in Lyon (5.17.4) (*PLRE* 1, 862–3 'Syagrius 2'; for the prosopographical conundrum of the very similar career of 'Syagrius 3', see van Waarden 2016, 63). He was a distant relative of Sidonius via Sidonius' wife Papianilla, who was a niece of Tonantius Ferreolus' wife, also called Papianilla. This Tonantius Ferreolus, a pivotal figure in Gallic politics in the 450s/460s, was a grandson of Flavius Afranius Syagrius, he and his family being intimate friends of Sidonius (*Carm.* 24.34–43, *Ep.* 7.12.1). Sidonius was probably Syagrius' senior and had first-hand knowledge of his grammatical education (§2 *pueritiam tuam ... memini*, 8.8.1 *Gallicanae flos iuuentutis*), with a wink stressing his humour (§4 *facetissime*) and refinement (*elegantissimus*). Prosopography: Mathisen 2020a, 122; John 2026, 230.

Date and Place

Pinpointing the letter's date is elusive. Arguing that '*Ep.* 5.5 ... usually is dated to 469 or 470, for no strong reason', Mathisen 2013, 244 is inclined to opt for a later date, perhaps 474, at the same time as 5.6, 5.7 and 5.8, all about Burgundian matters. Marolla 2023, 152–3, however, prefers an earlier date, prior to the bishopric, on account of what she feels as the letter's anti-Burgundian tenor, as Sidonius' attitude towards the Burgundians changed later on. If we can take the situation literally (rather than as an artful representation of a political dilemma), Syagrius would have been in Lyon and Sidonius elsewhere, for instance in the Auvergne.

Literature

Commentary: Marolla 2023, 142–67. Studies: Frauenhuber 2007; Egetenmeyr 2022, 347–51. Background (archaeology and history): *ODLA* 273 'Burgundians and Burgundian kingdom', *RGA*² 4, 224–71 'Burgunden', Krüger 1983, 2.361–79 'Burgunden'.

Commentary

1 Cum sis consulis pronepos: see Addressee. Ancestry is an essential asset of the nobility (cf. e.g. 1.3.1, 2.4.1, 7.12.1–2 etc.) and the first element of a person's *laudatio* in rhetorical theory (van Waarden 2010, 439–42). For the phrasing at the start of a letter, cf. Plin. 4.19.1 *Cum sis pietatis exemplum*, 8.14.1 *Cum sis peritissimus et priuati iuris et publici* (cf. Mart. 6.64.1, 6.77.1, 9.37.1). **idque per uirilem successionem:** the succession in the male line makes the case for *noblesse oblige* even stronger. Even the great Tonantius Ferreolus (see Addressee) was 'only' a descendant in the female line (1.7.4 *Afranii Syagrii consulis e filia nepos*). *idque* 'and what is more': *OLD -que* 11b. **ad causam subiciendam** 'to the case which I will present to you': *OLD subicio* 4. The gerundive serves as a passive future participle (see 1.9.6n. *admittendo*). **statuas dederant litterae:** as, for instance, Sidonius got in the Forum of Trajan for his Panegyric of Anthemius (Intro 1).

Indicative pluperfect in the apodosis of an unreal conditional vividly imagines the feasibility of the result; see 4.20.1n. *conciperes.* **trabeae:** the most distinguished form of the *toga* is the *trabea*, the plain one made of silk and dyed purple, worn by *consulares*, and the elaborate one, called *trabea triumphalis* or *toga picta*, worn by the emperor and consuls. It was made of purple cloth and heavily embroidered with gold thread and precious stones (see Delbrueck 1929, 130–3 with depictions on consular diptychs, pp. 470–98; *ODLA* 1506 'Toga picta'). **quod ... testantur:** his poetry is still read and appreciated. **culta uersibus uerba** 'words beautified by verse', i.e. couched in elegant verse, cf. e.g. Tac. *Dial.* 23.6 *cultum uerborum* 'elegance of diction'. **ne parum quidem** 'not even a little bit': for *parum* 'not particularly', 'not very', 'little', see L–S II (cf. 7.7.4n., 7.18.2n.). **quippe** 'especially': *quippe* develops from an explanatory discourse marker ('as is to be expected') to a connective one, establishing a close connection with what precedes (Schrickx 2011, 141). **immane narratu:** see 1.1.2n. *immane dictu.* **sermonis ... Germanici** has pejorative overtones, cf. *Carm.* 12.4 *Germanica uerba sustinentem*, 8.3.2n. *Getides anus* (cf. Ov. *Pont.* 4.13.19 *a, pudet, et Getico scripsi sermone libellum*); see Denecker 2017, 255–6, Intro 3.3 'Coexistence with "Barbarians"' and Discussion above. Further to Ovid and the Germanic language, see *Pont.* 3.2.40 (learning Gothic), *Trist.* 3.14.43–8 (unlearning and compromising one's Latin), 4.2.21–2 (even Homer would have been affected), 5.2b.23–4 (Latin and Greek sidelined), 5.12.57–8 (unlearning Latin while learning Gothic). **rapuisse** 'have mastered': *rapio* in the sense of 'to absorb', 'grasp ' with the senses or the mind, usually quickly or deeply (*TLL* 11/2.108.51–68, *OLD* 13d). The complexity of the first paragraph (one sentence!) draws out the eminent antecedents of the addressee, only to double down on his stupefying achievement in the brief concluding main clause.

2 atqui 'and yet' introduces the objection that Roman liberal education and interest in Germanic languages are mutually exclusive. The ideal of perfection at *Latine loqui* (e.g. Cic. *Brut.* 252, *Orat.* 79, Sidon. 2.10.1n. *meram linguae Latiaris proprietatem*, 3.14.2 *proprietas linguae Latinae*, 4.17.2 *sermonis pompa Romani*) is not about purity in any language. Against the background of the Stoic equation of 'speaking correctly' (εὖ λέγειν) with 'speaking (and thinking) the truth' (ἀληθῆ λέγειν) (Fögen 1998, 208–9), only Latin (for past generations also Greek) was considered the language adequate to express the full breadth of human thought. 'Barbarian' languages just were not good enough (Denecker 2015, 413–5). To attain this ideal, attention to even the minutest details of grammar and style was essential (Quint. *Inst.* 1.4–1.8, Fögen 1998, 202–4; see Discussion above). In the course of the fifth century, education in Gaul increasingly came to serve this limited elitist aim; see John 2026, 132–60.

scholis liberalibus 'liberal education', including a first stage with the grammarian studying grammar and poetry (Quint. 1.4.2 *recte loquendi scientiam et poetarum enarrationem*), with a selection of other subjects like music and geometry (Quint. 1.10), and a second one with the rhetor, reading orators and historians (Quint. 2.5) and practising public speaking (*progymnasmata, declamationes*). Cf. e.g. Plin. 1.10.1 *liberalibus studiis*, including philosophy among other subjects. **memini:** Sidonius remembers his study with the grammarian in Lyon and was informed (*habeo compertum*) about his rhetorical training (cf. Loyen 2, 235 n.8). **euphoniam gentis alienae:** obviously ironically as foreign languages by definition sound ugly (Denecker 2015, 416, cf. pp. 404–6). *euphonia* (*TLL* 5/2.1074.31–1075.41) is a technical term in grammatical treatises. **mihi** 'before my eyes' (Anderson): so-called ethical dative, indicating special interest in the action (G–L §351). **post ferulas lectionis Maronianae:** see 2.10.1n. *subduximus ferulae manum.* Being beaten by the grammarian was common practice, though disapproved of by Quintilian as ineffective and harmful (*Inst.* 1.3.14–17). Virgil (whose cognomen was Maro) was the principal subject of the *poetarum enarratio*. **desudatam uaricosi Arpinatis opulentiam loquacitatemque:** Cicero's speeches were a main concern of the rhetor's teaching. *desudatam* 'sweated over': cf. e.g. Claud. *Theod.* 11–12 *desudatis ... iudiciis*, Euseb. Gallic. *Hom.* 35.50 *laboribus desudatis*. *uaricosi* 'suffering from varicose veins': his ailment is also mentioned by Quint. *Inst.* 11.3.142, Dio Cassius 46.18.2, Macr. *Sat.* 2.3.5 (the disease is indeed an obvious topic of satire; see *OLD* s.v.). Together with *ferulas*, this qualification contributes to the somewhat boisterous tone of these school memories. Various explanations range from an occupational disease from always standing (Dalton, Anderson) and a malicious hint at impotence (at least in Macrobius' account; see Kaster in the Loeb edition, vol. 1, p. 339 n.32) to an ambiguity implicitly targeting his verbose style (Condorelli 2001, 105 n. 14). *Arpinatis:* Cicero was born in Arpinum (modern Arpino/Frosinone in S-E Lazio); cf. 5.13.3, also combined with Virgil: *nec oratorum princeps Marcus Arpinas nec poetarum Publius Mantuanus*. For *opulentia* (syn. *copia*), cf. Apul. *Apol.* 95 *neque ... requirat ... opulentiam Cicero*, Symm. 1.32.3 *opulentiam Tullianam*. *loquacitatem* 'long-windedness', often negative (van Waarden 2010, 192), but in this context student exaggeration (cf. *TLL* 7/1.1652.36 'in neutram vel malam partem' and 1653.36 'in bonam partem'). This longwinded phrase itself illustrates redundance. Already in his own day, Cicero's exuberant diction was targeted by the so-called Atticists who promoted sobriety in expression (Leeman 1963, 136–67); for the late antique perspective, see Macr. *Sat.* 5.1. Cf. Sidonius' stylistic assessments of Symmachus and Pliny in 1.1.1n. *rotunditatem* and *disciplinam maturitatemque*. **quasi de Harilao**

COMMENTARY: 5.5:2-3   173

uetere nouus Fago prorumpas 'initially a Charilaüs, so to say, you now suddenly turn into a Fago': quite unexpectedly, fed with a copious diet of the best of Roman education, you have now become an indiscriminate linguistic glutton; cf. the inverse imitation in Ruric. 1.3.1 *rusticitatis oblitus, quasi ex Arione in Orpheum repente mutatus*, about another such illogical change. Charilaüs was a friend of the archaic Greek poet Archilochus, who tells him 'a funny story ... you'll be delighted to hear it' (cf. §3 *risui*, §4 *facetissime* and *rideas*) about the homonymous gourmand, perhaps with a wink to the addressee himself (Archil. fr. 107D=168W; see Treu 1959, 96; as a motto, these lines inspired Catull. 56.1–4 (Courtney 1989, 160–2); it is plausible that Sidonius had access to grammatical or metrical repertories featuring examples taken from the Greek lyrical tradition, cf. Gualandri 2020, 285 n. 35). *Fago/p(h)ago* 'glutton' is found in Varro *Ling*. 7.61 as the title character of a (now lost) comedy by Plautus; further occurrences include Varro *Men.* 529 (cited in Non. p. 48.12 M.) and *Hist. Aug. Aurelian.* 50.4 (either a noun or a proper name). The passage under consideration is notorious and, in fact, not solved with certainty to date. The MSS read: (h)ilario α *PLeipMFVRT²N²*: (h)arilao *LR¹TN* | flacco α *LeipVT²*: falc(h)o *PMFRN*: fac(c)(h)o *LR*. The solution advocated here was devised by Wilhelm Heraeus (in Hofmann 1937, 107 n.1), but not noticed before except in *TLL* 6/3.2533.43–47 s.v. *harilaus*. Much ingenuity instead has been spent on *hilario/harilao* (thought to be either an eagle or an eyrie) in combination with *falco*, which almost everybody takes for granted (see Marolla 2023, 161–3). *Falco* as a bird species, however, is almost completely absent from (late) Latin (*TLL* 6/1.175.81–176.14 s.v. 2. *falco*) and scarcely qualifies for any telling comparison. As to *uetere nouus*, the opposition is a staple (indeed, almost an automatism) with Sidonius (see van Waarden 2010, 103, 279, 531). The attribute 'new' is not necessarily positive and often balanced, or legitimized, by recurring to what is 'old' and trusted, cf. 1.5.5n. *ueterem ... novumque*, 7.1.3n. *ad noua ... ueterum.*

3 risui: see §2n. *quasi de Harilao*. **barbarus barbarismum:** the ironic paradox is in full exposure at the end of the sentence – a barbarian afraid of making a mistake in his own language, which is in fact 'barbaristic' by definition. The opposite should be the case for barbarians, as illustrated by Arbogast, the count of Trier, of Frankish descent, who has remarkably attained the level of a native speaker of Latin: 4.17.1 *nescius barbarismorum*, though conversant with barbarians (*barbarorum familiaris*). *barbarismus* is impropriety in Greek/Latin, in speech or pronunciation (see *OLD*, cf. Quint. *Inst.* 1.5.7–10, hence also barbarian loanwords; see Condorelli 2001), repeatedly thematized by Sidonius as a danger to high-quality Latin; see 2.10.1n. *barbarismorum robigine* (and preceding *meram linguae*

Latiaris proprietatem). Cf., among Sidonius' friends, Claud. Mam. *Ep.* 2, lamenting the deplorable level of Latin speakers ruining their grammar, as if it were a barbarian one, with barbarisms (*barbaram barbarismi*). **curua ... senectus:** elders played a distinct, if not formalized, role within the Germanic nobility and at the royal courts. Members of the leading body of *principes/proceres* of the tribes at the time of Caesar (*Gall.* 4.11 *principes ac senatus*, 4.13 *principibus maioribusque natu*), they continued as advisers to the emergent kings well into the Middle Ages (*RGA*² 1, 63 'Adel 5a'); cf. for the Visigothic Kingdom in the 7th cent., *Lex Visig.* 3.1.5 *ex palatii nostri primatibus uel senioribus*, *Conc. Tolet.* 12 *a uenerandis patribus et clarissimis palatii nostri senioribu*s (*MGH LL nat. Germ.* 1, 127.3 and 476.39 respectively). A similar participation in legislation by the kingdom's most venerable men pervades the *Lex Burgundionum*: 1.1 *coram positis obtimatibus nostris*, 1.2 *habito consilio comitum et procerum nostrorum*, etc. (*MGH LL nat. Germ.* 2.1, 29.11 and 30.29; see Wood 2016, 8). The collocation *curua senecta* is first found in Ov. *Ars* 2.670 and Tib. 3.5.16, then in late antiquity. **arbitrum ... disceptatoremque:** the same (synonymous: *TLL* 5/1.1293.37–41) combination as in Cic. *Rep.* 5.3, Apul. *Flor.* 22, Amm. 14.11.26, Ambr. *Exc. Sat.* 1.58. **nouus** 'another', the embodiment of a predecessor (*OLD* 8d). **Solon:** the archetypical Athenian legislator, one of the Seven Sages, b. *c.* 640 BCE (*BNP* 'Solon'). **Amphion:** the mythical lyre player who, with his music, enchanted stones to build up into the wall of Thebes (*BNP* 'Amphion'). He here probably represents the development of the Burgundian polity, both as an organizational and as a cultural undertaking. **sed trichordibus** is open to interpretation. Lyres typically had seven strings (Varro *Ling.* 10.46 *e septem chordis citharae*), while virtuosos added more (*BNP* 'Musical instruments. V. Greece. 1. Lyres'). As little as three strings makes for a pretty simple instrument (as stated in Ps.-Plut. *Mus.* 18.2), which, at first sight, would belittle the extent of Syagrius' contribution: 'though only three-stringed' (*OLD sed* 7). This is the usual interpretation (see Marolla 2023, 164–5). However, the three- or four-stringed lyre is arguably the *phorminx* of epic singers in the eighth century BCE (West 1992, 52–3), which turns the phrase into a compliment (whether tongue-in-cheek or not): 'and a three-stringed one too', epic, proven and in the grand style (*OLD sed* 3). The adj. *trichordis* occurs here and Cassiod. *Anim.* 5.5 *harmoniam trichordem* 'triad'. Aug. *Serm.* 9 (*SL* 41, 120) compares the Ten Commandments to a ten-stringed lute (*decachordum*), composed of seven plus three (*trichordum*) strings. **temperandis** 'stringing' or 'tuning', cf. Ov. *Met.* 10.108 *citharam neruis ... temperat* (L–S IA2). **amaris ... audiris:** a fourfold asyndetic sequence of two verbs each, with a studied alternation of voices: pass./pass., pass./act., pass./pass., act./pass. It is the longest Sidonius provides (see van

Waarden 2010, 571–4), again aiming to poke fun at Syagrius' pride in his success. Cf. 6.12.9 *amaris laudaris, desideraris excoleris*. Geisler pointed out parallels in Pliny's correspondence: 2.9.6 *diligeris coleris frequentaris*, 6.34.1 *amaris suspiceris ornaris*. **decernis** 'you give your opinion' (cf. *OLD* 6); see 7.18.3n., 9.16.1n. **rigidi ... indolatilesque** 'primitive and uncultivated': *rigidi OLD* 4. *indolatiles* (L–S 'that cannot be fashioned') is a hapax from *dolare* 'to chip', 'shape'. **amplectuntur in te** 'they welcome, when dealing with you': *OLD* s.v. *amplector* 6; s.v. *in* 42. **sermonem patrium, cor Latinum:** there is hope that, via their own language, the Burgundians may also absorb Syagrius' Roman culture. For the phrase *cor Latinum* and its civilizing implications, cf. Paul. Nol. *Ad Nicetam* 261–4 Dolveck (*Carm.* 17 Hartel) *orbis in muta regione per te | barbari discunt resonare Christum | corde Romano placidamque casti | uiuere pacem*; cf. Ennius' *tria corda* (Oscan, Greek and Latin) in Gell. 17.17.1.

4 uir facetissime 'most humorous of men': see §2n. *quasi de Harilao*. **nihilo segnius** 'no more slowly', i.e. 'all the more eagerly': see *OLD nihilum* 4. Also 3.1.3, 5.8.3, 8.7.3; first instances Cic. *Mil.* 82 and Sall. *Iug.* 75.10. **uacabit** 'there will be a moment of relaxation' (*OLD* 6; cf. e.g. 8.6.18, Plin. 1.10.11). **temperamentum** 'equilibrium': see *OLD* 4, 7.18.1n. *temperamenti*. **ut ... rideas** forms two symmetrically shaped clauses, opposed in meaning: Syagrius should keep his Latin impeccable not to be laughed at by his equals and, at the same time, hone his Germanic in order to have a good laugh outdoing the natives. For the play on a passive and an active ending, cf. e.g. 8.12.7 *ut aut pascaris aut pascas*. For symmetry and parallelism, see Wolff 2020, 407–12, Intro 4.5. The letter ends on a double cretic *-atur ut rideas*, the third clausula in frequency.

LETTER 5.16: EXCELLENT NEWS FOR THE FAMILY

Outline

Sidonius informs his wife Papianilla that her brother Ecdicius has been awarded the title of patricius, *which further elevates the status of the family and provides moral support in the current time of war. Meanwhile, their daughter Roscia is in good health in the care of her grandmother, and sends greetings.*

Introduction

In Book 5, Sidonius touches upon different aspects of his life (see 5.5 Introduction). Letter 16 represents the family man, intent on the family's outward interest as well as on its private well-being.

Discussion

This is the only letter in Sidonius' correspondence addressed to a woman. Directed at his wife, it adheres to the pattern that female addressees in senatorial letter collections are typically related to the author and form a minority, e.g. Cicero's wife Terentia, daughter Tullia, mother and sister in *Ad familiares* Book 14, Pliny's wife Calpurnia (6.4, 6.7, 7.5), her aunt (4.19, 8.11), his mother-in-law (1.4) and three more female addressees (as against about 100 male; see Gibson and Morello 2012, 106 n. 10 and 141 n. 23), and Symmachus' anonymous daughter and son-in-law Nicomachus Flavianus who received the letters in Book 6 as a couple and are addressed as *Nicomachis filiis* throughout.

The political backdrop of the letter is the last year of Roman rule in Gaul. In the autumn of 474, the new emperor, Julius Nepos, decides to have done with the desperate situation in southern Gaul, now almost completely dominated by the Visigoths. Parallel to sending reinforcements and recapturing Arles, he sends one of his top diplomats, Licinianus, to pave the way for negotiations with Euric. Sidonius is forced into a balancing act. Whereas he himself has increasingly sought the support of the Burgundians, his family in Provence leans towards the emperor, allegedly supporting the so-called revolt of Vaison against the Burgundians (letters 5.6 and 5.7). Letter 5.16 is there to ease the family dispute by hailing the good news of Ecdicius' promotion, while glossing over the potentially bad news that critical negotiations are imminent (see Intro 3.2, Delaplace 2015, 253, Kulikowski 2020, 212).

At the time, Sidonius is travelling, visiting Vienne (5.6) and Lyon (5.16) and no doubt mediating in the family rift, possibly rallying further Burgundian support for Clermont and arguably meeting Licinianus or his aides to have the latest news from the diplomatic front – and receiving the imperial patent of the patriciate for his brother-in-law. While their daughter Roscia stays with her grandmother in Lyon, Papianilla has remained in Clermont/Aydat after another Visigothic offensive (the final one, as history will prove), the troops preparing to go into winter quarters. Sidonius returns before winter (3.7.4; Stevens 1933, 200).

Addressee

Papianilla was a member of the distinguished Auvergnat family of the Aviti, her father, Eparchius Avitus, being prefect of the Gauls in 439 and emperor 455–6, all the while having excellent contacts with the Visigoths (Harries 1994, 54–81. Mathisen 2020a, 84–5). She was a sister of Agricola (the addressee of 2.12, see introduction there and 2.12.2n. *tua soror*) and

Ecdicius (§1). In the early 450s, she married Sidonius from the related Apollinares family (Harries 1994, 31–3). They got four children, among them Severiana (2.12.2n. *Seueriana*) and Roscia (§5). For the family, see further Intro 1. Prosopography: Mathisen 2020a, 111.

Papianilla's dowry (or inheritance: Intro 1 n. 6) comprised the estate of Avitacum in the Auvergne where the couple settled. For her to have got it instead of her brothers may have been controversial (Stevens 1933, 20 n. 2, Harries 1994, 187). The estate was particularly dear to Sidonius 'because it is my wife's' (2.2.3 *quia uxorium*). Legally, any dowry remained the property of the wife and, although the husband had the right to use it, provided her with some degree of independence and made possible the creation of wealth in the female line (Arjava 1996, 143–54; Harper 2012, 672). It is conceivable that Papianilla kept running the estate after Sidonius became bishop and they perhaps made some marital arrangement of living apart together in accordance with the nascent requirement for clerics to practise sexual abstinence (Mascoli 2010, 41; on celibacy, see *ODCC*³ 'Celibacy of the Clergy', for Gaul in particular Barcellona 2012). Another indication of her agency concerning property is the story of her spat with Sidonius, who was in the habit of making gifts of their silver tableware to the poor. He then restored everything to the house, giving the equivalent value to the poor instead (Greg. Tur. *Hist*. 2.22).

Studies on women in Sidonius include Bonjour 1988; MacDonald 2000; Santelia 2008; Mascoli 2000; Mascoli 2010, 35–45; Mascoli 2014; Mathisen 2020c, 44–5. See also Intro 3.3 'Women'.

Date and Place

The letter is securely datable to the autumn of 474 (Loyen 2, 256 says October or November) after the accession of Nepos in July, as the Visigothic troops were about to retire to their winter quarters, lifting the blockade of Clermont, and Licinianus' negotiations with Euric in the winter of 474/5 were set to begin. Sidonius must have felt that he could absent himself for a time, and travelled to Lyon. See Stevens 1933, 155 and 198–201; Harries 1994, 231–2; Mathisen 2013, 222; Delaplace 2015, 253–4. It was probably written in Lyon, where Roscia stayed with her grandmother and aunts.

Literature

Commentary: Marolla forthcoming. Study: Mascoli 2010, 39–41.

Commentary

1 Rauenna ueniens: coming from the imperial court which was established there (see 2.2.5n. *Rauennam*). The name heralds official business. For opening sentences, see van Waarden 2010, 46–8. For geographical locations to open a letter, cf. e.g. 7.7.1 *Biturigas ... adueni.* Out of ten instances, four occur in Book 5: 5.13.1, 5.14.1, 5.16.1, 5.18.1 (further 1.2.1, 7.15.1, 8.9.1, 8.12.1, 9.7.1). Pliny features a comparable number of cases, though not with the name as the first word. **quaestor Licinianus** was sent by Julius Nepos, emperor from July 474 to August 475, to Gaul in order to negotiate with Euric concerning the Auvergne. In 3.7.2–4, from the autumn of 474, Sidonius actually had high hopes that he might relieve the beleaguered Arvernians. Prosopography: Mathisen 2020a, 104. The *quaestor sacri palatii*, in full, was a legally trained high official at court, charged with the task of drafting imperial constitutions (Jones 1964, 104, *ODLA* 1257–8). **Alpe transmissa:** Sidonius crossed the Alps in the opposite direction, see 1.5.2n. *per domicilia* and Map 3. The rare phrase could hark back to Prud. *C. Symm.* 1.467 *transmissis Alpibus*, where Constantine crosses the Alps to liberate Italy. **gerulum codicillorum:** for *gerulum*, see 3.9.2n. *gerulus*. *codicillorum* (pl.): an imperial diploma conferring a high office or title (*ODLA* 363, cf. *OLD* 3a). **in aduentu** repeats *aduentus*, stressing the official character, first of the arrival of the *quaestor*, then of the diploma (cf. *OLD* 3). **fratri etiam tuo Ecdicio:** *etiam*, to Ecdicius as well, for Sidonius himself was already a *patricius*, an honour conferred on him by the emperor Anthemius in 468 together with the function of prefect of Rome (Intro 1). Ecdicius acted as a warlord in defence of the Auvergne. Prosopography: Mathisen 2020a, 91, *PLRE* 2, 383–5 'Ecdicius 3' and stemma on p. 1317. **titulis ... gaudes:** *titulis*, *OLD* 7. Intertwined with status concerns of two families, a wife's profile depends on success in either. For titles and careers, see Intro 3.3. **honor patricius accedit:** for *patricius*, see 1.5.10n. *patricii Ricimeris. accedit* 'is given to', 'accrues to' (*OLD* 15). **si cogites eius aetatem:** cf. e.g. Plin. 6.31.13 *erat modica* [*cena*], *si principem cogitares*. His age was probably between 30 and 40, as Papianilla was about 35 at the time (assuming that she married Sidonius at, or soon after, the legal age of 12 in the early 450s). Age (*aetas*) counts among the criteria for determining social hierarchy alongside position (*priuilegium*) and seniority (*tempus*): see 1.9.5n. *senioris consularis*, 6.3.1, 7.9.6; Harries 1994, 25–7. **suffragium ... soluit** 'he paid for the support': *suffragium* is the support needed for appointment or promotion, secured by patronage or payment (*ODLA* 1425), cf. e.g. *Cod. Iust.* 2.7.23.2 *sine quadam suffragii solutione.* **in lance ... in acie** 'in the balance ... in the battlefield': Ecdicius had not paid for his advancement (for this metaphorical use of *lanx* to indicate bias or corruption, cf. Ennod. *Ep.* 9.23.1 *iniquum ponit aliquid in lance ueritatis*), but had merited it by the military support he provided, at his own expense, to Clermont; see 3.3.7 *collegisse te priuatis uiribus publici exercitus speciem*.

2 sancte 'duly' (*OLD* 4b), with ellipsis of something like *fecit*, not uncommon in sentences expressing a judgement (see K–S 2, 551). **Iulius Nepos**, the last emperor but one of the West, see §1n. *quaestor.* Prosopography: Mathisen 2020a, 109. **armis pariter ... ac moribus:** Julius Nepos had, by force of arms, overthrown the western emperor Glycerius (473–4, *PLRE* 2, 514), who was not recognized in the East, and probably recaptured Arles from the Visigoths (Delaplace 2015, 253 with n. 84). *pariter et/ac/ atque* 'both ... and' is a favourite of Sidonius, see 2.9.5n. **decessoris Anthemii:** *decessoris* 'predecessor', mainly late Latin (*TLL* 5/1.161.55–63). Anthemius, western emperor, 467–72, as an outsider introduced from the East, did not share any of the traditional ill feeling between Gaul and Italy (Kulikowski 2020, 210) and easily favoured the various Gallic factions (Intro 2.2), for instance also promoting Sidonius' friend and rival Magnus Felix (*PLRE* 2, 463–4) to the prefecture of Gaul and the patriciate in 469. Sidonius wrote the panegyric on Anthemius' second consulate, delivered in January 468 (*Carm.* 1–2), and had to thank him for his promotion to *patricius* and nomination as *praefectus urbi*; see letters 1.5 and 1.9 with commentary. **citerior** 'more recent': the conferral is all the more special as it was so long in coming. Cf. the general tension between merit and the timing of awards, 3.8.2 *rempublicam morari beneficia uos mereri*. For *citerior* of time, *OLD* 2, *TLL* 3.1195.32–54; cf. opp. *anterior*, Sidon. 8.1.2. Lütjohann unnecessarily proposed *citior*, followed by modern editors, against all manuscripts. **siquidem:** see 2.9.9n. **republica:** the concept of commonwealth plays an important role in Sidonius' thinking, occurring in seven letters. Whereas the state ought to be stable and a reliable remunerator of excellence for its citizens, worth exerting oneself for (as in this letter), in practice it is constantly threatened and deficient (e.g. 1.11.6 *uacante aula turbataque republica*, 2.1.4 *nullae a republica uires*, cf. van Waarden 2010, 355, 7.7.2n. the sarcastic *amore rei publicae*). **quia securus, hinc auidus:** *securus* 'confident' of their prospects (*OLD* 3). *hinc* 'hence' (*OLD* 8), as eagerness presupposes feeling confident, cf. Apul. *Met.* 8.11 *auide ac secure*. **mortuo ... principatus:** the sentence broadens as it reaches a conclusion, including the circumlocution *laborantum deuotioni*, which again stresses the great length to which people have gone, word order, parallelism, wordplay and clausula (Intro 4.5). **princeps ... principatus:** cf. Plin. *Paneg.* 6.1 *principi ... in principatu*, Alc. Avit. *Ep.* 13.1 M-R *loci principis principatum*. In last position in the sentence, these nouns are its focus (*OLS* 2, 1021–2). The clausula *principatus* is a double trochee, which is among the rhythms favoured by Sidonius. **redhibet** 'fulfils', 'honours' its commitments (late Latin, *TLL* 11/2.527.54–528.3).

3 interea tu marks the turn towards the addressee for the application of the above; see 2.10.2n. *interea tu.* **colligo** 'I judge', 'I estimate' (*OLD colligo*1 11). **hisce:** for *-ce*, see 1.1.4n. *hisce.* **solacium** 'comfort', but see also 1.9.6n. *solacium.* **inter aduersa maxima:** the ongoing aggression of the Visigoths against Clermont (*obsidionis terror* below; see letters 7.1, 7.10; Intro 3.2) reached its decisive stage in 474. **a tramite ... exorbitat** 'diverts from the path': *a tramite*, cf. 9.9.2 *a regula Sallustiani tramitis detortus exorbitat*, usually in the phrase *a tramite ueritatis exorbitat*, e.g. Aug. *Cur. mort.* 10.12. *exorbitat*: the verb is almost entirely confined to ecclesiastical writers, its meaning usually intr. 'to stray'; in Sidonius also 8.11.13 *catholicae fidei regulis exorbitaturum* (*TLL* 5/2.1553.37–1554.38, esp. 1554.27–9). The intricate phrasing carefully delineates the affective marital relation resisting outward duress. **quem ... participas** defines *meo ... honore. ex lege*: married women shared the rank or their husband (*Dig.* 1.9.8 *Feminae nuptae clarissimis personis clarissimarum personarum appellatione continentur*); see Hemelrijk 1999, 11. Papianilla, as Sidonius' wife, shared his advancement to the patriciate. **uxor bona, soror optima:** *uxor* and *soror* are essential roles of women in Roman society (along with the roles of *filia*, *mater* and *domina*), married women (*matronae*) cementing ties between their families (cf. e.g. 4.1.1 *soror mihi quae uxor tibi*), overseeing the household (as Papianilla can here be supposed to be doing at the family estate in the Auvergne), supporting their husband (see 2.10.5n.) and rearing the children. Conventional epithets of a praiseworthy woman – particularly frequent in funerary inscriptions – include *bona, casta, morigera, parca, pia, pudica, uniuira, utilis* among others (Riess 2012; cf. Sidonius' assessment of the deceased *matrona* Filimatia in poem 26 (letter 2.8.1; Mascoli 2003, Santelia 2008, 85–7) and Hindermann 2022b, 224–6, 239–42). For gender, see Intro 3.3 'Women'. **propitio deo Christo:** for similar pious qualifications, see 1.9.8n. *sub ope Christi.* By *deo Christo*, Christ is expressly defined as part of the Divine Trinity, cf. e.g. Prud. *Ham.* 931–2 *o Dee cunctiparens* [God the Father] *... o Dee Christe* [God the Son] | *... Deus Spiritus* [God the Holy Ghost]. **prosapiae tuae titulos:** *prosapia* 'lineage' is one of many archaic words revived in the second century. For the phenomenon, see Wolff 2020, 402. **gratatoriis apicibus** 'gratulatory letter': *gratatoriis*, hapax, *TLL* 6/2.2203.72–4, cf. *TLL* 6/2.2252.16–32 *gratulatorius. apicibus*: 1.5.2n. *sacris apicibus.* **festinus:** predicative adj., cf. 7.17.3n. **absoluens** 'taking away': see *TLL* 1.177.41–58, e.g. Liv. 8.13.17 *curam*, Ps.-Paul. Nol. *Carm.* 6.273 Hartel *metus*; cf. *OLD* 4b. **sollicitudinem ... pudorem:** Papianilla has been anxiously waiting for it, whereas modesty befits the recipient. The feeling of *pudor* ('modesty', 'reserve'; a related notion is *uerecundia*) will prevent someone from flaunting their success; see Intro 3.3 'Social Conventions' with n. 54.   **quem nil ... indicaturum ... si uerecundum ... nescires, nec sic impium iudicares:** the train of thought has two steps merged together: (1) he will not himself inform you (*indicaturum* predicating *quem*), because he is modest; (2) even if you did not know that he is modest (which is improbable), you would not think him unbrotherly (which is out of the question). *nec sic* 'not even so'. *impium*, i.e. deficient in his familial duties.

4 liberius 'without restraint', 'more openly': *OLD* 11; cf. e.g. 1.7.2 *libere queror*.   **concordia:** harmony is a necessary condition for the advancement of their families' mutual interests; see 2.2.3 *haec mihi cum meis ... concordia* [sharing Avitacum].   **suis** 'his own' (G–L §309.2).   **in commune:** see 3.12.3n.   **sicut nos ... patriciam ... ita ipsi ... consularem:** the last rung of the ladder is the consulate (*PLRE* 532–3), its glory since the Republic untarnished, though now no more than an honorary title. The office was accorded only to the most distinguished civil servants, usually members of the ancient noble families (cf. Intro 3.3 'Senators').   *nos ... ipsi*: Every generation hopes to do one better than the previous one. For this pervading principle in elite education, see *Carm.* 28.17–20n. (in 3.12) *titulis.*

5 Roscia salutat: cf. Cic. *Att.* 4.12 *domus te nostra tota salutat*, Sidon. 3.2.1 *Salutat populus Aruernus.*   **cura communis** 'our common object of care': cf. Symm. 1.48 *Paulina ... cura communis*, Sidon. 2.12.2n. *sollicitudo communis* (about daughter Severiana). *cura OLD* 8. The loving mention of their daughter counterbalances the career perspective just laid out. Yet, for Roscia's education too, ambition is leading (*informatur ingenium*).   **in ... sinu:** Roscia is being reared by her grandmother and aunts in Lyon (Sidonius' mother and sisters; see Mathisen 2020c, 59–60), possibly after Sidonius' consecration and due to the dangerous situation in Clermont.   **alienis** 'in other families': Sidonius pretends that such a warm nest away from home is rarely enjoyed by other grandchildren. Cf. Plin. 4.13.9 *liberi uestri ... alieni* 'your children ... [children] from elsewhere'. Sidonius thinks, and writes, very much in oppositions (Wolff 2020, 408; Intro 4.5). 'Own' vs 'other people's' is a frequent case in point, e.g. 1.9.4 *suae ... alienae*, 3.1.3 *tui ... alieni*, 8.16.1 *alieno ... meo*. Here the opposition is implicit. All manuscripts read *alienis* (so did *M*, who then erased *en*). There is no need to follow Wilamowitz' suggestion *alendis*, even if adopted by all later editors.   **cum seueritate** is not inconsistent with *indulgentissimo*, because – as the next sentence explains – her education, though ambitious, takes into account her tender age. *seueritas* is usually associated with the father's role, cf. e.g. Cic. *Cael.* 36 *patriam seueritatem*, Sidon. 7.9.22 *seueris patribus*, and often. Papianilla can rest assured that this role is also being played regardless of Sidonius' availability. **ingenium:** Roscia's education goes beyond the traditional limits of homestead and handicraft (e.g. *CIL* 6.15346 *domum seruauit lanam fecit*; Riess 2012, 494–5). Educated women were a luxury the elites could afford (Hemelrijk 1999), cf. 2.9.4n. *matronarum cathedras*, where the women enjoy the home library on a par with the men, reading Christian literature (for *doctrina* in women, see 2.10.5–6n.; see Intro 3.3 'Women'), *ingenium* significantly being the final word of the letter.

LETTER 6.11: RECOMMENDING A JEW

Outline

Recommendation letter for a Jew to lend support to a case he will set out himself.

Introduction

In Book 6 for the first time in the collection, the addressees are bishops, Sidonius' colleagues. Similar episcopal groups occur in 7.1–11, 8.13–15 and 9.2–11, covering twenty-three bishops in all (see Intro 4.1). Book 6 notably contains many recommendations (see 3.9 Introduction). Late antique bishops mediated and arbitrated in civil disputes as an alternative to the secular courts, in fact behaving like patrons taking care of their clients. This so-called *episcopalis audientia* or bishop's court originated in their authority within the Christian community and was incorporated into Roman law. The Church's capacity to become a decentralized legal entity was indeed one of its crucial success factors. See Intro 3.3 'Social Strata' with n. 41, 3.4 with n. 61, *ODLA* 252 'Bishops' court', Humfress 2011, Sirks 2013, Wojtczak 2021.

Discussion

In a letter of recommendation, the sender will spare the recipient as much as possible with regard to the idiosyncrasies of the beneficiary (see 3.9 Introduction). For Sidonius, Jews among others are a category that requires separate mention and justification: 3.4.1 *Gozolas natione Iudaeus, cliens culminis tui, cuius mihi quoque esset persona cordi, si non esset secta despectui*, and, concerning a converted Jew, 8.13.3 *cum sit gente Iudaeus, fide* [i.e. Christian faith] *tamen praeelegit censeri Israelita quam sanguine*. Sidonius' is the oldest record of Jews in Clermont. There as elsewhere in southern Gaul, the Jews were involved in trading (traditionally in competition with Christian 'Syrian' merchants – a view questioned by Grig 2024, 52–3) and moneylending, some of them becoming quite wealthy, particularly as landowners, and upwardly socially mobile (Bachrach 1977, 10–11; Brennan 1985, 328; Grig 2024, 53–6; see also van Waarden 2016, 203). Relations with the bishops of Clermont appear to have been friendly during the fifth century and well into the sixth, Sidonius being a case in point (Bachrach 1977, 3). Later in the sixth, tensions flared as pressure to convert mounted under bishop Avitus. According to Greg. Tur. *Hist.* 5.11, more than 500 Jews were baptized in 576 after an outbreak of mob violence, the rest relocating to Marseille (Brennan 1985). The number of 500, if trustworthy, indicates a considerable Jewish community in Clermont (Kaufmann 1995, 57 n. 79). On the Jews of Clermont, see also Fray 2000; on the position of the Jews in the post-Roman West, see *ODLA* 818; for their legal position in particular (their overall recognition as a religious minority (cf. *Cod. Theod.* 16.8 and 9) not preventing obstruction and violence), Bachrach 1977, 3–26 and 44–65, Brennan 1985, 333–5.

Addressee

Eleutherius was bishop of an unknown see. Prosopography: Mathisen 2020a, 91. Namesakes in Gaul include bishops of Auxerre (530s–540s; Duchesne 2, 446), Bourges (3rd/4th cent.?; 2, 26), Geneva (3rd/4th cent.?; 1, 226) and Tournai (*c.* 510 CE; 3, 114).

Date and Place

Written in Clermont, arising from Sidonius' obligations as bishop. The date is some point between Sidonius' ordination in 469/70 and the publication of Books 1–7 in 477/8 (see Intro 2.1).

Literature

Commentary: Westenholz forthcoming. Study: Westenholz 2023, 293–6.

Commentary

Sidonius domino papae Eleutherio salutem: for address line conventions, see Intro 4.2.

1 Iudaeum ... commendat: the bearer, unnamed, is reduced to his ethnicity. The opening immediately introduces the subject; cf. similar openings, with and without names: 6.2, 6.5, 6.8, 6.9, 6.10. For opening sentences, see van Waarden 2010, 46–8. **mihi:** singular of the sender, combined with *tu* (§2) of the addressee. Addressing a bishop with *tu*, despite the tendency towards an address in the plural or a *tu/uos* combination and an alternation of *ego/nos* for the 'I', flags the simple, businesslike nature of this letter (see van Waarden 2020e, 430 with n. 29). Address and farewell are the only formal traits of courtesy to the bishop. **error, per quem pereunt inuoluti:** *error* 'aberration', 'misguidance' of different or heretical religious convictions is standard Christian idiom (often combined with *inuolutus* 'entangled'; see Blaise s.v. (pass.)), cf. e.g. Tert. *Apol.* 46.18 *philosophus et christianus: amicus et inimicus erroris*, Sidon. 6.12.4 *a profundo gurgite erroris* (of the homoean barbarians, see Intro 3.4 'Christianity') (*TLL* 5/2.818.18–47). *pereunt* 'perish', i.e. do not obtain eternal life, in Christian parlance, cf. Vulg. *Ioh.* 3.15 *ut omnis qui credit in ipsum non pereat, sed habeat uitam aeternam*. Sidonius thematizes afterlife in 7.6.5, 9.4.3, 9.8.2. **ex asse damnabilem** 'completely beyond redemption' (Anderson): *ex asse* is originally a legal term ('whole', 'undivided', of an estate, *OLD* 4), later also used metaphorically (L–S IIB), cf. e.g. 9.2.1 *ex asse turbatus* 'completely nonplussed'. *damnabilem* has Christian overtones, cf. e.g. Aug. *Serm.* 237.1.1 *haeretici damnabiles*. **dum uiuit:** perhaps continues the legal atmosphere as it is the usual phrase for delimiting someone's property right, e.g. *Cod. Iust.* 3.33.16.1 *usum fructum ... habeat, dum uiuit, intactum*.

2 series 'tenor', 'purport' in patristic Latin, e.g. Ambr. *Fid.* 5.13 *apostolicae seriem lectionis* (see Blaise 2 'teneur', 'texte', 'contexte'). **praesentanea** 'available', 'in person': meaning in use from end of 4th cent. onward, cf. e.g. Claud. Mam. *Anim.* 2.9 *praesentaneis coram disputationibus*, Sidon. 7.11.2 *praesentaneo compendiosius ... memoratu* (about a letter bearer, see van Waarden 2010, 560) (*TLL* 10/2.852.55–66). **satis** 'very much', 'particularly': see 2.12.3n., 7.18.2n.; also *sat*(*is*) + superlative, 9.16.3n. **epistulari formulae debitam concinnitatem:** 'the economy required in writing letters': *epistulari formulae* 'epistolary style', 'the standard for a letter' (*OLD formula* 7 'rule', 'standard', 'pattern'), cf. Sidon. 7.2.9 *ignoscite praeter aequum epistularem formulam porrigenti*. *concinnitatem* 'elegance', achieved by being concise (*TLL* 4.49.84–50.3 'dicendi breuitas'). On epistolary brevity, see Intro 3.6. **sane** 'definitely' (*OLD* 3). **secundum uel negotia uel iudicia** 'according to the standards in business life as well as in court': cf. Mart. Cap. 5.550 *negotialis uel iudicialis assertio*. **huiuscemodi homines** 'this kind of people' is a negative qualification, see Blaise s.v. *huiusmodi*.

tu quoque: as his case is probably sound even by worldly standards, so much the more can you, as a bishop, defend this man's interests. **perfidiam ... personam:** the opposition closes the circle from where the letter began. *perfidiam* 'unbelief', 'heresy', e.g. the Jewish faith (Christian idiom: Souter 295, Blaise 611). For this distinction between somebody's peculiar or questionable ideas and their actual case and merits, cf. e.g. Symm. 1.64.1 *Commendari a me episcopum forte mireris. causa istud mihi, non secta persuasit* (cf. Symm. 9.57, pointing out that *non personas hominum sed uitae merita* should be considered in commending people). The carefully stylized closure, among other things, features the polyptoton *impugnas propugnare* and a striking *p-* alliteration (including repetition *per- per-*); see Intro 4.5. **memor nostri esse dignare, domine papa:** for valedictory conventions, see Intro 4.2.

LETTER 7.1: THE RESISTANCE OF CLERMONT AND THE ROGATIONS

Outline

The yearly attack of the Visigoths on the Auvergne and Clermont is about to start again. To boost the morale of his congregation in Clermont, Sidonius has introduced the ritual of the Rogations, inspired by their creator, Mamertus, the influential bishop of Vienne (§§1–2). Sidonius describes the dramatic events in Vienne leading up to their invention and their beneficial effect (§§3–6). Their introduction in Clermont is promising, he says, but more is needed. He begs for enduring (Burgundian) protection in exchange for the remains of Clermont's patron saint, which are preserved in Vienne – diplomacy and faith in one (§7).

Introduction

Book 7 is the climax in the collection for the drama that unfolds, politically and spiritually, in Clermont, under its bishop Sidonius (see Intro 3.2 and 4.1; for the role of bishops, 3.3 'Social Strata' with n. 41). Sidonius frames the last stand of Clermont as a crisis of *Romanitas* (traditional culture as against barbarism) and *Christianitas* (Nicene orthodoxy as against homoean heterodoxy, Intro 3.4) under threat from Visigothic aggression, resulting in the surrender of the Auvergne by the Empire. Letter 7.1 sounds the alarm for the Visigothic invasion and acknowledges Clermont's debt of mental balance to Mamertus, whose own town had recently gone through a transfer of power to the Burgundians. Soliciting Mamertus' support for his efforts, Sidonius tacitly courts broader

Burgundian support against the Visigoths – a balancing act which is as inevitable as it is dangerous (cf. 3.4.1, Clermont's people at the mercy of their rivalling neighbours, *suspecti Burgundionibus, proximi Gothis*; see 7.7.2n. *uicinorum*).

Discussion

Vienne and Mamertus

Once the principal town of the diocese of southern Gaul (Gallia Viennensis, later Septem Provinciae) and the capital of Viennensis, Vienne was now Burgundian territory (by 473, the Burgundians had progressed even further south: Harries 1994, 229, Delaplace 2015, 252; see also 4.20 Discussion). A rich metropolitan see and a border town, it had become a refuge for some of the nobles who escaped the Visigothic advance (among them Sidonius' relative Thaumastus (Mathisen 1984, 166 = Mathisen 1991b, 8; see also Intro 3.3 n. 38; for another relative who moved to Vaison for the same reason, see 2.9.1n. *Apollinarem*); besides, Sidonius' wife Papianilla was born there and the couple owned a pied-à-terre). Consequently, its bishop played an essential role in the communication between the Catholic church, the Burgundian authorities and the Gallo-Roman nobility. Together with the dramatic effect in the sudden invocation of crisis, Mamertus' key position in diplomacy must have been the reason for Sidonius to put this letter first in the book. Additionally, his name may well be significant (from Mars), as the preceding letter, the last of Book 6, is addressed to bishop Patiens ('the Hardy'), who had helped Clermont with supplies of grain (Harries 1994, 227): spiritual resilience shores up physical endurance.

Intertextuality

The description of the Visigothic campaign against the Auvergne as well as the events in Vienne is grafted onto Caesar's march on Rome and the capture of Rimini in Book 1 of Lucan's *Bellum ciuile* (Gualandri 1979, 43–9; van Waarden 2010, 75–7; Gualandri 2020, 309–10). Like Rimini, Clermont is the gateway to invasions (§1), and the defences of both towns are ramshackle (§2). The panic and havoc in Vienne resemble what happened next in Rome (§3). Lucan provides Sidonius with the bleak atmosphere and the general parallel (cf. 7.7 which also relies on Lucan in §2). Whether any more thematic allusivity is meant, is doubtful. One could think of a veiled political statement to the effect that a stronghold of Roman civilization is being threatened. For other applications of the motif of Caesar's civil war, see letters 1.5 and 3.12. For Sidonius' intertextuality, see Intro 3.5 and 4.4.

Rogation Days

Whereas Lucan suggests the overall structure, the conclusion is specifically Christian: prayers and tears of remorse make God save the people (§6) and shared relics seal the bond between Clermont and Vienne (§7). The centrepiece comprises the new Rogation ceremonies that were to become a characteristic element in Gallican liturgy: three days of collective fasting, prayers and processions, preceding Ascension Day (prescribed for the entire Frankish kingdom by the Council of Orléans, as early as 511; chronicled in Alcimus Avitus' *Homilies* 6–8, Gregory of Tours' *Histories* 2.34 (both 6th cent.) and Ado of Vienne's *Chronicon* (9th cent.)). The disasters that hit Vienne conform to the traditional Roman pattern of divine warnings and punishment. They also echo the fire in Lyon described by Seneca in his letter of consolation 91. It is difficult to decide in how far the mayhem in Vienne corresponds to historical reality. We are at the mercy of our sources: hagiography can be expected to stress the supernatural (Allen and Neil 2013, 71). Modern seismological catalogues do acknowledge the earthquakes in Vienne (Alexandre 1990, 1232; Guidoboni et al. 1994), but perhaps the narrative also reflects the disturbances caused by the arrival of the Burgundians. Further reading on the Rogations: Nathan 1998; van Waarden 2010, 77–80 with literature; van Waarden 2020c; Wolff 2021; Grig 2024, 160–2; on processions and community, Brubaker and Wickham 2021, 154–9; on episcopal crisis management, Allen and Neil 2013, 71–96 and 200.

Cult of Relics

The cult of the relics of saints is one of the pillars of episcopal authority, especially so in the evolving Christian landscape in Gaul after the demise of the Empire (see Intro 3.4). Writing as a bishop, Sidonius here plays this trump card in the existential crisis of his diocese in order to establish a religiously hallowed alliance with its neighbours in Burgundian territory.

Addressee

Mamertus was bishop of Vienne in the 460–70s. He and his family belonged to Sidonius' private circle. His elder brother and adviser, the priest-philosopher Mamertus Claudianus, was a lifelong friend (*Carm.* 39

in 4.11.6 is Sidonius' obituary of the latter). See van Waarden 2010, 70–4. Prosopography: Mathisen 2020a, 106.

Date and Place

Every year, from 471 to 474, the Visigoths attacked Clermont, cutting off the city from the outside world. This letter concerns the spring offensive of 473, which was particularly incisive, with the Goths not only threatening Clermont, but also taking Arles and Marseille and swathes of Spain, while the imperial government in Italy was absorbed in an internal power struggle (Stevens 1933, 145–53 and 198–201; Harries 1994, 226–8; Delaplace 2015, 251–3; Kulikowski 2020, 211–12). The dramatic date being the spring of 473, the time of writing will not differ much. There are flashbacks to the damage inflicted previously on the town and to the disruptions in Vienne which led Mamertus to introduce the Rogations, probably not long before. The place of writing must be Clermont.

Literature

Commentary: van Waarden 2010, 69–126. Study: Gualandri 1979, 43–9.

Commentary

1 Rumor est 'reports are coming in' is an uncommon variant of *fama est* (only Ter. *An.* 185, Cic. *Att.* 11.25.2, and Sidonius himself *Ep.* 2.1.4). The narrative in this letter includes several pieces of external information, here and in the nested flashbacks in §§3–6, which entails changes of perspective (see Hanaghan 2019, 167). The opening sentence states the letter's theme straightaway, bringing the emergency situation into stark relief; see van Waarden 2010, 46–8; cf. 8.3.1n. **Gothos in Romanum solum castra mouisse:** for the complex Visigothic offensive of 473, see above Date and Place. **nos miseri Aruerni ianua sumus** 'we poor Arvernians are the gateway': Sidonius typically frames the Auvergne and Clermont as the most vulnerable and undeserving warfront, ever since the opening of Book 3 where the war first appears in the correspondence; cf. 7.7.1n. *nostri ... infelicis anguli*. For the metaphorical use of *ianua*, see *OLD* 2. Sidonius echoes a passage in Lucan (1.244–57), where Caesar, coming from the Gallic provinces in the north, lays siege to Rimini. Its inhabitants deplore the fact that they live on the border to Gaul (1.248 *o male uicinis haec moenia condita Gallis*; cf. Sidon. 1.5.7n. *Ariminum*); they feel that *nos praeda furentum | primaque castra sumus* (250–1), their fate is *Latii ... claustra tueri* (253), and *hac iter est bellis* (257). **namque** 'namely', providing subsidiary information; see also 1.5.1n. *namque.* **hinc ... quia** 'because of the fact that' (*OLD hinc* 8a, H–S 512). **fomenta subministramus** 'we provide the fuel', 'we kindle': *fomenta* 'wood for kindling' (*OLD* 2). **quod** 'with regard to the situation that' (*OLD* 6: introducing a new subject for consideration). **necdum** 'not yet', preferred to *nondum* by Sidonius (cf. *OLD* 2). **terminos suos ... limitauerunt** 'they have established their borders': *terminos* is anologous to a cognate acc. (G–L §333.2). **ab Oceano in Rhodanum Ligeris alueo**: suggests that the Visigoths coveted the Loire (*Liger*) as their northern frontier, sealing off the territory between the Atlantic Ocean and the Rhône River against the Franks and Burgundians. Already in 471, Sidonius used similar words for this political constellation: 3.1.5 *illi* [the Visigoths] ... *metas in Rhodanum Ligerimque proterminant* (see Intro 3.2). As argued by Delaplace 2015, 253–4, this suggestion may be biased, as the Visigoths can be supposed to have simply adhered to the *foedus* with Rome in warding off Burgundian pressure. **sub ope Christi:** see 1.9.8n. **moram de nostra tantum obice patiuntur** 'they suffer a delay due only to the barrier we interpose': cf. 3.4.1 (from 471/2) *oppidum ... nostrum quasi quandam sui limitis obicem ... terrificant.* For *de* replacing *ex* and *ab*, see 1.5.1n. *de affectu.* The lack of a proper metrical clausula is striking: *óbice patiúntur* (–◡◡ ◡◡–×) is best explained as an accentual sentence ending (*cursus velox*; see Intro 4.5, van Waarden and Kelly 2020, 462–3); see §3 n. *mansuetudo ceruorum.* **spatia tractumque regionum** 'the length and breadth of the country', cf. Sen. *Dial.* 3.2.1 *spatia regionum* (also in a context of military destruction); Sidon. 2.11.1 *pro situ spatiisque regionum,* 9.4.1 *spatium viae regionumque.* Sidonius loves these minimalist shufflings (van Waarden 2010, 57, Intro 4.5). **regni minacis** 'the threatening realm', of the Visigoths; both the Visigothic and the Burgundians entities are dubbed *regna* (e.g. 7.6.4, 7.11.1), but so is the Roman state (7.6.10 *regni utriusque pacta* of the treaty between Rome and the Visigoths). *minax* is not frequent in Sidonius and quite emphatic: of the Huns in *Carm.* 2.245 *gens animis membrisque minax.* Could there be an echo of Hor. *Carm.* 2.12.12 *regum colla minacium* (in a comparable context of enemy kingdoms)? **importuna deuorauit impressio** 'is swallowed by the grim onslaught', an original and expressive conclusion, musically exploiting the assonance *importuna ... impressio,* and rhythmically reinforced by the double cretic of the clausula. For the verbal hyperbaton, see 2.12.1n. *germano* (cf. 1.9.1n. *spebus*).

2 In the cities of Gaul after the economic crisis of the third century, the walls surrounded only a limited area (*castrum*), excluding the less densely inhabited outskirts (*suburbium*). The walled town of Clermont was very small, comprising only three hectares, accommodating 700 inhabitants at most (see Loseby 1992, 150-1; Heijmans 2020, 54-5) and with no space for a proper *domus ecclesiae* – bishop's house and offices – adjacent to the cathedral (Greg. Tur. *Hist.* 2.21). A considerable part of its citizens would have lived outside the precinct, vulnerable to aggression. See van Waarden 2010, 12-13 with literature; for late antique Mediterranean cities in general, Loseby 2009. **animositati nostrae tam temerariae tamque periculosae**, 'our courage, so reckless and so dangerous': cf. the variation 7.5.2 *tam praecipitis animi ... tamque periculosi*, and see §1n. **spatia tractumque regionum.** The dative is governed by *opitulatura*; the phrase is the topic of the enunciation and hence placed at the beginning. For nouns in *-(i)tas*, see 1.9.1n. *serietatem*. **ambustam murorum faciem** 'the scorched surface of the ramparts': *facies* 'surface' (*OLD* 11) is the technical term for the outer layer (e.g. of stucco) on a wall (cf. Vitr. 2.8.8). Sidonius characteristically makes this piece of technical language function in an artificial context (for his attention to vocabulary, see Intro 4.5). This is the first of three parallel *cola*, the last of which is varied and longest; see Intro 4.5 n. 111. **putrem sudium cratem** 'the rotting wickerwork of the palisades' is a hint of Luc. 1.241-2 *nuda iam crate fluentes| ... clipeos*, as the inhabitants of Rimini grasp their tattered shields and other decrepit armour. Constructions of wickerwork for a wall are obviously inferior to stone (cf. Tac. *Ann.* 12.16). The walls of the *castrum* of Clermont remained intact at all times; it was the *suburbium* that bore the brunt of the attacks (Griffe 1965, 8 n.10). **propugnacula uigilum trita pectoribus** 'the battlements rubbed against by the breasts of the sentinels': *tero* 'to rub', 'press closely' (*OLD* 1, 2), cf. e.g. Stat. *Theb.* 7.499 *teris ... pectore matrem*. For the unwavering vigilance of Clermont's guards, cf. 3.7.4 where *non dies ... non nox* goes unattended. The whole of the sentence, with its sensorial pathos, mirrors the ruin and despair of the city and its defendants (Gualandri 1979, 45 n. 34; see Intro 4.5 'Hyperbole'). **opitulatura** 'will help', grammatically agrees with the nearest of the subjects *propugnacula*, logically with *faciem* and *cratem* as well (*OLS* 1, 1256-8). *confidimus opitulatura*, as often with main verb shifted back from the final position; clausula paeon IV + spondee. in this case foregoes the double cretic clausula *opitula-tura confidimus*. **tamen** 'though', 'indeed': besides denoting a contrast ('nevertheless'), *tamen*, in later Latin, may qualify the preceding sentence more broadly, introducing a restriction/concession ('at least', *autem*) or an explanation ('apparently', ≈ *nam, enim*) and even simply a continuation (Löfstedt 1911, 27-35; Spevak 2005, 208-9 and 222-3 (cf. Spevak 2006)). There is no need for Lütjohann's conjecture *iam* or for Mohr's *tantum*. Loyen rightly maintains the manuscript reading. **inuectarum te auctore** 'introduced on your initiative [in Vienne]'. **palpamur auxilio** 'we are comforted by the help': cf. 3.7.4 *palpate nos prosperis* 'comfort us

COMMENTARY: 7.1:2–3

with good news' in the same context of siege. **quibus inchoandis instituendisque** 'their beginning and establishment' marks the successive stages of the introduction of the Rogations in Clermont; cf. 5.14.2 *Mamertus ... inuenit, instituit, inuexit.* The case is dative, governed by *initiari.* **etsi non effectu pari, affectu certe non impari:** bicolon with parallelism (*effectu pari - affectu impari*), antithesis (*non effectu - affectu, pari - non impari*), homoeoteleuton (*effectu - affectu, pari - impari*) and paronomasia (*effectu – affectu*; same wordplay 3.14.1 and 9.2.2) is vintage Sidonius; the wordplay *par ... non impar* is found exclusively in Sidonius, see also 8.15.1n.; cf. 9.16.1n. *paria* (Intro 4.5). **coepit initiari:** stresses the hesitant beginning, but cf. 7.7.4n. *coepistis esse.* **circumfusis ... terroribus:** *OLD circumfundo* 6, cf. e.g. 3.4.1 *circumfusarum nobis gentium arma*, Liv. 34.38.7 *circumfuso undique pavore.* **necdum:** §1n. **dat terga** 'take to flight' is apt in a letter centring on war and an advancing army. The paragraph again ends on a double cretic and with alliteration *ter- ter-*.

3 We are now told the first part of the story of earthquakes and other terrifying incidents, which made the people of Vienne panic, and inspired Mamertus to react with a manifestation of faith. It extends over §§ 3, 5 and 6a. In between, in a still more distant flashback, is the memory of a fire at Vienne to which the bishop had withstood with uncommon courage (§4). The narrative perspective is complex: the original narrators are the people of Vienne (or Mamertus) who informed Sidonius (§3 *nostram sciscitationem*), but Sidonius, as a second narrator, provides the story with his own commentary as he retells it to Mamertus (and later readers; see Intro 4.3). **non enim latet nostram sciscitationem** 'it does not escape our notice, you know', answered by *quae omnia sciens* in §6. Unlike *nam, enim* is not a connector but an interactional particle, appealing to 'the involvement, cooperation and empathy of the addressee' (Kroon 1995, 171–209; Kroon 2011, 192; *OLS* 2, 1201–6): 'y'know', 'isn't it?', and similar. *sciscitationem* 'the making of enquiries' (*OLD*), found from Petr. 24.5 onward, in Sidonius also 4.11.3. It is the reading of *PLeipMF* (the other MSS of the δ-branch, the so-called 'fourth family', omit letters 1–5; see Intro 6), whereas the α-branch has *oscitationem* 'yawning'. The latter is sometimes defended on the basis of 5.14, an invitation to attend the Rogations in Clermont, where in §2 the old ceremonies that preceded the Rogations are called *oscitabundae supplicationes*. However, this would contradict the newly acquired optimism (*animositati, affectu*) described in the preceding paragraph. After *sciscitationem*, Lütjohann inserted *quod* 'the fact that', accepted by later editors. He evidently missed the correction in A, where the scribe himself or a contemporaneous hand inserted *quod* before *ciuitas* above the line (cf. Mohr's *quia* in the same place). *quod* may indeed have dropped out before the MS tradition divided, but is not indispensable. Sidonius elsewhere employs a similar loose construction, e.g., 6.12.9 *ilicet scias uolo: per omnem fertur Aquitaniam gloria tua*, 7.4.3 *accipe confitentem: suspicio quidem nimis seueros*. **harumce supplicationum institutarum** 'of the institution of these supplications', a so-called *ab urbe condita* construction, where the attributive participle conveys the leading thought of the phrase (K–S 1, 766–9). *harumce*: see 1.1.4n. *hisce*. **ciuitas caelitus tibi credita** 'the town entrusted to you by heaven': adverbs in *-(i)tus* like *caelitus* 'from heaven' (first attested Apul. *Pl.* 1.12, in Christian prose Cypr. *Ep.* 1.4) are frequent in later Latin. The *c*-alliteration may have favoured the choice of *caelitus* instead of classical *diuinitus*. **cuiuscemodi prodigiorum terriculamenta** 'alarming prodigies of every sort': *cuiuscemodi* in δ has been changed to *cuiusque modi* by editors since Lütjohann, but is perfectly sound (in use since the 2nd-cent. archaists Fronto, Gellius, and Apuleius, e.g. Apul. *Flor.* 15.2 *poculis et cuiuscemodi utensilibus*); *huiuscemodi* 'of the following sort' in α would also do, but *cuiuscemodi* is preferable on the principle of *lectio difficilior potior*. *prodigiorum terriculamenta* = *prodigia terribilia*: for this inverse genitive, see 1.5.8n. *amoena fontium*; cf. below *mansuetudo ceruorum, orationum frequentia* and often. *terriculamentum* 'terror' is an Apuleian neologism (e.g. *Apol.* 64.2 *omnia sepulchrorum terriculamenta*, perhaps echoed here). **uacuabatur:** the population fled the town of Vienne. Compare the panic and flight of people and senate in Rome, Luc. 1.486–8 *nec solum uolgus inani | percussum terrore pauet; sed curia et ipsi | sedibus exiluere patres*, 489 *fugiens ... senatus*. The pairing of *prodigia* and *supplicatio* is in accordance with traditional pagan Roman religion, e.g. Liv. 27.23.4 *horum prodigiorum causa diem unum supplicatio fuit*. The *prodigia* Sidonius has chosen come from the same tradition, viz. earthquakes (e.g. Liv. 4.21.5), strokes of lightning on public buildings (Liv. 24.10.9), fires (Liv. 27.4.12), and wild animals in towns (Liv. 3.29.9). The perplexity is driven home to the reader by means of a labyrinthine clause. Unlike in the preceding and the following paragraphs, the main verbs in §3 at first are firmly in final position. **nam** 'namely' is so-called 'backward-linking' *nam*, which provides subsidiary information (Kroon 1995, 148–9, *OLS* 2, 1194–7). **scaenae moenium publicorum** 'the fronts of the public buildings': *scaena* has the rare meaning 'facade', 'side', largely absent from dictionaries, cf. Symm. *Or.* 2.20 *scaena murorum*, Greg. Tur. *Mart.* 1.9 *in scaena montis aquosi* (cf. Verg. *Aen.* 1.164, *OLD* 1b; Gualandri 1979, 46 n. 37). Here, *moenia* 'buildings', 'structures' (*TLL* 8.1327.43–58) is to be distinguished from *murus* 'town wall' (e.g. Verg. *Aen.* 2.234 *diuidimus muros et moenia pandimus urbis*); cf. 1.5.1n. *moenium*. **concutiebantur**, imperfect, like *tumulabant*, and *collocabat*, paints the background situation of serious and repeated calamities, with which Mamertus' brisk resolution is contrasted in the perfect tense; see below *cum tu ... decurristi.* **saepe** 'repeatedly' is not seriously in doubt despite the misgivings of some editors (the MSS have *sepe* (*S seppe*), Pio 1498 first printed *saepe*). **caducas culminum cristas** 'the collapsing tiles of the rooftops': *cristae* are the round ridge tiles which cover the tops of the roofs (2.2.5 called *dorsa cristarum*); this is technical usage, *TLL* 4.1210.62–8 'culmen, cacumen', Niermeyer 5 'ridge tile'. **superiecto fauillarum monte tumulabant**, 'buried under a towering heap of ashes': cf. Amm. 29.5.18 *fauillarum ... aceruos.* The image of ashes as a burial mound (*tumulus*) is an innovation. Lucan says there was a great panic *as though* houses were burning and being rocked by an earthquake (Luc. 1.493–5). **stupenda ... ceruorum:** The shy deer enter the town and make their lair in the market place. The word order of the sentence is as intricate as the event is puzzling. Combining *audacium* with *ceruorum* 'reckless deer' and *pauenda* with *mansuetudo* 'terrifying meekness' in two chiastic oxymora, the author heightens the unreal effect of this nightly scene. Shanzer and Wood 2002, 382 n. 3 remark that, although this looks like a mere topos, in times of famine wild animals do search for food in centres of population in which they would not normally be found. *stupenda* and *foro* are fronted, stating the topic of bewildering events in the forum, of all places. *mansuetudo ceruorum* is an inverse genitive phrase: see *prodigiorum* n. above. It lacks a metrical profile (–◡— —×): perhaps an accentual *cursus planus* (*-túdo ceruórum*) should be felt; the succession of long syllables may also suggest the deer's tameness (cf. §1n. *obice patiuntur*). **pauenda:** *pauere* loses out against *timere* in later Latin (proportion 1 : 6 up to 200 CE, 1 : 20 in 200–500 CE, Sidonius however 1 : 3.5) and may be considered more forceful. *mansuetudo ceruorum = mansueti cerui*: see *prodigiorum* above. **cum tu ... decurristi** 'when you resorted': a so-called 'inverse *cum*' clause, containing the principal event, usually in the perfect tense, after a main clause in the imperfect which contains secondary events (H–S 623, *OLS* 2, 245–8). **discessu primorum populariumque** 'by the departure of the notables and the common people': the *primores* are the town council, *ordo decurionum*. **statu urbis exinanito** 'after the town's condition had been weakened', as a town's real strength are its citizens: 7.9.23 *si urbium status non tam murorum ambitu quam ciuium claritate taxandus est. status OLD* 6b 'state', 'condition'. **ad noua ... ueterum Niniuitarum exempla** 'to a new application of the example of ancient Nineveh': the story of Nineveh is a staple of the Jewish and Christian discourse of repentance, told in the biblical book of Jonah. God is angry at the city's wickedness and orders the prophet Jonah to denounce it. Jonah goes to Nineveh and proclaims its imminent destruction. The people of Nineveh take on mourning, they fast and pray and try to appease God. 'God saw what they did, and how they abandoned their wicked ways, and he repented and did not bring upon them the disaster he had threatened' (Jonah 3.10). For *noua ... ueterum*, see 1.1.5n., 5.5.2n. **tua quoque desperatio**: Mamertus' despair on top of (*quoque*) the general mayhem would have further reviled (*conuiciari* + dat.) God's warning. **conuiciaretur**, clausula cretic + spondee -*uīciārētur*.

4 Mamertus' defying the flames places him in the tradition of Martin of Tours: Sulp. Sev. *Mart*. 14.2 *obuium se aduenientibus flammis inferens ... ignem retorqueri* 'he confronted the approaching flames ... the fire retorted' (for miracles, see Intro 3.4). To visualize this story, compare Raphael's painting of pope Leo IV confronting the fire near St Peter's, in the Room of the Fire in the Borgo in the Vatican. The motif is related to miraculous escapes from fire by righteous men like the three men in the fiery furnace (Daniel 3.8–28), Aeneas fleeing Troy, Verg. *Aen*. 2.632–33 *ducente deo flammam inter et hostis | expedior; dant tela locum flammaeque recedunt*, and the story of the *pii fratres* in *Aetna* 603–45 (for the latter, Santelia 2012). **et uere** 'and indeed', adds a new argument (*OLD et* 2d). **iam de deo** 'especially when it comes to God': *iam* lends so-called 'counter-presuppositional' focus, things being different from what one might suppose (Kroon and Risselada 1998, 436–7). **post uirtutum experimenta** 'after you experienced his wonders': in Christian idiom, *uirtutes* (mostly plural) means 'deeds showing power', 'miracles' (Souter s.v.). Cf. 1.5.9n. *experimenta*, *Carm*. 33.9n. *uirtutum signa* (in 7.17). **uice quadam** 'once', 'on one occasion' (L–S *uicis* B1). **fides tua in illo ardore plus caluit** plays on literal and figurative 'burning'. *in* 'in the middle of', 'amid': cf. *OLD* 40c 'the action is surprising in the light of circumstances mentioned'. **obiectu solo corporis tui** reminds the reader of §1 *obice* and 2 *solo*: resistance is the base-line for the people as well as their spiritual leaders. **ignis recussus in tergum fugitiuis flexibus sinuaretur** 'rebounding, the fire writhed back in retreating curves' evokes a snake, the epitome of evil (Otto 1890, 25 *anguis*). The miracle worker and healer typically commands over serpents, cf. e.g. Greg. Tur. *Glor. conf.* 32 *serpentibus ... imperasse*. For *recutio* of repelling something dangerous, see *TLL* 11/2.468.73–469.14; for *ignis recussus*, cf. Coripp. *Ioh*. 6.122 *igne recusso*. **terribili nouo inusitato** 'startling, strange, unusual', an asyndetic triad (Intro 4.5). The near-tautology *nouus inusitatus* is not unusual, cf. e.g. Sen. *Contr.* 10 praef. 5, Amm. 14.7.14, Aug. *Ep*. 187.23; hence there is no need for Haupt's *inuisitato* (accepted by Lütjohann and Anderson), although these two words are frequently confused in the MSS. **affuit flammae cedere ... cui sentire defuit** 'the fire was able to retreat, though unable to understand': *adest* refers to the quality one has or the means at one's disposal (*TLL* 2.921.12–75), e.g. Apul. *Plat*. 2.13 *nec constantia illis* *adsit et diuturnitas desit. affuit ... defuit*: polyptoton. *cedere* specifically of demons, cf. *Carm*. 33.11n. (in 7.17). *sentire* is emphatically brought forward. **per reuerentiam ... per naturam**: there are two other instances, before Sidonius: Ambr. *Virg*. 3.3.14 *inrationabile animal per reuerentiam recognoscit quod per naturam ignorat* (about frogs being silent during prayer), after him Alc. Avit. *Ep*. 88.9 M-R *temperate et edomate per reuerentiam, quidquid ante uos indomitum fuerat per naturam* (addressed to the king, called upon to mitigate the heat).

5 Mamertus now proceeds to the expiation of the prodigies by means of fasting and impeccable conduct (on the part of the clergy, *paucis*), and prayer, mourning, and demonstrations of faith (on the part of the entire community, *omnibus*). **nostri ordinis uiris**: i.e. the clergy, see 9.16.2n. *nostrum*, 1.5.10n. *ordinum*. **et his paucis** 'who were few enough', both rare on the ground and an elite. *et* is epexegetic (*OLD* 11), specifying *uiris*. **indicis ieiunia, interdicis flagitia, supplicia praedicis, remedia promittis**: another frequent kind of asyndeton in Sidonius, two times two elements; note polyptoton, rhyme, and chiasmus; the 'music' often prevails over the exact meaning (cf. Gualandri 1979, 48 n. 48). *supplicium*, *OLD* 2 'a thing offered, act performed to propitiate a deity'. **nec poenam longinquam esse nec ueniam**: disaster is interpreted as divine punishment for man's iniquity (cf. 7.10.2 *per iniustitiae nostrae merita*; see on sin, Bailey 2020, 269–75), which God is prepared to forgive as soon as man repents. Like punishment, forgiveness is not 'far away', i.e. 'difficult to reach'; cf. the seminal text Deut. 30.11 *mandatum hoc ... non supra te est neque procul positum* 'this commandment is not above you nor is it far away'. **solitudinis** 'wasteland', 'devastation' (cf. *OLD* 4). **orationum frequentia** 'frequent prayers', inverse genitive; see *prodigiorum* n. above. **esse amoliendas** 'must be averted', possibly 'will be averted'; for the gerundive + *esse* as a periphrastic passive future tense, cf. 5.5.1n. *subiciendam*. and see 1.9.6n. *admittendo*. **aqua potius oculorum quam fluminum**: a studied opposition, *aqua oculorum* is not found elsewhere; *aqua* for tears is poetical (Prop. 3.6.10, Ov. *Tr*. 4.1.98); cf., in a different context, *Pan*. 2(XII).28.2 *hominum lacrimae, non amnium aquae*. **posse restingui** 'can be extinguished' or 'will be extinguished', as *posse* with present passive infinitive can replace the future passive infinitive with *iri* in later Latin (H–S 313–14, *OLS* 1, 441). Stylistically, this phrase creates a variation with *esse amoliendas* and *firmandam*. **terrae motuum conflictationem fidei stabilitate** opposes the physical and the metaphorical: 'the clash of earthquakes' and 'the stability of faith'. **firmandam**: 'to be stabilized', 'checked' (*OLD* 1c). There is soundplay on *m* (*mones, minacem, motuum*) and *f* (*conflictationem, fidei, firmandam*). Rhythmically, the first of the three parallel sentences ends in a double trochee, preceded by a spondee to mimic the difficult process: *ēss(e) āmōliĕndas*; the last two end in a cretic + spondee.

6 cuius ... consilii: conversion is characteristically abrupt ('immediately responding to this advice'), cf. e.g. in the gospel of Luke 18.43 *et confestim uidit et sequebatur illum*, Aug. *Conf.* 8.12 *et tali oraculo confestim ad te esse conuersum* [*Antonium*]. *sequax consilii* is a one-off phrase, as is *humilis turba* 'the lowly people': Sidonius can innovate with ordinary words. **maioribus ... suis:** the *humilis turba* set an example of piety for 'their superiors' (*maiores* are the upper class, cf. 3.3.7, 7.2.5; *TLL* 8.131.75–132.19, 2nd cent. and later), in accordance with the biblical precedence of the underdog, as in the Magnificat, Luke 1.52 *deposuit potentes de sede et exaltauit humiles*. The ritual is aimed to restore social cohesion in a city apparently torn apart between the interests of the leading body and those of the population (van Waarden 2020c, 206–7; cf. the process of return and reconciliation in Clermont, 3.2.2). **fuit incitamento** 'prompted': *esse* + predicative dative, as below *saluti, imitationi, praesidio, calamitati, formidini*. **piguisset ... puduit** 'had resented ... were ashamed': for the antithesis of *piget* and *pudet*, and the greater impact of *pudet*, cf. Cic. *Dom.* 29 *ut me non solum pigeat stultitiae meae, sed etiam pudeat*. Note alliteration, assonance, and chiasmus (with *fugere, redire*). **deuotione**, in the Christian sense of 'devotion', 'piety' (*TLL* 5/1.879.19–880.25). **inspector pectorum deus** 'God, the searcher of hearts': cf. e.g. Jeremiah 17.10 *ego Dominus scrutans cor et probans renes*. **obsecrationem uestram** 'your prayer' (*OLD* 1b). For the ternary structure of this sentence, see Intro 4.5. **denique illic deinceps** 'consequently there from then on': in Vienne, resilience has now greatly improved. *illic* as seen from Clermont: the narrative perspective changes. **uel ... uel:** *uel* (... *uel*) gradually supersedes *et* (... *et*) and is dominant in later Latin (H–S 501–2). **populus iste** 'the people here [in Clermont]': for *iste* = *hic*, see *Carm.* 27.29n. (in 2.10). **et accidisse prius et non accessisse posterius**, 'had indeed happened in the past and had not supervened later': stylistic ingenuity remains on a high level, this time with a double paronomasia. *accessisse*: see 3.12.5n. *accedat*. **uestigia tam sacrosanctae informationis amplectitur** 'embraces the footprints of [your] guidance so holy', i.e. 'follows in your wake', which could scarcely be said in a more ceremonious way. The formality in this letter to a close acquaintance reflects its official character. Parallels include Dido in Sil. 8.124–6 *mutae oscula, qua steteras, bis terque infixit harenae;* | *deinde amplexa sinu late uestigia fouit,* and the Sinful Woman who kissed Jesus' feet (Luke 7.36–50) in Sedul. *Carm. Pasch.* 4.66–8 *tunc mulier ...* | *... clementia supplex* | *corruit amplectens uestigia. sacrosanctus* is used often, and exclusively, for bishops in Sidonius. *informatio* 'instruction' is later Latin (*TLL*

COMMENTARY: 7.1:6-7

7/1.1474.20–45). **conscientiae tuae beatitudo** 'the blessedness of your conscience': i.e. 'you who are blessed through your good conscience' (cf. *Hier.* 119.10 *in eo habebunt beatitudinem, quod fruuntur bono conscientiae*), elaborating on the abstract title *Beatitudo Tua* 'Your Blessedness'. **mittat orationum suarum suffragia** 'grant the support of its prayers'.

7 The letter ends with an appeal based on the shared possession of the relics of the martyrs Ferreolus and Julian. **tibi soli:** the *solus* refrain a third time (see §§2 and 4). Greg. Tur. *Iul.* 2 cites this passage as follows: *praebet ... testimonium Sollius noster* [i.e. Sidonius], *ipsi Mamerto scribens his verbis:* '*Tibi soli concessa est in partes orbis occidui martyris Ferreoli solida translatio, adiecto nostri capite Iuliani*', as a proof of the historicity of Mamertus' discovery of the remains. **post auorum memoriam uel confessorem Ambrosium** 'since the time of our grandfathers or rather the confessor Ambrose': *uel* specifies (*OLD* 3). A *confessor* initially is a person who testifies to their faith as a martyr. The term is later applied to bishops on account of their firmness during persecution or against heresy, and finally more in general of bishops, abbots, and saints, without the connotation of martyrdom; see *Carm.* 33.9n. *confessorem* (in 7.17). Aurelius Ambrosius, *c.* 339–97, after a career in high office, bishop of Milan from 374 onward, was an influential theologian and a powerbroker in the secular and ecclesiastical politics of his day. His legacy includes hymns, theological works and a comprehensive letter collection (*ODCC* 49–50, *ODLA* 1, 58–9). **duorum martyrum repertorem:** Ambrose's discovery of the remains of Saints Gervasius and Protasius in 386 secured his control over a key church in Milan (present-day S. Ambrogio) in the ongoing dispute with Arians over church property. **in partibus orbis occidui** 'in the western world', cf. Luc. 4.63 *in occiduum ... orbem*, Claud. *Rapt. Pros.* 38 *occiduo ... ab orbe*; cf. Amm. 22.3.7 *in partes occiduas*. **martyris Ferreoli solida translatio adiecto nostri capite Iuliani** 'the complete transference of the martyr Ferreolus together with the head of our Julian': Ferreolus and Julian form a pair, like Gervasius and Protasius. Many late-Roman communities chose to opt for twin protector saints, such as Peter and Paul in Rome. The function of this phenomenon was essentially political and social concord (see Brown 1981, 96–7). According to tradition, Ferreolus, a military tribune, was martyred in Vienne *c.* 304 CE. Saint Julian was the local Clermontese saint par excellence, particularly venerated by Sidonius' family in the family shrine in Brioude (*c.* 60 km south of Clermont). A soldier in the company of Ferreolus, he was also martyred, his head being cut off. In Sidonius' days, this head, together with Ferreolus' remains, was owned by the church of Vienne. See further Harries 1994, 187–206; van Waarden 2010, 121–3; *Carm.* 41.78n. *patronorum* (in 9.16). *solida translatio* is obviously more prestigious than finding and securing partial remains; for *translatio*, see *ODCC* s.v. 'translation 1'. **nostri**, by its position, in slight relief. **istinc** 'from here', i.e. from Clermont/Brioude; cf. §6 *iste*. **turbulento ... persecutori** 'the unruly persecutor': the same phrase in 1.7.12. Julian had been advised by Ferreolus to flee to Clermont. There he was overtaken by his murderer (*carnifex*), who took his head back with him to Vienne, to present it to his superior (*persecutor*). **manus rettulit cruenta carnificis** 'the executioner's bloody hand brought back': the expressive spotlight is on the hand, acting as it were on its own initiative, enhanced by the word order, which, among other things, also brings together *cruenta* and *carnificis*, with *c*-alliteration. **quod ... deposcimus:** subject clause of *non iniurium est. quod = id quod.* **ut nobis inde ueniat pars patrocinii, quia uobis hinc rediit pars patroni:** specifies *quod ... deposcimus.* The letter ends with a sustained formal parallelism expressing an opposition. For a similar bargain, cf. *Carm.* 33.4n. (in 7.17) *partem regni portio martyrii*; for *patrocinii*, cf. 1.5.9n. *patrocinii.* In exchange for the relic of Julian ('a fragment of our patron saint'), Sidonius claims protection from Vienne's bishop ('a share in your patronage'), and thus implicitly from the Burgundian king and Roman *magister militum Galliarum* Chilperic (see above Introduction and Discussion). The cult of the saints is the continuation of diplomacy by other means (Intro 3.4).

LETTER 7.7: CLERMONT SURRENDERED

Outline

'No jokes this time, this is a sad letter (§1). The surrender of the city of Clermont, proud of its Roman roots, a courageous defender against the Visigoths and a principled imperial loyalist, is an outright shame (§§2–3). You, the Empire's negotiators, are selfish and irresponsible (§4). If possible, cancel this agreement. If not, prepare to offer us asylum to save at least our lives (§§5–6).'

Introduction

After having defended Clermont with unflagging energy for four seasons (471–4; see 7.1 Introduction), Sidonius, despite a certain degree of protection afforded by the Burgundians, had not been able to improve his strategic position in the war with the Visigoths. The central government in Ravenna decided that the Auvergne was lost, and staked everything on retaining Provence. From the end of 474 to the beginning of the next year, imperial envoys, apparently without involving representatives from the

Auvergne, made the essential diplomatic preparations for the final agreement in May/June 475 between Euric and a deputation of four Gallic bishops from Provence, which sealed the surrender of the Auvergne in exchange for Provence (see Stevens 1933, 158–60, Harries 1994, 233–7, Delaplace 2015, 253–6; also Intro 3.2 and letter 8.3 Addressee; for the role of bishops, 3.3 'Social Strata' with n. 41).

Discussion

In this letter to the most senior deputy, Graecus of Marseille, Sidonius vents his indignation on hearing the outcome of the negotiations. C. E. Stevens famously called this letter 'the Epitaph of the Western Empire' (Stevens 1933, 160). This is a sweeping statement: while the letter is certainly among the most telling testimonies of the ordeal Gaul went through in the fifth century, Sidonius' focus is local, on Clermont and the Auvergne about to lose their freedom despite their solidarity with the Empire and their heroic self-sacrifice. The Empire itself has not fallen – that is the fate of Clermont – but it betrays its essential mission of embodying and warranting freedom. It lets traitors go unpunished, its representatives do little more than further their own interests, and the emperor is conspicuous by his absence. These are the letter's key concepts: freedom vs slavery, solidarity vs treason, altruism vs egotism.

Two intertextual links in §2 underpin the message: a quotation from Lucan's *Bellum ciuile* for the pride the Gauls have always taken in being Romans, descendants of the Trojans, and an elaborate allusion to Silius Italicus' *Punica* about the resistance offered by Decius to the surrender of Capua to Hannibal. Another fleeting allusion to Lucan in §3 compares the plight of beleaguered Clermont to the hardships endured by Caesar's troops. The fifth-century present is firmly anchored in the heroic past of the Republic; see Intro 3.1 and 3.5. And Lucan's epic of civil war once more looms over the events as it had already done at the outset of Book 7 (see 7.1 Discussion 'Intertextuality' and Intro 4.4).

Addressee

Graecus, bishop of Marseille from the mid-460s until after 475, figures prominently in Sidonius' correspondence, the addressee of letters 6.8, 7.2, 7.7, 7.10, 9.4. In 475, he was the senior member of the episcopal embassy that negotiated with Euric, which resulted in the surrender of Clermont (see Intro 3.2; van Waarden 2010, 129–30 and 339). Prosopography: Mathisen 2020a, 99.

Date and Place

The dramatic date is mid 475, as the terms of the treaty became public. The date of writing follows immediately after, when Graecus has returned to Marseille (§1) and there is still some ephemeral hope of undoing the truce (§5 *statum concordiae tam turpis incidite*). See Mathisen 2013, 222; Kelly 2020, 179.

Literature

Commentary: van Waarden 2010, 334–78. Study: Mratschek 2013, 254–68.

Commentary

1 Amantius earned a living as a go-between, trading in the harbour of Marseille for his fellow townsmen in Clermont; he served as a lector in Sidonius' church and more than once took letters from Sidonius with him. Prosopography: Mathisen 2020a, 79. **nugigerulus** 'a peddler of trumpery' (*OLD*), hapax in Sidonius, found one more time in Plautus *Aul.* 525: comedy is in the air – seemingly; the word plays on *gerulus litterarum*, 'letter-bearer' (see Intro 3.3 'Social Strata'). *nugae* 'trifles' is the usual self-depreciatory description of one's own poetry (especially light verse, deriving from Catul. 1.4 *meas . . . nugas*) or prose. **Massiliam suam** 'his beloved Marseille', where he goes as a merchant and where he found his wife. **de manubiis ciuitatis** 'from the booty of that town', both the profits from his trade and his wife, as told in letter 7.2. In that letter, Amantius' successes are pictured as a kind of triumphant military campaign against the town, in a sphere of merrymaking. Now the message is completely different. **si tamen cataplus arriserit** 'if only an incoming ship smiles on him': for *tamen*, see 7.1.2n. *cataplus* (κατάπλους) is a graecism from daily life (Mart. 12.74.1, Auson. *Ordo* 127 Green; Gualandri 1979, 159, Wolff 2020, 405). *arrideo* metaphorically (*OLD* 1b), i.e. to bring profit. The text is uncertain and there is little to go by (the MS tradition of Book 7 is garbled and letter 7 is often lacking (see Intro 6); see also 7.1.3n. *sciscitationem*): the α-branch reads *si tamen aut cataplus arriserit*; so does *M*, who then deletes *aut*; *F* and *Leip* read *si tamen cataplus arriserit*. Keeping *aut* requires postulating a lacuna, as indeed does Lütjohann; I follow Savaron in leaving it out. **per quem ioculariter plura garrirem** 'through whom I would be chattering on various things in jest': letters are a substitute for meeting and talking to friends, *amicorum colloquia absentium* (Cic. *Phil.* 2.7); cf. §6 *sed ... laxamus?* (see Intro 3.6 with n. 79; this letter belongs to the blaming type; see 7.18.3n. *concitatiorem*). *ioculariter*: playfulness is one of the ingredients of cultivated conversation and letter-writing; cf. 7.18.2n. *dictaui ... iocando ... nonnulla*. For adverbs in *-(i)ter*, see Wolff 2020, 398. *garrirem*: the first person singular draws attention to the 'I'; the first and second persons plural in the rest of the letter can be seen as 'real' plurals (the inhabitants of Clermont and the bishops respectively) with the possible exception of §6 *laxamus* (see Intro 4.2 '"You" and "I"'). **exercere laeta ... tristia sustinere** 'indulge in happiness ... endure sadness': *exerceo* of feelings, *OLD* 4. For the topos, cf. 2.12.3n. [during the illness of his daughter] *si iocari liberet in tristibus* and e.g. Cic. *Att.* 5.5.1 *nec iocandi locus est, ita me multa sollicitant*. The chiasmus creates the ditrochaeic clausula *sustinere* (preceded by a dactyl) rounding off this idea (see Intro 4.5). The conclusion ('I am not going to jest now') is left to the reader; instead *siquidem* immediately points out the cause. **nostri ... infelicis anguli** 'our ... ill-fated corner': Sidonius typically frames Clermont as a remote corner and its inhabitants as undeserved underdogs, cf. 3.1.4 *inuidiosi huius anguli* (significantly at the beginning of Book 3, where the crisis of the Auvergne first becomes manifest; see Intro 4.1), 7.1.1 *nos miseri Aruerni* (characterizing Book 7 as a whole), *Carm.* 33.21n. (in 7.17) *angulus iste .... paupertinusque recessus*. **hic ... cuius** 'such ... that'. **ut fama confirmat**: Sidonius probably has been informed unofficially about the peace conditions. **melior**: the α-branch has *minus*, while δ is divided: *Leip* and *F* have *melior* (followed by Savaron and Sirmond), *M*¹ *minor* (*M min*.). If the text must be emended, Mohr's *<misera> minus* (an instance of haplography/ parablepsis) might show the way: in that case, *minus <misera>* is more idiomatic, as it may point back to Plaut. *Rud.* 185 *minus miserae* and Ov. *Trist.* 1.6.4 *minus misero*, both concerning the unhappy fate of people. **sub bello** 'during the war' is not attested elsewhere, but in Sidonius the stylistic urge to form a parallelism creates its own idiom (Intro 4.5).

2 facta est seruitus nostra pretium securitatis alienae 'our enslavement has become the price of the safety of others': the untenable situation, despite his exertions, cannot have escaped the author (Harries 1994, 236, Delaplace 2015, 255). His indignation is understandable, as ceding the region to the Germans 'cost the locals a very great deal. But the cost to the central government was negligible or non-existent, since it is unlikely that this area of Gaul was any longer providing significant tax revenues or military levies for the emperor' (Ward-Perkins 2005, 56). *facta est*: the verb in initial position opens this so-called 'presentative' sentence, '<what happened is that> it became'; see *OLS* 2, 844–6 and 1015. **pro dolor** 'the grief of it!' is found Stat. *Theb.* 1.77 and from the 4th cent. onwards. **seruitus** is a key concept in this letter: the essential sovereignty of Roman citizens is being sacrificed, extending, for Sidonius himself at least, to the inhibition of freedom of speech and thought; see §6n. *libertas* and 7.18.3n. *animi seruitutem*. **si prisca replicarentur** 'if past events were recalled': the metaphorical use of *replicare* (lit. 'to roll back a scroll'; *OLD* 2, L–S B1) is later Latin usage, beginning with Fronto and Apuleius; see 1.5.1n. *replicatione*, 2.9.10n. *replicatio*. **audebant se quondam fratres Latio dicere et sanguine ab Iliaco populos computare** is a near quotation of Lucan's *Bellum ciuile* 1.427–8 *Aruernique ausi Latio se fingere fratres, | sanguine ab Iliaco populi* 'the Arvernians were proud to think of themselves as brothers of Rome, people from Trojan stock'. It is a case of imitation in a contrastive context (see Gualandri 2020, 298–9): in Lucan, the Gallic tribes – the Arverni among them – rejoice at the departure of Caesar's oppressive garrisons, here the Arvernians mourn being abandoned by their Roman brothers (for Sidonius' adoption of either viewpoint, depending on his current objective, cf. *Carm.* 7.148–52; see Mratschek 2013, 255–6; Stoehr-Monjou 2020, 339). The claim of Roman brotherhood and Trojan descent is a typical feature of Gallo-Roman identity, testifying to the high degree of Romanization of the upper echelons, traditionalistic and attached to the old Roman ideals. Cf. the Gallic *Panegyrici Latini*, e.g. 5.2.4, 8.21.2, and Amm. 15.9 on the origin of the Gallic tribes. The concept can be followed via the Franks into the Middle Ages and early modernity: rulers, peoples and towns vied to trace back their history to the Trojans, among others, to establish their legitimacy and identity (Luiselli 1978; Borgolte 2001; Plassmann 2006; Enenkel and Ottenheym 2018). *Latio* is metonymical for *Romanis. populos* 'people', 'citizens' (*TLL* 10/1.2715.70–2716.2, cf. 2722.66). *computare* 'to consider' is found from the 2nd cent. CE onwards and repeatedly in Sidonius, e.g. 1.2.5, 7.9.17. **hi sunt ... occidere**: now follows a complex tripartite statement to characterize the people of Clermont, three paragraphs, marked by anaphora: *hi sunt qui ... hi sunt qui ... illi ...* (variation in the third member), each of them with a second, subsidiary member, which elaborates on it: *cui saepe populo ... de quorum tamen sorte ... quem conuictum deinceps ...* Their characteristics are as follows: (1) the people of Clermont took the initiative, without knowing fear, (2) they endorsed responsibility, without getting a reward, (3) they showed loyalty, without seeing any results. The structure and thought imitate a passage in Silius Italicus' *Punica* 11.155–90. In it Decius exhorts the citizens of Capua not to surrender to Hannibal, but to remain loyal to the Romans. Using the same anaphora of *hi sunt qui*, Decius points out the qualities of the Romans, their initiative and fearlessness, their unselfishness and adherence to the law (173–6). He underlines his appeal by stating his own inevitable loyalty because of the Trojan blood in his veins (177–9). His plea, however, is in vain. Capua concludes a treaty with the barbarian (189–90). In Sidonius' parallel, the roles of the good guys are exchanged – in Silius the Romans, in Sidonius Clermont (with Sidonius in the role of a new Decius). Note also the curious echo of *remorunt* (line 176) in *remorati sunt* (see van Waarden 2010, 350–2, elaborated in further detail by Mratschek 2013, 258–64). Silius left few traces, but Sidonius clearly knew him; see *Carm.* 9.260 and Geisler 1887, 393–4, 409–10. **uiribus propriis hostium publicorum:** the opposition *proprius* (= *priuatus*) – *publicus* recurs in §4 where the bishops are accused of promoting their own interests instead of the common good. **non fuit ... formidini, ... fieret ... terrori** 'did not frighten, ... terrified': the detailed parallel, among other elements, effectively lines up *formidini* and *terrori*, rounding off with the cretic + spondee clausula *castra terrori*. As to *terrori*, in letter 3.3 Sidonius describes a modest counter-attack by his brother-in-law Ecdicius. **intra moenia:** for Clermont's cramped city space, see 7.1.2n. **positis** see 1.5.1n. *positus.* **uicinorum,** i.e. the Visigoths; in 7.11.1, Sidonius describes how he is torn between *periculum de uicinis* 'threat from our neighbours [the Visigoths]' and *inuidiam de patronis* 'hostility from our protectors [the Burgundians]'; cf. 3.4.1 *suspecti Burgundionibus, proximi Gothis.* **tam duces fuere quam milites** 'were their own commanders as well as soldiers', whereas Rome should have provided the commanders. The topos ultimately goes back to Hom. *Il.* 3.179 ἀμφότερον, βασιλεύς τ' ἀγαθὸς κρατερός τ' αἰχμητής '[Agamemnon] both a good king and a strong soldier', a line which was a favourite of Alexander the Great, who recognized himself in it (Plut. *Mor.* 1.331c); cf. variations of the motif, e.g. Ov. *Fast.* 199–200 [the Fabii] *miles ... | ... dux fieri ... aptus,* Sal. *Cat.* 20.16 [Catilina available in either role] *uel imperatore uel milite me utimini,* and Luc. 9.401–02 [Cato promising the same] *dux an miles eam.* The double cretic clausula (*-ere quam milites*) is twice as frequent in this letter as on average, for no obvious reason. **de quorum tamen sorte certaminum si quid prosperum cessit** 'however, if any of the fights for their life was successful', opposed to the following *si quid contrarium.* Both ensuing main clauses are also perfectly parallel, with a variation in the verbs, *(ad)uersa fregerunt* again creating a cretic + spondee clausula. **solata sunt** 'relieved' (*OLD* 1c, 2), in later Latin also in the weakened sense of 'benefited', 'helped' (poorly documented in dictionaries, see Mossberg 1934, 68–9; cf. §4 *mederi* and §6 *medicari*); the same for *consolari,* see e.g. 4.11.4 *consolabatur,* 7.17.3n. *solari;* cf. 1.9.6n. *solacium.* **Seronatum barbaris prouincias propinantem** 'Seronatus who was handing over his provinces to the barbarians': around 469 CE, Seronatus (see Hanaghan 2019, 93–4; Mathisen 2020a, 120–1) had been one of the leading officials in southern Gaul and promoted a policy of intensified contacts and cooperation with the Visigoths. Because of that, he had been brought to trial in Rome at the instigation of the conservative elements in the Gallic nobility, especially the Auvergne. In Rome, he may have had considerable support, because his condemnation and execution did not take place immediately. Our only source is his opponent Sidonius, who paints an ugly portrait of him in letters 2.1 and 5.13. Wolfram 1988, 187 puts the accusation into perspective, indicating 'that much of what strikes us as high-level politics and Romano-Gothic animosity was in reality a function of intergroup rivalries within Gaul's leading stratum' (the Arvandus affair is another case in point, see Intro 1 and 2.9.1n. *Ferreolum*). For Gaul's factions, see Mathisen 1993; for the problem of cooperation and treason, see Harries 1992, Teitler 1992. **prouincias**: the diocese of the Septem Provinciae (see Map 1). **propinantem** 'making a complimentary present of' (*OLD* 1c), with the basic meaning of 'to drink to somebody's health' in the background – an instance of black humour as apparent from 2.1.1, where Sidonius accuses Seronatus of drinking and mixing the blood of his innocent victims (*sanguinem ... propinauerat ... misceret*). **legibus tradere** 'to hand over to justice'. **res publica**, i.e. the central government. **praesumpsit** 'dared', in later Latin (L–S G, *TLL* 10/2.961.5–22).

3 This section is divided into three rhetorical questions, expressing the feelings of bitter disappointment that all sufferings and losses have been made pointless by the treaty. The first sums up the diverse problems Clermont faced: famine, fire, killing, pestilence. The second highlights famine and its consequences. The third summarizes the other two. Stylistically, this is Sidonius at his most mannered: artifice is the benchmark for emotion, the bizarre mirrors the tragic; see Intro 4.5 'Hyperbole' and, for this passage in particular, Gualandri 1979, 40–3. **hoccine meruerunt ...?** 'is this the reward for ...?': *hoccine* (with the archaic form *hocc*) is found in the comedians and after that in the archaizing authors of the second century CE (see Intro 4.5). **flamma:** the policy of scorched earth (cf. 6.12.5). **pingues ... macri** 'satiated ... emaciated': *pingues* 'dripping' with blood (cf. *Carm.* 7.260 *lorica*). **huius ... inclitae pacis** 'this wonderful peace': for the sarcasm, cf. e.g. Cic. *Catil.* 1.26 *illam praeclaram patientiam.* **tamen** 'so', 'apparently': for the versatility of *tamen* in later Latin, see 7.1.2n. Lütjohann's emendation *tam* is unnecessary. **herbas in cibum traximus** 'we took the grass as food': *trahere in* + acc. is 'to apply for the purpose of' (*OLD* 21), e.g. Ov. *Met* 8.245 *in exemplum.* **indiscretis foliis sucisque** 'with nothing to distinguish their leaves or juices', all being equally green, whether healthy or noxious. **manus fame concolor legit** 'a hand plucked which had the same colour due to hunger', i.e. the pallor induced by starvation (cf. *OLD uiridis* 2c; Bohîlţea-Mihuţ 2024, 395). *concolor*: cf. 7.17.1n. *concolor* (and further *Carm.* 27.10n. *concolor* (in 2.10)); for 'manneristic'

COMMENTARY: 7.7:3-4   205

conceits at the most intense moments, Intro 4.5. The whole passage is reminiscent of Lucan 6.110–13 where Caesar's troops are starving during the siege of Dyrrhachium; cf. also Lucan 4.412–14. **deuotionis experimentis nostris** 'our proofs of loyalty': resumes what preceded and is the topic of the sentence that follows. Editors generally prefer the emendation *nostri* (objective genitive, governed by *iactura*), which has contrastive focus to an implied 'you' which is made explicit in the next sentence; see Intro 4.3. **facta iactura est** '(they) have been jettisoned', referring to the proofs of loyalty. *facta ... est* is split probably to create an effective clausula cretic + spondee (with elision *(e)st*).

4 precamur: the plural includes the author and the people of Clermont. **nec utilis nec decori** 'neither effective nor appropriate': *decori* is gen. of the adj. *decorus*. In Greek and Roman moral philosophy, *decorum* (Gr. πρέπον) 'propriety', 'seemliness', 'discretion', is the ethical category that undergirds all other virtues, being inherently in accordance with the overarching ideal of *honestum* (Gr. καλόν) 'moral perfection' (Cic. *Off.* 1.93); furthermore, nothing can be *utile* if it is not also *honestum* (Cic. *Off.* 3.34 *nihil ... utile quod non idem honestum*); see Morford 2002, 87–94. **per uos legationes meant** 'via you the delegations come and go': cf. 7.6.10 [to the same four bishops] *per uos ... pacta condicionesque portantur*. **quamquam principe absente:** this suggests that the bishops had plenipotentiary discretion (explained next in *tractata ... committitur*); albeit politically rational, this was of course exploited emotionally by the victims. After the relative abundance of references to emperors in the first book, and their subsequent gradual reduction, this is the low point of imperial engagement in Gaul and of their presence in the narrative (Hanaghan 2019, 104). **tractata reseratur ... tractanda committitur** 'is made known once negotiated ... is entrusted to be negotiated': note the parallel wording of the opposition. **ueritatis asperitas** 'the harsh truth' (= *aspera ueritas*): for this so-called inverse genitive, see 1.5.8n. *amoena*. **conuicii inuidiam** 'the reproach of abuse': see *OLD convicium* 2a. For his speaking-out to be pardonable (*ueniabilis*), Sidonius pleads that he is motivated solely by *dolor*, not by any intention to be abusive. Although somewhat softened in this way, the sharp criticism which follows is a far cry from the usual practice of extreme and verbose politeness. **parum in commune consulitis** 'you scarcely care for the common cause': *parum* (*OLD* 3, like *minus* and *uix*) is used as a euphemism for *non* (see L–S IIB, Hofmann 1951, 145–6; cf. Chahoud 2010, 49); cf. 5.5.1n., 7.18.2n. *in commune* 'in the public interest' (*OLD* 4a): cf. 3.12.3n. in a different context. **concilium** is quite vague: either their own meeting as envoys (thus Loyen 2, 191 n.36) or else (as Anderson 2, 329 n.4 points out) the provincial assemblies of bishops (see *comprouincialum* below) or the (remains of the) *Concilium Septem Prouinciarum*, the provincial council of Southern Gaul (cf. e.g. 1.3.3). **publicis mederi periculis** 'to solve the dangers the state is in': note again the parallel opposition to the next phrase. For the weakened metaphor of *mederi* (lit. 'to heal'), cf. §2n. *solata sunt.* **priuatis studere fortunis:** the envoys were bishops of Marseille, Aix, Arles and Riez, precisely the part of Provence that would be exchanged for the Auvergne (Intro 3.2). **utique** 'in any case' (*OLD* 5): whatever exactly is going on behind the scenes, it reflects badly on yourselves. **non primi comprouincialium ... sed ultimi:** instead of being the foremost bishops (in rank), they will be the last (in time) as they are not going to be succeeded (cf. 7.6.7 accusing Euric of barring the succession). *comprouincialis* 'colleague', a fellow bishop in an ecclesiastical province. Ecclesiastical geography largely coincided with the imperial administrative division into *prouinciae*, each subdivided into *ciuitates* (see Mathisen 1989, 5–6). **coepistis esse** 'you have become', equivalent to *facti estis. coepit* + inf. in later Latin is common as an alternative for the perfect tense; see H–S 319, 796, Fruyt and Orlandini 2008; cf. 7.1.2n. *coepit.*

5 at quousque istae poterunt durare praestigiae? 'well, how long are these tricks possibly going to last?': clearly an echo of Cic. *Catil.* 1.1 *quousque tandem, Catilina, abutere patientia nostra?* The innocent *praestigiae* of Amantius and letter 7.2 (see §1n.) are supplanted by the dangerous tricks of the bishops. *at* marks the 'reaction to the observed fact that someone is (still) not behaving as he is expected to do' (Kroon 1995, 360). **non ... habere:** as there is to be no offspring, the ancestors will no longer be ancestors. *enim* 'clearly' makes an 'appeal to interpersonal consensus' (Kroon 1995, 202). *incipiunt ... habere* 'will have': periphrastic future tense in later Latin, where the simple future is disappearing; see H–S 313, *OLS* 1, 429–42. **uel** 'at any rate': *OLD* 6, frequent in later Latin. **consilio, quo potestis** 'with all possible inventiveness' or 'by counsel, in which you have the power' (Anderson) or 'influencing the Council, where you are powerful' (Loyen, my translation). **statum concordiae ... incidite** 'put an end to the formal agreement'; for the juridical term *status* ('legal position', *OLD* 10), cf. 6.2.3 and 6.4.3, and see Heumann–Seckel 554 s.v. *incīdite*: *OLD* 6. **adhuc ... adhuc ... adhuc:** the triple anaphora makes for pathos. **delectat:** for the oxymoron of enjoying terrible things, cf. 7.13.3 *ieiuniis delectatur* 'he enjoys fasting'. **qui non potuimus uiribus obtineri** 'we who could not be taken by force', namely by the barbarian. **inuenisse uos certum est quid barbarum suaderetis ignaui** 'it is certain that it is you who thought up what mean thing you could recommend to the barbarian', i.e. the Visigoths could not defeat us by force; instead, we have been defeated by the dishonesty you suggested to them. *barbarum* is probably not neuter as often thought ('something barbarian') but masculine (as proposed by Shackleton Bailey 1982, 169–70; for *suadere alqm alqd*, see H–S 32–3). *ignaui* is usually taken as an apposition to *uos* ('you cowards' or 'in your cowardice'); taking it as a genitive with *quid* instead, apart from the more idiomatic phrasing (verbal hyperbaton, see 2.12.1n. *germano* and elsewhere), creates the more meaningful opposition (fair) force vs (unfair) bargaining, as applied by the barbarians (*OLD ignauus* 4).

6 sed cur dolori nimio frena laxamus? is a type of phrase with which epistolographers as it were interrupt and correct themselves, in imitation of colloquial language, cf. e.g. Cic. *Att.* 4.19.2, Plin. 8.14.24; for letters as conversations, see Intro 3.6 with n. 79. *frena laxare* 'to give free rein (to emotions)', cf., similarly, Plin. 5.21.6 *sed quid ego indulgeo dolori? cui si frenos remittas, nulla materia non maxima est*. The plural *laxamus* most probably refers to the singular writer, who, as it were, retires into the background, apologizing; see Intro 4.2 '"You" and "I"'. **ignoscite afflictis nec imputate maerentibus** 'pardon those who are ruined and do not blame those who mourn'. **namque** instead of *nam*: see 1.5.1n. *namque.* **sperat** 'can expect' (*OLD* 5). **medicari nostris ultimis:** *medicari* 'to help in', 'to save from', lit. 'to cure', aptly in connexion with following *sanguis uiuat*; for the metaphor, cf. §2n. *solata* and §4n. *mederi*. *nostris ultimis* 'our extremity': *OLD ultimus* 6b, neut. pl. as substantive. **prece sedula** 'by your urgent plea', humbly asking Euric for leniency. **ut sanguis uiuat** 'that our bloodline may live': a striking collocation if one looks back to §2, where the lineage of the Arverni was nothing less than *sanguine ab Iliaco*, now condemned to *seruitus* (here *moritura libertas*). The circle is complete. **quorum est moritura libertas** 'whose freedom is about to die': *libertas* 'the political status of a sovereign people', 'freedom', 'independence' (*OLD* 2), for Sidonius very much associated with being Roman: 1.6.2 [Rome] *patriam libertatis*; after glimpses of hope in the past (5.12.2 *libertatis fenestra*), civic liberty is about to die in Clermont (2.1.4 *ciuium extrema libertas*); cf. §2n. *seruitus*. Cf. Tac. *Ann.* 1.74.5 *uestigia morientis libertatis*, where *libertas* denotes senatorial autonomy and freedom of speech, threatened under the principate. For Tacitus and contemporaries like Pliny, the hope of revival of *libertas* under the emperor Trajan was a central theme (cf. e.g. Plin. 8.14.3 *reducta libertas*, and his entire panegyric of Trajan). Sidonius grafted much of his cultural identity on to the Trajanic era; see Intro 3.3 'Elite Status' with n. 48, Mratschek 2008. *moritura libertas* and *sanguis uiuat* are a chiasmus; clausula cretic + spondee. **parate exulibus terram:** for the fronted emphatic imperative, cf. 3.7.4 *mandate ... palpate*, see *OLS* 2, 1033–6. For *exulibus*, cf. the famous quote 2.1.4 *seu patriam dimittere seu* *capillos* 'to give up their home town or their hair', exile or becoming a cleric as the only feasible alternatives for the nobility if abandoned by the emperor. **capiendis redemptionem** 'ransom for those going to be taken captive': see Harries 1994, 216–17 on the role of the church in ransoming prisoners. For the gerundive taking over the function of the future passive participle in later Latin, see 1.9.6n. *admittendo*. **peregrinaturis** 'those going to travel away from home' (cf. *OLD* 1a). **si murus noster aperitur hostibus, non sit clausus uester hospitibus**: *murus ... uester*: the towns governed by the bishops or Graecus' Marseille specifically? The letter's conclusion is a dignified doublet, with opposition and chiasmus *noster aperitur–clausus uester*, and paronomasia *hostibus–hospitibus*; clausula cretic + tribrach.

LETTER 7.17 WITH POEM 33: CLERMONT AND THE MONKS

Outline

'You have asked me to write the text for a funerary inscription for the abbot Abraham. Apart from it being impossible to refuse you anything, my main motivation is the fervour with which count Victorius has taken the funeral in hand. As he has taken on the main responsibility, I am happy to be able to make the modest contribution of the epitaph.' (§§ 1–2)

POEM (Carm. 33): The monk Abraham, persecuted in Mesopotamia, flees to the West, performing miracles on the way. Disdaining the metropolises, he settles in Clermont, where he builds a church. Now here is an end to his wanderings: he has returned to his celestial home, to Abraham's bosom, to the rivers of paradise.

'There you are. In return, I ask you to undertake the speedy reform of Abraham's monastery along the lines of Lérins and Grigny. The new head, Auxanius, is too old and feeble to discipline the young monks in particular. He is a person who rather obeys than commands, so please let him oversee the congregation, but you should oversee him.' (§§ 3–4).

Introduction

Asceticism as an element of hope and an antidote to contemporary secular disappointments: that is what the second part of Book 7, letters 12–17, is about. Books 6 and 7, with their addressees consisting entirely of bishops and, in the second half of the latter, monks and aspiring clerics, present a cast of characters who are at the centre of a reinvented world. Letters

7.12–17, in particular, address a state of ferment in which the closely knit Gallo-Roman elite is shifting its moral and religious parameters along with its political certainties. The impetus for this to happen is asceticism.

Discussion

Letter 7.17 is the cornerstone of Sidonius' complex vision of a Christian society that is both new and traditional, ascetically sensitized and aristocratic, under Visigothic rule. The new political reality, represented by the Visigothic governor, *comes ciuitatis*, is recognized for what it is: inevitable and perhaps even useful. It is embraced with an ostentatiousness that disguises a degree of unease. The tacit power struggle unfolds via the deathbed mourning and funeral of the abbot Abraham of Clermont and is, with hindsight, part of the shift of control over the ritual from the family to the church in late antiquity (Rebillard 2009, Mogen 2020). Meanwhile, for Sidonius, poetry, which was rejected earlier as incompatible with the episcopal calling (see Intro 4.1), now finds a fitting voice in composing the epitaph of a saintly abbot. Letter and poetic insert mutually reinforce each other for the complex message conveyed (see Intro 3.6). Ausonius takes pride of place in the intertextual epitaph along with the Bible, interspersed with specks from Horace and Ovid. Letter and poem gain further colour from repeated reminiscences from Virgil.

The **abbot Abraham** of the monastery of Saint Quiricus in Clermont was purportedly a religious refugee from Persia, victim of the intermittent persecutions of Christians in the Sassanid empire in the fifth century. After a wide-ranging trek through the eastern monastic world, he may have been invited to Clermont by Sidonius' predecessor to propagate asceticism, bringing relics of the eastern child-saint Quiricus with him. Sidonius' letter is the essential account for his life; Gregory's hagiography in *Hist.* 2.21 and *Vit. patr.* 3 (*MGH SS rer. Merov.* 1,2: 222–3) heavily relies on it (cf. Intro 5). No doubt a charismatic figure, at his death his legacy was institutionalized – as apparent from this letter – in accordance with the trend in the development of monastic rules (see §3n. *regulam*). The abbot's namesake, the biblical patriarch Abraham, is among the figures with whom early western monasticism, and the Lérins community in particular, most strongly identified (further to Lérins, Intro 3.4 and *Ep.* 8.15 Discussion 'Saints' Lives'). A monk is equated with Abraham in an allegorical interpretation of Genesis 12.1 where God says to Abraham: 'Leave your own country, your kinsmen, and your father's house, and go to a country that I will show you'. A monk renounces possessions, family and the world as a whole: his fatherland is heaven (cf. Cassian *Conl.* 3.6.2).

Prosopography: Mathisen 2020a, 77, van Waarden 2016, 15 and 202–5; for asceticism, monasticism, miracles and relics, see Intro 3.4; for monastic rules, de Vogüé 1982, Rousseau 2000, 763–4.

Victorius was *comes et dux Aquitaniae Primae* in the service of the Visigoths from *c.* 471 to 479/80. He initially governed seven of its eight *ciuitates*, then, finally, in 475, Clermont as well, which he turned into his residence, becoming its *comes ciuitatis* (the local executive of the Visigoths, in charge of both military and civil affairs; Wolfram 1988, 211–17). Apparently chosen to reconcile the Auvergne to Visigothic rule, Victorius occupied an ambiguous position throughout this period. By accepting the appointment, he had *de facto* assumed full responsibility for the conquest of the Auvergne, ousting its last Roman military *dux*, Sidonius' brother-in-law Ecdicius, and endorsing the repressive measures against its bishops (see letter 7.6) including Sidonius. On the other hand, he helped obtain amnesty for Sidonius (4.10.2), built churches in Clermont (for St Germanus among others, who was promoted by Sidonius and the Lérins group; see 8.15 Discussion 'Saints' Lives' and van Waarden 2016, 206 n. 22) and enlarged the shrine of Julian, the local patron saint and favourite of the Aviti and Apollinares (cf. 7.1.1n. *martyris ... Iuliani*). The downside of this was, however, that it threatened the local patronage of these established families (van Waarden 2016, 207). In the present letter, Victorius appears keen to boost his moral authority by overseeing the burial of a popular abbot. In about 480, menaced in Clermont for sexual harassment, he fled to Rome, in the company of Sidonius' son Apollinaris, where he was killed (Greg. Tur. *Glor. mart.* 44). Prosopography: Mathisen 2020a, 126–7, van Waarden 2016, 205–9.

Addressee

The Volusianus, addressee of this letter, a *conuersus* (Intro 3.4) or an aspiring cleric at the time of writing (see commentary on *fratri*) and supervisor of Saint Quiricus monastery at Sidonius' behest, may be the same as two other contemporary Volusiani: a senator from Tours, owner of an estate at Bayeux (4.18.2), and the bishop of Tours from *c.* 490, exiled by the Visigoths on suspicion of collusion with the Franks. Prosopography: Mathisen 2020a, 127; discussion: van Waarden 2016, 200–1.

Date and Place

The dramatic date is the second half of 477, after Sidonius' return from exile (probably early that year; see Mathisen 2013, 223, van Waarden 2016, 201–2). It will have been written shortly after, before he finalized his collection of Books 1–7. This means that, also chronologically, this letter is the last but one in Book 7.

Literature

Commentary: van Waarden 2016, 198–251. Studies of *Carm.* 33: Condorelli 2013, 273–6, Consolino 2020, 361–2.

Commentary

fratri 'brother', 'fellow-Christian' (Blaise s.v., O'Brien 1930, 84) It is highly unusual, for persons other than bishops, not to be provided with the marker *suo* in Sidonius' address system (Intro 4.2), the only other exception being the preceding letter 7.16 to the abbot Chariobaudus: *Sidonius Chariobaudo abbati salutem*. The MSS reflect this anomaly: whereas, in 7.17, δ has *fratri*, α variously has *suo* (*CVat1661*), *suo* changed to *fratri* (A) and *fratri suo* (S). Both letters are addressed to figures in the monastic sphere. It is tempting to take *fratri* as 'monk' (Loyen 3, 195 n. 86) but this cannot be linguistically corroborated (van Waarden 2016, 40–5). Sidonius seems to stress his ties with Volusianus as an actively engaged Christian – probably a *conuersus* or an aspiring clergyman – as Book 7 ends in the *nec plus ultra* of monastic observation.

1 iubes: for the *iubes–pareo* motif, see Intro 4.2. **domine frater** 'my lord brother': a formula of respect among equals, see Intro 4.2 'Address'. **lege amicitiae** 'by the law of friendship': see Intro 3.3 'Social Conventions'. **diu desides digitos incudibus officinae ueteris imponere** 'to lay my long inactive fingers to the anvils of my old workshop' is a free reference to Vulcan's smithy, where the Cyclopes are instructed to put everything aside and start forging new armour for Aeneas: Verg. *Aen.* 8.451 *gemit impositis incudibus antrum* (cf. *Georg.* 4.173), perhaps with a hint of Hor. *Carm.* 1.4.7–8 *Cyclopum | Volcanus ... uisit officinas*. The reminiscence from Virgil explains the illogical plural *incudibus*. Sidonius has long been inactive as a poet (*diu desides, ueteris*) because a bishop is supposed to take his distance from (light) verse; poetry nevertheless reappears especially in Books 8 and 9 (see 2.10 Introduction). *digitos imponere* is a choice variation on *manum imponere* + dat. 'to try one's hand at', esp. of undertaking a literary work (e.g. Ov. *Pont.* 4.8.82). *incudibus*: the 'anvil' of poetry introduced by Horace *Ars* 441 *male tornatos incudi reddere uersus*; cf. 9.13.2 *Horatiana incude formatos Asclepiadeos*; Condorelli 2004. *officinae OLD* c, cf. 4.8.5 *intra officinam litteratorum carminis si quid incus metrica produxerit*. There is strong alliteration in *d*. **sancto** is a common epithet for all ranks of ecclesiastics (van Waarden 2010, 163, cf. 2.9.6n. *sancte*, 2.10.2n. *sancti*). **neniam sepulchralem** 'funeral song': for *nenia*, see 1.9.7n. *neniis*. *sepulchralis* (instead of *funebris*) is rare (first found Ov. *Ep.* 2.120), generally with nasty associations of doom and magic, which are absent here. **luctuosis carminibus inscribere** 'inscribe in elegiac verse', analogous to 2.8.2 *neniam funebrem ... per elegos ... marmori incisam*. It is not certain that this and similar literary epitaphs were meant to be engraved, but their length would certainly allow it (Wolff 2014, Consolino 2020, 361 with n.100; cf. Lauxtermann 2003, 215 for the Greek counterpart ἐπιτύμβιος, ἐπιτάφιος; see §2 *exaraturi*). Other verse epitaphs in the letters include *Carm.* 26 (in 2.8.3) on the lady Filimatia, 28 (in 3.12; see commentary in this volume) on his grandfather Apollinaris, and 30 (in 4.11) on his friend Claudianus Mamertus. The one on Abraham is the only one in the customary elegiac couplets (Hor. *Ars* 75–6 *uersibus impariter iunctis querimonia ... | ... inclusa est*), the others being in Sidonius' beloved Phalaecian hendecasyllables (Sidonius himself pointed out the anomaly at Filimatia's obituary, 2.8.2 (cited in part above) *non per elegos sed per hendecasyllabos ... dictaui*). **obsecundabo** 'I shall comply with' (*OLD* 1), an eager start in the first person singular (Intro 4.2 '"You" and "I"'); contrast below §2 *conferimus* and 3 *persoluimus*. **amplissimi uiri Victorii comitis:** the title *amplissimus* 'distinguished' is given to senators (e.g. 1.9.2 *in amplissimo ordine*) and to the highest offices of *consul, praefectus praetorio* and *praefectus urbi* (Heumann–Seckel s.v. *amplus*). Victorius is given his formal due as a top-level administrator, which only heightens the tension between Sidonius and him. **deuotione praeuentus** 'stimulated by the loyalty': *deuotio* 'allegiance', 'loyalty' is post-classical (*TLL* 5/1.879.19–75). *praeuenire* 'to precede' with the connotation of setting an example, cf. *TLL* 10/2.1101.23–30. **iure saeculari patronum, iure ecclesiastico filium:** Victorius is his superior in the *patronus–cliens* relationship 'according to secular law' (cf. 4.10.2 where Victorius, as Sidonius' *redux patronus*, has brought him back from exile; *ius saeculare* is Sidonius' own coinage to create a parallel with *ius ecclesiasticum*), but dependent on him in ecclesiastical terms. Both potentially antagonistic positions are clearly marked out before Sidonius begins the account of the funeral. The parallelism is followed by a chiasmus, *excolo ut cliens, ut pater diligo*. The ensuing deathbed scene is told in an overt narrative style, rather 'telling' than 'showing': the narrator interprets what is happening (pointing out Victorius' *cura* and his *dignitas*) and deploys a complex clause structure (see Intro 4.3). **quae ... aut qualis:** i.e. what he felt and how deeply, cf. Cic. *Mil.* 60 *quae erat aut qualis quaestio?* **sibi** is an ethic dative, conveying more 'warmth' than a genitive or a possessive pronoun (*NLS* §66, *OLS* 1, 919–23). **famulos Christi** 'the servants of Christ' (from 1 Cor. 4.1 ὑπηρέτας

Χριστοῦ) is a frequently occurring phrase, but only here in Sidonius. It is used to indicate the faithful, and priests in particular (Blaise s.v. *famulus* II). **torum circa** 'around the bed' is poetical (*torus* instead of *lectus*) and archaizing (anastrophe of *circa*, H–S 216) for a grand effect. The rare meaning 'sickbed', 'deathbed', recalls such heroic funerary scenes as Dido's in Verg. *Aen.* 4.508 and Misenus' in *Aen.* 6.220. **antistitis** here 'abbot': in Christian usage, *antistes* 'overseer' indicates any supervisor in the Church, in particular a priest or a bishop (Blaise s.v.). **non dignitatem minus quam membra curuatus** 'bent as to his dignity no less than to his limbs': *dignitatem* and *membra* are accusative of respect or Greek accusative (*NLS* §19, *OLS* 1, 1076), coupled in a zeugmatic way (abstract–concrete). Status being a main concern in this society (see Intro 3.3), every potential infringement is signalled, but, on the other hand, prestige is enhanced by condescension (cf. e.g. 7.4.2 'you do not break, but bend the high dignity of priesthood by your kindness', *non frangitis ... sed flectitis*). **propinqua morte pallentem:** cf. Verg. *Aen.* 8.709 *pallens morte futura* [Cleopatra] and 4.644 *pallida morte futura* [Dido], lending an epic ring to Abraham's death. As so often in Sidonius, emotion is filtered through the intertext (Gualandri 1979, 43). For colour, see Bohîlţea-Mihuţ 2024, 395. **concolor:** see *Carm.* 27.10n. *concolor* (in 2.10). **quid ... uellet** 'how he felt towards' (*OLD* 15). **lacrimis indicibus** 'telling tears': cf. e.g. *Paneg.* 5[8].9.6 *cum lacrimae illae pietatis essent indices, non doloris*. The clausula *-dicibus ostenderet* is the fairly rare paeon IV + cretic (∪∪∪– –∪×; van Waarden and Kelly 2020, 474).

2 Victorius clearly takes over the funeral, and Sidonius acquiesces, no doubt for strategic reasons, without so much as hinting at his own role as bishop in the liturgy, most importantly in administering the eucharist as *uiaticum* (Council of Orange (441) canon 3 (Munier 1963, 78–9); Mogen 2020, 16–18). **maximas humandi funeris partes:** the hyperbaton stresses the focus function of the clause (*OLS* 2, 1099). *humandi funeris*: for *funus* 'corpse', see *OLD* 2a. The collocation with *humare* is specific for Sidonius, cf. *Carm.* 16.121 *funeribus ... humandis*. **apparatu supercurrentis impendii** 'by providing ...' or 'by the sumptuousness of the surpassing expenditure' (*OLD* 1c, 2 respectively) is lavish in its own formulation. *supercurro* 'to exceed' is rare, first attested Plin. 7.18.3 (*OLD* 2) and then in 5th- and 6th-cent. authors experimenting with words. **ad obsequium** 'in fulfilment of my duty', 'obediently' (*OLD* 2–4), the provision of a proper burial in accordance with the wishes of the deceased being a moral and legal obligation (*Dig.* 5.3.50.1 *ad obsequium supremae uoluntatis*; Meyer 1990, 77–8). In addition, in the *patronus–cliens* relationship, *obsequium* 'deference' is also a concrete expression of *amicitia*, complementary to *officium* 'obligation' (7.2.4 *grandaeuos obsequiis, aequaeuos officiis obligare*; Intro 3.3 'Social Conventions'). **uerba conferimus:** whereas someone else organizes the funeral, Sidonius contributes (only) words – a version of the modesty topos, minimizing his own forte as a writer (the first person plural emphasizes this), cf. 4.11.7 *fecique ad epitaphium quod alii fecerunt ad sepulchrum*, and, in direct imitation, Ennodius *Ep.* 6.25 *uos beneficia, me uerba conferre*. The entire formulation might originate in Plin. 5.7.4 *illius hoc munus, illius liberalitas; nostrum tantum obsequium uocetur*. **exaraturi stili scalpentis impressu** 'going to inscribe by the impress of my carving pen', hinting at future inscription on the tomb (Shackleton Bailey 1997, 173; see proviso at §1n. *inscribere*). **ceterum** 'well' marks the transition to a new stage in the narrative or the argumentation (*OLS* 2, 1182–3). **uiri mores gesta uirtutes** 'the man's character, career, merits' are the essential elements in a *laudatio*: one's hereditary disposition (usually the ancestors are included) and how one makes use of it in the course of one's life (Quint. *Inst.* 3.7.10–18; van Waarden 2010, 439–42, van Waarden 2016, 66–7); cf. 8.15.1n. *mores merita uirtutes*. *uiri* and the following *meorum*, preceding their head nouns *mores* etc. and *dictorum*, are contrastive (the latter causing hyperbaton) (*OLS* 2, 859–62, 1072–4 and 1084–91). **uilitate dictorum:** self-depreciation again, cf. Ennod. *Dict.* 8 p. 78 l. 18 Vogel *eloquii uilitas*. **ponderabuntur** 'will be weighed up' (*OLD* 2); the clausula is a one-word cretic + spondee (Intro 4.5).

Poem 33: Epitaph

Near the end of Book 7, a poem breaks through the episcopal self-censure of not publishing poetry. It celebrates a 'holy man' (Brown 1971a), the embodiment of the ideal of a spiritual way of life for the literate nobility. Thoroughly Christian in its biblical imagery, it also pays homage to the classical tradition by way of a (Christianized and inverted) miniature *ordo urbium nobilium* in the vein of Ausonius (for the genre of city praise, Di Salvo 2000, 9–12). Ausonius (*Ordo*, no. 24 Green) celebrates first Rome, Constantinople and Carthage, then Antioch and Alexandria, third the imperial residences Trier and Milan among other towns and finally his hometown Bordeaux. Sidonius, significantly, starts with Rome, Constantinople and Jerusalem, the hallowed cities of the Christian empire, to continue with Alexandria, Antioch and Carthage, followed by the then residences Ravenna and Milan, and rounded off with his hometown Clermont. Not only is the order inverted, the topos itself is, as all these important cities are rejected but for tiny Clermont. The poem's structure is tripartite: verses 1–14 Abraham's origin and flight, marked by puns rounding off couplets, 15–24 Abraham's wanderings imitating

Ausonius in miniature, and 25–30 Abraham in heaven, full of biblical allusions.

Through its embedding in the letter, the poem acquires an undercurrent of resistance consisting in a political 'hidden message'. The letter conveys the lingering resentment and reluctant acceptance of the regime Sidonius once opposed. Opposition to a tyrant, imprisonment and exile (and homecoming as an exercise in humility) are as true for Sidonius as they had been for Abraham: dislocation and estrangement, a stolen *patria* and a precarious *peregrinatio* (as Sidonius calls his own exile at 4.10.1; cf. 1.5.1n. *peregrinationis*).

For detailed analysis, see Gualandri 1993, 209–12; Condorelli 2013, 273–6; van Waarden 2016, 222–8; Consolino 2020, 361–2. The metre is the elegiac couplet, common in funerary poems (*OCD* 'Elegiac poetry, Latin'; see also §1n. *luctuosis*). For embedded poems in prose letters, especially numerous in late antiquity, see letter 2.10 Introduction, with literature. On 'hidden messages', Schwitter 2015, 237–97. Comprehensively on epistolography, Intro 3.6.

1–2 sanctis merito sociande patronis 'rightly (going) to be united with your patron saints', i.e. buried next to them (the much sought after burial *ad sanctos*; for Abraham, they certainly included St Quiricus) as well as meeting them in heaven. Martyrs and saints have immediate access to heaven (Dresken-Weiland 2007, 292); extending this prerogative to ascetics and the clergy, as their right by merit (*merito*), contemporary epitaphs in Gaul are faithful to the traditional Roman belief that *merita* can claim *praemia* (Heinzelmann 1976, 87–8 and 97 on 'Asketenlob', praise of ascetics; Prinz 1988, 489–93 and 656–7 on aristocratic 'Selbstheiligung', self-sanctification; for contemporary theology, see Intro 3.4 with n. 63). Cf. Sidonius' own epitaph (see Appendix): *Sanctis contiguus sacroque patri | uiuit sic meritis Apollinaris*; for the roots of the motif, Ov. *Ars* 3.409–10 *Ennius emeruit … | contiguus poni, Scipio magne, tibi. sociande*: for the gerundive, see 1.9.6n. *admittendo*. Through the vocative, the epitaph speaks directly to the deceased. Epitaphs make use of the first, the second or the third person. As a rule of thumb, in a first-person epitaph, the deceased will muse on their life and death or, when a Christian, reach out for afterlife; formulated in the second person, the epitaph usually is a lament of the next-of-kin; in the third person, it typically commemorates the qualities of the deceased (Lauxtermann 2003, 215–16). Abraham's epitaph is a mixture of types two and three. **collegas:** commonly used to refer to fellow clergymen, it can also include apostles and saints, in a typical gesture of 'Selbstheiligung', as at 6.1.2 *quod dixit domino tuus ille collega* 'what that great colleague [the apostle Peter] of yours [bishop Lupus] said to the Lord'. **non trepidem** 'I would not hesitate': potential subjunctive (L&S §§257–9). The first person is a striking intrusion of the 'I' of the mourner (i.e. the author) speaking to the deceased.

3–4 sic 'in so far', 'to the extent', with restrictive *ut*-clause (*OLD* 8). **mox** 'next', 'close' (*OLD* 3). **partem regni portio martyrii**: Abraham's sufferings in the Persian persecution were a partial martyrdom, so that he now shares in the heavenly reward of the martyrs (Anderson n. 2). *regni*: the martyrs 'reign' with Christ in heaven (*Apoc.* 20.6 *et regnabunt cum illo*, Aug. *Civ.* 20.9 *regnant mortui, qui usque ad mortem pro ueritate certarunt*). For a similarly formulated bargain, cf. 7.1.7n. *pars patrocinii ... pars patroni*.

5–6 natus ad Euphraten is from Juv. 1.103–4 '*cur timeam dubitemue locum defendere, quamuis | natus ad Euphraten?*', words spoken by a vulgar and snobbish freedman, as he elbows aside any senator who happens to be less wealthy. Being 'born on the Euphrates' is clearly not an advantage in Rome. Unexpectedly, Sidonius turns this on its head: Euphrates is paradise, and Abraham is a saint. **ergastula** 'prison (for forced labour)' (*OLD* 1a, *TLL* 5/2.758.24). **quinquennali uincula laxa fame** 'the chains that grew loose due to five years of hunger': starvation and distress more than once inspire oxymoronic conceits like 'loose cuffs' (see Intro 4.5).

7–8 regi: the Persian king at the time was Yazdgird II (438–57); see *ODLA* 1601. **Susidis orae** 'the country of Susa': *Susis, -idis* is the feminine adjective of Susa (*Carm.* 34.47 *aulae Susidis*), one of Persia's royal residences (present-day Shush in south-west Iran with its archaeological site). Sidonius seems to mean the whole of Persia, but the province of Susa in particular accommodated several prisoner-of-war camps and the notorious state prison (*ODLA* 1431, Gropp 2005). **occiduum ... sŏlus ad usque sŏlum:** *occiduus* 'western' (*OLD* 3) is first found at Ov. *Fast.* 1.3.14 *occiduas ... aquas. sōlus ... sŏlum* 'alone ... ground' plays on the formula *sōlus ... sŏlum* 'one to one' from comedy (Pl. *Capt.* 602, *Trin.* 153, Ter. *Hec.* 557). The word order gives a vivid impression of the fugitive's vulnerability, *solus* in the middle, the far west at the line's extremes.

9–10 confessorem, because of his firmness in suffering persecution (the attribute is a rare accolade in Sidonius, for Ambrose (see 7.1.7n. *confessorem*) and St Martin (4.18.4) only). **uirtutum signa** 'signs of his miraculous powers': for *uirtutes*, see 7.1.4n. *post uirtutum experimenta*. **fers, fugitiue, fugam:** *ferre fugam* + dat. 'to put someone to flight' is Sidonius' own invention (elsewhere it is rather 'to endure flight', e.g. Ov. *Tr.* 3.1.74), facilitating a paradoxical and alliterative phrase.

11–12 Lemurum ... turba: Sidonius is the only late antique author, apart from antiquarians, to mention these nightly spectres – a piece of ancient lore he may have found in poetry or in Apuleius (see *OLD* s.v.), or in Varro's encyclopaedic works, which he still had in his library (see 2.9.4, 8.6.18). For demons besieging monks ever since Athanasius' *Life of Antony*, see Flint 1999, esp. 310–15, Brakke 2006. **se clamat cedere:** demons will recoil when confronted with divine power (cf. 7.1.4n. *ignis recussus* and *affuit flammae cedere*), crying out loud (cf. Jesus and the demons, Matth. 8.28–34, Luc. 8.26–34). **exul ... in exilium**, echoing the wordplay *fugitiue–fugam*.

13–14 This couplet (still relying on wordplay) serves as a transition to the section on the great cities that cannot keep Abraham, who instead prefers a modest abode in Clermont (Shackleton Bailey 1997, 174). **ambitus:** even massive courtship (*OLD* 7) does not get hold of him. **onerosus honor:** the proverbial *onus est honos* (Var. *L.* 5.73; cf. 7.9.7 *multum ... honoris, plus oneris*); see Otto 1890, 167.

15–16 Romuleos ... Byzantinosque fragores: the relatively rare adjectives (Kelly 2012) stress the antiquity of both Rome and Constantinople, for Rome possibly also its divine origin, like Ausonius in the first line of the *Ordo*: *divum domus ... Roma* 'house of the gods', including the deified Romulus (cf. *Carm.* 23.234–6 *Byzantina ... Romulea*). *fragor* is the roar of the big city, specifically of the audience in the (amphi)theatre and circus (*OLD* 2). **sagittifero ... Tito:** according to Suet. *Tit.* 5.2, in the final attack on Jerusalem (70 CE), the emperor Titus *duodecim propugnatores totidem sagittarum confecit ictibus* 'killed twelve defenders with as many bowshots'. The poetical adjective is striking of a Roman as it is normally applied to mythical figures or distant peoples (e.g. Catul. 11.6 *sagittiferosue Parthos*). Given that Jerusalem is the distinctively 'Christian' addition in Sidonius' list of cities (see introduction above), it might seem strange that it is evoked through the bloody exploits of a Roman conqueror. This is connected with the layout of the poem. Elsewhere, Sidonius shows himself well aware of the city's spiritual dimensions (7.6.4 *spiritalem Ierusalem*), but in this poem the religious and monastic elements come at the beginning and end, whereas this middle section focuses on the mundane, even brutal, aspects of the world to which Abraham refused to yield. Technically, there is the difficulty of fitting *Ierusalem/Hierosolyma* into verse.

17–18 The cities of Alexandria, Antioch and Carthage are evoked through their founders or those in whose honour they were named: Alexander the Great (332 BCE), Antiochus' son Seleucus I Nicator (300 BCE) and

Dido, respectively. Alexandria and Antioch were the two biggest eastern cities before the foundation of Constantinople. **Elisseae** is the adjective of Elissa, another name for Dido (Verg. *Aen.* 4.335 and later); Sidonius also uses it at *Carm.* 7.445 *Elisseae … Byrsae*; it is first attested in Silius Italicus. **Byrsica** is a hapax. Byrsa is the walled citadel of Carthage (Verg. *Aen.* 1.367).

19–20 The two imperial residences of Ravenna and Milan are surprisingly depicted as rural communities. Sidonius evidently wants them to appear second-rate compared to the preceding metropolises. Is this perhaps a political statement? Now that ties with the Roman empire have been severed, its iconic administrative capitals appear as superseded and definitely unhelpful for Clermont. **paludicolae … Rauennae:** situated amidst swamps and canals, the town is a stock target for satire on account of its frogs and mosquitoes (1.5.5–6nn.). *paludicola* 'marsh-dwelling' is a later poetic compound: cf. 4.1.4 *paludicolas Sygambros, De mens.* 2.6 *paludicolam … auem* (*Anth. lat.* 395 R), formed on the Ovidian model of e.g. *ruricola* (*Am.* 3.2.53) and *amnicola* (*Met.* 10.96). **lanigero de sue** 'from a hairy boar': Sidonius may have found this fanciful ancient etymology of Mediolanum from *lana* 'wool' in Claud. *Epith. Hon.* 182–3 *uolans ad moenia Gallis | condita, lanigeri suis ostentantia pellem*, cf. Rut. Nam. fr. A6 <*m*>*edium lanea terga suem.* Isid. *Orig.* 15.1.57 has: *uocatum autem Mediolanum ab eo quod ibi sus medio lanea perhibetur inuenta* 'it is called Mediolanum because it is held that a hairy sow was found in the middle of it'. An early medieval emblem of Milan is the *scrofa semilanuta* (https://en.wikipedia.org/wiki/Milan, Toponymy).

21–22 This is typical Lerinian discourse (see Intro 3.4). Vincent of Lérins begins his *Commonitorium* by saying that he has found the right place for writing, because 'I live in the seclusion of a monastery, on a remote country estate, far from the bustle and the crowds of the towns, where, without great distraction, one can do what is sung in the psalm: Be still, and know that I am God'. **angulus iste placet** derives from Horace, *Ep.* 1.14.22–3 *quod | angulus iste feret piper et tus ocius uua* (whereas the *uilicus* would rather leave his master's remote and barren 'little nook' for the pleasures of Rome) and *Carm.* 2.6.13–14 *ille terrarum mihi praeter omnis | angulus ridet* (to the poet, his little estate is the pinnacle of bliss); see Rimell 2015, 82–101. **paupertinus** is an archaism from Varro, picked up by Apuleius and Gellius (*OLD*; on archaisms, see Intro 4.5). **casa, cui culmo culmina pressa forent** hails back to the humble but hospitable abode of Philemon and Baucis, Ov. *Met.* 8.629–30 *tamen una* [sc. *domus*] *recepit, | parua quidem, stipulis et canna tecta palustri.* Most aptly, Philemon and Baucis entertained gods in disguise, while Clermont provides a refuge for a man of God. The concessive subjunctive *forent* 'were admittedly' (G–L §264) subtly retains the Ovidian *quidem*. Fourfold alliteration on *c* and paronomasia of *culmo* 'straw' and *culmina* 'roof' maintain the poem's high formal level.

23–24 It is not clear whether Abraham built a new church or enlarged an existing one, or with what means. The reference in the pentameter is to Paul's concept of the body as God's temple where His Spirit dwells (and which must be kept pure): 1 Cor. 3.16–17 *nescitis quia templum Dei estis et Spiritus Dei habitat in uobis?* (cf. 1 Cor. 6.19 and 2 Cor. 6.16). Compare the secular counterpart in Sidonius at *Carm.* 1.30 *nam noua templa tibi pectora nostra facis*, on the emperor Anthemius and his new subjects. See Herbert de la Portbarré-Viard 2023, 288–9.

25–26 finiti cursus is New Testament imagery for a believer, in old age, taking stock of his life: 2 Tim. 4.7 *bonum certamen certaui, cursum consummaui, fidem seruaui*. Life is like a foot race or a wrestling match for the prize of eternity: 1 Cor. 9.24–7. **uitaeque uiaeque** could be an echo of Claud. *Carm. min.* 20.22 *plus habet hic uitae, plus habet ille uiae*, where the man who stays all his life in his own country home is compared favourably to the restless traveller. A monk, conversely, is a traveller by definition towards perfection and eternity. **sudori ... dupla corona**: the prize for a Christian's effort, unlike an athlete's, is incorruptible: 1 Cor. 9.25 *illi quidem ut corruptibilem coronam accipiant, nos autem incorruptam*. The ascetic is the Christian athlete par excellence, cf. e.g. the discussion of a monk's struggle with the cardinal sins in Cassian. *Inst.* 5.19.1 *athletae Christi in corpore commoranti numquam defit conluctationum palma*. Abraham is awarded a *dupla corona* for being a victim of persecution and for exerting himself as an abbot; cf. Paul. Nol. *Natal.* 3.86–7 Dolveck (*Carm.* 14.89–91 Hartel), where St Felix receives *perpetuas duplici sub honore coronas, | ante sacerdotis, post martyris*. For secular examples, see *Carm.* 41.19–20n. **geminae ... coronae** (in 9.16).

27–28 milia: in the vision of paradise, thousands upon thousands of living beings surround the heavenly throne: Apoc. 5.11 *et uidi et audiui uocem angelorum multorum in circuitu throni et animalium et seniorum et erat numerus eorum milia milium*. **Abraham ... comperegrinus:** the patriarch Abraham receives the pious dead in his lap (the expression is: *in sinum Abrahae*, here: *te habet*) as an act of retributive justice for the sorrows that they have undergone in life; see the parable of Lazarus and the rich man in Luc. 16.19–31. The patriarch is also the archetype of the monk and the *conuersus* on their pilgrimage to heaven (*comperegrinus*).

29–30 patriam: a parallel is drawn between the heavenly and the earthly fatherland. Abraham was born on the Euphrates, which had its origin in the Garden of Eden (Gen. 2.14). He now enters an even better homeland: heaven. Cf. Hebr. 11.13–16 ... *confitentes quia peregrini et hospites sunt super terram.* ... *significant se patriam inquirere.* ... *nunc autem meliorem appetunt, id est caelestem.* **sed de qua decidit Adam:** the abbot Abraham is compared to none less than Adam, surpassing and vindicating him; cf. Brown 1988, 436–7: 'The perfected ascetic ... was thought to have recovered the glory of Adam'. *sed* 'however', 'but' after an affirmative clause (*OLD* 4a). **iam potes ad fontem fluminis ire tui:** Sidonius combines the literal sense (the river Euphrates, which irrigates Abraham's birthplace, coming from Paradise) with the figurative sense of God as the source of eternal life: Psalm. 36.9 *quoniam tecum est fons uitae*, Ioh. 4.14 *fons aquae salientis in uitam aeternam*; cf. also the heavenly river of water of life, Apoc. 22.1 *fluuium aquae uitae*. Cf. van Waarden 2011, 106.

3 ecce, ut iniunxeras: cf. 7.2.10 *ecce parui*, returning to the letter itself after having complied with the addressee's wish. **quae restant ... iusta persoluimus:** see §2 *quae remanserunt uerba*. For *iusta persoluimus*, see 3.12.6n. *iusta soluisse*; on offering the poem, the author keeps his tone low-key (first person plural), in contrast with §1 *obsecundabo*; see also §2 *conferimus*. **si** has a causal nuance: 'if (as is indeed the case)' (K–S 2, 427). **caritatis:** *caritas* is a synonym of *amor* and *amicitia* in the patronage system (Intro 3.3 'Social Conventions'). In this context, it may have the connotation of Christian love (Blaise s.v. 3) **fratres amicos commilitones:** *fratres* among social equals here probably has a religious colouring (above *fratri* n.); likewise *commilitones* 'fellow-soldiers (for Christ)', cf. Paul, Phil. 2.25 *Epaphroditum fratrem et cooperatorem et commilitonem meum*. For the asyndetic tricolon with increasing word length, see Intro 4.5 n. 111. **institutis** 'teachings' (*OLD* 3) or 'principles' (*TLL* 7/1.1994.38). The paronomasia with following *destitutorum* and *statuta* sketches out the entire process of reform, from vesting authority in Volusianus, through addressing the monks' unsettled state of mind, to the exemplary rule of Lérins. **aggredere solari:** *aggredere* 'proceed', 'begin' (imperative) with inf. (*OLD* 5); for *solari*, see 7.7.2n. *solata sunt*. **regulam** 'code of conduct', 'discipline' (cf. *OLD* 2), probably not yet any written monastic rule, as these were only just coming into existence (see Discussion above; Intro 3.4 n. 63). **fratrum** 'monks', e.g. *Carm.* 16.109 of the monks of Lérins. **statuta Lirinensium patrum uel Grinincensium** 'the rulings of the fathers of Lérins or Grigny': probably the orally transmitted prototypes of the oldest Gallican rules, the *Rule of the Four Fathers* and the *Second Rule of the Fathers* (see de Vogüé 1982, with texts). Given the profound influence of Lérins on the Rhône valley, it is highly probable that Grigny, for which we have no specific information, followed its lead in its internal organization. **patrum** in a monastic context are earlier, authoritative, hermits and monks (Pricoco 1978, 85–6). **Grinincensium**: from the fifth to the seventh centuries, Grigny, situated between Lyon and Vienne, on the right bank of the Rhône, comprised a conglomeration of monasteries and nunneries, including at one point the church and monastery of Ferreolus (for which see 7.1.7n.) and was instrumental in the advance of Nicene Christianity in the Burgundian kingdom (van Waarden 2016, 246–7). **festinus informa:** 'hasten to give shape to': *festinus* is used predicatively; cf. 5.16.3n. The clausula cretic + spondee is the first of three, together with *ipse castiga* and *ipse collauda*, bringing the message forcefully home. **cuius ... collauda:** a direct line can be traced from this to the twofold duty of an abbot formulated in the Rule of Benedict, chapter 2: *indisciplinatos et inquietos debet durius arguere, oboedientes autem et mites et patientes, ut in melius proficiant obsecrare*. **si qui rebelles:** for the lack of a verb, here and in the next clause, see 1.9.1n. *gratiae aditus*.

4 praepositus illis quidem uidetur 'admittedly seems to be at their head': *praepositus* is aptly ambiguous, as the term either indicates the *abbas* or his assistant (van Waarden 2016, 248). *quidem* concedes (*OLD* 4) that there may be a new head, at the same time suggesting that that is not the end of the matter. *uidetur* makes it a diplomatic turn of phrase, cf. 7.9.1 *orationem quam uideor ... sermocinatus*; alternatively, 'is seen to', 'clearly'. The long, winding sentence that follows reflects Sidonius' cautious approach. **Auxanius:** see Mathisen 2020a, 84 (the identification with the Auxanius of 1.7.6 is not certain, see *PLRE* 2, 203–4). **plusculum iusto** 'slightly more than acceptable': sustained politeness. **uerecundus** 'modest', almost 'shy', 'introverted: the socially valued quality of *uerecundia* (see Intro 3.3 'Social Conventions' with n. 54; 2.9.10n.) in this case is a disadvantage. **parendi quam imperandi promptior** is a frequent turn of thought, e.g. Cic. *Fin.* 2.46 *ad imperandum magis quam ad parendum accommodatum*, Liv. 21.4.3 *numquam ingenium idem ad res diuersissimas, parendum atque imperandum, habilius fuit*. **sub magisterio monasterii magister:** the soundplay strengthens the oxymoron. **si quis illum de iunioribus spreuerit**: according to the *Second Rule of the Fathers* (§§8 and 12), young monks ought not to speak unless asked to do so, and slighting an abbot's authority is an offence against God. **tamquam** 'on the ground of being' (*OLD* 7b). **pusillanimem** 'faint-hearted', 'timid': later Latin (first attested in Tertullian). The shy members of the Christian community deserve help: 1 Thess. 5.14 *consolamini pusillanimes* 'encourage the faint-hearted'. **unum** in pointed contrast to *utrumque*, cf. 6.2.3 *unam ...*

domum discordiosam, ... utramque discordem. **quid multa?** 'why say more?', 'to be brief': see 2.9.6n. **agnoscas:** *OLD* 7. **abbas** emphatically in first position: 'being the abbot'. **congregationem** 'monastic community' (Blaise 5). **uero:** *OLD* 7.

LETTER 7.18: ENVOI FOR THE SEVEN-BOOK COLLECTION

Outline

'*This collection began with you and it ends with you. At your request, I have edited a selection of letters from my archive in such a way as to strike a balance between their number and length. Such a collection is like a mirror of the author's soul and indeed you will find anything from advice and praise to sorrow and fun. The main thing for me is to think independently. I hope you will enjoy the result.*'

Introduction

The initial seven-book collection ends as it began, with a self-reflexive letter to Constantius, creating 'a frame for the whole seven books' (Harries 1994, 8). Looking back upon the collection, Sidonius points at the variety of emotions reflected in it, making it into a mirror of his soul. One thing stands out: his faith in honesty, in speaking out, and in not letting oneself be intimidated by one's environment (§3 *numquam me toleraturum animi seruitutem*). This defiant utterance is an important social and political statement, bearing witness to a degree of independence that must have strained the reinstated bishop's relationship with his new overlords to the limit (see 7.17 Discussion).

Discussion

The outlook in Book 7 is twofold: bleak for political affairs, confident for the promise held by asceticism. Its intensity befits the climax of the correspondence, whether or not the collection was initially meant to end here, with Books 8 and 9 as 'afterthoughts' (Intro 4.1 with n. 89).

The letter is remarkable for closing the collection by combining a reflection on its materiality and content (normally prefatory material) with a personal statement. Sidonius himself calls this an *epilogus* (see 9.1.2). It innovatively combines the self-conscious way in which Martial ends most of his books of epigrams (1.118, 2.93, 3.100, 4.89, 5.84, 7.99, 8.82, 10.104) with the personal *sphragis* or 'seal' (see *BNP* s.v.), a device inherited by the Augustan poets from Hellenistic models, e.g. Virgil concluding his *Georgics* (4.559–66), Horace his first three books of *Odes* (3.30) and the first book of *Epistles* (1.20.20–8), Propertius the first book of *Elegies* (1.22) and Ovid repeatedly, most notably the *Tristia* (4.10). In most cases further books follow these 'endings', as in Sidonius. Sidonius has an even more personal *sphragis* at the end of Book 9, where, in *Carmen* 41, he reviews his life and works (see commentary in this volume). For the layout of the collection being modelled on collections of Augustan poetry, see Intro 4.1.

Addressee

For Constantius, see 1.1 Addressee. He is the figure that presides over the whole letter collection as the dedicatee of Books 1–7 and, *honoris causa*, of Book 8 (letter 8.16). He also receives an honorific mention at the end of Book 9 (9.16.1).

Date and Place

The date of writing is 477/8, the date of the collective issue of Books 1–7 after Sidonius' return from exile (Intro 2.1). Place: Clermont.

Literature

Commentary: van Waarden 2016, 252–71.

Commentary

1 A te principium, tibi desinet 'With you it began, for you it will end', quoting Verg. *Ecl.* 8.11, where Virgil hands over the *Eclogues* to his patron Pollio who commissioned them, allegedly a modest piece of writing for a victorious general. Likewise, Sidonius aims to convey the ideas of patronage and commission, and of slight but (he hopes) attractive results, while emphasizing the greater merit of the addressee. Cf. Hor. *Ep.* 1.1.1–3 *Prima dicte mihi, summa dicende Camena,* | ... | *Maecenas*. There is a further possible allusion to *Ecl.* 3.60 *ab Ioue principium* ... | ... *illi mea carmina curae* (also applied in Stat. *Silv.* 1 praef. '*a Ioue principium*'). If so, Constantius is honoured as Sidonius' Jupiter – appropriately, as Sidonius himself posed as Phoebus among his comrades (for nicknames in Sidonius' circle, Mathisen 1991a). **petitum misimus opus** links back to 1.1.1 *diu praecipis ... ut ... uno uolumine includam*. The set must have comprised about 100 folios (200 pages) for the roughly 36,000 words of Books 1–7 (for an estimate of book lengths, see van Waarden 2016, 258–9). *misimus* is plural of modesty; for the epistolary perfect tense, 1.1.3n. *parui*. **raptim relectis exemplaribus:** *raptim* is the usual polite excuse when presenting a work for review, e.g. 9.16.2n. *raptim coactimque ... exscripsi*; cf. 8.3.1n. *festino*. For the restiveness of Sidonius' letter collection, see van Waarden 2020a, 165. *relectis* from *relĕgo* 'to (re)read (attentively) (with a view to correction)'; see *TLL* 11/2.894.18–31, cf. e.g. Ov. *Pont.* 1.5.15–17 *relego ... nec tamen emendo*, Auson. *Griph. ep.* 4 [*libellum*] *excussum relegi*, Sidon. 5.15.1 *librum ... relectum et retractatum*. *relectis exemplaribus* echoes 1.1.1n. *retractatis exemplaribus*. As to the MSS, *relectis* is warrranted by α and *P* among others (*electis* only in *LTN*). **in manus pauca uenerunt** echoes Plin. 1.1.1 *ut quaeque in manus uenerat*: Sidonius' close links back to Pliny's beginning (cf. 1.1 Discussion). In fact, Sidonius no doubt had a neatly ordered archive (Mathisen 2013, 234–5). **mihi nil de libelli huiusce conscriptione meditanti:** *mihi ... meditanti* is dative of agent (G–L §354). *libelli* is a modest diminutive, independently of the actual size of the volume (see van Waarden 2016, 32–40 and 1.1.2n. *uno uolumine*); cf. 9.16.1n. *libellus*. Here, it may refer to Book 7 alone (Loyen 2, xlvii), to the subset of Books 6 and 7 (as hypothesized at van Waarden 2016, 26–7) or to the entire correspondence to date. *huiusce*: see 1.1.4n. *hisce*. **hactenus incustodita ... inueniri** goes back to Plin. 1.1.2 *eas quae adhuc neglectae iacent requiram*; see 9.16.2n. *temere iacens*. **sane** 'admittedly' (*OLD* 8). **celeriter absolui:** for the notion of speed and improvisation (potentially either a good or a bad thing), cf. e.g. Stat. *Silv.* 1 praef. *gratiam celeritatis: nullum enim ex illis biduo longius tractum, quaedam et in singulis diebus effusa* (cf. 3.12.4n. *nocte proxima*). **quamquam incitatus semel animus necdum scripturire desineret:** cf. Plin. 5.11.3 *nescit enim semel incitata liberalitas stare*. *necdum* 7.1.1n. *scripturire* 'to long to write' (also 8.11.8 *scribebat assidue, quamquam frequentius scripturiret*), in this case, long to rewrite and embellish the original letters. Sidonius is fond of coining words (Wolff 2020, 398–9): for other coinages of verbs with a desiderative suffix, cf. *taciturire* 'to want to be silent' (8.16.3), *lecturire* 'to be eager to read' (below §4, 2.10.5n., 9.7.1). In his literary world, writing and reading can become something of an obsession (cf. the urge to write expressed by *garrulitas, prolixitas* and *loquacitas*, e.g. 1.9.7n. *prolixitatem* and *loquax*, 2.9.10n. *loquacitati*, 3.11.2 *garrulitas*). *desineret*: the subjunctive in concessive clauses with *quamquam* is found from the 1st cent. BCE onward and is common in later Latin (H–S 602–3). **seruans hoc ... genus temperamenti:** cf. Plin. 6.29.7 *hoc fere temperamentum ipse seruaui*. For *temperamentum*, see 5.5.4n. It is the balance struck between the relatively few letters selected for publication (*si numerus breuiaretur*) and their expansion in the process of editing (*ut epistularum produceretur textus*). Sidonius' letters as we have them are the result of artistic adaptation of the originals (Intro 4.1). A count confirms his claim: he has 16 letters on average per book unit at a median letter length of 229 words (324 words on average), Pliny 27 at 160 (226) and Symmachus 100 at 68 (80) (see van Waarden 2022b). **textus** 'fabric of words', 'text' is late Latin; Quint. 9.14.3 is an isolated early instance (see *OLD* 3, L–S 2.II, Blaise 3).

2 pariter et 'at the same time': see 2.9.5n. **lector delicatissimus** 'an extremely discerning reader': *delicatus* 'sensitive', 'fastidious' ('elegant' *OLD* 5) is mostly a positive quality in Sidonius, an aspect of aristocratic refinement, cf. Mart. 4.55.27 *delicate lector*, Plin. 4.14.7 *sapiens subtilisque lector*, Sidon. 2.2.20 *artifex lector* 'a reader of expert taste' (tr. Anderson). **desiderares** 'you desired, I suppose': subjunctive of the view of another person in the narrator's words (G–L §628; see focalization in Intro 4.3). **et satis habilem nec parum excusabilem** 'both perfectly wieldy and not poorly excusable', of the size of the book (not too big) vs the quality of its contents (not too bad). For *satis ... parum*, see 2.12.3n. Parallel contrasted phrases and homoeoteleuton are among Sidonius' most trusted stylistic devices (Intro 4.5; Wolff 2020, 411–12). **sensuum structurarumque leuitas** 'the light weight of its thoughts and structures', i.e. of the ideas and their wording; cf. 7.13.2 *magis ... medulla sensuum quam spuma uerborum* 'more the marrow of the thoughts than the froth of the words'. At 9.7.3, the *structura* of a text is praised for being *fortis et firma ... sed nec hinc minus lubrica et leuis*, 'strong and compact ... but nevertheless supple and smooth', a quality for which Sidonius particularly admired Symmachus (cf. 1.1.1n. *rotunditatem*). **membranarum certe fascibus minus onerarere:** the supposed *leuitas* of the text is made up for, if needed, by the (literal) light weight of the volume. *membranarum* 'parchment', as writing material (*OLD* 3), is first attested in Hor. *Sat.* 2.3.2. Sidonius will have sent Constantius a parchment codex (see §1n. *opus*; further on books and writing materials, *OCD* and *ODLA* 'Books'; cf. van Waarden 2022b, 62). *fascibus* 'bundles', 'loads' (*OLD* 2): the plural for exaggeration. *onerarere = onerareris*; for the idea of a 'load' of books, cf. e.g. Plin. 8.15.1 *Oneraui te tot pariter missis uoluminibus*. **commendo:** for verb initial, see Intro 4.3. **uarios ... motus:** the hyperbaton (discontinuity) of the noun phrase signals its being the focus of the clause, while the adjective, which precedes, carries emphasis (*OLS* 2, 1097–1101, Intro 4.3). For variety, see 2.9.6n. *uarietur*. **iudicio tuo nostri pectoris:** the singular *tuo* foregrounds the referee as opposed to the self-effacing plural *nostri* of the author (see Intro 4.2 '"You" and "I"'), reinforced by chiasmus. **quod ita mens pateat in libro uelut uultus in speculo** 'that one's mind is revealed in a book [of letters] like a face in a mirror': The idea is fully formulated in epistolary theory by Ps.-Demetr. *De eloc.* 227 σχεδὸν γὰρ εἰκόνα ἕκαστος τῆς ἑαυτοῦ ψυχῆς γράφει τὴν ἐπιστολήν 'in writing a letter, everybody almost paints a picture of their own soul' (Malherbe 1988, 18–19). Instances include Cic. *Fam.* 16.16.2 *te totum in litteris uidi*, Sen. *Ep.* 40.1 *quod frequenter mihi scribis … te mihi ostendis*, Paul. Nol. *Ep.* 13.2 *sermo uiri mentis est speculum*, Cassiod. *Var. praef.* 10 [if you don't publish your letters] *celas etiam, ut ita dixerim, speculum mentis tuae, ubi te omnis aetas uentura possit inspicere*. In Hor. *Sat.* 2.1.30–4, satires have the same function for the poet Lucilius who confided his innermost thoughts to them (*uelut fidis arcana sodalibus … | credebat libris*), revealing his personality as if drawn on a votive tablet (*omnis | uotiua patet ueluti descripta tabella | uita*); cf. Cic. *Pis.* 71 [in somebody's poetry] *tamquam in speculo uitam intueri*; Sen. *Ep.* 114.1 [on style as reflecting one's character] *talis hominibus … oratio qualis uita*. For writing and reading letters as a virtual meeting and 'seeing' each other, Intro 3.6 n. 79. The image of mirrors (among them letters and the body) reflecting the soul and the invisible in general is universal (Bartsch 2014, Gerolemou and Diamantopoulou 2020, Devriese 2021). **in libro** 'in a volume of letters' as opposed to individual letters, *chartae* (Gillett 2012, 833); among synonyms for 'book', *liber* highlights the content and the act of reading (van Waarden 2016, 34). **dictaui** 'I have written' is in topic position. *dictare* originally 'to dictate' to a scribe (e.g. Cic. *Att.* 2.23.1 *haec dictaui ambulans*), then 'to formulate', 'compose', 'write' (whether or not with the help of a scribe, e.g. Hor. *Ep.* 1.10.49 *haec tibi dictabam*), which is standard in late Latin (*TLL* 5/1.1011.62–1012.39); cf. 9.16.1n. **hortando, laudando … suadendo, maerendo … iocandoque:** letters of admonition, praise and advice, and ones which share grief or merriment are among the most frequent types of letters. Theorists would refine this almost indefinitely: Ps.-Demetrius distinguished twenty-one types and Ps.-Libanius no less than forty-one (see Intro 3.6). The aim is that of being attentive to different situations, moods and addressees. Pliny, for one, is conspicuous for such sensibility, particularly at 4.14.3, where he discerns a variety of emotions in his own poetry and judges it suitable for a diverse audience for this very reason: *his iocamur ludimus amamus dolemus querimur irascimur describimus* (cf. 4.27.1; see Intro 4.1 n. 90). Gibson and Morello 2012, 246 plausibly extend this statement to Pliny's conception of epistolary writing. Sidonius may well have had this passage in mind, with a significant twist as, whereas Pliny styles himself as timid (4.14.4 *timidiores*), Sidonius professes to be anything but servile, leaving it to the *timidi* to criticize this attitude (§3). *hortando* etc.: the ablative of the gerund, from Livy and Vitruvius onwards, increasingly replaces the present participle (H–S 380). *maerendo … iocandoque*: cf. Auson. *Epigr.* 1.3–4 Green *laetis | seria miscuimus*.

3 lectitauisti: see 1.5.9n. *scriptitans.* **in aliquos concitatiorem:** such an oubreak of vehement temper is, for instance, letter 7.7 with its scathing judgement of the treacherous peace negotiators (see commentary). **Christi dextera opitulante** 'with the help of Christ's right hand', a one-off reinforcement of Sidonius' usual devout phrase *sub ope Christi*; see 1.5.1n. *sub ope ... dei*, 1.9.8n. *sub ope Christi.* **numquam me toleraturum animi seruitutem:** the language of moral and spiritual resilience in the face of political and intellectual imprisonment. Sidonius is conscious of the dangers and limitations of freedom of opinion, as is particularly apparent in 4.22.5 where he refuses to write history; however, there is a pervading sense of optimism-against-all-odds, a fundamental tenacity in his letters (Intro 4.1, van Waarden 2010, 8; Gibson 2013, 218; see Ahl 1984 on (the limits of) freedom of speech). This spirit emerges in Gaul as early as the 410/20s as a reaction to the barbarian invasions (Roberts 1992). Just as material and spiritual destruction go together, spiritual regeneration will be followed by material revival. This is the spirit – the spirit of the *conuersi* – that Sidonius preserves well into the second half of the century. *Libertas* is among his fundamental values (see *Carm.* 38.12n. *liber* (in 3.12)), just as the Gallic aristocracy at large was focussed on both resistance and reconciliation (Mathisen 1979). **compertissimum tenens** 'being well aware': the superlative is a hapax, while only Fulg. Rusp. (6th cent.) has the collocation *tenemus ... compertum* (*ad Monim.* 1.10 and 2.6), instead of classical *compertum* or *pro comperto habere.* **super** = *de* (*OLD* 11). **censuram** 'judgement', *OLD* 2. **nam ut timidi me temerarium, ita constantes liberum appellant:** the stylistic figure of *distinctio*, the same quality being rated both positively and negatively, based on what Quintilian, on the authority of Aristotle, called *quaedam uirtutibus ac uitiis uicinitas* 'a certain proximity of virtues and vices' (Quint. *Inst.* 3.7.25, 9.3.65). The clause is an imitative remix of Plin. 9.26.13 [on stylistic matters] *aut enim tu me timidum aut ego te temerarium faciam. liberum* '(too) outspoken' (*OLD* 11). **decerno** 'I opine': cf. 5.5.3, 9.16.1. **iacere personam** 'his position is deplorable', 'his role is pitiful': *OLD iaceo* 5, *persona* 3. **latere sententiam:** the parallelism with *iacere personam* neatly rounds off this self-evaluation, before the author returns to the addressee.

4 interea tu 'as for you': see 2.10.2n. *interea tu.* **lectionis sacrae continuatione** 'the continuous reading of the Bible': sustained reading of the Bible (also called: *lectio diuina*), gradually replacing the reading of the pagan classics (*lectio uetustatis*), is a key indicator of the new Christian cultural paradigm (Eigler 2003, 130–46). Consequently, Constantius will have been a *conuersus* (see 1.1 Addressee). See Hier. 52.7 *diuinas scripturas saepius lege, immo numquam de manibus tuis sacra lectio deponatur;* Sidonius has the best of both worlds: 4.9.3 *sacrorum uoluminum lectio frequens* [the Bible], 4.17.2 *quae si frequenti lectione continuas* [the classics]; cf. 8.3.4n. *lectioni*. **his … neniis** 'this rubbish' (*OLD* 5): see 1.9.7n. **auocere** 'you may be distracted' (*OLD* 5), = *auoceris*, cf. e.g. 1.9.4n. *consequebare*. **nec faciet materia ut immensa fastidium:** Plin. 2.5.4 *fastidium legentium* (caused by an overlong speech) may be in the air; cf. Liv. 3.1.7 *fecit statim … fastidium copia*; cf. the proverbial μηδὲν ἄγαν 'nothing in excess', Horace's *aurea mediocritas* (*Carm.* 2.10.5). *ut* is causal (*OLD* 21a). **singulae causae singulis … epistulis:** preferably one subject for each letter, as prescribed by theorists, cf. Ps.-Demetr. *De eloc.* 4.231 περὶ ἁπλοῦ πράγματος ἔκθεσις '[a letter aims to be] an exposition of a single issue' (Malherbe 1988, 18–19). Sidonius' formulation harks back to Plin. 9.4.1 *nam singulis criminibus singulae uelut causae continentur*. The context there is (again) an overlong speech (*immodicam orationem*) sent by Pliny, palatable to the reader only because it is split into convenient units. Sidonius continues in the same way as Pliny (§2 *poteris ergo, undecumque coeperis ubicumque desieris, quae deinceps sequentur et quasi incipientia legere et quasi cohaerentia, meque in universitate longissimum breuissimum in partibus iudicare*). Readers are thus enabled to manage their own reading experience. **ante legere cessabis quam lecturire desistas** is not only a neat way of framing the addressee's reading expectations, but also provides a fitting ending to the volume as such at the point where every reader 'stops reading'. In addition, the letter elegantly comes full circle, with the addressee who will not 'stop wanting to read' (*lecturire desistas*) echoing the author who almost could not 'stop wanting to write' (§1 *scripturire desineret*). On *lecturire*, see above §1n. *scripturire*.

LETTER 8.3: SENDING A LIFE OF APOLLONIUS OF TYANA

Outline

'Here is a fresh copy from my library of a version of Philostratus' biography of the Pythagorean sage Apollonius of Tyana. Unfortunately, it is hurried and slipshod due to my confinement in Livia (many thanks, incidentally, for supporting my release). It was impossible to concentrate because of my assignments during the day and my despondency overnight. On top of that, the noise of a pair of drunken Gothic women disturbed my sleep. So, now, do take a break: stop writing poetry and prose, in particular your speech writing for the glorious King, whose influence ranges from the Rhine to Africa, and who is establishing the rule of law. No more court intrigues for now, but a profitable long read through Apollonius' travels to the Indian Brahmins and the Egyptian Gymnosophists. Like you, he was averse *to riches and immune to extravagance. His simple lifestyle exposed the decadence of eastern kings. He rather bestowed all the gifts he received on others. Apollonius' life probably got its appropriate narrator, but I am sure you, in any case, are its appropriate reader.'*

Introduction

Book 8 takes the reader to another phase of Sidonius' life and the history of Gaul (see Intro 4.1). The perspective is now decidedly post-Roman, which Sidonius memorably summarizes in 8.2.2: *iam remotis gradibus dignitatum, per quas solebat ultimo a quoque summus quisque discerni, solum erit posthac nobilitatis indicium litteras nosse* 'now that the old degrees of official rank are swept away, those degrees by which the highest in the land used to be distinguished from the lowest, the only token of nobility will henceforth be a knowledge of letters' (tr. Anderson). The atmosphere is one of reluctant acceptance of the new Visigothic order centred on themes including the preservation of the Roman intellectual heritage, the collision between aristocratic illusion and reality, and the unsteadiness of happiness (Zoeter 2018, 14–15). John Drinkwater memorably called this the era of 'un-becoming Roman' (Drinkwater 2013, 74).

Released from exile, Sidonius diplomatically acquiesces in Euric's rule (for Euric in Sidonius, see Egetenmeyr 2022, 307–29). In 8.3, he hails him as the 'glorious king' of whom foreign nations are in awe, and holds up to him the mirror of unselfish, responsible government. In 8.9, he pays a poetic tribute to the king (*Carm.* 34), whose court he pictures as the centre of the world. Tellingly, both addressees – Gallo-Romans like Sidonius himself and belonging to his intimates – are already close to the Visigothic court, Leo (letter 8.3) as Euric's counsellor, Lampridius (8.9) after having reached a profitable agreement for his estate. Sidonius hopes that they will sort out the last obstacles concerning his confiscated family property.

Unlike many others, Sidonius never came to support Visigothic rule wholeheartedly – at least according to his correspondence. There always remains an undercurrent of resistance, be it by way of high-end literature and sophisticated company, as mentioned above, or of the Catholic Church as an organizing principle that transcends local disruptions and perpetuates overarching Roman coherence. The three last letters but one (13–15) are thus addressed to fellow bishops. In letter 15 (where see commentary), the memory of the providential preservation of Orléans from the Huns at the town's bishop's prayer sheds light on the enduring centrality of the episcopate.

230   COMMENTARY: 8.3

   The very last word, in letter 16, is directed at the dedicatee of the entire correspondence, Constantius. Leaving behind all personal and political worries, it presents Book 8 as a work of literary art (including some poetry; see Intro 3.6 and 4.1 with n. 86; also letter 2.10 Introduction), written with the utmost care, knowing that perfection is elusive. May God – the author prays – grant it readers and recognition with posterity.

Discussion

This letter introduces us to the fascination for a Pythagorean lifestyle in Sidonius' circle as well as to the flow of manuscripts supporting this kind of pursuit, part and parcel of friendship networks (Intro 3.6). The peace of mind taught by the sage Apollonius contrasts with the din and fury of the present. This morphs into a political message conveying Sidonius' acquiescence with Euric's supremacy (see §3nn.), the closest he ever came (together with *Carm*. 34, see below) to professing his allegiance, but it is qualified by the indirect mirror of princes held up to Euric in §5.

Neoplatonism, Pythagoreanism, Apollonius, Philostratus

Late antique philosophy is largely synonymous with Neoplatonism, a synthesis of the ideas of Platonists, Stoics, Aristotelians and Pythagoreans (*ODLA* 1066–7 'Neoplatonism'). Pythagoras had come to be seen – unhistorically – as the central figure in the Greek philosophical tradition and was variously constructed as a metaphysician, as a mathematician and astronomer, as a magician or as a spiritual teacher and a sage upon whom we should model our lives. This reimagination of the early history of pagan philosophy originally served to counter Christian demonstrations of the antiquity of their own wisdom (*SEP* 'Pythagoreanism', *BNP* 'Pythagorean School', *ODLA* 1250 'Pythagoras in Late Antiquity'). In Sidonius' days, Pythagoreanism quietly coexisted with Christianity within an elite that valued it for enabling a less materialistic lifestyle, and providing, within the broader amalgam of Neoplatonism, a world view that extended across arithmetic, cosmology, astrology and music, including a tinge of mysticism (see Intro 3.4).

   One Pythagorean in particular captured the imagination: the first-century CE philosopher and pagan holy man Apollonius of Tyana. In the early third century, he became the subject of a fictionalized biography by the sophist Philostratus (cf. the Christian saints' lives, 8.15 Discussion). It was commissioned by the empress and patron of philosophy, Julia Domna, to whose circle of intellectuals Philostratus belonged. The biography describes Apollonius' travelling for knowledge to India and Ethiopia and his confrontations with the emperors Nero and Domitian. Favourably compared to Christ by pagan authors, Apollonius incurred severe criticism from Christians (*BNP* 'Apollonius 14 of Tyana', *ODLA* 99–100 'Apollonius of Tyana in Late Antiquity'). In Sidonius' circle, polemic had given way to admiration for the wisdom of the past. Leo's interest in Sidonius' copy of Apollonius' biography was a logical consequence of his being a prominent adept of this way of thinking (see further below; cf. Loyen 1943, 15–16; van Waarden 2010, 17–19).

Sidonius' Copy of the Life of Apollonius of Tyana

The exchange of books, copied from the sender's own library by his staff and duly revised by himself, was both a proof of friendship and an indispensable support of intellectual life (Intro 3.3 'Elite Status' and 'Gift-Giving' with n. 55). Sidonius had been asked by his friend Leo for a copy of a specific, apparently rare, edition of Philostratus' *Life of Apollonius of Tyana* sitting in Sidonius' library. It harked back – Sidonius does not fail to spell out – to the editorial activities of the interlinked families of the Symmachi and the Nicomachi. These late-fourth-century families famously, among much else, produced a revised version of Livy's first decade, still extant, signed off with colophons (*subscriptiones*) mentioning the editor-in-chief Tascius Victorianus and the family members involved (see at length Cameron 2011; for the colophons and what the *emendatio*, performed by these men, entailed, see Zetzel 1980). Sidonius possessed Victorianus' edition of the *Life of Apollonius*, which derived from an older version made by Nicomachus Flavianus *père*.

Why does Sidonius begin his letter with these complexities? As a member of the Neopythagorean circle of Narbonne and a scientific authority (*Carm.* 14.*ep.* 1 and *ep.* 2; see Intro 3.4), Leo was no doubt aware of the gist of this famous biography. He may even have owned the older (fuller?) version. Does Sidonius imply that Leo was interested in the novelties provided by Victorianus? Or is it the other way round: does he apologize for not having the 'real thing', i.e. the original version? On top of this vagueness, Sidonius leaves us in the dark as to the nature of both versions and of the copy he has made for Leo (are they in Greek or in Latin, are they abbreviated, annotated? Leo read and wrote Greek: see *Carm.* 40.19–22 in 9.15; cf. John 2021, 857–63), because he uses terms (*exscripsit, translatio*) that can mean anything from 'to copy' to 'to edit' and 'to translate', thus creating one of the unsolved puzzles of classical philology.

The three main reconstructions of what happened are as follows: (1) Nicomachus translated Philostratus into Latin, Victorianus revised this translation, Sidonius made a second revision of it (Mommsen

1887, 420 'Apollonius'; Pecere 1986, 60–1 with n. 230 on pp. 232–3; Prchlík 2007; Mathisen 2020a, 104; Nardelli 2022; Giannotti 2023); (2) Nicomachus owned a copy of Philostratus, Victorianus copied it and added a colophon, Sidonius somehow had access to Victorianus' version (which may have been sent to Gaul by Symmachus together with copies of Livy and Caesar; see Traube 1904, 16) and made his own copy of it, all in Greek (Sirmond, *Notae* 81; Anderson 2, 404 n. 5; Cameron 2011, 546–54; Mratschek 2020a, 247 with n. 71; Van Hoof and Van Nuffelen 2020, 36–58; John 2023, 306–10); (3) Nicomachus made an edition of Philostratus in Greek, Victorianus revised it, Sidonius translated the latter (Pricoco 1965a; Loyen 3, 196–7 n. 5 (Loyen 1943, 27 had left the matter open)). Any of these editions (revisions, translations) may have included selection and reduction (see especially Bleckmann 2022, ii–iv).

Much depends on one's estimate of Sidonius' command of Greek. Traditionally, this is thought to be poor like most people's in his circle, with the exception of a few luminaries such as Mamertus Claudianus who mastered *triplex bybliotheca ... | Romana, Attica, Christiana* (*Carm.* 30.4–5 in 4.11.6), Sidonius' being just about enough to check a Latin comedy against its Greek counterpart (4.12.1). A classic representative of this scepticism is Loyen 1943, 26–30, followed in a slightly more generous vein by Courcelle 1969, 251–62 (French original 1948, 235–44). Currently, however, Sidonius tends to be credited with a fuller command of Greek (John 2023, 305–16, John 2026, 167–8), which would bring a translation of Philostratus within his reach (see Intro 3.3 'Elite Status'; cf. 2.9.5n. *interpretatus*).

The complex account of the successive copies of the *Life* – both detailed and vague; all the more prominent as it opens the letter – raises the question why Sidonius left the matter unresolved when he published the letter. It may have been clear (and important) to Leo, but it was certainly not so to later readers. Was it to flaunt the depth of his library holdings in relation to the Roman tradition represented by the Symmachi and Nicomachi, while suggesting a more essential role for himself than was perhaps justified?

Politics

Via Leo, Sidonius comes to speak of Euric (without mentioning his name, calling him 'the glorious King') and acknowledges his territorial gains and diplomatic successes. At this stage, it has become imperative for Sidonius, in hopes of resuming his work in Clermont, to forge an entente with the winner. He encourages Leo to take some time off from his duties at court and take to heart Apollonius' example who kept aloof from the excesses of kings and coveted simplicity. This is as much a piece of friendly advice for Leo as it is, indirectly, a mirror of princes held up to the king (see further §5n.). It is a personal qualification of the allegiance sketched moments ago. This same ambivalent attitude is in evidence further on, in letter 8.9, which Sidonius writes to another friend close to Euric, Lampridius. He complains that he himself is wasting his time in Bordeaux trying to get access to Euric to reach a material agreement after his exile, whereas Lampridius is all settled. In the poem included there, often called Euric's panegyric (*Carm.* 34; Fo 1999; Fo 2002), Euric is portrayed as the *dominus* to whom the whole *subactus orbis* resorts (vv. 19–20), as the saviour of the Roman empire (vv. 42–4). So, another accolade for the new ruler, but again provided with a counterpoint, in this case that, at a personal level, Sidonius' – i.e. a Roman's – individual needs are being disregarded.

Sidonius' enduring distrust of Euric in the correspondence – openly in Book 7 during the raids on Clermont, tacitly after the exile – is scarcely to be missed. Some would stress an element of active resistance against a barbarian overlord hidden in the intertextuality of Books 8 and 9, the letters being encrypted political messages (Fo in the articles just mentioned and Overwien 2009). It is striking, however, that Euric, is not being dismissed for being a barbarian. He is, in any case, an effective ruler. The point is rather one of renewed self-positioning on Sidonius' part. There is subtle irony in the later Books: Sidonius is looking for openings while not forgetting his former criticism (Fascione 2019, 62–72; Egetenmeyr 2022, 180–2 and 307–29). Sidonius' praise of Euric is neither heartfelt nor insincere, but tentative and diplomatic.

Addressee

Leo of Narbonne, a *uir spectabilis*, a title that points to a previous imperial career, a jurist (*Carm.* 9.314, 23.447–9) and a poet (*Carm.* 23.450–6, 36.20 (in 9.13.2), 40.19–20 (in 9.15.1)), served as an adviser and speech writer of the Visigothic king Euric, among other key tasks, welcoming the 474/5 Roman embassy at the court in Toulouse (Ennod. *VEpiph.* 85; see letter 7.7 Introduction) and arguably engaged in drafting Visigothic legislation (Harries 2001 with some caveats, John 2026, 115; see letter 5.5 Discussion for another Gallo-Roman, Syagrius, playing a similar role at the Burgundian court in Lyon). While Sidonius was in exile, he suggested that he write history after publishing his correspondence, which Sidonius declined as being too compromising (letter 4.22 to Leo; Mratschek 2020a, 246–7). He was instrumental in securing Sidonius' release from confinement, and shortly after received from him the copy of the *Vita Apollonii* which is the subject of this letter. He was a member of the circle of *complatonici* of Narbonne (*Carm.* 14.*ep.* 1–2; see Intro 3.4), engaged in Neoplatonist/Neopythagorean philosophy and scientific speculation, which included many of Sidonius' relations (a similar group existed in Aquitaine, which counted Lampridius of Bordeaux among its members: see 8.11.10). He continued his function at court under Euric's successor Alaric II from 484 onwards. Prosopography: Mathisen 2020a, 104; see also Kaufmann 1995, 61 n. 93.

Date and Place

Late 476 or 477, after Sidonius' return to Clermont (Loyen 3, 216).

Literature

Studies: Mommsen 1887, 420; Loyen 1943, 27; Pricoco 1965a; Pecere 1986, 60–1; Prchlík 2007; Overwien 2009, 98–100; Cameron 2011, 546–54; Fascione 2019, 69–70; Mratschek 2020a, 247; Van Hoof and Van Nuffelen 2020, 36–58; Bleckmann 2022, ii–iv; Nardelli 2022; Egetenmeyr 2022, 180 and 319–21; John 2023, 324; Giannotti 2023.

Commentary

1 Apollonii Pythagorici uitam: The first words state the theme, see 7.1.1n. On Apollonius, see Discussion above. Pythagoras figures in 4.3.6 in a list of four emblematic philosophers along with Socrates, Plato and Aristotle and in *Carm.* 2.171, in a longer list, coupled with Democritus and Heraclitus representing laughter and tears respectively, to represent silence (see van Waarden 2010, 445–7). *Carm.* 15.51–78 lists him among the Seven Sages and provides an extensive exposé of his concept of the universe and the music of the spheres. For (Neo)pythagoreanism, see Discussion above. **non ut … sed ut:** either Leo had specifically asked for the Victorianus version or Sidonius apologizes for not having the original version (see Discussion above). **Nicomachus senior:** *PLRE* 1, 347–9 'Virius Nicomachus Flavianus 15'. Born in 334, he became praetorian prefect of Italy 390–2, and, as a convinced opponent of Christianity, rallied to the usurper Eugenius 393–4, becoming consul in the West in 394. He committed suicide in 394 after Eugenius' defeat by the emperor Theodosius on 5 September at the River Frigidus, which had been the last hope for pagans to stop Christianity. He was a friend of Symmachus (the recipient of Symmachus' letters 2.1–91), whose daughter married his son Nicomachus Flavianus, who, in their turn, were the recipients of

Symmachus' letters 6.1–81. According to Sidonius' testimony here, he either made a Greek adaptation or a translation into Latin of the *Life of Apollonius of Tyana* by Philostratus. He is a character in the *Saturnalia* of Macrobius. See Cameron 2011. **Philostrati:** one of up to four Philostrati active in the late second century and the first half of the third as so-called 'sophists', i.e. public speakers on both fictional and real-life subjects, for entertainment as well as on official occasions. The Philostratus who wrote the *Life of Apollonius* may also have written *Lives of the Sophists*, coining the term 'Second Sophistic' for the period. One of the others authored the description of paintings entitled *Images* (Gr. Εἰκόνες). See *ODLA* 1187–8 'Philostrati', *BNP* 'Philostratus 5–8'. See further Discussion above. **Tascius Victorianus:** *PLRE* 2, 1160–1 'Tascius Victorianus 2'. Little is known about him except from the *subscriptiones* to the first decade of Livy (see Discussion above). According to them, he was a senator (*uir clarissimus*) and 'editor-in-chief' of the editorial project of classic texts of the Symmachi and Nicomachi. Here it appears that he also edited Philostratus' *Life of Apollonius* in the version of Nicomachus the Elder, be it in Greek or Latin – a kind of 'second edition'. **e Nicomachi schedio exscripsit:** *schedium* means 'manuscript' or 'copy', to judge from 9.7.1 *copiosissimo ... declamationum tuarum schedio*, 9.16.2 *si quod schedium temere iacens chartulis putribus ac ueternosis continebatur, raptim coactimque translator festinus exscripsi*. The noun surfaces in Sidonius' last two books, possibly inspired by Auson. *Biss.* 2.5 Green *Bissula in hoc schedio cantabitur*. It seems to have lost the connotation of improvisation (Petr. 4.5, Apul. *Socr.* pr.1; cf. Lucil. fr. 1279 *qui schedium fa*[—], but may have retained that of draft (Pecere 1986, 60–1); see *OLD*). *exscripsit* means 'transcribed', 'wrote out' (*OLD* 1), not necessarily verbatim, potentially covering copying, adapting and translating; cf. of a (free) translation 2.9.5 *ut nec Apuleius Phaedonem ... neque Tullius Ctesiphontem sic ... in usum regulamque Romani sermonis exscripserint*, and of a neat, edited copy (9.16.2 see above) (*TLL* 5/2.1831.1–24). **quia iusseras, misi:** The phrase characterizes the letter as a covering letter (see Intro 4.2 '*Iubes–pareo*'). For gift-giving, see Intro 3.3. **parēre festino:** *festino* (and the following *celeriter*) is the usual editorial (and epistolary) excuse of haste at odds with carefulness, cf. 9.9.2 *parere properanti*, 9.16.1–3n. with exactly the same series of apologies; cf. 7.18.1n. *raptim*. **celeriter eiecit in tumultuarium exemplar turbida et praeceps et Opica translatio:** the impersonal way of putting this may stress that scribes, not Sidonius himself, did the copying, chaotically and without understanding; cf. 9.16.2, where, as Sidonius is preparing Book 9 for dispatch, he is in charge (*exscripsi* 'I had it written out') but a secretary struggles with pen and ink. *tumultuarium*: a modesty topos, see 1.9.6n. *tumultuariis fidibus*. One wonders what use a 'chaotic copy' would have been to an insider like Leo if this were more than modesty. *turbida* and *praeceps* belong together in the description of storm, torrential rain and flooding (Verg. *Aen*. 12.684–5, Sil. 17.121–2); cf. 7.8.1 (of character) *turbidus per superbiam ... praeceps per iuuentutem. Opica*, meaning 'Oscan' (i.e. provincial), 'ignorant' (esp. linguistically), 'uncultured' (see *OLD*), may here have the later nuance of 'abstruse', 'outlandish' (Auson. *Prof*. 22.3 Green *chartas, Ep.* 27.99 Green *papyri*); see *TLL* 9/2.702.74–703.19. The qualification is proverbial: Otto 1890, 256–7 #1297. *translatio* 'transposition' (the neutral rendition suggested by Giannotti 2023, 123; similarly *transferre, translator*) is any alteration applied to or undergone by a text from version A to B: 'copy' (e.g. 9.11.6 *copiam transferendi*, Ruric. 1.8.2 *codicem ... transtulisse me fateor*), 'adaptation' (e.g. 9.16.2 *schedium ... translator exscripsi*, Paul. Petric. *Mart*. 4.5.1 *Finierat ... translatio ... uolumen*) or 'translation' (e.g. 2.9.4n. *ad uerbum sententiamque translatus*, Hier. *Ez*. 7.29 *quid sonent in hebraeo expressit nostra translatio*). For a similar context, favouring the notion of adaptation, cf. Boeth. *In Herm. comm. sec.* 1.1 *nisi quod Vetius Praetextatus priores postremosque analyticos non uertendo* ['translating'] *Aristotelem Latino sermoni tradidit, sed transferendo* ['adapting'] *Themistium*. Compare the discussion on orthodoxy and translation in 2.9.5n.; see also Intro 3.4 'Christianity'. **credito diuturnius** 'longer than expected': this use of *credito* is unique; cf. the abl. of comparison of other adjectives used as substantives like *aequo, iusto* and *solito* (G–L §398 N.1). The comparative *diuturnius* is rare, but is used several times by Sidonius (also 2.14.1, 9.9.9; *TLL* 5/1.1647.6–15). **mora moenium Liuianorum:** *mora* 'barrier', 'confinement' (cf. *OLD* 6, 8, 10); cf. Ovid. *Trist.* 3.14 *custodia muri* (where the walls, conversely, serve to keep the Goths out). The stronghold of Livia or Liviana, probably present-day Capendu/Douzens, between Carcassonne and Narbonne (*Barrington Atlas* 25.H2, *Peut. Tab.* 1.b.2, Miller 1964, 109), was the place of Sidonius' banishment in 475–6 after the Visigothic takeover (see Intro 1). **post opem Christi tibi debeo:** cf. 5.1.3 *solus post opem Christi ... sufficis*; see 1.5.1n. *sub ope ... dei* and 1.9.8n. *sub ope Christi*. Leo had interceded with Euric for Sidonius' release. **curis ... aeger** recalls Verg. *Aen*. 1.208 *curisque ingentibus aeger. cura* covers a range of meanings from 'worry' to 'task' (*OLD* 1, 7) (e.g. 1.3.1 *curis peruigilibus* of pursuing a career, 2.13.4 *mole curarum* of the emperor's burden). **saltim saltuatim tradenda percurrere** 'to review at least cursorily what I was going to send you' (i.e. check the copy), or else 'what was to be put on paper' (i.e. check the original or a draft; *OLD* 9, Mart. 3.20.2 *chartis tradidit ille ... legenda*). *saltuatim* is an archaism, one of many words from early Latin revived in the second century CE (Wolff 2020, 402, Intro 4.5). **nunc per nocturna suspiria, nunc per diurna officia distractus** is a neatly formulated (parallel, rhyme) variation on the topos of protracted anxiety or sorrow lasting all day and night, e.g. Cic. *Tusc.* 1.48 *diurno ac nocturno metu*, Stat. *Silv.* 3.5.1–2 *Quid mihi maesta die, ... quid noctibus, ... | ... ducis suspiria?*

2 excubiis 'tasks', *excubiae*, in later Latin, undergoing a shift from 'watch' to 'obligation', 'hard work' (van Waarden 2010, 168 with 7.2.5n., *TLL* 5/2.1287.46 'i.q. cura, labor'; Anderson translates 'my post of duty', Mascoli 'posto di lavoro'). Sidonius had apparently been assigned a job during the day. We can only guess at the severity of the curbs imposed on him. Episcopal exile could vary in distance and severity, from creating a cooling-off period to removing the victim indefinitely (Stevenson 2014; Barry 2019; Stadermann 2023, 226 n. 63). Euric applied this instrument to silence political opponents such as Crocus and Simplicius (7.6.9, each with a different prospect of return), and Faustus of Riez (exiled from 477 to 485 at quite some distance, see Faust. 6.1, 9.1, 12.1; Ruric. 1.2.3; Kaufmann 1995, 209 with n. 639). Sidonius' exile did not last too long and he was confined just across the border of Auvergne, not far from Narbonne where he had many friends. **crepusculascens hora**, a one-off periphrasis of *crepusculum*. **luminibus inflexis** 'my drooping eyelids' (tr. Anderson), cf. Ambr. *Isaac* 6.50 *cum oculis requieuisset inflexis* (cf. Ambr. *Abr.* 2.2.6 *mens ... aliquando se inflectat* ['relaxes']). **paruula quies:** cf. *parua quies* in Luc. 5.504, Claud. *Eutr.* 2.121. The clausula is the rare dactyl + iamb (–⏑⏑ ⏑×), which enjoys some favour in Sidonius together with comparable rhythms (see Marolla 2023, 33). In this § there is an accumulation: also *Getides anus* (anapaest + iamb), *-macius erit* (dactyl + iamb) and *otii fuit* (cretic + iamb). The effect is a parlando style. **nam fragor ilico:** with ellipsis of a verb meaning 'to arise'; cf. K–S 2, 553–4. **impluuio cubiculi** 'the courtyard where my bedroom was located'. **Getides anus**: the Greek adjective *Getes, -idis* is very rare (Ov. *Pont.* 4.13.18 *poeta Getes*). In the third and fourth centuries, the name *Getae*, Goths, was attached to populations living on the northern Black Sea coast. In the fifth century, different groups made their way west, eventually resulting in the Visigothic and the Ostrogothic successor states (*ODLA* 673). **litigiosius bibacius uomacius:** *bibax* is a rare archaic adjective (cf. Gell. 3.12.1) and *uomax* 'given to vomiting' is a creation of Sidonius, for the rhyme (see Wolff 2020, 398–9 for *hapax legomena*); for similar asyndetic sequences, see van Waarden 2010, 571–4. The drunken old woman is a stock type in comedy, e.g. Leaena in Plautus' *Curcullio* (77 *multibiba atque merobiba*, 79 *uinosissima* 109 *sitit haec anus*) and the brothelkeeper in *Cistellaria* who is chatty too (149 *utrumque haec, et multiloqua et multibiba, est anus*; cf. Hier. 53.7 *garrula anus*); see Gualandri 1979, 169; cf. Barrow 2018. It coincides with the stereotype of the barbarian as an intemperate eater and drinker (cf. *Carm.* 12.6 *Burgundio cantat esculentus*, there too hampering

Sidonius' creativity; Fascione 2019, 70). It is also the very opposite of the educated aristocrat who cannot but be appalled; cf. Ovid's archetypical experience in the *Tristia*, e.g. 3.13–5 *me sciat in media uiuere barbarie:* | *Sauromatae cingunt, fera gens, Bessique Getaeque,* | *quam non ingenio nomina digna meo!* **reduci** sc. *mihi*: Sidonius has returned from exile, which provides a date for this letter in late 476 or in 477. **semicrudum** 'half-raw', 'underdone' may be a hint at the impalatable past year, as barbarians ate their meat half-raw (Hier. *Adv. Iovin.* 2.7, *Vita Malchi* 4). **ut aiunt, tamquam musteum:** *ut aiunt* not only marks the proverb, but, above all, the allusion; this is the so-called 'Alexandrian footnote', see Hinds 1998, 1–5. The metaphor of unfermented wine (*mustum*) for an immature book is derived from Plin. 8.21.6 *hunc adhuc musteum librum*, cf. Plin. 9.16.2 *pro nouo musto ... uersiculos ... mittemu*s. **plus desiderii tui quam officii mei memor obtuli:** Sidonius sends the copy without revising it (as he should have done), because Leo is so keen to have it. *-i memor obtuli* is the rare dactyl + cretic clausula (–⏑⏑ –⏑×).

3 sepone ... suspende ... sepone articulate Leo's various activities to be put aside for an instant, summarized by 4 *exuere ... curis*. Cf. Mart. 7.33 *paulisper ... doctos sepone libellos*. **Pythicas lauros Hippocrenenque:** i.e. Apollo and the Muses. Hippocrene is a spring below Mt Helicon in Boeotia, made, according to myth, by Pegasus with a blow of his hoof (hence its name Ἱπποκρήνη, 'Horse Spring'), cultivated as a home of the Muses and poetic inspiration (*BNP* 'Hippocrene'). Leo receives a similar accolade in 9.13.2 (*Carm.* 36.20) for being the most prominent poet, *rex Castalii chori*. **illos carminum modos:** Sidonius praises Leo for his metrical expertise at *Carm.* 23.450–1 (hexameter) and *Carm.* 40.19–20 in *Ep.* 9.15.1 (iambic trimeter). **doctis, ut es ipse, personis:** the notion of *doctrina* is essential for understanding Roman poetry. The Hellenistic age created the *poeta doctus* with his display of erudition and refined language, embraced in Rome by Catullus and later poets (on Sidonus himself as *poeta doctus*, see Condorelli 2008). See also Intro 3.3 'Elite Status'. **non tam fonte quam fronte:** cf. the bon mot 'Genius is 1 per cent inspiration and 99 per cent perspiration'. Even a gifted poet (*fonte* alludes to Hippocrene) has to work hard, which is what Sidonius wants Leo to stop doing for a while. For the paronomasia, cf. *Carm.* 28.14n. (in 3.12). **perorandi ... flumen:** *perorare* basically denotes public speaking in general (*TLL* 10/1.1604.64), especially an advocate's pleading, e.g. Nep. *Phoc.* 4.2 *perorandi ... facultas ... et dicendi causam*, Sidon. 6.3.2 *togatorum ... perorantum peritiam* (*OLD* 1). Cf. Sidonius' characterizations of Leo as *catus* 'shrewd' (*Carm.* 9.314) and *doctiloquus* as a jurist (*Carm.* 23.446–9). See above Addressee for Leo's role as a juridical adviser at the Visigothic court. *flumen*, metaphorically of the copious supply of eloquence already in Cicero (e.g. *Brut.* 325; *OLD* 3); cf. 9.7.2 *flumen in uerbis.* It logically complements the flow of Leo's poetic inspiration described in the preceding clause. **non solum gentilicium sed domesticum** combines Plin. 6.15.1 *gentilicium* (cf. 9.22.1–2), about poetical talent inherited from distant generations, with Plin. 5.8.4 *domesticum,* about an example close at hand, in the person of Pliny's stepfather. Cf. the proverbial *domi habuit unde discere* (Ter. *Ad.* 413, Sidon. 7.9.19). **per succiduas aetates** 'through successive generations' (tr. Anderson): *succiduas* in this sense is later Latin usage; cf. e.g. Oros. *Hist.* 7.34.4 *per succiduas ... generationes* (Souter s.v.; van Waarden 2010, 324). *aetates*: *OLD* 8. **ab atauo Frontone:** Marcus Cornelius Fronto, *c.* 95–*c.* 166, orator, tutor of the emperor Antoninus Pius' sons Marcus Aurelius and Lucius Verus. Celebrated for his oratory (*Paneg.* 8[5].14.2 *Romanae eloquentiae non secundum sed alterum* [i.e. on a par with Cicero] *decus*), he is nowadays principally known for his correspondence with the imperial family, esp. Marcus (*OCD* 'Cornelius Fronto, Marcus'). Stylistically, he belongs to the archaizing movement of the second century; see 1.1 Discussion. **pauxillulum:** see 1.5.9n. **conclamatissimas declamationes** 'much acclaimed discourses': *conclamatus* in this sense is new with Sidonius (*TLL* 4.71.45–9). The prolonged acclamations are mimed by the wording itself (two long words, *a*-sounds, polyptoton; see Wolff 2020, 411). *declamationes* 'speeches', in Sidonius not necessarily connected with the notion of rhetorical exercise, see 9.7.1 *declamationum tuarum schedio* (probably sermons); cf. 5.2.1 *oratoria declamat.* **oris regii uice:** Leo is the king's spokesman and speech writer, cf. Cassiodorus for king Theoderic: *Var.* 11.praef.6 *decem libris ore regio sum locutus.* **rex inclitus:** *inclitus* 'glorious' is an honorific given to Roman emperors from the fourth century onwards and to the successor kings, e.g. Theoderic (*Inscr. christ.* Diehl 35.1), Childebert (*MGH SS rer. Merov.* 3, *Vita Avit. Aurel.* 12), Guntram (*SS rer. Merov.* 2, *Lib. Hist. Franc. rec. B* 35) (*TLL* 7/1.960.59–961.5). Sidonius now recognizes Euric's authority and the range of his impact. In 4.22.3, also to Leo from about the same period, he calls him *potentissimi ... regis*, with interests across the whole world (*totius ... orbis*). **gentium transmarinarum:** the Vandals in North-Africa. In the past two decades, Visigothic territory had expanded across Spain, which made them neighbours of the Vandals. Euric's policy was to maintain Gothic hegemony in Spain, if ultimately in vain (Kulikowski 2020, 213 with literature). **de superiore** 'from on high', 'sovereignly' or similar; not elsewhere attested, except Ps.-Charisius, *Synon. Cic.* p. 440 l. 17 *pro tribunali*: *de summo loco; de superiore.* **barbaris ad Vachalin trementibus:** *barbaris* from a Roman point of view (the narrator's perspective). The river Waal (*Vac(h)alis, Vac(h)alus*), a branch of the Rhine delta, typical demarcator of the northern border

(*Carm.* 5.209, 13.31, 23.244), was at the time in Frankish territory; cf. a similar stretch between the Germanic north and the Spanish south, Ven. Fort. *Carm.* 6.5.350 *perstrepit hoc Vachalus, illud Hiberus aquis*. **foedus ... innodat:** the verb *innodare* 'to fasten with a knot' appears in the fourth century (*TLL* 7/1.1710.28–65), this visual expression being a Sidonian unicum. In conjunction with the cession of the Auvergne to the Visigoths in 475, which made the Loire into their northern border, they had also made peace with the Burgundians and deterred the Saxons and Salian (western) Franks, thus creating an equilibrium of forces in Gaul. Details, however, escape us. In *Carm.* 34 (in letter 8.9), the Saxons, the tribes of the Lower Rhine and the Burgundians are depicted, begging for peace at Euric's court, but Sidonius is no doubt exaggerating in his own interest (see Delaplace 2015, 288). **per promotae limitem sortis** 'everywhere within the confines of his enlarged territory': for *promotae*, see *OLD promoueo* 2b. *sortis* is the 'share' or 'territory' that had been assigned to the Goths in the 418 treaty, which they now owned, in an enlarged form, as an independent state; cf. 7.6.4 *Euarix ... limitem regni sui rupto dissolutoque foedere antiquo ... promouet* and 10 *limes Gothicae sortis*. On the question of the *sortes Gothicae* and the distribution of land and tax revenues between Goths and Romans, see Intro 3.3 'Coexistence' with n. 37. **ut populos sub armis, sic frenat arma sub legibus:** in this otherwise original epigram, Luc. 7.123–5 *arma | permittit populis frenosque furentibus ira | laxat* (though saying something different) may have triggered the combination of *populos, armis* and *frenat*. For the sense, cf. Cic. *Off.* 1.77 '*Cedant arma togae*'. Euric's Visigothic law code can be partly reconstructed; it was complemented by a collection of Roman law, applicable to the Roman population of the Visigothic Kingdom, the *Lex Romana Visigothorum* (also called *Breviarium Alarici*), issued in 506 (see *ODLA* 'Alaric, Breviarium of'). Euric's code for Visigothic subjects was replaced in the seventh century by the *Liber iudiciorum* (edited, together with the *Codex Euriciana*, by Zeumer 1902). Leo played his part in Euric's project: see above Addressee.

4 exuere utcumque continuatissimis curis et otium tuum molibus aulicis motibusque furare: this passage is modelled on Stat. *Silv.* 4.4.28–9 *exue curis | pectus et assiduo temet furare labori* after Verg. *Aen.* 5.845; the collocation *otium furari* is also in Gell. praef. 12 *negotiorum interualla, in quibus furari otium potui. exuere* is medio-passive imperative singular (see G–L §218). *molibus ... motibusque*: wordplay (paronomasia) with rhyme. For syndetic pairs of words, see van Waarden 2010, 575. **ad Caucasum Indumque ... ad Aethiopum gymnosophistas Indorumque bracmanas:** Apollonius' trek through the Caucasus (i.e. the Hindu Kush) and India is described in the *Life* books 2 and 3 (3.15.1 'I saw the Indian Brahmans living on the earth and not on it, walled without walls, owning nothing and owning everything', tr. Jones), his travels in Egypt in book 6 (6.6 'Setting out from there at sunrise, before noon they reached the Naked Ones' ashram. ... In wisdom they are more inferior to the Indians than they are superior to the Egyptians. They wear as little clothing as do sunbathers at Athens'). Cf. Hier. 107.8 *Indorum Bragmanae et Aegyptiorum gymnosophistae*; in 53.1, Jerome describes at length Apollonius' wanderings: *transiuit Caucasum ... Indiae regna penetrauit ... peruenit ad Bragmanas ... Aethiopiam adiuit, ut gymnosophistas ... uideret*, of one among many who went abroad *ut eos quos ex libris nouerant coram quoque uiderent*; on autopsy and travelling by proxy, see 1.5.1n. *fideliore didicisse memoratu* and below. See *BNP* 'Brahmin' and 'Gymnosophists'. **totus lectioni uacans:** *totus* of full concentration, cf. e.g. Hor. *Sat.* 1.9.2 *totus in illis*. *lectioni* is a key word of intellectual activity, both for pagan (e.g. 5.5.2 *lectionis Maronianae*) and for Christian (e.g. 7.18.4n. *lectionis sacrae*) study. The theme of reading returns at the very end of the letter. *uacans* + dat. 'open to' (*OLD* 7b): cf. e.g. Sen. 88.35 *totum pectus illi* [i.e. the subject of study] *uacet*. **ipse quodammodo peregrinere:** an instance of 'armchair travelling'; see Carruthers 1998, Staat 2023; cf. 1.5.1n. *inspexerint*. *peregrinere* (= -*ris*) is present subj., stating a possibility or likelihood (see G–L §§257, 596).

5 This paragraph can be read as a mirror of princes for Euric (see above Discussion 'Politics'). In conjunction with the preceding accolade of the *rex inclitus*, it is not so much an encrypted appeal to Leo to distance himself from the king (as Overwien 2009, 98–100 thinks, rightly toned down by Egetenmeyr 2022, 180–2 and 319–20) as a piece of moral and political advice for the king, via his trusted adviser, to distance himself from despotism. Leo impersonates this responsible lifestyle (*uirum* [i.e. Apollonius] ... *in plurimis similem tui*); Euric – it is implied – is to follow under his influence. It is centred on the related virtues of *sobrietas* and *largitas* and the corresponding vices of *luxuria* and *auaritia*, the latter particularly in evidence in eastern despotism and extravagance. From republican times, these were felt to be the vital threats to the commonwealth: Sall. *Catil.* 5.8 *corrupti ciuitatis mores, quos pessuma ac diuorsa inter se mala, luxuria atque auaritia, uexabant*, Liv. 34.4.2 *diuersisque duobus uitiis, auaritia et luxuria, ciuitatem laborare*. In a Christian context, they figure prominently alongside superstition, lust, violence, pride and discord (see Prud. *Psych*. 310–628, occupying one third of the poem). See *BNP* 'Virtue' and 'Luxury'; on the difficult Roman relationship with luxury, Toner 2019. Stylistically the paragraph relies on the technique of parallelism and variation at phrase level, cf. 7.9.*contio* in van Waarden 2010, 442 and 576–84; see Wolff 2020, 407–9. **fidei catholicae pace praefata** 'with due respect to the Catholic faith': i.e. the universal and orthodox faith as opposed to Christian heresies; the first occurrences of *catholicus* in this sense are in the third century (Tertullian, Cyprian); this phrase Cypr. 25.2 *secundum catholicam fidem* (see Blaise s.v. *catholicus*). For *pace* 'with due respect', in various combinations, cf. e.g. 1.4.2 *bonorum pace praefata*, 1.9.2 *seruata pace reliquorum*, 5.14.2 *salua fidei pace*, 7.9.12 *reliquorum pace*. **a diuitibus ambitum nec diuitias ambientem:** variations on the idea of being well-liked without being pushy include 3.2.1 *non ambitiosus ... sed ambiendus*, 7.9.22 *maxime ambiendus, quia minime ambitiosus*. **cupidum scientiae continentem pecuniae:** for the opposition desire/greed vs restraint, cf. e.g. Cic. *Verr.* 2.4.34 [in one and the same person] *et cupiditatis et continentiae*, Ambr. *Off.* 3.2.10 *continentem esse ... alieni cupidum non esse. cupidum scientiae*: cf. e.g. Cic. *Fin.* 4.2.4 *cupiditatem scientiae*. Leo was a member of the philosophical circle of Narbonne (see Addressee above). *continentem pecuniae*, also Cassiod. *Var.* 5.4 *pecuniae continens*, cf. Sidon. 3.5.2 *alieni non appetens, sui parcus*. **inter epulas abstemium:** the first of three observations concerning luxury. Fasting (often combined with treating guests to a meal – or else, eating only a little not to offend them) is part of the ascetic aristocratic lifestyle promoted by the Lérins community (see Intro 3.4 'Christianity', van Waarden 2016, 2–22). It is a constant in Sidonius' correspondence, e.g. 6.2.1 *non minus se ieiuniis quam cibis pauperes pascit*, 7.9.10 *eum qui pascendo ieiunet*, 7.13.3 *ieiuniis delectatur, edulibus adquiescit*, 8.4.1 *ager tuus ... hospites epulis, te pascit hospitibus*. **inter purpuratos linteatum:** *purpuratos* 'clothed in purple', of emperors and royals (*TLL* 10/2.2707.8–17; see 1.9.2n. *post purpuratum*), here probably more generally 'grand people', cf. 7.6.4 *ut ... diues ... purpura ... ueletur* (from the parable of the Rich Man and Lazarus). *linteatum* 'wearing linen clothes', e.g. Sen. *Dial.* 7.26.8 *linteatus senex*, cf. Sidon. *Carm.* 7.455 *lintea* 'linen shirts' worn by the impoverished Visigothic senators. **inter alabastra censorium:** *alabastra* 'perfume bottles' (*OLD* 1), in Sidonius also *Carm.* 9.324, 37.63 (in 9.13.5). *censorium* 'austere' (*OLD* 3a). **concretum hispidum hirsutum** 'matted, shaggy, rough' of the unpretentious Apollonius is set off against *delibutarum* of eastern peoples as, chiastically, is *uenerabili squalore* against *murrhatos pumicatos malobathratos* of eastern satraps. This unkempt sturdiness is also an essential trait of the early republican ideal of the true commander who comes from, and returns to, his farm (Camillus and Cincinnatus among others), an ideal applied by the panegyricists in their praise of the emperors (e.g. Claud. *IV Hon.* 415–8, Sidon. *Carm.* 2.526–30, 5.298–304, 7.378–87). **nationum delibutarum:** *delibutarum* 'smeared' with a liquid, e.g. perfumes, Cic. *Rep.* 4.5 *delibutum unguentis.* In Prud. *Psych.* 311–2, the vice of Luxuria is *delibuta comas.* For the stereotype of eastern (Persian) decadence in the context of ethnic images in antiquity, see Nippel 2007, esp. p. 39. **tiaratorum** 'wearing a tiara' (Persian headdress): the participle is first encountered here. **murrhatos pumicatos malobathratos** 'wearing myrrh perfume, pumice-rubbed and doused with cinnamon oil': in *Carm.* 2.415, *malobathrum myrrhas* are among the scents in Aurora's mythical eastern paradise; cf. Hor. *Carm.* 2.7.7–8 *nitentis | malobathro Syrio capillos.* These grecisms *murrhatos* and *malobathratos* (the latter a hapax forged by Sidonius) help to create an exotic atmosphere (Gualandri 1979, 162). Pumice stone was used as a depilatory. Cf. the description of Arvandus (see Intro 1, 1.5 Introduction) confronted with his accusers in 1.7.9, the former arrogant, *detonsus pumicatusque*, the latter in their role as victims, *semipullati atque concreti.* The words in the asyndetic triad are in ascending order of syllables (see 4.5 n. 111). **uenerabili squalore pretiosum:** the clause ends in an oxymoron; cf. Hor. *Carm.* 2.1.22 *non indecoro puluere sordidos* [at the battle of Pharsalus]. For the combination of unkemptness (*squalor*) and venerability, cf. the Visigothic elders: *squalent uestes* and *honora pauperies* (*Carm.* 7.454 and 458–9). **proprio nihil esui aut indutui de pecude:** Pythagoreans were vegetarians and protective of animals, motivated by the doctrine of the transmigration of souls (see also Intro 3.4 and Discussion 1 above). *proprio* is emphatically fronted. *esui* and *indutui* are datives of the object for which (G–L §356). **regnis ob hoc, quae pererrauit, ... suspicioni ... fuisse suspectui:** for the double dative, see G–L §356. *ob hoc* summarizes the preceding reason clause; its unemphatic second position causes hyperbaton of head noun and relative clause, which is striking (cf. the usual pattern of noun phrase hyperbaton, *OLS* 2, 1101–8). For parallelism and paronomasia, cf. 4.22.1 *suspicere ... suscipere.* The infinitive *fuisse* somewhat awkwardly breaks the series of adjectives defining *uirum* and is bracketed by Lütjohann. The MSS, however, are unanimous. **mage ... praestare quam sumere**: for the proverb, cf. Vulg. *Act.* 20.35 *beatius est magis dare quam accipere*; for the formulation, Symm. 2.77 *beneficium te non ... praestare sed sumere.* *mage* is an alternative of *magis.* Sidonius uses *mage* before consonants, *magis* before consonants and vowels, both in his prose (with a clearcut preference for *magis*, 6 to 1) and his verse (almost equally distributed).

6 quid multis? is a formula for summing up (also 1.2.6, 4.3.9, 8.9.2); alternatives include *quid multa?* and *quid plura?*; see 2.9.6n. **si uera metimur aestimamusque:** the conclusion seems to be a variation on Livy's ending to Book 8, chapter 40.4–5. Livy states that he has difficulty in deciding what is true and what is not in the sources and continues as follows: *nec quisquam aequalis temporibus illis scriptor extat quo satis certo auctore stetur* 'nor is there extant any writer contemporary with that period on whose authority we may safely take our stand' (tr. B. O. Foster). The context of this passage is probably not coincidental to Sidonius' borrowing for a letter in Book 8 concerned with an edition by the Symmachi and Nicomachi: at the end of Livy's Book 8 and immediately preceding its colophon (see Introduction 'Sidonius' copy'). *metimur aestimamusque*: redundancy is a result of Sidonius' love of verbal abundance (Wolff 2020, 409). **fors fuat an** 'it might be that', 'perhaps' (*OLD* 5): found in Plautus and Terence, then, as an archaism, in Apuleius, Fronto and the correspondences of Symmachus and Sidonius (also 2.2.17). What follows is a comparative system, aimed to finish the letter in a memorable way (for this technique, see Wolff 2020, 413; cf. e.g. 8.15.2n.). **philosophi uitae scriptor aequalis maiorum temporibus accesserit:** 'the times of our ancestors found an author congenial with the philosopher's life': *philosophi uitae* is topic of this and the following clause, while *scriptor* and *lector* have contrastive focus. The dative *uitae* goes with *aequalis* 'commensurate with', 'up to the standard of' (see *OLD* 5b; cf. Cic. *Orat.* 123 *erit rebus ipsis par et aequalis oratio*). For *accedere* + dat. 'accrue to', 'be given to' (with as its complements *maiorum temporibus* and *saeculo meo*, respectively), see 3.12.5 *accedat*. The past *presumably* got an insightful biographer in the person of Philostratus, but Sidonius' own time *certainly* gets its sensitive reader in Leo (thus Loyen, Bellès, Mascoli). The point is the degree of certainty, which characteristically ends in a compliment for Leo. Linking instead *maiorum temporibus* to *aequalis* 'on a level with (the writers of) our ancestors' time' and *accesserit* to *uitae* (Anderson, Köhler) works less well as it diverts attention from the author being up to his task to the author competing with his generation. Yet another solution is taking *scriptor* as 'transcriber' (cf. *OLD* 1), 'revisor', which shifts the comparison to Sidonius and Leo and creates the usual modesty topos (Giannotti 2023, 126). In his imitation of Livy, Sidonius strikingly deviates from the meaning of *aequalis* there (indeed the normal one): 'contemporary'. **certe par saeculo meo per te lector obuenit** strengthens the similarity by means of *certe* (Sidonius)–*certo* (Livy), *lector* (Sidonius)–*auctore* (Livy) and the synonymous pair *accesserit–obuenit* replacing Livy's wordplay *extat – stetur*. *meo … te* emphasizes Sidonius' closeness to Leo, whereas *nostro … te* would have been a more distanced alternative (see van Waarden 2020e, 435–6). For the theme of readerly collaboration as a key to late antique intertextuality, see Pelttari 2014, Gualandri 2020, 313–16. The clausula *lector obuēnit* (pf.) is the number-one cretic + spondee (Intro 4.5).

LETTER 8.15: IN PRAISE OF THE BISHOP OF ORLÉANS

Outline

Bishop Prosper is anxious to glorify his eminent predecessor in the see of Orléans, Anianus. He begs Sidonius to write the history of the war against Attila, in which Anianus memorably saved his city from plunder. Sidonius declines a full history as too cumbersome, but promises to write a eulogy of the bishop.

Introduction

This letter combines two threads: the commonplace refusal, on the part of the sender, to write a piece of poetry or prose – here, history – and a promise to write a saint's Life, a Christian form of panegyric intended to influence church politics as much as to edify.

Discussion

Refusal to Write History

Misgivings over writing history, or refusing outright (*recusatio*) to do so, are an epistolary trope. In Sidonius' own correspondence, letter 4.22 to Leo, the adviser of king Euric (see 8.3n.), shows how this works. Leo had asked Sidonius to write the history of their time. As the frictions between Visigoths and Romans would of necessity be a prominent theme and his own role in them would lead to unpleasant confrontations, Sidonius declined (cf. Overwien 2009, 112–13). A core argument is (§5): *praeterita infructuose praesentia semiplene, turpiter falsa periculose uera dicuntur* '[the] account of things past is profitless, that of things present is only half-complete; and while it is shameful to utter falsehoods, it is dangerous to tell the truth' (tr. Anderson). Cf. similar arguments in Cic. *Fam.* 5.12 and Pliny 5.8.12. In the autocracy that the Empire was, the only feasible option was writing panegyric – or hagiography. Cf. Eutr. 10.18.3, Amm. 31.16.9. On the theme, see Cugusi 1990, Kaldellis 2017.

Saints' Lives

The fourth century witnessed the rise of a distinct genre of hagiography, the *Vita* or Life of Christian holy men and women, a mixture of biography and pious fiction (see *ODLA* 1320–2 'Saints' Lives'; for its pagan counterpart, see 8.3; cf. Brown 1971a). The classic example is the Life of the Egyptian monk Antony by Athanasius of Alexandria (*ODLA* 89–90 'Antony the Great, S.', *ODCC* 'Antony, St, of Egypt'). Sulpicius Severus introduced the ascetic Life in the West by means of his *Life of St Martin*, the defiantly ascetic bishop of Tours, written in the 390s (*ODLA* 972 'Martin, S.', *ODCC* 'Martin, St'). In fifth-century Gaul, the austere spirituality of Aquitaine, with St Martin as its figurehead, competed with the more moderate sphere of Provence and the Rhône delta (see Intro 3.4). Bishops' Lives played an essential role in profiling these currents. The 'east' sought to promote bishop Germanus of Auxerre as its champion. His Life, *Vita Germani*, was written in the late 470s by Constantius of Lyon, the dedicatee of Sidonius' correspondence, as part of 'a co-ordinated effort [by Auxerre and Lyon] to counter the vigorous promotion of St Martin by Perpetuus of Tours' (Harries (1994) 121–22). Not only was it written by one of Sidonius' intimates, it also broadly coincides with the publication of Book 8 (Gillett 2003, 282–3). The promise, in the present letter, of writing a eulogy (§2 *praeconio*) of Anianus, legendary bishop of Orléans – on an equal footing with Germanus (§1 *Germanoque non imparem*) – ties it in with the 'eastern' project and embraces his role as a defender of his city as model for the bishops involved. The eulogy has not been preserved – if it was written in the first place (see Intro 2.2; we do have a later Life, see §1n. *Anianum*). Incidentally, Sidonius' overall position is quite balanced. He also supports Perpetuus by contributing a text for the walls of the enlarged basilica of St Martin in Tours (*Carm.* 31 in letter 4.18) and engaging him to audit the procedure for the nomination of a new bishop in Bourges (letter 7.9) (see van Waarden 2016, 254 n. 8).

Addressee

Prosper, bishop of Orléans, figures only here and in the eleventh-century bishops' list of Orléans. Prosopography: Mathisen 2020a, 116.

Date and Place

There are no external dating criteria for this letter except that Sidonius is clearly a bishop (Kelly 2020, 188). Prosper's years in office are unknown. The earliest preserved bishops' list of Orléans (11th cent., Vat. Reg. lat. 465, 84r; see Duchesne 2, 457–64) knows of four bishops preceding him after Anianus' death in the late 450s (see §1n. *decessit*). An internal criterion could be its concurrency with Constantius' *Life of Germanus* (see above). Loyen 2, 217 thinks that it was a new letter, written for the first additional instalment to the correspondence, hence between 477 and

478/80 (for the date of publication of Book 8, see Intro 2.1). The place of writing is presumably Clermont.

Literature

Studies: Cugusi 1990, Overwien 2009, 112–13.

Commentary

1 sanctum Anianum: *sanctum* 'holy', 'blessed' is a common epithet for bishops, cf. 2.9.6n. *sancte*, 2.10.2n. *sancti*. Anianus was bishop of Orléans when the Huns of Attila ravaged Gaul in 451 and laid siege to the town. According to the hagiographical sources (the early-sixth-century *Vita Aniani* and Greg. Tur. *Hist.* 2.7), he had gone to Arles to secure the aid of the Roman *magister militum* Aëtius and had fortified the town walls. At the last moment, after repeated prayers of the citizens, Aëtius arrived to drive off Attila. The historical core is an instance of ecclesiastical crisis management in an age of governmental discontinuity. Other cases include, for instance, bishop Patiens of Lyon supervising corn distributions (see 2.10 Addressee) and Mamertus of Vienne warding off the panic caused by earthquakes (see 7.1 Discussion 'Rogations Days') (see *CAH* 14, 511–13 (Ian Wood), Allen and Neil 2013). Previously, Aëtius had been on good terms with the Huns and even directed their forces against Gaul for his own ends, but in 451 changed circumstances led him to counter them with the help of the Visigoths, procured through a long-standing trustee of their king Theoderic, Eparchius Avitus, Sidonius' future father-in-law (see Harries 1994, 67–75; Sidonius magnifies Avitus' role at the expense of Aëtius in *Carm.* 7.316–56). The episode ended with the defeat of the Huns in the Battle of the Catalaunian Fields, near Troyes. For Sidonius' secular treatment of the episode as against the *Vita*'s spiritual take, see Barnish 1992, 38 and 44; for the *Vita*, Loyen 3, 203 n. 63, Keefer 1996; for the history of Gaul in Sidonius' early years, Kulikowski 2020, 203–6; for the Huns, e.g. *ODLA* 748–9 'Huns', C. Kelly 2008, Maas 2015; prosopography of Anianus: Mathisen 2020a, 79. **consummatissimum** is first found in Plin. 2.7.6 *consummatissimum iuuenem*, then from the early 5th cent. onwards. Out of four occurrences in Sidonius, three concern bishops of the highest status (also 4.17.3, 7.2.1). **Lupo parem Germanoque non imparem:** the uncontested doyen of the Gallic episcopate in Sidonius' time (6.1.3), Lupus was bishop of Troyes from *c.* 426 to 478. He had close connections to Lérins, where he had been a monk. In 429, he accompanied Germanus on a mission to Britain to combat the heterodoxy of Pelagianism. He is mentioned throughout the correspondence and received letters 6.1, 6.4, 6.9 and 9.11. Prosopography: Mathisen 2020a, 105. Germanus was a jurist and governor (*dux*) of Brittany before becoming bishop of Auxerre, where he served from *c.* 418 to 446/8. He was associated with members of the Lérins group through contacts with Lyon and Arles. See further Discussion above 'Saints' Lives'. Prosopography: Mathisen 2020a, 98; see also Harries 1994, 41–2. For *parem ... non imparem*, see 7.1.2n.   **uis:** Prosper is addressed in the second person singular throughout, which makes for a straightforward personal letter (van Waarden 2020e, 429–30; see below on *famulemur*).   **fidelium** 'the faithful', 'believers': see *TLL* 6/1.657.73–658.61, Blaise 2.   **uiri talis ac tanti:** the collocation *talis ac tantus* (or *vice versa*) literally 'of such calibre and importance', often defining persons (*uir, homo,* etc.; see *OLD* 3), is frequently found in later Latin; early examples include Cic. *Fam.* 13.66.1, *Nat. deor.* 3.92, Plin. *Nat.* 29.75, Apul. *Met.* 11.4.   **mores merita uirtutes** 'character, achievements, qualities': cf. 7.17.2n. *mores gesta uirtutes*. For asyndetic triads, often consisting of members of increasing length, see Intro 4.5 with n. 111. This clausula (paeon IV + spondee) and all others in this letter belong to the classic core, lending it stability.   **cui ... gloriae datur** 'who is credited with': *gloriae* is predicative dative, as e.g. Plin. *Nat.* 7.186 *gloriae,* Lucil. 1333 *honori,* Cic. *Cluent.* 51 *laudi* (*OLD do* 17, G–L §356); alternatively, it can be taken as a partitive genitive with *illud*.   **non absque** 'not without ...' > 'with full ...': this litotes (G–L §700) belongs to late Latin idiom.   **te successore decessit** 'he died with you as his successor': nominally a compliment for Anianus, actually for Prosper. *decessit* combines the notions of dying and being succeeded, cf. 7.2.4 *uobis decessit.* See above Date and Place.   **Attilae bellum** 'the <story of the> war with Attila': see above and van Waarden 2016, 69 on 7.12.3n. *Attilam Rheni hostem ... Aëtium Ligeris liberatorem.*   **stilo ... intimaturum** 'would make known by means of my pen': see L–S *intimo* IIB. For *stilus,* see 1.1.2n. *in stilo epistulari.*   **quo ... continebatur** 'which contained': one expects a subjunctive ('which would contain'), but the indicative conveys the fact Sidonius had already done something, as is apparent from the following *coeperam scribere.*   **Aurelianensis urbis:** present-day Orléans. Originally called Cenabum, central *oppidum* of the Carnutes, it was burnt down by Caesar in 52 BCE (Caes. *Gall.* 7.11). It remained a regional market place which was turned into a fortified *castrum* in the late third century by an emperor with the *gentilicium* Aurelius, possibly Probus (276–82). The common assumption that it was Aurelian in 273 is false (see Debal 1974, 20; further, Mathisen 2020d, 157).   **obsidio oppugnatio, irruptio nec direptio** 'siege and storming, invasion but no pillage': the last being the usual conclusion of the capture of a city, as when Caesar took the town: *Gall.* 7.11.9 *oppidum diripit atque incendit, praedam militibus donat.* For the pair *obsidio oppugnatio,* cf. e.g. Caes. *Civ.* 3.9.4, Liv. 5.2.1; for syndetic and asyndetic sequences van Waarden 2010, 571–5. **uulgata ... uaticinatio:** *uulgata* 'famous' (*OLD* 2a). *caelitus* 'from heaven' is later Latin for *diuinitus* or *caelo,* first found in Apul. *Pl.* 1.12 and Cypr. *Ep.* 1.4. For *sacerdos* 'bishop', see 3.12.3n. *uaticinatio* is the confidence radiated by Anianus in the upcoming relief of the city (*Vita Aniani* 10 *quod bonus praedixerat uatis ... adfuit Agetius,* Greg. Tur. *Hist.* 2.7 *confisus in Deo ... suspicabatur ... Aetium aduenire*). The phrase is symmetrical, with *caelitus* in the middle.

2 operis arrepti fasce: for the workload of writing history, cf. e.g. Cic. *Fam.* 5.12.2 *oneribus ... susceptarum rerum,* Plin. 5.8.12 *onerosa collatio.* The phrase is adopted by Ennod. *Dict.* 9.15 *sub fasce suscepti operis.* For *fascis,* metaphorically 'weight', 'burden', see *TLL* 6/1.307.62–308.18; in Sidonius also 5.20.3, 7.4.1. **taeduit:** the perfect tense is rare and limited to ecclesiastical writers. Fourth-century grammarians (Charisius, Diomedes) said that it is impossible: *dici non potest.* **nullis auribus credidi** 'I did not entrust to anyone's ears': for critical assessment, cf. 8.16.1 *cuius auribus non peperci, dum tuis parco* (cf. e.g. 4.3.1 *examen aurium tuarum*). **me censore damnaueram:** *censore* '(literary) critic', e.g. Hier. 125.18 *criticum ... censoremque Romanae facundiae,* Sidon. 8.6.9 *ad puncta censoris.* For *damnaueram* 'I had disapproved', 'I had rejected', of a literary work, cf. e.g. Mart. 4.86.9, Quint. 3.64. For the commonplace refusal to write history, see Discussion. **dabitur ... precatui** 'your request will be satisfied', with *dari* in the sense of 'to be granted', e.g. Sen. *Contr.* 9.2.1 *gratiae ... precibus,* Plin. 1.22.9 *precibus ... lacrimis* (L–S M, *OLD* 16). **quatenus ... famulemur:** *quatenus* 'inasmuch as' (*OLD* 8). The plural *famulemur* – the only deviation from the straightforward *ego–tu* of this letter – emphasizes Sidonius' obliging attitude. **praeconio suo:** instead of historiography, Sidonius will write a eulogy (*OLD praeconium* 1c), perhaps a poem as for bishop Faustus (*Carm.* 16) or rather a prose hagiography like Constantius' *Vita Germani* (see above). For *suo* instead of *eius,* which are interchangeable in late Latin, see H–S 175–6. **celeri occasione** is a one-off collocation, cf. Curt. 8.6.1 *matura obuenit occasio.* **creditor iustus:** in the spirit of the law that a creditor should treat the interest of the debtor as he would his own: Ulp. *Dig.* 46.3.34.9 *aequissimum enim uisum est ita creditorem rem agere debitoris, ut suam ageret.* **insolubile ... inreposcibile:** *insolubilis* 'that cannot be repaid' is first found at Sen. *Ben.* 4.12.1. *inreposcibilis* (MSS reading unassimilated *inr-* instead of *irr-,* parallel to *ins-;* cf. §1 *irruptio;* see Intro 6 n.124) is elsewhere only at Apul. *Apol.* 92.8 (see Wolff 2020, 400). The closure of a letter often consists of a comparative system (like 8.3.6n.); see Wolff 2020, 413. Placed chiastically against *insolubile, inreposcibile* rounds off the sentence with a cretic + tribrach clausula.

LETTER 9.16 WITH POEM 41: HIS SPIRITUAL TESTAMENT

Outline

At Firminus' request, Sidonius has added another book of correspondence to the eight already inscribed to Constantius. Back from a tour of his diocese, he braves the cold to copy out anything he can find before spring. He apologizes for the inevitable inaccuracies and takes the opportunity to present Firminus with a poem in Sapphics. The poem muses on the reputational risk for an author of both poetry and prose in publishing his work, which Sidonius has safely managed to do. He has won the state accolades of a statue in Rome and the city prefecture for his panegyrics and written quantities of light verse of which, as an older man, he is now largely ashamed. As a bishop he rejects trivial poetry, but might be tempted to write poems about the martyrs. There follows a short hymn on the earliest martyr of Toulouse, Saturninus. The letter ends in prose so as not to violate Horace's rule of artistic unity.

Introduction

Book 9 is the second addition to the letter collection, which aligns it with Pliny's nine-book collection, bringing to a close the grand arc of the correspondence (see Intro 4.1). Firminus' promising youthfulness, coupled with the experience of the overall dedicatee Constantius (see §1n. *Constantium*), adds a note of hopefulness to the closure. The younger generation will carry on with Sidonius' legacy. In the economy of Book 9, at the end, this generation stands out in at least three young addressees (apart from Firminus in 9.16, Tonantius in 9.13 and Gelasius in 9.15; strikingly, Sidonius' son Apollinaris Jr – their peer and friend – is relegated to a critical aside in 9.1.5: see Intro 3.3 n. 46) and the unashamed reappearance of poetry in the letters they receive, numbers 13–16 prefaced by 12 (Mathisen 2013, 238–9, Neger 2020, 87–101; see Intro 4.1 n. 86). Letters 1–11, in counterpoint, are addressed to bishops, among them Lupus who receives the last episcopal letter in the collection (9.11) as he did the first (6.1) (Mratschek 2020b, 220). In addition, letter 9.11 looks back on the collection of Books 1–7/8 (Kelly 2020, 187).

Discussion

The letter and its embedded poem constitute a *sphragis* rounding off Sidonius' collected correspondence and his career as a *littérateur* (as done previously at the end of Book 7; see 7.18 Discussion). It is one of the letters specifically written, or adapted, for the collection (Kelly 2020,

181–5), drawing on Pliny's last letter 9.40 for the setting in (metaphorical) winter (see Gibson 2013, 218–19). Counterbalancing this, Pliny's addressee is young and promising (see Plin. 6.11), and Sidonius elaborated on this (see further in Intro 4.1 n. 82). For the embedded poem, comparable pieces come to mind like Hor. *Carm.* 3.30 and Ov. *Trist.* 4.10. A notable model for this 'spiritual testament' is Prudentius' *Praefatio*, which thematizes youth and sadder and wiser old age, high office and the turn towards singing the martyrs (see e.g. Gualandri 1979, 4–7; for the poem as autobiography, Kaufmann 2022). In the concluding prose §4, Sidonius works out the metaphor of pottery for literary output in the vein of Horace's *Ars poetica*, in notable contrast to Prudentius' *Epilogus* (Mratschek 2017, 321–2). Both Prudentius and Horace are in fact omnipresent, by the poetic form itself and in many details, as pointed out in the commentary (see also 2.9.4n.). Another poetical model is Ovid, while Statius and the ecclesiastical writer Eucherius offer hypotexts in the prose part. The very last words refer back to Cicero.

Addressee

Firminus is a young man who presumably lived in Arles, if he is the Firminus mentioned in the *Vita Caesarii* 1.8. He was a friend of Apollinaris Jr (9.1.5 *Apollinaris tuus*), Gelasius, the addressee of 9.15 (see §3; Mathisen 2020a, 98) and Tonantius, the addressee of 9.13 (see 9.15.1; Mathisen 2020a, 124). He is possibly identical with Firminus, a relative of Ennodius of Pavia (Ennod. 1.8, 2.7). Prosopography: Mathisen 2020a, 96.

Date and Place

The interconnected letters 12–16 can be dated to the years 480–2, following the indication in 9.12.2 that Sidonius has not written poetry for twelve years (*tres olympiadas*) after his consecration in 469/70. Accordingly, letter 16 is usually dated to 481 or 482 (e.g. Loyen 2, 219 (on p. 178: 'Clermont, February 482'), Mathisen 2013, 238), though Kelly 2020, 188–9 considers the winter of 478/9.

Literature

Studies of the letter: Gibson 2011, Stoehr-Monjou 2024. Of the poem: Gualandri 1979, 4–7; Ravenna 2004; Condorelli 2008, 228–39; Egelhaaf-Gaiser 2010; van Waarden 2011, 107–8; Mratschek 2017, 319–22; Consolino 2020, 367–9; Condorelli 2020a, 459–61; Kaufmann 2022.

Commentary

1 Si recordaris: evoking shared memories is one of the ways of creating an informal epistolary exchange, also 4.24.1; cf. e.g. Cic. *Att.* 13.49.1 *si meministi* (cf. Cugusi 1983, 79–81; see Intro 3.6 n. 79: a letter as one half of a conversation). The verb also creates a first tentative link to Pliny's last letter 9.40, which thematizes *memoria* (cf. Whitton 2019, 346–52). **domine fili** 'esteemed son': see Intro 4.2 'Address'. The correspondence ends with a letter to – and indeed an entire book commissioned by – a junior member of the nobility after it began with one to a senior aristocrat. It is striking that this cultural torch-bearer is not Sidonius' son Apollinaris, who has other interests (see Introduction). Condorelli 2015, 503–7 points out that this is an inverse parallel to Symmachus' collection, which was indeed edited by his own son. **libellus:** see 7.18.1n. **dictatus** 'composed': see 7.18.2n. It echoes Plin. 9.40.2 *illa quae dictaui*. **copularetur:** cretic + spondee is the dominant clausula in §§1–2. **ad Constantium:** for the dedications and Constantius' engagement with the cause of Clermont, see 1.1, 3.2, 7.18 and 8.16; for his prosopography, 1.1 Addressee. **ingenii, consilii** 'talent' and 'discernment' respectively: essential personal characteristics, often combined in Cicero, e.g. *Q. Rosc.* 48 *miseri ingeni, nullius consili*. As pointed out by Quintilian, *ingenium* (Quint. 10.1.130, 10.2.12) requires *consilium* (syn. *iudicium*: Quint. 6.5.3, 10.1.130) for it to be applied in a sensible way. **in tractatibus publicis** 'in public discussions': *OLD tractatus* 3a. **seu diuersa siue paria decernat:** *diuersa ... paria* is characteristic of the antithetic style, see 7.1.2n. *pari ... non impari*. For *decernat* 'speaks in favour of', see 5.5.3, 7.18.3. **facundiae dotibus:** *dotibus* + gen. 'talents of', 'gifts of' (*OLD* 3), often weakened 'by virtue of', 'thanks to', cf. e.g. 2.6.1 *morum dotibus*, 9.9.12 *animi litterarumque dotibus*; Ov. *Ars* 2.112 *ingenii dotes*, Plin. 3.3.4 *cum ceteris naturae fortunaeque dotibus*. The emphatic accolade of Constantius, even as the focus is on Firminus' request, proves how large his shadow looms across the entire correspondence, not only in the first seven books dedicated to him, but also in Book 8, which is dedicated to a certain Petronius but concludes with a letter to Constantius, leaving Petronius with the *correctionis labor*, while giving Constantius the *honor editionis* (8.16.1). **exacte ... instanter** 'perfectly ... promptly' (tr. Anderson): *exacte* 'accurately', 'carefully' (*OLD exacte*), also 'artfully' (as in 7.9.2 *exacte perorantibus*, see van Waarden 2010, 421; cf. 8.11.5 *uersus ... exactos*). *instanter* has the specific sense of 'hastily', 'immediately' (*TLL* 7/1.2006.10–15) rather than the usual 'vehemently' (*OLD*; see 1.2.7 *mittit instanter*). The request of the addressee has to be fulfilled as soon as possible: cf. 7.18.1n. *raptim*, and *celeriter*. For the topical opposition of care and haste in editing, see §3 below and 8.3.2n. *festino ... in tumultuarium exemplar*.

2 diocesibus 'parishes': Sidonius has made an inspection tour in his diocese, possibly for administrative reasons. For the practice, cf. *Concilium Tarraconense* (516 CE) can. 8 *decreuimus, ut … annuis uicibus ab episcopo dioceses uisitentur*, with the injunction to restore any churches fallen into disrepair (Vives Gatell 1963, 36). For the noun, cf. 7.6.8 *in … diocesibus parochiisque*: in the fifth and sixth centuries, *dio(e)cesis* and *parochia* were still interchangeable for both (episcopal) diocese and (local) parish; see van Waarden 2010, 319, Herbert de la Portbarré-Viard 2023, 64 nn. 360–1. **schedium temere iacens:** For *schedium*, see 8.3.1n. The sender pretends that his archive is a mess of crumbling documents, cf. 7.18.1n. *pauca* [*exemplaria*] *… quia … incustodita nequeunt inueniri* (letters), 9.13.6 *in imo scrinii fundo muribus perforatas* (poems). Models include Plin. 1.1.2 *eas quae adhuc neglectae iacent* (letters) and Auson. *Griph. ep.* l. 3 Green *situ chartei pulueris eruissem* (poems). For epistolary archives, see 1.1.1n. *exemplaribus.* **chartulis putribus ac ueternosis:** although neglected archives are a commonplace, *chartulis putribus* probably recalls Stat. *Silv.* 4.3.141 [*dicta*] *putribus euoluta chartis* '[sayings] unrolled from mouldering sheets', of the Sibylline oracles. Combined with *ueternosis* 'worn-out', this should remind the reader of 8.16.4 *uerba … Sibyllina … quae … ueternosus … aenigmatista patefecerit* 'Sibylline oracles expounded by some antiquated riddler'. The point there is the sought-after archaic style, which Sidonius pretends not to be able to master. Occurring three times in Sidonius, in the last letters of Books 8 and 9, as well as in the first of Book 1 (see 1.1.2n.), *ueternosus* is an important marker of the stylistic, archaizing unity of the correspondence and its defence of tradition. **raptim coactimque:** see 7.18.1n. *raptim*, 8.3.1n. *festino*, both being instances of the polite depreciation of speed as being incompatible with carefulness and quality (see also §3 below). *coactim* is a *hapax legomenon*: 'concisely', 'briefly' (L–S) or 'under compulsion (pressure)' (Souter); cf. *TLL* 3.1534.15. For neologisms in -*tim*, see Wolff 2020, 398. **translator festinus exscripsi** 'I hastily edited and had it written out': see 8.3.1n. *exscripsit* and *translatio*. For the phrasing, cf. 5.16.3 *festinus … inscripsi*, 7.18.1n. *celeriter absolui.* **tempore hiberno:** the season is inspired by Pliny's writing in winter in 9.40. Nor is winter the best time for travelling, as Sidonius just did (except, paradoxically, in war conditions, cf. 3.2). The seasonal context strongly suggests the mood of a metaphorical winter (Hanaghan 2019, 181–2: 'These comments highlight Sidonius' mortality. Winter time is symbolic of death'). Sidonius winds up his legacy with one more book of letters and his spiritual testament (the included poem). It is up to the next generation, in the person of Firminus, when spring comes (*Fauonius* below), to take over. The correspondence ends on a note of hope. For the progression of Sidonius' age in the correspondence and its darkening mood, see van Waarden 2018, 191–6; for the last books in particular, and the final ray of hope, see Gibson 2013, 211–19; for the next generation, Intro 4.1 with n. 82; for the structuring role of the seasons, see Hanaghan 2019, 73–5, Marolla 2023, 9–11 (cf. time in narrative, Intro 4.3). **antiquarium moraretur:** *antiquarium* 'scribe', 'calligrapher' (Souter), specializing in restoring books (*Cod. Theod.* 14.9.2); see *TLL* 2.174.1–18. The delaying of the scribe is a reversal of Auson. *Ep.* 9a Green *Oblata per antiquarios mora* – the scribes causing delay. **insiccabilis** 'never drying' is late Latin, otherwise only attested in Aug. *In psalm.* 41.2 *insiccabilis fons* (Wolff 2020, 402); for the proliferation of neologisms by means of -*bilis*, see ibid. 398. **calamo durior gutta:** oxymoronic hyperbole, cf. for frozen liquid, Coripp. *Iust.* 3.283 *fit durior unda metallis*; for over-thick ink, Pers. 3.12 *crassus calamo quod pendeat umor.* **non fluere sed frangi** is the kind of opposition dear to Sidonius, cf. e.g. 7.4.2 *non frangitis ... sed flectitis* (van Waarden 2010, 228). **compotem officii ... agere** 'to discharge my duty': this noun phrase elsewhere only 4.7.3 *me officii uotiui compotem fecit* 'he has enabled me to discharge my incumbent duty' (tr. Anderson), Alc. Avit. *Ep.* 89.3 M-R *me ... legistis officii mei compotem*, 'you have read that I am in charge of my office'. See *OLD ago* 26. **duodecimum nostrum ... Numae mensem uos:** as the Roman year originally began in March, February is the twelfth month (Varro *Ling.* 6.13). Even so, it is strange for Sidonius to *call* it the twelfth. The clue might be found in his episcopal mindset. Eucherius of Lyon, at *Instr.* 2 p. 204, 295 *Adar in libro Esther Februarius qui apud nos duodecimus*, brings together the twelfth month of the Roman and of the Jewish religious calendars: in the month of Adar, the Feast of Purim is celebrated, commemorating the Jews' being saved from annihilation in Persia, as told in the Bible book of Esther. Sidonius knew and no doubt read Eucherius, a defining presence in the southern Gallic church, monk in Lérins and bishop of Lyon until his death *c.* 449 (see Intro 3.4, van Waarden 2016, 6–8; mentioned 4.3.7). If this passage is also what Sidonius had in mind, *nostrum* refers to his own milieu of ecclesiastics (cf. 7.1.5n.), whereas *uos* refers to the laity. One further step would be to take it as a quip at the Visigothic dominance over the Roman population on the analogy with Persia threatening the Jews. The collocation *Numae mensem* 'Numa's month', i.e. February, was coined by Ausonius (*Ecl.* 7.7, 8.13, 9.2 Green; Sidonius also 2.14.2 *Iani Numaeque ninguidos* ['snowy'] *menses*), but is slightly misleading. Numa, the second king of Rome after Romulus, was credited with numerous legal and religious institutions, among them the addition of *two* months, January and February, to the calendar (Ov. *Fast.* 1.44; cf. Auson. *Ecl.* 3.3–4 Green), February thus closing the year (Ov. *Fast.* 2.49). Because in everyday usage the month would be simply called February, the reference to ancient lore seems to reinforce the case for Firminus being identical with Ennodius' later correspondent, a learned and eloquent man, according to Ennodius (see Addressee). **Fauonius:** the west wind, the beginning of spring (*OLD* 2); cf. e.g. Hor. *Carm.* 1.4.1 *Soluitur acris hiems grata uice ueris et Fauoni.* Spring also figures in Plin. 40.9 (along with the other seasons). **flatu teporo:** cf. Plin. *Nat.* 16.93 *uento Fauonio ... maritantur uiuescentia.* For *teporus* of spring, cf. Auson. *Ecl.* 10.1 Green *a teporo ueris aequinoctio.* **pluuiisque natalibus maritaret:** cf. Claud. *Rapt. Pros.* 2.89 *glaebas fecundo rore maritat* [*sc. Zephyrus*]. *natalibus* exceptionally probably means 'life-giving', as suggested by Warmington (in Anderson's Loeb edition, 2, 598), rather than 'native' (for unusual meanings, see Wolff 2020, 403).

3 restat, ut 'it remains to' frequently signposts the shift of responsibility for the next stage to the addressee; also *quod restat, superest ut, quod superest*; Cicero and Pliny only use *superest* (e.g. Plin. 1.1.2). **reposcamur res omnino discrepantissimas:** for the syntax of verbs of asking in the passive, see *OLS* 1, 164–5; for *reposcor*, see e.g. Quint. *Inst.* 6.3.10, Plin. 7.12.6. The first-person plural creates 'background': the 'I', as it were, ducks away to avoid the claim (see Intro 4.2 '"You" and "I"', van Waarden 2020e, 420–2). *omnino* reinforcing the superlative is first seen in Gell. 14.1.13 *omnino ignarissima* (L–S 2, 478–9; cf. *sat*(*is*) + superlative below). The superlative of *discrepans* occurs only one more time, Sol. 52.19. **maturitatem celeritatemque:** for an elaborate example of this topos, see Apul. *Socr.* prol. fr. 1.3. **honorem ... ab obsequio:** in an *amicitia* relationship, the act of mutually granting each other's requests is essential (see Intro 3.3 'Social Conventions'), cf. e.g. Symm. 7.130 *mihi honorem fieri obsequio litterario*, Sidon. 6.8.2 *litterarum mearum obsequium*. **Gelasium** is the addressee of the preceding letter (9.15) and a friend of Firminus: see above Introduction and Mathisen 2020a, 98. **uirum sat benignissimum** 'the very kindest of men': see 2.12.3n. *satis*; cf. *omnino* + superlative above; the earliest example is Plin. *Nat.* 17.12 *satis utilissimum.* For *benignus* (*OLD* 1a), cf. e.g. 4.17.3 *benignus ... sed et iustus*, 4.24.3 *humanitas* ['hospitality'] *... sic benigna quod frugi.* **missos iambicos:** Sidonius included a poem in stichic iambic trimeters in 9.15, having been challenged by Gelasius to write in a different metre from his favourite hendecasyllables (*Carm.* 40; see Condorelli 2020a, 455–7). For *iambicos* instead of *iambos*, cf. e.g. Prud. *Epil.* 7 *citos iambicos* (*TLL* 7/1.130.51–61). **te quoque:** Firminus gets his poem, like Gelasius, and likewise in a divergent metre. **Mytilenaei oppidi uernulas** 'little natives of the town of Mytilene': i.e. Sapphic stanzas, Sappho coming from the town of Mytilene on Lesbos; cf. Claud. *Nupt.* 235 *Mytilenaeo modulatur pectine Sappho.* The personification *uernulas* is gleaned from Mart. 5.4 *praeter libellos uernulas nihil misi.*

Poem 41: Retrospect and Outlook

1–16 The mission of Sidonius' twin production of poetry and prose is accomplished.
17–32 His official poetry has earned him public honours.
33–48 He prefers not to be reminded of most of his light verse.
49–64 He has turned his attention to letter writing and renounces all poetry, except perhaps in honour of the martyrs.
65–84 Sample of a hymn to St Saturninus. More could follow, if not in verse form, at least in his heart.

For the Sapphic stanza, see Condorelli 2020a, 459–61.

1–4 alternum pelagus loquendi: verse and prose; cf. line 3 *bipertito ... fluento, Carm.* 36.7 (9.13.5) *in utraque disciplina.* This refers to letter 1.1.4, where he hesitates to publish his letters, risking criticism at the very moment that his poetry has proved a success. Now the circle is closed. For the navigation metaphor, see 1.1.3n. *famae pelagus,* 1.1.4n. *in portu, post ... Scyllas enauigatas* and *ancora sedet.* **mea cymba** 'my boat': metaphor for the poet's creativity, cf. Prop. 3.3.22, Ov. *Ars* 3.26, *Trist.* 1.1.85, 2.330, Quint. 12.10.37. **flectere clauum:** metaphor imitated by Ennod. *Carm.* 1.7.47 *flecte ... clauum*; literally in Luc. 3.555, Sil. 14.403 *flectenti ... clauo.*

5–8 soluit antemnas, legit ... uela is a coupling and elaboration of Verg. *Aen.* 4.574 *soluite uela citi* and 3.532 *uela legunt socii.* The caesura underlines the sequence of activities, as at v. 13 *uerberant ... quatiunt*; cf. e.g. Hor. *Carm.* 2.10.13 *sperat ... metuit.* **osculandam:** for kissing home ground upon arrival, cf. Ov. *Met.* 3.24 (upon departure ibid. 13.420). **saltus harenam:** cf. Ov. *Met.* 3.599 *doque leues saltus udaeque immittor harenae.*

9–12 mussitans 'muttering': a suppressed expression of displeasure, as at 7.9.3 (see van Waarden 2010, 428); the verb is an archaism (Wolff 2020, 402). **chorus inuidorum:** cf. *Carm.* 27.25n. *chorus helciariorum* (in 2.10.4). **hirritu ... canino:** a sign of envy, cf. 1.1.4n. *liuidorum latratuum*, dogs being a metaphor for spiteful aggression (Otto 1890, 69). **nil palam sane loquitur:** like the spiteful candidates for the bishopric at 7.9.3 *palam ne mussitantibus quidem.* **puncta:** see 1.9.7n.

13–16 This stanza and the next remind the reader of Ovid's desperate outcry in *Trist.* 1.4 as the ship taking him away from Rome is battered by a storm (vv. 5–10) and knocked off course. But, unlike Ovid's captain, Sidonius remains in control (v. 17 *rectam comite arte proram* vs Ovid 12 *non regit arte ratem*) and straight away reaches his destiny (v. 19 *sistimus portu* vs Ovid 18 *in loca iam nobis non adeunda ferar*). **uentilant spondas** 'blow against the frames': *uentilo* is more usually said of fanning movable objects (e.g. hair, fire); in connection with seafaring, cf. Stat. *Silv.* 4.3.106 *carbasa uentilatis aurae. sponda*, usually the frame of a bed (*OLD* s.v.), is applied differently by Sidonius, occurring only twice and in his two last poems (linking them chronologically): *Carm.* 40.10 (in 9.15.1) for a metrical pattern and here for the frame of a ship's side (see Souter s.v.); cf. Verg. *Aen.* 1.122 *laterum compagibus*. **rotundas** typically occupies the last position in a verse. **arborem** 'mast' (*OLD* 4b). **uolitant** is associated both with the flight of Fama (Verg. *Aen.* 7.104 *uolitans iam Fama per urbes*, 9.473) and with the fluttering of sails (Luc. 5.595–6 *fragilemque super uolitantia malum | uela*. **sinistrae ... linguae:** of hostile criticism, a sensitive subject endlessly varied: 1.2.9 *mordacis linguae*, 7.9.8 *linguarum ... latratus*, 7.9.11 *pungentibus linguis maledicorum*, 8.1.2 *linguas cote liuoris ... acuminatas*; cf. Plin. 1.9.5 *sinistris sermonibus carpit*. **sibila:** cf. Sen. *Nat.* 2.28.3 *uentus qui circa arborem finditur sibilat*.

17–20 rectam comite arte 'steered by my skill': cf. Ov. *Ars* 2.433–4 *rector | ... arte retentet equos*. For *comite* + abstract noun, cf. e.g. Cic. *Att.* 10.4.5 *conscientia comite*, Apul. *Socr.* 24 p. 38 *sapientia comite*. **proram ... sistimus portu** 'I bring my ship into port': cf. e.g. Verg. *Aen.* 3.117 *classem ... sistit*, Sulp. Sev. *Dial.* 1.3.2 *nauem ... sistunt* (see *OLD* 4b). Metaphorical applications of *portus* abound, e.g. 1.2.8, 4.3.2, 6.3.2, 8.2.1. **geminae ... coronae:** in recognition of his panegyrics of the emperors Avitus and Anthemius; earliest examples of the collocation include Claud. *Carm.* 10.203 *geminas, Concordia, necte coronas*, Paul. Nol. *Natal.* 3.112 Dolveck (*Carm.* 14.115 Hartel) *gemina belli pacisque corona*; cf. Verg. *Aen.* 1.655 *duplicem gemmis auroque coronam*; see *Carm.* 33.26n. *dupla corona* (in 7.17.2).

21–24 populus Quirini ... senatus: an elaboration of the formula *Senatus Populusque Romanus*. The god Quirinus was identified with the deified Romulus (see *OLD Quirinus*[1]). For the phrase, see Hor. *Carm.* 1.2.46 *populo Quirini*, Ov. *Fast.* 1.69 *patribusque tuis populoque Quirini*; in Sidonius' own words in *Carm.* 8.9, he got his accolade *populo simul et plaudente senatu*. **blattifer** 'wearing purple': senators wore a distinctive purple-seamed toga (see *OCD* 'Toga'); the adjective is a *hapax legomenon* (see Wolff 2020, 398). **uel =** *et:* see 4.20.1n. **peritorum ... ordo consors iudiciorum:** 'the group that shares expert opinions', i.e. knowledgeable poetry critics. For *ordo* 'social class', see 1.5.10n. *ordinum*.

25–28 statuam perennem harks back to Hor. *Carm.* 3.30.1 *monumentum aere perennius*, thus linking Sidonius' poetic performance to Horace's.

Sidonius was awarded a bronze statue with honorific inscription (*titulis* in line 26) in the poets' corner of Trajan's Forum after delivering his panegyric in honour of Avitus in 456: *Carm.* 8.8 V*lpia quod rutilat porticus aere meo* (see Intro 1, van Waarden 2020b, 17 n.34, Mratschek 2020b, 214 with n. 1). **Nerua Traianus:** Trajan was adopted by Nerva and reigned as emperor from 98 to 117. He is also called *Nerua Traianus* in Tac. *Agr.* 3.1. The optimism associated with Trajan there may also transpire in our passage (for the times of Trajan as a golden age in Sidonius' work, see Mratschek 2020a, 237–48; Mratschek 2020b, 215–16; Intro 3.3 n. 48). Trajan's Forum contained a *basilica*, libraries for Greek and Latin (hence *utriusque ... bybliothecae*), and the famous Column (see *OCD* 'Trajan'). **inter auctores ... fixam:** he is assured of an enduring position in the literary canon. For his concern for his legacy, see 8.16.5, and for his conviction that others will live on by being included in his correspondence, 8.5.1.

29–32 The other honour conferred upon him was the city prefecture of Rome in 468 after the successful panegyric in honour of Anthemius (*Carm.* 1–2; see letter 1.9 with commentary, in particular 1.9.8 *cum ad praefecturam ... stili occasione peruenerim*). For the political context, see Kulikowski 2020, 210. **post:** the first *post* is adverb, the second preposition. **uisus prope** probably means 'received in audience', cf. *Carm.* 34.17 (8.9.5) *semelque uisos* 'and received once' [Sidonius by Euric]. **post bilustre tempus:** actually, twelve years later. *bilustre* to convey final success after a long wait, as in the ten-year Trojan War, comes from Ov. *Am.* 2.12.9 *Pergama ... bello superata bilustri* and is specific for Sidonius (*Carm.* 23.299 *ad Pergama ... bilustre bellum*, *Ep.* 4.24.1 *per bilustre ... tempus*). **patrum ac plebis** varies *populus ... senatus*. **unus:** other offices were held by two or more colleagues. **iura gubernat:** 'exercises authority': the *praefectus urbi* chaired the senate and was responsible for public affairs, including food provision and police surveillance (see *ODLA* 1222 'Praefectus Urbi Romae'). For *iura* 'authority', 'jurisdiction', cf. e.g. Ov. *Fast.* 2.851–2 *capit annua consul | iura*; in Sidonius also *Carm.* 2.480 *mea iura gubernet* (see *OLD* 13a).

33–36 heroos: i.e. dactylic hexameters, the metre of heroic verse, also used in panegyric. **ioca** 'light verse', such as Martial's epigrams (Mart. 5.15.1 *nostrorum liber est ... iocorum*; *TLL* 7/2.288.47–65). **multis | texui pannis** is a variation on Hor. *Ars* 15–16 *unus et alter | assuitur pannus*. *pannus* 'piece of fabric' metaphorically stands for a poetic digression, embellishment or other tour de force. Here the emphasis is on a diversity of metres, first of all his preferred ones, the elegiac couplet and the Phalaecian hendecasyllable (for metrics in Sidonius, see Condorelli 2020a). Sidonius also alludes to Horace's *Ars poetica* in §4. **elegos frequenter ... rotaui:** *elegos* means 'pentameters', as at *Carm.* 23.24 *per quinos elegi pedes ferebant*; cf. Diom. *Gramm.* 1.503.20 Keil *geminum comma, id est elegus, hexametro subiungitur* (*TLL* 5/2.339.67–70; Gualandri 1993, 212–13 with n. 85). The elegiac couplet is used fourteen times across Sidonius' oeuvre (in the present selection, *Carm.* 33). The verb *rotaui* 'I made go round', 'I alternated' is unique in this context (compare, however, Sen. *Nat.* 2.35.2; *OLD* 2a); for the usual designation *alternus*, see Diom. *Gramm.* 1.484.17 Keil *hexametro uersu pentametroque alternis <in> uicem positis*, Ov. *Epist.* 15.5–6 *mea ... alterna ... | carmina* 'my elegies'. **subditos senis pedibus:** cf. Diomedes' definition (prev. n.); Hor. *Ars* 75 speaks of *uersibus impariter iunctis* (whence Sidon. *Carm.* 23.23 *uestigia iuncta*). **commate** 'halfline': again cf. Diomedes' definition, Ter. Maur. 1753 *scandunt pentametrum, duo sint quasi commata, quidam*; cf. 1.9.1n. *uersibus commata ... facit*.

37–40 nunc 'on other occasions' (*OLD* 8c). **per undenas ... syllabas:** Phalaecian hendecasyllables, used in twelve out of Sidonius' forty-one poems (in the present selection, *Carm.* 27). He qualifies them as *dulces* (*Carm.* 23.27), *rotundatos* (8.4.2), *lubricos et enodes* (8.11.5), *teretes* (9.13.2). As to *undenas*, the use of distributive instead of cardinal numerals is a poeticism (H–S 212–13). **equitare suetus ... lusi celer:** his familiarity with this metre made writing in it an 'easy ride'. For *equitare* 'to gallop' in the metaphorical sense of 'to be carried away', see *TLL* 5/2.729.65–73. *lusi* is the *mot juste* for writing light verse in a variety of metres, introduced by the neoteric poets: Catull. 50.4–5 *scribens uersiculos uterque nostrum | ludebat numero modo hoc modo illoc* (see *OLD* 8); cf. Plin. 4.14.2–3 *hendecasyllabos nostros ... his iocamur ludimus*. **creber:** actually, this is the only poem in Sapphic stanzas that he selected for preservation. The phrase 8.11.7 *in sapphico inflatus* probably points to their lofty gait (see Condorelli 2020a, 459–61). **citato rarus iambo:** cf. 8.4.2 *citos iambos*, cf. Hor. *Carm.* 1.16.24 *celeres iambos*, *Ars* 251–2 *iambus, | pes citus*, Ter. Maur. 1384 *pes uirilis et raptim citus*. The qualification *rarus* chimes with his complaint in 9.15.1 *nam metrum diu infrequentatum durius texitur*. *Carm.* 40, contained in that letter, is in iambic senarii at the express request of the addressee, and is the only one in the collection.

41–44 quanta: in *Carm.* 9.9–13, Sidonius disparages his own youthful production as vast and a waste of paper. **primo iuuenis calore:** cf. Symm. 7.9 *decet enim loqui exultantius iuuenalem calorem*, Hier. 52.1 *pro aetate tunc lusimus ... calentibus adhuc rhetorum studiis*; cf. Tac. *Dial.* 2.1 *ardore iuuenili*.

45–48 senectutis propiore meta: Sidonius' sense of getting old emerges about the age of 45 (see 5.9.4 *in annis iam senectutis initia pulsantibus*, written *c.* 476/7) and marks the end of the collection, for himself (8.4.3 *modo tempus est seria legi, seria scribi deque perpetua uita potius quam memoria cogitari*) and for his worldview (8.6.3 *per aetatem mundi iam senescentis*); see van Waarden 2018. For *meta* in a temporal sense (*OLD* 5), cf. e.g. Verg. *Aen.* 10.472 *metas ... aeui*, Auson. *Prof.* 20.13–14 Green *pulchra senecta ... | et ... uitae congrua meta.* Cf. Prud. *Praef.* 4–5 *instat terminus, et diem | uicinum senio iam Deus adplicat.* **pudet ... reminisci:** cf. Ov. *Pont.* 1.5.15 *cum relego, scripsisse pudet.* **si quid leue lusit:** cf. Mart. 12.94.8 *ludo leuis elegos.*

49–52 cultum 'polish' (*OLD cultus*² 7). **curae:** typically for the care devoted to writing artful letters; see Intro 3.6 with n. 76. **ne reus cantu petulantiore | sim reus actu:** being guilty of questionable poetry, he is now intent on not also becoming guilty of questionable conduct (*OLD actus* 7), in particular as an ecclesiastic, cf. 9.12.1 *si me occupasset leuitas uersuum quem respicere coeperat grauitas actionum* (see Gualandri 1979, 6–7). For *petulans* 'insolent', 'wanton' of light verse, cf. Plin. 4.14.4 *si non nulla tibi petulantiora paulo uidebuntur.* Cf. Prud. *Praef.* 11–12 *luxus petulans (heu pudet ac piget) | foedauit iuuenem.* Prudentius, conversely, sees it as his vocation to praise God by writing poetry (*Praef.* 36 *uoce*) because by his deeds (*meritis*) he cannot.

53–56 puter is present subjunctive passive of *putare.* **solui** 'become enervated' (*OLD* 8c). **schema ... phalerasque:** see 1.9.1n. *schemata* and 1.9.7n. *phaleris.* For the tense relationship between poetry and oratorical bravado on the one hand and clerical status on the other, see Intro 4.1 with n. 86.

57–60 epigramma: broadly 'poetry', see Intro 2.1 n. 24 (also 2.10.4n. *epigrammata*). **teneroque metro uel graui** 'in light or heavy metres': i.e. in lyrical or epic/encomiastic verse. Cf. about poets in various genres: *Carm.* 23.168 *arguti, teneri, graues, dicaces,* covering epigram, lyric, epic and satire; cf. 8.11.5 [of a poet] *tener multimeter ... erat.* Cf. the more narrow origin of *tener* in (love) elegy, e.g. Catull. 35.1 *poetae tenero*, Ov. *Ars* 2.2.73 *teneros ... uersus.* For *grauis,* cf. e.g. Cic. *Planc.* 59 *grauis ... poeta* [the tragic poet Accius].

61–64 persecutorum ... quaestiones 'examinations by persecutors': *persecutor* 'persecutor (of Christians)' is already found in the New Testament, 1 Tim. 1.13. Put in first position, the noun is topic, receiving the added weight of a full half verse. Both nouns together dominate the line and announce the theme of martyrdom as a feasible motive for writing poetry. The three stanzas that follow constitute a martyr's hymn in the style of Prudentius' *Liber peristephanon* (Consolino 2020, 368). **forsitan dicam:** although this is often seen as a polite way of refusing to write Christian poetry (e.g. Kaufmann 2022, 78), the sum of the evidence could point in a different direction: see Intro 2.2. **meritosque caelum:** earning a place in heaven has a classical pedigree (where it describes apotheosis), e.g. Mart. 5.65.15 *pro meritis caelum tantis ... dederunt*. There is a suggestive wordplay meritos in combination with the following martyras mortis. **mortis pretio:** cf. Prud. *Perist.* 4.125 *mortis pretium*, ibid. 3.39–40 *sanguinis in pretium* | *mortis amore*. **praemia uitae:** cf. e.g. Ambr. *Exc. Sat.* 2.45 *ipsa mors martyrum praemium uitae est*, i.e. eternal life. Chiasmus, alliteration and paronomasia emphasize the oxymoronic opposition with *mortis pretio*.

65–68 psallat hymnus: cf., in the same position, Paul. Petric. *Mart.* 3.270 *psalleret hymnis*. In ecclesiastical Latin, *psallere* is the term for singing psalms and hymns, and glorifying God or the martyrs (L–S II). Singing hymns is yet another link with Prudentius' *Praefatio*, line 37 *hymnis continuet dies*. **Tolosatem ... cathedram:** the reason for choosing St Saturninus of Toulouse must be that the town was the capital of the Visigothic Kingdom. Sidonius' veneration may have found further expression in his liturgical writings (see Intro 2.2), and he may have been buried in St Saturninus church in Clermont (Harries 1994, 205–6 and 221). According to tradition, Saturninus was Toulouse's first bishop and died a martyr during the persecution of Decius (250 CE). He was widely venerated across southern Gaul and Iberia. See the fifth-century *Passio Saturnini* (Piras 2002), Greg. Tur. *Hist.* 1.30 and Venantius Fortunatus' hymn to Saturninus (Ven. Fort. *Carm.* 2.7; for a comparison, Condorelli 2020b, 386–9); see Duchesne 1, 306, *BEEC* 'Toulouse', *ODLA* 'Toulouse'. *cathedram* 'bishop's seat', 'bishop's office' (L–S IIB, Blaise 4). **Capitoliorum:** the temple of the Capitoline Triad, Jupiter, Juno and Minerva, near the forum in Toulouse, presumably built on a steep pediment (see Heijmans 2006, 28–9); cf. Greg. Tur. *ad Capitolium duceretur*, Ven. Fort. v. 19 *ad Capitolia duxit*. **praecipitatum** is a key word filling the last line, cf. Greg. Tur. *de Capitolio praecipitatus*. To the reader who, in line 25 *statuam perennem*, has been alerted to Horace's *Carm.* 3.30, this stanza paints the inverse movement to Horace's proud *dum Capitolium* | *scandet ... pontifex* (lines 8–9). Humility and self-sacrifice suit the Christian bishop – though not necessarily also the Christian writer: see §4.

69–72 confitentem 'confessing', 'acknowledging' (God, Christ, the Holy Spirit), common in ecclesiastical Latin (L–S III). **iniugati** 'unyoked' is a *hapax legomenon*; cf. Greg. Tur. *tauri furentis*, Ven. Fort. v. 26 *tauri indomiti*. **plebs furibunda:** cf. Ven. Fort. 17–19 *plebs ... mala sana*.

73–76 ut ... cadauer: cf. Ven. Fort. 31–2 *hinc ferus impatiens mox curua per auia raptus | passim membra pii fundit in urbe uiri*. In mythology, the fate of Dirce is comparable: Plaut. *Pseud.* 199–200 *Dircam ... deuinxere ad taurum*, Ov. *Ib.* 535 *perque feros montes tauro rapiente traharis* (depicted in the 'Farnese Bull' sculpture from the Baths of Caracalla in Rome). **cautibus ... cerebri:** the graphic detail is inspired by a host of battle scenes from Virgil to Silius Italicus, e.g. Verg. *Aen.* 5.413 *sparsoque infecta cerebro*, Stat. *Theb.* 8.760 *effracti perfusum tabe cerebri*. For *puls* 'pulp', see 1.5.6n. *pulte*.

77–80 Saturninum: the short *a* is a metrical licence, as in Prud. *Perist.* 4.163 *Saturninos* (see Condorelli 2020a, 443; see further below). **plectra cantent:** for *plectra* as the maker of the music, cf. Prop. 4.7.62 *sonant ... plectra*. The usual construction is with an ablative, cf. e.g. Ov. *Met.* 10.150 *cecini plectro*, and in Sidon. *Carm.* 14.27 and 16.70. **patronorum reliquos:** St Julian of Brioude and St Just of Lyon, for example, come to mind, the former the patron saint of Auvergne, and of Sidonius' family in particular (see 7.1.7n. *Iuliani*), the latter the venerated former bishop of Lyon (see the feast on his name day in 5.17; for his church and cemetery, 3.12.2n. *e supercilio uicini collis*). On Clermont and the expanding cult of saints, see Harries 1994, 52 and 187–206, Intro 3.4. **probaui** 'I have experienced': a development of later Latin, see *TLL* 10/2.1472.47–1473.4. **duros ... per labores:** in particular, the war in the Auvergne.

81–84 non ualent uersu cohibere: cf. Hor. *Sat.* 1.5.87 *mansuri oppidulo quod uersu dicere non est* (with Kiessling-Heinze ad loc. for other examples of the topos). It is filtered through Prud. *Perist.* 4.161–4, who does not care and inserts the unmetrical name *Saturninos*, as he says: *renuente metro*. Sidonius goes even further than Prudentius: not only does he replicate *Saturninum*, he extends the excuse to other saints whom he might in future write about. He had used it before, at *Carm.* 23.485–6 *horum nomina cum referre uersu | affectus cupiat, metrum recusat*. The third(?)-century grammarian Terentianus Maurus has *Metr.* 1368 *tertium detrecto nomen: lege nam metri uetor*, 1481–2 *nomen ... in hoc referre metro | longae prohibent*. **chordae ... corda:** for the paronomasia, cf. Aug. *Serm.* 243.8 *concordibus cordibus melius quam citharae chordis dicimus laudes Deo, cantamus alleluia*, *In psalm.* 32.2.1.5 *tange chordas in corde*; cf. Paul. Nol. *Natal.* 4.28 Dolveck (*Carm.* 15

Hartel) *cordis testudine* 'the lyre of the heart'. Praising God in an outward movement from heart to sound is a motif that goes back to the Psalms, e.g. Vulg. *Psalm.* 28 (27).7 *Dominus adiutor meus ... et exultauit cor meum et in cantico meo confitebor ei*, and is a commonplace of Christian literature, e.g. Ambr. *In psalm.* 43.24.2 *qui enim hymnum dicit, puro corde et spiritaliter dicit* (see Condorelli 2008, 237). **sonabunt:** Ravenna 2004, 322 sees an allusion to *canemus*, the final word of Horace's last ode (4.15) which equally is divided into two parts, representing two attitudes towards poetry, and contains the promise of celebrative lyric verse.

4 in finem 'by way of conclusion': *OLD in* 21c; Lütjohann's *in fine*, however, has found broad approval. Concluding letters containing a poem with a prose paragraph is normal practice. The fact that it is thematized here points to the wider horizon of Book 9 or the collection as a whole. **oratorium stilum** 'prose style', 'prose': cf. 3.3.2 *oratorio stilo* and 4.14.2 *oratores*, both opposed to poetry; cf. also *Carm.* 36.26 *oratoris opus* (in 9.13.2). **ordine** 'way', 'system', 'plan' (*OLD* 14/15). **epilogis musicis opus prosarium clauserimus:** closures, and indeed structure, are of particular concern to Sidonius, also in the composition of the correspondence which, more or less against his will, ends in *triplices epilogos* (the closures of Books 7, 8 and 9; see 9.1.2). Cf. Martial, concluding the prose preface of his first book of epigrams with a poem: *uideor mihi meo iure facturus si epistolam uersibus clusero*. On the mixture of genres and closure, see Intro 3.5 with n. 68. *musicis* 'poetic' (*OLD* 1). *opus prosarium* is a Sidonian collocation, also found 3.14.1 *opere prosario*. There is no metrical clausula (—⏑-–⏑⏑×), perhaps to imitate the near-breach of protocol. **secundum regulas Flacci:** *Flaccus* is Horace (see 2.9.4n. *Horatius*). **amphora ... urceus:** the injunction is for artists to carry out their plan consistently, as expressed in Hor. *Ars* 21-2 *amphora coepit | institui: currente rota cur urceus exit?* Someone plans a nice big amphora, but, because he gets lost in irrelevant details and on side paths, ends up with a little pitcher. The same quotation appears in Hier. 107.3. Pelttari 2016, 329-31 points to the irony of Sidonius' statement, as what he actually does is combine styles, tones and genres (unlike Mratschek 2017, 321-2 who stresses the unity in diversity). Apart from stylistic propriety, it also carries an ethical message, as is apparent from a comparison with Prudentius' *Epilogus* (see Mratschek 2017, 322). Prudentius compares his poetic legacy to an *obsoletum uasculum* in a house full of prestigious crockery. However – he says – any vessel is useful that is acceptable to Christ. Quite differently, Sidonius, in rounding off his work, has no place for pious modesty but strives for the highest literary standard, an *urceus* being definitely not good enough. **exisse uideatur:** preceded by *coepit* and accompanied by *in finem, terminaturi, epilogis* and *clauserimus*, Horace's *exisse* is supremely apt as a closure. Horace is joined by Cicero in the Ciceronian clausula *-isse uideatur* (paeon I + spondee; cf. Tac. *Dial.* 23, Quint. *Inst.* 9.4.73, who both criticize Cicero's imitators for overdoing it: cf. the petty imitators in Sidon. 1.1.2), where Sidonius could easily have written *exeat*, like his model Horace. The clausula is a final, silent salute to the greatest orator of all – silent, for *de Marco Tullio silere melius puto* (1.1.2n.).

APPENDIX

SIDONIUS' (PRESUMED) EPITAPH AND DEATH DATE

Two MSS belonging to the α branch conclude with Sidonius' epitaph, according to the title in one of them. In 1991, two stone fragments of this epitaph were identified in Clermont-Ferrand. The two MS versions are slightly different, most notably in vv. 10–11 and in their dating. The death date in the Madrid codex is unhelpfully unspecific: '21 August, in the reign of Zeno', i.e. 474–91. The Paris codex is unclear: '21 August in the consulate of Zeno', as Zeno was consul three times. Only his last consulate in 479 could be relevant. The attribution to Sidonius has been questioned (if only because he was never referred to as Apollinaris – some would indeed attribute it to his son) and the question is still undecided.

Madrid, BNE 9448, f. 162v		Paris, IRHT CP 347, ff. 132v–133
Epithaphium Sidonii		[no title]
Sanctis contiguus sacroque patri		Sanctis contiguus sacroque patri
uiuit sic meritis Apollinaris,		uiuit sic meritis *appo*⌐*l*¬*inaris*,
illustris titulis, potens honore,		illustris titulis, potens honore,
rector militie forique iudex,		rector mili*ti*e forique iudex,
mundi inter tumidas quietus undas,	5	mundi inter tumidas quietus undas,
causarum moderans subinde motus		causarum moderans subinde motus
leges barbarico dedit furori;		leges barbarico dedit furori;
discordantibus inter arma regnis		discordantibus inter arma regnis
pacem consilio reduxit amplo.		pacem consilio reduxit amplo.
haec inter tamen et philosophando	10	haec inter tamen *et facundus ore*
scripsit perpetuis habenda seclis		*libris excoluit uitam parentis*
et post talia dona gratiarum		et post talia dona gratiarum
summi Pontificis sedens cathedram		summi *p*ontificis sedens cathedram
mundanos †sobali refudit actus.		mundanos †sobali refudit actus.
quisque hic dum lacrimis deum rogabis,	15	quisque hic dum lacrimis deum rogabis,
dextrum funde preces super sepulcrum:		dextrum funde preces super sepulcrum:
nulli incognitus et legendus orbi		nulli incognitus et legendus orbi
illic Sidonius tibi inuocetur.		illic Sidonius tibi inuocetur.
XII kal septembris Zenone imperatore.		*Duodecimo* kal*endas S*eptembris *z*enone *consule*

Literature: Prévot 1993, Furbetta 2015a, Stoehr-Monjou 2017, Montzamir 2023, Wood 2023, John 2026, 113–15; see further Intro 1 with n. 20 and the epitaph section of the Sidonius website. Compare the epitaph of Apollinaris the Elder, *Carm.* 28 in *Ep.* 3.12.

BIBLIOGRAPHY

For a full, and regularly updated, bibliography of Sidonius, see the Sidonius website, www.sidonapol.org. Since 1 May 2025, it is continued in cooperation with the Propylaeum Platform of Heidelberg University Library and the Bavarian State Library in Munich. The sections *News* and *What's up?* remain on the original website, while *Bibliographies*, *Aftermath* and *Publications* have moved to the Propylaeum Platform, www.propylaeum.de/themen/sidonius-apollinaris. The original website links to the various sections that have moved. For a reasoned research bibliography, see Condorelli 2020c. Journal titles are abbreviated according to *L'Année philologique*.

Ahl, F. 1984. 'The Art of Safe Criticism in Greece and Rome', *AJPh* 105, 174–208.

Alexandre, P. 1990. *Les séismes en Europe occidentale de 394 à 1259: Nouveau catalogue critique*, Brussels.

Allen, P., and B. Neil 2013. *Crisis Management in Late Antiquity (410–590 CE): A Survey of the Evidence from Episcopal Letters*, Leiden.

Amherdt, D. 2001. *Sidoine Apollinaire, Le quatrième livre de la correspondance: Introduction et commentaire*, Bern.

Anders, F. 2010. *Flavius Ricimer: Macht und Ohnmacht des weströmischen Heermeisters in der zweiten Hälfte des 5. Jahrhunderts*, Frankfurt am Main.

Arjava, A. 1996. *Women and Law in Late Antiquity*, Oxford.

Audin, A. 1952. 'Sur la géographie du Lyon romain: la population, les voies et les quartiers d'après les documents épigraphiques', *Géocarrefour* 27, 133–9.

Bachrach, B. S. 1977. *Early Medieval Jewish Policy in Western Europe*, Minneapolis.

Bailey, L. K. 2020. 'Sidonius and Religion', in Kelly and van Waarden 2020, 261–75.

Balmelle, C. 2001. *Les demeures aristocratiques d'Aquitaine: Société et culture de l'Antiquité tardive dans le Sud-Ouest de la Gaule*, Bordeaux.

Banniard, M. 1992. 'La rouille et la lime: Sidoine Apollinaire et la langue classique en Gaule au Ve siècle', in L. Holtz and J.-C. Fredouille, eds., *De Tertullien aux Mozarabes: antiquité tardive et Christianisme ancien. Mélanges offerts à Jacques Fontaine*, Paris, 413–27.

Baratte, F. 2019. 'Vaisselle d'argent, nourriture et service de table', *AT* 27, 223–39.

Barcellona, R. 2012. 'Clero e sessualità: I percorsi della continenza', in R. Barcellona, *Una società allo specchio: la Gallia tardoantica nei suoi concili*, Soveria Mannelli, 15–65.

Barnish, S. 1988. 'Transformation and Survival in the Western Senatorial Aristocracy, c. A.D. 400–700', *PBSR* 56, 120–55.

Barnish, S. 1992. 'Old Kaspars: Attila's Invasion of Gaul in the Literary Sources', in Drinkwater and Elton 1992, 38–47.

Barrow, R. 2018. 'The Ageing Body: Drunken Old Woman', in R. Barrow, *Gender, Identity and the Body in Greek and Roman Sculpture*, Cambridge, 62–75.

Barry, J. 2019. *Bishops in Flight: Exile and Displacement in Late Antiquity*, Oakland, CA.

Bartsch, S. 2014. *The Mirror of the Self: Sexuality, Self-Knowledge, and the Gaze in the Early Roman Empire*, Chicago.

Bérard, F. 2012. 'Les corporations de transport fluvial à Lyon à l'époque romaine', in M. Dondin-Payre and N. Tran, eds., *Collegia: Le phénomène associatif dans l'Occident romain*, Bordeaux, 135–54.

Birch, D. J. 1998. *Pilgrimage to Rome in the Middle Ages*, Woodbridge.

Birks, E. M. 2004. *Britons in the Gaul of Sidonius Apollinaris*, Australian National University, Canberra.

Blanck, H. 1992. *Das Buch in der Antike*, Munich.

Bleckmann, B. 2022. 'Eine Fragmentsammlung spätlateinischer Historiker', *Histos* 16, i–xxix.

Bohîlţea-Mihuţ, F. 2024. 'Classical Authors in Sidonius Apollinaris' Letters', *C&C* 19, 389–99.

Bonjour, M. 1988. 'Discrétion mondaine ou réserve chrétienne? Les femmes chez Sidoine Apollinaire', in D. Porte and J.-P. Néraudau, eds., *Res Sacrae: Hommages à Henri Le Bonniec*, Brussels, 40–52.

Borgolte, M. 2001. 'Europas Geschichten und Troia: Der Mythos im Mittelalter', in *Troia: Traum und Wirklichkeit*, Stuttgart, 190–203.

Bowersock, G. W., P. Brown, and O. Grabar, 1999a. 'Introduction', in Bowersock et al. 1999b, vii–xiii.

Bowersock, G. W., P. Brown, and O. Grabar, eds., 1999b. *Late Antiquity: A Guide to the Postclassical World*, Cambridge, MA.

Brakke, D. 2006. *Demons and the Making of the Monk: Spiritual Combat in Early Christianity*, Cambridge, MA.

Brennan, B. 1985. 'The Conversion of the Jews of Clermont in AD 576', *JThS* 36, 321–37.

Brödner, E. 1983. *Die römischen Thermen und das antike Badewesen*, Darmstadt.

Brown, P. 1971a. 'The Rise and Function of the Holy Man in Late Antiquity', *JRS* 61, 80–101.

Brown, P. 1971b. *The World of Late Antiquity*, London.

Brown, P. 1981. *The Cult of the Saints: Its Rise and Function in Latin Christianity*, Chicago.

Brown, P. 1988. *The Body and Society: Men, Women, and Sexual Renunciation in Early Christianity*, New York.
Brown, P. 2012. *Through the Eye of a Needle: Wealth, the Fall of Rome, and the Making of Christianity in the West, 350–550 AD*, Princeton, NJ.
Brown, P., and S. C. Levinson 1987. *Politeness: Some Universals in Language Usage*, Cambridge.
Brubaker, L., and C. Wickham 2021. 'Processions, Power, and Community Identity: East and West', in W. Pohl and R. Kramer, eds., *Empires and Communities in the Post-Roman and Islamic World, c. 400–1000 CE*, Oxford, 121–87.
Bruggisser, P. 1993. *Symmaque ou le rituel épistolaire de l'amitié littéraire: Recherches sur le premier livre de la correspondance*, Fribourg.
Brun, J.-P. 2005. *Archéologie du vin et de l'huile en Gaule romaine*, Paris.
Cameron, A. 1970. *Claudian: Poetry and Propaganda at the Court of Honorius*, Oxford.
Cameron, A. 1992. 'Observations on the Distribution and Ownership of Late Roman Silver Plate', *JRA* 5, 178–85.
Cameron, A. 1999. 'Remaking the Past', in Bowersock et al. 1999b, 1–20.
Cameron, A. 2011. *The Last Pagans of Rome*, New York.
Cameron, A. 2012. 'Anician Myths', *JRS* 102, 133–71.
Cameron, Av., and P. Garnsey, eds., 1997. *Cambridge Ancient History*, vol. 13 *The Late Empire*, A.D. *337–425*, Cambridge.
Cameron, Av., B. Ward-Perkins and M. Whitby, eds., 2000. *Cambridge Ancient History*, vol. 14 *Late Antiquity: Empires and Successors*, A.D. *425–600*, Cambridge.
Carrié, J.-P. 2010. 'Le *deversorium* dans les *villae* occidentales tardives: Éléments pour une identification archéologique', *AT* 18, 277–96.
Carruthers, M. J. 1998. *The Craft of Thought: Meditation, Rhetoric, and the Making of Images, 400–1200*, Cambridge.
Cavuoto-Denis, N. 2022. 'De l'épigramme au billet: La contagion du style épigrammatique dans les lettres de Symmaque', in D. Vallat and F. Garambois-Vasquez, eds., *Stylistique et poétique de l'épigramme latine. Nouvelles études*, Lyon, 37–47.
Chahoud, A. 2010. 'Idiom(s) and Literariness in Classical Literary Criticism', in E. Dickey and A. Chahoud, eds., *Colloquial and Literary Latin*, Cambridge, 42–64.
Charles-Edwards, T. M. 2000. 'Law in the Western Kingdoms between the Fifth and the Seventh Century', in Cameron et al. 2000, 260–87.
Christiansen, P. G., and J. E. Holland 1993. *Concordantia in Sidonii Apollinaris carmina*, Hildesheim.
Chronopoulos, T. 2020. 'Glossing Sidonius in the Middle Ages', in Kelly and van Waarden 2020, 643–64.

Clark, E. A. 1992. *The Origenist Controversy: The Cultural Construction of an Early Christian Debate*, Princeton, NJ.
Colafrancesco, P. 2013. 'Sidon. *epist.* 3, 12: Note a margine', *InvLuc* 35-6 (2013-14), 71-6.
Collins, R. 2000. 'The Western Kingdoms', in Cameron et al. 2000, 111-34.
Condorelli, S. 2001. 'Una particolare accezione di *barbarismus* in Sidonio Apollinare', in U. Criscuolo, ed., Mnemosynon: *Studi di letteratura e di umanità in memoria di Donato Gagliardi*, Naples, 101-9.
Condorelli, S. 2004. 'L'*officina* di Sidonio Apollinare: Tra *incus* metrica e *asprata lima*', *BStudLat* 34, 558-98.
Condorelli, S. 2008. *Il* poeta doctus *nel V secolo D.C.: Aspetti della poetica di Sidonio Apollinare*, Naples.
Condorelli, S. 2013. 'Gli epigrammi funerari di Sidonio Apollinare', in M.-F. Guipponi-Gineste and C. Urlacher-Becht, eds., *La renaissance de l'épigramme dans la latinité tardive*, Paris, 261-82.
Condorelli, S. 2015. 'L'inizio della fine: l'epistola IX 1 di Sidonio Apollinare tra *amicitia* ed istanze estetico-letterarie', *BSL* 45, 489-511.
Condorelli, S. 2020a. 'Metrics in Sidonius', in Kelly and van Waarden 2020, 440-61.
Condorelli, S. 2020b. 'Sidonio e Venanzio Fortunato', in A. Di Stefano and M. Onorato, eds., *Lo specchio del modello: Orizzonti intertestuali e* Fortleben *di Sidonio Apollinare*, Naples, 361-406.
Condorelli, S. 2020c. 'Sidonius Scholarship: Twentieth to Twenty-First Centuries', in Kelly and van Waarden 2020, 564-617.
Condorelli, S. 2023. 'Le *nugae* di Sidonio: La *vita lunga* di una *brevis charta*', in Santelia and Condorelli 2023, vii-xc.
Consolino, F. E. 2015. 'Le mot et les choses: *epigramma* chez Sidoine Apollinaire', in P. F. Moretti and et al., eds., *Culture and Literature in Latin Late Antiquity: Continuities and Discontinuities*, Turnhout, 69-98.
Consolino, F. E. 2020. 'Sidonius' Shorter Poems', in Kelly and van Waarden 2020, 341-72.
Conte, G. B. 1986. *The Rhetoric of Imitation: Genre and Poetic Memory in Virgil and Other Latin Poets*, Ithaca, NY.
Corsi, C. 2000. *Le strutture di servizio del cursus publicus in Italia: Ricerche topografiche ed evidenze archeologiche*, Oxford.
Courcelle, P. 1969. *Late Latin Writers and their Greek Sources*, tr. H. Wedeck, Cambridge, MA (original *Les lettres grecques en occident de Macrobe à Cassiodore*, rev. edn, Paris 1948).
Courtney, E. 1989. 'Two Catullan Questions', *Prometheus* 15, 160-4.
Crogiez-Pétrequin, S. 2010. 'Sidoine Apollinaire et le col du Petit Saint Bernard', in F. Delrieux and F. Kayser, eds., *Des déserts d'Afrique au pays des Allobroges: Hommages offerts à François Bertrandy*, Chambéry, 35-44.

Crogiez-Pétrequin, S. 2021. 'Les bénéficiaires du *cursus publicus*: des privilégiés?', *RH* 698, 447–62.

Cugusi, P. 1983. *Evoluzione e forme dell'epistolografia latina nella tarda repubblica e nei primi due secoli dell'impero*, Rome.

Cugusi, P. 1990. 'Un'*epistola recusatoria* di Sidonio', *BStudLat* 20, 275–80.

Curtius, E. R. 1990. *European Literature and the Latin Middle Ages*, 7th ed., Princeton, NJ.

Dalton, O. M. 1915. *Sidonius Apollinaris: Letters*, Oxford.

de Jong, I. J. F. 2014. *Narratology and Classics: A Practical Guide*, Oxford.

de Vogüé, A., ed., 1982. *Les règles des Saints Pères*, Paris.

Debal, J. 1974. 'De Cenabum à Orléans', *Bulletin SAHO* Suppl. 44.

Delaplace, C. 2015. *La fin de l'Empire romain d'Occident: Rome et les Wisigoths de 382 à 531*, Rennes.

Delbrueck, R. 1929. *Die Consulardiptychen und verwandte Denkmaeler*, Berlin.

Demandt, A. 1984. *Der Fall Roms: Die Auflösung des römischen Reiches im Urteil der Nachwelt*, Munich.

Demandt, A. 1997. 'Die Spätantike als Epoche', in L. J. Engels and H. Hofmann, eds., *Neues Handbuch der Literaturwissenschaft*, vol. 4 *Spätantike*, Wiesbaden, 1–28.

Demandt, A. 2007. *Die Spätantike: Römische Geschichte von Diocletian bis Justinian, 284–565 n. Chr.*, 2nd ed., Munich.

Denecker, T. 2015. 'Language Attitudes and Social Connotations in Jerome and Sidonius Apollinaris', *VChr* 69, 393–421.

Denecker, T. 2017. *Ideas on Language in Early Latin Christianity: From Tertullian to Isidore of Seville*, Leiden.

Devriese, L., ed., 2021. *The Body as a Mirror of the Soul: Physiognomy from Antiquity to the Renaissance*, Leuven.

Di Salvo, L. 2000. *Decimo Magno Ausonio, Ordo urbium nobilium: Introduzione, testo critico, traduzione e note di commento*, Naples.

Dickey, E. 2002. *Latin Forms of Address: From Plautus to Apuleius*, Oxford.

Dolveck, F. 2020a. 'A Census of the Manuscripts of Sidonius', in Kelly and van Waarden 2020, 508–42.

Dolveck, F. 2020b. 'The Manuscript Tradition of Sidonius', in Kelly and van Waarden 2020, 479–507.

Dräger, P. 1997. '*Alisontia*: Eltz oder Alzette? Der Nebenflußkatalog und ein unentdecktes Strukturprinzip in Ausonius' *Mosella*', *Kurtrierisches Jahrbuch* 37, 11–38.

Dresken-Weiland, J. 2007. 'Vorstellung von Tod und Jenseits in den frühchristlichen Grabinschriften der Oikumene', *AT* 15, 285–302.

Drinkwater, J. F. 2013. 'Un-becoming Roman: The End of Provincial Civilisation in Gaul', in S. Diefenbach and G. M. Müller, eds., *Gallien in Spätantike und Frühmittelalter: Kulturgeschichte einer Region*, Berlin, 59–77.

Drinkwater, J. F., and H. Elton, eds., 1992. *Fifth-Century Gaul: A Crisis of Identity?*, Cambridge.

Egelhaaf-Gaiser, U. 2010. 'Bleibende Klänge: Das hymnische Briefsiegel des Bischofs Sidonius (*epist*. 9,16)', *Millennium* 7, 257–92.

Egelhaaf-Gaiser, U. 2014. 'Who Reads What? Intended Plurality of Addressees in the Epistolary Votive of Bishop Sidonius (*Epist*. 2,10)', in J.-C. Julhe, ed., *Pratiques latines de la dédicace. Permanences et mutations, de l'Antiquité à la Renaissance*, Paris, 369–93.

Egetenmeyr, V. 2021. 'Sidonius Apollinaris' Use of the Term *Barbarus*: An Introduction', in M. Friedrich and J. M. Harland, eds., *Interrogating the 'Germanic': A Category and its Use in Late Antiquity and the Early Middle Ages*, Berlin, 145–65.

Egetenmeyr, V. 2022. *Die Konstruktion der 'Anderen': Barbarenbilder in den Briefen des Sidonius Apollinaris*, Wiesbaden.

Eigler, U. 1997. 'Horaz und Sidonius Apollinaris: Zwei Reisen und Rom', *JbAC* 40, 168–77.

Eigler, U. 2003. *Lectiones vetustatis: Römische Literatur und Geschichte in der Literatur der Spätantike*, Munich.

Eigler, U. 2013. 'Gallien als Literaturlandschaft: Zur Dezentralisierung und Differenzierung lateinischer Literatur im 5. und 6. Jh.', in S. Diefenbach and G. M. Müller, eds., *Gallien in Spätantike und Frühmittelalter. Kulturgeschichte einer Region*, Berlin, 399–420.

Elsner, J. 2002. 'Introduction: The Genres of *Ekphrasis*', *Ramus* 31, 1–18.

Elsner, J. and J. Hernández Lobato 2017. 'Notes towards a Poetics of Late Antique Literature', in J. Elsner and J. Hernández Lobato, eds., *The Poetics of Late Latin Literature*, New York, 1–22.

Enenkel, K. A. E., and K. A. Ottenheym, eds., 2018. *The Quest for an Appropriate Past in Literature, Art and Architecture*, Leiden.

Evans, E. C. 1935. 'Roman Descriptions of Personal Appearance in History and Biography', *HSPh* 46, 43–84.

Evans-Grubbs, J. 2009. 'Marriage and Family Relationships in the Late Roman West', in Rousseau 2009, 201–19.

Ewig, E., and U. Nonn 2006. *Die Merowinger und das Frankenreich*, 5th ed., Stuttgart.

Fascione, S. 2018. 'Finding Identities on the Way to Rome', in C. Ferella and C. Breytenbach, eds., *Paths of Knowledge: Interconnection(s) between Knowledge and Journey in the Greco-Roman World*, Berlin, 177–87.

Fascione, S. 2019. *Gli 'altri' al potere: Romani e barbari nella Gallia di Sidonio Apollinare*, Bari.

Fernández López, M. C. 1994. *Sidonio Apolinar, humanista de la antigüedad tardía: Su correspondencia*, Murcia.

Février, P.-A., J.-C. Picard, C. Pietri, and J.-F. Reynaud 1986. *Province ecclésiastique de Lyon* (Lugdunensis prima), Topographie chrétienne des cités de la Gaule des origines au milieu du VIIIe siècle, vol. 4, Paris.
Fischer, S. and L. Lind 2017. 'Late Roman Gaul – Survival amidst Collapse?', in T. Cunningham and J. Driessen, eds., *Crisis to Collapse: The Archaeology of Social Breakdown*, Leuven, 99–130.
Fitzgerald, W. 2016. *Variety: The Life of a Roman Concept*, Chicago, IL.
Flint, V. 1999. 'The Demonisation of Magic and Sorcery in Late Antiquity: Christian Redefinitions of Pagan Religions', in B. Ankarloo and S. Clark, eds., *Witchcraft and Magic in Europe*, vol. 2 *Ancient Greece and Rome*, London, 277–348.
Fo, A. 1991. 'Percorsi e sogni geografici tardolatini', *Aion*, 13, 51–71.
Fo, A. 1999. 'Sidonio nelle mani di Eurico (*Ep.* VIII 9): Spazi della tradizione culturale in un nuovo contesto romanobarbarico', in M. Rotili, ed., *Memoria del passato, urgenza del futuro: Il mondo romano fra V e VII secolo*, Naples, 17–37.
Fo, A. 2002. 'Arginare la decadenza da "minore": Sidonio Apollinare', in S. Ronchey, ed., *La decadenza: Un seminario*, Palermo, 154–90.
Fögen, T. 1998. 'Bezüge zwischen antiker und moderner Sprachnormentheorie', *Folia philologica* 121, 199–219.
Fögen, T. 2018. 'Ancient Approaches to Letter-Writing and the Configuration of Communities through Epistle', in P. Ceccarelli, ed., *Letters and Communities: Studies in the Socio-Political Dimensions of Ancient Epistolography*, Oxford, 43–80.
Fögen, T. 2024. '*Ars adeo latet arte sua:* Die "epigrammatischen" Briefe des Jüngeren Plinius', in T. Fögen and N. Mindt, eds., *Brief und Epigramm: Bezüge und Wechselwirkungen zwischen zwei Textsorten in Antike und Mittelalter*, Berlin, 167–96.
Fontaine, J. 1977. 'Unité et diversité du mélange des genres et des tons chez quelques écrivains latins de la fin du IVe siècle: Ausone, Ambroise, Ammien', in M. Fuhrmann, ed., *Christianisme et formes littéraires de l'antiquité tardive en occident*, Vandoeuvres, 425–72.
Formisano, M. 2007. 'Towards an Aesthetic Paradigm of Late Antiquity', *AT* 15, 277–84.
Fournier, M., and A. Stoehr-Monjou 2014. 'Cartographie géo-littéraire et géo-historique de la mobilité aristocratique au Ve siècle d'après la correspondance de Sidoine Apollinaire: Du voyage officiel au voyage épistolaire', doi.org/10.4000/belgeo.12689.
Fournier, M., and A. Stoehr-Monjou 2015. 'Représentation idéologique de l'espace dans la lettre I, 5 de Sidoine Apollinaire: Cartographie géo-littéraire d'un voyage de Lyon à Rome', in P. Voisin and M. de Béchillon, eds., *L'espace dans l'antiquité*, Paris, 267–85.

Franceschelli, C., and P. L. Dall'Aglio 2014. 'Entre voies de terre et voies d'eau: L'évolution du voyage en Italie Padane, entre l'*Itinerarium Burdigalense* et le témoignage de Sidoine Apollinaire', doi.org/10.4000/belgeo.12877.

Frauenhuber, A. 2007. 'Kontinuität und Wandel. Karrieren und Lebensbilder im Gallien des 5. Jahrhunderts: Betrachtungen zu zwei Briefen des Sidonius Apollinaris an Syagrius', *Diomedes* 4, 11–21.

Fray, J.-L. 2000. 'La présence juive au très haut Moyen Age', in D. Jarrassé, ed., *Les juifs de Clermont: Une histoire fragmentée*, Clermond-Ferrand, 17–23.

Fruyt, M., and A. Orlandini 2008. 'Some Cases of Linguistic Evolution and Grammaticalisation in the Latin Verb', in R. Wright, ed., *Latin vulgaire – latin tardif*, vol. 8, Hildesheim, 230–7.

Frye, D. 1990. 'Gundobad, the *Leges Burgundionum* and the Struggle for Sovereignty in Burgundy', *C&M* 41, 199–212.

Furbetta, L. 2013. 'Tra retorica e politica: Formazione, ricezione ed esemplarità dell'epistolario di Sidonio Apollinare', in S. Gioanni and P. Cammarosano, eds., *La corrispondenza epistolare in Italia: Forme, stili e funzioni della scrittura epistolare nelle cancellerie italiane (secoli V–XV)*, Rome, vol. 2, 23–65.

Furbetta, L. 2015a. 'L'epitaffio di Sidonio Apollinare in un nuovo testimone manoscritto', *Euphrosyne* 43, 243–54.

Furbetta, L. 2015b. 'La lettre de recommandation en Gaule (Ve–VIIe siècles) entre tradition littéraire et innovation', in A. Bérenger and O. Dard, eds., *Gouverner par les lettres, de l'Antiquité à l'époque contemporaine*, Metz, 347–68.

Furbetta, L. 2020. 'Sidonius Scholarship: Fifteenth to Nineteenth Centuries', in Kelly and van Waarden 2020, 543–63.

Geisler, E. 1887. 'Loci similes auctorum Sidonio anteriorum', in C. Lütjohann, ed., *Gai Sollii Apollinaris Sidonii epistulae et carmina*, Berlin, 351–416.

Gerolemou, M., and L. Diamantopoulou, eds., 2020. *Mirrors and Mirroring from Antiquity to the Early Modern Period*, London.

Giannotti, F. 2016. Sperare meliora. *Il terzo libro delle* Epistulae *di Sidonio Apollinare: Introduzione, traduzione e commento*, Pisa.

Giannotti, F. 2020. 'Sidonius Reception: Late-Nineteenth to Twenty-First Centuries', in Kelly and van Waarden 2020, 705–29.

Giannotti, F. 2021a. '*Levigata pagina:* Riconsiderando l'epitaffio di Sidonio per il nonno Apollinare (*ep.* 3.12)', *InvLuc* 43, 7–22.

Giannotti, F. 2021b. Scrinia Arverna: *Studi su Sidonio Apollinare*, Pisa.

Giannotti, F. 2023. 'Translation vs Decadence: Revisiting Sidonius Apollinaris' *Ep.* 8, 3', *PAN* n.s. 12, 115–29.

Gibson, R. K. 2003. *Ovid, Ars Amatoria, Book 3*, Cambridge.

Gibson, R. K. 2011. '<*Clarus*> Confirmed? Pliny, *Epistles* 1.1 and Sidonius Apollinaris', *CQ* 61, 655–9.

Gibson, R. K. 2012. 'On the Nature of Ancient Letter Collections', *JRS* 102, 56–78.

Gibson, R. K. 2013. 'Reading the Letters of Sidonius by the Book', in van Waarden and Kelly 2013, 195–219.

Gibson, R. K. 2015. 'Not Dark Yet ...: Reading to the End of Pliny's Nine Book Collection', in I. Marchesi, ed., *Pliny the Bookmaker: Betting on Posterity in the Epistles*, Oxford, 185–222.

Gibson, R. K. 2020a. *Man of High Empire: The Life of Pliny the Younger*, Oxford.

Gibson, R. K. 2020b. 'Sidonius' Correspondence', in Kelly and van Waarden 2020, 373–92.

Gibson, R. K., and R. Morello 2012. *Reading the Letters of Pliny the Younger: An Introduction*, Cambridge.

Gillett, A. 2001. 'Rome, Ravenna, and the Last Western Emperors', *PBSR* 69, 131–67.

Gillett, A. 2003. *Envoys and Political Communication in the Late Antique West, 411–533*, Cambridge.

Gillett, A. 2012. 'Communication in Late Antiquity: Use and Reuse', in Johnson 2012, 815–46.

Girke, G. 1922. *Die Tracht der Germanen in der vor- und frühgeschichtlichen Zeit*, Leipzig.

Goffart, W. A. 1980. *Barbarians and Romans, A.D. 418–584: The Techniques of Accommodation*, Princeton, NJ.

Grafton, A., G. W. Most, and S. Settis, eds., 2010. *The Classical Tradition*, Cambridge, MA.

Green, R. 2020. 'Translating Sidonius', in Kelly and van Waarden 2020, 618–27.

Griffe, É. 1965. *La Gaule chrétienne à l'époque romaine*, vol. 3 *La cité chrétienne*, Paris.

Grig, L. 2024. *Popular Culture and the End of Antiquity in Southern Gaul, c. 400–550*, Cambridge.

Gropp, G. 2005. 'Susa v. The Sasanian Period', in *Encyclopaedia Iranica*, https://www.iranicaonline.org/articles/susa-v/.

Gualandri, I. 1979. *Furtiva lectio: Studi su Sidonio Apollinare*, Milan.

Gualandri, I. 1993. '*Elegi acuti*: Il distico elegiaco in Sidonio Apollinare', in G. Catanzaro and F. Santucci, eds., *La poesia cristiana in distici elegiaci*, Assisi, 191–216.

Gualandri, I. 2020. 'Sidonius' Intertextuality', in Kelly and van Waarden 2020, 279–316.

Guastalla, G. 2017. *Word of Mouth:* **Fama** *and its Personifications in Art and Literature from Ancient Rome to the Middle Ages*, Oxford.
Guidoboni, E., A. Comastri, and G. Traina 1994. *Catalogue of Ancient Earthquakes in the Mediterranean Area up to the 10th Century*, Rome.
Gwynn, D. M. 2012. 'Episcopal Leadership', in Johnson 2012, 876–915.
Haarhoff, T. J. 1958. *Schools of Gaul: A Study of Pagan and Christian Education in the Last Century of the Western Empire*, Johannesburg.
Halsall, G. 2007. *Barbarian Migrations and the Roman West, 376–568*, Cambridge.
Halsall, G. 2013. *Worlds of Arthur: Facts and Fictions of the Dark Ages*, Oxford.
Hanaghan, M. P. 2017a. 'Latent Criticism of Anthemius and Ricimer in Sidonius Apollinaris' *Epistulae* 1.5', *CQ* 67, 631–49.
Hanaghan, M. P. 2017b. 'Micro Allusions to Pliny and Virgil in Sidonius's Programmatic Epistles', *IJCT* 24, 249–61.
Hanaghan, M. P. 2019. *Reading Sidonius'* Epistles, Cambridge.
Hanaghan, M. P. 2020. 'Competing at *otium*? A Juxtaposed Reading of Sidonius' Baths', *JLA* 13, 117–36.
Hardie, P. 2012. *Rumour and Renown: Representations of 'Fama' in Western Literature*, Cambridge.
Hardie, P. 2019. *Classicism and Christianity in Late Antique Latin Poetry*, Oakland, CA.
Harnett, B. 2017. 'The Diffusion of the Codex', *ClAnt* 36, 183–235.
Harper, K. 2012. 'Marriage and Family', in Johnson 2012, 667–714.
Harries, J. D. 1992. 'Sidonius Apollinaris, Rome and the Barbarians: A Climate of Treason?', in Drinkwater and Elton 1992, 298–308.
Harries, J. D. 1994. *Sidonius Apollinaris and the Fall of Rome AD 407–485*, Oxford.
Harries, J. D. 1996. 'Sidonius Apollinaris and the Frontiers of Romanitas', in R. W. Mathisen and H. S. Sivan, eds., *Shifting Frontiers in Late Antiquity*, Aldershot, 31–44.
Harries, J. D. 2001. 'Not the Theodosian Code: Euric's Law and Late Fifth-Century Gaul', in R. W. Mathisen and D. Shanzer, eds., *Society and Culture in Late Antique Gaul: Revisiting the Sources*, Aldershot, 39–51.
Harrison, S. J. 2007a. *Generic Enrichment in Vergil and Horace*, Oxford.
Harrison, S. J. 2007b. 'The Primal Voyage and the Ocean of Epos: Two Aspects of Metapoetic Imagery in Catullus, Virgil and Horace', *Dictynna* 4, https://doi.org/10.4000/dictynna.146.
Heather, P. J. 1991. *Goths and Romans 332–489*, Oxford.
Heather, P. J. 2005. *The Fall of the Roman Empire: A New History of Rome and the Barbarians*, London.
Hecquet-Noti, N. 2013. 'Le temple de Dieu ou la nature symbolisée: La dédicace de la cathédrale de Lyon par Sidoine Apollinaire (*Epist.* 2,10)',

in F. Garambois and D. Vallat, eds., *Le lierre et la statue: La nature et son espace littéraire dans l'épigramme gréco-latine tardive*, Saint-Étienne, 217–31.

Heijmans, M. 2006. 'La place des monuments publics du Haut-Empire dans les villes de la Gaule méridionale durant l'Antiquité tardive (IVe–VIe s.)', *Gallia* 63, 25–41.

Heijmans, M. 2020. 'The Late Roman City Walls in Southern Gaul', in E. E. Intagliata, S. J. Barker, and C. Courault, eds., *City Walls in Late Antiquity: An Empire-Wide Perspective*, Oxford, 51–62.

Heinzelmann, M. 1976. *Bischofsherrschaft in Gallien: Zur Kontinuität römischer Führungsschichten vom 4. bis zum 7. Jahrhundert. Soziale, prosopographische und bildungsgeschichtliche Aspekte*, Munich.

Hellegouarc'h, J. 1963. *Le vocabulaire latin des relations et des partis politiques sous la république*, Paris.

Hemelrijk, E. A. 1999. *Matrona Docta: Educated Women in the Roman Élite from Cornelia to Julia Domna*, London.

Henke, R. 2012. 'Der Brief 3,12 des Sidonius Apollinaris an Secundus: Eine Novelle in einer Epistel?', *Hermes* 140, 121–25.

Henning, D. 1999. *Periclitans res publica: Kaisertum und Eliten in der Krise des weströmischen Reiches 454/5–493 n. Chr.*, Stuttgart.

Henriksén, C. 2012. *A Commentary on Martial, Epigrams Book 9*, Oxford.

Herbert de la Portbarré-Viard, G. 2014. 'Les descriptions et évocations d'édifices religieux chrétiens dans l'œuvre de Sidoine Apollinaire', in Poignault and Stoehr-Monjou 2014, 379–406.

Herbert de la Portbarré-Viard, G. 2023. *Naissance du discours sur les édifices chrétiens dans la littérature latine occidentale, d'Ambroise de Milan à Grégoire de Tours*, Turnhout.

Hernández Lobato, J. 2010. 'La écfrasis de la catedral de Lyon como híbrido intersistémico: Sidonio Apolinar y el "Gesamtkunstwerk" tardoantiguo', *AT* 18, 297–308.

Hernández Lobato, J. 2012. *Vel Apolline muto: Estética y poética de la Antigüedad Tardía*, Bern.

Hernández Lobato, J. 2020. 'Sidonius in the Middle Ages and the Renaissance', in Kelly and van Waarden 2020, 665–85.

Herrin, J. 2020a. *Ravenna: Capital of Empire, Crucible of Europe*, Princeton, NJ.

Herrin, J. 2020b. 'Sidonius Apollinaris in Ravenna', in Herrin 2020a, 72–6.

Higham, N. J. 2018. *King Arthur: The Making of the Legend*, New Haven, CT.

Hindermann, J. 2020a. 'At Leisure with Pliny the Younger: Sidonius's Second Book of the *Epistulae* as a Book of *Otium*', *JLA* 13, 94–116.

Hindermann, J. 2020b. 'La lettre comme lieu de publication des épigrammes: Les épigrammes dans les épîtres de Sidoine Apollinaire et son modèle Pline le Jeune', in L. Furbetta and C. Urlacher-Becht, eds.,

Les 'lieux' de l'épigramme latine tardive: Vers un élargissement du genre, RET Suppl. 8, 75–95.

Hindermann, J. 2022a. '*Lucubratio* (Night Work) and the *Candelabra* as a Symbol of Marriage and Inspiration in Sidonius Apollinaris (*Epist.* 2,10,5)', in H. Harich-Schwarzbauer and C. Scheidegger Lämmle, eds., *Gender Studies in den Altertumswissenschaften: Women and Objects in Antiquity*, Trier, 205–22.

Hindermann, J. 2022b. *Sidonius Apollinaris' Letters, Book 2: Text, Translation and Commentary*, Edinburgh.

Hinds, S. 1998. *Allusion and Intertext: Dynamics of Appropriation in Roman Poetry*, Cambridge.

Hofmann, J. B., ed., 1937. *Kleine Schriften von Wilhelm Heraeus zum 75. Geburtstag am 4. Dezember 1937*, Heidelberg.

Hofmann, J. B. 1951. *Lateinische Umgangssprache*, 3rd ed., Heidelberg.

Holford-Strevens, L. 2003. *Aulus Gellius: An Antonine Scholar and His Achievement*, rev. ed., Oxford.

Hopman, M. G. 2012. *Scylla: Myth, Metaphor, Paradox*, Cambridge.

Humfress, C. 2011. 'Bishops and Law Courts in Late Antiquity: How (Not) to Make Sense of the Legal Evidence', *JECS* 19, 375–400.

Hunsucker, R. G. R. 2025. *Refounding Rome: Ktistic Renewal in the Augustan Age and Late Antiquity*, Nijmegen.

Inglebert, H. 2012. 'Introduction: Late Antique Conceptions of Late Antiquity', in Johnson 2012, 3–28.

Janson, T. 1964. *Latin Prose Prefaces*, Stockholm.

John, A. 2021. 'Learning Greek in Late Antique Gaul', *CQ* 70, 846–64.

John, A. 2023. 'Greek in the Literary Circles of Sidonius' Gaul', in Meurer and Egetenmeyr 2023, 303–30.

John, A. 2026. *Learning and Power: A Cultural History of Education in Late Antique Gaul*, Cambridge.

Johnson, S. F., ed., 2012. *The Oxford Handbook of Late Antiquity*, Oxford.

Johnson, W. A. 2010. *Readers and Reading Culture in the High Roman Empire: A Study of Elite Communities*, New York.

Johnson, W. A. 2011. 'Constructing Elite Reading Communities in the High Empire', in W. A. Johnson and H. N. Parker, eds., *Ancient Literacies: The Culture of Reading in Greece and Rome*, Oxford, 320–30.

Jones, A. H. M. 1964. *The Later Roman Empire, 284–602: A Social, Economic and Administrative Survey*, Oxford.

Kaldellis, A. 2017. 'How Perilous Was It to Write Political History in Late Antiquity?', *SLA* 1, 38–64.

Kaster, R. A. 1988. *Guardians of Language: The Grammarian and Society in Late Antiquity*, Berkeley.

Kaster, R. A. 2005. *Emotion, Restraint, and Community in Ancient Rome*, Oxford.
Kaufmann, F.-M. 1995. *Studien zu Sidonius Apollinaris*, Frankfurt am Main.
Kaufmann, H. 2017. 'Intertextuality in Late Latin Poetry', in J. Elsner and J. Hernández Lobato, eds., *The Poetics of Late Latin Literature*, New York, 149–75.
Kaufmann, H. 2022. 'Identity in Latin Verse Autobiography', in L. Roig Lanzillotta, J. L. Brandão, C. Teixeira, and Á. Rodrigues, eds., *Roman Identity: Between Ideal and Performance*, Turnhout, 71–90.
Keefer, T. D. 1996. 'Anianus of Orleans and the *Vita Aniani* I: A Critical Study of the Codex Parisiensis 11748', Sonoma State University.
Kelly, C. 2008. *Attila the Hun: Barbarian Terror and the Fall of the Roman Empire*, London.
Kelly, G. 2008. *Ammianus Marcellinus: The Allusive Historian*, Cambridge.
Kelly, G. 2012. 'Claudian and Constantinople', in L. Grig and G. Kelly, eds., *Two Romes: From Rome to Constantinople*, New York, 241–64.
Kelly, G. 2016. 'Claudian's Last Panegyric and Imperial Visits to Rome', *CQ* 66, 336–57.
Kelly, G. 2020. 'Dating the Works of Sidonius', in Kelly and van Waarden 2020, 166–94.
Kelly, G., and J. van Waarden, eds., 2020. *The Edinburgh Companion to Sidonius Apollinaris*, Edinburgh.
Kenney, E. J. 1982. 'Books and Readers in the Roman World', in E. J. Kenney and W. V. Clausen, eds., *The Cambridge History of Classical Literature*, vol. 2 *Latin Literature*, Cambridge, 1–32.
Ker, J. 2004. 'Nocturnal Writers in Imperial Rome: The Culture of *Lucubratio*', *CPh* 99, 209–42.
Ker, J. 2023. *The Ordered Day*, Baltimore, MD.
Kleberg, T. 1967. *Buchhandel und Verlagswesen in der Antike*, Darmstadt.
Köhler, H. 1995. *C. Sollius Apollinaris Sidonius, Briefe Buch I: Einleitung, Text, Übersetzung, Kommentar*, Heidelberg.
Köhler, H. 2014. *C. Sollius Apollinaris Sidonius: Die Briefe*, Stuttgart.
Krautheimer, R. 1980. *Rome: Profile of a City, 312–1308*, Princeton, NJ.
Kroon, C. H. M. 1995. *Discourse Particles in Latin: A Study of* nam, enim, autem, vero *and* at, Amsterdam.
Kroon, C. H. M. 2011. 'Latin Particles and the Grammar of Discourse', in J. Clackson, ed., *A Companion to the Latin Language*, Oxford, 176–95.
Kroon, C. H. M., and R. Risselada 1998. 'The Discourse Functions of *iam*', in B. García-Hernández, ed., *Estudios de Lingüística Latina*, Madrid, 429–45.
Kroon, C. H. M., and R. Risselada 2002. 'Phasality, Polarity, Focality: A Feature Analysis of the Latin Particle *iam*', *BJL* 16, 65–78.

Krüger, B., ed., 1983. *Die Germanen: Geschichte und Kultur der germanischen Stämme in Mitteleuropa*, Berlin.
Kulikowski, M. 2020. 'Sidonius' Political World', in Kelly and van Waarden 2020, 197–213.
Lake, J. 2023. 'The Malicious Barking of Critics: A Literary-Historical Approach to the topos of Anticipated Criticism', in E. Kooper and S. Levelt, eds., *The Medieval Chronicle* 16, 128–55.
Lançon, B. 2017. *La chute de l'empire romain: Une histoire sans fin*, Paris.
Lansford, T. 2009. *The Latin Inscriptions of Rome: A Walking Guide*, Baltimore, MD.
Lausberg, H. 1990. *Handbuch der literarischen Rhetorik: Eine Grundlegung der Literaturwissenschaft*, 3rd ed., Stuttgart.
Lauxtermann, M. D. 2003. *Byzantine Poetry from Pisides to Geometres: Texts and Contexts*, Vienna.
Leatherbury, S. 2019. *Inscribing Faith in Late Antiquity: Between Reading and Seeing*, Abingdon.
Leeman, A. D. 1963. *Orationis ratio*, Amsterdam.
Le Guennec, M.-A. 2017. 'Espaces de l'hospitalité gratuite, espaces de l'accueil marchand dans l'Occident romain (République et Haut-Empire): Distinctions et porosités', *Hypothèses HospitAm*, https://hospitam.hypotheses.org/1167.
Lenoble, M. 2019. *Atlas topographique de Lugdunum*, vol. 1 *Lyon-Fourvière*, *RAE* Suppl. 47.
Lieberg, G. 1969. 'Seefahrt und Werk: Untersuchungen zu einer Metapher der antiken, besonders der lateinischen Literatur, von Pindar bis Horaz', *GIF* 21, 209–40.
Liebeschuetz, W. 2015. '*Habitus Barbarus:* Did Barbarians Look Different From Romans?', in W. Liebeschuetz, *East and West in Late Antiquity: Invasion, Settlement, Ethnogenesis and Conflicts of Religion*, Leiden, 151–66.
Liebs, D. 1998. 'Die Juristenwelt bei Sidonius Apollinaris: Römische Juristen 420 bis 500 n. Chr. im südlichen Gallien', in M. Humbert and Y. Thomas, eds., *Mélanges de droit romain et d'histoire ancienne: Hommage à la mémoire d'André Magdelain*, Paris, 259–73.
Lintott, A. 2023. *Violence, Justice, and Law in Classical Antiquity: Collected Papers of Andrew Lintott*, ed. E. H. Bispham and J. A. Rosenblitt, Leiden.
Lizzi Testa, R. 2009. 'The Late Antique Bishop: Image and Reality', in Rousseau 2009, 525–38.
Löfstedt, B. 1985. 'Sprachliches und Textkritisches zu Sidonius' Briefen', *ALMA* 44–45, 207–11.
Löfstedt, E. 1911. *Philologischer Kommentar zur* Peregrinatio Etheriae: *Untersuchungen zur Geschichte der lateinischen Sprache*, Uppsala.
Löfstedt, E. 1956. Syntactica: *Studien und Beiträge zur historischen Syntax des Lateins*, vol. 1, Lund.

Longobardi, C. 2014. 'Il *memoratus*, la dimensione scritta del ricordo', in Poignault and Stoehr-Monjou 2014, 195–203.
Loseby, S. T. 1992. 'Bishops and Cathedrals: Order and Diversity in the Fifth-Century Urban Landscape of Southern Gaul', in Drinkwater and Elton 1992, 144–55.
Loseby, S. T. 2009. 'Mediterranean Cities', in Rousseau 2009, 139–55.
Lowe, D. 2015. *Monsters and Monstrosity in Augustan Poetry*, Ann Arbor, MI.
Loyen, A. 1943. *Sidoine Apollinaire et l'esprit précieux en Gaule aux derniers jours de l'Empire*, Paris.
Lucarini, C. M. 2002. 'Congetture a Sidonio Apollinare e al *Carmen adv. Marcionitas*', *SCO* 48, 378–92.
Lucht, B. 2011. *Gastfreundschaft und Landleben bei Sidonius Apollinaris am Beispiel von* epist. *2,9 (an Donidius): Text, Übersetzung, Kommentar und Interpretation*, Münster.
Luiselli, B. 1978. 'Il mito dell'origine troiana dei Galli, dei Franchi e degli Scandinavi', *RomBarb* 3, 89–121.
Maas, M., ed., 2015. *The Cambridge Companion to the Age of Attila*, Cambridge.
MacCormack, S. 1981. *Art and Ceremony in Late Antiquity*, Berkeley, CA.
MacCormack, S. 2013. 'Cicero in Late Antiquity', in C. Steel, ed., *The Cambridge Companion to Cicero*, Cambridge, 251–305.
MacDonald, E. 2000. *Representations of Women in Sidonius Apollinaris and Gregory of Tours:* coniuges et reginae, University of Ottawa.
Machado, C. 2019. *Urban Space and Aristocratic Power in Late Antique Rome: AD 270–535*, Oxford.
Malherbe, A. J. 1988. *Ancient Epistolary Theorists*, Atlanta, GA.
Mannheimer, I. 1975. *Sprachliche Beziehungen zwischen Alt- und Spätlatein*, Zürich.
Marolla, G. 2022. 'Who Was Sidonius' Correspondent Simplicius? An Identification Problem in the Letters', *CQ* 72, 889–901.
Marolla, G. 2023. *Sidonius, Letters Book 5, Part 1: Text, Translation and Commentary*, Edinburgh.
Marolla, G. 2024. 'The Names of Sidonius' Addressees and the Manuscript Tradition of the Letters', *Mnemosyne* 77, 796–817.
Marolla, G. forthcoming. *Sidonius, Letters Book 5, Part 2: Text, Translation and Commentary*, Edinburgh.
Marrou, H.-I. 1977. *Décadence romaine ou Antiquité tardive? (IIIe–VIe siècle)*, Paris.
Mascoli, P. 2000. 'Personaggi femminili in Sidonio Apollinare', *InvLuc* 22, 89–107.
Mascoli, P. 2003. 'L'elogio funebre di Filomazia (Sidon. *epist*. 2,8): Saggio di commento', *InvLuc* 25, 153–67.
Mascoli, P. 2010. *Gli Apollinari: Per la storia di una famiglia tardoantica*, Bari.

Mascoli, P. 2014. '*Multum est quod debemus et matribus:* Le donne della famiglia degli Apollinari', in Poignault and Stoehr-Monjou 2014, 33–9.
Mascoli, P. 2021. *Sidonio Apollinare, Epistolario: Introduzione, traduzione e note*, Rome.
Mathisen, R. W. 1979. 'Resistance and Reconciliation: Majorian and the Gallic Aristocracy after the Fall of Avitus', *Francia* 7, 597–627.
Mathisen, R. W. 1981. 'Epistolography, Literary Circles and Family Ties in Late Roman Gaul', *TAPhA* 111, 95–109.
Mathisen, R. W. 1984. 'Emigrants, Exiles and Survivors: Aristocratic Options in Visigothic Aquitania', *Phoenix* 38, 159–70.
Mathisen, R. W. 1988. 'The Theme of Literary Decline in Late Roman Gaul', *CPh* 83, 44–52.
Mathisen, R. W. 1989. *Ecclesiastical Factionalism and Religious Controversy in Fifth-Century Gaul*, Washington D.C.
Mathisen, R. W. 1991a. 'Phoebus, Orpheus and Dionysus: Nicknames and the Literary Circle of Sidonius', in Mathisen 1991b, 29–44.
Mathisen, R. W. 1991b. *Studies in the History, Literature, and Society of Late Antiquity*, Amsterdam.
Mathisen, R. W. 1993. *Roman Aristocrats in Barbarian Gaul: Strategies for Survival in an Age of Transition*, Austin, TX.
Mathisen, R. W. 1999. *Ruricius of Limoges and Friends: A Collection of Letters from Visigothic Gaul*, Liverpool.
Mathisen, R. W. 2013. 'Dating the Letters of Sidonius', in van Waarden and Kelly 2013, 221–48.
Mathisen, R. W. 2018. 'The "Publication" of Latin Letter Collections in Late Antiquity', in G. M. Müller, ed., *Zwischen Alltagskommunikation und literarischer Identitätsbildung: Studien zur lateinischen Epistolographie in Spätantike und Frühmittelalter*, Stuttgart, 63–84.
Mathisen, R. W. 2020a. 'A Prosopography of Sidonius', in Kelly and van Waarden 2020, 76–154.
Mathisen, R. W. 2020b. 'Sidonius' Earliest Reception and Distribution', in Kelly and van Waarden 2020, 631–42.
Mathisen, R. W. 2020c. 'Sidonius' People', in Kelly and van Waarden 2020, 29–75.
Mathisen, R. W. 2020d. 'Sidonius' Places: A Geographical Appendix', in Kelly and van Waarden 2020, 155–65.
Mauskopf Deliyannis, D. 2010. *Ravenna in Late Antiquity*, Cambridge.
Mazzoli, G. 2006. 'Sidonio, Orazio e la *lex saturae*', in L. Cristante, ed., *Il calamo della memoria: Riuso di testi e mestiere letterario nella tarda antichità*, vol. 5, Trieste, 171–84.
McEvoy, M. 2010. 'Rome and the Transformation of the Imperial Office in the Late Fourth-Mid-Fifth Centuries AD', *PBSR* 78, 151–92.

Merchie, E. 1922. 'Confiteor errorem: Sidoine Apollinaire, *Ep.* III, 12, 2', *Musée belge* 26, 145–9.
Meslin, M. 1970. *La fête des kalendes de janvier dans l'empire romain: Étude d'un rituel de Nouvel An*, Brussels.
Meurer, T. L. and V. Egetenmeyr, eds., 2023. *Gallia docta? Education and In-/Exclusion in Late Antique Gaul*, Tübingen.
Meyer, E. A. 1990. 'Explaining the Epigraphic Habit in the Roman Empire: The Evidence of Epitaphs', *JRS* 80, 74–96.
Meyer, E. A. 2004. *Legitimacy and Law in the Roman World: Tabulae in Roman Belief and Practice*, Cambridge.
Miller, K. 1964. *Itineraria romana: Römische Reisewege an der Hand der Tabula Peutingeriana*, Rome.
Miller, P. C. 2009. *The Corporeal Imagination: Signifying the Holy in Late Ancient Christianity*, Philadelphia.
Mitchell, J. 2018. 'The Eastern and Western Consulship in the Later Roman Empire', *Hiperboreea* 5, 5–16.
Mogen, S. L. M. 2020. *Mourning the Dead in Christian Late Antiquity*, University of Calgary.
Mommsen, T. 1887. 'Index personarum', in C. Lütjohann, ed., *Gai Sollii Apollinaris Sidonii epistulae et carmina*, Berlin, 417–38.
Mondin, L. 2008. 'La misura epigrammatica nella tarda latinità', in A. M. Morelli, ed., *Epigramma longum: Da Marziale alla tarda antichità*, vol. 2, Cassino, 397–494.
Mondin, L. 2019. 'The Late Latin Literary Epigram (Third to Fifth Centuries CE)', in C. Henriksén, ed., *A Companion to Ancient Epigram*, Hoboken, NJ, 575–95.
Montone, F. 2017. 'Vita e svaghi di un aristocratico del V secolo: Il secondo libro dell'epistolario di Sidonio Apollinare', *Salternum* 21, 23–45.
Montzamir, P. 2023. 'Sidonius' Presumed Epitaph: Two Manuscripts, Two Fragments of Stone, and Many Questions', doi.10.11588/propylaeumdok.00006720.
Morford, M. 2002. *The Roman Philosophers*, London.
Morvillez, É. 2017. '"Avec vue sur jardin": Vivre entre nature et paysage dans l'architecture domestique, de Cicéron à Sidoine Apollinaire', *Mondes anciens* 9, doi.org/10.4000/mondesanciens.1926.
Mossberg, K.-Å. F. 1934. *Studia Sidoniana critica et semasiologica*, Uppsala.
Mratschek, S. 2008. 'Identitätsstiftung aus der Vergangenheit: Zum Diskurs über die trajanische Bildungskultur im Kreis des Sidonius Apollinaris', in T. Fuhrer, ed., *Die christlich-philosophischen Diskurse der Spätantike: Texte, Personen, Institutionen*, Stuttgart, 363–80.
Mratschek, S. 2013. 'Creating Identity from the Past: The Construction of History in the Letters of Sidonius', in van Waarden and Kelly 2013, 249–71.

Mratschek, S. 2017. 'The Letter Collection of Sidonius Apollinaris', in Sogno et al. 2017a, 309–36.
Mratschek, S. 2020a. 'Creating Culture and Presenting the Self in Sidonius', in Kelly and van Waarden 2020, 237–60.
Mratschek, S. 2020b. 'Sidonius' Social World', in Kelly and van Waarden 2020, 214–36.
Mratschek, S. 2024. 'Caesar in Late Antiquity: From Portrait to Symbol', in N. Lenski, R. Rees, and O. van Nijf, eds., *From East to West in Late Antiquity: Studies in Honor of Jan Willem Drijvers*, Bari, 255–67.
Munier, C., ed., 1963. *Concilia Galliae A. 314–A. 506*, Turnhout.
Mynors, R. A. B., ed., 1963. *C. Plini Caecili Secundi epistularum libri decem*, Oxford.
Nardelli, J.-F. 2022. 'Nicomaque Flavien Senior et la Vie d´Apollonios de Tyane: Essai de résolution du témoignage de Sidoine Apollinaire', *Exemplaria Classica* 26, 33–83.
Nathan, G. 1998. 'The Rogation Ceremonies of Late Antique Gaul: Creation, Transmission and the Role of the Bishop', *C&M* 49, 275–303.
Nathan, G. 2000. *The Family in Late Antiquity: The Rise of Chrisitianity and the Endurance of Tradition*, London.
Neger, M. 2020. '*Lascivire vetat mascula dictio:* Metaliterary Reflections on Poems in Late Antique Prose Letters', in J. Hernández Lobato and Ó. Prieto Domínguez, eds., *Literature Squared: Self-Reflexivity in Late Antique Literature*, Turnhout, 83–109.
Nehlsen, H. 1978. 'Der Grabfrevel in den germanischen Rechtsaufzeichnungen', in H. Jankuhn, H. Nehlsen, and H. Rorth, eds., *Zum Grabfrevel in vor- und frühgeschichtlicher Zeit*, Göttingen, 107–68.
Neri, M., ed., 2009. *Ruricio di Limoges, Lettere*, Pisa.
Nippel, W. 2007. 'Ethnic Images in Classical Antiquity', in M. Beller and J. Leerssen, eds., *Imagology: The Cultural Construction and Literary Representation of National Characters. A Critical Survey*, Amsterdam, 33–44.
Noble, T. F. X., and J. Van Engen, eds., 2011. *European Transformations: The Long Twelfth Century*, Notre Dame, IN.
Nutton, V. 1983. 'The Seeds of Disease: An Explanation of Contagion and Infection from the Greeks to the Renaissance', *Medical History* 27, 1–34.
O'Brien, M. B. 1930. *Titles of Address in Christian Latin Epistolography to 543 A.D.*, Washington, D.C.
Olson, K. 2008. *Dress and the Roman Woman: Self-Presentation and Society*, London.
Olson, K. 2017. *Masculinity and Dress in Roman Antiquity*, London.
Onorato, M. 2020. 'The Poet and the Light: Modulation and Transposition of a Prudentian Ecphrasis in Two Poems by Sidonius Apollinaris', in F.

Hadjittofi and A. Lefteratou, eds., *The Genres of Late Antique Christian Poetry: Between Modulations and Transpositions*, Berlin, 75–92.

Oppedisano, F. 2020. 'Sidonio, Antemio e il senato di Roma', in F. Oppedisano, ed., *Procopio Antemio, imperatore di Roma*, Bari, 97–119.

Oppedisano, F. 2022. 'Une note sur la *legatio Arverna* à Rome (467 ap. J.-C.)', in M.-P. Chambon, S. Crogiez-Pétrequin, A. Ferdière, and S. Janniard, eds., *L'Antiquité tardive dans le centre et le centre-ouest de la Gaule (IIIe–VIIe siècles)*, *RACF* Suppl. 82, 69–75.

Otto, A. 1890. *Die Sprichwörter und sprichwörtlichen Redensarten der Römer*, Leipzig.

Overwien, O. 2009. 'Kampf um Gallien: Die Briefe des Sidonius Apollinaris zwischen Literatur und Politik', *Hermes* 137, 93–117.

Pabst, B. 1994. *Prosimetrum: Tradition und Wandel einer Literaturform zwischen Spätantike und Spätmittelalter*, Cologne.

Painter, K. 1993. 'Late-Roman Silver Plate: A Reply to Alan Cameron', *JRA* 6, 109–15.

Pasquali, G. 1942. 'Arte allusiva', *L'Italia che scrive* 25, 185–7.

Pecere, O. 1986. 'La tradizione dei testi latini tra IV e V secolo attraverso i libri sottoscritti', in A. Giardina, ed., *Società romana e impero tardoantico*, vol. 4 *Tradizione dei classici, trasformazioni della cultura*, Rome, 19–81.

Pellizzari, A. 2003. *Servio: Storia, cultura e istituzioni nell'opera di un grammatico tardoantico*, Florence.

Pelttari, A. 2014. *The Space That Remains: Reading Latin Poetry in Late Antiquity*, Ithaca, NY.

Pelttari, A. 2016. 'Sidonius Apollinaris and Horace, Ars poetica 14–23', *Philologus* 161, 322–36.

Percival, J. 1992. 'The Fifth-Century Villa: New Life or Death Postponed?', in Drinkwater and Elton 1992, 156–64.

Percival, J. 1997. 'Desperately Seeking Sidonius: The Realities of Life in Fifth-Century Gaul', *Latomus* 56, 279–92.

Piacente, L. 2005. 'In viaggio con Sidonio Apollinare', in A. Gargano and M. Squillante, eds., *Il viaggio nella letteratura occidentale tra mito e simbolo*, Naples, 95–106.

Pinkster, H. 1999. 'The Present Tense in Virgil's Aeneid', *Mnemosyne* 52, 705–17.

Piras, A., ed., 2002. *Passio sancti Saturnini (BHL 7491)*, Rome.

Plassmann, A. 2006. *Origo gentis: Identitäts- und Legitimitätsstiftung in früh- und hochmittelalterlichen Herkunftserzählungen*, Berlin.

Poignault, R., and A. Stoehr-Monjou, eds., 2014. *Présence de Sidoine Apollinaire*, Clermont-Ferrand.

Pollmann, K. 2017. *The Baptized Muse: Early Christian Poetry as Cultural Authority*, Oxford.

Porena, P. 2023. 'Simmaco, Sidonio Apollinare e la gloriosa genealogia dei Syagrii di Lione', in L. Furbetta, F. Oppedisano, and C. Urlacher-Becht, eds., *Mouvements de personnes, circulation littéraire et rapports politiques*, Pisa, 137–65.

Prchlík, I. 2007. 'Sidonius or Flavianus: By Whom Was Philostratus' *Vita Apollonii* Translated into Latin?', *Graecolatina Pragensia* 22, 199–210.

Prévot, F. 1993. 'Deux fragments de l'épitaphe de Sidoine Apollinaire découverts à Clermont-Ferrand', *AT* 1, 223–9.

Prévot, F. 2004. 'Faut-il réhabiliter le fils de Sidoine Apollinaire?', in C. Balmelle, P. Chevalier, and G. Ripoll, eds., *Mélanges d'antiquité tardive: Studiola in honorem Noël Duval*, Turnhout, 251–60.

Pricoco, S. 1965a. 'Sidonio Apollinare traduttore della "Vita di Apollonio di Tiana" di Filostrato', in Pricoco 1965b, 71–98.

Pricoco, S. 1965b. 'Studi su Sidonio Apollinare', *ND* 15, 69–150.

Pricoco, S. 1978. *L'isola dei Santi: Il cenobio di Lerino e le origini del monachesimo gallico*, Rome.

Prinz, F. 1988. *Frühes Mönchtum im Frankenreich. Kultur und Gesellschaft in Gallien, den Rheinlanden und Bayern am Beispiel der monastischen Entwicklung (4. bis 8. Jahrhundert)*, Munich.

Raga, E. 2009. 'Bon mangeur, mauvais mangeur: Pratiques alimentaires et critique sociale dans l'oeuvre de Sidoine Apollinaire et ses contemporains', *RBPH* 87, 165–96.

Raga, E. 2016. 'Le vocabulaire de l'hospitalité dans l'Antiquité tardive occidentale: Le cas d'*humanitas* et les nouveaux enjeux de l'hospitalité à l'âge de l'ascétisme chrétien', *Hypothèses HospitAm*, https://hospitam.hypotheses.org/265.

Raga, E. 2019. 'Romans and Barbarians at the Table: Banquets and Food as Tools of Distinction According to Sidonius Apollinaris (Fifth-Century Gaul)', in Y. Fox and E. Buchberger, eds., *Inclusion and Exclusion in Mediterranean Christianities, 400–800*, Turnhout, 239–58.

Rapp, C. 2005. *Holy Bishops in Late Antiquity: The Nature of Christian Leadership in an Age of Transition*, Berkeley, CA.

Ravenna, G. 1990. *Le nozze di Polemio e Araneola (Sidonio Apollinare, Carmina XIV-XV): Introduzione, testo, traduzione e commento*, Bologna.

Ravenna, G. 2004. '*Quos tamen chordae nequeunt sonare, / corda sonabunt*: Sidon. epist. IX 16,3 vers. 83–84 (Sidonio Apollinare giudica la sua poesia)', in *Incontri triestini di filologia classica* vol. 3, Trieste, 315–26.

Rawson, E. 1985. *Intellectual Life in the Late Roman Republic*, London.

Raynaud, C. 2006. 'Le monde des morts', *Gallia* 63, 137–56.

Rebillard, É. 2009. 'The Church, the Living, and the Dead', in Rousseau 2009, 220–30.

Regato, P. 2022. 'Southern Europe: Northern Italy Stretching to the Shore of the Adriatic Sea', in *WWF Ecoregions*, www.worldwildlife.org/ecoregions/pa0432.

Reynaud, J.-F. 1998. Lugdunum christianum: *Lyon du IVe au VIIIe s.: Topographie, nécropoles et édifices religieux*, Paris.
Reynaud, J.-F. 2014. 'Les lieux de culte et la renaissance burgonde à Lyon et à Vienne, textes et données archéologiques', *HAM* 20, 170–82.
Reynaud, J.-F., and F. Prévot 2014. 'Province ecclésiastique de Lyon (*Lugdunensis prima*)', in *Quarante ans d'enquête (1972–2012): Topographie chrétienne des cités de la Gaule des origines au milieu du VIIIe siècle*, vol. 16, Paris.
Rich, A. 1901. *A Dictionary of Roman and Greek Antiquities*, 3rd ed., London.
Richardson, L. 1992. *A New Topographical Dictionary of Ancient Rome*, Baltimore, MD.
Riess, W. 2012. '*Rari exempli femina:* Female Virtues on Roman Funerary Inscriptions', in S. L. James and S. Dillon, eds., *A Companion to Women in the Ancient World*, Malden, 491–501.
Rimell, V. 2015. *The Closure of Space in Roman Poetics: Empire's Inward Turn*, Cambridge.
Risselada, R. 2013. 'Applying Text Linguistics to the Letters of Sidonius', in van Waarden and Kelly 2013, 273–303.
Roberto, U. 2020. 'La corte di Antemio e i rapporti con l'Oriente', in F. Oppedisano, ed., *Procopio Antemio, imperatore di Roma*, Bari, 141–76.
Roberts, M. 1989. *The Jeweled Style: Poetry and Poetics in Late Antiquity*. Ithaca, NY.
Roberts, M. 1992. 'Barbarians in Gaul: The Response of the Poets', in Drinkwater and Elton 1992, 97–106.
Roberts, M. 2011. 'Light, Color, and Visual Illusion in the Poetry of Venantius Fortunatus', *DOP* 65/66, 113–20.
Rohrbacher, D. 2010. 'Physiognomics in Imperial Latin Biography', *CA* 29, 92–116.
Roller, M. B. 2018. *Models from the Past in Roman Culture: A World of Exempla*, Cambridge.
Rousseau, P. 2000. 'Monasticism', in Cameron et al. 2000, 745–80.
Rousseau, P., ed., 2009. *A Companion to Late Antiquity*, Chichester.
Rowe, G. O. 2001. 'Style', in S. E. Porter, ed., *Handbook of Classical Rhetoric in the Hellenistic Period 330 B.C. –A.D. 400*, Leiden, 121–57.
Rummel, P. von. 2007. Habitus barbarus: *Kleidung und Repräsentation spätantiker Eliten im 4. und 5. Jahrhundert*, Berlin.
Russell, D. A. and N. G. Wilson, eds., 1981. *Menander Rhetor*, Oxford.
Sallares, R. 2002. *Malaria and Rome: A History of Malaria in Ancient Italy*, Oxford.
Salzman, M. R. 2017a. 'Emperors and Elites in Rome after the Vandal Sack of 455', *AT* 25, 243–62.
Salzman, M. R. 2017b. 'Latin Letter Collections before Late Antiquity', in Sogno et al. 2017a, 13–37.

Samson, R. 1992. 'Slavery, the Roman Legacy', in Drinkwater and Elton 1992, 218–27.
Santelia, S. 2000. 'Sidonio Apollinare e i *bybliopolae*', *InvLuc* 22, 217–39.
Santelia, S. 2002. *Sidonio Apollinare, Carme 24 Propempticon ad libellum: Introduzione, traduzione e commento*, Bari.
Santelia, S. 2005. Per amare Eucheria, *Anth.Lat. 386 Shackleton Bailey: Saggio introduttivo, traduzione e note*, Bari.
Santelia, S. 2007. 'Sidonio Apollinare autore di una epigrafe per l'ecclesia di Lione: *epist.* 2,10,4 (= Le Blant *ICG* 54)', *VetChr* 44, 305–21.
Santelia, S. 2008. '"Storie" di donne nella Gallia di età romanobarbarica', in P. Brunel and G. Dotoli, eds., *La femme en Méditerranée*, Fasano-Paris, 85–95.
Santelia, S. 2011. 'Modelli femminili nella tarda antichità', *VetChr* 48, 335–57.
Santelia, S. 2012. *La* miranda fabula *dei* pii fratres *in* Aetna *603–645*, Bari.
Santelia, S., and S. Condorelli 2023. *Sidonio Apollinare:* Carmina minora, Naples.
Schetter, W. 1992. 'Zur Publikation der *Carmina minora* des Apollinaris Sidonius', *Hermes* 120, 343–63.
Schindler, C. 2009. Per carmina laudes: *Untersuchungen zur spätantiken Verspanegyrik von Claudian bis Coripp*, Berlin.
Schrickx, J. 2011. *Lateinische Modalpartikeln:* nempe, quippe, scilicet, videlicet *und* nimirum, Leiden.
Schwitter, R. 2015. Umbrosa lux: Obscuritas *in der lateinischen Epistolographie der Spätantike*, Stuttgart.
Shackleton Bailey, D. R. 1982. 'Notes, Critical and Interpretative, on the Letters of Sidonius Apollinaris', *Phoenix* 36, 344–57.
Shackleton Bailey, D. R. 1997. *Selected Classical Papers*, Ann Arbor, MI.
Shanzer, D., and I. Wood 2002. *Avitus of Vienne, Letters and Selected Prose*, Liverpool.
Sheerin, D. J. 1982. '*Celeuma* in Christian Latin: Lexical and Literary Notes', *Traditio* 38, 45–73.
Sherwin White, A. N. 1966. *The Letters of Pliny: A Historical and Social Commentary*, Oxford.
Sirks, A. J. B. 2013. 'The *episcopalis audientia* in Late Antiquity', *Droit et cultures* 65, 79–88.
Sloane, T. O., ed., 2001. *Encyclopedia of Rhetoric*, Oxford.
Snyder, J. M. 1989. *The Woman and the Lyre: Women Writers in Classical Greece and Rome*, Carbondale, IL.
Sogno, C. 2017. 'The Letter Collection of Quintus Aurelius Symmachus', in Sogno et al. 2017a, 175–89.

Sogno, C., B. K. Storin, and E. J. Watts, eds., 2017a. *Late Antique Letter Collections: A Critical Introduction and Reference Guide*, Berkeley, CA.
Sogno, C., B. K. Storin, and E. J. Watts 2017b. 'Introduction', in Sogno et al. 2017a, 1–10.
Soler, J. 2005. *Écritures du voyage: Héritages et inventions dans la littérature latine tardive*, Paris.
Spevak, O. 2005. *La concession en latin*, Brussels.
Spevak, O. 2006. '*Tamen:* Essai d'une description syntaxique', *Glotta* 82, 221–48.
Spevak, O. 2014. *The Noun Phrase in Classical Latin Prose*, Leiden.
Staat, K. 2023. 'Between Reading and Viewing: Mapping and Experiencing Rome and Other Spaces', *JOLCEL* 8, 7–42.
Stadermann, C. 2023. 'Between Rome and Toulouse: The Catholic Episcopate in the *regnum Tolosanum* (418–507)', in D. Castro and F. Ruchesi, eds., *Leadership, Social Cohesion, and Identity in Late Antique Spain and Gaul (500–700)*, Amsterdam, 215–55.
Stein, C. 2015. 'Épigraphie et mise en scène de la domination sociale dans la Gaule méridionale tardive (IVe-VIe s.): A propos de la tombe du grand-père de Sidoine Apollinaire', in S. Agusta-Boularot and E. Rosso, eds., *Signa et tituli: Monuments et espaces de représentation en Gaule Méridionale sous le regard croisé de la sculpture et de l'épigraphie (Mélanges Michel Janon)*, Paris, 191–205.
Stevens, C. E. 1933. *Sidonius Apollinaris and His Age*, Oxford.
Stevenson, W. 2014. 'Exiling Bishops: The Policy of Constantius II', *DOP* 68, 7–27.
Stoehr-Monjou, A. 2013. 'Sidonius and Horace: The Art of Memory', in van Waarden and Kelly 2013, 133–69.
Stoehr-Monjou, A. 2017. 'L'épitaphe funéraire en l'honneur de Sidoine Apollinaire, entre manuscrits, fragments de la stèle et tradition littéraire: à qui l'hommage est-il rendu?', *Bulletin de l'Association Antiquité tardive* 26, 74–9.
Stoehr-Monjou, A. 2020. 'Sidonius' Panegyrics', in Kelly and van Waarden 2020, 317–40.
Stoehr-Monjou, A. 2021. 'Enjeux mémoriels d'un récit de voyage de Lyon à Rome: Sidoine Apollinaire (Lettre 1, 5)', *Viatica HS* 4, doi .org/10.52497/viatica2059.
Stoehr-Monjou, A. 2024. 'Poetics of Conclusion in Sidonius' Letters (Books 7–9, *Epist.* 9.12–16)', in C. Guerra, M. Kersten, and A.-K. Stähle, eds., *The Dynamics of Paratextuality in Late Antique Literature: Stumbling Texts*, London, 53–70.
Susini, G. 1973. *The Roman Stonecutter: An Introduction to Latin Epigraphy*, Oxford.
Sykutris, J. 1931. 'Epistolographie', in *RE* Suppl. 5, 186–220.

Teitler, H. C. 1992. 'Un-Roman Activities in Late Antique Gaul: The Cases of Arvandus and Seronatus', in Drinkwater and Elton 1992, 309–18.
Toner, J. 2019. 'Decadence in Ancient Rome', in J. Desmarais and D. Weir, eds., *Decadence and Literature*, Cambridge, 15–29.
Toynbee, J. M. C. 1973. *Animals in Roman Life and Art*, London.
Traube, L. 1904. 'Bamberger Fragmente der vierten Dekade des Livius', in L. Traube, *Palaeographische Forschungen*, vol. 4, Munich, 3–44.
Treu, M., ed., 1959. *Archilochos*, Munich.
Uggeri, G. 1987. 'La navigazione interna della Cisalpina in età romana', *AAAD* 29, 305–54.
Uggeri, G. 1990. 'Aspetti archeologici della navigazione interna nella Cisalpina', *AAAD* 36, 175–96.
Urlacher-Becht, C. 2023. '"Gaule" et "Italie" dans les épîtres de la fin Ve-début VIe siècle: Stratégies littéraires et enjeux identitaires', *ASNP* s. 5, 15, 309–53.
Valditara, G. 2018. 'Roman Law and Civil Law Reflections upon the Meaning of *Iniuria* in *Damnum Iniuria Datum*', in P. J. du Plessis, ed., *Wrongful Damage to Property in Roman Law: British Perspectives*, Edinburgh, 224–54.
Valentini, R., and G. Zucchetti, eds., 1942. *Codice topografico della città di Roma*, 2nd ed., Rome.
van Dam, H.-J. 2008. '*Vobis pagina nostra dedicatur*: Dedication in Classical Antiquity', in I. Bossuyt et al., eds., *Cui dono lepidum novum libellum? Dedicating Latin Works and Motets in the Sixteenth Century*, Leuven, 13–34.
van den Hout, M. P. J. 1999. *A Commentary on the Letters of M. Cornelius Fronto*, Leiden.
Van Hoof, L., and P. Van Nuffelen 2020. *The Fragmentary Latin Histories of Late Antiquity (AD 300–620): Edition, Translation and Commentary*, Cambridge.
van Waarden, J. A. 2010. *Writing to Survive: A Commentary on Sidonius Apollinaris, Letters Book 7*, vol. 1 *The Episcopal Letters 1–11*, Leuven.
van Waarden, J. A. 2011. 'Sidonio Apollinare, poeta e vescovo', *VetChr* 48, 99–113.
van Waarden, J. A. 2016. *Writing to Survive: A Commentary on Sidonius Apollinaris, Letters Book 7*, vol. 2 *The Ascetic Letters 12–18*, Leuven.
van Waarden, J. A. 2018. '"Il tempo invecchia in fretta": La biografia di Sidonio Apollinare nella sua corrispondenza', *InvLuc* 40, 187–98.
van Waarden, J. 2020a. '*Amicitia, Otium*, and the Chronotope of Sidonius's Correspondence', *JLA* 13, 149–72.
van Waarden, J. 2020b. 'A Biography of Sidonius in Photo-Negative', in Kelly and van Waarden 2020, 13–28.
van Waarden, J. 2020c. 'The Emergence of the Gallic Rogations in a Cognitive Perspective', in N. M. Vos and A. C. Geljon, eds., *Rituals*

in Early Christianity: New Perspectives on Tradition and Transformations, Leiden, 201–20.
van Waarden, J. 2020d. 'Sidonius Reception: Sixteenth to Nineteenth Centuries', in Kelly and van Waarden 2020, 686–704.
van Waarden, J. 2020e. '"You" and "I" in Sidonius' Correspondence', in Kelly and van Waarden 2020, 418–39.
van Waarden, J. 2021. 'Symmachus and the Metamorphosis of "You and I" in Epistolary Usage', in A. Bruzzone, A. Fo, and L. Piacente, eds., *Metamorfosi del classico in età romanobarbarica*, Florence, 145–61.
van Waarden, J. 2022a. 'Leafing through Pliny with Sidonius: Sidon. *Ep.* 1.1, Plin. *Ep.* 1.1, 1.2, and 1.5, and Satire', *Mnemosyne* 75, 1021–43.
van Waarden, J. 2022b. 'The Proportions of Latin Letter Collections: A Probe', in S. Fascione, ed., *Concatenantur sibi epistulae nostrae: Reading Ancient Latin Letter Collections*, Foggia, 57–70.
van Waarden, J. 2023. 'A Gentleman Weighs His "You and I": Inclusion in the Letters of Faustus, Mamertus Claudianus, Ruricius, Avitus and Ennodius', in Meurer and Egetenmeyr 2023, 91–115.
van Waarden, J. 2024. 'The Death and Public Rehabilitation of Apollinaris the Elder: Intertextuality with Lucan in Sidonius Apollinaris, *Epist.* 3.12', *CQ* 74, 309–14.
van Waarden, J. forthcoming. 'Sidonius' Journey to Rome and Ockham's Razor: An Essay', in S. DiGiulio and D. Machado, eds., *Poeticis magis decora? Latin Prose and the Limits of Intertextuality*.
van Waarden, J. A., and G. Kelly, eds., 2013. *New Approaches to Sidonius Apollinaris*, Leuven.
van Waarden, J., and G. Kelly 2020. 'Prose Rhythm in Sidonius', in Kelly and van Waarden 2020, 462–75.
Vives Gatell, J. 1963. *Concilios visigóticos e hispano-romanos*, Barcelona.
Vogel, C. 1962. '*Sol aequinoctialis:* Problèmes et technique de l'orientation dans le culte chrétien', *RSR* 36, 175–211.
Wallraff, M. 2004. 'Gerichtetes Gebet: Wie und warum richten Juden und Christen in der Spätantike ihre Sakralbauten aus?', in A. Gerhards and H. H. Henrix, eds., *Dialog oder Monolog? Zur liturgischen Beziehung zwischen Judentum und Christentum*, Freiburg, 110–27.
Ward-Perkins, B. 2005. *The Fall of Rome and the End of Civilization*, Oxford.
Webb, R. 2009. *Ekphrasis, Imagination and Persuasion in Ancient Rhetorical Theory and Practice*, Abingdon.
Weiler, I. 1981. *Der Sport bei den Völkern der alten Welt*, Darmstadt.
West, M. L. 1992. *Ancient Greek Music*, Oxford.
Westenholz, W. 2023. 'When You Have Nothing Nice To Say …: Some Unkind Letters of Recommendation from the Pen of Sidonius Apollinaris', in Meurer and Egetenmeyr 2023, 283–300.

Westenholz, W. forthcoming. *Gaining and Wielding Influence: A Commentary on Book 6 of the Letters of Sidonius Apollinaris*, Edinburgh.
White, P. 2010. *Cicero in Letters: Epistolary Relations of the Late Republic*, Oxford.
White, P. 2018. 'Senatorial Epistolography from Cicero to Sidonius: Emergence of a Genre', *BICS* 61, 7–21.
Whitton, C. 2013. *Pliny the Younger, Epistles Book 2*, Cambridge.
Whitton, C. 2019. *The Arts of Imitation in Latin Prose: Pliny's Epistles/ Quintilian in Brief*, Cambridge.
Wickham, C. 2005. *Framing the Early Middle Ages: Europe and the Mediterranean, 400–800*, Oxford.
Wickham, C. 2009. *The Inheritance of Rome: A History of Europe from 400 to 1000*, London.
Williams, G. 2002. 'Ovid's Exile Poetry: *Tristia, Epistulae ex Ponto* and *Ibis*', in P. Hardie, ed., *The Cambridge Companion to Ovid*, Cambridge, 233–45.
Williams, J. 2014. 'Letter Writing, Materiality, and Gifts in Late Antiquity: Some Perspectives on Material Culture', *JLA* 7, 351–59.
Winterbottom, M. 1974. 'Introduction', in M. Winterbottom, ed., *Seneca the Elder. Declamations*, Cambridge MA, vii–xxiv.
Winterbottom, M. 1982. 'Literary Criticism', in E. J. Kenney and W. V. Clausen, eds., *The Cambridge History of Classical Literature*, vol. 2 *Latin Literature*, Cambridge, 33–50.
Wojtczak, M. 2021. '*Audientia sacerdotalis*? Remarks on the Legal Nature of Dispute Resolution by Ecclesiastics in Late Antiquity', *ZAC* 25, 108–49.
Wolff, É. 2012. 'La description par Sidoine de son voyage à Rome (Lettres I, 5)', *Itineraria* 11, 1–12.
Wolff, É. 2014. 'Sidoine Apollinaire et la poésie épigraphique', in A. Pistellato, ed., *Memoria poetica e poesia della memoria: La versificazione epigrafica dall'antichità all'umanesimo*, Venice, 207–18.
Wolff, É. 2016. 'Sidoine Apollinaire voyageur', *AT* 24, 193–201.
Wolff, É. 2020. 'Sidonius' Vocabulary, Syntax, and Style', in Kelly and van Waarden 2020, 395–417.
Wolff, É. 2021. 'Quelques remarques sur la lettre V, 14 de Sidoine Apollinaire et les rogations', in M. Simon and É. Wolff, eds., *Operae pretium facimus: Mélanges en l'honneur de Charles Guittard*, Paris, 759–65.
Wolfram, H. 1988. *History of the Goths*, Berkeley, CA.
Wood, I. N. 2000. 'The North-Western Provinces', in Cameron et al. 2000, 497–524.
Wood, I. N. 2012. 'Family and Friendship in the West', in Johnson 2012, 416–36.
Wood, I. N. 2014. *The Merovingian Kingdoms 450–751*, Abingdon.

Wood, I. N. 2016. 'The Legislation of *Magistri Militum*: The Laws of Gundobad and Sigismund', *Clio@Themis* online 10, 1–16, doi .org/10.35562/cliothemis.1191.
Wood, I. N. 2017. 'Burgundian Law-Making, 451–534', *IRLH* online 3, 1–27, doi.org/10.13130/2464-8914/12878.
Wood, I. N. 2022. *The Christian Economy of the Early Medieval West: Towards a Temple Society*, Binghamton, NY.
Wood, I. N. 2023. 'The Silence of Sidonius', in A. Campus, A. Chahoud, G. Lusini, and S. Marchesini, eds., Tempus tacendi: *Quando il silenzio comunica*, Verona, 213–28.
Wuilleumier, P. 1953. *Lyon, métropole des Gaules*, Paris.
Yegül, F. 2009. *Bathing in the Roman World*, Cambridge.
Young, F. M. 1997. *Biblical Exegesis and the Formation of Christian Culture*, Cambridge.
Zelzer, M. 1997. 'Die Briefliteratur', in L. J. Engels and H. Hofmann, eds., *Neues Handbuch der Literaturwissenschaft*, vol. 4 *Spätantike*, Wiesbaden, 321–53.
Zetzel, J. E. G. 1980. 'The Subscriptions in the Manuscripts of Livy and Fronto and the Meaning of *Emendatio*', *CPh* 75, 38–59.
Zetzel, J. E. G. 2018. *Critics, Compilers, and Commentators: An Introduction to Roman Philology, 200 BCE–800 CE*, Oxford.
Zeumer, K., ed., 1902. *Leges nationum Germanicarum*, vol. 1 *Leges Visigothorum*, Hanover.
Zoeter, M. 2018. *Reading the Future, Writing the Present: A Literary and Interpretive Commentary on Sidonius Apollinaris Letter 8.11*, doi.org/10.11588/propylaeumdok.00006792.
Zöllner, E. 1979. *Geschichte der Franken bis zur Mitte des sechsten Jahrhunderts*, Munich.

INDEX

PLACES

Adda, river 77
Adige (*Athesis*), river 77–8
Adriatic Sea 77, 79, 81–2
Aix 206
Alexandria 141, 214, 217–18
Allier, river 139
Alps, mountain range 70, 74–6, 78, 87, 178
   Alpis Cottia Pass (Mont-Genèvre) 76
   Alpis Graia Pass (Petit-Saint-Bernard) 76
Angers 163
Anio, river 84
Antioch 214, 217–18
Aquileia 78
Aquitaine (*Aquitania*) 105, 116, 149, 234, 246
Aracynthus, mountain 106
Arles 60, 80, 105, 176, 179, 188, 206, 247–8, 251
   capital of the Gauls 1, 157
Arpinum 135, 172
Athens
   Athenaeum 109
Auvergne 2–3, 8, 17, 71, 92, 122, 139, 144, 150, 152, 170, 177–8, 185, 198, 204, 210, 237, 262
Auxerre 59, 183, 246, 248

Bayeux 210
Boeotia 238
Bordeaux 7, 214, 233–4
Bourges 12, 144, 183, 246
   election speech 4–5
Brescello (*Brixillum*) 79
Brioude 60, 197–8
Britain 144
Brittany (*Armorica*) 144, 248

Capua 199, 202
Carcassonne 3, 236
Carthage 7, 214, 217
   citadel Byrsa 218
Catalaunian Fields 247
Caucasus (Hindu Kush), mountain range 240

Clermont (*Augustonemetum, Aruerni*) 2 and *passim*
   cathedral church 129
   church of St Saturninus 3, 261
   monastery of St Quiricus 209–10
Clitumnus, river 84
Constantinople 8, 73, 96, 214, 217–18
Cremona 78–9

Dalmatia, province 82
Déols 144
Dyrrhachium 205

Egypt 241
Ethiopia 231
Euphrates, river 216, 220

Fabaris, river 84
Fano (*Fanum Fortunae*) 82
Frigidus, river 234
Fucinus, Lake 83

Gardon, river 107, 118
Gaul 1 and *passim*
   Cisalpine 80
   dioceses
     Galliae 157
     Septem Prouinciae 157, 186, 204
     Viennensis (later *Septem Prouinciae*) 157, 186
   Prefecture of the Gauls 157
Geneva 162, 164, 183
Gibraltar, Strait of 8
Grigny 208, 220–1
   monastery of St Ferreolus 221

Helicon, mountain 238
Hippocrene, spring 238

India 230, 240
Italy 8, 10, 71, 78, 81, 93, 98, 104, 151, 178–9, 188, 234
   Prefecture of Italy and Africa 157
   provinces and regions
     Aemilia et Liguria 79
     Apulia et Calabria 82

Flaminia et Picenum 82
Puglia 82
Tuscany 84
Tuscia et Umbria 82
Umbria 83–4
Venetia et Histria 79

Jerusalem 214, 217
Jura, mountain range 13

Lambro, river 77
Lérins, monastery 13, 60, 113, 208–10, 220–1, 247–8, 254
Lesbos 255
Livia/Liviana, fortress 3, 228, 236
Loire (*Liger*), river 8, 144, 162–3, 189, 240
Lyon (*Lugdunum*) 1–4, 8, 59–60, 70, 72, 75, 107, 122–3, 127, 139, 148, 150, 161–4, 169–70, 172, 176–7, 181, 221, 233, 246–8, 254, 262
    Burgundian court 163
    cemeteries (Trion, St Irenaeus, St Just) 149–50, 152
    Fourvière Hill 149, 152
    port 133
    road to Narbonne 149
    road to the Auvergne 149–50, 152
    St Irenaeus' (St John's) 149
    St John the Baptist (cathedral) 125, 132, 149
        dedication 59, 120–1, 128
    St Just's (Maccabees) 149
    St Stephen's (baptistry) 125

Mantua 78–9
Marseille 13, 183, 188, 200, 206
Metaurus, river 82, *see also* Topics: History: Roman Empire
Milan (*Mediolanum*) 7, 197
    emblem a sow 218
    imperial residence 79, 214, 218
    S. Ambrogio 197
Mincio, river 77
Mytilene 255

Nar, river 84
Narbonne (*Narbo*) 1, 5, 73, 106, 236–7, *see also* Topics: Philosophy

Nîmes (*Nemausus*) 101, 103–5, 107, 112, 118
Nysa, mountain 106

Orléans (*Cenabum, Aureliani*) 229, 245–8
    bishops' list 246

Padua 78
Persia 209, 216, 254
Philippi *see* Topics: History: Roman Empire
Piacenza (*Placentia*) 78
Po (*Padus, Eridanus*), river 70, 77–80
Provence 3, 8, 13, 75, 150, 176, 198–9, 206, 246

Ravenna 7, 70–2, 77, 79–81, 178, 198
    Caesarea 79
    Classis 79
    Fossa Augusta 79
    imperial residence 79, 214, 218
    Via Caesaris 79
Rhine, river 7, 239–40
Rhône (*Rhodanus*), river 13, 75, 118, 189, 221, 246
Rieti 84
Riez 206
Rimini (*Ariminum*) 77, 81–2, 186, 188–90
Rodez 105
Rome 2, 7–8, 11, 17–18, 59, 63, 70–3, 75, 77, 79, 81–5, 88, 92–3, 98, 105, 109, 156–7, 164, 166, 186, 189, 192, 197, 202–4, 207, 210, 214, 216–18, 238, 256
    comitium 98
    Forum of Trajan 2, 170, 258
    imperial residence 79
    Janiculus Hill 132
    Mausoleum Hadriani 84
    Muri Aureliani 85
    Naumachia Traiani (or *Vaticana*) 84
    new Christian buildings 72
    pilgrim guides 85
    pomerium 84–5
    public spaces and buildings still in use 72
    'refoundation' 85
    rostra 98

Rome (cont.)
  S. Agnese fuori le mura 126
  S. Maria Maggiore 126
  S. Sabina 126
  S. Sebastiano on the Via Appia 85
  St Paul's (S. Paolo fuori le mura) 85
  St Peter's (S. Pietro) 84–5, 194
  Vatican Hill, 85
Rubicon, river 76, 81

Salona 82
Saône (*Arar*), river 133, 149
Sapaudia (Savoy) 162
Spain (*Iberia*) 7, 104, 188, 239, 261
Susa 76, 216

Tiber, river 84–5
Toulouse 7, 70, 122, 261
  Capitoline temple 261
  Visigothic court 86, 169, 233, 261
Tournai 183
Tours 210
  basilica of St Martin 121, 126, 129, 246
Trier 173
  capital of the Gauls 157
  imperial residence 214
Troy 159, 194
Troyes 247

Vaison 105, 186, *see also* Topics: History: Gaul
Valois 13
Velinus, Lake 84
Verona 78
Vicus Helena 23, 167
Vienne 22–3, 25, 76, 105, 162, 164, 176, 185–8, 190–1, 196–8, 221
  capital of *Viennensis* 186
  disasters 191–2
  nunnery 140

uillae
  Auitacum (Aydat?), Papianilla's estate 2, 10, 101–2, 115, 118, 120, 142, 176–7, 180, 1
  Laurentinum, estate of Pliny the Younger 101, 104, 106, 115
  Prusianum, Tonantius Ferreolus' estate 101, 105, 115, 120
  Treuidon, estate of Tonantius Ferreolus 105
  Tusci, estate of Pliny the Younger 101, 106, 115
  Vorocingus, Apollinaris' estate 101, 105, 115, 120

Waal (*Va(c)halis*), river 239

PERSONS

Abbreviations: *cos.* = *consul*; MVM = *Magister Vtriusque Militiae*; PPG = *Praefectus Praetorio Galliarum*; PPO = *Praefectus Praetorio*; PVR = *Praefectus Vrbi Romae*

Abraham, abbot of Clermont 208–9, 212–17, 219–20
  epitaph 4, 209, 214–15
Abraham, patriarch 209, 219
Achilles 143, 159
Adam 220
Ado of Vienne
  Chronicon 187
Aegidius, MVM (456/7–63) 162
Aeneas 83, 194, 211
Aëtius, MVM (433–54) 7, 247
Agricola, son of Eparchius Avitus, addressee of *Ep.* 2.12 138–9, 176
Agroecius, bishop of Sens 124
  Ars de orthographia 168

Alaric I, king of the Visigoths (d. 410) 7, 77
Alaric II, king of the Visigoths (484–507) 234
Alcima, daughter of Sidonius 2
Alemans, people 162
Alexander the Great 148, 159, 203, 217
Alypia, daughter of Anthemius 70, 86, 88
Amantius, tradesman from Clermont 200, 206
Ambrose, bishop of Milan 137, 197, 216
Amphion 174
Anianus, bishop of Orléans 245–9

INDEX

Anonyma (Avita?), mother of Sidonius 1, 10, 175–7, 181
Anonymae, Sidonius' sisters 10, 177, 181
Anonymi, uncles of Sidonius 156
Anonymus (Alcimus?), father of Sidonius 1, 7, 156
Anthemius, emperor (467–72) 2, 8, 70–1, 82, 86, 90, 93, 96, 98, 100, 178–9, 219
  second consulship (468) 72, 89
Antoninus Pius, emperor (138–61) 239
Apollinares, family 10, 155, 177, 210
Apollinaris the Elder, grandfather of Sidonius 7, 149–51, 154, 156–7, 212
  PPO (408–9) 1, 7, 148, 151
  rehabilitation 148
  tomb and epitaph 4, 148–52, 154, 156, 266
Apollinaris, cousin (?) of Sidonius 101, 103, 105, 108, 115–17, 156
Apollinaris, son of Sidonius 2, 149, 210, 250–2
Apollo 238
Apollonius of Tyana 13, 228–32, 234, 240–2
Apuleius 22, 112, 135, 192, 202, 217–18, 244
  translation of Plato's *Phaedo* 112
Arcadius, eastern emperor (383–408) 166
Archilochus 173
Argentaria Polla 137
Aristotle 16, 227, 234
Arvandus, *PPG* (464–8) 2, 71, 89, 105, 150, 155, 204, 243
Athanasius
  Life of Antony 246
Attila, king of the Huns 2, 93, 105, 245, 247–8
Augustine of Hippo 14–15, 18, 92, 110–11, 137, 143, 158
Aurelian, emperor (270–5) 248
Ausonius 22–3, 65, 67, 122, 125, 209, 214–15, 217, 254
  Mosella 71, 73, 77, 118
  Ordo urbium nobilium 73
Auxanius, abbot of Clermont 208, 221
Avienus, Gennadius, Roman senator 90, 93–5

Aviti, family 1, 10, 102, 176, 210
Avitus, Alcimus, bishop of Vienne 25, 140, 187
Avitus, bishop of Clermont 183
Avitus, Eparchius, emperor (455–6), Sidonius' father-in-law 1–2, 7–8, 70, 72, 78, 86, 93–4, 96, 99, 138, 156, 176, 247

Basilius, Caecina, Roman senator 88, 90, 93–5, 97
Beroaldo, Filippo 26
Bonifatius, *MVM* (432) 7
Britons, people 145, 147–8
Brutus 79
Burgundians, people 3, 13, 144–5, 150, 162–4, 170, 175, 185–7, 189, 198, 203, 240
  Lex Burgundionum 169
  Lex Romana Burgundionum 9, 169

Caesar, C. Iulius 8, 81–2, 94, 148, 159, 174, 186–8, 199, 202, 205, 248
  copy of his works 232
Caesennia 137
Calpurnia 135–6, 176
Camillus 242
Cassian of Marseille 13, 113, 129, 209, 219
Cassiodorus 239
Cassius 79
Cato the Elder (*Censor*) 61
Cato the Younger (*Uticensis*) 94, 135
Catullus 22, 125, 136–7, 238
Chilperic II, king of the Burgundians (472–93) 169, 198
Chiron 143
Cicero 15–16, 22–3, 25, 57–9, 64–6, 100, 112, 114, 134–5, 141, 144, 172, 239, 251–2, 255, 264
  translation of Demosthenes' *On the Crown* 112
Cincinnatus 157, 242
Claudian 4, 22–3, 77–8, 125
  Carmina minora 4
  Panegyricus de VI consulatu Honorii 71
Clio 99
Consentius the Elder of Narbonne 124, 168
  Ars de barbarismis et metaplasmis 124, 168

Consentius of Narbonne, dedicatee of
  Carm. 23 13, 124, 168
Constans, *caesar* (408–9/10) 7
Constantine (Constantinus III),
  usurper (407–11) 7
Constantine I, emperor (306–37) 178
Constantius II, emperor (337–61) 164
Constantius III (Flavius Constantius),
  MVM, emperor (421) 7
Constantius of Lyon
  dedicatee of the correspondence 12,
    17–18, 57, 59–60, 63, 127,
    139, 222–3, 225, 227, 230,
    250, 252
  Life of Germanus 59, 122, 246, 249
Corinna 136
Cratia 135
Cyclopes 211
Cynthia 137
Cyprian 242

Dardanus, Claudius Postumus, *PPG*
  (412–13) 7
Decius 93, 199, 202–3, 261
Delia 137
Democritus 234
Demosthenes 58, 64
  On the Crown 12
Dido 128, 196, 213, 218
Diocletian, emperor (284–305) 6
Diogenes 143
Dion of Prusa 115
Domitian, emperor (81–96) 59, 231
Domnitius, addressee of *Ep.* 4.20
  162–3
Donidius, addressee of *Ep.* 2.9 103,
  120

Ecdicius, son of Eparchius Avitus 138,
  175, 177–8, 203, 210
  promotion to *patricius* 142, 176
Eleutherius, addressee of *Ep.* 6.11 183
Elissa *see* Persons: Dido
Ennodius, bishop of Pavia 25, 251, 255
Eucherius, bishop of Lyon 251, 254
Euganei, people 78
Eugenius, usurper (393–4) 234
Eulalia, cousin of Sidonius 110
Euric, king of the Visigoths (466/7–
  84) 3, 8, 13, 20, 70, 169,
  176–8, 199, 206–7, 229–30,
  232–4, 236–7, 239–41, 245,
  258

Eusebius of Caesarea 12
  Church History 111

Fago, stage character 173
Faustus, bishop of Riez 2, 12–13, 81,
  125, 141, 145, 150, 237
  praise in *Carm.* 16 249
Ferreolus and Julian, pair of martyrs
  197
Ferreolus, saint 197–8
Filimatia 180, 212
Firminus, dedicatee of Book 9 12, 17,
  250–3, 255
Florentinus, addressee of *Ep.* 4.19 160
Franks, people 144, 162–4, 166, 189,
  202, 210
  Ripuarian 162
  Salian 162, 240
Fronto 15–16, 22, 58, 61, 65–6,
  135, 141, 144, 192, 202, 239,
  244

Gaetulicus 137
Galen 83
Galla Placidia, imperial regent
  (425–37) 7, 80
Gaudentius, *uicarius* 150, 154
Gelasius, correspondent 250–1, 255
Gellius, Aulus 22, 67, 81, 192, 218
  Noctes Atticae 61
Germanus, bishop of Auxerre 60,
  246–8
Gerontius, usurper (407–11) 7
Gervasius and Protasius, pair of
  martyrs 197
Glycerius, emperor (473–4) 179
Graecus, bishop of Marseille,
  addressee of *Ep.* 7.7 199–200,
  208
Gregory, bishop of Tours 3, 5, 25, 122
  Histories 25, 187
Gundioc, king of the Burgundians
  (436–73) 162, 164, 169
Gundobad, king of the Burgundians
  (c. 474–516) 169

Hannibal 76, 82, 199, 202
Harilaüs/Charilaüs 173
Hasdrubal 82
Hector 159
Heraclitus 234
Heronius, addressee of *Epp.* 1.5 and
  1.9 72, 75, 89–90, 92, 98, 100

INDEX 299

Hesperius, addressee of *Ep.* 2.10 120–
  2, 124, 127, 134
Hippocrates 83
Homer 73, 82, 159
Honoratus, bishop of Arles 13
Honorius, emperor (395–423) 7, 81,
  156, 166
Horace 14, 17, 22–3, 64, 79, 81–2,
  111, 122, 142, 209, 211, 218,
  228, 250–1, 257, 261, 263–4
  Ars poetica 98, 105, 112, 114, 125,
    136, 212, 251, 259, 263
  closure *Epistles* Book 1, 223
  closure *Odes* Books 1–3 223
  interuallum lyricum 18
  voyage to Brindisi (*Sat.* 1.5) 71
Hortensius 135
Huns, people 2, 7, 105, 189, 229, 247

Jerome (Hieronymus) of Stridon 18,
  67, 111–12, 124, 241
Jesus 133
  Christus medicus 143
  and the demons 217
  and the Samaritan woman 81
  and the woman kissing his feet 196
Jews, people 14, 182–3, 254
John Chrysostom 15
Jovinus, usurper (411–13) 7, 151
Julia Domna, empress 230
Julian of Brioude, saint 2, 60, 197–8,
  210, 262
Julius Nepos, emperor (474–5) 8,
  176–9
Just (Justus), bishop of Lyon 123, 132,
  149, 163, 262
Justus, physician 143
Juvenal 22

Ketelaer and van Leempt
  editio princeps 1473/4 26

Lampridius 91, 229, 233–4
Leaena, stage character 237
Leo IV, pope 194
Leo of Narbonne, addressee of *Ep.* 8.3
  3, 9, 13, 86, 93, 169, 229,
  231–4, 236, 238–42, 244–5
Lesbia 136
Libanius 15
Licinianus 176–8
Livy 22–3, 81, 226, 244
  closure of Book 8 243–4

  revision 231–2
  subscriptiones (colophons) 231, 235,
    244
Lucan 7, 22–3, 131, 137, 148, 154,
  159, 186–8, 193, 199, 202,
  205
  Bellum ciuile 199
Lucilius 62, 71, 226
  Voyage to Sicily 71
Lucius Verus, co-emperor (161–9) 239
Lupus, bishop of Troyes 153, 215, 247,
  250

Machaon 143
Macrobius 113, 137, 172
  Saturnalia 235
Magnus Felix, *PPG, patricius* (469) 5,
  179
Majorian, emperor (457–61) 2, 8, 86,
  93, 96, 155, 162
Mamertus Claudianus 12, 23, 91, 137,
  187, 212, 232
  De statu animae 2, 23
Mamertus, bishop of Vienne,
  addressee of *Ep.* 7.1 9, 105,
  185–8, 191–2, 194–5, 197,
  247
Marcellinus, *patricius* 94, *see* Topics:
  History: Auvergne/Clermont
Marcia 135
Marcus Aurelius, emperor (161–80)
  66, 141, 239
Mars 167, 186
Martial 4, 22–3, 94, 98, 108, 121–2,
  125, 133, 137, 162, 222, 258,
  263
Martianus Capella
  Philologia 122
Martin, bishop of Tours, saint 13, 60,
  194, 216, 246
Mercury 122
Muses 238

Namatius, admiral of Euric 12
Namatius, bishop of Clermont 129
Nero, emperor (54–68) 58–9, 231
Nerva, emperor (96–8) 258
Nicomachi, family 231–2, 235, 244
Nicomachus Flavianus the Younger
  176, 234
Nicomachus Flavianus, Virius, cos.
  (394) 231–2, 234–5
Numa, king of Rome 254

Odoacer, *patricius* 8
Origen of Alexandria 14, 101, 111–13
  On First Principles 111
  (un)orthodoxy, 111–12
Ovid 22–3, 65, 117, 136, 146, 171,
    209, 236, 238, 251, 256
  Epistulae ex Ponto 168
  Tristia 168, 223

Papianilla, wife of Sidonius, addressee
    of *Ep.* 5.16 1–2, 10, 138–40,
    142, 158, 169, 175–8, 180–2,
    186
Papianilla, wife of Tonantius Ferreolus
    169
Patiens, bishop of Lyon 59–60, 120–3,
    126, 128–30, 148, 150, 153–
    4, 186, 247
Paul, apostle 143, 219
Paulinus, bishop of Nola 18
  church of St Felix 129–31, 134,
    219
Paulus, Gennadius, Roman senator 88,
    90–1
Pegasus 238
Perpetuus, bishop of Tours 60, 129,
    246
Peter and Paul, pair of apostles 70,
    85, 197
  earliest memorial site 85
Petrarch (Petrarca) 25, 64
Petronius, dedicatee of Book 8 252
Phaethon 77
Phaethon's sisters 77
Philemon and Baucis 218
Philostratus 228, 230–2, 235, 244
  Life of Apollonius of Tyana 13, 112,
    228, 235
  Sidonius' copy 231
  Lives of the Sophists 235
Pio, Giovanni Battista 26, 193
Plato 234
  Phaedo 112
Plautus 22, 81, 100, 114, 173, 200,
    237, 244
  Miles gloriosus 100
Pliny the Elder (C. Plinius Secundus)
  Historia naturalis 63
Pliny the Younger (C. Plinius Caecilius
    Secundus) 4, 15–18, 22–3,
    57–60, 63–7, 70, 74, 88–90,
    102, 104–6, 109, 111–13,
    115, 121, 124–5, 134–6, 138,
    141, 144, 149, 160, 172,
    175–6, 178, 207, 224–6, 228,
    239, 245, 250–3, 255
  Vesuvius letters 71
  villa letters 101
Pompey 7, 148, 154
  lament in Lucan's *Pharsalia* 154
Probus, emperor (276–82) 248
Propertius 104, 137
  closure *Elegies* Book 1 223
Prosper, bishop of Orléans, addressee
    of *Ep.* 8.15 245–6, 248
Prudentius 14, 22–3, 85, 111, 251,
    261–3
  Liber peristephanon 261
  Praefatio and *Epilogus* 251, 263
Ps.-Demetrius, epistolary theorist 226
Ps.-Libanius, epistolary theorist 226
Pudentilla 135
Pyrgopolinices, stage character 100
Pythagoras 13, 230, 234

Quintilian 172, 227, 252
Quiricus, saint 209, 215, *see also* Places:
    Clermont
Quirinus, *see* Persons: Romulus

Raphael, painter 194
Regulus 58–9
Ricimer, *patricius*, MVM (456–72) 2,
    8, 71–2, 77–8, 82, 86–7, 90,
    93, 162
  wedding 70, 86, 88
Riochatus 145
Riothamus, chieftain of the Britons,
    addressee of *Ep.* 3.9 144–5,
    147
  identified with King Arthur 145
Romulus 85, 217, 254, 257
Romulus and Remus, patrons of Rome
    85
Roscia, daughter of Sidonius 2, 140,
    142, 175–7, 181–2
Rufinus of Aquileia 111–12
Ruricius, bishop of Limoges 12, 25,
    122, 138–9
Rusticiana, wife of Symmachus 135
Rutilius Namatianus
  De reditu suo 71

Sallust 22, 65, 100
Salutati, Coluccio 25
Salvianus of Marseille 105

Saturninus of Toulouse, saint 3, 250, 256, 261–2
Savaron, Jean, 26, 85, 142, 152, 163, 200–1
Saxons, people 144, 240
Scylla 68–9
Secundinus, poet 127
Secundus, nephew of Sidonius, addressee of *Ep.* 3.12 16, 63, 148–50, 155–6, 158
Seleucus I Nicator 217
Seneca the Younger (L. Annaeus Seneca) 15
Seronatus, *uicarius VII prouinciarum* (469? –72?) 203–4
Severiana, daughter of Sidonius 2, 21, 138–40, 177, 181
Sidonius
  baptism 2, 81
  biography 1
  bishop of Clermont 3, 150
  Carmina minora (*Carm.* 9–24) 4–5, 62, 105, 110
  changing side to the Burgundians 8, 176, 186
  dating works 4–5, 22, 60, 72, 89, 103, 123, 139, 145, 150, 160, 163, 165, 170, 177, 183, 188, 200, 210, 223, 234, 246, 251
  death and burial 2, 3, 261
    epitaph 157–8, 169, 215, 265
    tombstone 3, 265
  embassy to Rome 2, 22, 71, 88, 96, 139
  Epistulae 4, *see also* Topics: Letter writing
    aims 18
    letters to bishops 182
    mirror of princes (*Ep.* 8.3.3) 241
    publication 18
    refusal to write history (*Ep.* 8.15) 245
    structure 16, 57, 89
    age as metaphor 253, 260
    Book 1 17
    Books 1–7 5, 16–17, 62, 183, 211, 222–3, 250
    Books 8 and 9 5, 18, 222–3, 229, 233, 250
    closure/*sphragis* 4, 18, 222–3, 250, 263, 264
  Epithalamium of Polemius and Araneola (*Carm.* 14–15) 134

Epithalamium of Ruricius and Hiberia (*Carm.* 10–11) 134
exile 3, 5, 210, 212, 215, 223, 229, 233, 237–8
honorific statue 2, 170, 250, 258
knowledge of Greek 232
missae 5
network 60, 75, 92, 169
Panegyric of Anthemius 2, 71, 86, 99, 170, 257–8
Panegyric of Avitus 2, 96, 257–8
Panegyric of Majorian 2, 96
Panegyrics, *Carm.* 1–8 4
patricius 2, 178
pessimism vs hope in youth 1, 10, 17, 121, 149, 207–8, 227, 250, 253
poems in the letters (*Carm.* 25–41) 4
poetry and the bishop 17, 209, 211, 214, 230, 250–1, 260–1
PVR 2, 71, 105, 178–9, 250, 258
retirement into *otium* 2, 103, 139, 155
Sigismer, Frankish (?) prince 21, 161–2, 164–5, 167
Sigismund, king of the Burgundians (516–24) 169
Silius Italicus 23, 199, 202–3, 218, 262
Simplicius, cousin (?) of Sidonius 105, 156, 237
Sirmond, Jacques 26, 143, 201, 232
Socrates 234
Solon 169, 174
Statius 22–3, 118, 131, 137, 251
  Siluae 4
Stilicho, *MVM* (394–408) 7, 87
Suetonius 22
Sulpicius Severus
  Life of St Martin 246
Syagrius, addressee of *Ep.* 5.5 9, 124, 167–70, 174–5, 233
Syagrius, Fl. Afranius, *cos.* (382) 169–70
Symmachi, family 16, 62, 135, 231–2, 235, 244
Symmachus 4, 15–16, 22, 57–8, 63–4, 66, 134–5, 141, 144, 160, 172, 176, 225, 232, 234–5, 244, 252

Tacitus 81, 207
Tantalus 81
Terence 22, 81, 100, 244
  Eunuchus 100

Terentia 135, 176
Terentianus Maurus 262
Tertullian 221, 242
   De spectaculis 87
Thaumastus, cousin (?) of Sidonius
   105, 156, 186
Theoderic I, king of the Visigoths
   (418–51) 7, 247
Theoderic II, king of the Visigoths
   (453–66/7) 8, 70, 113, 165
Theoderic the Great, king of the
   Ostrogoths (475–526) 81,
   239
Thrasea Paetus 59
Thraso, stage character 99
Tibullus 137
Titianus 58–9, 65–6
Titus, emperor (79–81) 217
Tonantius Ferreolus, *PPG* (451–2/3)
   101, 103, 105, 108, 115, 169,
   170
Tonantius, son of Tonantius Ferreolus
   115, 250–1
Trajan, emperor (98–117) 63, 89, 102,
   115, 207, 258
Tullia 141, 176

Valentinian III, emperor (425–55) 7,
   94, 156
Vandals, people 7–8, 71, 93–4, 239

Varro 14, 22, 110–11, 118, 173,
   217–18
   Libri logistorici 12
Veneti, people 78
Venus 167
Victorianus, Tascius 231–2, 234–5
Victorius, *comes ciuitatis* (*c.* 471–79/80)
   3, 208, 210, 212–13
Vincent of Lérins 218
   Commonitorium 218
Virgil 22–3, 64, 68, 78–9, 84, 100,
   136, 143, 172, 209, 211, 223,
   262
   closure *Georgics* 222
Visigoths, people 3, 7–10, 13, 17, 23,
   60, 71, 104–5, 163, 176,
   179–80, 185–6, 188–9, 198,
   203, 206, 210, 240, 245, 247
   Codex Euriciana 240
   Lex Romana Visigothorum 9, 153, 169,
   240
Vitruvius 141, 226
Volusianus, bishop of Tours 210
Volusianus, addressee of *Ep.* 7.17
   210–11, 220
Vulcan 117, 211

Yazdgird II, king of Persia (438–57)
   216

TOPICS

Architecture
   aedes 125–6
   apse 126, 129–31
   atrium 131–2
   basilica (church) 125, 127
   basilica (hall) 258
   colour and radiance 130–1
   dimensions 129
   domus ecclesiae 129, 190
   ecclesia 125
   marbles 116, 131–2
   mosaic 14, 126–8, 131
   orientation 130, 133
   porticus 131–2, 258
   vault 131

Books
   codex 18, 110, 225
   libellus 62, 224, 252

   liber 62, 226
   opus 62, 223, 225, 263
   opusculum 62, 68
   papyrus 119
   translatio 236
   translation 101, 111–12, 124, 135,
   235–6
   uolumen 62, 236

Catalogues/lists
   authors 63–4, 135
   events 24, 87
   fish 118
   laudes urbium 73, 214, 217
   learned women 134, 136
   philosophers 234
   properties 24, 91, 93
   rivers 73, 77, 83
   subjects 91

INDEX 303

travelogue 73
troops 83
Christianity, 13
  Arianism 13, 197
  asceticism 12–13, 17, 208, 215, 242
  baptism 158
  Bible 22, 111, 209, 227–8
    Book of Esther 254
    story of Tobias 23, 102, 107
  confessor 141, 197
  conuersus, 14, 59, 81, 126, 139, 154, 210–11, 219, 227
  Council of Orange (441) 213
  Council of Orléans (511) 187
  cult of relics 14, 187, 197, 209–10
  cult of saints 14, 85, 129, 187, 197–8, 215, 262
    translatio 197
  demons 217
  ecclesiastics 13, 86, 148, 212, 254
  episcopal authority and crisis management 186–7, 247
  episcopal exile 237
  episcopalis audientia 182
  hagiography 5, 14, 187, 209, 230, 245, 249
  holy (wo)men 214, 230, 245
  homoean heterodoxy 13, 184–5
  laity 113, 254
  liturgy 133, 187, 213
    Gallican 187
  martyrs 85, 197, 215–16, 250–1, 256, 261
  miracles 14, 194, 208, 210
    uirtutes 'miracles' 194, 216
  monastic rules 13, 209–10, 220–1
    Rule of Benedict 221
  monasticism 13, 113, 209–10
  Nicene Creed and orthodoxy 13, 90, 101, 111–12, 122, 158, 185, 221, 236, 242
  paradise 105, 121, 208, 216, 219–20
  Pelagianism 248
  predestination 122
  Rogationes 3, 185, 187–8, 191, 247
  (sacro)sanctus 59, 114, 153, 196
  Semipelagianism 13
  sin 195
  soul, nature of 12–13
  spirituality Aquitaine vs Provence 13, 60, 246
Climate
  air and vapours 83, 141

  Atabulus (sirocco) 82
  health and countryside 138–9, 141–2
  malaria 83, 141
  miasma theory 141
  natural disasters 187–8, 247
  seasons as metaphor 253, 255
Crafts and transport
  barge haulers on the Saône 9, 132–3
  corpse bearers 152
  crews on the river Po 9, 79
  cursus publicus 72, 75–7
  merchants 183, 200
  stone-cutter 155
  Tabula Peutingeriana 75
  Via Aemilia 77
  Via Domitia 104
  Via Flaminia 82, 84, 132
  Via Popilia 79
  Via Salaria 132
  Via Triumphalis 85
Culture
  ascetic lifestyle 13, 229–30, 241–2
  Christianitas 72, 185
  defence of Roman culture and language 19, 124, 168, 253
  disciplina 63, 92, 124, 172
  doctrina 11, 90, 92, 111, 158, 182, 238
  exempla 120–1, 134, 159, 193
  exemplary times of Trajan 11, 102, 207, 258
  knowledge of Greek 11, 112, 231–2
  libertas 157, 201, 207, 227
  maturitas 63, 172
  musical instruments 174
  otium, aristocratic leisure 2, 11, 101, 103, 113, 127, 240
  theme of Book 2 17, 101, 122
  republican virtues 157
  res publica (commonwealth) 179
  Romanitas 11, 72, 102, 185, 202
  scientia 92, 110, 138
  Trojan descent of the Gallo-Romans 202, 207

Grammar
  attrib. adj. vs gen. of noun 78, 95, 107, 143, 151
  epistolary perfect tense 67, 224
  gerundive as fut. pass. part. 97, 134, 142, 170, 195, 208, 215
  inverse genitive 83, 192–3, 195, 205

INDEX

Grammar (cont.)
  pronouns
    hic = *huc* 80
    iste = *hic* 133, 196
  suffixes
    -(i)tas 90
    -alis 151
    -bilis 81, 128, 146, 161, 254
    -c(e) 69, 128
    -urire 69, 224
    suus = *eius/eorum/earum* 153
  verb endings
    -ēre = *-ērunt* 81
    -re = *-ris* 95
  verbal infix *-tit-* 86, 90

History
  Auvergne/Clermont
    coniuratio Marcelliniana (457) 94
    Jewish community 183
    negotiations with Euric 198–9, 206
    surrender 3, 185, 198–9, 207, 240
    Visigothic offensive 180, 186, 188, 198, 201
  Gaul 8, 247
    cooperation with the Visigoths 1, 3, 70, 176, 203–4, 229, 232
    Council of the Seven Provinces 8, 206
    factions 3, 8, 13, 89, 150, 162, 176, 204
    foedus 7–9, 189
    Gallic loyalties 2, 7, 59, 71, 101, 105, 148, 151
    hospitalitas (Visigoths) 8
    post-Roman 1, 229
    Vaison, revolt against the Burgundians 176
  Roman Empire
    Battle of Philippi (42 BCE) 79
    Battle of the Metaurus (207 BCE) 82
    capture of Jerusalem (70 CE) 217
    demise of the West 1, 3, 6, 8, 176, 187, 199
    Second Punic War 82
  Sassanid Empire
    persecutions of Christians 209, 216

Language
  barbarismus 125, 173
  deficiency of Germanic 171
  grammarians 109, 124, 168, 249, 262
  purity of Latin 168, 171
  schools of grammar and rhetoric 171
  soloecismus 125
Late antiquity 6, 15, 209
Letter writing 15, *see also* Persons: Sidonius: *Epistulae*
  breuitas 97, 119, 184
  coded communication 20, 69, 91, 215
  colloquial tone 91, 114, 134, 167, 207
  dates of event, writing, reading 4, 22, 72, 140, 163, 188, 200, 210
  embedded poetry 4, 16, 120–2, 148, 156, 215, 250–1
  formulas of greeting and signing off 19, 61, 70, 125, 183, 185
  half a conversation 16, 69, 104, 161, 167, 207, 252
  letter bearers 9, 144, 146, 152, 161, 178, 184
  like a face in a mirror 225–6
  pious formulas 75, 100, 119, 142, 180, 189, 227, 236
  primary and secondary reader 22, 103, 134
  self-fashioning 18, 102
  senatorial 16
  theorists 16, 61, 225–6, 228
  titles
    domine fili 19, 252
    domine frater 19, 211
    domine maior 19, 61
    (domine) papa 19, 125
  types and topics 16, 226
    admonition 168
    cover letters 5, 12, 16, 89–90, 98, 235
    dedicatory 57
    health and illness 138, 141
    invitation 138
    recommendation 144, 182
    salutatio 159
Literature
  coded communication 77, 215
  comparatio/synkrisis 94
  criticism and envy 57–9, 68–9, 155, 249, 256–7

INDEX

editing and publishing 12, 62, 67
  haste vs carefulness 97, 126, 235, 252–3
ekphrasis 14, 121, 129, 131, 162
epigram/*epigramma* 4, 128, 159, 260
  prose epigram 159
epitaph 1, 3, 60, 99, 151, 156–7, 208–9, 215, 265
  engraving 212
intertextuality 15, 22, 82, 122, 154, 159, 187, 199, 209, 233, 244
  classical vs late antique 15
late antique, 14
laudatio 93, 170, 214
metaphor of sailing 67, 256
mixture of genres 16, 120, 263
nugae 'light verse' 200
writing panegyric 245

Manuscript tradition 3, 5, 26, 28, 80, 84, 88, 100, 163, 173, 179, 181, 190–1, 193–4, 200, 211, 224, 243, 249, 265
  Dolveck's stemma 26–7, 66–7

Naming conventions 1, 96
  nicknames 111, 122–3
  signum 1
Narrative 21–2, 74, 83, 96, 98, 103, 112, 119, 187–8, 191, 196, 205, 212, 214
  cliff-hanger 72, 88
  focalization 22, 103, 128
  narrator and narratee 21–2, 103, 128, 191, 212, 225, 239
  space 22
  time 22, 103, 151, 153
    verb tenses 102

Particles 21
  autem 21, 68, 151, 190
  enim 21, 64, 190–1, 206
  iam 139
  nam(que) 21, 64, 74, 94, 127, 146, 188, 190–2, 207
  quippe 21, 171
  scilicet 21, 66
  tamen 21, 99, 110, 117, 152, 190, 200, 203–4
  uel 116, 164, 196–7, 206, 257
  uidelicet 21, 66
Philosophy
  Aristotelianism 12, 230

Narbonne, circle of Neoplatonists/Neopythagoreans 13, 231, 234, 242
Neoplatonism 12, 135, 230, 234
Platonism 12, 230
Pythagoreanism 12, 230, 243
Second Sophistic 235
Seven Sages 234
soul, nature of 12
Stoicism 12, 58–9, 171, 230
Politeness 19, 205, 221
  diminutives 67, 97, 114, 125, 224
  iubes–pareo 20, 58, 61, 97, 125, 211, 235
  modesty 6–8, 89–90, 97, 119, 124, 127, 165, 181, 214, 235–6, 244, 263
  pudor 11, 146, 181
  speed 69, 252
  uerecundia 11, 119, 127, 146, 181, 221
  'You' and 'I' 19–20, 61, 67, 69, 84, 119, 124, 141, 160, 184, 201, 212, 214, 220, 224, 248–9, 255

Senators
  clarissimus 11
  consulate 181
  illustris 11
  patricius 11, 175
  Roman senate 11
  spectabilis 11
Society
  amicitia 11, 74, 93, 104, 124, 142, 211, 220, 255
  gift-giving 11–12, 103, 140, 230–1
  networks 9, 11–12, 60, 230
  officium 11, 107, 134, 213
  aristocratic poise 126
  barbarians 6, 8–9, 22, 71, 147, 162, 173, 184, 203, 207, 233, 237–8
  apparel 164–6
  council of elders 174, 243
  calendar
    Adar, Jewish month 254
    Feast of Purim 254
    January and February 254
    Kalendae Ianuariae 96
  concordia 181, 206
  enslaved people 9, 103, 106, 116, 135, 144, 147, 153

Society (cont.)
  food and fasting 107–8, 113–15,
      119, 187, 195, 242
  hospitalitas 90, 106
  marriage
    deductio 87
    dextrarum iunctio 88
    dowry 2, 10, 142, 177
    pronuba 88, 127
    '*T(h)alassio*' cry 87
  ordo 'class' 86, 146, 257
  patronage 9, 11, 85–6, 90, 92–5,
      144, 178, 198, 210, 220, 223
  seniority 95, 108, 154, 178
  Sidonius' vision 209, 250
  social strata, 9
  status 10–11, 109, 124–5, 137, 147,
      155, 162, 165, 178, 213
  villa life 11, 101, 104, 108, 111, 132
    ball playing 108–109, 163
    baths 102, 115–6, 118, 131
    idealized countryside 105
    library and reading 108–9
    playing at dice 108–9, 163
    table talk 107, 114
  virtues and vices 241
  women 10, 86, 88, 110, 116, 135–6,
      138, 176–7, 180, 182, 237
    devotional reading 110, 182
Style 135
  alliteration 24, 94, 130, 185, 191–2,
      196, 198, 211, 219, 261
  archaism 22–3, 61, 65, 69, 86–7,
      99–100, 110, 134–5, 146,
      204, 213, 218, 236, 239, 244,
      253, 256
  assonance 24, 189, 196
  chiasmus 24, 92, 104, 152, 195–6,
      201, 207–8, 212, 225, 261
  concordia discors 18
  direct speech 96
  homoeoteleuton 24, 191, 225
  hyperbole 24, 66, 254
  isocolon, 23, 73
  law of rising members 24, 63, 87,
      114, 125, 220, 243, 248
  litotes 95, 117, 155, 248

  'mannerism' 24, 65, 70, 82, 204
  metre in poetry 4, 63, 91, 126, 215,
      255, 258–60
  unmetrical names 262
  oxymoron 81, 88, 104, 107, 114,
      142, 146, 165, 206, 216, 221,
      243, 254, 261
  parallel sequences (pairs, triplets)
      23–4, 62, 73, 78, 83, 87, 91,
      93, 125, 134, 147, 163, 220,
      237, 248–9
  paronomasia 24, 93–4, 97, 104, 142,
      158, 191, 196, 208, 219–20,
      238, 240, 243, 261–2
  polyptoton 24, 92, 94, 104, 106,
      110, 113, 147, 153, 185, 195,
      239
  prose rhythm 24, 118
    clausula 24, 61–3, 66–7, 69, 74–5,
      88, 92, 94, 101, 108, 111,
      125, 134, 140–3, 152, 159–
      60, 164, 167, 175, 180, 189–
      90, 194–5, 201, 203, 205,
      207–8, 213–14, 221, 237–8,
      244, 248–9, 252, 263–4
    metrical vs accentual 24
  rhyme 24, 63, 68, 78, 99, 106, 195,
      236–7, 240
  rotunditas 63, 172
  smoothness vs complexity 23–4, 70,
      116, 171, 193
  uarietas 18, 114, 131

Text linguistics 20
  focus 20–1, 66, 142, 164, 180, 194,
      213, 225
    contrastive 21, 205, 244
  hyperbaton (discontinuity) 21, 67,
      76, 80, 97, 106, 140, 151,
      213–14, 225, 243
    verbal 21, 92, 140, 189, 207
  topic 20–1, 66, 74, 105, 151,
      164, 190, 193, 205, 226,
      244, 260
    contrastive 21, 104, 106
  word order 20, 152
    verb initial 21, 87, 97, 225

For EU product safety concerns, contact us at Calle de José Abascal, 56–1°, 28003 Madrid, Spain or eugpsr@cambridge.org.

www.ingramcontent.com/pod-product-compliance
Ingram Content Group UK Ltd.
Pitfield, Milton Keynes, MK11 3LW, UK
UKHW020812180326
469097UK00017B/1145